Lone Star Politics

PAUL BENSON

Tarrant County College

DAVID CLINKSCALE

Tarrant County College

ANTHONY GIARDINO

Tarrant County College

Longman

Boston   Columbus   Indianapolis   New York   San Francisco   Upper Saddle River
Amsterdam   Cape Town   Dubai   London   Madrid   Milan   Munich   Paris   Montreal
Toronto   Delhi   Mexico City   São Paulo   Sydney   Hong Kong   Seoul   Singapore   Taipei   Tokyo

Executive Editor: Reid Hester
Development Editor: Elizabeth Alimena
Senior Marketing Manager: Lindsey Prudhomme
Supplements Editor: Corey Kahn
Media Supplements Editor: Regina Vertiz
Production Manager: Denise Phillip
Project Coordination, Text Design, and Electronic Page Makeup: Electronic Publishing
  Services Inc., NYC
Cover Design Manager: Wendy Ann Fredericks
Cover Designer: Kay Petronio
Cover Photos: *Background photo:* © Shutterstock.com; *mosaic images:* © Glowimages/Getty
  Images
Photo Researcher: Poyee Oster
Senior Manufacturing Buyer: Roy L. Pickering, Jr.
Printer and Binder: R. R. Donnelley & Sons/Crawfordsville
Cover Printer: The Lehigh Press/Phoenix Color Corporation

Library of Congress Cataloging-in-Publication Data
Benson, Paul.
  Lone Star politics / Paul Benson, David Clinkscale, Anthony Giardino.—1st ed.
    p. cm.
  Includes bibliographical references and index.
  ISBN 978-0-13-605769-7
  1. Texas—Politics and government. I. Clinkscale, David. II. Giardino, Anthony. III. Title.
JK4816.B45 2011
320.4764—dc22

2010041453

Longman
is an imprint of

www.pearsonhighered.com

ISBN-13: 978-0-13-605769-7
ISBN-10:   0-13-605769-1

BRIEF CONTENTS

Contents   *iv*
Preface   *xiv*

Chapter **1**   Texas Society and Political Culture   2

Chapter **2**   Federalism and the Texas Constitution   34

Chapter **3**   Political Participation: Voting and Elections   64

Chapter **4**   Political Parties   88

Chapter **5**   Interest Groups in Texas Politics   116

Chapter **6**   The Legislature in Texas Politics   146

Chapter **7**   The Governor   184

Chapter **8**   The Plural Executive and the Bureaucracy   206

Chapter **9**   The Texas Courts System   230

Chapter **10**   The Judicial System and Due Process   250

Chapter **11**   Local and County Governments and Special Districts   270

Chapter **12**   Finance, Budgeting, and Public Policy   296

Appendix I: *The Constitution of the United States of America*   *330*
Appendix II: *Selected Excerpts from the Texas Constitution*   *348*
Glossary   *369*
Credits   *373*
Index   *374*

CONTENTS

Preface *xiv*

CHAPTER 1 Texas Society and Political Culture   2

The Historical Pieces 5

The Explorers 5

   The Spanish 5

   The French 6

The Colonists 7

   The Hispanics 7

   The Anglos 8

The Texans 10

   The Republic 10

▶ **TEXAS MOSAIC** Rough Justice: Order in the Court 10

   The Confederacy 11

▶ **INSIDE THE FEDERALIST SYSTEM** A Federal Government
Ally in the Texas Governor's Mansion 12

The Americans 14

   A Frontier State 14

   A Modern State 15

The Geographic Pieces 18

The Gulf Lowlands 18

   The Coastal Plains 18

   The Piney Woods 19

   The Post Oaks and Prairies 19

   The South Texas Prairie 19

The Western Highlands 20

   The Edwards Plateau 20

   The Llano Uplift 20

   The Wichita Prairie 20

The High Plains   20
The West Texas Basins and Ranges   21

The Economic Pieces   21
The First Stage—Take It   21
The Second Stage—Make It   23
The Third Stage—Serve It   23

The Demographic Pieces   24
Population Size   24
Population Growth   24
Population Distribution   25
Population Diversity   26

▶ **WHAT CAN YOU DO?**   27

Putting It Together: The Picture of Texas   28
Political Culture   28

Political Culture and Policy   30
The Changing Face of Texas   30

Summary   31

CHAPTER 2   Federalism and the Texas Constitution   **34**

Federalism   36
Federalism Applied   36
Constitutional Limits on States   37
▶ U.S. Constitutional Limits on State Power   37
▶ U.S. Constitutional Provisions Regarding Interstate Relations   38
Shared Powers   38

Constitutions   39

National Gains   39
Constitutional Amendments   39

Budgetary Powers   40
▶ U.S. Congressional Powers   *40*
The Federal Courts   41
A Brief History of Federalism   42
The "New" New Federalism   42

State Constitutions   44
State Constitutional Structure   44

The Seven Constitutions of Texas   46
Coahuila y Tejas   46
The 1836 Constitution   46
The 1846 Constitution   46
The 1861 Constitution   47

The 1866 Constitution 47
The 1869 Constitution 47

▶ **TEXAS MOSAIC** Early Diversity in Texas: African Americans in 19th-Century Texas Politics 49

▶ **TEXAS MOSAIC** Diversity of Thought: E. J. Davis 51

The 1876 Constitution 52

▶ **INSIDE THE FEDERALIST SYSTEM** A Comparison of U.S. and Texas Bill of Rights 55

▶ **THE TEXAS CONSTITUTION** A Closer Look 56

Amending the Constitution 57
Constitutional Revision 57

▶ **WHAT CAN YOU DO?** 58

The 1974 Constitutional Convention 58
Prospects for Revision 59

Summary 61

CHAPTER 3 Political Participation: Voting and Elections   **64**

A History of Voting Rights 66
White Primary 66

Poll Tax 67
Federal Court Intervention 67
The Voting Rights Act 67

▶ **TEXAS MOSAIC** Increasing Diversity in Elective Politics: Barbara Jordan 68

Qualifications 68

▶ **THE TEXAS CONSTITUTION** A Closer Look 69

Registration 69

▶ **WHAT CAN YOU DO?** 69

Turnout 70
Who Turns Out 72
Texas Factors in Registration and Turnout 73

Types of Election 75

Primary Election 75
General Election 75
Special Election 76

▶ **MY TURN** Down-Ballot Races *Tom Wilder* 78

Campaigning 81

▶ **INSIDE THE FEDERALIST SYSTEM** State and Federal Campaign Contribution Limits 82

Summary 85

CHAPTER 4 Political Parties   **88**

Political Parties   90

Party Structure   90

Conventions   92

    The Precinct Level   *92*
    The County (or District) Level   *93*
    The State Level   *94*

▶ **WHAT CAN YOU DO?**   94

Elected Offices   95

    The Precinct Level   *95*
    The County Level   *96*
    The State Level   *97*

▶ **MY TURN** Why I Am a Democrat *Kelly Becker*   98

The Democratic Party   99

    Foundations   *99*
    Dominance   *99*
    Retrenchment   *101*

▶ **INSIDE THE FEDERALIST SYSTEM** A Look at the State Democratic and Republican Party Platforms   102

The Republican Party   103

    Post-Reconstruction   *103*
    John Tower, Lyndon Johnson, and a U.S. Senate Seat   *103*

▶ **MY TURN** Why I Am a Republican *Joshua Barber*   104

▶ **TEXAS MOSAIC** John Tower   106

Slow Growth   107

The Reagan Revolution   107

    A Two-Party State   *108*
    How Not to Run a Campaign   *109*
    Republican Gains   *109*

Party Politics in the New Millennium   110

▶ **THE TEXAS CONSTITUTION** A Closer Look   111

Summary   *113*

CHAPTER 5 Interest Groups in Texas Politics   **116**

The Roles of Interest Groups   118

    Interest Groups Defined   *118*
    Interest Groups: Okay   *119*

▶ **THE TEXAS CONSTITUTION** A Closer Look   119

Interest Groups: Not Okay   120

The Types of Interest Groups   121

Business Interests   122
Labor Interests   123
Professional Interests   123
Ethnic Interests   124
Other Interests   124

The Methods of Interest Groups   126

▶ **INSIDE THE FEDERALIST SYSTEM** Interest Groups in Texas   128

▶ **TEXAS MOSAIC** A Lobbyist's Tale   131

▶ **MY TURN** Lobbyists and the Texas Legislature *George S. Christian*   132

Membership Mobilization   135
Interim Oversight   136
Regulating Interest Groups   137

▶ **WHAT CAN YOU DO?**   137

Money and Interest Groups   138

Internal Funding   138
External Funding: PACs   139

The Iron Triangle   140

Interest Groups and You   142

Summary   143

CHAPTER 6   The Legislature in Texas Politics   **146**

▶ **THE TEXAS CONSTITUTION** A Closer Look   148

The Legislature in Texas   149

Structure   149
Membership   149
Apportionment   151

The Presiding Officers   157

The Lieutenant Governor   157

▶ **TEXAS MOSAIC** The Killer Bees: Rattling the Texas political cage   159

The Speaker of the House   161

"The Team"   163

The Committee System   165

Standing Committees   166

Special Committees   167

How Committees Work   168

How a Bill Becomes a Law   170

Introduction of a Bill   170

Committee Action   171

▶ **WHAT CAN YOU DO?**   171

Floor Action   172

Ways to Kill a Bill   175

▶ **TEXAS MOSAIC** There Oughta Be a Law . . . : And now there is!   176

The Legislature in the Political Arena   177

Legislative Support   177

Other Players   178

▶ **INSIDE THE FEDERALIST SYSTEM** The 2009 Stimulus Act   179

The Legislature and You   179

Summary   180

| CHAPTER 7 | The Governor | 184 |

Qualifications, Term, and Salary   186

The Governor's Powers   187

Executive Powers   187

Appointment Powers   188

Military Powers   189

Law Enforcement Powers   189

Legislative Powers   190

Session-Calling Power   190

Message Power   191

Veto Power   191

▶ **INSIDE THE FEDERALIST SYSTEM** Comparative Power of the Veto   192

Budgetary Powers   194

Line Item Veto Power   194

Budget Creation Power   195

Judicial Powers   195

Appointment Power   195

Clemency Power   195

▶ **THE TEXAS CONSTITUTION** A Closer Look   196

Informal Powers   197

Partisan Leader   197

Persuasive Power   197

▶ **TEXAS MOSAIC** Two for the Price of One: James E. Ferguson   198

Congressional Liaison   199

International Relations   199

Leadership Style   200

The Governor's Staff   201

▶ TEXAS MOSAIC Increasing Gender Diversity: Ann Richards   201

Options for Reform   202

▶ WHAT CAN YOU DO?   203

Summary   204

CHAPTER 8   The Plural Executive and the Bureaucracy   **206**

▶ INSIDE THE FEDERALIST SYSTEM United States   208

Elected Officials   209

The Lieutenant Governor   209
The Attorney General   210

▶ TEXAS MOSAIC Old-Style Texas Politics: Bob Bullock   211

▶ MY TURN Open Government *Greg Abbott*   213

Comptroller of Public Accounts   215

▶ WHAT CAN YOU DO?   216

The Commissioner of the General Land Office   217
The Commissioner of Agriculture   217

▶ WHAT CAN YOU DO?   218

▶ THE TEXAS CONSTITUTION A Closer Look   218

▶ TEXAS MOSAIC Increasing Diversity in the Executive Branch: The Secretaries of State   219

Appointed Offices   220

Secretary of State   220
Insurance Commissioner   220
Adjutant General   220

The Bureaucracy   220

Size   221
Hierarchy and Expertise   222
Accountability   222
Elected Boards and Commissions   223
Administrative Boards   224
University Boards and the Coordinating Board   225
Occupational Licensing Boards   225
Regulatory Boards   225

The Sunset Advisory Commission   226

Summary   227

CHAPTER 9 The Texas Courts System   **230**

The Texas Court System 232

Determining Jurisdiction 232
Two Types of Law 232
Other Distinctions Between Civil and Criminal Law 233
Can an Act Be Both Civil and Criminal? 234
Two Types of Courts 234

Structure of the Texas Courts System 234

Trial-Level Courts 236

▶ TEXAS MOSAIC Judge Roy Bean 238

Appellate Courts 240

▶ THE TEXAS CONSTITUTION A Closer Look 241

▶ WHAT CAN YOU DO? 242

The Court's Role in Public Policy Making 242
Selection of Judges 243

▶ INSIDE THE FEDERALIST SYSTEM 244

First Assumed Office 245

▶ TEXAS MOSAIC Justice Wallace B. Jefferson 245

The Call for Judicial Reform 246

Summary 247

CHAPTER 10 The Judicial System and Due Process   **250**

Crime and Punishment 252

Reporting Crime 252

▶ WHAT CAN YOU DO? 252

Crime in Texas 252
Factors in the Crime Rate 253
Corrections 253

Law Enforcement 256

Various Levels of Law Enforcement 256

Due Process 259

▶ INSIDE THE FEDERALIST SYSTEM Search and Seizure 260

Stages of Due Process 261
Grand Jury and Indictment 262

▶ THE TEXAS CONSTITUTION A Closer Look 263

Trial 263

▶ MY TURN Essay from a Texas Death Row Inmate *Martin Allen Draughon* 265

Summary 267

CHAPTER 11 Local and County Governments
and Special Districts   **270**

▶ **TEXAS MOSAIC** Increasing Texas Diversity: Henry Cisneros   272

Municipal Government   **274**

    Types of Municipalities   *274*

▶ **THE TEXAS CONSTITUTION** A Closer Look   275

    Forms of Municipal Government   *276*

▶ **WHAT CAN YOU DO?**   278

    Municipal Elections   *278*
    Types of Municipal Elections   *279*
    The Effects of Group Participation   *279*
    Municipal Finance   *280*

▶ **INSIDE THE FEDERALIST SYSTEM** In Step   284

County Government   **284**

▶ **MY TURN** Is County Government Antiquated? *Dionne Bagsby*   285

    Structure of County Government   *285*
    Other Elected Officials   *286*
    County Government Finance   *288*
    Criticism of County Government and Proposed Reform   *289*

Special Districts   **290**

    The Nature of Special Districts   *291*
    Types of Special Districts   *291*

Councils of Government   **292**

Summary   *293*

CHAPTER 12 Finance, Budgeting, and Public Policy   **296**

Public Policy   **298**

    Types of Policy   *299*
    The Policy Model   *300*
    Agenda Setting   *300*
    Formulation   *300*
    Adoption and Implementation   *301*
    Evaluation   *301*

▶ **WHAT CAN YOU DO?**   302

The Texas Budget   **302**

    Constraints on Budgeting   *302*
    Balanced Budget Provision   *302*

▶ **THE TEXAS CONSTITUTION** A Closer Look   303

The Biennial Budget System   304
Public Sentiment   304
Dedicated Funds   304
Congressional and Court Mandates   305

The Budget-Making Process   306

State Revenue   307

Tax Collection   308
Tax Notes   313
Taxation Summary   314
Reforming Texas Taxes   315
The Casino Option   315
Other Revenue Raising Options   317

▶ **INSIDE THE FEDERALIST SYSTEM** Left on the Table   319

Expenditures   321

The Big Three   321
Education   321
Higher Education   323
Health and Human Services   323
Business and Economic Development   325
Other Expenditures   326

Nonfiscal Policy   326

Summary   327

Appendix I: The Constitution of the United States of America   330

Appendix II: Selected Excerpts from the Texas Constitution   348

Glossary   369

Credits   373

Index   374

As we write this, in the summer of 2010, public approval ratings of government officials are at all-time lows. With the economy still in the grips of a lingering recession and voters so exercised that many elected officials across the nation have stopped holding town hall meetings to avoid public wrath, one wonders who would pursue elective politics as a life calling. Yet none of the 150 seats in the Texas House or the 31 seats in the Texas Senate are wanting for a candidate; most major state offices have candidates from both political parties.

As a thoughtful observer, though, it would be difficult not to feel a little compassion for members of the state legislator. In a best-case scenario, they enter the 2011 legislative session having to close a $10 billion gap in the budget simply to maintain current state services. If the nation has a double-dip recession, an outcome largely out of the hands of Texas lawmakers, the gap could be twice that, or even more. And they take on this challenge, leaving their homes, families, and better-paying jobs behind, for the princely sum of $600 a month. So, while we view vigorous, constructive criticism as a prerequisite for a healthy democracy, have some sympathy for the bedeviled legislator, and maybe a little gratitude that many citizens are still willing to take on such a challenge. Unless you think you can do better, in which case the filing deadline is approaching faster than you think. . . .

Much has changed in Texas politics since the initial edition of *Lone Star Politics* launched a decade and a half ago. Democrats still held a significant number of state offices and enjoyed a narrow majority in the Senate and a wide one in the House. Now, as we write, Republicans control all state offices and have a narrow margin in the House and a wider margin in the Senate. Most of those who we originally highlighted as state leaders are elsewhere. Former Governor George W. Bush served as president, of course, then retired from politics. The great Bob Bullock passed away. Legislative leaders like Republican Bill Ratliff and Democrat Rob Junell have retired. Former House Speaker Pete Laney was reduced to just another member of the House when his party lost its majority status, then he retired. Likewise, his replacement, Tom Craddick, was relegated to the back row after a political coup. Former Attorney General Dan Morales spent time as a guest of the federal prison system because of illegal activities while in office. These former politicians have been replaced by a new crop of leaders, all jockeying for power. That competition has led to many of the conflicts noted in the opening paragraph. Furthermore, Texas politics has become more partisan over the last 15 years, but there is still nowhere near the level of acrimony that permeates politics at the national level. Both parties face internal challenges as they try to exert influence in the Lone Star political arena. All in all,

Texas politics is still a fun game to watch, and something to which we pay attention because the contest is being played with your money and your rights.

Our approach in writing this book is simple. First, be realistic. Texas politics is less a debate about ideology and theory than it is pragmatic—finding what works. We will show how different government officials use their powers to achieve their goals. Second, we want to give students the opportunity to become involved in the political process. You will find "What Can You Do?" boxes located throughout the text, giving the reader suggestions on ways to get involved in the political process. Finally, since we think Texas politics is the most exciting game in town, we wrote this book to be as entertaining and fun as possible, while still delivering all the information you need. You might even find it funny in places—that's just the nature of Texas government.

We would like to acknowledge Dickson Musslewhite, Eric Stano, Elizabeth Alimena, and Angela Boone at Pearson, without whom this book would not be possible. Many people at Tarrant County College had an important role in the development of *Lone Star Politics*, including Division Deans Judith Gallagher and Arrick Jackson and department chairs Wanda Hill and Jessica Patton; we would like to thank them for their patience and support during the writing process. The library staff, especially Sandra McCurdy and the now retired Anna Holzer, made our job much easier. Kudos to the numerous students who made valuable suggestions over the last couple of years. Finally, and most importantly, we want to thank our families. This book would not have happened without our spouses—Carolyn Benson, Karen Clinkscale, and Lisa Giardino—who made it possible, and our children, who made it necessary. They all thank you for reading *Lone Star Politics*.

Resources

Instructor's Manual and Test Bank (ISBN 0-13-605770-5) Instructor's Manual offers learning objectives, chapter outlines, chapter summaries, lecture starters and teaching tips, and assignments and class activities. Test Bank contains over 40 questions per chapter in multiple-choice, true-false, and essay format.

MyTest Test Bank (ISBN 0-205-11265-X) All questions from the Test Bank can be accessed in this flexible, online test generating software.

PowerPoint Presentation (ISBN 0-205-11276-5) Slides include a lecture outline of each chapter, including images and figures from the book.

Texas Government Study Site Online package of practice tests, flashcards and more organized by major course topics. Visit www.pearsontexasgovernment.com.

Texas Society and Political Culture

1

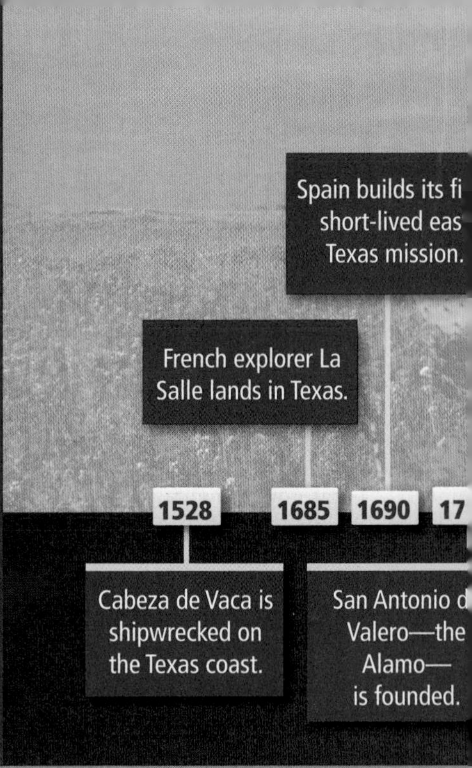

Spain builds its fi
short-lived eas
Texas mission.

French explorer La
Salle lands in Texas.

| 1528 | 1685 | 1690 | 17 |

Cabeza de Vaca is
shipwrecked on
the Texas coast.

San Antonio d
Valero—the
Alamo—
is founded.

By the end of this chapter on Texas society and political culture, you should be able to . . .

★ Differentiate between government and politics.
★ Explain the historical pieces of the Texas mosaic.
★ Differentiate among the geographic regions of the state.
★ Analyze the economic forces in Texas.
★ Analyze the influences of major demographic groups in the state.
★ Identify the dominate political cultures in Texas.

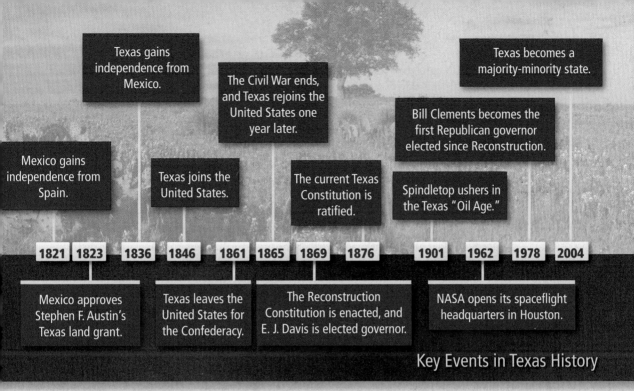

Key Events in Texas History

1821	Mexico gains independence from Spain.
1823	Mexico approves Stephen F. Austin's Texas land grant.
1836	Texas gains independence from Mexico.
1846	Texas joins the United States.
1861	Texas leaves the United States for the Confederacy.
1865	The Civil War ends, and Texas rejoins the United States one year later.
1869	The Reconstruction Constitution is enacted, and E. J. Davis is elected governor.
1876	The current Texas Constitution is ratified.
1901	Spindletop ushers in the Texas "Oil Age."
1962	NASA opens its spaceflight headquarters in Houston.
1978	Bill Clements becomes the first Republican governor elected since Reconstruction.
2004	Texas becomes a majority-minority state.

> *If I owned Hell and Texas,*
> *I'd rent out Texas and live in Hell*

—PHILIP H. SHERIDAN, U.S. ARMY GENERAL, c. 1855

> *God Bless Texas*

—THE LATE BOB BULLOCK, TEXAS LIEUTENANT GOVERNOR, c. 1992

Since this book is about politics in Texas, we will begin by defining the term. There are probably as many definitions of this word as there are political scientists eager to establish a reputation by defining it. However, when you strip away the verbal clutter that often accompanies such efforts, a basic working definition emerges. Simply put, **politics** is who gets what, when, and how.[1]

The term "politics" and its first cousin, "politician," aren't the most popular words around. Yet politics is an integral part of human society and the human condition. In even the most rudimentary cultures, people will seek to benefit themselves by acquiring needed or desired things. The process by which this acquisition occurs is politics, and it can occur outside of government as well as inside of it. If you need evidence of this, watch a group of 3 year olds on a playground. They may be complete strangers when the play period begins, but within five minutes somebody will have determined the distribution of those things that are valuable to 3 year olds.

Having already mentioned government, we need to define it as well. "Government" (like "politics") is one of those terms that everyone bandies about, but whose

politics
The process of seeking or maintaining power.

definition can prove elusive. It calls to mind the story told about U.S. Supreme Court Justice Potter Stewart, who was asked to define the term "obscene." He remarked that while he could not, in fact, define it, he knew it when he saw it! We know government when we see it, and we would like to offer a working definition of the term. **Government** is composed of public institutions that have the authority to mandate the collection of revenue and to allocate valuable things for a society. Public institutions can include such disparate entities as the Texas legislature, the Office of Governor, the Higher Education Coordinating Board, the Houston City Council, the El Paso County Commissioners Court, and so on. Mandatory revenues constitute money payments that must be rendered by citizens. Valuable things can include money, land, natural resources, individual freedoms—even life itself. And an allocation made with authority simply refers to a division or distribution that is recognized as legitimate.

government
Composed of public institutions acting with authority to levy taxes and to allocate things for society.

Politics and government are inextricably intertwined with one another. You will never have government without politics, but politics pervades everything we do. It's in our jobs, our churches, our civic clubs, our schools, our families, our soccer leagues—it's anywhere and everywhere humans interact with one another. Rather than simply dismissing politics as unsavory or corrupt, why not try to understand its dynamics and how you can use it in a positive way? Rest assured that if you don't, someone else is going to, and they may not have your good intentions. Besides, politics in Texas is fascinating. Let's take a closer look.

Any study of the panorama of Texas politics must begin with an understanding of the land and its people. As seen by the sentiments expressed at the beginning of this chapter, Texas and Texans generate a wide range of opinions and reactions. This should come as no surprise, because Texas is many things to many people. This rather large piece of real estate has been a refuge, an escape hatch, a land of opportunity, a dream maker, and a heartbreaker for countless thousands who have called themselves "Texans" (or "Texians" or "Tejanos" or even, simply, "the People"). By turns, Native Americans, Spaniards, Africans, French, Mexicans, Germans, Irish, Italians, Asians, and scores of others have made their way to Texas and made themselves Texans in the process. This incredible ethnic and cultural diversity makes defining a "Texas" society and a uniformly "Texan" culture an exercise in futility to some extent. As the tuxedo-clad young urban professional sits in his Lexus awaiting valet parking before attending the Van Cliburn International Piano Competition at the Bass Performance Hall in downtown Fort Worth, Bubba, on his way to a Robert Earl Keen concert at Billy Bob's Texas, drives by in a mostly blue '62 Chevy pickup, complete with a dog of manifold and indeterminate lineage as well a bumper sticker proclaiming, "Keep Honking, I'm Reloading!" Neighborhoods of abject poverty and random violence stand in stark contrast to enclaves of unimaginable wealth and political power, often in the same city. On a given day, the temperature may be 95°F in Brownsville and 25°F in Dalhart. Yet it is this sheer diversity and variety that may, in the final analysis, define Texas and Texans more than anything else.

mosaic
The joining of small pieces of material, varied in shape and color, to produce a whole image; often used describe the social and cultural diversity that defines Texas.

On reflection, it seems clear that there cannot possibly be only one Texas society and one Texas culture. This state's society and its culture constitute a **mosaic**, a picture made up of many parts and fragments. There are historical, geographic, economic, and demographic pieces. Only by attempting to understand these individual pieces and their relationship to one another can we begin to see the whole picture of Texas, its people, and its politics.

Cattle drivers were once a vital part of the Texas economy. How has the glorification of that era added to the Texas mystique?

The Historical Pieces

Some of the more interesting pieces in the Texas mosaic emerge from history. Certain historical events have helped to shape political attitudes as well as political actions in this state. While the following brief survey of Texas history can only be considered cursory, it nevertheless highlights some of these important elements.

The Explorers

The Spanish

When the first Europeans came to that part of the so-called New World now known as Texas, the land was already occupied. Numerous Native American groups—bands, tribes, even confederations—lived here, representing a wide range of social organization and lifestyle. Much of what is known about these groups is derived from reports made by some of the early European explorers. One of the first, a Spaniard named Alvar Nuñez Cabeza de Vaca, arrived in Texas (by way of Florida) in November 1528, and spent the next seven years wandering over a large portion of Texas and the American Southwest. After numerous encounters with various native people, he eventually found his way to a Spanish outpost on the Gulf of California, and thence to Mexico City, where he recounted his adventures to Spanish colonial officials.[2]

This painting of Coronado is by famed artist Frederic Remington.

Cabeza de Vaca's report prompted these officials to outfit a full-scale expedition to explore systematically the area he had traveled and, in particular, to search for several "golden cities" that he claimed to have observed at a distance. This expedition, led by Francisco Vásquez de Coronado, spent several years wandering through parts of present-day Arizona, New Mexico, and Texas (one group made it as far as Kansas) in a fruitless search for wealth before returning to Mexico City.[3] At about the same time, a remnant of the ill-fated de Soto expedition wandered into East Texas and encountered the relatively sophisticated Caddo cultures there. Despite these early contacts, the rather pessimistic reports filed by these would-be *conquistadores*, depicting Texas as barren, inhospitable, and lacking accessible natural resources, cooled the Spanish desire to see more of Texas for the foreseeable future. However, even though these early explorations proved to be an economic disappointment for Spain, they did establish for that nation an important territorial claim to Texas that went largely unchallenged for the next century and a half.

The French

The Spanish, with their policy of benign neglect toward the empire's northern reaches, received a rude shock when a small French expedition, led by René-Robert Cavelier, Sieur de La Salle, landed on the Texas coast in 1684 and claimed the area for the king of France. La Salle had strayed from his original target (he had intended to land at the mouth of the Mississippi River) and his expedition never amounted to much, at least from the French perspective. He was murdered, and most of his compatriots died of disease, of starvation, or as a result of Indian attacks. This French "settlement" lasted barely three years, yet it had significant long-term consequences. As a result of the abortive La Salle expedition, Spain saw the need to reassert a more vigorous claim to the part of its empire that included Texas. The Spanish made plans to establish a permanent presence in these desolate northern provinces in order to deter future incursions by other European powers. Ironically, the greatest legacy of La Salle and his ill-fated band was to ensure Spain's continuing attempts to occupy Texas for the next 130 years.[4]

The Colonists

The instrument Spain used to establish a permanent presence in Texas was the mission.

The mission system had worked well in other parts of Spain and her empire as a means of subduing conquered or indigenous peoples and converting them into both faithful Christians and loyal Spanish subjects. The results of their efforts in Texas, however, were mixed at best.

The Hispanics

The first Spanish missions to Texas proper were established in east Texas near present-day Nacogdoches. They did not prosper because the Caddo Indians living there, among the most highly developed and sophisticated in Texas, saw no real advantage to relocating to the missions. After several attempts over a period of years during the early 1700s, the east Texas mission effort was largely abandoned.

Similarly, Spanish efforts to establish missions among the Plains Indians during the middle years of the 18th century proved fruitless. Missions near present-day Brady and Menard lasted less than two years before they were attacked and destroyed by Comanche bands. The message to Spain was painfully clear: the People (as the Comanche called themselves) wanted no part of the Spanish or their institutions, except as a source of horses to be stolen and captives to be seized.

Only in south Texas did the missions truly prosper, and it would be here, in an area bounded by the Rio Grande River and the Gulf of Mexico, that Spanish culture would put down its deepest, most persistent roots. These south Texas colonial outposts blended the native cultures of the area's Coahuiltecan Indians with elements from Spain, the Canary Islands, and, increasingly, an emerging Mexican culture.

Many Texans today see the most obvious influence of this culture in the hundreds of Spanish place names throughout Texas, but these Hispanic colonists also made significant contributions to Texas's legal heritage in such diverse areas as community property and water rights. In addition, ranching communities established along the Rio Grande in the 1750s provided the basis for a growing cattle trade with the Hispanic settlements to the north and to the south. This cattle culture would later provide most of the tools, terminology, and technology for an emerging Anglo cattle industry in the 19th century.

Born of the melding of Spanish and native Indian bloodlines, the Mexican people rose up in revolution against their colonial overlords on September 16, 1810. After ten years of bloody fighting, Spain abandoned her colonial empire and the Republic of Mexico was born. Yet even as this young country struggled to establish its place among the community of nations, a new and ultimately divisive force appeared in its northernmost state: Anglo settlers began to arrive in Texas.

Cowboys ride in front of the Alamo, a mixing of two iconic Texas images.

The Anglos

The first organized Anglo settlement of Texas occurred under the leadership of Stephen F. Austin, whose father, Moses, had negotiated a settlement agreement with the Spanish.

After his father's death, Stephen Austin confirmed this agreement with the new government of Mexico and began issuing land grants.[5] In the 1820s, land was a precious commodity and a powerful magnet, and the deal Austin offered was too good to pass up. Farmers received 177 acres of land; ranchers, 4,428 acres. (It is truly amazing how hundreds of Southern dirt farmers were transformed into ranchers by passing through or over the waters of the Red or Sabine Rivers.) This land came with relatively few restrictions. The prospective landowner had to occupy the land within two years, have it surveyed, make improvements to it, and become a Catholic (the only religion recognized as legal by the Mexican Constitution). While the typical Anglo settler, coming from the upland areas of the Old South, was not a Catholic, the possibility of possessing more than 4,400 acres of prime river bottom land acted as a powerful, if superficial, agent of conversion.

So the Anglos came. They came by the hundreds and, eventually, the thousands. They brought their families, their livestock, and, most significantly, their attitudes toward society and government, attitudes that ran counter to those of the prevailing Hispanic culture. These Anglos—poor, proud, fiercely independent, and enormously intolerant of those unlike themselves—gradually became more and more estranged from the government in faraway Mexico City. And that government, in turn, became more and more concerned about the increasingly rebellious attitudes of these newcomers. In order to stem this foreign tide, Mexico enacted tough restrictions on immigration beginning in 1830, but this merely heightened the tension between these two proud cultures. In 1832, a minor skirmish at Anahuac was quickly settled, but it would prove to be a harbinger of much more serious conflict in the future.

The election of Antonio López de Santa Anna as president of Mexico in 1833, and his subsequent assumption of virtually dictatorial powers, added another element to the increasingly combustible mix in Texas. Santa Anna's flaunting of democratic principles, he maintained that Mexico was not yet ready for democracy, alienated many of the old families of Hispanic Texas. These true "native Texans" (known as "Tejanos") included such venerable families as the Ruizes, the Navarros, the Veramendis, and the Seguins, and their opposition to Santa Anna soon led them to make common cause with their Anglo neighbors to the east. In October 1835, fighting broke out between Anglo settlers near Gonzales and Mexican cavalry troops from San Antonio. The battle was soon being referred to as the "Lexington of Texas," and within weeks the Anglo colonists and their allies from the Hispanic communities revolted against the government of President Santa Anna. This alliance was somewhat shaky from the start, as many of the Anglos openly manifested the typically American attitude of racial superiority common in that day. However, such underlying divisions were temporarily put aside in the face of a more immediate threat. By early 1836, Santa Anna had responded, entering Texas at the head of a large army and promising to destroy these rebellious interlopers.[6]

As wars go, the Texas Revolution was rather brief. It lasted a mere seven months and saw relatively few major battles, although the one fought at the old mission San Antonio de Valero (better known as the Alamo) would almost immediately become the stuff of legend and would help create a popular and persistent image of the fearless Texan standing tall against insurmountable odds. General Santa Anna's counterpart was Sam Houston, a free-spirited politico from Tennessee who had come to Texas. He had spent considerable time with his Cherokee friends, who called him the Big Drunk, in Indian Territory, before coming to Texas to start life anew. He was reluctant to fight against superior odds, but when he finally took the field against Mexican troops at San Jacinto (near present-day Houston) on the afternoon of

GENERAL D. ANTONIO LOPEZ DE SANTA-ANNA.
PRESIDENT OF THE REPUBLIC OF MEXICO.
By **A. Hoffy**, from an original likeness taken from life at **Vera-Cruz.**

Santa Anna would continue to be an important figure in Mexican politics, off and on, for two decades after Texas Independence.

April 21, the element of surprise, the emotional memories of the massacres of friends and compatriots at the Alamo and Goliad, and no small amount of luck led to victory for the "Texians" and defeat and capture for Santa Anna.[7]

After San Jacinto and the subsequent withdrawal of Mexican forces from Texas (in exchange for the return of Santa Anna, who had been captured), the victors found themselves in something of a dilemma. No longer a part of Mexico, they were not yet part of anything else. Popular opinion among Anglo Texans favored admission to the United States as a state, but unwilling to antagonize Mexico or to upset the free state–slave state balance that then existed in Congress, the U.S. government rebuffed Texas. In the face of these political realities, Texans did what was completely in keeping with their independent nature: acting on the Declaration of Independence they had penned back in March, they became their own nation.

The Texans

The Republic

Republic of Texas

The independent nation created by Texans that lasted from 1836 to 1846; its status as an independent country has contributed to (and continues to influence) an independent spirit in its politics.

The **Republic of Texas** existed for almost ten years. This decade was marked by a growing population, an expanding frontier, a deteriorating economy, a chronically bankrupt government, Indian attacks, Mexican invasions, European immigration, and politics that made your typical barroom brawl look like a Sunday School picnic by comparison. Despite an enormous influx of people, including, near the end of the Republic's life, a large number of Germans who settled in the Hill Country of central Texas, times were tough for this young nation and its citizens. Inflation was rampant and the economy in many areas came to be based on barter. Cash was scarce and was usually outrageously inflated.

The economy was not the only area where controversy and confusion reigned.

Political parties did not yet exist, but the clash of egos between Sam Houston, hero of San Jacinto and first president of the Republic, and his successor, a latter-day

Texas **MOSAIC**

Rough Justice
Order in the Court

Just exactly how rough was it for government officials during this time? Look at what happened to The Honorable Robert McAlpin Williamson, circuit court judge for the Republic of Texas. Williamson was nicknamed "Three-Legged Willie" because a bout with childhood polio left him with a withered left leg to which he attached a wooden peg. As a circuit judge, he would ride to various counties and hold court. One of the counties on his "circuit" was Gonzales County, known for its brazen disregard for the law. On one memorable trip to Gonzales County, Judge Williamson was attempting to hold court outdoors. His judicial

bench was a board held up by two kegs of whiskey and his seat was a keg of nails. He leaned his cane and a long rifle against a nearby tree and tried repeatedly to bring the unruly mob to order. As the crowd became more menacing, the judge leaned over, picked up his rifle, placed it before him on the bench, and loudly cocked it. "This court is coming to order," he said. "If it doesn't come to order—right now—I am by God gonna kill somebody, and I'm not particular who I kill." Court came to order.

SOURCE: C. F. Eckhardt, *Texas Tales Your Teacher Never Told You* (Plano, TX: Wordware, 1992), p. 144.

cavalier and poet from Georgia with the colorful name of Mirabeau Buonaparte Lamar, sparked an endless series of political pyrotechnics centering on the personalities of the people involved. A growing estrangement between Anglo and Tejano further fueled the political turmoil, as public policies and cultural practices began to turn against the latter. Moreover, Indians were likely to raid frontier settlements at the drop of an arrow, and Mexico sent armies to invade Texas not once but twice. Although not exactly what 17th-century English philosopher Thomas Hobbes spoke of in his description of the presocietal state of nature ("nasty, brutish, and short"), life in Texas during the period of the Republic was certainly difficult, as the Texas Mosaic suggests. Thus, the failures of the Republic served to intensify a tendency by these evolving Texans to regard government and authority as superfluous at best and dangerous at worst.

Ultimately, the way out of the many dilemmas confronting the Republic lay in union with the United States.[8] By the mid-1840s, U.S. public opinion and a political agenda based on "Manifest Destiny" combined to bring about the annexation of Texas and, in February 1846, the government of the Republic of Texas ceased to exist. Yet the shadow cast by this dubious decade of nationhood would stretch far into the future, and as subsequent generations of Texans looked back on the Republic, they would tend to ignore its failures and see instead a kind of golden era during which Texas stood tall among the community of nations. This attitude of uniqueness, often labeled "Texas Exceptionalism," manifests itself as an enormous sense of pride on the part of Texans that, in turn, has become an integral part of the Texas social, cultural, and political equation. However, those less generous in their evaluation would see Texas Exceptionalism as evidence of a bloated self-centeredness that has led to the kind of arrogance, violence, and racism sometimes associated with things Texan.

The Confederacy

Texans had hardly gotten used to calling themselves Americans before they once again shifted their political allegiance. Barely 15 years after becoming the 28th state in the Union, Texas joined 10 other Southern states in attempting to sunder that union by forming the Confederate States of America. Not all Texans wanted this and, reflecting the diversity that is so characteristic of this state, opposition would continue to simmer throughout the Civil War in such areas as the German Hill Country and several of the Red River counties of north central Texas. As early as the summer of 1862, opposition to the Confederacy in and around Gainesville in Cooke County was so strong that a large group of citizens plotted to remove the area from Confederate control. The scheme was uncovered and more than 40 participants were hanged. In the same year, a cavalry troop slaughtered a number of German Texans on the Nueces River as they were making their way to Mexico and thence to join the Union army. The bodies were left where they fell as a warning to others of the same sentiment. However, a solid majority of Texans supported the Confederacy, and although few major battles were actually fought on Texas soil, the state became a major supplier of men and materiel to the South's war effort.[9]

That effort, of course, would prove futile, and when the Confederacy finally capitulated, Texas found itself economically devastated, politically decimated, and

INSIDE THE FEDERALIST SYSTEM

A Federal Government Ally in the Texas Governor's Mansion

There are occasions when the long arm of the federal government extends unusually deep into a state through an individual whose political interests demonstrate a greater loyalty to the federal government than to the citizens he was elected to govern. Oftentimes, that governor is charged with implementing rules, regulations, and programs endorsed by the federal government but which are completely adverse to the beliefs and sentiments of most of the state's citizens. Such was the fate—-and the choice—-of Edmund J. Davis, who governed the state during the highly controversial period known as Reconstruction.

Davis, Texas's first post-Civil War governor, was a former Union army officer. Like all children of wealthy families, Davis was well-educated long before his family move to Texas in 1848. He became a lawyer one year later. During the early part of professional career, Davis served as an inspector and deputy customs collector. In 1853, he became district attorney of the Twelfth Judicial District at Brownsville. Three years later, Governor Elisha M. Pease named him as a judge of the same district, where he served until 1861. Davis joined the Democratic Party in 1855, but he renounced his affiliation with the party shortly before the end of the Civil War. Because he vigorously opposed secession, the state eliminated his judgeship. After Texas voted to secede, Davis left the state in May 1862. The following October, he met with Abraham Lincoln, who commissioned Davis as a colonel responsible for recruiting cavalrymen on behalf of the Union. His leadership in a number of successful missions led to his promotion to brigadier general.

At the conclusion of the Civil War, Davis participated in state politics as a Unionist and Republican. His political exploits, however, paled in comparison with his military successes. While he served in the Constitutional Convention of 1866, he was defeated in his attempt to win a state Senate seat. However, he was chosen as the president of the Constitutional Convention of 1869. In this capacity, David favored the restriction of political rights of former secessionists and expanded rights for blacks. In addition, he supported a proposal to divide Texas into several Republican-controlled states. Clearly, Davis represented every characteristic favored by Union sympathizers and resented by Democrats who were, at the time, prohibited from voting.

In the election of 1869, Davis successfully ran for governor as a Radical Republican, but his election was highly contentious. As the state's fourteenth governor, Davis loyally served as the national government's crony and seemed intent on punishing Texas Democrats during Reconstruction. His most controversial actions included: using the state's militia to physical subject political opponents; suppressing the publication of newspapers critical of his leadership; and bolstering the rights of newly-free slaves. Davis' tenure in office was characterized by excessive public spending, significant property tax increases, appropriation of public funds for the benefit of the governor's political and financial allies; and strict control of voter registration by the occupying Union military. Regardless of any favorable policies or programs implemented during his administration, Davis is often considered to be the most controversial of all Texas governors.

Despite his obvious unpopularity, Davis ran for reelection in December 1873. By then, many Democrats had denounced their loyalty to the Confederacy and had, as a result, regained the right to vote. Democratic voters contributed heavily to the election of Davis' Democratic opponent, Richard Coke. Davis attributed his defeat in part to the vindictive policies of the Republican national government and the resulting strain that

(continued)

existed between the state and Washington. From 1875 until his death, Davis led the weakened Republican party in Texas. However, because of his perceived but now disputed loyalty to the national government, which appeared to most Texans as oppressive during Reconstruction, he was soundly rejected by voters in every subsequent election for state and federal office. Over one-hundred years elapsed before Texans elected another Republican governor.

SOURCE: The Handbook of Texas (citing Ronald N. Gray, Edmund J. Davis: Radical Republican and Reconstruction Governor of Texas (Ph.D. dissertation, Texas Tech University, 1976). William C. Nunn, *Texas Under the Carpetbaggers* (Austin: University of Texas Press, 1962). Charles W. Ramsdell, *Reconstruction in Texas* (New York: Columbia University Press, 1910; rpt., Austin: Texas State Historical Association, 1970)).

militarily occupied. When he stepped ashore on June 19, 1865, at the head of 1,800 Federal troops, General Gordon Granger brought more than military occupation. He also brought with him a copy of the Emancipation Proclamation, which first had been issued by President Lincoln in 1863. His public pronouncement that those who had been slaves were now free spread quickly among African Americans in Texas. Eventually, black Texans began to celebrate June 19 ("Juneteenth") as a holiday, and the practice continues today in many Texas communities. The arrival of General Granger and his federal troops at Galveston in June 1865, signaled the beginning of a new and uncertain period in the history of Texas: **Reconstruction**.

Reconstruction
Post-Civil War period (1865–1877) during which former Confederate states had restrictive laws applied to them by the federal government; it (and E. J. Davis) led to Texas becoming a one-party Democratic state.

Reconstruction was a time of great stress and turmoil in Texas. The withdrawal of federal troops at the beginning of the Civil War had left Texas's extensive western frontier vulnerable to repeated attacks by Plains Indians. The Union blockade of Southern ports had helped to destroy the state's economy. Wartime deaths and injuries had devastated a generation of Texans. The initial policies of Reconstruction were not terribly onerous, though they certainly aggravated many Texans who clung stubbornly to the values that had given birth to the Confederacy. Yet harsher policies implemented by the Radical Republicans in Congress resulted in many Confederate supporters and wartime state officials being barred from voting and holding elective office. These laws, along with others that gave a modest measure of civil rights to those black Texans who had been slaves, helped bring about the election of the state's first Republican governor, E. J. Davis, in 1869.[10]

Davis's governorship has been much discussed by scholars. Given extraordinarily broad powers by the Texas legislature, Davis struggled to bring order out of the economic and political chaos that confronted him. But he and the Republican-dominated legislature were forced to raise taxes (never a popular move with Texans), and his vigorous use of the state's militia and police forces to combat widespread lawlessness earned him growing hostility from a population weary of military rule.

By 1873, many former Confederates had their voting rights restored. They returned to the polls with a vengeance, bent on removing the hated Davis and his fellow Republicans from office. In an election marred by widespread voter fraud on both sides (the basic political strategy employed by the two parties seems to have been "vote early and often"), Davis was swept from office. However, he refused to go quietly and sought to overturn the election by appealing to the Texas Supreme Court and its justices, all of whom Davis had appointed. Davis won the appeal, but faced with a mostly Democratic mob that besieged him in the state capitol, he finally relented and gave up his office.

The departure of E. J. Davis marked the effective end of Reconstruction in Texas, but the legacy of this period would live on for 100 years. In truth, Davis probably wasn't as bad as his political successors made him out to be, but unfortunately, what happened in history is never as important as what people think happened. And those who came to power immediately after Davis and beyond had a low opinion of him and of all Republicans. This attitude would make the Democratic Party the only real political force in Texas for a century and would doom the Republican Party to 100 years of electoral frustration and futility.

The Americans

A Frontier State

The last years of the 19th century in Texas were marked by expansion, recovery, and, as we've come to expect, political upheaval. The return of federal troops to the frontier in the early 1870s helped to ensure the ultimate demise of the Plains Indians as a free-roaming people. Their forced removal from the High Plains, coupled with the eradication of the buffalo herds on which their culture depended, set the stage for a rapid expansion of settlement into the western parts of the state.[11] And people weren't the only newcomers. Spreading out from the south Texas brush country came Texas longhorns in numbering in the millions. By the mid-1880s, vast areas of west Texas had been divided into huge ranches and cotton had a rival for economic dominance in Texas. Texas's long frontier experience with hostile Indians, border bandits, and a general lack of law and order contributed significantly to the development of an individualistic political culture that is so evident in the state today (as discussed in the "Individualistic" section below). It also encouraged self-reliance, the importance of land ownership, and a belief in material progress and growth as positive forces in a community. A general attitude of friendliness and a willingness to help others—even strangers—is also sometimes associated with the legacy of the frontier in Texas.

As Texas's population grew and moved westward, railroads were built and eventually spread to the farthest reaches of the state. The railroads meant life and prosperity for those communities through which they passed, and they provided Texas with a sorely needed network of dependable transportation. But many people were angered at the preferential treatment given railroads by the legislature (e.g., free public land) as well as by some of the questionable practices and tactics of these companies. Growing economic troubles and political dissatisfaction, chiefly among small farmers and shopkeepers, led to the election of Governor James Stephen Hogg in 1890, and to the beginning of the **Progressive Era** in Texas politics.[12]

After taking office, Hogg made good on a campaign promise when he persuaded the legislature to establish the Texas Railroad Commission. This act (which created one of the first state agencies in the nation to regulate an industry effectively and which the railroads vehemently opposed), was only one in a series of laws that sought to redress some of the grievances that had been festering among many

Progressive Era
A period of time (1890–1910) during which Texas enacted numerous laws designed to protect ordinary citizens and to prevent their being taken advantage of by large monopolies such as the railroads.

ordinary Texans. Acts regulating insurance companies, restricting child labor, and restructuring the state's prisons (sound familiar?) as well as local government soon followed. The kind of activism that produced these laws runs counter to the "leave me alone" approach that most Texans take toward government, but it is an undercurrent that manifests itself on occasion. These periods of activism often muddy our attempts to analyze the waters of Texas politics. In reality, Texas at this time was a state in transition: from country to city, from farm to factory, from the 19th century to the 20th. It should come as no surprise that its society and its politics would reflect the turmoil of this transition.

A Modern State

Big Oil followed the 20th century into Texas by ten days. On January 10, 1901, A. F. Lucas brought in a huge well south of Beaumont and the Spindletop field became the most productive in the world.[13] Although there were still plenty of cattle, lots of cowboys, and the wide vistas associated with the traditional images of a frontier state, Texas would never be the same.

The early decades of the century saw an accelerated movement of people from rural to urban areas. Cheap, readily available fuel powered a growing drive toward industrialization that moved Texas farther away from its agrarian past. After all, many people found that working in an oil refinery in Texas City was vastly better than following the north end of a southbound mule down a rock-filled furrow for 16 hours a day!

In the midst of this change, Ferguson leaped to the center of the political stage. In 1914, Jim Ferguson ("Farmer Jim") won the governorship. Ferguson claimed to represent "the boys who live back at the forks of the creek." Touting programs that benefited farmers and other rural residents, he enjoyed a successful first term and growing public approval. After his reelection in 1916, however, Farmer Jim made a fatal political mistake: he crossed political swords with the University of Texas. In a feud with faculty and administration, many of whom had supported his political opponents, Ferguson rashly used the line item veto to eliminate all funding for the university from the 1917 general appropriations bill (see the discussion of the line item veto in Chapter 7). Ferguson tried to make amends, but it was too late. After repassing the appropriation for University of Texas, the Texas House of Representatives charged the governor with 21 articles of impeachment and the Senate convicted him on ten counts, most related to the questionable diversion of state funds to the Temple State Bank, which Ferguson had helped establish. Farmer Jim thus became the only governor of Texas to be impeached and removed from office (though he tried to avoid this "honor" by attempting to resign prior to the delivery of the Senate's decision).[14]

Despite these antics, Ferguson remained enormously popular with rural Texans. After all, how many of those boys who lived back at the forks of the creek sent their kids to University of Texas? Barred from holding elected office, he nevertheless moved into the governor's mansion by way of the back door in 1924, when his wife Miriam ("Ma") ran for and won the governorship. Running on the slogan "Two Governors for the Price of One," she sought vindication for her husband. Although she is sometimes cited as a kind of pioneer for women in Texas politics, "Ma" was governor in name only. Jim continued to call the shots.

While Miriam Ferguson was largely a figurehead for her husband's thwarted political ambitions, a true leader in the fight for political equality waged by Texas women was Annie Webb Blanton. Ms. Blanton lobbied long and hard to help win the vote for women in this state and was active in politics for most of her life. She was the first woman to serve as president of the Texas State Teachers Association as well as the first woman to hold a statewide elected office in her capacity as state superintendent of public instruction from 1918 to 1922.

As the Fergusons' political soap opera, as well as other issues such as Prohibition and the resurgence of the Ku Klux Klan, diverted people's attention, Texans on the national political scene were quietly gaining substantial power. Seniority led to power in the U.S. Congress, and because Texas was essentially a one-party state, its congressmen and senators were routinely reelected until they died or retired. This guaranteed them long tenure and, after the Democratic electoral victories of 1932, a growing number of key committee chairs and leadership positions in both houses. Men like John Nance Garner, Sam Rayburn, and Lyndon Johnson followed this path to prominence and power.

The Depression hit Texas hard, largely due to the collapse of farm prices, and this hastened the exodus of many rural Texans to urban areas, where they sought work. However, new oil discoveries in east Texas and the Permian Basin of west Texas eased the economic pain somewhat, and jobs in defense plants created during and after World War II made many Texans financially secure by the 1950s. This cozy relationship between the federal government and Texas defense industries would continue to be an economic mainstay throughout the 20th century.

Unfortunately, this prosperity was not uniform. A legacy of social and economic racism meant that many Texans of color did not share life in the mainstream. *De jure* (legal) segregation and other discriminatory laws and social practices prevented many African Americans from gaining access to public education, housing, and other accommodations. Moreover, a long history of *de facto* (practiced) racial prejudice against Hispanics resulted in the denial of basic rights to these citizens. However, political activism among both Hispanic and African American Texans began to increase at this time, especially under the leadership of minority veterans who returned from the war unwilling to accept the segregated status quo of the past.

One of the most important leaders of the postwar movement for civil rights among Hispanics was Dr. Hector P. Garcia, who had fought in Europe during World War II. He organized Hispanic veterans who encountered barriers to receiving the financial and medical benefits that were due to all veterans. This group, the American GI Forum, was one of the first to boldly challenge the second-class status that had long been accorded Hispanic Texans. The Forum's clash in 1949 with a funeral home in Three Rivers, TX, over the home's refusal to bury a decorated Hispanic soldier who had been killed in the war brought national attention to the organization and its goals.

The 1960s witnessed the accession of the first self-acknowledged Texan to the White House when Vice President Lyndon Johnson succeeded John F. Kennedy after Kennedy's assassination in Dallas.[15] Ironically, Kennedy was in Texas trying to patch up a political feud among factions within the state's Democratic party. Johnson's tenure was controversial and was noted both for a wide-ranging agenda of domestic legislation (the programs of the Great Society) and for increasingly bitter opposition to the Vietnam War. Faced with a divided party, Johnson chose not to seek reelection in 1968, and retired to his Hill Country ranch.

The decades of the 1970s and 1980s in Texas were a veritable roller coaster of politics, economics, and demographics. Stunned by the Sharpstown Scandal of the early 1970s (which saw a number of elected state officials convicted or implicated in the stock fraud scheme of Houston financier Frank Sharp), Texas voters "threw the rascals out" in 1972.[16] Almost half of the members of the 1973 legislature were new, but reforms enacted as a result of the scandal were modest at best. By the mid-1970s, economics began to overshadow politics as the Arab oil embargo of 1973–1974 produced a tripling of oil prices worldwide and an incredible revenue windfall for the state of Texas. A large portion of the state's revenue was generated directly or indirectly by petroleum, and as oil prices rose, so did the state's income. The biggest "problem" facing the Texas legislature during this time was, "How are we going to spend all this money?"

Convinced that oil prices would hit $50 a barrel by the mid-1980s, Texans went crazy. Loans for oil drilling and production were as common and as readily available as prickly pear in south Texas. Profits from the "oil patch" fueled speculative real estate ventures. Many were making money hand over fist and there seemed to be no end in sight. People migrated to Texas by the thousands each week to get in on the action. However, as Sir Isaac Newton first taught, "What goes up must come down." When the Organization of Petroleum Exporting Countries (OPEC) failed to agree on a worldwide oil price structure in early 1984, Saudi Arabia flooded the market with oil. The result was a disaster for Texas. Oil prices plunged from $36 a barrel to $10 a barrel in 18 months. The state of Texas lost billions of dollars in revenue. Soon the Texas economy was in critical condition. The effect of defaulted energy loans rippled through the real estate market, bringing down banks and other lending institutions on a weekly basis. Unemployment in the energy sector soared. U-Haul trucks heading north on I-35 and I-45 represented an exodus of biblical proportions.

These upheavals in the economic world seared the Texas psyche greatly. And as if these events weren't enough, seismic activity began to register on the political Richter scale as well. In 1978, William P. Clements became the first Republican since E. J. Davis to win the governorship of Texas, thus effectively signaling the beginning of the end of one-party rule in Texas.[17] The 1980s saw more and more Republicans being elected each year, culminating in what many consider to be the arrival of two-party politics in Texas with the election of George H. W. Bush as president in 1988. The defeat of popular Democrat Ann Richards by Republican George W. Bush in the 1994 governor's race clearly showed a state moving quickly beyond two-party politics and toward GOP domination. This trend was subsequently confirmed in the landslide reelection of Bush as governor in 1998, as well as in the continuing Republican dominance of statewide elected offices in Texas in the elections of 2002 and 2006. In the state house and in urban counties, though, Democrats made notable gains in 2006 and 2008.

As you can see, the portrait of Texas that emerges from this admittedly selective historical survey is varied and complex. History has helped to make Texans proud, generous, abrasive, intolerant, resilient, persistent, loved, and hated—often at the same time! It has fostered conservatism as the hallmark of the state's politics, and yet it has also produced an occasional recurrence of populist reform. It has, in short, contributed many important pieces to the Texas mosaic.

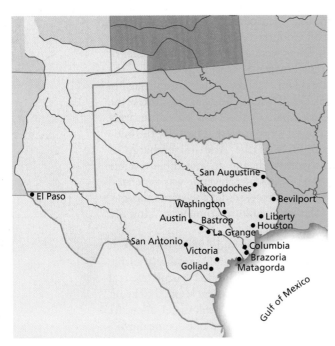

Tourist shops in Texas used to sell postcards of Texas crowding other states into the Atlantic and the Pacific Oceans. Size is a major factor in the geography of Texas.

The Geographic Pieces

That mosaic also includes pieces shaped by the land itself, and any understanding of this state must acknowledge the pivotal role that geography has played in the lives of Texans.[18]

Indeed, such geographic factors often have created political issues in and of themselves. Take, for example, the annexation of Texas by the United States. The sheer size of Texas at the time (the Republic had claimed all of present-day Texas, half of New Mexico, the Oklahoma panhandle, slivers of Kansas and Colorado, and a thin slice of Wyoming) led Congress to include a unique provision in the annexation agreement. Texas was granted the right to divide itself into as many as five states whenever it wished to do so. This provision, although of dubious constitutionality, clearly shows that Congress recognized geography as a political fact of life in Texas.

Approximately 267,000 square miles are contained within its borders. The state spans 773 miles east to west and stretches 801 miles north to south. The geographic center of Texas is situated near Mercury in northeast McCulloch County. (A marker on U.S. Highway 377 between Brownwood and Brady identifies the spot, and a local entrepreneur bought the adjacent five acres a number of years ago and began selling title to one-inch squares of land "deep in the heart of Texas"!) Within this vast area is an enormous variety of landform, climate, and vegetation. Because for most of human history, land has dictated lifestyle and livelihood, this geographic diversity has left an indelible mark on the people of Texas. It is possible to make some generalizations about these elements (for example, as you move from east to west across Texas, elevation increases and rainfall decreases), but Texas geography is better understood by examining it in smaller pieces.

The Gulf Lowlands

Texas is divided geographically by the Balcones Escarpment. Running roughly from Del Rio to San Antonio, then north through Austin to Waco, this ancient fault line separates the higher, drier areas to the west from the lower, more humid lands to the east. The eastern area, the Gulf Lowlands, contains four geographic subdivisions.

The Coastal Plains

These flat grasslands interwoven with coastal marshes extend in an arc along the Gulf of Mexico coast from near Corpus Christi to the Louisiana border. The Gulf coast itself is sheltered by a series of barrier islands (among them is Padre Island, which is popular among college students). These help create a fertile nursery for marine life, which in turn plays a large role in the coastal economy. The Coastal Plains receive adequate rainfall, and the generally treeless topography is ideally suited to raising rice, cotton, and grain sorghum crops. Here, too, are found significant oil and natural gas fields, especially in the highly urbanized reaches of the upper coast from Houston to Beaumont.

The Piney Woods

Lying north of the Coastal Plains, this area of forested, rolling hills receives the greatest amount of annual rainfall in Texas (nearly 60 inches per year in some areas). As the name indicates, pine trees predominate in this area, which is the westernmost extension of the great pine forests that once spread across the entire South. Timber products from the Piney Woods have long been an economic mainstay in east Texas, and since the 1930s, oil and gas production have been added to that equation. This area also contains the Big Thicket, a unique meeting place of several different ecosystems and a biological and botanical treasure trove now protected by federal law.

The Post Oaks and Prairies

As you move west out of the Piney Woods, you encounter a geographic amalgam of rolling prairies and wooded areas. Pine trees give way to oaks and hickories, and the rich soils of the area's Black and Grand Prairies are where most of the state's cotton was grown in the 19th century. Some oil is found in the region, but the Barnett Shale natural gas deposits are a major source of economic activity now. This increasingly urbanized area includes the cities of Austin, Dallas, Fort Worth, San Antonio, and Waco.

The South Texas Prairie

This southernmost geographic area of Texas is characterized by an arid climate and extensive brush country. One 19th-century settler complained that every bush he encountered was armed! As pointed out earlier, this area did give birth to the western cattle industry when Spanish settlers along the Rio Grande began raising cattle here in the mid-1700s. Today, agriculture plays a major role in the area's economy. An extended growing season (nearly 11 months in some places) combined with modern irrigation techniques have made the Winter Garden area around Crystal City as well as the lower Rio Grande Valley area major centers for the production of vegetable, fruit, and cotton crops. Over the years, the area has developed a booming tourist business, playing host annually to thousands of "snowbirds" (winter visitors from the Frost Belt states) and "birders" (bird watchers), as well as to an increasing number of retirees.

The Western Highlands

North and west of the Balcones Escarpment, the land becomes more rugged, more varied, and more arid. There are five geographic subdivisions in these Western Highlands.

The Edwards Plateau

This large area of central and southwest Texas is characterized by rugged limestone hills, dense thickets of mesquite and juniper, and spring-fed streams and rivers. The Edwards Plateau has never been a haven for farming, but sheep and goat ranches have fared well, along with some cattle ranches in the less hilly areas. In recent years, the cultivation of wine grapes and the breeding of exotic game animals have added diversity to the area's economic fabric.

The Llano Uplift

While limestone of relatively recent geologic vintage is the most common type of rock found in Texas, much more ancient granite and marble formations characterize the Llano Uplift.

This beautiful area of scenic hills, quiet valleys, and crystal clear rivers accounts for much of the state's solid mineral production (the state capitol in Austin is constructed of the area's distinctive pink granite). Although agriculture has always been a tough row to hoe in this part of Texas, German immigrants in the mid-19th century managed to turn some parts of the Llano Uplift into productive farm- and ranch lands, and this area of Texas remains the center of that German culture.

The Wichita Prairie

This rolling grassland rises in waves as you move westward. Good soils in the eastern portions of the area, sometimes aided by irrigation, produce wheat and cotton crops (Hall County, at the edge of the Panhandle, claims to be the "Cotton Capital" of Texas). The western portions of the Wichita Prairie are more rugged. It was here that many of the famous ranches from Texas history (such as the Four Sixes) were established.

The High Plains

Another escarpment, the Caprock, marks the beginning of this high, flat, grassy plateau that covers most of the Texas Panhandle and the South Plains. As noted earlier, this is where the buffalo roamed (and the deer and the antelope played!). Huge ranches in the late 1800s gave way to extensive irrigated as well as dry-land farming in the 20th century. Today, the rich soils of this high plateau, irrigated with water from the Ogallala underground aquifer, produce more cotton and grain crops (so-called cash crops) than any other area in Texas. Oil production is also found throughout the area, especially in the Permian Basin region around Midland and Odessa. The eventual depletion of the region's water resources presents a thorny and potentially contentious economic and political problem in both the near and the long term. For evidence of this, one needs look no further than the activities of multimillionaire T. Boone Pickens, who in recent years has begun buying up large tracts of water rights in West Texas in anticipation of future water shortages.

The West Texas Basins and Ranges

This huge area, lying generally west of the Pecos River, is the most sparsely populated, least developed part of the state. It contains the county with the smallest population (Loving, population 66) as well as the county with the greatest area (Brewster, 6,193 square miles). It also contains numerous mountain ranges (including Guadalupe Peak, Texas's highest point at 8,749 feet), wide elevated basin areas in between, and rainfall amounts in the 10-inch-per-year range. Although some irrigated farming takes place here, notably in the Stockton Plateau area, most of the area is desolate, wild, and starkly beautiful. Big Bend National Park and its neighbor Big Bend Ranch State Natural Area draw visitors from around the country, and the annual chili cook-off at Terlingua attracts visitors and participants from around the world. A new feature has begun to pop up on the seemingly endless horizons of the landscape in recent years. Wind-powered turbines capable of generating electricity without pollution have contributed to an economic rebirth in some areas of this otherwise desolate region. However, for those Texans who think a neighbor every 40 miles or so is close enough, this remains heaven.

The Economic Pieces

The First Stage—Take It

Until fairly recently, the economy of Texas was firmly grounded in activities that can best be described as extractive—that is, they involved taking something directly from the land. Specifically, Texas in the past largely depended on the three Cs (cattle, cotton, and crude)—representing livestock, cash crops, and petroleum products—to provide its basic economic underpinning. These have receded in importance today, but they were crucial during Texas's formative years.

Cattle came to Texas with the Spanish. Mission expeditions included herds of cattle and horses, and Indians living at the missions were taught the basic skills of animal husbandry. As previously noted, towns established by Spanish settlers along the Rio Grande River in the mid-1700s quickly became centers for a regional ranching culture throughout what is today south Texas. The social and political upheavals of the first half of the 19th century disrupted some of this ranching activity, but they didn't keep the cattle in this brush country from reproducing at a great rate. By the 1860s, it was said that there were six head of cattle for every one person in Texas.

This abundance, along with a growing American appetite for beef after the Civil War, made it possible for a lot of people in Texas to make a lot of money. Rounding up these ill-tempered, essentially wild animals, these early-day "ranchers" herded them to railheads in Kansas and elsewhere. If a steer in which you'd invested as little as $3 sold for around $30 at market, you didn't have to be Warren Buffett to figure out you could make a pile of money this way. Eventually, this cattle culture spread north and west onto the High Plains, following the demise of the Plains Indians and the buffalo. Texas cattle became the boom market in the second half of the 19th century, attracting desperately needed investment capital from all over the United States as well as from foreign countries. You could say that Texas rode these ornery animals to economic recovery following the Civil War.

The 19th century also saw the growth of agriculture as a primary economic factor throughout Texas. Crops, especially cotton, rivaled cattle and other livestock as economic mainstays. Cotton had also come to Texas with the Spanish, but it didn't gain a major foothold in the state's economy until the advent of Anglo settlement in the 1820s. These settlers came primarily from the Old South, and they brought that region's cotton culture with them and planted it deeply in the fertile soils of east central Texas and the Coastal Plains. After the Civil War, cotton production rose drastically, increasing by more than 1000 percent between 1860 and 1900. By the 1920s, cotton production had spread to the High Plains. There, ranching began to give way to both irrigated and dry-land farming, and today this area leads the state in the production of cash crops.

As stock raisers and farmers moved west, the railroads followed them and soon became a major agent for the state's economic growth. Thousands of miles of track were laid in Texas between 1860 and 1900, and by the turn of the century, Texas contained more railroad miles than any other state. This expansion in turn fueled the exploitation of the east Texas forests and gave rise to an immense timber industry.

The last of the great extractive economies to develop in Texas was oil. A few oil wells were drilled in Texas after the Civil War (the first at Melrose near Nacogdoches in 1866), and a fairly profitable field was developed at Corsicana in the early 1890s. But it was the discovery of the huge Spindletop field near Beaumont early in 1901 that signaled a new economic era for Texas. There, the drilling crew had stopped to take a break when, suddenly, a tremendous explosion shook the earth. Mud, rocks, drill pipe, and derrick parts shot high into the air, followed by oil, oil, and more oil. So forceful was the flow that it took workers almost two weeks to cap the well. Within a year, Spindletop had become the most productive oil field in the world.

The rapidly expanding automobile market and the shift to oil-fired (later diesel-powered) locomotives fed a growing demand for oil and its products. Other major oil fields were soon being discovered and developed all across the state, and these fields would lay the groundwork for a major shift in the Texas economy. It wasn't long before refineries appeared, particularly along the Gulf Coast where the Houston Ship Channel was in full operation by 1925. Neither was it long before Texas was home to industry leaders in the realm of oil field equipment. New technologies in oil exploration seemed

The Spindletop gusher ushered in a new economic era in Texas. How might the state have been affected if not for its vast oil resources?

to come about as frequently as did the gushers, major cities sprang up where only sleepy towns had been before, and economic opportunity seemed endless. State government came to depend increasingly on oil and the revenue derived from it as a major budgetary foundation. Oil and Texas seemed like a match made in heaven.

The Second Stage—Make It

Fueled by this oil boom, the Texas economy in the middle years of the 20th century began to expand beyond its agrarian origins. By the late 1930s, manufacturing was becoming a more important part of the state's economic picture. This expansion went into full swing in the 1940s with the advent of World War II and the ensuing growth of defense manufacturing in Texas. By the end of the decade, more Texans than ever before were employed either directly or indirectly by the myriad defense contractors across the state.

After the war, Texas became a leading manufacturer of petroleum-based chemicals and compounds such as plastics and synthetic rubber. Steel production and metal smelting began to assume a larger role in the state's economy and by the early 1970s, electronics manufacturing, led by such industry pioneers as Texas Instruments, was becoming a major economic player in Texas. Once again, the future seemed bright and limitless.

The Third Stage—Serve It

The 1980s were an economic disaster for Texas. The collapse of the oil industry, coupled with severe cuts in defense spending brought about by the end of the Cold War, left Texas reeling and grasping for any kind of economic future. But the 1990s saw the Lone Star State make a comeback, and as Texas entered the new millennium, economic optimism was widespread. By most measures of economic vitality, the last decade of the 20th century had been a good one for Texas. The state outstripped the national average in such areas as job growth, income growth, and consumer confidence. The fastest-growing segment of this revitalized economy was the service sector, as reflected in such key indicators as retail and wholesale trade and general business services. A booming entertainment industry, an increasingly important film community, as well as expanding tourism also contributed to this trend. At the end of the decade, service-related employment accounted for the lion's share of the state's total nonfarm jobs.

However, by early 2001, there were signs that this unprecedented period of economic growth in both Texas and the United States was coming to a close. Terrorist attacks, corporate misdeeds such as the Enron fiasco, and a questionable government regulatory climate all combined to make the economic outlook decidedly grimmer. Eventually, investor confidence in the once-invincible stock market began to evaporate, and by the fall of 2008, the subprime mortgage crisis triggered a worldwide collapse of financial institutions the like of which had not been seen since at least the Savings and Loan debacle of the 1980s, if not the Great Depression.

As the first decade of the 21st century comes to a close, members of the Texas business community, public policy makers, and the people of Texas continue to confront the daunting task of rebuilding confidence in the economy while navigating its treacherous waters. The Texas legislature will continue to confront both an erratic flow of state revenue and a need for long-term revitalization and redirection of the state's economy, yet experience has shown that simple answers to these challenges do not abound. For example, the persistent mantra of "deregulation" that echoed through the halls of Congress and the Texas legislature during the 1990s and the early years of the 21st century proved to be quite alluring, but has resulted in public policies that have been mixed. One need look no farther than the deregulation of the electric service industry to see controversy such policies can create. Add to this reality the increasingly interrelated and global aspects of the state's economy, and Texans face still more and greater challenges and opportunities. The cold, hard fact of 21st century economic reality is that states and even nations can no longer exist and, perhaps more importantly, make policy in an economic vacuum.

Most scholars agree that the key to future economic growth in Texas and the United States will lie in developing an educational infrastructure that can meet the demands of a constantly evolving, 21st century economy. The most important product of such an infrastructure will be an educated (not merely skilled) employee, able to adapt to a rapidly changing, highly competitive, increasingly global economic reality. As a college student reading this textbook, you can look forward to changing careers several times over the course of your work life and, in all likelihood, to retiring from a job that does not even exist at this time!

The Demographic Pieces

The picture of Texas becomes even clearer when you examine the various peoples collectively called "Texans." The population of this state can be analyzed in terms of both size and diversity. Let's look first at the number of people in Texas.[19]

Population Size

According to estimates of the Texas State Data Center, 25,373,947 people will call Texas their home in 2010. That figure will keep Texas the second most populous state in the union, trailing only California, and represents an almost 22 percent increase over the official 2000 Census total.

Population Growth

Unlike some states in the Northeast and Midwest, Texas has enjoyed continuous growth since the first federal census was taken here in 1850. In fact, the percentage of growth each decade has never been less than 10 percent, and during the "take the money and run" period of 1970–1980, population in the Lone Star State grew at a rate in excess of 27 percent.

Much of that decade's growth was due to people moving to Texas. The 1980s saw a different pattern emerge. Growth continued at a substantial pace, but most of the thrust of that growth came in the first half of the decade before the oil bust of 1984–1986. During the second half of the decade, growth slowed considerably (less than 1 percent increase in 1987–1988, for example), and only a substantial natural increase (Texans having little Texans) was able to offset out-migration. This trend has now been reversed and the 1990s saw a return to a more robust pattern of growth. Thus, whether by natural increase or in-migration, most demographers are

TABLE 1.1 Texas Population Projections *(Scenario 2000–2007)*

YEAR	TOTAL	ANGLO	BLACK	HISPANIC	OTHER
2000	20,851,820	11,074,716	2,421,653	6,669,666	685,785
2005	22,973,810	11,281,608	2,665,825	8,129,049	897,328
2010	25,373,947	11,441,595	2,925,751	9,847,852	1,158,749
2015	28,015,550	11,555,667	3,191,394	11,793,119	1,475,370
2020	30,858,449	11,612,122	3,447,896	13,940,031	1,858,400
2025	33,936,986	11,604,901	3,691,742	16,321,616	2,318,727
2030	37,285,486	11,525,269	3,922,900	18,973,424	2,863,893
2035	40,927,000	11,383,525	4,140,279	21,900,808	3,502,388
2040	44,872,038	11,196,427	4,341,627	25,090,745	4,243,239

SOURCE: Texas State Data Center and Office of the State Demographer, *Projected Population 2000–2040* (San Antonio, TX: University of Texas at San Antonio, 2008). http://txsdc.utsa.edu/tpepp/2008projections/2008_txpoprj_txtotnum.php.

confident in projecting steady, sustained population growth for Texas well into this century (see Table 1.1).

This growth will not be uniform throughout the state, however. For several decades now, a number of Texas's 254 counties have lost population, with most of the losses recorded in counties west of I-35. Even in those west Texas counties that did not lose population, the pattern of "growth" has often been stagnant at best. It appears that the hardest-hit counties in terms of population loss have been those that have depended heavily on agriculture, oil, or both. However, some areas in and to the west of the Fort Worth–Dallas Metroplex saw a resurgence in energy exploration at mid-decade (primarily in the form of extensive drilling for natural gas in the Barnett Shale formation), and continuing high prices for oil products worldwide may continue to drive this venerable economic engine for a while longer.

Population Distribution

The popular image of Texas around the world includes the notion that all Texans live on huge ranches with wide-open spaces and that they herd cattle when they're not drilling for oil. This vision, reinforced and exaggerated in film and literature, flies in the face of reality.

In fact, the closest most Texans come to oil is when they have their car's changed at the 10-Minute Lube down the street, and their most direct contact with cattle is when they order a Whataburger with cheese (with jalapeños and no onions). Of course, the biggest fallacy in this image is that of Texas as a rural state. In reality, more than 80 percent of the state's population resides in metropolitan areas, and almost 58 percent of all the people in Texas can be found in ten urban counties (those with a projected 2010 population in excess of 500,000; see Table 1.2). The fact that Texas is the only state with three cities (Houston, San Antonio, and Dallas) among the ten largest in the nation gives further evidence of its essentially urban character, and recent census data note that the Dallas–Fort Worth metropolitan area is the fastest-growing such area in the nation.

Because the overwhelming majority of Texans live in cities and suburbs, we can expect the political agenda to be dominated by issues vital to these areas. In fact, a complaint commonly voiced by state legislators from rural districts is that the needs of their constituents are increasingly overlooked in the formulation of public policy. The issues with which Texas must deal in the future—transportation and how these needs will be addressed (mass transit? toll roads?) and the related problems of air

TABLE **1.2** **Projected Population of Largest (500,000 or more) Urban Counties in Texas, 2010**

COUNTY	POPULATION
Harris	4,096,052
Dallas	2,435,919
Tarrant	1,825,548
Bexar	1,636,642
Travis	992,773
Collin	842,364
Hidalgo	793,137
El Paso	773,125
Denton	706,103
Fort Bend	577,444
TOTAL	14,679,107
Texas	25,373,947

SOURCE: Texas State Data Center and Office of the State Demographer, *2008 Population Projections: Texas Counties* (San Antonio, TX: University of Texas at San Antonio, 2008). http://txsdc.utsa.edu/tpepp/2008projections/2008_txpoprj_txtotnum.php.

pollution, crime, and juvenile violence; as well as the continued deterioration of big-city school systems—are all related to some degree to a highly urbanized population.

Population Diversity

The people of Texas are not only many in number, they are diverse in their ethnic and cultural heritage. You could spend an entire semester studying the scores of such groups found in Texas, but time and space constraints force us to look specifically at only the three largest of these: Anglos, Hispanics, and African Americans.

ANGLO TEXANS By the middle of the first decade of the 21st century, Texas had reached a demographic milestone: *No* ethnic group constituted a majority of the state's population. The largest group of Texans in the population remains (for the moment) Anglos, with the 2010 population estimates showing some 45 percent of the state's population in this category. However, that percentage has been steadily decreasing over the last several decades (the 1980 population was 68 percent Anglo; the 1990 population, 56 percent) and projections for the future indicate a continuation of that pattern. Demographers estimate that by the year 2040 Anglos will account for about 25 percent of the whole population. While this group has traditionally dominated the political (and economic and social) life of Texas, these statistics seem to indicate that, in the future, Anglos will have to share this control with other Texans.

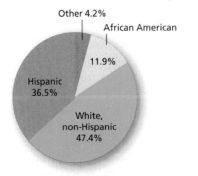

2008 Texas Population.

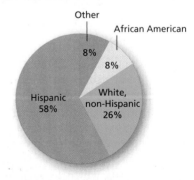

Estimated Texas Population, 2040.

HISPANIC TEXANS The second largest ethnic group in Texas, and the largest and fastest-growing minority group in the state, is Hispanic Texans. In 2010, it is estimated that 39 percent of the state's population will be Hispanic, the result of a phenomenal growth rate over the course of the previous decades. Much of the Hispanic population lives in the state's urban areas, and if you were to draw a line on a Texas map from Victoria to Odessa, a majority of the people living south and west of the line would be Hispanic.

Politically, Hispanics were present at the creation of Texas. In fact, it is ironic that the only "native Texans" to sign the Texas Declaration of Independence were José Antonio Navarro and Francisco Ruiz. Until fairly recently, Hispanic Texans have been generally excluded from the political process, but that is changing. The elections of Raul Gonzalez to the Texas Supreme Court and Dan Morales to the office of Attorney General of Texas were earlier portents. In particular, Morales, a former state legislator, seemed destined for a much larger role in Texas politics. However, his surprise announcement that he would leave office after his term expired in 1998 dealt a blow to those who had looked to him as the future standard-bearer for Hispanics in the political arena. His failure to win the Democratic Party's gubernatorial nomination against fellow Hispanic (and political novice) Tony Sanchez in 2002, and his subsequent legal woes brought to an end what appeared to be a bright political future. On the other hand, Sanchez's candidacy created a historic political contest in Texas. The first Hispanic to win a major party nomination to the office of governor, this Laredo businessman engaged in one of the most expensive campaigns in Texas history. His candidacy likely signals changes to come in Texas. In 2008, State Representative Rick Noriega became the Democratic Party nominee for U.S. Senate, and although he lost to incumbent John Cornyn, no doubt he will be followed by more and more Hispanics in the coming years. By 2040, Hispanics will constitute a solid majority (56 percent) of the state's population. These changes seem certain to be reflected in both the electoral politics and the public policy debates of Texas.

WHAT CAN YOU DO?

If you really would like to find out more about the rich cultural heritage of Texas, there's no better place to visit than the Institute of Texan Cultures in San Antonio. Built as part of the 1968 Hemisfair Exposition, the Institute operates now under the auspices of the University of Texas and showcases the dozens of ethnic and cultural groups that have helped make up the Texas mosaic. And if you like music, don't miss the Institute's Texas Folklife Festival, held each summer on the third weekend in June. For more information on this Texas treasure, call (210) 458-2300 or go online at http://www.texancultures.utsa.edu.

AFRICAN AMERICAN TEXANS The third largest ethnic group in Texas is composed of African American Texans. In 2010, black Texans will represent 11 percent of the state's population, a percentage that is little changed from 1980. Much of the state's African American population is found in the eastern half of Texas, with highest concentrations in southeast and north central Texas. Like Hispanics, a majority of African American Texans live in urban areas. Unlike Hispanics, however, the African American portion of the state's population is expected to decrease somewhat (to 10 percent in 2040) over the next several decades.

African American Texans have also been subjected to political, economic, and legal discrimination (see the discussion of voting barriers in Chapter 3). Yet this pattern is slowly changing. When Judge Morris Overstreet was elected to the Texas Court of Criminal Appeals, he became the second African American to hold a statewide elective office in Texas. Judge Louis Sturns had been appointed to the same position a year earlier; Overstreet beat him when the seat went up for election.

Notable public policy makers like Sylvester Turner, a state representative from Houston, and Royce West, a state senator from Dallas, have begun to play a more visible role in Texas politics, building on the accomplishments of predecessors like Mickey Leland, Barbara Jordan, and Wilhelmina Delco. The nomination of former Dallas mayor Ron Kirk as the Democratic candidate for the U.S. Senate in 2002 was unprecedented in Texas political annals. In the state's first general election of the 21st century, a black Texan headed a major party ticket, something unheard of in previous generations. On the Republican side, Railroad Commissioner Michael Williams has positioned himself well for a future run at higher office, and Chief Justice Wallace Jefferson and Justice Dale Wainwright serve on the Texas Supreme Court.

OTHER TEXANS All other ethnic groups in Texas will account for approximately 4 percent of the state's population in 2010. This amounts to a significant increase over the last two decades, and census projections indicate that by 2040, these other Texans will represent 9 percent of the people in the state. Within this diverse group, Asian American Texans are growing in significant numbers. While we may lump these groups together for statistical purposes, the richness and variety of their cultures have made important contributions to what we as Texans are today.

Putting It Together: The Picture of Texas

Modern Texas is truly a multicultural state. As proof of its extraordinary diversity, no single prevailing culture or single dominant theme could serve to encompass the entire population. Yet even though this great mosaic called "Texas" was created by the hands of many people, we can identify some consistent similarities in the fabric from which it has been fashioned.

Political Culture

For years, historians and political scientists have grappled with the concept of identifying and distinguishing the political nuances that exist among the states. They knew, as do we, that Texas is "different" from, say, New York. Although we are all Americans in terms of nationality, most Texans embrace an outlook on politics and government that is part southern, part western, and in many respects unique. Throughout this book you will find evidence that Texas is, as the Texas Tourism Board commercials once proclaimed, "like a whole other country." The differences among the various states can best be explained in terms of variations in political culture, which take into account the many factors that make a group of people distinctive in the way they talk, act, and approach politics.

political culture
The attitudes, beliefs, and behavior that shape an area's politics; often a product of various historical and social factors unique to that area.

Political culture, then, can be defined as the attitudes, beliefs, and behaviors that shape how people act politically. Interestingly, the political cultures of Texas have not changed much since the creation of the state. This is significant when you consider the explosive population growth and the tremendous economic and social changes this state has experienced in the past century. It tells us that political culture is a fundamental part of the makeup of a people, and that as newcomers arrive, they tend to adopt the prevailing political culture to which they are exposed. Thus, to understand any group of people, we have to understand their political culture. In a classic study of American politics, political scientist Daniel J. Elazar identified three predominant political cultures in the United States—individualistic, traditionalistic, and moralistic. Elazar's assessments are widely accepted by political scientists, and they help us gain insight into that strange and wonderful creature, the Texan.[20]

INDIVIDUALISTIC The individualistic political culture is rooted in the notions of individualism, independence, limited government, and free enterprise. This component of the Texas "psyche" emphasizes the traits associated with rugged self-reliance that many non-Texans have in mind when they think of this state. Politics is regarded as a necessary evil and politicians as generally arrogant and self-serving leeches. This doesn't mean that Texans are not a charitable people, because charity and a willingness to help your neighbor were integral parts of the frontier experience. Rather, it means that, in the minds of many Texans, the government should have no part in redistributing wealth and should generally leave folks alone. For many Texans, helping others should be done by the private sector, not governmental bureaucracies. The iconic (although largely mythical) image of the cowboy in many ways captures the deep-seated notion of individual achievement and self-sufficiency that is felt by many to be at the heart of what it means to be a Texan.

Examples of this individualistic political culture abound. In fact, this is likely the most widely manifested political culture in the Lone Star State. Texas is the only state that was an independent nation. The state's constitution reflects the general distrust of government held by the framers. Legislators' salaries are low and the governor's office is relatively weak. Even the judicial system is fragmented, presumably to prevent a single court from possessing too much power. There is, moreover, a kind of contrarian streak among Texans that such individualism breeds, which manifests itself occasionally, as in 2006 when not one but *two* independent candidates for governor made their way onto the ballot. This culture has often nurtured economic opportunity and individual initiative, but it has also engendered an attitude that assumes whatever is good for the business community is good for the greater community that is Texas. In short, Texas government is set up to be limited and to have as little impact on individual prerogative as possible.

TRADITIONALISTIC The traditionalistic political culture emphasizes maintaining the prevailing order and is extremely resistant to change. The role of government is to preserve the status quo and to refrain from innovation. Moreover, leadership tends to be restricted to a privileged few, and participation by ordinary citizens is discouraged. Politics tends to be played out in a decidedly social context, with ties among "old" families often determining the power structure. In such an atmosphere, corruption can easily flourish and often does. Moreover, the traditionalistic culture makes it very easy to ignore real human needs, which can in part account for the fact that Texas regularly ranks at or near the top in such dubious social policy categories as high school dropout rates, incidence of teenage pregnancy, and number of children living in poverty. These data mirror the reluctance of Texans to accept change of almost any kind.

Texas was one of the last states to introduce legalized gambling in any form and one of the last to abolish the "blue laws," which prevented individuals from purchasing a wide array of items, ranging from building materials to panty hose, on Sundays. Texas laws have also reflected this traditionalism by limiting participation in the political process in general and by attempting to keep minorities "in their place" through the use of such devices as the poll tax and the white primary. And even though Democrats ruled Texas unchallenged for 100 years, make no mistake about it—this state is and always has been conservative. Traditions and customs rightly are held in high regard by all cultures, but for Texans they often become sacred. It wouldn't be an exaggeration to say the seven most important words for many a Texan are "We just don't do things that way!"

MORALISTIC The moralistic political culture derives its basic attitudes toward politics and, in a larger sense, toward society from the viewpoint that human cultures and communities are a commonwealth. That is, our society and its component parts are interrelated, interconnected, and integrated. Because of this attitude, the role of government in a moralistic political culture is one of activism and that of politics one of inclusion. Citizens are encouraged to involve themselves in their own governance, and a plethora of activist political organizations is usually the hallmark of this culture. Along these same lines, the moralistic culture emphasizes public good over private gain and is therefore quite intolerant of governmental or political corruption. This culture is usually open to new ideas and forms of public participation.

The foregoing outline of Texas and its people clearly shows little indication of the kind of attitudes that would incubate a moralistic political culture. While this culture finds expression in many New England states as well as in certain areas of the upper Midwest (think Minnesota and Wisconsin), its basic elements simply do not fit comfortably with the beliefs and mores that characterize Texas. Some might argue that a nascent moralistic culture can be seen in places like Austin, but the fact is that the attitudes, habits, and behaviors of Texans clearly manifest themselves as expressions of the traditionalistic and, especially, the individualistic cultures at the expense of the moralistic.

Political Culture and Policy

Texas's individualistic political culture manifests itself in the state's public policy. Texas provides lower levels of public assistance than almost any other state and even these limited benefits are difficult to obtain. Only three states have a lower level of union membership than Texas[21] Voter turnout is relatively low, particularly in local elections that have the most profound impact on individual communities. Texans are likely to be "joiners" only when it comes to church, the National Rifle Association, and in support of the local professional sports franchise, with the latter significantly influenced by the fortunes of the current season. The strong "go it alone" bent to Texas culture oddly gives government greater latitude, because the average Texan pays only limited attention to things political.

At the same time, the traditionalistic cultural influences have shown some signs of waning. Texas politicians and voters have shown an increased willingness to consider new ideas, solutions, and compromises as they address difficult political challenges. The selection of Joe Straus as Speaker of the House in 2009 was a significant departure from the usual practice of electing an entrenched insider to that post.

The Changing Face of Texas

As we write this (and as you read it) Texas continues its kaleidoscopic evolution as a society and a culture. Yet as we have seen, it probably is simplistic to speak of "a" culture when referring to this state and its people. Diversity is the hallmark of our history, our geography, our economy, and our population. Even when a certain veneer of uniformity is applied to Texas, as is the case when we somewhat arbitrarily describe its political culture as individualistic and traditionalistic, we can nevertheless rub through such a layer and uncover the rich mosaic that underlies it. And while our general political culture will continue to reflect the importance of both the individual and tradition, new people and new opportunities will challenge the way things have been. Texas politics will mirror these realities and challenges in the coming years.

Lone Star Politics: A User's Guide

Throughout this text, we have created several features that will help foster understanding of and participation in Texas politics. The Texas Mosaics highlight various people and groups who have had a profound impact on shaping the state. The Texas Constitution: A Closer Look ties a portion of Texas's governing document into the applicable chapter. Likewise, Inside the Federalist System highlights how the state fits into the broader federal system. The My Turn essays invite Texas political practitioners to give their take on what they do and how they do it. What Can You Do features suggest ways you can become involved in Texas politics. In addition, you will find the entire U.S. Constitution, and major portions of the Texas Constitution, in the appendix at the end of the book. We have also provided key terms, chapter review questions and critical thinking questions at the end of each chapter.

Summary

Politics is who gets what, when, and how. Government is composed of public institutions acting with authority to mandate the collection of revenue and to allocate valuable things for society. Understanding the politics and government of Texas requires an understanding of the many diverse elements (the mosaic) of our society. The history of Texas is marked by conflict between tradition and change. Our economy has reflected that same kind of conflict, as Texas has evolved from a sparsely populated, rural, agrarian state to a large, urban, postindustrial, service-oriented conglomeration that isn't quite sure where it's headed. Our land is as varied in form and feature as the people who inhabit it. Our political culture values individuality and tradition, yet faces a future where interdependence and change are increasingly the measure of our society. Working out the tensions created by this fascinating mosaic lies at the heart of Texas politics.

Chapter Test

1. According to Harold Lasswell, politics can be described as
   a. the act of governing.
   b. who gets what, when, and how.
   c. mandating revenue collection.
   d. institutions that allocate valuable things.

2. The earliest Europeans to explore the area that is Texas were
   a. French.
   b. Dutch.
   c. Spanish.
   d. English.

3. The primary result of the La Salle expedition to Texas was to
   a. establish French control over Texas for the next 100 years.
   b. allow Spain to conquer all of Louisiana and control the Mississippi River.
   c. provide an opportunity for English settlers to arrive in Texas in the 1790s.
   d. cause Spain to establish a permanent presence in Texas.

4. The first person to actually settle Anglo Americans in Texas was
   a. Stephen F. Austin.
   b. Phillip Nolan.
   c. Moses Austin.
   d. Sam Houston.

5. One result of Reconstruction in Texas was to make Texas a
   a. one-party state dominated by Republicans for the next 100 years.
   b. highly competitive two-party state for the next 100 years.
   c. state where neither major party was able to control elected offices.
   d. one-party state dominated by Democrats for the next 100 years.

6. During the 1980s, more and more _____ began to be elected in Texas.
   a. Democrats
   b. Libertarians
   c. Republicans
   d. Populists

7. The Texas geographic subregion that has an 11-month growing season is the
   a. Piney Woods.
   b. High Plains.
   c. Llano Uplift.
   d. South Texas Prairie.

8. According to official U.S. Census Bureau data, Texas ranks _____ in population.
   a. first
   b. second
   c. third
   d. fourth

9. By 2040, _____ are projected to make up 56 percent of the Texas population.
   a. Anglos
   b. African Americans
   c. Asians
   d. Hispanics

10. The political culture that seems to be the most widespread in Texas is the
    a. individualist culture.
    b. traditionalistic culture.
    c. moralistic culture.
    d. legalistic culture.

Answers: 1. b 2. c 3. d 4. a 5. d 6. c 7. c 8. b 9. d 10. a

Critical Thinking Questions

1. If Texas is a "mosaic" made up of many different elements, show how various events from the state's history reflect that mosaic.

2. Discuss the evolution of the Texas economy and show the direction such evolution may take in the 21st century.

3. Discuss the various types of political culture found in the United States and in Texas and explain how these also reflect elements of the Texas mosaic.

Key Terms

government, **p. 4**
mosaic, **p. 4**
political culture, **p. 28**
politics, **p. 3**

Progressive Era, **p. 14**
Reconstruction, **p. 13**
Republic of Texas, **p. 10**

Notes

1. Harold Lasswell, *Politics: Who Gets What, When, How* (New York: Meridian Books, 1958). This is the classic definition of politics given by Professor Lasswell, one of the giants of 20th century American political science.

2. "Alvar Nuñez Cabeza de Vaca," in Ron Tyler, Editor-in-Chief, *The New Handbook of Texas* (Austin: The Texas State Historical Association, 1996), Vol. I, pp. 882–883.

3. "Coronado Expedition," in Tyler, *The New Handbook of Texas*, Vol. II, pp. 328–329.

4. "René-Robert Cavelier, Sieur de La Salle," in Tyler, *The New Handbook of Texas*, Vol. IV, p. 82.

5. William C. Davis, *Lone Star Rising: The Revolutionary Birth of the Texas Republic* (New York: Free Press, 2004), pp. 58–59.

6. Ibid., pp. 202–03.

7. Ibid., pp. 270–272.

8. "Annexation," in Tyler, *The New Handbook of Texas*, Vol. I, pp. 192–193.

9. "Civil War," in Tyler, *The New Handbook of Texas*, Vol. II, p. 121.

10. "Edmund Jackson Davis," in Tyler, *The New Handbook of Texas*, Vol. II, pp. 526–527.

11. "Ranching," in Tyler, *The New Handbook of Texas*, Vol. V, pp. 430–431.

12. " James Stephen Hogg," in Tyler, *The New Handbook of Texas*, Vol. III, pp. 652–653.

13. "Spindletop Oilfield," in Tyler, *The New Handbook of Texas*, Vol. VI, pp. 29–30.

14. The most thorough account of the Ferguson impeachment and conviction can be found in Bruce Rutherford, *Ferguson: The Impeachment of Jim Ferguson* (Austin, TX: Eakin Press, 1983).

15. "Lyndon Baines Johnson," in Tyler, *The New Handbook of Texas*, Vol. III, pp. 958–959.

16. A meticulous presentation of the Sharpstown Scandal and its aftermath can be found in Charles Deaton, *The Year They Threw the Rascals Out* (Austin, TX: Shoal Creek Publishers, 1973).

17. "Republican Party," in Tyler, *The New Handbook of Texas*, Vol. V, p. 535.

18. The following discussion of Texas geography is based on Keene Ferguson, *The Texas Landscape: The Geographic Provinces of Texas* (Austin, TX: Texas Mosaics Publishing, 1986).

19. The population figures in this section are derived from the Texas State Data Center and Office of the State Demographer, *Projected Population 2000–2040* (San Antonio, TX: University of Texas at San Antonio, 2008). http://txsdc.utsa.edu/tpepp/2008projections /2008_txpoprj_txtotnum.php. The model used reflects growth rates that occurred between 2000 and 2007.

20. Daniel J. Elazar, *American Federalism: A View from the States*, 3rd ed. (New York: Harper and Row, 1984).

21. U.S. Bureau of Labor Statistics, *Union Members in 2008*, (January 28, 2009).

Federalism and the Texas Constitution

2

Texas's first state constitution, as a part of the Mexican Federation.

1827   1836

The Constitution of the Republic of Texas is modeled after the U.S. Constitution.

By the end of this chapter on federalism and the Texas Constitution, you should be able to . . .

★ Explain how state power is constrained by federalism and by the national and state constitutions.

★ Analyze how the national government has gained power within the federalism equation.

★ Explain why state constitutions tend to be long and restrictive.

★ Differentiate between constitutional law and legislative law.

★ Differentiate among the seven constitutions of Texas.

★ Analyze how the current document is partially a reaction to the previous Reconstruction-era document and partially a return to pre–Civil War policies.

★ Explain why those who benefit from the current constitution will work to make comprehensive reform difficult.

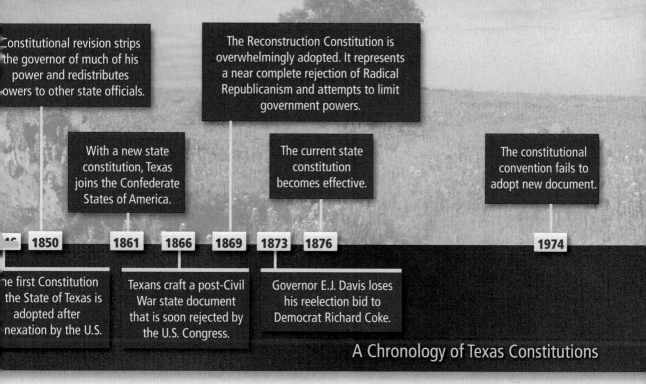

Constitutional revision strips the governor of much of his power and redistributes powers to other state officials.

The Reconstruction Constitution is overwhelmingly adopted. It represents a near complete rejection of Radical Republicanism and attempts to limit government powers.

With a new state constitution, Texas joins the Confederate States of America.

The current state constitution becomes effective.

The constitutional convention fails to adopt new document.

1850 — 1861 — 1866 — 1869 — 1873 — 1876 — 1974

The first Constitution the State of Texas is adopted after annexation by the U.S.

Texans craft a post-Civil War state document that is soon rejected by the U.S. Congress.

Governor E.J. Davis loses his reelection bid to Democrat Richard Coke.

A Chronology of Texas Constitutions

We know that the convention has relatively but a few able men in its composition . . .

—SEPTEMBER 16, 1875, *SAN ANTONIO HERALD*
ON THE DELEGATES TO THE 1875 CONSTITUTIONAL CONVENTION

Texans like to do things their own way. It's part of our state's individualistic and traditionalistic nature. Texans want to generate their own answers to issues such as crime and punishment, speed limits, and allocation of university funds. Most Texans believe that if a majority of voters agree on an issue, that view should prevail. In reality, there are two major constraints on pure majority rule. First, Texas is part of the federal system and national government actions often limit the state's options. Second, both the U.S. and Texas constitutions limit the power of the majority.

Federalism

federalism
A constitutional sharing of powers between the national and state governments.

In the United States, states and the national government share power under a unique structure called **federalism**. Federalism is a dual system of government. Two systems operate concurrently, one at the national level, another within each of the states. Both levels have authority over their citizens, meaning that you have to obey both the laws of the United States and of the state of Texas, as well as the ordinances of local governments, which are technically subdivisions of the state. At first glance—and maybe at second as well—there appears to be a duplication of many government functions. Both the state and national governments have their own executive, judicial, and legislative branches. The president serves as the nation's chief executive; the governor holds the equivalent office in Texas. The U.S. House and U.S. Senate comprise the national Congress, while the state house and state senate serve as the Texas legislature. The national government and the state each have their own court systems. The national court system considers alleged violations of national law and handles civil suits involving residents of different states. Texas courts handle state criminal matters and civil suits in which both parties are from Texas.

Federalism Applied

Federalism is one of the most confusing, and least understood, aspects of American government. Citizens often find it difficult to distinguish between national and state functions. Many are unaware of the dual legislative systems, often lumping congress members and legislators together in one large pot. It doesn't help matters that the U.S. Congress and Texas legislature often deal with the same basic issues, such as crime control and welfare policies.

Originally, the delineation of duties between the national and state governments was clearer. The national government dealt with problems of national importance. Military and foreign policy issues are to this day the primary responsibility of the U.S. government. Issues with a larger local impact, such as education and aid to the poor, have traditionally fallen under the control of the state. Although the national government has taken a considerable role in setting standards for education, most decision making and funding come from the state and local levels. For all the campaign rhetoric about the importance of education that you hear from candidates for the president and U.S. Congress, 85 percent of funding for the Texas education system is generated within the state. It is not the same in social services. Most of what Texas spends on aid to the poor comes from federal grant programs, with the national government setting minimum standards of service that the state must provide.

An important aspect of our American system of federalism is that the delineation of power—who does what—is set out in the U.S. Constitution. This is what makes federalism "federalism," so to speak. In theory, the only way to alter that balance of power is to change either the Constitution or the U.S. Supreme Court's interpretation of that document. In practice, the equation involves other factors, which we'll discuss later.

Nonetheless, federalism is a departure from the more traditional unitary or central government, where power is concentrated at the national level. Under a centralized system, the national legislature can lend power to the local level, but it retains the authority to take this power back. Real power, then, never leaves the central government. That's an important distinction. Under federalism, the U.S. government can't wake up one day and do away with the state of Texas.

Constitutional Limits on States

In our system, many of the limits on states are found in Article I, Section 10 of the U.S. Constitution (see U. S. Constitutional Limits on State Power). States, for example, are prohibited from levying taxes on goods arriving from other states. A state may not enter into treaties on its own, neither may it engage in war independently unless it is attacked. States cannot coin money.

Article IV establishes how states must treat one another. For example, when an accused or convicted felon escapes from Texas to Oklahoma, Oklahoma is obligated to return the fugitive to Texas. Likewise, Texas must give full faith and credit to civil proceedings emanating from Oklahoma. A person cannot skip from state to state in order to avoid paying civil damages (see U.S. Constitutional Provisions Regarding Interstate Relations). Other significant limits are found in the constitutional amendments and will be discussed later.

U.S. Constitutional Limits on State Power

ARTICLE I

Section 10

No State shall enter into any Treaty, Alliance, or Confederation; grant Letters of Marque and Reprisal; coin Money; emit Bills of Credit; make any Thing but gold and silver Coin a Tender in Payment of Debts; pass any Bill of Attainder, ex post facto Law, or Law impairing the Obligation of Contracts, or grant any Title of Nobility.

No State shall, without the Consent of the Congress, lay any Imposts or Duties on Imports or Exports, except what may be absolutely necessary for executing its inspection Laws: and the net Produce of all Duties and Imposts, laid by any State on Imports or Exports, shall be for the Use of the Treasury of the United States; and all such Laws shall be subject to the Revision and Controul of the Congress.

No State shall, without the Consent of Congress, lay any Duty of Tonnage, keep Troops, or Ships of War in time of Peace, enter into any Agreement or Compact with another State, or with a foreign Power, or engage in War, unless actually invaded, or in such imminent Danger as will not admit of delay.

U.S. Constitutional Provisions Regarding Interstate Relations

ARTICLE IV

Section 1

Full Faith and Credit shall be given in each State to the public Acts, Records, and judicial Proceedings of every other State. And the Congress may by general Laws prescribe the Manner in which such Acts, Records and Proceedings shall be proved, and the Effect thereof.

Section 2

The Citizens of each State shall be entitled to all Privileges and Immunities of Citizens in the several States.

A Person charged in any State with Treason, Felony, or other Crime, who shall flee from Justice, and be found in another State, shall on Demand of the executive Authority of the State from which he fled, be delivered up, to be removed to the State having Jurisdiction of the Crime.

No Person held to Service or Labour in one State, under the Laws thereof, escaping into another, shall, in Consequence of any Law or Regulation therein, be discharged from such Service or Labour, but shall be delivered up on Claim of the Party to whom such Service or Labour may be due.

Section 3

New States may be admitted by the Congress into this Union; but no new State shall be formed or erected within the Jurisdiction of any other State; nor any State be formed by the Junction of two or more States, or Parts of States, without the Consent of the Legislatures of the States concerned as well as of the Congress.

The Congress shall have Power to dispose of and make all needful Rules and Regulations respecting the Territory or other Property belonging to the United States; and nothing in this Constitution shall be so construed as to Prejudice any Claims of the United States, or of any particular State.

Section 4

The United States shall guarantee to every State in this Union a Republican Form of Government, and shall protect each of them against Invasion; and on Application of the Legislature, or of the Executive (when the Legislature cannot be convened), against domestic Violence.

Shared Powers

To add to the confusion of federalism, many government powers are shared. Both states and the national government, for example, collect taxes. Both work jointly to implement many programs, such as the social services we've discussed. Long ago, the limited social assistance programs were administered almost exclusively by state and local governments. Beginning with the economic chaos of the Great Depression, the national government assumed a larger role in welfare policy. By the 1960s and 1970s, the national government had a primary role in social services. State governments still administer most aid programs, but the national government mandates minimum standards.

Furthermore, the national government provides much of the money for social programs. In Texas, federal grants generate more than half of welfare spending. Education, transportation, and health care are all examples of programs administered concurrently by federal and state governments. We traditionally think of distinct divisions between national and state powers and responsibilities, but in practice there is much overlap and interaction.

Constitutions

The purpose of a **constitution** is to provide a framework in which government operates. It is, in essence, the blueprint for government. Ideally, it should specify which branch of government has what responsibilities. It should grant power to these branches but also set limits on what government can do. An important aspect of the American system of government is that a constitution should establish a system of checks and balances that keeps any branch from possessing too much power. The document should also provide a method for amendment so the constitution can be updated.

constitution
The basic document under which a state or nation's government operates.

Most Americans learn at an early age to value democratic ideals. Politicians repeatedly invoke the notion that their actions reflect "the will of the people." In a pure representative democracy, the majority rules. Elected officials, in theory at least, carry the views of the people forward to the legislature. The coalition that can form a majority on a particular issue will have its policy enacted.

However, we don't live in a pure democracy. We live in a constitutional republic, where constitutional law is supreme, as are acts of Congress and treaties created in accordance with the national constitution. Laws created by either the U.S. Congress or the Texas legislature that conflict with the U.S. Constitution can be struck down, despite what the majority might want. Texas cannot, for instance, place import taxes on goods coming in from Oklahoma. Portions of a state constitution are void if courts determine that they conflict with the U.S. Constitution.

The U.S. Constitution gives 18-year-olds the right to vote, therefore Texas could not set 21 as the voting age in state elections. Similarly, a state legislature is prohibited from enacting laws that violate its state constitution. Through a process called **judicial review**, courts decide when laws are unconstitutional. Both state and national courts can exercise this power with the U.S. Supreme Court having the ultimate say if there is a dispute.

judicial review
The power of the courts to strike down laws that violate the state or national constitution.

National Gains

Over the past 200 years, the balance of power has shifted significantly to the national government at the expense of the states. **Amendments** to the national constitution have played a role in this power shift, but other factors have also had an impact.

amendments
Additions or deletions to the constitution; passed in a prescribed manner.

Constitutional Amendments

Since the passage of the **Bill of Rights**, which was aimed at limiting national government power, many constitutional amendments have restricted state action. After the Civil War, the Thirteenth and Fifteenth Amendments ended slavery and gave

Bill of Rights
The portion of the constitution limiting the government and empowering the individual.

African American males the right to vote. The Fourteenth Amendment required state governments to extend due process and equal protection under the law to all their citizens. Over the past five decades, the U.S. Supreme Court has used the Fourteenth Amendment to apply significant portions of the Bill of Rights to state governments as well. For example, the state of Texas could not successfully prosecute Gregory Lee Johnson for burning the American flag because the First Amendment of the U.S. Constitution guarantees freedom of speech. In 1989, the U.S. Supreme Court struck down the Texas statute prohibiting flag burning, finding that it unconstitutionally infringed on this right. The Seventeenth Amendment stripped state legislatures of the power to appoint U.S. senators. The Nineteenth, Twenty-fourth, and Twenty-sixth amendments prohibited states from restricting voters' rights. They respectively granted women the right to vote, ended poll taxes, and extended voting rights to 18-to 20-year-olds.

Budgetary Powers

The national government has gained greater control over the states through its taxing and spending policies. The national budget exceeds $3.5 trillion a year. A large part of that spending is returned to the states through various grant programs. About a third of Texas's state budget comes from federal government sources.

It is important to understand that when the national government sends money to states, it comes with strings attached. The U.S. Constitution constrains Congress just as it constrains the states; limiting Congress to powers explicitly listed in Article I, Section 8 (see U.S. Congressional Powers). Congress, however, can get around this roadblock and compel the states to pass legislation by threatening to withhold federal grants.

U.S. Congressional Powers

ARTICLE I

Section 8

The Congress shall have Power To lay and collect Taxes, Duties, Imposts and Excises, to pay the Debts and provide for the common Defence and general Welfare of the United States; but all Duties, Imposts and Excises shall be uniform throughout the United States; To borrow Money on the credit of the United States; To regulate Commerce with foreign Nations, and among the several States, and with the Indian Tribes; To establish an uniform Rule of Naturalization, and uniform Laws on the subject of Bankruptcies throughout the United States; To coin Money, regulate the Value thereof, and of foreign Coin, and fix the Standard of Weights and Measures; To provide for the Punishment of counterfeiting the Securities and current Coin of the United States; To establish Post Offices and post Roads; To promote the Progress of Science and useful Arts, by securing for limited Times to Authors and Inventors the exclusive Right to their respective Writings and Discoveries; To constitute Tribunals inferior to the supreme Court; To define and punish Piracies and Felonies committed on the high Seas, and Offences against the Law of

(continued)

Nations; To declare War, grant Letters of Marque and Reprisal, and make Rules concerning Captures on Land and Water; To raise and support Armies, but no Appropriation of Money to that Use shall be for a longer Term than two Years; To provide and maintain a Navy; To make Rules for the Government and Regulation of the land and naval Forces; To provide for calling forth the Militia to execute the Laws of the Union, suppress Insurrections and repel Invasions; To provide for organizing, arming, and disciplining, the Militia, and for governing such Part of them as may be employed in the Service of the United States, reserving to the States respectively, the Appointment of the Officers, and the Authority of training the Militia according to the discipline prescribed by Congress; To exercise exclusive Legislation in all Cases whatsoever, over such District (not exceeding ten Miles square) as may, by Cession of particular States, and the Acceptance of Congress, become the Seat of the Government of the United States, and to exercise like Authority over all Places purchased by the Consent of the Legislature of the State in which the Same shall be, for the Erection of Forts, Magazines, Arsenals, dock-Yards, and other needful Buildings;—And To make all Laws which shall be necessary and proper for carrying into Execution the foregoing Powers, and all other Powers vested by this Constitution in the Government of the United States, or in any Department or Officer thereof.

Studying just one area of the budget, transportation, provides insight into the magnitude of the money and power involved. Approximately half of state highway fund revenue comes from federal funds, totaling over $3 billion in both 2008 and 2009. In order to receive all of that money, the state has to abide by a series of restrictions placed on it by Congress and the U.S. Department of Transportation. In the 1970s, states were required to set maximum speed limits at 55 miles per hour in order to receive highway funds. This particular restriction has since been lifted, but the precedent for congressional control remains.

In the 1980s, states were forced to raise the drinking age to 21 in order to receive federal money for transportation. Moreover, it was in connection with the drinking age provision—in *South Dakota* v. *Dole*—that the U.S. Supreme Court explicitly upheld Congress's prerogative to withhold grant money, provided its direction was related to the "general welfare" of the nation. Later that decade, the Department of Transportation threatened to cut off funds to states that did not adopt seat belt laws. Federal grants are available in most areas of state government spending, and similar restrictions affect almost every area of state government.

It is equally important, when discussing these grants, to understand that this is "Texas money" in the first place. The federal government's budget comes primarily from taxes on the income of individuals within the several states. In other words, Washington will give Texas back *some* of its money, but only if the state abides by their rules.

The Federal Courts

As a result of federal laws and the Fourteenth Amendment to the U.S. Constitution, federal courts often have jurisdiction in areas once completely under state control. Over the last several years, Texas politicians have found themselves constrained by federal court orders involving issues such as prison control, mental health and retardation services, higher education funding and minority recruitment programs, and school desegregation.

A Brief History of Federalism

dual federalism
Well-defined divisions between national and state powers and responsibilities.

From the beginning of the Republic through the 1920s, **dual federalism** defined the operation of the U.S. constitutional system. Under this interpretation, each level of government had its own sphere of influence, separate and distinct. States exercised great power in areas of local concern, which meant practically anything outside of national defense and trade policy. The end of dual federalism began with the advent of the Great Depression.

Citizens and politicians, desperate for economic relief, were unconcerned with philosophical questions over the nature of federalism. The problem seemed too large for states to solve independently, so power collected at and programs flowed from the national level.

cooperative federalism
Era of expanded national government power, mandates, and funding.

Under **cooperative federalism**, the role of the national government expanded significantly. Power that migrated to the national level during the depths of the Great Depression and World War II remained there after the chaos ended. Cooperative federalism was supposed to define an era under which national and state governments worked together in the administration and implementation of programs. Many state leaders, however, believed that more coercion than coopera- tion took place. The greatest expansion of national power occurred in conjunction with President Lyndon Johnson's Great Society programs. The national govern- ment had learned that it could force state and local compliance with national wishes by threatening to withhold government grants.

The significance of this approach bears reiteration. The national government found a way to enforce policy it has no constitutional power to mandate. Relevant rule- making power is clearly reserved to the states in many of these policy arenas. Nonetheless, national grants make up at least a third of most state budgets. In order to receive grant money back from Washington, states must accede to the national govern- ment's will. Often, the parameters have nothing to do with the purpose of the pro- gram. Rather, they are intended to achieve social goals deemed worthy by Washington. Proponents of national government intervention argue that the threat of sanctions has reduced discrimination, helped clean the air and water, and created a safer nation. Opponents paint the restrictions as a power play by the national government.

new federalism
Greater discretion to state governments in the use of federal grants.

Several modern-day presidents, beginning with Richard Nixon, have claimed to favor a **new federalism**. Generally, new federalism entails a significant reduc- tion in the use of categorical grants—which can only be used for narrowly defined purposes—opting for less restrictive block grants. During Ronald Reagan's admin- istration, these block grants were used more frequently and many of the regula- tions that went along with them were eased. Nonetheless, the overall size and power of the national government continued to increase.

The "New" New Federalism

When the Republican Party took control of the U.S. House and Senate in 1995, members promised to reduce the scope of national government. Republican leaders argued that decision making should be returned to the states.

However, the proponents of this "new" new federalism movement proved less than committed to substantive change. States have gained some limited control under this scenario. The rapid expansion of national government funding slowed, although it picked up again in the 21st century. **Devolution**, the transfer of programs from the national to state levels, occurred in some areas. Speed limits, for instance, are once again the responsibility of state governments. Federal grants may come with fewer strings attached, but the states will pay for this freedom by having to pick up a larger share of many social service programs. On the other hand, restrictions may have just shifted. States that didn't adopt federal blood-alcohol levels for driving while intoxicated lost some federal transportation funds, a policy backed by some of the same Republican members of Congress who decried national interference on the issue of speed limits. And if we measure government by the size of its expenditures, it grew more rapidly during the Bush administration than at any time during recent memory. Federal grants have grown in tandem with the larger federal budget, even faster than the federal budget during the early portion of the Obama administration.

Over the last decade, however, the U.S. Supreme Court has issued decisions that have limited the power of the national government. Two major decisions have breathed life back into the Tenth Amendment to the U.S. Constitution, which reserves to the states powers not denied them by the national document. In *United States* v. *Lopez* (1995), the Court struck down a law passed by the U.S. Congress that banned guns in the vicinity of schools. Congress argued that, because it regulates interstate commerce, it had the power to pass the law. The Court rejected the argument, saying that if Congress is granted such a broad reading of the clause, "We are hard pressed to posit any activity by an individual that Congress is without power to regulate." In 1997, the Court struck down a key provision of the Brady Bill, which required local law enforcement agencies to perform background checks on people attempting to purchase handguns. The Court ruled that Congress didn't have the power to force these governments to help administer this federal program. In the 2000 case of *United States* v. *Morrison*, a divided Court took a second step toward narrowing the commerce clause, striking down an act of Congress that allowed women who had been sexually assaulted to recover damages against the perpetrator in federal court. Congress had used the commerce clause to justify the act, reasoning that a hostile sexual environment could damage business opportunities for women. The Court struck down the law, finding again that such an expansive reading of "commerce" would give virtually limitless power to Congress. These rulings signal a willingness on the part of the U.S. Supreme Court to cap the national government's expansion of power. Some recent decisions have not sided with state rights, as evidenced by the 2005 case of *Gonzales* v. *Raich*, which affirmed the Drug Enforcement Administration's authority to prosecute medicinal marijuana cases despite state laws allowing such use.

States have shown increasing frustration with national government **mandates**. The U.S. Congress often passes regulations that set standards for state conduct. For example, states, and the businesses that operate in them, were required to meet accessibility standards under the 1990 Americans with Disabilities Act. Enlarging doorways, building additional wheelchair ramps, and making other such improvements cost state and local governments millions of dollars. Congress provided no money to help meet these requirements, making this an **unfunded mandate**. The national government has set such standards in

devolution
The transfer of government programs from the national to the state level.

mandates
Regulations set by Congress that state and local government must meet.

unfunded mandates
Congressional directives that are issued without corresponding federal funding.

areas ranging from voter registration to water quality and from hazardous waste disposal to asbestos removal. These mandates force state officials to spend funds they would rather use elsewhere. Unfunded federal mandates increase the tax burden on the state's citizens.

State Constitutions

The U.S. Constitution is a model of brevity. At 8,500 words, it established not only the national government, but the federal system as well. State constitutions, on the other hand, tend to be lengthy. Thirty-three state constitutions exceed 20,000 words and several others exceed 17,000. Alabama's constitution is the longest at 340,000 words. The Texas Constitution contains more than 80,000 words.[1] See Table 2.1 for a comparison of selected state constitutions.

TABLE **2.1 Length and Effective Date of Select State Constitutions**

STATE	EFFECTIVE DATE	NUMBER OF WORDS
Alabama	1901	340,136
California	1879	54,645
Delaware	1897	19,000
Indiana	1851	10,379
Louisiana	1975	54,112
Kansas	1861	12,296
Maine	1820	16,276
Massachusetts	1780	36,700
Minnesota	1858	11,547
New York	1894	51,700
North Carolina	1971	16,532
Oklahoma	1907	74,075
Texas	1876	90,000
Vermont	1793	10,286

Note: States that are in boldface are close to the national model for constitution length.
SOURCE: *The Book of the States 2007* (Lexington, KY: Council of State Governments, 2007), p. 9.

State Constitutional Structure

Most state constitutions are similar in structure. Separate articles empower the executive, legislative, and judicial branches. The legislative branch makes the laws, the executive branch carries out the laws, and the judicial branch determines the constitutionality of and interprets the laws. Another article contains the state's Bill of Rights, which protects individuals from unreasonable government action. Most constitutions include a separate article detailing the powers of and limitations on local government.

    Ideally, the state constitution serves as a blueprint from which government emerges. In other words, it answers the question Who does what? Theoretically, the structure of government should be more difficult to change than the laws governing the day-to-day operations of government. In reality, though, most states blur constitutional law and **legislative law**—the bills passed by the legislature and enacted by the governor. Issues that go well beyond governmental structure are contained in many constitutions. Most state constitutions include policy matters as well.

legislative law
Law passed by the legislature.

This mixing of constitutional law and legislative law is quite evident in the Texas Constitution. Take, for instance, the cases of pari-mutuel gambling and the state lottery. Both are avenues through which the state profits from gambling. Neither pari-mutuel gambling nor the state lottery has a role in determining the government's framework, so ideally both should be dealt with in the state's statutes. However, while a state law forbade horse racing, a constitutional provision banned a lottery. Legalizing betting on the horses took a simple majority vote in the House and Senate and approval from the governor. Authorizing the lottery required the much more difficult process of amending the state constitution.

Because state constitutions contain so many legislative provisions, they tend to be restrictive. There are exceptions. Vermont's constitution, which follows the national model, has only 10, 286 words. It has been in effect for 200 years.[2] More often, these documents handcuff government, giving it little room in which to operate. Because of this, the typical state constitution has been amended many times. Alabama holds the record. Adopted in 1901, its constitution had already been amended 799 times by 2010. California follows close behind, exceeding 500 amendments. Twenty-seven other states have more than 100 amendments. Texas is at the extreme, being one of four states with a constitution that has been amended more than 300 times. Contrast that with Vermont's constitution, amended just 53 times in the last 215 years,[3] and the U.S. Constitution with 27 amendments, only 17 of which occurred after 1791.

Table 2.2 shows the great variance in frequency of constitutional amendment. The U.S. Constitution has been amended the least frequently. Although the Texas document has been amended often, it pales in comparison to South Carolina, California, and Alabama. At the other extreme, Kentucky, Rhode Island, Vermont, and Delaware have averaged fewer than one amendment every two years.

TABLE **2.2** Frequency of Constitutional Amendment in Selected States

STATE	TOTAL AMENDMENTS	AMENDMENTS PER YEAR*
Alabama	794	7.5
Arkansas	91	1.0
California	511	4.0
Delaware	138	1.3
Hawaii	108	2.8
Idaho	119	1.0
Kentucky	41	0.4
Massachusetts	120	0.5
Maine	171	0.9
Nebraska	224	1.7
New York	216	2.0
North Dakota	149	1.3
Rhode Island	10	0.3
South Carolina	492	4.4
Texas	432	3.3
Vermont	53	0.2
Wyoming	97	0.8
United States	**27**	**0.1**

*Amendments per year is derived from dividing the number of amendments adopted by the number of years the constitution has been in existence. The table includes all amendments passed through January 2007.

Note: The U.S. Constitution has been amended much less frequently than the average state document.

SOURCE: *The Book of the States 2007* (Lexington, KY: Council of State Governments, 2007), p. 9.

The Seven Constitutions of Texas

Coahuila y Tejas

Texas has had seven constitutions. Only Georgia and Louisiana have had more. The first of these, created in 1827, governed Texas while it was still a part of the Mexican Federation. Texas was joined with Coahuila as one state, although Coahuilan representatives dominated the legislature. Texans lobbied to have their own state within the Mexican Federation. This and other issues created tensions between Texas and Mexico that led to war. Texans twice asked Mexico for separate statehood, but Mexico denied both requests. To the Texans, it represented a simple request for self-government, understandable when viewed from their American background. To Mexico, the request was slightly short of treason. Their national constitution prohibited an area with a population as small as that of Texas from becoming its own state.

The 1836 Constitution

The 1836 Constitution of the Republic of Texas emerged between the fall of the Alamo and Sam Houston's stunning victory at San Jacinto. The constitution was written quickly because it had to be. Convention members were fleeing in the face of Santa Anna's advancing troops.

The 1836 Constitution generally followed the U.S. model. It created a house of representatives, a senate, and a president. Limits were placed on the president's term—he was not allowed to succeed himself. In an effort to reduce religious influences, the constitution prohibited clergy from holding office. Slavery was legalized and the head of each household was given a sizable land grant.[4]

You can read the Texas Declaration of Independence at http://www.lsjunction.com/docs/tdoi.htm.

The 1846 Constitution

After a decade-long struggle as a republic, Texas reached an annexation agreement with the United States at the end of 1845. No longer independent, Texas needed a new constitution.

The legislature retained a house and a senate to make state laws. A governor and lieutenant governor headed the executive branch. Term limits prohibited the heads of state from serving for more than four years of any six-year period. The governor

Congressman, General, President, Senator, Governor. Sam Houston did it all.

appointed other executive officials, such as the attorney general and the treasurer.[5] As in the current Texas Constitution, limits were placed on the powers of government. State debt was severely restricted, and the legislature was scheduled to meet every other year. Slavery was permitted.

In a wave of "Jacksonian democracy," selection of the attorney general, comptroller, and treasurer was transferred to the voters through an 1850 amendment.[6] Jacksonian democracy, based on the political philosophy of Andrew Jackson, asserts that power should reside with the people. As a result, citizens should elect, rather than have the governor appoint, as many government officials as possible.

The resolution admitting Texas to the United States can be found at http://www.lsjunction.com/docs/annex.htm.

The 1861 Constitution

Fifteen years after its successful struggle to become part of the United States, Texas seceded from the union and became part of the Confederate States of America. As a part of a new nation, the state needed another constitution. In reality, changes from the amended version of the 1846 Constitution were not substantive; they merely acknowledged the state's place in the Confederacy. One provision did, however, forbid slaveholders from emancipating slaves without permission from the state government.

The Texas Ordinance of Secession is available at http://www.lsjunction.com/docs/secesson.htm.

The 1866 Constitution

After the Confederacy lost the Civil War, Texas was forced back into the Union. As a conquered power, Texas was expected to write a new constitution making slavery illegal. In essence, though, the 1866 Constitution was nothing more than an amended 1846 document.

The term of the elected executives was lengthened and government officials received pay raises.[7] The constitution denied African Americans the right to vote. Also, the newly freed slaves were not allowed to hold office or testify in court unless African Americans were party to the case.[8] Operating under this constitution, the new Texas legislature further restricted the rights of African Americans through the passage of a series of **Black Codes**. Such legislation limited job opportunities for and social interaction of the newly freed slaves. In effect, the Texas Constitution and legislature had created a caste system in the state, under which African Americans were trapped in a limbo between freedom and servitude.

Black Codes
Post–Civil War laws restricting the freedom of African Americans.

The 1869 Constitution

The U.S. Congress vehemently opposed the efforts of the former Confederate states to keep African Americans downtrodden. In March 1867, all southern state governments were disbanded and the former Confederacy was divided into five military districts. A new constitution that guaranteed African American suffrage had to be written in each state, and each had to ratify the Fourteenth Amendment of the U.S. Constitution.

Democrats were the predominant political party in Texas at the time, but members were so angered by the federal government's action that most boycotted the elections leading to the creation of the new constitution. Therefore, Republicans, both Radical and moderate, dominated the 1868 Constitutional Convention. Many of the delegates were African American, as detailed in the Texas Mosaic on African American leaders. The Radicals and moderates divided over three main issues. The first was called *ab initio* and dealt with the question of whether all actions of the state government during the time of rebellion should be made null and void. Moderates, who would prevail, believed that only those actions taken in direct rebellion should be voided. The second issue was *division*. Texas's annexation agreement with the United States allows it to divide into up to five states at any time. Although there are serious constitutional questions about the viability of this provision, Radicals launched a plan to create the separate state of West Texas. Radicals knew that they could not compile an elective majority in Texas after the Democrats returned to the political process, so they figured they would create a state out west where there weren't many people, move the Radicals and their African American brethren there, and be able to control *that* state government. Obviously, the moderates won on that issue, too. **E. J. Davis**, a Radical who served as the convention chair, succeeded in his efforts to grant African American men the right to vote. The extension of voting rights was substantial. Although Davis had among his loyal supporters the freedmen, there is evidence that his concern for racial equality was genuine. As a state legislator in the 1850s, Davis had introduced legislation calling for bilingual ballots, effectively extending voting access to Hispanic men. One can surmise that this was not a particularly popular cause, in light of the rampant racism of the time. On issues other than voting rights, though, Davis saw the convention slipping away from the Radicals. Rather than submit, the chair adjourned the convention. It was left to the state's military commander to compile the document into a workable constitution and submit it to the voters.

E. J. Davis
The Republican governor of Texas during the era of Reconstruction.

In 1869, the new state constitution was adopted by an overwhelming margin: 72,446 to 4928. Progressive and modern, the document centralized much power in the hands of the governor. The state's chief executive not only had the power to appoint key executive officials, such as the attorney general, but judges as well. He was also empowered to fill vacancies in local government. Ordinarily, that would not be significant. However, hundreds of vacancies had been created when prior officeholders who had fought for the Confederacy lost their right to vote, making them ineligible to hold office. Looking toward the future, the convention created the Permanent School Fund, which earmarked money generated from public lands for education. Black men, as well as most white ex-Confederate males, were guaranteed the right to vote.[9] The document itself provided a framework under which a strong government could operate. The factors that led to its relatively quick demise had more to do with the actions of Governor E. J. Davis, both real and attributed, than with the constitution itself.

After the constitutional convention, Davis was elected governor, winning a hotly contested race against A. J. Hamilton, a fellow Republican. Still slow to organize, the Democrats failed to field a candidate, although many eventually supported Hamilton as the lesser of two evils. Both sides claimed their opponent participated in fraud and intimidation during the election. Despite claims of corruption by the Hamilton backers, Davis might have won by a larger margin had African Americans been granted freer access to the polls. African American turnout actually dropped from the 1868 to the 1869 elections, due to intimidation in the registration and voting process.[10]

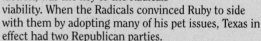

Texas MOSAIC

Early Diversity in Texas:
African Americans in 19th-Century Texas Politics

George Ruby was a carpetbagger, which simply means that he came South after the Civil War to seek his fortune. He came to Texas in the post–Civil War era to reconstruct the recently rebellious state and help the former slaves integrate into society. Ruby was a well-educated teacher from Maine who arrived with the occupying forces shortly after the war ended. On the way to New Orleans, Ruby had been denied first-class passage on a ship for one reason: he was African American. This blatant discrimination, a kind that he had not before encountered, was an experience he would never forget.

Ruby quickly became the dominant African American in Texas politics. Residing in Galveston, he became an active leader in both the Union League and the state's infant Republican Party. The party's leaders knew that they must reach out to the African American community in order to remain politically viable in Texas. As a result, the majority of the delegates to the party's first state convention in 1867 were African American. Ruby was named vice president of the convention.

If Anglo party leaders thought that Ruby would be content with a token position within the party, they were mistaken. Ruby effectively controlled the Galveston branch of the Union League by the fall of 1867. He used this power to win election as a delegate to the 1868 state constitutional convention. He campaigned for the convention with an unwavering promise to work for the protection of African American rights. A savvy politician, Ruby worked to keep his bloc of African American delegates positioned between the other factions, siding with whichever group best protected his interests on an issue-by-issue basis.

In June 1868, Ruby became president of the statewide Union League. The league had started as a secretive, white, pro-union organization at the beginning of Reconstruction. It aimed to galvanize the newly freed slaves behind the idea of union. Having Ruby as its head was not what league founders had in mind, but Ruby was able to convince the African American delegates to oust the sitting white president and elect him instead.

Ruby's most important role in a busy 1868 involved splitting the state party into radical and moderate factions. The moderates controlled the regular state Republican convention. E. J. Davis led his Radicals out of the convention when it failed to address issues that he considered important. Davis knew that his band of white Radicals was not large enough to have an impact upon state politics on its own. Ruby, who controlled a sizable African American faction, was the key to the Radicals' viability. When the Radicals convinced Ruby to side with them by adopting many of his pet issues, Texas in effect had two Republican parties.

Moderate Republicans, attempting to discredit Ruby, resorted to a campaign of character assassination. They accused him of taking a bribe. African Americans rallied around their leader, sensing a conspiracy. Ruby and the Radicals would back Davis in his bid for governor. Davis won a close race and rewarded those who had helped him with appointments to important offices. Davis's superintendent of schools, for instance, appointed Ruby and his protégé, Norris Wright Cuney, to the Galveston County school board. Ruby also served as a state senator during the Davis administration.

Ruby, whose time at the political forefront was coming to an end, would use his power to help Cuney ascend. With Ruby's aid, Cuney became chair of the executive committee of the National Labor Convention of the Working Men of Texas, a major African American interest group. Cuney, also an African American, was born in Texas. He was sent north prior to the Civil War to acquire an education. He later studied law in

George Ruby was a prominent African American Republican in post Civil War Texas. He wielded significant power during Reconstruction.

(continued)

(continued from page 49)

Galveston and, at the age of 26, served as a delegate to the Republican National Convention in 1872. Cuney would serve as a delegate to all Republican national conventions through 1892.

When Davis died in 1883, Cuney became chair of the state Republican Party. In 1886, Cuney would add the position of Republican National Committeeman to his resume after being elected by the African American majority at the party's state convention.

In the last two decades of the nineteenth century, the Republican Party in Texas was essentially a patronage vessel: it dispensed federal jobs to loyal party members whenever Republicans controlled the White House. Outside of a few local positions, Republicans had no chance to win elections. Cuney exploited the patronage aspect in 1889 and obtained the position of customs collector in Galveston, a high-paying and prominent job.

By the end of the 1880s, white Republicans began a concerted effort to regain control of the party from African Americans. By organizing, they were able to control the party and garner nominations for their slate of statewide candidates in 1890. At the 1892 state convention, Cuney was able to retain control for his faction by railroading the convention and running over the "lily white" Republicans. As a result, white

Republicans held a separate "rump" convention and selected their own national delegates and gubernatorial ticket. At the national convention, Cuney's delegation was seated and he was elected to another four-year term on the Republican National Committee.

Cuney's faction of the party chose not to run a gubernatorial ticket in 1892. In 1894, there were again two Republican state conventions. This time, each side opted to run its own gubernatorial ticket. While the Democrats easily won the governor's race, Cuney's candidate outpolled the "lily white" candidate by a 10-to-1 margin.

By 1896, however, as a result of an intraparty battle over the Republican presidential nomination, Cuney found himself left out of the process because he had backed the wrong candidate. He was shut out of the national convention, lost his national committee position, and, finally, was ousted as party chair. He would be replaced by another African American, H. C. Ferguson, but the days of African American control of the state's Republican Party were all but over.

SOURCES: Carl H. Moneyhon, *Republicanism in Reconstruction Texas* (Austin, TX: The University of Texas Press, 1980); Paul Douglas Casdorph, "Norris Wright Cuney and Texas Republican Politics, 1883–1896," *Southwestern Historical Quarterly* 67(1963): 68, 455–464.

THE DAVIS ADMINISTRATION The Davis administration is infamous in Texas for its alleged abuses. Chief among the complaints was the governor's implementation of the **"Obnoxious Acts,"** the name given by opposing Democrats to the cornerstone of Davis's legislative agenda.

Obnoxious Acts
The derisive name given to the legislation included in E. J. Davis' agenda.

First, the governor and the Republican legislature created a state militia and a state police force. In Texas legend, the purpose of these forces was the intimidation and harassment of poor white Texans. In reality, the organizations were formed to protect the frontier from Indian incursion, to stop the lynching of African Americans, and to halt the general lawlessness that engulfed Texas. The militia and police were generally effective at achieving their goals. Three factors, however, led to the negative perceptions held by generations of white Texans. First was the enormous cost of the endeavor. Second, the forces included African American militia and policemen. Anglo Texans were not thrilled with the prospect of armed former slaves patrolling the state.[11] Finally, Davis had forced the enacting bill through the legislature in a high-handed way. When some Senate opponents of the militia bill realized they didn't have the votes to stop it through traditional methods, they skipped out on the session, thereby preventing a quorum. The governor had the missing senators arrested for contempt. The authorities returned only four of the nine absent senators to the chamber, achieving a quorum while at the same time holding opposition to a minimum, thus guaranteeing passage of the bill.[12]

Another of the "Obnoxious Acts" gave the governor broad power to fill vacancies created at the state or local level. Because readmittance to the Union resulted in the removal of many officeholders of questionable loyalty, Davis had the power to fill thousands of political offices. He also postponed elections for state and congressional offices, thereby guaranteeing extended terms for Radical officeholders. You can read more on Davis in the Texas Mosaic detailing his career.

THE DEMOCRATS RETURN TO POWER The Democrats regained control of the legislature after the 1872 elections. They immediately began to dismantle the Radical programs. Davis went along with some changes, agreeing, for instance, to decentralize the school system. When he vetoed efforts to repeal portions of the "Obnoxious Acts," Democrats found enough sympathetic Republicans to help override the vetoes.[13]

In late 1873, Davis lost his bid for reelection to Democrat Richard Coke. Some Republicans, seeing an alleged technical discrepancy between the state constitution and the execution of the 1873 election, argued that the election was unconstitutional. Democrats believed that Davis, who had previously stated he would not contest the election, would use the controversy to stay in office.

Texas **MOSAIC**

Diversity of Thought:

E. J. Davis

Edmund J. Davis, the Republican governor of Texas during Reconstruction, was one of the most controversial figures in Texas history. The son of an attorney, Davis arrived in Texas when he was twenty. He served as a clerk at the Galveston post office while studying law. The next year, he was admitted to the bar in Corpus Christi. He used connections within the Democratic Party to secure a job as customs inspector in Laredo. Later, he was an elected Democratic district judge and, in 1857, a delegate to the Democratic state convention. Davis, a Union officer in the war, joined the Republican Party after the rebellion ended.

Davis's wife, Anne Elizabeth Britton Davis, was the daughter of Major Forbes Britton, a powerful Jacksonian Democrat who had served in both houses of the Texas Legislature. Lizzie was a strong, influential woman. She was a driving force behind her husband's political career and, no doubt, helped shape his political outlook. She considered his election as governor to be the first step toward the White House. While he was governor, she addressed the legislature, giving a speech for her husband almost fifty years before women were granted the vote in Texas.

Davis's Programs. Despite all the controversy surrounding his administration, Davis had a vision for Texas. He believed the state needed to educate its citizens. Toward that end, the governor and his legislative supporters created a centralized and free public education system. Such a program was costly and increased the state's debt. The centralization was so complete

that the governor's patronage power actually extended to hiring teachers. School employees could therefore be counted upon for their loyalty to the governor.

Likewise, the state's railroad construction program, consisting partially of monetary grants to railroad companies, was expensive. Davis was a supporter of extending the rail lines and would ultimately be blamed for the debt incurred, but the legislation authorizing the monetary grants was passed over his veto. Davis favored land grants and other innovative enticements to the railroad companies. As a result of his perseverance, the state's debt was significantly less than it otherwise might have been.

After his term as governor, Davis did not fade quietly from the political scene. He controlled the state Republican Party until his death in 1883. He made one last run for the governor's office in 1880, but captured less than 25 percent of the vote. In the end, he believed that the national party had abandoned the Republicans of Texas.

E.J. Davis was the last Republican governor for almost 100 years. How did perceptions of the Davis administration play into Democratic domination?

SOURCES: Carl H. Moneyhon, *Republicanism in Reconstruction Texas* (Austin, TX: The University of Texas Press, 1980); Ronald N. Gray, "Edmund J. Davis" (Ph.D. diss. Texas Tech University, 1976).

They demanded that the governor relinquish power immediately rather than wait until his term ended in April. The Democrats convened the legislature and inaugurated Coke as governor. Davis continued to serve in office as well. In January 1874, the Republican-controlled Texas supreme court sided with Davis, declaring the elections invalid.[14]

Davis asked for federal intervention, requesting that President Ulysses S. Grant send U.S. troops to Texas to help him keep order until the election matter could be resolved. Grant refused. On January 19, before his term officially ended, Davis resigned, determined to prevent violence, which he feared might occur should the impasse continue.

The 1876 Constitution

Firmly in control of both the legislative and executive branches, the Democrats moved to consolidate power. As governor, Coke was not as enthusiastic as some other Texans to downgrade his office. The Democratic leadership in 1874 authored a series of amendments to the constitution that would have retained many governmental powers. The legislature would continue to meet each year. While state debt was limited, it was ten times more than the debt allowed under the 1846 Constitution. No ceiling was placed on state or local taxes, neither were there restrictions on the uses of state tax revenue. The governor's term of four years was retained, as was the office of state superintendent of schools.[15] While the proposed constitution differed from the 1869 document, it retained the basic tenet of centralized state power. The legislature failed to act on the proposal, however, and a constitutional convention became inevitable.

The convention changed the playing field. No longer would the process be controlled by party leaders. Instead, independently elected delegates would be free from leadership constraints. The most influential group, comprising a 38-member plurality of the 90-delegate convention, was the Texas **Grange**.[16] Grangers were a populist farmers' group whose members blamed their economic decline on railroad companies, Radical Republicans, and the newly freed slaves. They believed the government was spending too much money and they sought to rein in state debt.

The easiest interpretation of the document produced by the 1875 convention is that it represented a simple backlash against Radical Republican rule and the perceived abuses of the Davis administration. Certainly, this was a major factor. In many vital ways, however, the **1876 Constitution** would mirror the pre–Civil War document. Furthermore, the new document was similar to state constitutional development throughout the nation at the time.[17] Other constitutions enacted during that period, even those created outside of the post-Reconstruction South, sought to limit government control.

The 1846 Constitution had called for biennial legislative sessions, relatively low legislative salary, a two-year term limit for the governor and six-year terms for an elected member of the Texas supreme court. It also placed strict limits on state debt and prohibited state grants to banks or railroads.[18] All these provisions reappeared in the 1876 document. The Grangers' insistence on a reduction of government power was at least partially aimed at the Democratic leadership in 1874–75, because the 1876 Constitution restricted Democrats' power as well.

Grange
A populist farmers' alliance influential in the creation of the 1876 Constitution.

1876 Constitution
The current Texas Constitution, written after Reconstruction.

It is somewhat surprising that the 1875 Constitutional convention commissioned a poster, given that their purse strings were so tight that they didn't hire an official record keeper to chronicle the proceedings.

Many Grangers were leery of the governor and other party leaders who pushed the 1874 revision attempt in the legislature, ignoring the traditional method of changing constitutions through the convention process. This was viewed as an effort to retain power for the government by those already in office. The perception, of course, was correct.

LIMITS ON GOVERNMENT POWER The 1876 Constitution aimed to restrict the power of the government. It did not seek to limit the executive branch alone; it limited all branches. The power of the legislature was limited by the return to biennial sessions. The reasoning is simple: the less time the legislature is in session, the fewer opportunities it has to pass laws. The salary was low, encouraging members to limit service. Senate terms were cut from six years to four. Expense money dropped as the session went on so that legislators would finish their business quickly and go home. Any increase in legislative salary required a constitutional amendment, which required voter approval. The legislature was prohibited from calling itself into special session. By giving this responsibility exclusively to the governor, power is further dispersed.

The most significant limit on the legislature, though, was the balanced budget provision, which greatly restricted the state's ability to go into debt. This was certainly a reaction to the spending habits of the Radical Republicans. Limiting the amount of money available to the legislature limits its ability to enact programs. But it was nothing new for Texans, as it echoed similar stipulations in the 1846 document.

The governor's office was restricted through stripping his appointment powers. No longer could he appoint his cabinet. Rather, other executive heads, such as the attorney general, lieutenant governor, and comptroller, would be elected independently. Each executive officer would have his own constituency. His loyalty would be owed to the voters, not the governor. The governor's salary was reduced as well.

The size of the judicial branch was reduced as the number of district courts decreased. The term of judges was reduced and they were chosen by popular election, not appointment.

THE BILL OF RIGHTS One of the most significant portions of the 1876 Constitution was its long, detailed Bill of Rights (see Appendix 2, and the Texas Constitution box nearby). This was a bold response to the Davis administration. Texans wanted to ensure that individual liberties would never be trampled again, even if those liberties, as was the case in 1876, extended only to white males. Again, the Bill of Rights cannot be viewed entirely as a reaction to Reconstruction. Most of the key components of the 1876 document are derived directly from the 1846 Constitution. Many provisions in the Bill of Rights date back to the 1836 Republic of Texas Constitution.[19]

A state Bill of Rights is important for two reasons. First, the U.S. Bill of Rights does not explicitly extend protections to the relationship between a state and its citizens. It wasn't until the 1940s that the U.S. Supreme Court began applying most provisions of the U.S. Constitution's Bill of Rights to state and local governments, almost 70 years after the Texas Constitution was created see the Inside the Federalist System box nearby.

Second, while a state cannot give less protection to its citizens than is allowed through U.S. Supreme Court interpretations, it can give more. For instance, the effort to include an Equal Rights Amendment in the U.S. Constitution, which would have banned gender-based discrimination, was defeated. The Texas Constitution, however, contains such a provision as a result of a 1972 constitutional amendment (art. 1, sec. 3a).

INSIDE THE FEDERALIST SYSTEM

A Comparison of U.S. and Texas Bill of Rights

The Texas Constitution tends to be wordier and more detailed than the U.S. document. Here, notice the contrast between the brief treatment of freedom of religion and speech in the U.S. version and the longer Texas Constitution.

Freedom of Religion

United States

Congress shall make no law respecting an establishment of religion or prohibiting the free exercise thereof. (*First Amendment*)

Texas

All men have a natural and an indefeasible right to worship Almighty God according to the dictates of his own consciences. No man shall be compelled to attend, erect or support any place of worship, or to maintain any ministry against his consent. No human authority ought, in any case whatever, to control or interfere with the rights on conscience in matters of religion, and no preference shall ever be given by law to any religious society or mode of worship. But it shall be the duty of the legislature to pass such laws as may be necessary to protect equally every religious denomination in the peaceable enjoyment of its own mode of public worship. (*art. 1, sec. 6*) No money shall be appropriated or drawn from the Treasury for the benefit of any sect, or religious society, theological or religious seminary, nor shall property belonging to the State be appropriated for such purposes. (*art. 1, sec. 7*)

Freedom of Speech and the Press

United States

Congress shall make no law . . . abridging the freedom of speech or of the press. *(First Amendment)*

Texas

Every person shall be at liberty to speak, write or publish his opinions, on any subject, being responsible for the abuse of that privilege; and no law shall ever be passed curtailing the liberty of speech or of the press. In prosecutions for the publication of papers, investigating the conduct of officers or men in public capacity, or when the matter published is proper for public information the truth thereof may be given in evidence.

And in all indictments for libels, the jury shall have the right to determine the law and the facts under the direction of the court, as in other cases. *(art. 1, sec. 8)*

Whereas the national constitution's Bill of Rights contains only 10 provisions, the Texas Bill of Rights has 30. In addition to protections against unreasonable searches and seizures and double jeopardy, as well as guarantees of freedom of the press and freedom of speech, it also ensures that individuals will not be imprisoned for debt and that monopolies will not be allowed in the state. Texas may not deport a citizen from the state for any offense committed in Texas.

Two portions of the Bill of Rights seem most directly attributable to a reaction against Reconstruction. Article I, Section 1 says, "Texas is a free and independent state, subject only to the Constitution of the United States." The language tries to create powers for Texas that were denied to it during Reconstruction. Its placement at the beginning of the Bill of Rights emphasizes its importance. The second item is a direct strike against Davis: it prohibits the use of state money for religious purposes. Its aim was to dismantle the education structure erected by the Republicans, which included state funding for parochial schools. Neither of these two provisions had appeared in previous Texas constitutions.[20]

The Texas Bill of Rights extends many protections to those accused of crime. A person cannot be held without charges, has the right to confront accusers, and has a right to a trial by jury. Unlike some states, no person can be tried for a felony crime without first being charged by a grand jury. On the other hand, a 1989 amendment extended rights to crime victims, including the right to confer with a representative from the prosecutor's office and the right to restitution from the perpetrator.

You can find the entire Texas Constitution on the Web at http://tlo2.tlc.state.tx.us/txconst/toc.html.

The Texas Constitution: A Closer Look

The creators of the 1876 Constitution wanted to restate their independence and distance themselves from Reconstruction policies. The first three sections of Article I illustrate this well.

ARTICLE I. BILL OF RIGHTS

Sec. 1. FREEDOM AND SOVEREIGNTY OF STATE. Texas is a free and independent State, subject only to the Constitution of the United States, and the maintenance of our free institutions and the perpetuity of the Union depend upon the preservation of the right of local self-government, unimpaired to all the States.

Sec. 2. INHERENT POLITICAL POWER; REPUBLICAN FORM OF GOVERNMENT. All political power is inherent in the people, and all free governments are founded on their authority, and instituted for their benefit. The faith of the people of Texas stands pledged to the preservation of a republican form of government, and, subject to this limitation only, they have at all times the inalienable right to alter, reform or abolish their government in such manner as they may think expedient.

Sec. 3. EQUAL RIGHTS. All free men, when they form a social compact, have equal rights, and no man, or set of men, is entitled to exclusive separate public emoluments, or privileges, but in consideration of public services.

Amending the Constitution

Amending the Texas Constitution is a two-step process. First, both the House and the Senate must approve the proposed amendment by at least a two-thirds vote. This is the most difficult step in the process because 51 House members or 11 senators have the ability to block an amendment. Even with today's Republican majorities, any amendment vote that divides along party lines will be defeated.

Ratification of amendments approved by the legislature requires majority approval from the voters. Most of the time, voters approve proposed amendments. From 1985 through 2009, Texans had the opportunity to vote on 227 amendments. All but 29 passed. In other words, 87 percent of all proposals that reach the voters were ratified. In 1987, when 25 amendments were offered, 8 were defeated see Figure 2.1. When so many issues are presented at one time, some voters find it easier to vote "no" than to research each amendment carefully. When fewer issues are presented at one time, the voters have a better chance to study each proposition. However, in 2001, all 19 proposed amendments passed, as did all 22 in 2003, all 17 in 2007, and all 11 in 2009.

The governor has no formal role in the amendment process. Informally, he or she can use the visibility of the office to campaign for or against an amendment. The governor's support does not always help. In May 1993, Governor Ann Richards worked hard for the passage of the "Robin Hood" school reform amendments, which would have redistributed money from property-rich school districts to poorer ones. The amendments went down to overwhelming defeats, foreshadowing Richards's own ouster from office a year and a half later.

The Texas Constitution had been amended 467 times as of 2010. During this period, only 12 amendments have been added to the U.S. Constitution.

29
Failed
13%

188 Passed
87%

FIGURE **2.1   Proposed Constitutional Amendments, 1985–2009** The overwhelming percentage of proposed amendments are passed by the voters.

Constitutional Revision

The Texas Constitution of 1876 was written for a backward, agrarian, racist state recovering from the humiliation of a military defeat and subsequent Reconstruction. The 19th-century document did not provide for an efficient governmental system in the long term, especially with myriad amendments that have served to make the document even bulkier and more confusing. There have been numerous efforts to revise or rewrite the Texas Constitution. Most have failed completely. Voters have shown little interest in the process. When they have been given an opportunity to ratify significant structural reform, they have defeated the propositions.

The document itself is a model of disarray. It contains sentences that seem to go on forever. One stretches to several hundred words. This particular instance of incompetence cannot be blamed on the Grange. It was part of an amendment allowing for the creation of the Dallas/Fort Worth International Airport.

A 1999 constitutional amendment eliminated three outdated passages. For purposes of privilege against arrest, the original document had assumed a legislator could only travel 20 miles a day (art. 3, sec. 14). The governor had been allowed to call out the militia to "protect the frontier from hostile incursions by

WHAT CAN YOU DO?

If you think you might get married, and if you're considering purchasing property, review Chapter 41 of the Texas Property Code and Article XVI, Section 15 of the Texas Constitution at the Texas Legislature Online Web site. Chapter 41 of the Texas Property Code specifically defines homestead. Article XVI, Section 15 of the Texas Constitution provides that all property of a spouse that is owned or claimed before that individual marries, and all property that individual acquires by gift, devise or descent after the person marries is the separate property of that spouse. Otherwise, Texas law presumes that the property acquired by a married couple after they marry is community property. It is important to address the ramifications of both of these provisions as you consider purchasing property and whether you own (or will own) separate and community property if you marry.

Indians" (art. 4, sec. 7). The legislature had specifically been granted the power to "aid to indigent and disabled confederate soldiers and sailors" (art. 3, sec. 51). But many problems remain. Article III, Section 52 contains parts a, b, and d, but not c. The legislature was confused as to the numbering sequence when it submitted the amendment to the voters.[21] Article VII has two section 16s: one dealing with terms of office in school systems, the other pertaining to taxation of university lands.

In 1969, several obsolete provisions, such as one dealing with Spanish and Mexican land titles, were removed. Instead of renumbering the document to reflect the changes, blank sections and articles now litter the constitution. Prior to a 1991 amendment, all bond issues approved by the voters became a permanent part of the Texas Constitution. Those issues remain in the document, adding greatly to its bulk. Although bonds must still be approved through the same amendment process, they no longer appear in the document. As a result, the rapid expansion of the constitution's size has slowed.

The 1974 Constitutional Convention

The last major attempt to revise the constitution occurred in the 1970s. During a period of dissatisfaction with government in general, Texas politics entered an era of reform. The legislature embarked on an effort to give the state a new governing document. A constitutional amendment, approved by the voters in 1972, called for the creation of a revision commission that would submit its recommendations to a constitutional convention scheduled for January 1974. The convention's delegates were the elected members of the House and Senate, sitting as one body. In the wake of Watergate and an increasingly unpopular war at the national level, and the Sharpstown scandal at the state level (see Chapter 1), there was genuine hope for reform.

The revision committee produced a much shorter document, which would have drastically changed the structure of government in Texas. The proposal was only 17,500 words long. The revision would have required annual sessions of the legislature and provided for the appointment of judges.

After haggling over proposed changes from January to July 1974, the convention killed its own document. Needing two-thirds approval from the 181 members, the delegates fell three votes short. Had it succeeded, there is no guarantee that the voters would have approved the new constitution. A controversial right-to-work provision, which guaranteed that a Texan could not be required to join a union in order to get a job, contributed to the defeat. Representatives and senators from labor strongholds were pressured to vote against the document.

The 1974 constitutional convention expended significant time, money, and political resources on crafting a better constitution, but opposing forces defeated the effort. Who would benefit from a revised constitution?

School funding equalization, a topic that would dominate Texas's political focus from the mid-1980s through the mid-1990s, was also a factor. Delegates from property-poor areas wanted more state money devoted to education. Nonetheless, a significant majority of delegates believed that the proposed constitution was better than the present one. In 1975, reconvened as the legislature, the House and Senate submitted it to the voters in the form of eight separate propositions.

With the vocal opposition of the governor, who claimed the new document could result in a state income tax, voters overwhelmingly defeated all the provisions. Ironically, there was no clause in the 1876 Constitution at that time that would have prevented an income tax. Since then, an amendment has been added that requires voter approval before such a tax can be levied (see Chapter 12).

Prospects for Revision

For 20 years after the collapse of the last major revision effort, no serious attempt to achieve reform emerged. Given the expenditure of time, energy, and money on the futile last effort, it is easy to understand why state leaders were not motivated to revisit the convention process.

There are major obstacles to revision. Any effort to change the constitution will garner opposition from groups that benefit from the way things are. The Republican Party, for instance, now confident of its ability to win statewide judicial races, as well as judgeships in many urban counties, is likely to oppose any reform mandating judicial appointment. Likewise, the University of Texas and Texas A&M University System, as well as their powerful alumni associations, would oppose a further division of the Permanent University Fund (PUF) revenue if they were forced to share with all public colleges and universities.

Those who would lose benefits under a new constitution would be more committed to its defeat than those who might gain would be committed to its adoption. To the prospective winners under reform, promises of long-term benefit some time in the future would be less tangible and less concrete. Furthermore, constitutional revision isn't a hot topic with most Texans. Families don't talk about it around the dinner table.

Nonetheless, prospects for change are not hopeless. A realization that the old constitution just doesn't work seems to be taking hold among many Texas political actors. Major newspapers have called for revision. About a decade ago, Republican Senator Bill Ratliff and Democrat House Member Rob Junell collaborated on a proposed constitution. Their document was less than a quarter of the length of what we now have. It contained several significant changes for Texas government. Legislative terms would be lengthened, for instance, but terms would be limited. The governor would appoint a cabinet, including the agriculture and land commissioners, but the attorney general and comptroller would still be elected. The biggest change would be in the judiciary. The highest civil and criminal courts would be combined. Judges at the district court level and above would initially be appointed by the governor, then subjected to periodic retention elections, where voters could give a thumbs-up or thumbs-down to their continued service. Their proposal died in committee, but such is the fate of most innovative ideas on their first introduction to the Texas legislature. Since then, both Ratliff and Junell have retired from public office, depriving the movement of its leadership.

Then-Governor Bush's response to the 1999 effort was lukewarm at best, but who could blame him? Looking toward a 2000 presidential run, he had little to gain from weighing in on the issue. If he got behind it and it passed, no one outside Texas would care. If he failed, the national press would jump on him for his failure to control politics in his home state. In essence, that is the root of the problem for constitutional reform in Texas. It is difficult, time-consuming, and costly, and the political rewards are limited at best. If you achieve your goal, only people who write government books will remember your name. Your reward will be a better Texas, but you're likely to make more enemies than friends simply by making the attempt.

Summary

Texas is part of the American federalist system of government. As such, the state's policies are often shaped by forces beyond its control. Acts of Congress, federal funding, federal mandates, and federal judicial decisions all affect the way Texas transacts its business.

Every state has its own constitution. Most tend to be much longer than the national document and tend to restrict state action, containing provisions that go well beyond shaping the government's structure. Despite an early history of changing constitutions often, Texas has been under the present document since 1876. Written for another century, the constitution was intended to restrict the power of government. It achieves this goal well. As a result of its restrictive nature, the constitution must be frequently amended.

All efforts to rewrite the current Texas Constitution have failed. Attempts to create a new document have consistently garnered opposition from those groups that benefit from the current document.

Chapter Test

1. The document that provides a framework in which a government operates is a
   a. law.
   b. declaration.
   c. statute.
   d. constitution.

2. The transfer of programs from the national to state governments is called
   a. devolution.
   b. mandates.
   c. reversal.
   d. none of the above.

3. Most states
   a. seldom amend their constitutions.
   b. cannot amend their constitutions.
   c. do not have formal constitutions.
   d. amend their constitutions more often than the national government.

4. All are true of Texas Constitution amendments *except*
   a. they must be approved by two-thirds of the House.
   b. they must be approved by two-thirds of the Senate.
   c. the governor must sign them.
   d. they must be approved by the voters.

5. State constitutions tend to
   a. be flexible.
   b. be short.
   c. include "legislative" law.
   d. be amended infrequently.

6. The current Texas Constitution was partially a reaction to
   a. the Civil War.
   b. Reconstruction.
   c. the Great Depression.
   d. devolution.

7. Radical Republican Reconstruction policies included all *except*
   a. suffrage for African American males.
   b. creating balanced budgets.
   c. integration of the races.
   d. developing railroads.

8. The sharing of powers by the national and state government is
   a. bicameralism.
   b. federalism.
   c. utopianism.
   d. liberalism.

9. All of the following statements about the Texas Constitution are correct *except* that it
   a. has been amended more than 400 times.
   b. is more than 120 years old.
   c. has been amended more than the average state document.
   d. provides for a powerful executive branch.

10. The 1876 Constitution did all *except*
    a. cut salaries of government officials.
    b. call for annual legislative sessions.
    c. cut the governor's term of office.
    d. provide a detailed Bill of Rights.

Answers: 1. d 2. a 3. d 4. c 5. c 6. b 7. b 8. b 9. d 10. b

Critical Thinking Questions

1. Should Texas call a state constitutional convention? What forces would oppose such a revision?

2. How has the national government gained power over the last 200 years? Should states be given more power in the federalist equation?

3. How is the 1876 Constitution a reaction to Reconstruction?

Key Terms

1876 Constitution, **p. 52**
amendments, **p. 39**
Bill of Rights, **p. 39**
Black Codes, **p. 47**
constitution, **p. 39**
cooperative federalism, **p. 42**
devolution, **p. 43**
dual federalism, **p. 42**
E. J. Davis, **p. 48**

federalism, **p. 36**
Grange, **p. 52**
judicial review, **p. 39**
legislative law, **p. 44**
mandates, **p. 43**
new federalism, **p. 42**
"Obnoxious Acts," **p. 50**
unfunded mandates, **p. 43**

Notes

1. *The Book of the States, 2004* (Lexington, KY: Council of State Governments, 2004), p. 10.
2. Ibid.
3. Ibid.

4. Rupert N. Richardson, Adrian Anderson, and Ernest Wallace, *Texas: The Lone Star State* (Englewood Cliffs, NJ: Prentice Hall, 1993), p. 110.

5. Ibid., p. 151.

6. Ibid.

7. *Seymour* v. *Conner, Texas: A History* (Arlington Heights, IL: Harlan Davidson, 1971), pp. 216–217.

8. Richardson, p. 227.

9. Ibid., p. 294.

10. Carl H. Moneyhon, *Republicanism in Reconstruction Texas* (Austin, TX: University of Texas Press, 1980), pp. 123–124.

11. Ibid., p. 139.

12. Richardson, p. 236.

13. Moneyhon, pp. 184–185.

14. Ibid., pp. 192–193.

15. John Walker Mauer, "State Constitutions in a Time of Crisis: The Case of the Texas Constitution of 1876," *Texas Law Review* 68 (1990): 1625–1626.

16. J. E. Ericson, "The Delegates to the Convention of 1875, A Reappraisal," *Southwestern Historical Quarterly* 67 (1963):22.

17. Mauer, p. 1624.

18. Ibid., pp. 1625–1626.

19. Arvel Ponton, "Sources of Liberty in the Texas Bill of Rights," *St. Mary's Law Journal* 20 (1988):97.

20. Ibid., pp. 102–107.

21. Mike Kingston, ed., *The 1994–95 Texas Almanac* (Dallas, TX: Dallas Morning News, 1993), p. 363.

Political Participation: Voting and Elections

3

Primary elections and the white primary, both of which replace the pa[rty] caucus, are adopted by the Democrat[ic] Party and debut in the state.

Most African American males are eligible to vote for delegates to the Constitutional Convention.

The poll tax is passed into law.

| 1867 | | 1900 | 1902 | 1903 |

Texas has 650,000 potential African American voters, but less than one in thirty are eligible to vote.

By the end of this chapter on voting and elections, you should be able to . . .

★ Identify past restrictions on voting rights in Texas.

★ Explain voter registration requirements in Texas.

★ Analyze causes of low voter turnout in Texas.

★ Differentiate among primary, general, and special elections.

★ Explain the obstacles to running a campaign in Texas.

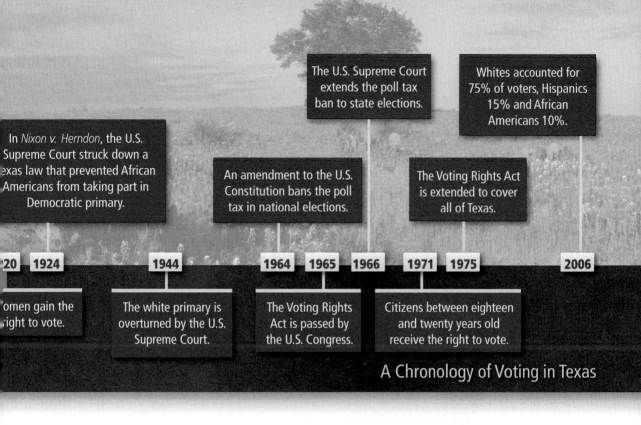

A Chronology of Voting in Texas

In *Nixon v. Herndon*, the U.S. Supreme Court struck down a Texas law that prevented African Americans from taking part in Democratic primary.

The U.S. Supreme Court extends the poll tax ban to state elections.

Whites accounted for 75% of voters, Hispanics 15% and African Americans 10%.

An amendment to the U.S. Constitution bans the poll tax in national elections.

The Voting Rights Act is extended to cover all of Texas.

20 · 1924 · 1944 · 1964 · 1965 · 1966 · 1971 · 1975 · 2006

Women gain the right to vote.

The white primary is overturned by the U.S. Supreme Court.

The Voting Rights Act is passed by the U.S. Congress.

Citizens between eighteen and twenty years old receive the right to vote.

*When "the people" is master of the vote,
it becomes master of the government.*

—ARISTOTLE

*Some people shouldn't vote;
they should just go eat ice cream*

—PAUL STOCKARD, TARRANT COUNTY REPUBLICAN ACTIVIST,
ON THE IMPACT ON UNINFORMED VOTERS

In order for a democracy to work, educated, enlightened, and informed citizens must be able and willing to take part in the political process. Today Texas has **universal suffrage**. Almost all citizens 18 and older have the right to register and vote. Registration is relatively easy and early voting laws effectively extend election periods dramatically. Despite its voter-friendly regulations, Texas's voter turnout is low.

universal suffrage
The concept that holds that virtually all adult citizens (felons and illegal aliens are excluded) have the right to vote.

A History of Voting Rights

Before the Civil War, of course, slaves in Texas had no voting rights. When Texas fell under martial law after the Civil War, the state had to extend voting rights to African American males in order to regain full statehood. This extension was short-lived, however. After the Democrats regained control of the state, both intimidation and government action were used to restrict minority voter access. By 1900, the state had 650,000 potential African American voters, but only 25,000 were qualified to vote.[1]

Women, meanwhile, had no voting rights until the Nineteenth Amendment to the U.S. Constitution passed in 1920. Texas was the first southern state to approve the amendment and had allowed women to participate in primary elections as early as 1918.

White Primary

In Texas, from the end of Reconstruction until the early 1960s, Democratic nomination was tantamount to election. Republicans never won. By the beginning of the 20th century, Democrats held every office in the state. Therefore, the Democratic Party made the real decisions as to who would win which office.

In 1903, under the auspices of progressive reform, the Texas Democratic Party adopted the primary system to replace the party caucus. Under the caucus method, party leaders selected Democratic nominees for elective office, choosing officeholders, not merely nominees. Under the primary system, voters chose nominees—tantamount to officeholders—in the Democratic primary. The so-called progressives wanted to shift nomination power to some, but not all, Texas citizens. They did not favor racial equality and adopted a **white primary** system, whereby African Americans were prohibited from participating. Once African Americans were excluded from the primary, they were, effectively, excluded from the political process. Even if they were permitted to vote in the general election, the winning candidate had already been chosen.

African American leaders contended that such a system violated the Fifteenth Amendment to the U.S. Constitution, which guarantees that race cannot be used to prevent a person from voting. In 1924, in *Nixon* v. *Herndon*, the U.S. Supreme Court struck down a Texas law that prevented African Americans from taking part in a Democratic primary. (Note that the law did not ban Hispanics from participating. Whether Hispanics could vote in the primary was determined locally.) Texas Democrats reacted to the 1924 decision by passing a party resolution granting primary election suffrage only to whites. Minority leaders objected and took the state and party to court. The U.S. Supreme Court rejected their argument in *Grovey* v. *Townsend*.

The Court sided with the Democratic Party, which maintained that as a private organization, it could include or exclude people at its discretion. This argument ignored the party's domination of Texas government. The party and the government were, for all practical purposes, the same.

By 1944, the character of the U.S. Supreme Court had changed. President Franklin Roosevelt's appointees had made the Court more liberal. In ***Smith*** v. ***Allwright***, the Court overturned *Townsend*. Because primary elections are conducted under state authority and because state courts can review conflicts arising from primary elections, the Court ruled that political parties are "an agency of the state." As such, they must abide by federal law regarding political participation and suffrage.[2]

white primary
The practice of allowing only whites to vote in the Democratic primary (discontinued).

Smith* v. *Allwright
U.S. Supreme Court case that overturned the white primary.

Although African American voter registration numbers increased rapidly, the last vestiges of the white primary continued in some parts of Texas. With the state Democratic resolution struck down by the court, some county Democratic organizations passed their own white primary resolutions. It took a few additional years before federal courts struck down these provisions as well.[3]

Poll Tax

Another device that worked to hold down voter turnout was the **poll tax**, passed into law in 1902. A citizen had to pay this tax in order to register to vote. While this worked to reduce minority turnout, it also negatively affected all economically disadvantaged and politically unaware people. The greatest impact was, as intended, on the minority community, where poverty was concentrated. This tax was part of the same "progressive" reforms that brought about the primary. The progressives wanted to formalize the election registration process to help root out corruption. Also, by reducing the number of poor voters, they could increase their chances of bringing about a prohibition on the sales of alcoholic beverages. By limiting alcohol sales and voting rights, progressives believed that they were "saving" the poor from their own excesses.

Faced with having to pay the tax to register, many poor people decided their votes were not important enough to sacrifice limited financial resources. Prior to *Smith* v. *Allwright*, this was particularly true for African Americans. Barred from the Democratic primary, where the actual election occurred, they had no compelling reason to pay the tax. Another problem with the poll tax stemmed from the requirement that it be paid before the end of January in each election year. No reminder notices were sent into minority and poor communities to urge on-time registration. If a person missed this deadline, he lost his right to vote.

In 1964, the Twenty-fourth Amendment was added to the U.S. Constitution to ban poll taxes in federal elections, specifically for president, vice president, and the U.S. Senate and U.S. House of Representatives. Texas tried a way to get around the ban. It created a dual-ballot system. Everyone received a federal ballot, but only those who paid their poll taxes received state ballots. Even though the Twenty-fourth Amendment referred specifically to federal elections, not state offices, the U.S. Supreme Court struck down the Texas law in *United States* v. *Texas*[4] in 1966.

poll tax
A tax paid for registering to vote (this tax no longer exists).

Federal Court Intervention

After the poll tax decision, federal courts became more active in regulating state voting requirements. In a series of rulings, these courts struck down provisions requiring annual registration and a year of residence in Texas before a person could vote. As the Texas Mosaic on Barbara Jordan shows, the impact was almost immediate. Federal courts also rejected a provision of the Texas Constitution allowing only property owners to vote on bond issues.

The Voting Rights Act

The **Voting Rights Act (VRA) of 1965** had a significant impact on minority voter turnout. Although not fully extended to Texas until its renewal in 1975, the act protects minorities from discrimination in the registration or voting process. Additionally, it requires all affected states and municipalities to submit redistricting plans to either

Voting Rights Act of 1965
National act protecting minorities from discrimination in the voting or the registration process.

Texas MOSAIC

Increasing Diversity in Elective Politics:
Barbara Jordan

One thing is clear to me: We, as human beings, must be willing to accept people who are different from ourselves.

—Barbara Jordan

"First" might not have been Barbara Jordan's last name, but it could have been. The adjective followed her surname in so many instances that the words tended to appear in tandem.

Born in 1936 to a working-class family in Houston's Fifth Ward, Jordan refused to settle for a "second-class" life. After attending segregated public schools and a segregated state university—Texas Southern—she obtained her law degree from Boston University. She returned to Houston in 1960, opening a law office and working in Lyndon Johnson's presidential campaign. Among her duties in the Johnson campaign was helping register African American voters. She would continue with these efforts after that campaign was finished. In 1962, and again in 1964, she ran unsuccessfully for the Texas Senate, as the odds were stacked too heavily against her. Black voter registration was still low, and Texas House and Senate districts were gerrymandered in such a way as to splinter and dilute the minority vote. By 1966, however, federal court intervention, as well as voter registration efforts by Jordan and others like her, had sufficiently leveled the playing field. Jordan became the first African American elected to the Texas Senate since 1883. Reelected in 1968, she would become president pro tempore of the state senate and served as "governor-for-the-day," an honor that accompanies the office.

In 1972, Jordan became the first African American woman from the South elected to the U.S. Congress. Two years later, Jordan came to national prominence for her eloquent, hard-hitting questioning during the Watergate hearings, which helped end the Nixon administration. Coupled with her distinctive voice, Jordan became a political star and was chosen to deliver the keynote speech at the 1976 Democratic National Convention. She was the first woman to deliver the keynote address.

After three terms in Congress, Jordan returned to her home state and took a professorship at the LBJ School of Public Affairs at the University of Texas. She would later serve as an ethics adviser to Governor Ann Richards. She delivered a second Democratic National Convention keynote address in 1992; the Democrats were 2 to 0 in presidential elections following keynote speeches by Jordan. She passed away in 1996.

the U.S. Justice Department or a federal court for approval. This provision of the VRA weakened the ability of the state to engage in racial gerrymandering—the process of drawing district lines to dilute minority voting strength. As a result, the number of minority officeholders in Texas has increased dramatically. Minority political power has increased as well.

Three African American Republicans held statewide positions after the 2008 elections, and it was minority Democrats who helped tip the balance toward Republican Tom Craddick in the race for Speaker of the House in both 2003 and 2007, and, to a lesser extent, Joe Straus in 2009.

Qualifications

In order to vote in Texas today, a person must be at least 18 years old by election day, a U.S. citizen, and a Texas resident, as indicated in the *Texas Constitution* box. (A person can apply at age 17, 10 months.) The prospective voter must be a resident of his county 30 days prior to the election and must register to vote 30 days in

The Texas Constitution: A Closer Look

The Texas Constitution grants its citizens near universal suffrage:

ARTICLE VI. SUFFRAGE

Sec. 1. CLASSES OF PERSONS NOT ALLOWED TO VOTE.

(a) The following classes of persons shall not be allowed to vote in this State:
   (1) persons under 18 years of age;
   (2) persons who have been determined mentally incompetent by a court, subject to such exceptions as the Legislature may make; and
   (3) persons convicted of any felony, subject to such exceptions as the Legislature may make.

(b) The legislature shall enact laws to exclude from the right of suffrage persons who have been convicted of bribery, perjury, forgery, or other high crimes.

advance as well. Convicted felons are not allowed to vote until two years after their sentences, including probation and parole, are completed.

Registration

Registering to vote in Texas is simple. You only need to fill out a postcard-size form. Additionally, a voter can register a spouse, parent, or child, provided that the second person meets voting qualifications. In Texas, registration is permanent. As long as a person maintains the same address, registration will be automatically renewed. (Some counties will remove you from the rolls if you don't vote for several years.) If you move, you need to reregister. Furthermore, it is not necessary to have your registration card in order to vote. If you have misplaced your card, simply produce another form of identification, such as a driver's license. If you never received a card, you may be asked to sign a sworn affidavit confirming that you did properly register.

Under the "motor voter" law passed by the U.S. Congress, a person can also register to vote when applying for a driver's license without even filling out a form. The law requires that a person be allowed to register to vote when they apply for a driver's licenses, public assistance, or other public services. By simply affirming they wish to register, citizens are added to the registration rolls. In the first month the process was in effect, Texas added 80,000 new potential voters.[5] One criticism of the law was that legally unqualified voters, such as noncitizens, may be registered in

WHAT CAN YOU DO?

By becoming a volunteer deputy registrar, a person can help register citizens to vote. Many college student organizations participate in this activity as a service to the community. To become involved, contact the voter registrar in your country, which you can find here: http://www.sos.state.tx.us/elections/voter/votregduties.shtml.

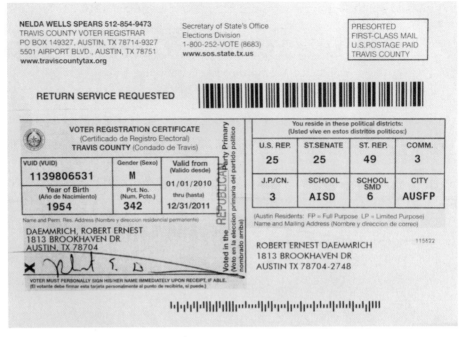

A Texas voter registration card.

error simply by answering yes to the registration question. In response, Texas became one of the first states to require agencies that register voters to determine their eligibility using records at their disposal.

Turnout

turnout
Percentage of registered voters who cast ballots.

The irony of **turnout** in the United States is that, despite the long fight for the right, relatively few people vote, especially in comparison to other Western democracies. Descendants of the groups that fought the hardest and longest to secure the right to vote are among the least likely to turn out. Additionally, many eligible citizens do not register. Because these people are not counted in traditional turnout percentages, actual voter participation is even lower than it appears.

The greatest single factor in determining turnout is level of education. In fact, if education and income levels are controlled, minorities and whites vote at roughly the same rate. The more educated a person is, the more likely he or she is to vote. Nonetheless, there is a correlation between race and turnout. Anglos are more likely to vote than minorities. In the 1998 Texas governor's race, 72 percent of the voters were white. African Americans comprised 10 percent of the voters, slightly less than their percentage of the state's population. Hispanics accounted for just 16 percent of voters. In 2002, the percentage of Hispanic voters increased to 17 percent. In contrast, African American voters dropped to 7 percent and white voters to 71 percent. In 2006, as noted in figure 3.1, whites accounted for 75 percent of voters, Hispanics 15 percent, and Africans Americans 10 percent.

A huge factor, second only to level of education, is family tradition. Citizens from families that support the idea that voting is a civic duty are much more likely to turn out than those from a nonvoting family. If your parents vote, you will probably turn into a voter, even if you aren't one now. Voters are also likely to be older and wealthier than nonvoters.

Another factor in turnout is the type of election. Presidential elections, the most prominent, draw the most media attention and the highest turnout. State elections, such as the governor's race, are next. Local elections attract low turnout, usually bringing out less than 10 percent of registered voters. School board races routinely draw even fewer voters.

Voter turnout numbers in Texas have varied in recent years. In 1986, only 47.2 percent of registered voters cast a ballot in the governor's race. By 1990, turnout increased to 50.5 percent. In 1994, it edged up to 50.8 percent. The number of ballots cast increased from 3,441,460 in 1986 to 3,892,746 in 1990 and 4,392,580 in 1994. In 2006, only 34 percent of voters turned out, which translated to 4,399,068 ballots.[6]

Texas had about 9 million registered voters in 1994 and has a little over 13 million today. These numbers show not only that the percentage of registered voters has increased, but also that the number of registered voters has increased. Prior to 1994, less than two-thirds of voting age Texans were registered to vote. From the mid-1990s forward, registration has hovered close to 80 percent of the voting age population. At least part of this increase was due to relaxed early voting laws and an intense effort by the last several secretaries of state to enlarge voting rolls. The motor voter law also had an effect, although many of those registered under the act never intended to vote. When comparing turnout before and after the act, raw numbers provide a better comparison than percentage.

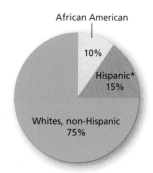

*Hispanic turnout was well below its share of the population.

FIGURE **3.1** **Texas Voter Turnout, 2006.**

In most urban areas, voting is conducted primarily on computerized machines, which bypass paper ballots. Is this a better way to vote?

The last two elections of the 1990s reversed that trend, however, as numbers dropped, both in terms of total number of voters and percentage of registered voters turning out. In the 1996 general election for president, only 5,611,644 voters cast ballots. This equals 53.2 percent of registered voters. In the 1998 governor's race, turnout was 3,738,078, or 32.4 percent. Much of the downtrend might be attributable to the fact that the 1996 and 1998 races were seen as noncompetitive. Although Bob Dole carried Texas in 1996, it was widely believed that Bill Clinton would win reelection. George W. Bush was so clearly ahead in the 1998 governor's race that the contest was considered over by early summer. Only 52 percent of those registered voted in 2000. Again, the presidential race wasn't competitive because Bush was heavily favored in his home state. In the 2002 governor's race, only 36 percent of voters showed up at the polls. Like good football games, highly competitive races draw more interest than dull blowouts. In 2004, turnout was back up to 57 percent. However, as we mentioned above, just over one-third of registered voters participated in 2006. In 2008, 59.5 percent of eligible voters cast ballots.[7] In the 2010 midterm election, just under 5 million voters produced a 37.5 percent turnout.

Who Turns Out

Who turns out has a huge impact on who is elected. In 1994, 88 percent of African Americans and 71 percent of Hispanics who turned out voted for Ann Richards for governor, yet together these ethnic groups made up only 22 percent of voters. If Hispanics and African Americans had voted in a percentage equal to their share of the population, and if their margins of support for Richards had held, she would have been reelected by about eight percentage points. This is almost identical to the margin by which she lost.

Lower turnout in minority communities is a product of several factors. First, persons from disadvantaged socioeconomic groups often have had fewer positive interactions with government than middle- or upper-class voters. This can lead to distrust of government in general, causing citizens to question why they should bother voting. Such people often feel **disfranchised**, believing their votes either do not matter, since there is little concrete connection to their day-to-day lives, or do not count, due to perceived "corruption" within the system.

disfranchised
Persons who cannot vote, or who believe their votes don't count.

Second, family tradition has an impact on voter participation. A person who grows up in an environment in which voting is important is more likely to participate. In Texas, there has been a history of barriers placed between minorities and the voting booth. In addition to governmental blocks, minorities faced barriers from society at large. Violence and intimidation were used to discourage minority voting. In south Texas, many Hispanic voters faced the loss of a job if they cast a ballot. If past generations were prohibited from participating, it is more difficult to establish a family tradition that views voting as a civic duty.

Third, especially within the Hispanic community, language can be a barrier to participation. Even though ballots and registration cards are bilingual—trilingual in Harris County, which now prints ballots in Vietnamese as well—it is more difficult for non-English-speaking citizens to obtain information on registration, voting, issues, and candidates. Nonetheless, the efforts of the Southwest Voters Education and Registration Project to encourage Hispanics to participate have resulted in significant increases in registration and voting within the Latino community. More Hispanics now serve in elected office than at any time in the state's history.

Turnout among young people is historically low. Many consider government issues too far removed from their everyday existence to be important. More register and vote as they become older and more aware of the issues. However, government policies—from setting college tuition rates to speed limits, and from the drinking age to student loan programs—have a profound impact on young people. If anyone wants to influence the future, there is no better way to start than by registering, paying attention to the political world, and voting.

States with a traditionalistic political culture tend to have lower-than-average turnout. In addition, one-party states tend to have lower turnout because many believe their votes won't matter. While Texas no longer falls under the one-party state classification, years of Democratic domination still negatively affect turnout because voting is a learned trait and parents who don't value the political process tend to produce children who don't vote. Besides, Republicans now dominate statewide politics—except for the House of Representatives—in a manner similar to the domination of the Democrats a generation ago. Finally, low voter turnout can point to general voter satisfaction. When citizens are angry about something, they tend to let their voices be heard. But when things are going well, some citizens become apathetic about exercising their political rights.

Texas Factors in Registration and Turnout

A major factor that affects turnout is the large number of elections in Texas. During a single year, a citizen may be asked to vote in a party primary, a party primary runoff, a city election, a city election runoff, a local bond election, a local recall election, a tax rollback election, a special election, a special election runoff, and a general election. Even when cities, school boards, and junior college districts hold their elections on the same day, a voter might be asked to visit three different polling places in order to participate in all three elections. Texas voters can develop **election burnout**, and only the most dedicated citizens vote every time they have the opportunity to cast a ballot.

election burnout
Occurs when citizens believe there are too many elections, and thus, fail to vote.

The **long ballot** that confronts Texas voters also has a detrimental effect on turnout. In large urban counties, a voter might be asked to select the best person for 30 or more different judicial positions, from the Texas Supreme Court to justice of the peace. It is unlikely that the average Texan is familiar with more than one or two of the judicial candidates. In addition, voters are asked to fill several positions the responsibilities of which are misunderstood. For instance, the Texas Railroad Commission has little to do with railroads. Few Texans can identify the duties of the comptroller or land commissioner, yet these offices appear on the ballot. Selecting the best person to fill the positions becomes a near impossibility under the circumstances. Instead of picking the wrong candidate, some choose not to vote at all. Many voters don't know that they are not required to vote for every office in order to have a valid ballot. They can vote for only one candidate, or just those candidates with whom they are familiar.

long ballot
A system under which many officials are up for election at the same time.

Another aspect of Texas law that discouraged voter registration was that, prior to 1992, jury duty summons lists were compiled from voter registration rolls. Many people chose not to register because they did not want to be called for jury duty. Although jury selection lists now comprise virtually all adult citizens (see Chapter 10), many people still believe that registering to vote is, in essence, registering for jury duty. Even those aware of the change have not necessarily bothered to register.

Some reforms would make participation easier. Several states now allow Election Day registration. A person may decide to participate at the last minute, instead of having to register 30 days prior to the election. Other states have experimented with an expanded ballot by mail. In Texas and most other states, a person who is out of the state or disabled can vote by mail. Oregon, however, filled the seat vacated by U.S. Senator Robert Packwood in a primary and general election carried out completely through the mail and has transitioned exclusively to mail in ballots. Many other states have liberalized their voting rules, allowing voters to cast ballots by mail merely by asking.

Voter turnout would be higher, it is argued, if all a voter had to do was pick up a ballot from the mailbox, fill it out at his or her convenience, and return it through the mail. Likewise, the prevalence of the Internet offers an opportunity to create easier access to the ballot.

Both Election Day registration and alternative ballots have their critics. In each case, opportunity for fraud exists. A 30-day registration window allows election officials to check records for fraud. States that use same-day registration, however, have not reported significant problems. With a mail-in or Internet ballot, it would be easy for "helpful" campaign workers to give illegal assistance. This has already occurred in nursing homes in this state, where some overenthusiastic campaign workers have "saved" elderly Texans trouble by filling out the ballots for them. In fact, the elimination of such fraud is another suggested reform. Giving significant prison time to those who engage in such activity, it is argued, would increase the perception that your vote is a sacred, protected right that is not easily manipulated. In fact, a bill passed the Texas House in 2005 that would have made voting more difficult—it would have required all voters to have a picture ID before casting a ballot. The bill was killed in the Senate, but it underscored a concern with the potential for illegally cast ballots. Critics of the bill saw it as an attempt to suppress minority turnout. The bill failed again in 2007 and in 2009, but by late 2010 the issue was already on the informal agenda for the 2011 session.

Opponents of lenient registration and voting laws believe there is a cost to making it too easy to vote: uninformed citizens might be more likely to cast ballots. As long as registration and voting require some affirmative act, the process tends to weed out the least prepared voters. This makes a difference if you believe that an informed public makes better choices than an uninformed one. One reform already enacted in Texas that has increased turnout is the state's no excuse early voting policy. In most states, voters can only vote absentee—or early—if they are going to be out of town on Election Day. In Texas, however, voters can vote early without such a restriction. For primary and general elections, the period for early voting begins 15 to 17 days—and ends 4 days—prior to the election. The county clerk or elections administrator determines starting dates.

Voters can go to any of a number of designated locations across the county and cast their ballots. Early voting is popular in Texas. Of those who turn out for elections, upward of 30 percent routinely vote during the preelection period. In 2008, early voters comprised 42 percent of total voters. In 2004, an astounding 51 percent of those who cast a presidential vote in Texas voted early. Such numbers influence campaigns because consultants realize the importance of getting the candidate's message out early. It doesn't help to connect with voters after they have cast their ballots.[8]

You can access a vast amount of information on registration, voting, and turnout at the secretary of state's Web site at http://www.sos.state.tx.us.

Types of Election

Primary Election

Texas holds partisan elections for all state offices from governor to constable. Before the Democrat and Republican can run against each other in a general election, the parties must determine their nominees for each office. These nominees are chosen through the **primary election**. The direct primary allows all registered voters to help select the nominees for the party of their choice.

Voters do not register as Democrats or Republicans in Texas. Rather, official party affiliation is not determined until the day of the primary election. In this sense, the Texas system is open. A person can be standing in line to vote in the Democratic primary, change his or her mind, and go to the Republican primary. A person voting in one primary may not vote in the other party's primary—it's against the law. Furthermore, a person who votes in one party's primary cannot cross over and vote in the other party's runoff, if one is necessary. In this very limited way, from the primary election date until the runoff four weeks later, a voter is bound by party affiliation. A quirk in state election law, however, allows a citizen who did not vote in either primary to cast a ballot in the runoff of his or her choice.

In Texas, primary elections are held on the first Tuesday of March. This was intended to coincide with the Super Tuesday primary on which several predominately southern states held their presidential primaries, but Texas kept the date even as several other states moved theirs earlier. Some states separate the presidential vote from their other elections, holding the primary for state offices closer to the actual election in November. Texas, however, in order to avoid expenses incurred by holding two elections, holds all primary elections in March, even in nonpresidential years. To win a primary election, a person must receive the majority of the votes cast. If no one receives more than 50 percent, a runoff election is held between the top two vote getters for that particular office. The party's nominee will be the person who wins the runoff. With two active, strong political parties, some runoffs are inevitable. So many candidates file for some offices in the primaries that it is unlikely that any person will receive a majority.

Not all parties in Texas are required to hold primaries. Minor parties, such as the Libertarian Party, have not proven strong enough to warrant the expense of statewide elections. Unless its candidate received at least 20 percent of the vote in the last governor's race, a party is entitled to select its candidates through its state convention.

General Election

General elections determine who will hold office. The winners of the primaries, as well as the nominees of minor parties, have their names placed on the general election ballot. It is very difficult for a third party to qualify for ballot access in Texas, particularly in statewide elections. Unless one of your candidates received at least

primary election
The process through which major parties choose their nominees for the general election.

general election
The process through which officeholders are elected from among party nominees.

5 percent of the vote in the last general election, you need the signature of almost 50,000 citizens (1percent of the last general election total for that office) who did not vote in either the Republican or Democrat primary. And you have only 30 days after the primary to collect your signatures. For all practical purposes, this means that in Texas, only the Republicans, the Democrats, and the Libertarians have a permanent spot on the ballot. The Green Party used the petition method to qualify for the 2010 ballot. (See Chapter 4 for more on third parties.)

plurality

Exists when a candidate has more votes than any other candidate, even if the total is less than 50 percent.

General elections require a **plurality** of the votes, not necessarily a majority, to win. Plurality means more votes than any other candidate. In the 1990 governor's race, for example, Ann Richards did not receive a majority of the vote. Her 1,925,670 votes represented just 49.5 percent of the total. Her opponent, Clayton Williams, received 47 percent of the vote. The rest was divided among Libertarian Party candidate Jeff Daiell, who received 3.3 percent, and a number of write-in candidates. Richards took office without a runoff.

gubernatorial election

The election for governor and other executive offices.

Gubernatorial elections, in which the governor and other executive officials are picked, are held during even-numbered years between presidential elections. The off-year elections mean that voters pay more attention to these statewide executive races. If they were to be held during presidential years they would receive less media coverage due to the intense focus on national politics. Also, turnout tends to be lower in nonpresidential years, meaning that more-dedicated voters show up for gubernatorial elections. This makes a party's ability to turn out its voters a key factor in winning. Parties tend to concentrate on those voters who participated in their primary as they attempt to get out the vote. They reason that primary voters are both loyal to the party and more likely to turn out than the average citizen.

The winning party in the governor's race is listed first on the ballot in elections for the following four years. While this might not be significant at the top of the ballot, it can have an influence on lower-level races. When voters don't recognize either name, they are more likely to vote for the first one on the list.

Finally, Texas allows general election voters to fill in one mark at the top of the ballot and thereby vote for a party's entire slate of candidates. Additionally, a voter can fill in the mark at the top and then mark candidates from another party for individual offices, thereby voting predominately for one party with noted exceptions. While straight-ticket voting initially benefited the Democrats, that advantage has generally flowed to the Republicans in recent elections.

Special Election

special election

An election held to fill a vacancy, ratify a state constitutional amendment, or approve a local bond issue.

Special elections are held to fill vacancies, ratify state constitutional amendments, or approve local bond issues. Special elections to fill vacancies are "nonpartisan," require a majority to win, and usually occur outside of the traditional March and November dates.

The best-known special election was held to fill the U.S. Senate seat vacated when former Senator Lloyd Bentsen resigned to become President Bill Clinton's treasury secretary in 1993. Former Governor Ann Richards appointed fellow Democrat Bob Krueger to fill the position until a special election could be held. Krueger joined a field of 23 other candidates that included prominent Texas politicians such as congressmen Jack Fields and Joe Barton, business leader (and future Dallas Federal Reserve President) Richard Fisher, and state Treasurer Kay Bailey Hutchison. A number of political unknowns were on the ballot as well. With so many candidates, it was not a surprise that no one received a majority of the votes during the initial round of balloting. Hutchison and Krueger emerged from the pack and made it into the runoff. Hutchison easily won the runoff, garnering two-thirds of the votes.

Referring to special elections as nonpartisan is somewhat misleading. In 1993, everyone interested in the political process knew that Hutchison, Fields, and Barton were Republicans and that former state Attorney General Jim Mattox, Fisher, and Krueger were Democrats. All appealed to their traditional party bases as they ran for election. The race was nonpartisan in the sense that candidates did not have to go through the primary process in order to appear on the ballot.

Kay Bailey Hutchinson would convert this special election victory into almost two decades of service in the US Senate.

my turn

Down-Ballot Races

by Tom Wilder, Tarrant County District Clerk

Tom Wilder, who has been active in the Republican Party since 1962, has served as District Clerk for Tarrant County since 1995. Since that time, Tarrant County has twice been recognized for "best practices" by the Texas Association of Counties. The Texas Attorney General has commended Wilder for having the best run clerk's office in the state.

For the purposes of this essay, we will somewhat arbitrarily define down-ballot races to mean those races that appear on local ballots only and are not statewide in nature.

Immediately, it should be recognized that there are two distinct tiers in local, down-ballot races. These would be legislative races and then everything else including the local judiciary, county races such as county judge, district attorney, district clerk, sheriff, tax assessor-collector, county clerk, county commissioner, and constables.

Even within the first tier, there is a substantial difference between congressional races and races for the Texas legislature. Congressional races attract many more contributors and volunteers than candidates for the Texas legislature as well as free media, especially where the incumbent is concerned. Nationwide, incumbent congressional officeholders win over 90 percent of the time due to their ability to raise money and are basically in campaign mode every year due to their two-year terms.

It is ironic that congressional and state legislative candidates run in districts drawn with substantially fewer people than any candidate who must run countywide in the urban areas. Even a congressional district, which must contain about 500,000 residents, is only about one-third the size of the population of countywide candidates who must run in counties such as Bexar and Tarrant, which have about 1.5 million people. Of course, Harris and Dallas are much larger than that, creating an even greater disparity. Congressional candidates often spend $500,000 to $1,000,000, each in an urban area. Candidates for the Texas legislature often generate substantial contributions for their campaigns, especially state senators. However, the fact that almost all of them have to supplement their officeholder accounts with campaign funds

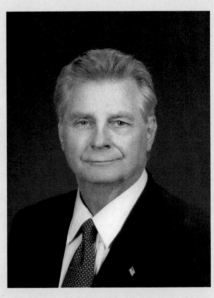

Tom Wilder worked his way through the political ranks before becoming district clerk.

over and above what they are given for office expenses is a drag on their resources available for campaigns. Arbitrary limits on legislative staff salaries contribute to this shortfall and help cause the big turnover in legislative personnel.

The top tier of down-ballot candidates are usually able to build large campaign organizations that are most helpful for get-out-the-vote efforts (GOTV) and additional fund-raising capabilities. Free media or earned media, as it's often called, flows freely to legislative races. In most instances, the other candidates who must run countywide have smaller organizations and only get free media if there is some sort of scandal or other unusual controversy.

Further complicating the ability of the second tier of down-ballot candidates to run effective campaigns is the fact that offices such as district attorney, district and county clerk, sheriff, tax-assessor, and the judiciary are full-time jobs requiring the daily presence and involvement of the elected official. It's always tough to find time to make fund-raising calls that must be done outside the office and to handle the daily campaign management, since second-tier candidates usually can't afford salaried campaign staff as can the top-tier candidates.

Another problem facing down-ballot candidates is the drop-off factor. This phenomenon occurs in every election and is easily seen when comparing the number of people who vote in top of the ticket races and those who vote in down-ballot races. Often the drop-off will approach 20 percent. This means that thousands of voters will vote only partway down the ballot, skipping some or all of the races. This is a nightmare for down-ballot candidates, especially in the general elections where the pool of prospective voters is much larger than the pool of primary voters. This generates an additional variable that is very difficult to handle. Another fact magnifies this effect, that of voter turnout. It is quite common to see twice the turnout in presidential years versus gubernatorial years. The race for president always draws more interest than the race for governor. While congressional races occur every two years and have the money to be better able to deal with these problems, contestants for sheriff, tax-assessor, two members of commissioners court, and some judicial races that are up for election in presidential years must be ever mindful of these factors and plan accordingly.

Another factor that heavily influences all races is party affiliation. In some counties such as Tarrant, being the nominee of the dominant party is tantamount to winning the election. Republicans currently hold all countywide offices in Tarrant County and almost all the legislative offices. In some other mainly rural counties, only democrats can win local down-ballot races. In counties where one party dominates, the other party will often only file token candidates that are hoping the dominant parties' candidates die before the November general election or are caught "in flagrante delicto" or some major scandal that can damage the dominant

party's nominee. The down-ballot nominees of a dominant party must guard against not only the drop-off factor but must be prepared to appeal to new voters who have moved into the county and don't know them. While there are techniques to communicate with these voters, they are expensive.

Thus, there is some good news for the down-ballot candidate in counties dominated by one party, since they only have to win their party primary election instead of having to run two full-scale races in counties where democrat and republican voting strength is more evenly matched. While the dominant party candidate would be prudent to make some kind of limited effort in the general election as an insurance policy against the unforeseen, most of this candidate's money and effort will be spent in their party primary election, which often will have only 10 to 15 percent of the those who vote in the general election. Usually, this means less money to be raised, since the potential voter pool will be much smaller and easier to identify. As an example, I spent over $90,000 in the GOP Primary election in 2002 and spent less than $20,000 in the general election due to the strength of GOP voters.

Since the different strategies and tactics used by top-of-the-ticket and down-ballot candidates are so complex, only a general discussion will be made here. Television advertising is the mainstay of the top-of-the-ticket campaign while direct mail is the tool used most successfully in down-ballot races. The millions spent on television by up-ballot campaigns gives these candidates the ability to move public opinion and respond quickly to an opponent's attacks. Buying the large media markets in Texas will reach about 80 percent of the electorate. While direct mail is used, it is mainly for fund-raising and to approach various specific voter groups. The down-ballot candidate must depend almost solely on direct mail since buying the electronic media is simply not cost effective. Most of the large media markets in Texas cover multiple counties and advertising is priced accordingly. A down-ballot candidate wouldn't want to pay to reach voters in other counties out of their own voting area even if they could afford it. Direct mail to specific voters allows down-ballot candidates to put their money on target but does have some limitations. It is much harder to respond to last-minute attacks and is subject to poor mail delivery, which can be disastrous. By example, in my initial race for district clerk, I had a procedure in place to monitor the delivery of direct mail. I discovered that the entire city of Arlington failed to receive any of my first mail piece. While I was able to remail that area since we

(continued)

(continued from page 79)

were just starting the mail program, which consisted of four mailings, I would have been out of luck had this happened on either of the last two mailings because direct mail must be repetitive and properly spaced to have the desired effect. Candidates would also be well-advised to hire professional help to design and manage any direct mail campaign since ill-conceived and poorly designed mail can cost votes no matter what an opponent might do. In the larger counties, four mailings will cost about between $85,000 and $110,000 total in the primary alone. Nondelivery to any large degree could be the difference between victory and defeat.

Phone banks and campaign signs are often used heavily in down-ballot races but are becoming more problematical with the passing of each election year. Once these were the main tools of down-ballot candidates, because they were generally cheaper than other types of campaign vehicles. Now, due to changes in the law and public acceptance, they are less effective. This is a shame, since our volunteer phone bank made over 20,000 completed calls in my first race. It was chaired by my wife, Charlene, and contributed mightily to the victory we achieved in 1994. It only cost about $5,000, which is a fraction of what just one mailing would cost in a countywide race. Good sign locations are becoming tougher to find, and city ordinances on signs are even more complex, not to mention increasing vandalism and theft.

Traditional "retail politics," such as speeches at forums and door knocking, are giving way to large e-mail campaigns and Web sites since it is just not possible to reach the number of voters required in the limited time when the voters are paying attention, which can be a matter of only a few weeks at best and a few days at worst.

Actually, most down-ballot candidates would probably admit that fund-raising is the biggest challenge they face. They are often surprised that they must fund their race with their own money, to a large degree, especially in a contested primary where multiple, credible candidates have filed. In the aforementioned dominant party scenario, little money will flow to the nondominant party's candidates for the general election. Of course, these realities heavily favor incumbents who already have name recognition and an established donor base. However, even where the incumbent chooses not to run again, any challenger will usually have to pony up thousands of dollars of their own money to have any chance of success. This has happened in many local, second-tier races, including my own in 1994,

where there were nine candidates running for the Republican nomination since the incumbent chose not to run again. I had to spend more than $25,000 of my own money to completely fund my game plan, which correctly included allowing for a run-off election, since I didn't think I could defeat eight opponents by getting a majority of the votes outright. There were a number of very credible candidates in the race, and like most multicandidate races in second tier, down-ballot contests, a run-off election is usually necessary. Run-off elections rarely have more than 15,000 to 30,000 votes even in countywide races and are real nail-biters due to the lack of interest. This is where a candidate with a good GOTV organization usually wins, as person-to-person contact to encourage voters to go back out to vote is all important.

It must be emphasized that any candidate must have the support of their spouse and "fire in the belly" to serve successfully in public life. The demands of campaigning and holding office are too great otherwise. A number of county officials like mine have tremendous personal liability, which puts added stress on an elected official. Anyone who works in the courthouse is also subject to some personal risk from disgruntled litigants and family members. However, if one has the proper motivation and qualifications, it can be deeply rewarding to hold the public trust and participate in the rule of law. No society has endured without it.

In the final analysis, it is important to continue to elect down-ballot candidates since it is necessary to retain our system of checks and balances. The idea that the best government is the one closest to the people has been proven over and over. Devolution of power from federal and state governments down to local offices began several years ago and hopefully will continue, as local offices are often more responsive and cost efficient than their larger brethren. Citizens also have the opportunity to get to know their local down-ballot candidates personally and can contact them much more easily than up-ballot officeholders. While all campaigns are stressful and expensive, down-ballot races present great challenges to the candidates. Voters would be well advised to meet them and make an assessment of their skills and qualifications, which they can do with local candidates. Electing local officials has proven to produce less corrupt, more responsive, cost-efficient government, as opposed to a system of appointing these officials as is done in a number of foreign countries.

Campaigning

Campaigning for office in Texas can be a daunting undertaking. While many races for local offices, such as city council or school board, still allow for a great deal of person-to-person contact, especially in small towns and cities, the process of seeking elective office in the state's large metropolitan areas is one that is increasingly distant from the people. As Tom Wilder's *My Turn* essay illustrates, running for office takes a significant commitment of time and resources.

This problem of distance between candidates and voters is even more acute when the political race is regional or statewide. Many state senate districts, especially in west Texas, sprawl over huge areas encompassing many counties. For example, the 19th District stretches from the southern part of Bexar County (San Antonio) to the southern part of El Paso County—a distance of almost 550 miles and an area that includes all of 21 counties in addition to the two already noted! A candidate may have to travel thousands of miles in order to make personal appearances during the course of a campaign. While urban Senate districts are not as geographically far-flung as those in the rural areas of Texas, campaigning in them can be as expensive if not

Campaigning can take many forms, some as simple as setting up a booth to create enthusiasm.

more so. It is not unusual for a closely contested race for the Texas Senate to require a candidate to spend between a million and two million dollars (and even such astronomical sums do not necessarily guarantee victory). Even a race for a seat in the Texas House (which usually involves an even more circumscribed geographic area) can be startlingly expensive. Candidates for such seats in Houston, Dallas–Fort Worth, or San Antonio can easily spend $500,000 or more, and even incumbents without opponents may spend as much as $250,000 in an election. In a state with virtually no limits on campaign contributions, raising money is imperative. Take a look at the differences between U.S. and Texas campaign laws in the Inside the Federalist System box nearby.

If you'd like to find out more information on candidates and their expenditures, log on to the Texas Secretary of State's Web site http://www.sos.state.tx.us, or the Web site of the Texas Ethics Commission http://www.ethics.state.tx.us.

Races for statewide offices, such as U.S. senator, governor, and other executive positions, or the state's highest appellate courts require candidates to roam the length and breadth of the state, often traveling farther in a single day than the distance from Texarkana to Chicago or from El Paso to San Diego. In light of these

INSIDE

THE FEDERALIST SYSTEM

State and Federal Campaign Contribution Limits

A stark difference between the federal and state law is demonstrated through the different approaches to campaign finance law. This chart shows limits on contributions to people running for U.S. Congress:

Contribution Limits 2009–2010
(Source: http://www.fec.gov.)

	To each candidate or candidate committee per election	To national party committee per calendar year	To state, district, and local party committee per calendar year	To any other political committee per calendar year[1]	Special Limits
Individual may give	$2,400*	$30,400*	$10,000 (combined limit)	$5,000	$115,500* overall biennial limit: • $45,600* to all candidates • $69,900* to all PACs and parties[2]
National Party Committee may give	$5,000	No limit	No limit	$5,000	$42,600* to Senate candidate per campaign[3]
State, District and Local Party Committee may give	$5,000 (combined limit)	No limit	No limit	$5,000 (combined limit)	No limit
PAC (multicandidate)[4] may give	$5,000	$15,000	$5,000 (combined limit)	$5,000	No limit
PAC (not multicandidate) may give	$2,400*	$30,400*	$10,000 (combined limit)	$5,000	No limit
Authorized Campaign Committee may give	$2,000[5]	No limit	No limit	$5,000	No limit

*These contribution limits are increased for inflation in odd-numbered years.

[1] A contribution earmarked for a candidate through a political committee counts against the original contributor's limit for that candidate. In certain circumstances, the contribution may also count against the contributor's limit to the PAC. 11 CFR 110.6. See also 11 CFR 110.1(h).

[2] No more than $45,600 of this amount may be contributed to state and local party committees and PACs.

[3] This limit is shared by the national committee and the Senate campaign committee.

[4] A multicandidate committee is a political committee with more than 50 contributors that has been registered for at least 6 months and, with the exception of state party committees, has made contributions to five or more candidates for federal office. 11 CFR 100.5(e)(3).

[5] A federal candidate's authorized committee(s) may contribute no more than $2,000 per election to another federal candidate's authorized committee(s). 2 U.S.C. 432(e)(3)(B).

(continued)

Texas, on the other hand, has no practical limits. Corporations and labor unions may not contribute directly to candidates, but their political action committees can (see Chapter 5). The only contribution limits are in judicial races. Other candidates can accept unlimited contributions as long as they properly disclose their source.

geographically imposed constraints, campaigning in Texas has become increasingly based on the electronic media, targeted mass mailings and, more recently, the Internet. Television and radio have become the major avenues for candidates to reach voters. But the price for gaining access to the airwaves is steep, especially in the major metropolitan areas and especially if you want to ensure that your ad makes it onto the airwaves. Media outlets are required to offer advertising time to political candidates at what is referred to as the lowest unit rate (LUR). This is, as the name implies, a relatively economical rate. However, time purchased at this rate is subject to preemption. So, to ensure that their ads do appear at the most desirable times, most candidates purchase time at a higher, non-preemptable rate, especially during the final weeks of a campaign. For example, the cost of a half-minute prime-time political advertising spot on KTVT Channel 11, the CBS affiliate in the Fort Worth–Dallas metropolitan area, ranges from $4,000 to $15,000, depending on the ratings of the program during which the ad appears. But there's more involved than the cost of a single ad.

Political consultants know that in a world where voters are increasingly inundated with a veritable avalanche of electronic blandishments (such as the very real possibility of potential voters having hundreds of cable or satellite TV channels from which to choose), a candidate's message must be repeated many times in order to penetrate the mind of those voters. Running *one* 30-second political ad four times daily Monday through Friday on *one* major TV affiliate in *one* major media market in Texas could cost a candidate anywhere from $300,000 to $500,000. Multiply that, then, by the number of other major market buys necessary to mount a statewide campaign and it's no surprise that media expenses list as the largest item in the campaign budgets of most high-profile candidates.

As media costs have risen, many candidates have begun to rely more on targeted mass mailings. Of course, campaign "junk mail" has been a part of American politics almost as long as there has been a postal service, and you've probably used such material to line the birdcage or train the puppy. Today, though, mass mailing has become incredibly sophisticated, targeting specific voting blocs with messages designed to energize and mobilize.

Instead of mailing one generic campaign flier to all voters, candidates produce numerous tracts focusing on specialized topics or issues and send them to specific groups, usually using computer-generated mailing lists compiled and marketed for just such purposes.

Thus, a member of the National Rifle Association will receive a pamphlet that extols the candidate's stalwart support of gun ownership (complete with a photograph of said candidate blasting away at some sort of winged game fowl), while a member of the Sierra Club will open a mail-out that proclaims that same candidate's undying devotion to sound ecological principles (complete with a photograph of said candidate petting a spotted owl).

Of course, the more groups a candidate tries to reach, the greater the costs of a campaign. Well-financed campaign phone banks have begun using the aforementioned tactics developed for mass mail-outs. For example, you might receive a call telling how Representative Righteous shares your concerns about the need to reintroduce public prayer in our schools. These and other cost-intensive strategies have greatly increased the price of getting elected and have served to narrow the field of candidates who can realistically undertake such high-dollar campaigns. A perfect example of such electoral costs can be seen in the race for Texas governor in 2002, which broke all previous spending records for statewide races in Texas. Fueled by a massive infusion of his own money, Democrat Tony Sanchez exceeded Republican Rick Perry in spending, and both candidates combined to lay out about $100 million dollars. Many students of Texas politics had scoffed at the idea of a $60 million gubernatorial campaign in Texas, but clearly Sanchez and Perry have taken the race to places where candidates for that office have never been before.

However, hope for those who don't own the Hope Diamond (or a modestly productive gold mine) may lie in the Internet, which many candidates are using as a relatively cost-effective way to get their message(s) to the public. In 2006, virtually every candidate for statewide office maintained slick, user-friendly Web pages loaded with information about the candidates and their campaigns. Of course, such an approach will not reach low- to moderate-income voters who often don't have ready access to computers. But it may help generate voter turnout among younger people who have not been receptive to more traditional campaign strategies, and as more of our society gain access to the information superhighway, such electronic campaigning will only become more commonplace.

As more people become more comfortable with the Web as a source of political information, the very real possibility exists that candidates who don't necessarily have Ross Perot's billions (or Tony Sanchez's millions) may be able to compete and even win in today's electoral arena.

Along with the increase in the monetary costs of campaigning has come a concomitant rise in the emotional costs of seeking office. A particularly troublesome manifestation of this has been the tendency of campaign advertising to portray opponents in a negative light, often focusing more on personal traits and alleged character flaws than on a person's ability to govern or legislate. Although nothing is new in American (and especially Texas) politics, this trend seems to have become almost standard operating procedure for many candidates. The reason for this is relatively simple, though rather cynical. It's easier to malign a candidate in 30 seconds or a minute than it is to delve into the intricacies of most of the issues with which a candidate must deal while seeking office. And because many voters cannot or will not take the time to familiarize themselves with these issues, they tend to respond to the candidate who hurls the most eye- and ear-catching accusations against an opponent. Most of us as voters say we deplore the use of such negative tactics, but because history as well as survey research shows us responding to them, most candidates either choose to or are forced to resort to them at one time or another. Some recent electoral results, however, indicate that positive campaigning might be in vogue once again.

Many analysts believe that one reason George W. Bush was able to defeat popular incumbent Ann Richards in 1994 was his use of an essentially positive campaign style as opposed to her more combative approach, which may have been perceived by voters as negative. In the 1998 elections, the brothers Bush (George W. and Jeb) both ran positive, inclusive types of campaigns and were able to win significant victories, while other candidates with similar resources and similar groups of core supporters ran negative, divisive campaigns and lost. Still, the 2002 election seems to have produced a return to a more attack-oriented style of campaigning, at least in the Lone Star State, and by the 2006 gubernatorial race, mud and an almost eager willingness to sling it had become the order of the day for most of the candidates. Candidates for statewide office didn't hesitate to resort to negative ads in an attempt to paint their opponents as everything from accidental officeholders to big-spending liberals.

Another factor that has an impact on Texas political campaigns is the rather lax campaign contribution laws that adhere in the Lone Star State. As one would expect in a state where the individualistic political culture is such a dominant force, these laws for the most part are predicated on the notion that requiring candidates to publish the contributions that they receive is all the "regulation" that is needed in this area of the political arena. Yet these data are often cursory in the extreme, and are characterized by a vagueness as to actual source and specific amount that makes it quite difficult for a layperson to gain a practical understanding of just how much a particular candidate has received and from whom the candidate has received it.

In the final analysis, money is the engine that sits under the hood of most political campaigns. As campaign costs have risen, candidates must devote more and more time and energy, both before and after an election, to fund-raising. In fact, it is not unusual to see a losing candidate spend months seeking funds to pay off a huge campaign debt. Little wonder that more and more citizens who might consider public service are choosing not to enter the political arena, or are doing so only reluctantly. Win or lose, it takes a lot of money to play politics in Texas.

Summary

Democracy only works when citizens are involved in the political process. At the beginning of the 20th century, many Texans were barred from participating through a series of laws and state practices. Almost all these barriers have been lifted, as Texas has few restrictions on voting. Unfortunately, large segments of society voluntarily fail to participate in the system, thereby giving up a right that others fought long and hard to achieve.

To win most offices in Texas, a person must survive two elections. First, he or she must win a party primary. Second, the primary winners meet in a general election.

When a vacancy occurs in office, the primary is not used and all candidates run against each other in a special election.

Campaigning for office is a difficult and costly endeavor. Candidates have to endure personal attacks and must be adept enough fund-raisers to bring in the money to launch counterattacks against their opponents. Campaigning has become more sophisticated as politicians have learned how to target groups effectively based on their individual interests.

Chapter Test

1. Turnout is low among all *except*
   a. the poor.
   b. the wealthy.
   c. minorities.
   d. the uneducated.

2. The term that describes citizens who fail to vote because there are so many elections is
   a. overkill.
   b. devolution.
   c. suffrage.
   d. election burnout.

3. Winning a general election requires
   a. a majority of the vote.
   b. a minority of the vote.
   c. a plurality of the vote.
   d. first winning a special election.

4. Factors in low voter turnout in Texas include all *except*
   a. language barriers.
   b. the emergence of a second major party.
   c. the state's traditionalistic culture.
   d. past discrimination.

5. The most important asset in a political campaign is
   a. money.
   b. television ads.
   c. radio spots.
   d. free media.

6. The most important factor in determining whether a person votes is
   a. age.
   b. race.
   c. education.
   d. income.

7. The practice of keeping African Americans from voting in Democratic primaries was called the
   a. grandfather clause.
   b. poll tax.
   c. primary process.
   d. white primary.

8. A registered voter can vote in the Republican primary by
   a. registering as a Republican.
   b. declaring as a Republican 30 days prior to the primary.
   c. attending the Republican precinct convention.
   d. showing up at the primary on election day.

9. The Voting Rights Act of 1965
   a. set aside legislative seats for minorities.
   b. applied to the entire state from its inception.
   c. sought to protect minorities in the registration and voting processes.
   d. all of the above.

10. The election likely to draw the largest turnout would be
    a. city council.
    b. school board.
    c. governor.
    d. President.

Answers: 1. b 2. d 3. c 4. b 5. a 6. c 7. d 8. d 9. c 10. d

Critical Thinking Questions

1. What are the key factors in determining voter turnout?

2. What are the chief differences among primary, general, and special elections?

3. Describe the evolution of voting rights in Texas.

Key Terms

disfranchised, **p. 72**

election burnout, **p. 73**

general election, **p. 75**

gubernatorial election, **p. 76**

long ballot, **p. 73**

plurality, **p. 76**

poll tax, **p. 67**

primary election, **p. 75**

Smith v. *Allwright*, **p. 66**

special election, **p. 76**

turnout, **p. 70**

universal suffrage, **p. 65**

white primary, **p. 66**

Voting Rights Act of 1965, **p. 67**

Notes

1. Carl H. Moneyhon, *Republicanism in Reconstruction Texas* (Austin, TX: University of Texas Press, 1980), p. 194.

2. *Smith* v. *Allwright*, 321 U.S. 649 (1944).

3. Rupert N. Richardson, Adrian Anderson, and Ernest Wallace, *Texas: The Lone Star State* (Englewood Cliffs, NJ: Prentice Hall, 1993), p. 394.

4. *Texas* v. *United States*, 384 U.S. 155 (1966).

5. Stephen Power, "'Motor Voter' Law Tied to Registration Climb," *Dallas Morning News*, 9 April 1995, p. 31A.

6. Office of the Secretary of State of Texas, *Election History, 1992–current*, http://elections. sos.state.tx.us/elchist.exe.

7. Ibid.

8. Office of the Secretary of State of Texas, *Early Voting*, http://www.sos.state.tx.us/elections/ earlyvoting/index.shtml.

Political Parties

Republicans control executi[ve]
and legislative branches
during Reconstruction.

The Democratic Party
organizes in Texas for U.S.
presidential election.

1848   1859   186[0]

Union Party candidate
Sam Houston elected
Governor.

4

**By the end of this chapter on political parties,
you should be able to . . .**

★ Differentiate between ideological and coalitional parties.
★ Describe the levels of political party organization.
★ Explain the long and successful history of the Democratic Party
  in Texas.
★ Explain the Republican Party's recent gains.
★ Analyze the challenges facing each major party in the 21st Century.

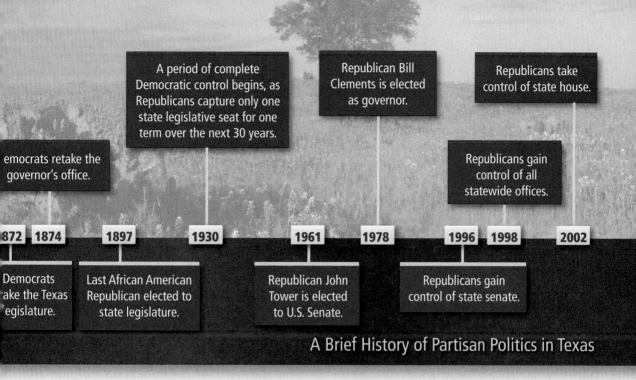

A Brief History of Partisan Politics in Texas

Timeline entries:

A period of complete Democratic control begins, as Republicans capture only one state legislative seat for one term over the next 30 years.

Republican Bill Clements is elected as governor.

Republicans take control of state house.

...emocrats retake the governor's office.

Republicans gain control of all statewide offices.

Democrats ...ake the Texas ...egislature.

Last African American Republican elected to state legislature.

Republican John Tower is elected to U.S. Senate.

Republicans gain control of state senate.

Timeline dates: ...872 · 1874 · 1897 · 1930 · 1961 · 1978 · 1996 · 1998 · 2002

We used to envy the Democrats the luxury of having those little squabbles and still winning. Now it's our turn.

—FORMER GOP NATIONAL COMMITTEE MEMBER ERNEST ANGELO ON TEXAS POLITICS, *HOUSTON CHRONICLE*, OCTOBER 6, 1995

Political parties form for the simple purpose of winning elections. Why else would people come together to wear funny hats, listen to all-too-often boring speeches, and engage in name-calling and insult-trading at political conventions? Some party members can't stand each other. They unify because their distaste for the opposition party is greater than their differences with fellow party members. Politics is a continuing game. We keep score by how well a party did in the latest election.

For more than a century, Texas was dominated by the Democrats, and Republicans had little chance of winning an election. But times have changed. In the 2002 elections, Republicans won every statewide seat, plus a majority in both the Texas House and Senate. Democrats retained strength along the border and in many urban areas, but the party's longtime dominance, at least for now, has been ended.

Political Parties

Although everyone would probably agree that voting is the easiest way for citizens in a democracy to voice their opinions and express their choices, it is certainly not the only way. Political parties provide another medium through which we can act. And although in recent years parties have fallen into some disfavor with many people, they still represent an important avenue of access within the political system. If you've never thought of a political party as a way to get involved, think again. And pay attention—this chapter will show you how.

A **political party** is a group of people who share a common body of principles or goals and who attempt to control government by gaining and controlling public offices. A political party differs from an interest group in that it is usually larger, it addresses a broader array of issues, and it nominates and formally runs candidates for office (for a discussion of interest groups, see Chapter 5). Parties were not part of the original scheme of government and politics envisioned by the nation's founders and are not mentioned in the Constitution. James Madison realized that parties were inevitable and believed that the constitutional system of checks and balances could help alleviate their worst aspects. He wrote to a friend, "There is nevertheless sufficient scope for combating the spirit of party, as far as it may not be necessary to fan the flame of liberty, in efforts to divert it from the more noxious channels; to moderate its violence, especially in the ascendant party; to elucidate the policy which harmonizes jealous interests; and particularly to give to the Constitution that just construction, which, with the aid of time and habit, may put an end to the more dangerous schisms otherwise growing out of it."[1]

political party
A group of people who share common goals and attempt to control government by winning elections.

Party Structure

The basic structure of the two major political parties in the United States (and in Texas as well) can best be described as **coalitional**. This means that each party comprises a number of different subgroups that band together for the main purpose of winning elections. Today, political scientists refer to such subgroups as factions. This is a more restricted meaning of the term than that used by Madison. These groups usually agree on some sort of basic, often vaguely defined set of ideas, but there is also a fair amount of tension and rivalry. Sometimes with this kind of political party, the discord is so great that there is little beyond the decision to form a coalition holding it together.

coalitions
Alliances consisting of a variety of individuals and groups in support of a particular candidate for elected office.

Parties in other countries, as well as many minor (or so-called third) parties in this country, frequently exhibit a structure that can be labeled **ideological**. An ideological party is united by a single principle or a narrowly defined set of principles to which all members are expected (and often required) to adhere. Factionalism tends to be rare and fidelity to principle is often deemed more important than the expedient of winning an election. These people would rather be "right" (as *they* define it) than president, or governor, or state representative, or county tax assessor-collector. As we've already implied, ideological parties have a pretty hard time in United States as well as in Texas politics. The chief reason lies in the heterogeneous nature of our population. We've already noted that Texas is made up of many different cultural, economic, and political groups. No one single group is likely to control

ideological
A group or party built around a unifying set of principles.

what happens. In order to be successful, political parties have to appeal to a broad array of groups. This also tends to force the resolution of most issues to the middle of the political road. The "true believers" in each party find such pragmatism distasteful. Former Texas Agriculture Commissioner Jim Hightower, a noted ideologue, once scornfully remarked, "The only things in the middle of the road are yellow stripes and dead armadillos!" However, that pragmatism he mocks turns out to be the key to victory in most contests, including the one in which he was defeated for reelection.

It is these very factors—a broadly based model of political party structure as well as a general political climate that encourages centrist solutions—that often lead one or the other (and sometimes both) major parties to literally steal the core idea or ideas that underpin many ideological parties. In doing so, the major parties hope to woo the smaller group's supporters into their respective folds. The net effect is to broaden the base of the major party while rendering the ideological party politically superfluous. Examples of such action can be seen in the Democrats' appropriation of most of the Populist Party platform (and even William Jennings Bryan, their presidential candidate!) in 1896, in the eventual incorporation of many elements from the Progressive Party's **platform** into the New Deal agenda; and in the adoption by both Democrats and Republicans of a sizable portion of the issue base of George Wallace's American Independent Party in the early 1970s.

platform
The statement of principles passed by a political party's convention.

Texas has had its fair share of ideological political parties—the Libertarian Party is the most prominent contemporary example. As we mentioned in Chapter 3, the Libertarian Party is the only third party to regularly appear on the Texas ballot. Elections rules all but prohibit another party from joining them. Libertarians are likely to remain on the ballot because—given recent Republican domination in statewide elections—Democrats don't run candidates for every office. Texas voters are contrarian enough that at least 5 percent of them are going to vote against *any* incumbent, given a choice. Contesting every race and thereby knocking the Libertarians from future ballots would not be in the Democrats best interest, as most Libertarian voters would cast Republican ballots if not given a third choice. Sometime in the future, in a close election, that could make a difference.

Conversely, by securing a place on the 2010 ballot, the left-leaning Green Party should marginally aid Republican candidates, as they would logically draw votes from the Democratic Party. If Greens can hit the 5 percent threshold in any statewide race, they can secure a place on future ballots. An intriguing aspect of the Green's petition success in 2010 is that much of the effort's funding seems to have come from contributors normally associated with Republican candidates. It is easy to see why they might want a Green candidate on the ballot. To find out more about Texas Libertarians, log on to their Web site at http://www.tx.lp.org. To find out more about the Texas Green Party, visit their Web site at http://txgreens.org.

So while such parties can and may on occasion tip the results of an election to one or the other major party, the chances of their winning across the board are about as remote as those of a snowball lasting through an August day in McAllen. We, therefore, will concentrate on explaining the structure of the two major parties in Texas, because that's where the vast majority of Texans who are inclined to get involved with a political party will find themselves. The internal structure of the Republican and Democratic parties in Texas is similar enough to allow for a single description that will generally apply to both parties.

Both parties have internal structural elements that allow for short-term as well as long-term participation by citizens. The short-term elements are essentially a series of **conventions** in which party supporters participate; the long-term elements comprise a series of elected offices within the parties that party supporters try to win. These conventions and elected party offices exist at several levels within the party structure.

conventions
Formal party meetings to select leadership, delegates, and create a platform.

Conventions

The Precinct Level

precinct
A political subdivision through which elections are carried out.

The voting **precinct** is a small geographic area created to facilitate the conduct of elections. Every county in Texas is divided into such precincts, so the political parties have made this the basic entry level into their organizations. The easiest way for most people to get involved within a political party is by attending a precinct convention. This meeting is held (in most cases) on the evening of the party's primary election, and the only thing you have to do in order to participate is vote in the party primary. Those who attend the precinct convention will be helping to direct the activities of their party and will also have an opportunity to help identify and develop the party's stance on major issues.

precinct convention
The basic or grassroots level at which delegates are selected to the county party convention.

A typical **precinct convention** will begin with the election of a convention chair and secretary, then participants move on to selecting delegates. Delegates are people attending the convention who will go on to the next level within the convention process and who in essence will represent and speak for their precinct there. Each precinct convention is allocated delegates based on how much support the precinct gave to the party's last candidate for governor. For the more mathematically inclined, this is determined by a ratio: 1 delegate for every 25 votes cast in the precinct at the last general election for the party's nominee for governor. It sounds complicated, but it really boils down to this: the more people in the precinct who voted for your party's candidate for governor, the more delegates your precinct convention will be allowed to select. (It should be noted that, in an effort to bolster participation in these conventions, the Democrats have instituted a revised ratio of 1:15.)

resolutions
Proposed planks in the party platform; formed and submitted through the convention system.

After the delegates are chosen, anyone participating in the convention may offer **resolutions**. These are statements that express the party's stance on an issue and are a way for you to try and get the party to see things your way. If, for example, you would like to see more state (or federal) funds be made available for college loans and grants, you could introduce a resolution to that effect at your precinct convention. Resolutions are approved by majority vote of those attending the convention and become a kind of platform for that precinct. They are sent, along with the precinct's delegates, to the next convention.

Precinct conventions are one of the best-kept secrets in Texas politics. They're close at hand, take up very little time, and are remarkably accessible. In fact, the odds are that if you were to go to your next precinct convention, you'd probably wind up a delegate! It's not unusual for there to be fewer people at a precinct convention than there are delegates to be chosen. So if you've ever said to yourself, "I wish the Democrats (or the Republicans) would talk about *my* issues," here's your chance.

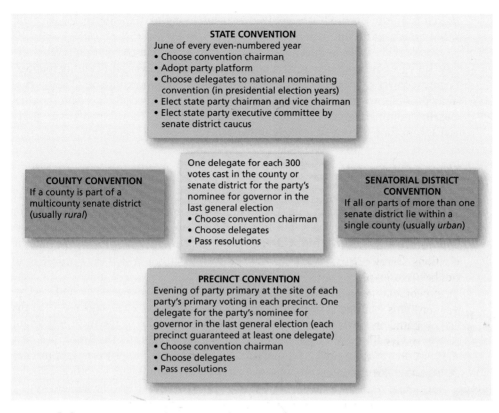

FIGURE **4.1** The Conventions of Texas Political Parties.

The County (or District) Level

Delegates selected at the precinct conventions go on to either a county convention or a **state senatorial district convention**. How do you determine which one? Essentially, it's a function of where you live: generally speaking, rural counties hold county conventions and urban counties hold district conventions. To be more specific, counties that lie completely within a state senate district hold county conventions. Counties that contain more than one or parts of more than one state senate district hold a district convention in each district or part of a district within that county.

At these county or district conventions, essentially the same agenda and rules apply as did at the precinct convention. First, a convention chair and a secretary are elected. Then delegates are selected, much as they were at the precinct convention. The only difference is that the ratio for determining the number of delegates chosen is changed. Each county or district convention is granted one delegate for every 300 votes cast in the county or part of a district with the county at the last general election for the party's nominee for governor. (As was the case with the precinct conventions, in an effort to bolster participation in these conventions, the Democrats have instituted a revised ratio of 1:180.) After this, attendees debate and vote on resolutions brought from the precinct conventions and approved by the convention's resolutions committee, as well as new ones

state senatorial district convention
Mid-level party meeting between precinct and state; same level as county convention.

offered from the floor. Those approved are sent, along with the delegates selected, to the party's state convention.

As we said earlier, being chosen a delegate at a precinct convention is relatively easy. Being chosen a delegate at a county or district convention is a bit tougher. There are fewer chosen per capita and the competition is more intense. But it is certainly possible, and if you can convince enough people (especially those on the convention's nominating committee) that you're part of that "new blood" every party needs from time to time, it is likely to happen.

The State Level

The highest level of the parties' conventions, and the place to be for most party activists, is the state convention, held in June of even-numbered years. The sites for these conventions are usually the state's major cities, with Dallas, Houston, Fort Worth, Austin, and San Antonio frequently being chosen. Delegates selected in the county or district conventions attend the state convention, which usually lasts from two to three days.

Those who participate in this convention begin by choosing a chair and a secretary. At this level, a fair amount of time may be devoted to discussing changes in the party's rules and other administrative responsibilities. One of the most important actions taken here will be to finalize the state party platform, the list of ideas and issues that the party deems important. Voters may use the platform as a mechanism for assessing the party's candidates for office. The elements that make up this platform (the "planks") are usually those resolutions that rank-and-file party supporters got passed at the precinct conventions and then at the county or district conventions. Ideas born at the precinct convention in March may very well become a part of the platform by June. An example of this process at work can be seen in recent Republican state party platforms, which have reflected many of the issues embodied in resolutions that evangelical Christians within the party passed at their precinct conventions. For Democrats, it can be seen in recent platform resolutions urging protection of gay rights.

To compare the most recent platforms of both Texas Democrats and Texas Republicans, visit the party Web sites at http://www.txdemocrats.org or http://www.texasgop.org.

A couple of other state convention chores have to be taken care of in presidential election years. They include electing delegates to the party's national nominating convention and selecting a list of potential presidential electors. These people become the official electors of the state only if the party's candidate for president carries Texas in the November general election. Finally, the state convention delegates must elect the state chair, other state party officials, and state executive committee members before adjourning. We'll say more about this when we turn to a discussion of the elected offices within the party.

WHAT CAN YOU DO?

Texas political parties afford a number of opportunities for you to become involved in their many activities.

The Republican Party of Texas (http://www.texasgop.org/) Web site enables those interested in party work to discover how to get involved by learning about the Republican Party structure and the political process. The Republican Party also invites members to join auxiliary groups in your area, or send your thoughts on an issue to the party. The Web site provides updates of activities you can attend during the current month.

The Texas Democratic Party (http://www.txdemocrats.org/) Web site includes a Take Action link which allows the party faithful to, among other activities, participate through Find an Event, Organize with MyTDP, Sign Up to Volunteer, Intern at the TDP, and Get Democratic Updates.

If you prefer to support an alternative political party in the state, the Green Party of Texas (http://txgreens.org/drupal/) and the Libertarian Party of Texas (http://lptexas.org/) provide similar activities for you.

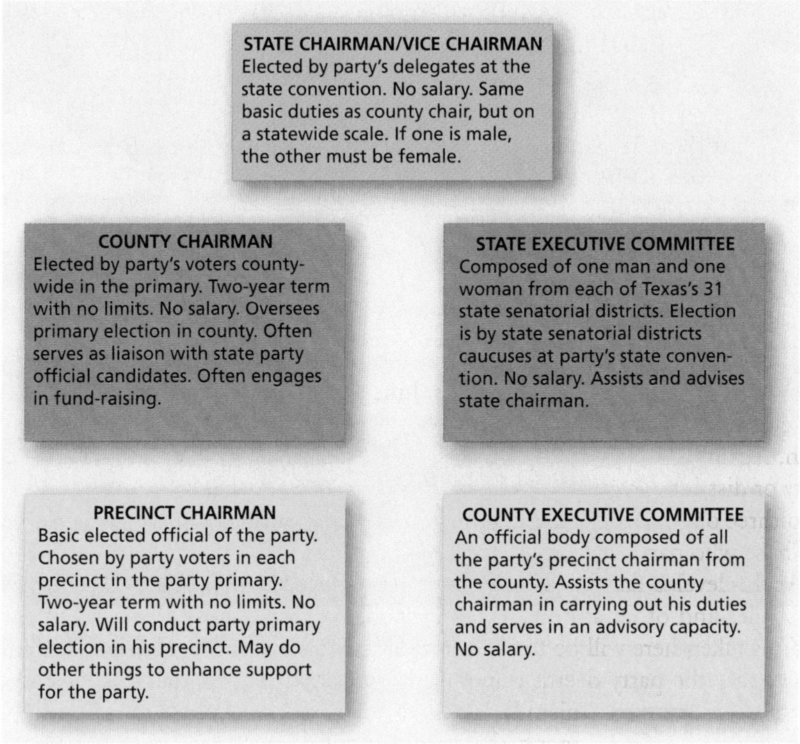

FIGURE **4.2** Elected Offices within Texas Political Parties.

Elected Offices

The Precinct Level

The jumping-off point for involvement with the elected offices within the party organization also can be found at the precinct level, in the office of precinct chair. This person is the basic point of contact between the party and the people who support it. The precinct chair is elected by the party's voters in the primary election and serves a two-year term. There is no limit on the number of terms you may serve and many precinct chairs are routinely reelected, often without opposition. This is an unpaid position, so those who seek it tend to be political junkies.

Just exactly what does a precinct chair do? The Texas Election Code lists a number of responsibilities for this party official, but essentially, a chair does as much or as little as he or she wants to. Because the position provides its holder no compensation, activity levels vary greatly from precinct to precinct. If nothing else, the precinct chair will usually be responsible for holding the party's primary election in his precinct. This includes overseeing the polls on primary election day, lining up workers to help, and reporting results to the party's county office. Beyond this rather rudimentary task, some precinct chairs actually promote the party by registering people to vote, mailing out newsletters, soliciting campaign contributions,

During the 2008 Democratic Senate District conventions, even the process of voting was open to debate. Such conventions can bog down for hours over rule interpretations.

and arranging for transportation on election day. In this office, the personalities of the people involved and their commitment to the party's principles are crucial in determining how much and what will get done.

Should you become a precinct chair? There's no filing fee to get on the ballot and it involves a relatively small number of voters, so it's not a terribly difficult office to attain. And if you'd like to have a little more to say in the political world, it might be a good place to start. The job of the precinct chair is often a thankless one, yet the person who holds it can have a significant effect on the political process. In a precinct where the two major parties are roughly equal in strength, the difference in a given election may very well be the efforts put forth by the precinct chair. If going to a precinct convention has whetted your appetite for things political, a logical next step might be to run for precinct chair.

The County Level

At this level, you'll find a couple of offices within the party's structure. The first of these, the county chair, oversees the party's activities across the county. The person who holds this office, like the precinct chair, is elected by the voters of the party in the primary election. The term of office is two years with no limits on reelection, and again, no regular salary accompanies this office. The county chair's job is considerably broader than that of the precinct chair.

Here the responsibility for conducting the primary election is countywide, and the chair must make sure every precinct has someone to oversee the election. The county chair plays a much larger role in fund-raising than does the average precinct chair. Also, those who direct the campaigns of state or area office seekers often single out the county chair as a point of contact. So if the party's candidate for governor wants to visit Tyler, the county chair of Smith County often arranges for a meeting hall, coordinates transportation, and makes sure an enthusiastic throng of supporters greets the candidate.

The county executive committee helps the county chair carry out these tasks. Who are they? They're all the party's precinct chairs in that county. Every precinct chair is automatically an ex officio member of the county executive committee. They meet regularly with the county chair and perform whatever tasks may be delegated to them. This group is especially important in urban counties where the demands on the county chair can at times be overwhelming. There, you often see subcommittees formed within this body to provide for a more effective division of labor. You may also see in such urban counties the formation of senatorial district committees for the same reason. The office of county chair requires a significant commitment of time and effort. There is no pay, and the hours can be long, especially in highly urbanized areas where the position is, for all practical purposes, a full-time job. Not many people can afford to invest that much of themselves in what is essentially a voluntary act. Nevertheless, those willing to do so have a proportionally greater voice in their party's affairs.

The State Level

Choosing the party's highest elected officials takes place at the party's state convention. All delegates to that convention vote for the state chair and, in separate ballots, various other state party offices. These officials serve two-year terms, with no limit to the number of terms they may serve. Like the other party offices we've discussed, these do not come with a salary. Yet their duties can be time consuming and, in the case of the state chair, can be a full-time job and more. All of the things done by the county chair will be done by the state chair, but on a much larger scale. This is especially the case with regard to raising money for the party, something that in itself could easily occupy the time and energy of the chair to the exclusion of all other tasks. Additionally, the state chair must often serve as a liaison with the national party and its presidential campaign.

The state chair presides over the state executive committee, which includes one man and one woman from each of the state's 31 senatorial districts. Chosen by state convention delegates who divide into senatorial district caucuses (meetings) for this purpose, state executive committee members serve two-year terms, may be reelected without limit, and (you guessed it!) receive no salary. This body assists the state chair in carrying out his or her many duties, one of the most important of which is planning and holding the next state convention.

The executive committee convenes several times a year, and though the job is not as demanding as that of the state chair, members invest a good bit of their own time and money in meeting their responsibilities. Realistically, holding any state office within the party is going to lie beyond the realm of possibility for many Texans. But those who can serve will have much to say about the direction and goals of their party.

my turn

Why I Am a Democrat

by Kelly Becker

Ms. Becker graduated summa cum laude from R. L. Paschal High School in Fort Worth. She finished high school in three years and was a Texas Scholar. She is a Cornerstone Honors student at Tarrant County College South campus, where she is a member of the Phi Theta Kappa. Ms. Becker is majoring in political science and plans to earn a postgraduate degree so that she can become a professor of government.

My generation is one that feels the need to give a label to everyone, to make them fit in some familiar category. In high school, our labels were based on superficial things like someone's style of dress or the type of music to which one listened. We labeled people and ourselves because we felt the need to be a part of a group (whether we admitted it or not). Now that we have reached college, our labels have become fewer and less frivolous. It seems that now we are searching for a label that truly means something, one that will last. We base those labels on our convictions because they are what we value the most, and because we want to be a part of a like-minded body. In America, the best way to let people know what beliefs and ideas we prize is through affiliation with a political party. I am a Democrat. When I classify myself as such, people know what principles I hold closest to my heart.

I have known for quite some time that I am a Democrat. But how did I come to choose this political party? To be honest, it is difficult for me to limit myself with the label of one party, for fear of being a hypocrite. If an issue is presented, and I don't agree with the Democratic platform, does that make me any less of a Democrat? Also, there are topics that I feel strongly about that are more actively addressed by third-parties than by either of the major parties. So how did I make the big decision to call myself a Democrat, despite these lingering questions?

The truth is that the majority of people don't fit into any one political party. However, we live in a democracy that is dominated by only two major parties. As cynical as it may sound, if we want the majority of our issues to be addressed we can't go with a third-party candidate on election day. We've got to choose the major party that most closely represents our beliefs. For some, that may feel like choosing the lesser of two evils. But the important thing is that we do in fact make the choice.

The reason I am a Democrat comes down to the party's stance on several key issues: abortion, welfare, education, health care, and the environment.

As a woman, I support the platform Democrats hold in regards to abortion and welfare. Traditionally, Democrats support a woman's right to choose, and therefore continue to fight to keep *Roe* v. *Wade* from being overturned. Though welfare does not only pertain to women, a large number of the people who receive welfare are single mothers, and I am sympathetic to their situation. Despite the abuse that does take place, I am a definite supporter of the welfare system, as is the Democratic party.

Both major parties agree that education is of the utmost importance. The Democratic party supports funding for research and development of new educational programs, especially those designed to help bridge the gap between white and minority students' academic achievement, which I think is of extreme importance. Every child, regardless of race or gender, deserves to be successful in school, and I support the development of programs that work to make that happen. Also, the Democratic party advocates relief from rising college tuition costs, a cause close to any college student's heart and wallet.

I have a hard time accepting the fact that America is the wealthiest nation in the world and yet some of our citizens don't have access to quality, affordable health care. This same issue has been a part of the Democratic platform for quite some time, and Democrats continue to seek a resolution to this problem.

(continued)

The protection of the environment is an issue greatly championed by the Green Party, and is an issue that I am adamant about. I believe that the fate of our world depends on responsible steward-ship of the environment, and this is the stance that Democrats take as well.

There are other subjects that are important to me, and my views coincide with the Democratic view of the majority of the time. As I said before, I choose to label myself as a Democrat because of my convictions and values. "Democrat" and "Republican" are labels that should not be given arbitrarily, so don't choose a party because your friends or parents choose it. Decide what matters the most to you, and make your decision accordingly.

The Democratic Party

Foundations

The Democrats were one of the first political parties to organize in Texas, establish-ing themselves formally in 1854. They tended to dominate the political scene, although they occasionally saw challenges from the dying Whig Party and the secre-tive Know-Nothing Party during the 1850s. And although the issue of secession divided Texas Democrats, it did not tear them apart as was the case with the national party organization. When Texas did secede in February 1861, most officeholders who took the new oath to the Confederacy were Democrats, and this pattern contin-ued throughout the course of the Civil War.

During Reconstruction, virtually all people who had held office in Confederate or state government were barred from holding further office, and most were dis-franchised.

Republicans (and occasionally, Independents) therefore held the majority of elected offices during the period. Only in the early 1870s were former officeholders' rights to vote and hold office restored, but once this happened, they reemerged with a vengeance. By 1873, as a reaction to the perceived excesses of Reconstruction (and the identification of those "excesses" with the Republican Party), most Republicans had been routed from office, and for the next 100 years, the Democrats, for all prac-tical purposes, would be the only game in town.

Dominance

The fact that there was only one viable political party in Texas after Reconstruction did not mean that there was no political competition. Although Texas was devoid of any real interparty competition, its politics for the next century would be decidedly intraparty. Simply put, Democrats fought other Democrats for political dominance. The key players in this drama would be **factions**, which would arise from time to time. Factions, as we noted above, are identifiable subgroups within a political party. These groups are united by a commonly held belief, issue, or personality, although they generally are not tightly organized and may vary greatly in size and influence. The first factions to emerge among Democrats after Reconstruction were primarily economic in their orientation. The Redeemers, so-called because they wanted to "redeem" the South from the Republicans, slashed government spending,

factions
Divisions within a political party.

cut back on state support for education, and rewrote the state's constitution. They hoped these actions would create a climate favorable to business and industry in Texas. To this end, they enacted laws that allowed public land to be given to various railroad companies as an inducement to extend their tracks across Texas. This practice, along with the increasingly pro-business attitude of the Redeemers, gave rise to an opposing faction among Texas Democrats.

Growing discontent among farmers had led to a number of protest movements in Texas during the 1870s and 1880s, including the Grange and the Farmers' Alliance. These various movements began to coalesce as an identifiable "Agrarian" wing within the Democratic party. With James Stephen Hogg as their standard-bearer, these Agrarians gained control of the party in 1890, and inaugurated a period of reform that would last more than 20 years. They sought to regulate business, protect the farmer, and enact reforms that would make things easier on the "little guy." Under their leadership, Texas passed its first child labor law and made extensive changes in the way elections were conducted.

By the second decade of the 20th century, the lines between these early economic factions had begun to blur. The election of Jim Ferguson in 1914 gave rise to a new intraparty matchup. For the next 20 years, politics in the Democratic Party would revolve around "Farmer Jim" and his wife Miriam (see Chapter 1 for a discussion of their political careers). The factions that emerged were more or less personality-based, with one group strongly supporting Ferguson and others opposing him. Of course, these skirmishes continued during his wife's several campaigns for office, but after her second term as governor (1933–1935), Ferguson and his personality politics began to recede.

By the mid-1930s, two reformulated groups began a decades-long struggle for control of the Democratic Party. Liberals and conservatives emerged as relatively ideological factions that initially revolved around support of or opposition to the policies of Franklin Roosevelt and the New Deal. Liberals supported Roosevelt and enthusiastically endorsed the more activist role for government that the New Deal programs set up. Texas politicians like Lyndon Johnson, Ralph Yarborough, and James Allred were among this group. They were opposed by the conservatives, whose dislike of Roosevelt and his New Deal bordered on hatred and whose supporters included John Nance Garner and Coke Stevenson.

During the 1930s, the liberals seemed to control the Texas political agenda. This can best be seen in the programs advocated by Governor Allred during his two terms (1935–1939). These programs complemented the work of various federal agencies that were created during that period. However, by the early 1940s, the factional winds were shifting. Texas conservatives found a rallying point by opposing a third-term nomination for Roosevelt, and when he won nomination to a fourth term in 1944, they briefly deserted the party and organized themselves as the **"Texas Regulars."** Eventually these dissidents returned to the party fold and by the late 1940s had gained almost complete control of the party machinery. The death of Roosevelt in 1945, combined with the increasingly conservative mood of the country following World War II, played a large part in this power shift.

Liberals made several attempts to mount a comeback over the next several decades. In the mid-1950s they formed the **"Democrats of Texas"** in order to back Ralph Yarborough in his race for Texas governor. Yarborough lost in the primary, but with help from liberals won a special election for a U.S. Senate seat in 1957,

"Texas Regulars"
A conservative faction of the Democratic party during the 1940s.

"Democrats of Texas"
A liberal faction of Democrats formed in the 1950s.

a seat he would hold until 1971. That was about the extent of the good news for this group. The 1950s weren't exactly the best of times to be a liberal in Texas, and though liberals enjoyed a brief resurgence in the 1960s (at least nationally), the generally conservative nature of the average Texan has made it difficult for this faction to enjoy much success. In recent years, only Jim Hightower's election as agriculture commissioner in 1982 could be construed as a victory for an out-and-out liberal.

Retrenchment

The victory of Republican Bill Clements in the 1978 governor's race ended 105 years of Democratic control of that office. It also had the effect of a slap in the face to Texas Democrats, who began to realize that they no longer could enjoy the luxury of fighting among themselves. In the years since, intraparty divisions have been somewhat muted, particularly as many more overtly conservative Democrats have left to join the Republican Party. And though the party did recapture the governor's office in 1982 and again in 1990, the ascendancy of the Republicans since the early 1990s means that Texas's days as a one-party Democratic state are gone forever.

In this new millennium, Texas Democrats face a daunting task. The party must hold on to its traditional supporters while broadening its appeal statewide. Those who have traditionally supported the party have included minorities, members of labor unions, blue-collar workers in general, and rural conservatives (the so-called yellow dog Democrats). In recent elections, Republicans have made some potentially significant inroads into these core constituencies. For example, then Governor Bush's landslide reelection in 1998 saw him rack up a larger percentage of Hispanic votes than any Grand Old Party (GOP) candidate ever. Union support also wavered, at least as measured in the 1998, 2002, and 2006 gubernatorial election. It remains to be seen whether this shift is temporary or fundamental. In races for the Texas legislature, Democrats still do well among both African Americans and Hispanics. In fact, many of the seats in the legislature in south and southwest Texas remain in the Democratic column. The nomination of Tony Sanchez for governor and Ron Kirk for U.S. Senate in 2002 was a significant effort for the Democrats as they tried to retain their bases of support in the Hispanic and African American communities of Texas. While it failed to achieve the desired results in that election (and while the 2006 general election saw no similar attempt to nominate minority candidates to statewide office by the Democrats), such a strategy is sure to be an important part of future party efforts, especially in light of the demographic trends discussed earlier. Democrats have managed to hold on to some of their union supporters in areas such as Beaumont–Port Arthur and the petrochemical suburbs of the Houston-Galveston area. Likewise, some rural voters continue to pull the Democrat lever with regularity. But the fastest-growing areas of Texas, the booming suburbs, represent a challenge to the party that it has only begun to address. Calling for stronger families, better public education, and economic "fairness" seems to be the way Democrats have chosen to go after this crucial bloc of voters. This, of course, represents an attempt to recapture the middle ground of the Texas political landscape, which, as we have already seen, you must control if you are going to win. Unfortunately for Democrats, election results seem to indicate that they have not been able to get these issues and ideas across to suburban voters, as the party has, in the last several elections, lost every major statewide office on the ballot.

While 21st-century Texas Democrats might be inclined to agree with Thomas Paine that "These are the times that try men's souls," developments at the national level of politics in 2008 may have the effect of reinvigorating and renewing the Democratic Party and its supporters. The unprecedented candidacies of Hillary Clinton and Barak Obama seem to have galvanized Texas Democrats in a way not seen in many a year. Participation in the Democratic Party primary election in March of 2008 broke all kinds of records for voter turnout. But perhaps of more significance were the heretofore unheard of rates of participation in the party's precinct conventions as both Clinton and Obama enthusiasts sought to gain an

INSIDE
THE FEDERALIST SYSTEM

A Look at the State Democratic and Republican Party Platforms

In Texas, as within the United States in general, there is a distinctive difference in the major political parties' interpretation of federalism. In general, Republicans believe that decision making should be closest to the people, with significant powers dispersed to state and local governments. Democrats believe in a strong national government that protects the interest of individuals while promoting a stronger union. These excerpts from the 2008 state party platforms, although not exactly parallel, help illustrate the different philosophies. The Democratic platform calls for increased national government spending; the Republican alternative calls for downsizing the federal government.

Democratic Platform

To rebuild our American infrastructure, Texas Democrats support a requirement that public funds and contracts be awarded to American companies that use American workers who have a vested interest in the security and prosperity of our nation. For a generation, America has neglected its public infrastructure: roads, bridges, railroads, ports, water and sewer systems, schools, parks and libraries. We support a federal initiative to foster a sustained increase in public capital investment. We must not only increase funding to maintain aging infrastructure, but also to build new and more reliable public works.

SOURCE: 2010 Texas Democratic Platform, p. 11.

Republican Platform

Fiscal Responsibility—We urge state and federal legislators to reduce spending. We urge a commission composed of citizens and business owners to identify cost savings and reductions in state government. We also support a "cap" on government spending at all levels, with adjustments based only on average family income and population change.

Unfunded Mandates—We oppose all unfunded mandates by the federal and state governments including unreasonable requirements on voluntary emergency response personnel. State mandates without full funding should be included in the government body's annual increase spending limits.

Downsizing the Federal Government—We support abolishing all federal agencies whose activities are not granted in the Constitution, including the Departments of Education and Energy. We support a sunset provision law at the federal level.

SOURCE: 2010 Republican State Platform, p. 17.

edge for their respective candidates in the all-important drive to acquire delegates to the national nominating convention. Will this enthusiasm be translated into electoral success in the general election of 2008 and beyond? That is a question to which all Democrats eagerly await the answer.

To see what today's Texas Democratic Party is all about, take a look at their Web site at http://www.txdemocrats.org.

The Republican Party

Post-Reconstruction

Prior to 2003, the last time the Republican Party controlled Texas was during the reign of E. J. Davis. After Reconstruction ended, the Democrats quickly consolidated their grip on state government. Republicans survived primarily as a radical and African American party. Legislative representation, albeit in relatively low numbers, continued until the beginning of the 1900s, when African Americans were successfully purged from the voting rolls through several methods discussed in the previous chapter.

The resurgence of the party did not begin until the advent of presidential Republicanism in 1952. Despite Democratic domination of all statewide executive and judicial offices and absolute Democratic control of the legislature, the state began turning to Republican presidential candidates. Two factors helped create this trend. First was the disparity between the national and state Democratic organizations. The national party was becoming more liberal, but the state party continued its conservative tradition. Texans still elected conservative Democrats within the state, but balked at the prospect of electing a liberal Democrat to national office.

A second factor was the differences between the Republican and Democratic presidential candidates in 1952. Republican Dwight D. Eisenhower was a war hero. Popular and grandfatherly, he was moderately conservative. Importantly, Eisenhower backed Texans on the "Tidelands" controversy. Texas and California claimed the right to issue oil and gas leases for the areas immediately off their coasts. Democratic nominee Adlai Stevenson, a liberal, disagreed. He backed a 1947 U.S. Supreme Court ruling that granted these rights to the national government.[2] This issue not only meant a lot of money to the state of Texas, it was also important for state sovereignty. In 1956, the Stevenson-Eisenhower confrontation repeated itself. Texas again backed Eisenhower. Between 1952 and 1996, Democratic presidential candidates would carry Texas only four times. Factor out the 1960s and only one Democratic presidential nominee has carried the state since Harry Truman.

Despite successes on the presidential level, Republicans failed to pose any serious threat to the Democrats in races for state or local offices throughout the 1950s. The Grand Old Party managed to elect one U.S. congressman, Bruce Alger, from Dallas in 1954, but retaining that seat was essentially the limit of Republican success.

John Tower, Lyndon Johnson, and a U.S. Senate Seat

In 1960, U.S. Senator Lyndon Baines Johnson (LBJ), a Democrat who may have been the most powerful figure in the history of Texas politics, wanted to run for president. LBJ faced a problem, however: 1960 was the year in which his Senate seat was up for reelection. State law prohibited a person from running for two

my turn

Why I Am a Republican

by Joshua Barber

Joshua Barber penned this essay while a senior at the University of North Texas. A product of the Cornerstone Honors program at Tarrant County College–Northwest, Mr. Barber served as a White House intern for President George W. Bush in fall 2008.

It's mainly due to the fact that I am first an American.

I don't mean "I am an American" in the terms that I am a flag-toting, war-mongering, imperialist (which are all false accusations). I am an American in my conviction that freedom is congenital and universal in the fiber of *Homo sapiens*. While many in opposition throw around "strict constructionist" as an insult in the political arena, I implore, "What is wrong with life, liberty, and the pursuit of happiness?"

Life is worth the fight. I didn't have to be taught to preserve my life. Liberty and the pursuit of happiness go hand-in-hand. We are given the freedom to pursue happiness. There is no authority to decide where I work, what I do, whom I shall marry, how many children I believe will complete my family, Whom I worship, or how I worship, just to name a few. Although around 30 percent of my earnings are taken out in Social Security, Medicare, Medicaid, and the other taxes that my employer and I pay, I still have the choice where and how my money is invested.

While I endure the financial, social, and physical drudgery of the college scholar, I keep focused on the proverbial "light at the end of the tunnel." What is it there waiting for me when I clasp my diploma in my hand? I'll be thousands of dollars in debt, in an hourly wage job for which I will be overqualified and underpaid, and I'll still have the same '03 Kia Rio that is falling apart at the seams.

This is opportunity! Through my own devices at this juncture do I make my own accords and choose where to allocate my money. I can sell myself as a skilled laborer, or I may invest in myself and start my own business through my own innovation.

I've learned very quickly, through the graces of Mark Twain, to not let my schooling get in the way of my learning. I knew a guy from high school whose father had spoiled him—I despised him. He was vulgar, wore the most expensive clothes, and came off as stupid; his grades seemed to prove it, but most of all, he was loud. He would drive a different luxury car to school everyday. I soon found out that his father owned a used-car lot.

Then it struck me: While my perception had been that he didn't deserve or earn any of his expensive toys, I made an error in judgment, and I was embarrassed at myself for buying into the perceived class struggle. His father had founded that company, made money, and provided for his own. His father had secured an environment in which his son could now keep the company prosperous. While I believe that he may have failed to groom him to be a gentleman or socially savvy, the father had successfully used private land to create family security and wealth. More importantly to you, the consumer, he continues to provide used cars at affordable prices. I saw him at college for one semester. I didn't see him after that, but I had heard through the grapevine that he was virtually running the car lot now.

While I believe that liberty is built into our biological system, many quickly give up their freedom for security. "Any society that would give up a little liberty to gain a little security will deserve neither and lose both," per Benjamin Franklin. President Ronald Reagan aptly stated "Freedom is never more than one generation away from extinction. We didn't pass it to our children in the bloodstream. It must be fought for, protected, and handed on for them to do the same."

I believe the free enterprise system to be the only long-term arrangement congruous with civil liberty. Republicans are always accused of not caring about the poor, impoverished, or the unemployed. Maybe Republicans need to better articulate their platform. The goal of Republicans is to make the disadvantaged autonomous. Remember the childhood book *If You Give a Mouse a Cookie*

(continued)

by Laura Joffe Numeroff? Silly as it may sound, it illustrates the frustration that Republicans have with the welfare system. The Personal Responsibility and Work Opportunity Act of 1996, signed by President Clinton (and more importantly devised by a Republican Congress), brought economic prosperity unseen following its signing.

What I want you, my peers, to understand is that our generation's future is being talked about, played with, kicked around, taxed, subsidized, and manipulated. I see no young adults from either side in the national spotlight pronouncing our thoughts and considerations. Sexism and racism are often heralded as the most terrible traits. Ageism, on the other hand, is seldom discussed because there are none representing our age group at the national level. There are movements without faces, but there is no formal leadership representing tomorrow's American.

The GOP has also been labeled as the old, white man's party. Republicans have the opportunity to advance their cause through all young Americans. Freedoms of our tomorrow are being taken away on a daily basis as the tax code expands directly or indirectly. Our freedom as Americans, young Americans, and humans are slipping away swifter every moment. I am a Republican because I believe in helping the poor help themselves. I am a Republican because I believe personal responsibility is the key to prosperity. I vote Republican because our liberty remains in a limited government. I side with the GOP because when I do succeed, I do not want my burden increased. I remain loyal to the party because while I pursue happiness on my own accord, I also have the ability to fail. Because I have the ability to fail, I am motivated to do everything with excellence to be a testament to my inevitable success.

I call myself a Republican because I am young.

offices at the same time, and Johnson was not sure he could win the presidency. As majority leader of the U.S. Senate, LBJ was neither ready nor willing to give up sure power in return for an opportunity to hold higher office.

Johnson confronted the problem in a way only he could; he pressured the Texas legislature into changing the law. It now prohibits a person from running for two offices at the same time unless one is U.S. senator and the other is president or vice president of the United States. As it turned out, LBJ lost the Democratic presidential nomination to John F. Kennedy and settled for the second spot on the ticket, vice president.

In the Senate race, the GOP chose as its standard-bearer John Tower, a political science professor at Midwestern State University in Wichita Falls. See the Texas Mosaic on Tower nearby. LBJ won easily, but Tower still managed to garner more than 40 percent of the vote, an unexpectedly high percentage against the popular Johnson.

Kennedy and Johnson captured the White House. Johnson had the ability to manipulate Texas law, but even he was unable to overcome the U.S Constitution's prohibition against serving in both the executive and legislative branches. As a result, a U.S. Senate seat opened in Texas, and a special election was called to fill the vacancy. Concurrently, many conservative Democrats formally broke ties with their old party after the 1960 elections.

Tower was the only serious Republican candidate to opt into the race. Several well-known Democrats threw their hats into the ring, including liberal stalwart Henry B. Gonzales and future U.S. Speaker of the House Jim Wright, but the front-runner was William Blakely. Governor Price Daniel Jr. had appointed the ultraconservative Blakely to fill the open seat until the election could be held. A total of 71 candidates appeared on the ballot. No one received a majority of the vote in the initial round of balloting.

Tower led with 31.5 percent. Blakely joined him in the runoff with 18.3 percent, edging Wright, who received 16.4 percent.[3] Conventional wisdom was that

Democrats would put aside their differences and back Blakely, allowing him to retain the Senate seat. Liberal Democrats had other ideas. By withholding support for Blakely, they hoped to defeat him and, as a result, force conservatives out of the party. Many liberals voted for Tower, others opted not to vote at all.

Tower was also aided by the Bay of Pigs fiasco. Many Texans blamed the recently elected president for the failure of the abortive invasion of Cuba. Kennedy had called off U.S. air support of the anti-Communist Cuban nationalists' invasion. The nationalists were routed by Fidel Castro's superior forces. Some Texans believed that Kennedy was soft on communism: a serious charge in Texas. They could not vote against the president, so many voted against the nearest Democrat, who happened to be Blakely. Tower won by about 10,000 votes out of almost 900,000 cast.[4] Suddenly, a party that had no representation in the state legislature and only one representative in the congressional delegation had one of two U.S. senators from Texas.

Texas **MOSAIC**

John Tower

John Tower was the father of the modern Republican Party in Texas.

He created the foundation upon which the party was built. A political science professor at Midwestern State University in Wichita Falls before entering the political arena, Tower was the son and grandson of Methodist ministers. From the time of his 1961 special election victory, he was instrumental in the party's emergence. As a high profile, successful officeholder, he helped recruit candidates and raise money for the party. For almost twenty years, Tower was *the* face and *the* voice of the Texas GOP.

He made it easier for other Republicans to raise funds and win elections. During his time in office, the Republican Party was transformed from a minor irritant to the Democrats into a viable entity that had elected a governor and a significant number of legislators. Tower helped guide the party through its formative years.

A longtime member of the Senate Armed Services Committee and its chair after Republicans took control of the Senate in 1981, Tower was a "hawk" when it came to foreign policy. He favored a strong military; a large, viable defense industry; and a proactive role for the United States in foreign affairs. He was an ardent anti-Communist. These views, shared by many Texans, helped him win reelection three times.

The conservative Tower believed that with the exception of the Department of Defense, government should be small. He feared government power and opposed unnecessary government interference in both business and personal endeavors. This view would

cause him problems with some Texas Republicans late in his career. Tower supported abortion rights, at one time even voting for federal funding of abortions for poor women. As a result, some GOP extremists in Texas tried to deny the former senator a seat at the Republican National Convention in 1988. The incident drips with irony. First, without Tower, the Republican Party in Texas might never have left the ground. Second, most of the people involved in the movement to oust Tower had roots in the Democratic Party, leaving only after their views were continually ignored.

U.S. Senator John Tower was the first Republican elected statewide since E.J. Davis.

Therefore, they were not involved with Republican politics during the time when Tower was building the GOP. Yet in 1988 they argued that Tower was not a true Republican. Ultimately, their effort would fail, and Tower would be present when his old friend George Bush—George W.'s father—was nominated to be president of the United States.

It is another irony that the election of Bush would bring a bitter end to Tower's political career. Upon his election, Bush appointed Tower to be his secretary of defense.

Because of his long tenure on the Armed Services Committee, most political observers believed that his nomination would fly through the Senate. Despite some Democratic grumbling over the high income

(continued)

Tower had made as a defense consultant after leaving the Senate, it appeared he had enough votes to win confirmation.

It has been said that politics makes strange bedfellows. Never was this truer than during the 1989 confirmation hearings. Some radical Republican activists were troubled enough by Tower's stand on abortion rights that they were determined to derail his nomination. They began to leak stories about Tower to both the media and select Democrats. Some Democrats had legitimate reservations about Tower, others disliked him, and still others were anxious to get back at Republicans after their rough handling of Michael Dukakis during the 1988 presidential campaign.

Tower was an easy target. While many of his tastes were simple, he liked to dress in expensive clothes. Twice divorced, he had a reputation as a ladies' man. He was known to throw back a drink or two. (Every Texas Independence Day, Tower would gather his staff in his office at noon, close the door, and break the seal on a good bottle of bourbon. Tower would then read

William B. Travis's moving "I will never surrender" letter from the Alamo. There was seldom a dry eye in the room as the staff would drink a toast to Texas heroes long since gone.)

Some of the charges were ridiculous, particularly the one alleging that he and a Russian ballerina had disrobed on a grand piano at a posh River Oaks party. Others may have had some substance. Tower played into his enemies' hands when he agreed to give up liquor during his tenure in office. This implied, in the eyes of many, that he did have a problem with alcohol. The allegations, coupled with the Senate's increasing partisanship, doomed the nomination. Tower refused to step back from the nomination, though, forcing a Senate vote. He lost and returned to a defense consulting and teaching at Southern Methodist University in Dallas.

Tower, along with a daughter, was killed in a plane crash on April 5, 1991.

SOURCE: John G. Tower, *Consequences* (Boston, MA: Little, Brown and Company, 1991).

Slow Growth

Senator Tower's 1961 victory laid the foundation for the growth of the Republican Party. He was reelected in 1966, but Republicans held only 3 of 150 seats in the Texas House.[5] In 1972, Tower won again. With a popular President Richard Nixon heading the ticket, Republicans managed their best showing yet. Tower won by the largest margin of his career. The Sharpstown Bank Scandal also hurt the Democrats as Republican membership in the Texas House grew to 17, including future Speaker of the House Tom Craddick.[6]

What happened in 1978 was a total surprise. Not only was Tower reelected, but Texas also chose a Republican governor for the first time since Reconstruction. Tower's campaign against Democrat Bob Krueger was one of the dirtiest in the history of Texas—a state not exactly known for clean campaigns. Both candidates found their personal lives the subject of attack and innuendo. Tower survived his final election bid by a margin of a little more than 12,000 votes.

The election of Bill Clements as governor was a huge upset. Polls showed Democrat John Hill leading by as much as eleven percentage points. On Election Day, the conservative Clements edged the liberal Hill by almost 17,000 votes. Even Republicans were surprised. Democrats, however, still controlled the legislature; holding 27 of 31 Senate seats and 128 of 150 House seats.

The Reagan Revolution

Ronald Reagan's conservatism resonated with Texans in 1980, as he rode a landslide victory into the White House. On his coattails, and as the national party took on a decidedly more conservative bent, Republicans made substantial inroads into the state house and senate, electing 35 representatives and 8 senators, both post-Reconstruction highs.

In 1982, Republicans took a step backward as they lost the governor's office. In 1984, they rebounded quickly. Reagan and Bush again led the ticket. Tower surprised everyone by opting out of the U.S. Senate race, but Democrat-turned-Republican Phil Gramm was overwhelmingly elected to the open seat. GOP gains were most pronounced in the Texas House, where Republican representation leaped to 52 seats. By exceeding one-third of the House's membership, Republicans gained the ability to block constitutional amendments.

The year 1986 marked the political resurrection of Bill Clements. Playing to his advantage were the political misfortunes of Mark White. The Democrat had the unfortunate distinction of being governor when oil prices collapsed. White bore the brunt of the blame for the economic decline in Texas. Worse, he had earned the wrath of the state's high school football coaches, having been an integral part of the school reforms that had included the "no pass–no play" rule. The provision prohibited students who failed a course from participating in extracurricular activities for six weeks. When this began to affect Texas high school football, many were outraged. Meddling with high school football was definitely "messing with Texas." The Bubba faction joined with the football coaches and displaced oil workers to oust White from office. The Republicans held their strength in the Senate and gained four seats in the House, bringing their total to 56. For the first time since Reconstruction, Republicans had both the governor and more than a third of the seats in the House. In effect, this insulated the governor's veto from override.

down-ballot races
Statewide races below the level of president, U.S. Senator, or governor.

Texas, however, could not be considered a two-party state in 1986. Republicans showed an absolute inability to win statewide down-ballot races. **Down-ballot races** are contests below the level of president, governor, or U.S. senator. The designation includes such offices as lieutenant governor, attorney general, Supreme Court justice, railroad commissioner, and comptroller. In 1986, Texas was still a Democrat-dominated state with a Republican governor and a significant number of Republicans in the House. That year, the GOP did not even run a serious candidate for lieutenant governor—widely considered to be the most powerful office in the state—in part because no one wanted to run against Bill Hobby. Gubernatorial candidate Clements refused to share the podium with the man who was the Republican nominee for that office, viewing him as a far-right extremist.

A Two-Party State

Texas became a two-party state on Election Day 1988. The top of the ballot told part of the story: Texans overwhelmingly voted for Republican George Bush for president over Democrat Michael Dukakis, despite the fact that Dukakis's running mate was Texas Senator Lloyd Bentsen. On the next line of the ballot, many of the same voters chose Bentsen over his Republican rival for the Senate by about the same large margin. (Bentsen had taken advantage of the "LBJ law" in order to run for both offices.) The bigger story, though, was in the down-ballot races. Republicans won three Supreme Court seats, including the chief justice's position. Additionally, a Republican captured a railroad commission seat. Democrats awoke the next morning to the hard fact that they could no longer take the down-ballot races for granted.

How Not to Run a Campaign

Students of politics still view the 1990 Texas gubernatorial race as a case study in how to lose an election. Republican Clayton Williams' political gaffes cost him an early lead of 20 points.[7] The GOP did manage to elect two rising stars: Kay Bailey Hutchison was elected as treasurer, and Rick Perry won the race for agriculture commissioner. Republicans also won two Supreme Court races.

Republican Gains

The biggest victory for the Republican Party in 1992 was not in the ballot box, but in the courtroom. Three Republican-appointed federal judges ruled that the Democrat-controlled state senate had illegally gerrymandered its 1991 redistricting plan. The judges created their own new districts and ordered that the 1992 elections be held under a plan much more favorable to the Republicans. GOP Senate strength soared from 8 to 13.

In 1993, Hutchison won her U.S. Senate seat in the June special election runoff. As a result, Republicans now hold both U.S. Senate seats from Texas, with John Cornyn elected in 2002 to succeed Phil Gramm in the Tower seat.

In 1994, Republican George W. Bush, son of the former President George H. Bush, was elected governor. While Democratic incumbents retained all five statewide executive offices, Republican incumbent Rick Perry held on to his office as well. Significantly, the GOP took control of the state Supreme Court for the first time since Reconstruction. Republicans also won an additional railroad commissioner's seat. In fact, Republicans captured all down-ballot races in which the Democrats didn't have an incumbent.

Of major interest to Texas political observers was the outcome of the state senate races. After the 1992 elections, Democrats had successfully appealed their redistricting case to a higher federal court. As a result, the 1994 Senate elections were run under the original Democrat-drawn districts. Most experts expected the GOP to lose at least some of their 1992 gains. Surprisingly, Republicans picked up a seat, increasing their representation to 14, two short of Senate control. Republican success can be attributed to two factors. First, the incumbency factor held. The GOP was able to hold onto seats it won in 1992, even though the districts were not drawn as favorably in 1994. Second, President Clinton's lack of popularity in Texas hurt all Democrats. In 1996, Republicans did what would have been unthinkable a decade before: they carved out a 17–14 advantage in the Texas Senate. In the House, Republicans held 64 seats after the 1994 elections, a 1995 special election, and defections by former Democratic representatives.

From 1996 through the 2006 elections, Republicans won all statewide races on the ballot. This trend marks a fundamental shift in Texas politics. Twenty years ago, when average Texans reached the point on the ballot where they were no longer familiar with the candidates, they automatically voted Democratic. Today, faced with the same proposition, they vote Republican. In statewide elections, that spells trouble for Democrats, who now must overcome obstacles of both incumbency and partisan preference. Republicans hold every statewide office, including all seats on the state Supreme Court and Court of Criminal Appeals.

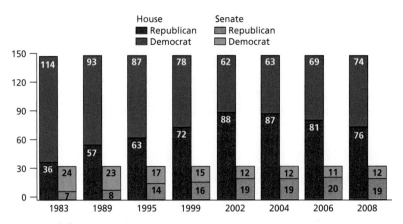

FIGURE **4.3** **Growth of the GOP**.

The 2002 election saw Republicans post remarkable gains in the legislature as well. They extended the barest of majorities in the Senate to a 19:12 advantage. More importantly, they went from minority status in the House to a huge 88:62 advantage, giving Republicans the Speaker's position for the first time since Reconstruction. (See the "Growth of the GOP" chart above.) Democrats kept their advantage in the Texas delegation to the U.S. Congress, holding a 17:15 edge. Republicans picked up the two new seats dictated by congressional reapportionment. The biggest factor here was incumbency; every member of Congress from Texas who ran again was reelected.

That Democratic edge would evaporate in 2004 as a result of one of the most controversial partisan actions in recent Texas history, leaving Republicans with a 21:11 advantage in the congressional delegation (see the redistricting section in Chapter 6 for the details). Democrats came out of the 2004 elections with at least one small reason to celebrate. Although Republicans maintained their 19:12 advantage in the Senate, the Democrats picked up a seat in the House, cutting the Republican advantage to 87:63. It was the first time Democrats had gained a seat in a generation. In 2006, Democrats made up more ground, as the Republican edge shrank to 81:69. And in 2008, the Democrats almost recaptured the House, leaving Republicans with a bare two-seat majority.

You can visit the Web site of the Republican Party of Texas at http://www.texasgop.org.

Party Politics in the New Millennium

Texas politics has entered a remarkable phase in the early 21st century. Its long Democratic heritage, coupled with its conservatism—an idea best expressed by the modern Republican Party—will make elective politics one of the most interesting games in town for years to come.

The Texas Constitution: A Closer Look

For a document as verbose as the Texas Constitution, it may seem odd that there is but one passing reference to parties in the entire text. Article III, Section 24 requires that each party be represented on the Texas Ethics Commission.

The overwhelming success of the Republicans over the last several elections does not mean that the party is without potential problems. In 2008, for instance, Republicans lost seats in both the Texas house and senate. When Democrats controlled Texas politics, the party was overrun with intraparty struggles and factionalism. Weak and generally ineffective, Republicans tended to unite in an effort to win the few offices the party managed to capture. As the Republican Party has ascended, it has become plagued by similar factionalism. This is another one of the ironies of Texas politics: Republicans who once laughed at the divided Democrats now find themselves in the same boat. Republicans are divided among economic conservatives, who believe lower taxes and less business regulation is the key to the state's prosperity; libertarian conservatives, who fear government intrusion on an individual's life; and social conservatives, who believe our biggest problems are caused by the nation's moral decay. Each faction wants to be the driving force in the party, as Republicans have achieved true majority status. The problem for each is that none of the three constitutes a majority of the party. Furthermore, not all Texas Republicans fall easily into one of the three categories. The faction that controls the state party apparatus, the social conservatives, does not represent the viewpoint of most Republican primary voters, as evidenced by the difficulty far-right candidates face in winning nominations. Yet that faction tries to speak for all party members on substantive matters. As long as the factions can unify, either around a group of strong candidates or against a common enemy, the coalition can hold together.

Democrats, on the other hand, face the problem of being perceived as liberal in a conservative state. Although liberals are certainly a large, influential, and important faction of any Democratic majority, it is almost impossible for a truly liberal candidate to win a major statewide race. Therefore, it is important for the party to ensure that conservative Democrats, such as former Supreme Court Justice Raul Gonzalez and former Comptroller John Sharp, remain comfortable in the party. If Republicans move farther to the right, Democrats need to be prepared to occupy the vast middle ground between the extremes.

And as the Republican Party tries to portray the Democrats as the party of liberalism, the Democrats need to portray the Republicans as the party of the extreme right. Furthermore, Democrats must work hard to encourage minority voter turnout. Minorities comprise over 50 percent of the Texas population, but this has not translated into a proportional number of minority voters. Turnout is the key to future Democratic Party success in Texas.

Despite its transformation into a two-party state, at least prior to the 2003 redistricting fight, Texas managed to remain remarkably nonpartisan. For instance, in the U.S. Congress, and in most states, the party that controls a House of the legislature also has one of its members as each committee's chair. In Texas, however, state leaders have worked to ensure that the best person is named chair, leading to many Republican chairs in the formerly Democrat-controlled House and Democrat chairs in the Republican-controlled Senate. Most votes in the Texas legislature are not along party lines. Republican governors have worked well with Democratic leaders as most involved have placed policy above partisanship. While state party chairs and executive committees have become increasingly partisan and divisive, elected politicians have continued to work together. One of the unique—and good—things about Texas politics through the 1990s was that hard work and good ideas were rewarded regardless of political party. It led to the great working relationship among Governor George W. Bush, Lieutenant Governor Bob Bullock, Speaker Pete Laney, and a host of other state leaders who worked across party lines. The 2003 sessions left that spirit gravely wounded. Will those injures prove fatal?

We got a better sense of that over the last three sessions. Two key questions gave a fairly clear indication. First, would the Republican leadership continue to appoint Democrats to chair key committees? Second, would the two-thirds rule be reinstated in the Senate? The answer to the first question is yes. There is a long history of bipartisan appointments, stretching back to the days when Democrats firmly controlled both chambers. (Republican leaders even helped raise campaign funds for select Democrats who had been in leadership position in 2003, although some of those lost their primary elections.) The quorum-breaking actions, however, gave the Republicans an excuse to punish Democrats by withholding some key appointments. Although the prime chairs went mainly to the Republicans, at least some semblance of bipartisanship survived.

The answer to the second question was, for the most part. The two-thirds rule was reinstated in 2005 and 2007. In 2009, however, the rule came with a stipulation: It would not apply to the voter ID bill, which stalled out in the House. Senate rules are determined by a majority of the Senate. Since Republicans comprise that majority, Republicans can create whatever rules they want. By tradition, those rules have included a provision requiring two-thirds concurrence for a bill to reach the Senate floor. And, since the lieutenant governor's legislative powers are set by that same majority vote, did Dewhurst open a Pandora's box that might ultimately lead the majority to strip his office of its powers, vesting them instead in some type of a Majority Leader position? If a Republican majority finds itself crosswise with the Republican lieutenant governor, might they recall this incident as a way to strip his or her office of its vast powers? Or, when Dewhurst vacates the office, senators might see that as a logical time for a change. That would shake up things in Texas politics much more than a shift in partisan control. Whatever momentum the Democrats had in Texas after 2008 was reversed in 2010. Republicans trounced Democrats in all races for statewide office, while picking up 22 seats in the Texas House and three congressional seats. Although Democrats held their county gains in Dallas County, Republicans reasserted themselves in Harris County and took control of Galveston County government for the first time since Reconstruction.

Summary

The major political parties in Texas form for the purpose of winning elections. They are coalitional. Ideological parties, which are more philosophical in nature, are seldom a factor in Texas politics. A party is composed of groups of people, sharing common goals, who attempt to gain control of government through winning elective offices. In Texas, the major parties are the Republicans and the Democrats.

Despite their policy differences, the major parties share the same internal structures. Both elect state delegates through a series of precinct and district conventions. Both parties establish state platforms. And both select the permanent elements of their structure: the party's state chair and state executive committee.

Democrats dominated Texas politics completely from the end of Reconstruction until the early 1960s. Despite divisions within the party, the Democrats carried every office. In the 1960s, things started to change with the election of Republican U.S. Senator John Tower. Republicans elected a governor in the 1970s, but true party equity didn't occur until the late 1980s. By the late 1990s, Republicans dominated statewide races.

Since the 2002 contests, Republicans have controlled the state house and senate as well. The future of Texas politics will depend on which party is most successful at holding its various factions together and keeping them active in the political system.

Chapter Test

1. Which is a coalitional party?
   a. Republican.
   b. Green.
   c. Libertarian.
   d. Socialist.

2. A senatorial district convention is on the same level as a
   a. precinct convention.
   b. county convention.
   c. state convention.
   d. national convention.

3. A party's state chair is chosen by
   a. state delegates.
   b. the state executive committee.
   c. the party's national chair.
   d. primary voters.

4. Liberals controlled the Texas Democrats' political agenda
   a. from Reconstruction to today.
   b. from 1940 until today.
   c. during the 1930s.
   d. during the 1950s.

5. All is true of John Tower *except* he
   a. was a Democrat senator.
   b. lost to LBJ.
   c. had been a political science professor.
   d. gained office through a special election.

6. The most important goal of a major political party is to
   a. win elections.
   b. influence policy.
   c. run the government.
   d. frame important issues.

7. Prior to the 1960s, Texas was a
   a. two-party state.
   b. three-party state.
   c. Republican-leaning state.
   d. solid Democratic state.

8. Today in Texas
   a. Republicans dominate statewide offices.
   b. Democrats carry Texas in most presidential elections.

   c. Democrats control the House and Senate.
   d. the state is moving toward a three-party structure.

9. State executive committee members are paid
   a. $1,000 a month.
   b. $7,200 a year.
   c. $100,000 a year.
   d. no salary.

10. After Reconstruction, Democrats held the governor's office for about
   a. 10 years.
   b. 25 years.
   c. 50 years.
   d. 100 years.

Answers: 1. a   2. b   3. a   4. c   5. a   6. a   7. d   8. a   9. d   10. d

Critical Thinking Questions

1. Defend the platform of either the Democratic or Republican Party.

2. Which party will dominate Texas politics 20 years from now?

3. Which party best represents the interests of the average Texan?

Key Terms

coalitions, **p. 90**
conventions, **p. 92**
"Democrats of Texas," **p. 100**
down-ballot races, **p. 108**
factions, **p. 99**
ideological, **p. 90**
platform, **p. 91**

political party, **p. 90**
precinct, **p. 92**
precinct convention, **p. 92**
resolutions, **p. 92**
"Texas Regulars," **p. 100**
state senatorial district convention, **p. 93**

Notes

1. James Madison, Letter to Henry Lee, 25 June 1824.

2. Rupert N. Richardson, Adrian Anderson, and Ernest Wallace, *Texas: The Lone Star State* (Englewood Cliffs, NJ: Prentice Hall, 1993), p. 393.

3. John R. Knagg, *Two-Party Texas* (Austin, TX: Eakin Press, 1986), p. 9.

4. Ibid., pp. 12–15.

5. Ibid., p. 107.

6. Ibid., pp. 174–176.

7. *The Texas Almanac, 1992–93* (Dallas, TX: *Dallas Morning News*, 1991), p. 424.

Interest Groups in Texas Politics

5

The term "lobbyist" is first used to describe Civil War–era government contractors who accosted congressmen in the lobby areas outside the legislative chambers.

1863

189

Texas railroads try to prevent government regulation by urging legislators to oppose the new Tex Railroad Commission proposed b Governor James S. Hogg.

By the end of this chapter on interest groups, you should be able to . . .

★ Explain the role of interest groups.
★ Identity the types of interest groups.
★ Analyze the methods of interest groups.
★ Explain the relationship between money and interest groups.
★ Understand the impact of interest groups on the political environment.
★ Explain how you can become involved with interest groups.

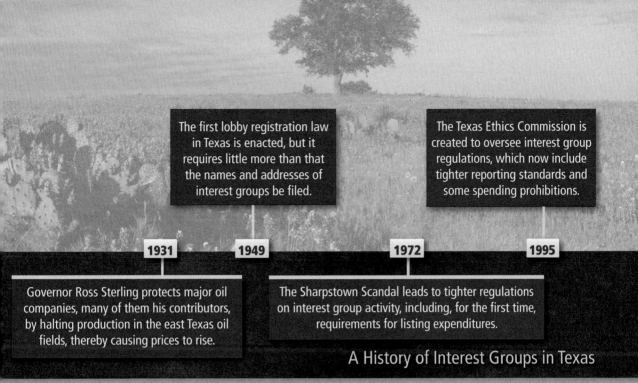

The first lobby registration law in Texas is enacted, but it requires little more than that the names and addresses of interest groups be filed.

The Texas Ethics Commission is created to oversee interest group regulations, which now include tighter reporting standards and some spending prohibitions.

1931 **1949** **1972** **1995**

Governor Ross Sterling protects major oil companies, many of them his contributors, by halting production in the east Texas oil fields, thereby causing prices to rise.

The Sharpstown Scandal leads to tighter regulations on interest group activity, including, for the first time, requirements for listing expenditures.

A History of Interest Groups in Texas

You can't sling a cat around your head without hitting a lobbyist!

—VETERAN HOUSE MEMBER DURING A SESSION
OF THE TEXAS LEGISLATURE

At times, interest groups and the people who represent them seem to be crawling all over the political landscape. While this appears to be especially true during a session of the Texas legislature, interest groups are full-time participants in this state's politics, and many of these groups work year-round to advance their causes. Interest groups are among the most powerful forces in Texas politics. They also generate strong opinions about what they do and how they do it. Some people view interest groups as a vital and even necessary element in our political equation, but others see them as divisive and self-seeking, placing private gain before public good. Tell people you serve as legislative liaison for a state trade association and they might be impressed. Confess that you're a lobbyist for an interest group and they may treat you as a swine flu carrier!

The Roles of Interest Groups

Interest Groups Defined

interest group
A collection of individuals who share a common set of ideas or principles and who attempt to advance those ideas or principles by influencing public policymakers.

In order to explain the role of interest groups in Texas politics, we should begin by defining this creature. An **interest group** is composed of people who share a common set of ideas or principles and who attempt to advance those ideas or principles by influencing public-policy makers. This definition shares some of the same components as that of a political party (see Chapter 4) in that both entities are united (albeit sometimes rather loosely) around a core of ideas or principles and both are organized (again, to widely varying degrees). However, interest groups differ significantly from political parties in at least two ways.

First, interest groups do not run candidates for office. At first glance, this may seem to be an artificial distinction. After all, haven't we heard elected officials proudly proclaim that they are life members of the NRA, the PTA, or some other group ending in "A"? Obviously, members of interest groups can run for and win political office. But when they seek public office, they are identified on the ballot as the candidate of a political party, not of the interest group to which they happen to belong. Their path to the general election leads through the party primary and their campaign benefits from the support of the party that has nominated them. Moreover, in those elections where party designations on the ballot are forbidden (including races for school board, city council, community college board of trustees, and others at local levels of government), no group label whatsoever will appear by the candidate's name.

Rather than formally trying to capture elected office by running candidates, an interest group focuses on attempting to persuade those who already hold office (or positions of administrative responsibility) to see things their way. They also may mobilize their members to work on behalf of particular candidates who are friendly toward the group and its goals. They may even help raise money for a candidate's campaign. But they don't nominate their members for political office, so you aren't going to see a candidate from the National Rifle Association Party on the ballot.

A second difference between interest groups and political parties can be found in their focus. Parties, especially in the United States and Texas, usually address a broad array of issues in their attempt to build a winning coalition among voters. They may take positions on such topics as abortion, free trade, gun control, environmental action, business regulation, crime prevention, and many other political subjects. The party's position on these topics sometimes appears to be superficial because the breadth of their appeal limits the depth to which they can develop their stances. Simply put, parties try to say a little about a lot.

Interest groups, on the other hand, focus on a single issue or a narrowly related group of issues. Because they are not preoccupied with coalition building, they can afford to expend most of their efforts on the subject that is of prime concern to their members. They don't have to (and usually aren't inclined to) take a position on nonrelated issues. Thus, the National Rifle Association probably won't take a public stance on the issue of abortion. Likewise, the Texas State Teachers Association does not express a group position on the issue of emissions testing for automobiles in metropolitan areas. By focusing on a narrow range of topics, interest groups can develop more in-depth levels of information than can a political party. Simply put, interest groups try to say a lot about a little.

Interest Groups: Okay

While it may not be popular to say so publicly, an argument can be made for the notion that interest groups are a vital part of our political process. For one thing, they probably have a kind of backhanded blessing from both the U.S. and Texas constitutions (see the Constitution Box in this chapter).

Constitutional considerations aside, interest groups are useful for a couple of reasons: they magnify voices and they multiply choices. By magnifying voices, these groups make it more likely that your opinions and your ideas will be heard. One person walking back and forth in front of the capitol in Austin carrying a sign that says "Save the Paluxy" might get a curious glance and a fleeting reflection on just what kind of endangered species a "Paluxy" is from a passing legislator. An organized group of a thousand people e-mailing, writing, and calling that same legislator urging her to enact legislation to protect the Paluxy River from development will likely get more of her attention, especially if they include her constituents. Why, they may even be able to enlist her support. Each of those thousand people has a personal belief in that group's goal, but collective action through an interest group allows each person to voice that belief more effectively.

Interest groups also multiply choices. To illustrate this, let's look at the two-party system in this state. If you don't like the Republican Party position on an issue, you can always turn to the Democrats. But what if you don't like what the Democrats have to say on that issue? If neither of the two parties takes a position with which you agree, you can end up extremely frustrated. You may in fact

The Texas Constitution: A Closer Look

The U.S. Constitution seems to allude to something that could be described as interest group activity in the First Amendment when it states, in part, that "Congress shall make no law . . . abridging . . . the right of the people peaceably to assemble, and to petition the Government for a redress of grievances."[1] Those who supported adoption of this proposed new Constitution saw benefit in the actions of what we would today call interest groups. In *Federalist No. 10*, James Madison made the point that competition among such groups (whom he referred to as "factions") would likely prevent one single group from cornering the market on political and governmental power. In like manner, the Texas Constitution specifically guarantees that "citizens shall have the right, in a peaceable manner, to assemble together for their common good and apply to those invested with the powers of government for redress of grievance or other purposes, by petition, address or remonstrance."[2] At the very least, this means that you and your friends or fellow believers can get together and, as long as you do not participate in violent behavior, can try to make some senator or representative see your point of view and help you get what you want.

Ben Sargent's cartoon suggest that lobbyists crowd out the interests of others. How is that an exaggeration of real world politics?

conclude, as did early-20th-century humorist Will Rogers, that choosing between Democrats and Republicans is an exercise in futility. As Rogers wryly stated, "The more you read and observe about this Politics thing, you got to admit that each party is worse than the other."[3] To someone in this situation, interest groups may provide just the avenue along which to advance a heartfelt cause. Also, interest groups can (and usually do) address questions that parties often ignore as being too trivial. For example, neither major party may be overly concerned with saving the Paluxy River, but an interest group could easily make that issue one of its paramount concerns. If that's the issue that most concerns you, then that interest group becomes a more likely choice for realizing your political aims. However, interest groups not only multiply choices for citizens, they also multiply choices for policy makers. As interest groups ply their "wares" (information) among legislators, regulators, and other decision makers, the competing viewpoints thus presented afford a broader array of possible policy options.

Interest Groups: Not Okay

Of course, some will argue that interest groups have a negative side as well. It is often pointed out that the proliferation of special interest groups in the political arena seems to have contributed to the much-publicized fracturing of American culture. This school of thought holds that the division and redivision of our society into groups that are often hostile toward other competing groups helps to create a politics of confrontation and somehow heightens the struggle for what often are perceived as scarce public services and resources. Those who are leery of interest groups suggest that in a society such as ours, which is already ethnically and culturally diverse (and all too often divided along these lines), these added internal divisions only make it more difficult for people to come together and to find consensus. When the social fabric seems always to be badly frayed, if not outright shredded, such divisiveness is seen as something without which we would be better off.

Another possible problem that interest group politics may pose is the disparity that often occurs among such groups in terms of their actual ability to organize, inform, and influence policy makers. All interest groups are not created equal, and differences in the size and wealth of various groups often create a political playing field that is anything but level. Moreover, the added dimension of representation afforded citizens by interest groups may be largely mitigated if the citizen in question is not aware (or does not particularly care) that he or she is a member of such a group. Most Americans (and most Texans) belong to, are affiliated with, or have some connection to more than one interest group, but that American (or that Texan) needs to be aware of that link and its potential benefits in order to take *full* advantage of what the group has to offer. Of course, one of the good things we've already pointed out about pluralism is that, with so many groups out there, most people's views are represented whether or not they choose to participate (or are even aware of their group ties). But lack of membership awareness can mean that some potentially powerful or influential groups may not be successful in achieving their ends, especially if such success is predicated on mobilizing large numbers of group members in support of policy goals (see the "Membership Mobilization" section below).

The Types of Interest Groups

There are literally thousands of actual (not to mention potential) interest groups in Texas. This is partly because there are a lot of people in Texas. However, a large population alone does not guarantee a bumper crop of interest groups. That large population has to be sufficiently diverse in its composition to produce identifiable subgroupings of people who may share common ideas. These groups then have the potential to organize themselves as true interest groups. Obviously, Texas has such diversity within its large population, and this helps account for the many interest groups here.

This plethora of groups also exhibits an interesting variety of organizational forms. Some of these groups are highly **centralized** in their organization. They concentrate decision making at or near the top of the group's structure and exercise leadership through a small group at that level. An example of such a group is the Texas Community College Teachers Association. Although this group has approximately 6,000 members, a legislative committee of 15 members proposes its public policy agenda, which is then ratified by a 6-member executive committee. Its president and its professional staff make most of the group's political contacts, although in recent years the association has hired a professional lobbyist (see the discussion of the role of lobbyists below) to serve as a point of contact with policy makers. While rank-and-file members are occasionally called on to engage in large group activities, the association tends to avoid demonstrative or confrontational politics, focusing instead on providing timely information to key decision makers in the legislature and in certain executive agencies.

Other groups have a more **decentralized** internal structure. In these, decision making and leadership are often widely dispersed among the membership, and the members focus on a good bit of regional and local political activity in addition to dealing with issues before the state legislature. The Chamber of Commerce in Texas is a good example of this type of organizational structure. Although there is a state-level chamber, there are also numerous regional and local bodies that pursue their own political agendas in addition to working with the state office. These local organizations are

centralized
Groups with decision making concentrated near the top.

decentralized
Groups with decision making widely dispersed.

often very active in contacting legislators and other policy makers in support not only of their general group goals, but also of their own more local agendas as well.

Some groups in Texas lack even the most rudimentary of organizational structures. The people who make up these groups may have only a tenuous connection to the group and may only occasionally act as a group. We could best describe the structure of such groups as **amorphous**. The homeless and welfare recipients might well fit into this category. Communication among the "membership" of such groups is difficult and sporadic, and they rarely are able to orchestrate action in support of specific policy goals. Political activities by such groups are usually spontaneous and in response to some immediate perceived threat to the group.

amorphous
Groups with tenuously connected interests.

A classic example of this kind of spontaneous group activity was seen in the events that preceded the World Cup soccer matches in Dallas in the summer of 1994. In an attempt to bolster the image of Dallas as a "world-class" city, local authorities forcibly removed many homeless people from under one of the city's freeway overpasses, where visitors to the games could see them. In response, an interesting amalgam of social, religious, and human rights groups came together to represent the interests of the individuals being displaced. Some would argue that such loose collections of people really shouldn't be called interest groups. However, like more formally structured interest groups, amorphous groups do exhibit collective activity on occasion and, in this particular instance, did attempt to influence public policy. When they do, they are functioning as if they were an interest group. A major problem, of course, lies in the lack of knowledge and experience regarding the policy-making process that characterizes many such groups. And in interest group politics, as in playing baseball or the guitar, practice makes perfect.

Business Interests

Groups that represent the business community in Texas are among the most powerful and influential in the state. Texas's political climate is quite friendly toward its large business community, as you would expect in a state where the individualistic political culture is so prevalent (for a discussion of political culture, see Chapter 1). These groups, often called trade associations, can consistently gain the ears of policy makers because of their numerical (and financial) strength and because most have access to a vast amount of information that legislators can use (see the "Methods of Interest Groups" section below). Armed with that information, most of these groups try to maintain a friendly regulatory climate, promote a tax structure that is favorable to the business community, and lend their support to legislation that can benefit their own particular enterprises.

One perennial power among business interest groups is the Texas Good Roads and Transportation Association. With a membership drawn primarily from construction contractors, the group works hard to promote the extension and renovation of the state's highway system, one of the largest in the nation. This of course results in more state contracts, which in turn helps keep the association's members busy.[4]

Another group in this category is the Texas Taxpayers and Research Association (TTARA). This innocuous-sounding organization began operating more than 70 years ago as the Texas Research League. Several years ago, it merged with the Texas Taxpayers Association, and its membership includes a veritable who's who among the Texas business community. The TTARA specializes in generating data related to the state's tax structure and is particularly interested in helping to develop the state's overall fiscal policies. The legislature and many state agencies make routine use of this powerful group's information, enabling its members to enjoy an advantage in shaping policy from the very beginning of the process.[5]

Labor Interests

Interest groups that act on behalf of organized labor have not fared well in Texas politics. The same political climate that favors groups from the business community often generates an attitude of antipathy toward labor groups. When you look at the issues that labor emphasizes, they often conflict with those that might help produce a "healthy business climate." Labor groups, usually organized as unions, tend to push for enhanced workplace safety, preservation of rights under worker's compensation laws, and, in the case of farm laborers, limitations on the use of pesticides. These views on such issues are not the sort to set a businessman's heart singing. The AFL-CIO and the Oil, Chemical and Atomic Workers of Texas are among the more effective labor organizations in the state. The latter group has had some impact on the political agenda in southeast Texas, especially in the Galveston Bay–Beaumont area. Because of the many oil refineries and petrochemical plants located there, the union workers in those plants have, on occasion, been able to flex some political muscle. However, in most cases, unions and other labor interest groups wind up fighting a kind of rearguard action, hoping to minimize losses but rarely ever enjoying a clear-cut victory.[6]

Professional Interests

Most professions—doctors, teachers, lawyers, accountants, and others—form and maintain interest groups. These groups also are some of the most powerful forces in Texas politics and often rival business groups in their influence on public policy formulation. Most of these groups focus on issues that relate directly to their fields of expertise, such as determining the criteria for admission to the profession or setting the operational boundaries of that profession.

Some of the more influential of these groups include the Texas Medical Association, the Texas Trial Lawyers Association, and, on a somewhat lower power plane, the Texas State Teachers Association.[7] Much of their power, especially in the policy areas of medicine and the law, flows from the fact that those topics often involve issues that are complex and esoteric. The specialized knowledge that members of those two professions can bring to bear on such issues gives them a decided advantage in most cases. As a matter of practical reality, most legislators who are neither doctors nor lawyers either have to take the word of one or the other of these groups on such issues or reject their information out of hand.

When groups like these clash with each other or with groups from the business community, sparks fly, political tensions increase dramatically, and money flows like a Hill Country river after a thunderstorm. Some of the fiercest interest-group battles in the legislature have been waged over issues such as medical malpractice, which can pit lawyers, doctors, and insurance companies against one another. And in the now-classic Pennzoil-Texaco battle over antitrust legislation, millions of dollars were spent in a period of days, and both sides hired so many lobbyists that you needed a scorecard just to keep track of who was working for whom. More recent examples of these kinds of titanic interest group struggles can be seen in legislative battles over deregulation of the telecommunications and public utilities industries. Because almost all of us buy gas, use telephones, turn on lights, and go to the doctor, such confrontations among and between business and professional groups can have long-lasting impact on all the citizens of Texas.

Ethnic Interests

A number of interest groups have formed to represent ethnic groups in the political process, but most have not fared well in their attempts to influence public policy. Although Texas presents a mosaic of ethnic and cultural communities, this diversity is not reflected among the major purveyors of influence in Austin.

African American Texans have for many years had their concerns voiced by the National Association for the Advancement of Colored People (NAACP). This group's legislative successes have been rare, but its willingness to use the courts has resulted in significant gains for the African American community, notably in the areas of public access and accommodation as well as voting rights. (See, e.g., the struggle to eliminate the use of the white primary described in Chapter 3.)[8]

In like manner, groups such as the League of United Latin American Citizens (LULAC) and the Mexican American Legal Defense and Educational Fund (MALDEF) have sought to protect and advance the interests of Hispanic Texans over the years. As with the NAACP, these Latino interest groups have often sought to influence policy through court action rather than through legislative activity. Recently, MALDEF has become heavily involved in court cases arising out of the passage of local anti-immigrant ordinances in such cities as Farmers Branch, and the group has won several preliminary legal battles to enjoin the enforcement of such local laws.[9]

In reality, such ethnic interest groups are often frustrated, not only by the vestiges of racism and cultural bias that still mark our political system, but also by a sometimes stubborn unwillingness to work together on issues of common concern, such as equal pay for equal work and equal access to higher education opportunities. Intergroup jealousies frequently have led to a squandering of political influence and opportunity. By the time these groups finish fighting each other, they often have nothing left to expend on other opponents, many of whom had them outmanned and outgunned (monetarily) from the beginning.

Other Interests

single-issue groups
Interest groups, such as the NRA and MADD, that devote their energies to pursuing a single, narrowly defined policy goal.

Many other kinds of interest groups abound in Texas. Some of the most zealous in pursuit of their aims are what can be called **single-issue groups**. Business, labor, and professional groups may address issues in several areas related to their primary field of concern, but these single-issue interest groups—as their name suggests—focus on one issue only. One of the most consistently influential of these groups is the National Rifle Association (NRA). The NRA wields national influence, but it has been especially successful in pursuing its goals in Texas. The group advocated for the passage of a concealed handgun law in this state for years, and in the 1995 legislative session they saw this goal realized. The most recent session of the legislature saw this group supporting a measure that would have allowed possessors of concealed handgun licenses to carry their weapons onto public college and university campuses.[10]

Another single-issue group that has gained a fair amount of attention over the years is Mothers Against Drunk Drivers (MADD). A true grassroots organization, MADD worked for years to toughen DWI laws in Texas, often with little success. For example, the group failed in its attempt to ban all open containers of alcoholic beverages in vehicles during the 1995 session of the legislature. But groups like MADD lie outside the Texas power zone of business and the professions and therefore rarely get what they want the first time around. The primary lesson such groups must learn is that you've got to "suit up and show up" at every legislative session. MADD's dogged persistence in pursuit of its legislative agenda was rewarded during the 1999 session when the House and Senate agreed to lower the blood-alcohol limit for determining legal intoxication from .10 to .08. Two years later, MADD returned, once more seeking to ban all open alcohol containers in vehicles. This time, they won.[11]

Environmental organizations are another example of single-issue interest groups. For many years, they've been a voice crying in the wilderness of the Texas political landscape. Traditional Texans, who tends to view nature as something to be conquered and subdued, have little regard for those they often derisively refers to as "tree huggers." However, the continued population growth in the state has generated new concerns over such issues as air and water quality, gridlock, open space, and urban sprawl. Many environmental groups have attempted to address these concerns from a lifestyle, rather than a purely environmental, perspective. This shift in strategy has opened up discussions with many who formerly disdained them (e.g.,, alliances between environmentalists and hunting and fishing enthusiasts are becoming more common). The Nature Conservancy, for one, has proved innovative in avoiding the more confrontational strategies often favored by such groups. They have pioneered the building of partnerships among disparate communities of interest—particularly businesses, sportsmen, and environmentalists—that have led to creative programs of public-private land acquisition and management. These programs have, in turn, saved some of the most fragile and unique natural areas in the state of Texas.[12]

Some interest groups form out of a desire to provide public service to the general citizenry. The League of Women Voters works to advance political awareness and informed decision making on the part of voters (and by the way, you don't have to be a woman to join the league). The league routinely publishes information about candidates (usually in the candidates' own words) prior to most elections. Another such group, Common Cause, strives to promote ethical behavior by elected officials as part of an overall aim to bring about open and responsible government. Both of these organizations maintain Web sites that provide more details about their history and their purposes.[13]

Then there are groups promoting particular points of view with regard to morality and lifestyle. The Christian Life Commission of the Baptist General Convention of Texas, a staunch and consistent opponent of legalized gambling, also frequently speaks out on family issues. Groups like the Parent Teacher Association (PTA) focus on children's issues, and numerous pro-life (e.g., Project Rescue) and pro-choice (Texas Abortion Rights League) organizations regularly confront each other and lawmakers on the issue of abortion. Finally, a growing number of groups representing the gay and lesbian communities of Texas are speaking up and working to advance their goals. If you haven't found a group somewhere out there to represent your interests, chances are you just haven't looked hard enough.

Lobbyist Suzii Paynter of the Christian Life Commission speaks against the expansion of legalized gambling in Texas. Do you believe that such events are aimed more at legislators or the public at large?

The Methods of Interest Groups

Interest groups attempt to gain their ends in a number of different ways. Many of their methods focus on the Texas legislature because that body is the primary policy-making agent in Texas politics. The nature and structure of the legislature itself help to shape the methods used by interest groups and enhance the role of these groups as some of the most powerful forces in Texas politics. Let's look closer at how the legislature's methods of operation make interest groups so effective.

The Texas legislature meets in regular session for a maximum of 140 days beginning in January of every odd-numbered year. In that five-month period, between 6,000 and 7,000 pieces of legislation likely will be introduced. The entire two-year (biennial) budget for the state of Texas must be hammered out and adopted. Complex issues such as tort reform, electric utility deregulation (or, more recently, reregulation), casino gambling, toll road construction, and equitable funding for public education often are the focus of the legislature's attention. All of this is to be done by so-called citizen-legislators who are paid $600 per month before taxes and who have extremely limited in-house research and staff resources available. Merely reading all the bills that are introduced in a legislative session is virtually impossible; being able to understand the subtleties of every piece of legislation simply cannot be done without help.

This volume of work is compounded by the short period of time allotted for a session. Over the course of the 140 days in which the legislature meets, events move at an accelerated pace, reaching a frenetic climax during the last month. Although many have described Texas as having a "part-time legislature," a more accurate description would be to call it a "full-time legislature part of the time." That's not merely a semantic difference. For these five months, lawmakers tend to be consumed by the tasks confronting them. Workdays often begin at dawn or before and end at midnight or beyond. It is this combination of too much to do and too little time in which to do it that enhances the power of interest groups.

In this kind of pressure-cooker environment, the most important commodity available to legislators isn't gold, silver, oil futures, or pork bellies. It's information. Legislators with information usually get to call the shots. Legislators with information usually get what they want. Those without information usually get left out and left behind. Given this reality, what kind of entity is in a position to generate the sort of specialized information crucial to the legislative process? If you said a legislator's own staff, sorry, you lose. If you said an interest group, then you get to play in the championship round.

Interest groups exert the kind of influence they do in Texas politics in large part because they give legislators the one thing they need the most and have the least: information. Successful interest groups spend a great amount of time in **information dissemination**. This process will likely begin months before a legislative session actually convenes. Once a particular issue is identified as being on the front burner politically, groups on all sides of that issue will delve into the topic, research its pros and cons, and look for compelling evidence that reinforces their stance. Please note that we said all aspects of the issue will be explored by the groups concerned. Not only do you need to know the facts that will help your group, you also need to know what will hurt it. And you need to know the legitimate points that are likely to be made by opposition groups.

information dissemination
The ability of a lobbyist to provide information to elected officials.

Harvesting information is probably the least glamorous and most burdensome aspect of interest group activity. It involves slogging through various and sundry legal codes, compilations of state law, administrative rules and regulations, as well as the hundreds of other sources relevant merely to one issue. Yet it is this kind of persistent digging that can provide a group with its best ammunition. Of course, the continuing evolution of the Internet as a source of broadly accessible information has meant that interest groups no longer may exert almost exclusive control over facts and figures. Yet, despite this apparent "democratization" of information access, most legislative staffers have such large workloads that they find it impossible to compete with large, well-financed interest groups in generating in-depth information of a specialized nature. Therefore, it is not an exaggeration to say that most groups' successes (or failures) on a given issue will be determined in large part by the kind of research they do and the resultant information they are able to generate.

ESTABLISHING A LINK Once a group has researched a particular topic and staked out a position on a particular issue, it has to be able to deliver the information to policy makers. The best information in the world is worthless if you don't have **access** to those who can help your cause. Gaining this access is one of the most important things a group can do to ensure its success.

access
The ability of an interest group to contact policymakers in an attempt to enlist their help. Access is crucial, for without it an interest group's information is largely useless.

lobbyist
A person who works on behalf of an interest group and who serves as a point of contact between the group and policymakers.

Most interest groups try to gain access through the activities of a lobbyist. A **lobbyist** is a person who works on behalf of an interest group and serves as the point of contact between the group and policy makers. It is the responsibility of the lobbyist to take the information gathered by (or for) the group and use it to persuade legislators and other public officials to the group's point of view. While some lobbyists volunteer their services (usually to the groups of which they are a member), more and more groups are hiring lobbyists today than ever before, as noted in the Inside the Federalist System box nearby. These lobbyists are paid (and often paid extremely well) for their professional services. Not surprisingly, the number of lobbyists in Austin and elsewhere throughout Texas has increased sharply over recent years.

Who are these people? Where do lobbyists come from and how do they operate? Anybody can rent office space in Austin and hang out a sign announcing that they are a "legislative advocate," but the most successful lobbyists come from several readily identifiable groups. Some of the busiest lobbyists are former members of the Texas legislature. That stands to reason: a man or woman who has actually served in the House or the Senate is likely to know not only how the legislative process is *supposed* to work but also how it *actually* works. In most cases, knowledge of the latter is much more important. For example, knowing that a certain senator is chair of a key committee is well and good. However, knowing that senator has not one clue as to what goes on in the committee, and that the really knowledgeable person you need to talk to about a bill is the clerk of the committee, can be crucial. This kind of insider's knowledge along with a generally well-developed network of friends within the legislature makes the retired House or Senate member an excellent lobbyist. Examples of such lobbyists include Gib Lewis (a former Texas House Speaker), former State Senator Kent Caperton (who in 2005 joined the Ben Barnes Group, an influential lobbying firm headed by former Texas lieutenant governor

---

INSIDE THE FEDERALIST SYSTEM

Interest Groups in Texas

It is worth noting again that because our government operates at both the state and national level, interest groups work in both Austin and Washington. When most people think about lobbyists, they think of K Street in Washington, and of their interaction with the national government. In Texas, though, interest groups might hold even more power, as legislators have less access to unbiased information than members of U.S. Congress do. Although there are more lobbyists in the District of Columbia, Texas has more per dollar of government expenditure. According to the Texas Ethics Commission, there are 1,814 registered lobbyists in Texas in 2009. The Center for Responsive Politics lists 15,223 federal lobbyists in 2008.

Lobbyists for Partners in Mobility, a business oriented group advocating greater roadway spending, gather before a meeting with Texas Highway Department officials. Why are lobbying activities particularly effective in Texas?

Ben Barnes), and former State Representative Mike Toomey, featured in this chapter's Texas Mosaic.

Of course, not all lobbyists are ex-legislators. Many entered the field after being involved in politics as a staff member of an elected official. This kind of background allows for building a network almost as good as that of a former legislator. Examples of such advocates include the late George Christian, whose son and partner, George Scott Christian, provides the My Turn essay in this chapter. The elder Christian, a fixture in Texas politics for three decades, was a former press secretary to President Lyndon Johnson with a vast network of contacts across the Texas political landscape. George the younger also served a staff apprenticeship as a legislative aide to former State Senator Ray Farabee. Another example of a staff member-turned-lobbyist is Russell "Rusty" Kelley, who was chief aide to the late Billy Clayton during Clayton's tenure as Speaker of the House. These lobbyists, as well as many who are former legislators, are sometimes referred to as **hired guns**. This simply means that anyone can engage their services (if they can afford to). The client pays a fee to have the lobbyist represent the group on an issue. When the issue is settled, the job is done, and lobbyist and client may part company until another issue brings them together. However, these lobbyists work hard to retain their most lucrative clients on a continuing basis, and consistent success in representing these clients is usually the best guarantee of such retention.

Then there are lobbyists who are lawyers and who use their legal training to represent their clients. Of course, it's not unusual for a hired-gun lobbyist to be a lawyer, but the fact is that more and more law firms across the state are using attorneys from their staffs for the sole or primary responsibility of lobbying for the firm's clientele. One of the most successful such lobbyists in Austin is Gaylord Armstrong. His firm, McGinnis, Lochridge, and Kilgore, employs numerous staff attorneys to serve the

"hired gun"
Refers to a professional, outside lobbyist employed by an interest group to represent its interests on a particular issue. The relationship lasts until the issue is settled.

legislative interests of a number of important corporate clients. Over the years, Armstrong has represented such clients as American Express, Exxon Mobil Corporation, Texas Cable and Telecommunications Association, and Texas Instruments before the legislature. Other giant law firms from around the state, like Baker Botts in Houston and Hughes and Luce in Dallas, maintain scores of lawyers on staff to do this sort of lobbying exclusively, and some firms try to maximize their efforts by hiring lawyers who are also former legislators.

Some interest groups still use the services of their own members as lobbyists, but this practice is not as widespread as it once was. The rising costs of lobbying and the fact that such advocacy has in many cases become a year-round activity has made it much more difficult to use amateurs. For example, the Texas Community College Teachers Association will usually offer testimony on issues of concern to the group through its elected president and occasionally through various committee chairs, all of whom are members of the organization. But it can be very difficult (and sometimes impossible) for someone who must be in the classroom every day also to be available, often at a moment's notice, to run to Austin and speak on the group's behalf, so in recent years, TCCTA has employed the services of a professional lobbyist, Beaman Floyd. Many groups who use their own members as lobbyists are constrained by their small membership or lack of sufficient operating funds. Obviously, a group's size and relative affluence can be crucial factors in its overall influence.

FORMAL CONTACTS Most interest groups will attempt to make some kind of formal contact with legislators in order to win their support. Usually, this will mean that the lobbyist for the group will sit down and talk directly to the legislator, outlining the issue as the group sees it, and answering any questions the legislator may have. In these meetings, the lobbyist will try to be as brief as possible and still get his or her point across. Timing can be very important in this process. If contact is made too far in advance of debate on an issue, any information given tends to be forgotten. Wait too long and you may not have time to explain your position fully. Often, when you share the information is as important as what you share.

It has been our experience that many students assume lobbyists will routinely misrepresent the truth to legislators in order to get them to go along with their group's ideas. In fact, that rarely happens, not because all lobbyists are as pure as the driven snow with regard to their ethics, but because most fear the consequences of this behavior. If a senator or representative discovers that a lobbyist has deliberately lied, what are the chances that legislator will ever believe that lobbyist again? Those lobbyists who have been the most successful over the years know that their success rests in large part on their credibility and that one lie can destroy that credibility. Now this doesn't mean that a lobbyist won't present the facts in a way that is most favorable to the group represented. That, after all, is the nature of the job. But deliberate lies are not part of the arsenal of reputable lobbyists. In fact, many lobbyists will also allude to the arguments that might be offered up against their position by opposing groups, if only to be able to deal with those arguments in a preemptive manner and thus neutralize their effect.

Beyond individual meetings with legislators, interest groups may try to influence policy formation during the meeting of legislative committees. Committees are the heart of the legislative process and the fate of most legislation is decided there (for a fuller discussion of legislative committees, see Chapter 6). In many

Texas MOSAIC

A Lobbyist's Tale

Had Chaucer included a lobbyist among his pilgrims, Mike Toomey could have spun a most interesting tale for his fellow travelers. One of the most active and successful lobbyists in Austin today, Toomey took a typical road to his current occupation. After representing the Houston area for several terms in the House, he then served as chief of staff for Governors Bill Clements and Rick Perry before going into the lobbying business. He is a prototypical lobbyist who has parlayed his legislative experiences and expertise into an extremely lucrative postgovernment career. Toomey numbers among his clientele a wide array of powerful business and professional entities in Texas. The following list highlights some of his better-known clients as well as the range of the fee each contracted to pay Toomey and the time frame of the contract:

Associated Builders and Contractors of Texas
$25,000–$49,999.00
01/28/09–12/31/09

AT&T
$50,000–$99,999.99
01/28/09–12/31/09

CIGNA
$50,000–$99,999.99
02/12/09–12/31/09

Citigroup Global Capital Markets
$25,000–$49,999.00
04/03/09–12/31/09

Distilled Spirits Council of the United States
$50,000–$99,999.99
01/28/09–12/31/09

Green Mountain Energy
$50,000–$99,999.99
01/28/09–12/31/09

Hewlett Packard
$50,000–$99,999.99
02/12/09–12/31/09

Merck & Co.
$50,000–$99,999.99
01/28/09–12/31/09

State Farm Mutual Automobile Insurance Co.
$100,000–$149,999
01/28/09–12/31/09

Texans for Lawsuit Reform
$50,000–$99,999.99
01/28/09–12/31/09

Texas Association of Realtors
$50,000–$99,999.99
01/28/09–12/31/09

Texas Instruments
$25,000–$49,999.00
01/28/09–12/31/09

SOURCE: Texas Ethics Commission, *2009 Lobby Activity Reports.*
http://www.ethics.state.tx.us/dfs/loblists.htm.

instances, the best opportunity for a group to get a bill passed (or killed) will be here. Lobbyists routinely testify before committees and subcommittees and often try to work with committee members and staff to alter wording, add amendments, or delete offensive clauses in proposed legislation. This can be a very time-consuming (not to mention frustrating) ritual. Lobbyists may spend hours waiting to offer testimony only to have a hearing canceled at the last minute. Often the committee's work has to be monitored daily (and sometimes hourly) to make sure nothing contrary to the group's interests has been added to a bill. Factor in having to monitor several (or several score) bills at the same time and you can see what a formidable task effective lobbying can be.

my turn

Lobbyists and the Texas Legislature

by George S. Christian

George S. Christian is a political consultant and lawyer. A native of Austin, Christian holds undergraduate and law degrees with highest honors from the University of Texas. He was legislative aide to State Senator Ray Farabee of Wichita Falls from 1983 to 1985, and has practiced law in New York and Texas. Christian joined his late father's public affairs firm in 1990, after four years with the Austin office of Hughes & Luce. He has been engaged primarily in legislative lobbying since 1986, with extensive involvement in state finance, tort reform, worker's compensation, health care, public and higher education, and various business-related issues. Business clients of the firm include the Texas Taxpayers and Research Association, Texas Civil Justice League, Texans for Judicial Election Reform, Shell Oil and other oil and gas producers, Texas Utilities, Brown & Root, Owens Corning, American General Insurance Co., and Eli Lilly.

As an attorney and independent lobbyist, I am often asked whether the stories about lobbyists wining and dining state legislators to try to get their votes are true. My honest answer is that I don't know, because every lobbyist and legislator I know works such long hours every day during the legislative session that the last thing most of them want to do is go out to eat with lobbyists and legislators.

Lobbying is a different animal than it used to be. The state of Texas has grown so much, so fast, since the 1970s that the entire political and economic landscape has been transformed. Not long ago the Texas legislature was dominated by representatives from rural areas. The big businesses in the state were agriculture and oil and gas. Texas had a small government, provided only limited welfare or human services, and was under no court mandates to spend billions of dollars on new prisons or public education funding. Everyone was a Democrat, and the only question was whether you were conservative or liberal.

The issues were important and sometimes controversial (especially where taxes were concerned), but the legislature basically met to write a state budget, to make sure the hunting season was in good shape, and to pass congratulatory resolutions for 50th wedding anniversaries and high school football champions.

There are a lot of stories about wining and dining, but most of them are from these "good old days" of Texas government. Recent changes to lobbyist regulation (which most lobbyists welcomed) have made it so burdensome to report expenditures to entertain members of the legislature that the better lobbyists don't think it's worth the effort.

More to the point, any lobbyist worth his or her salt knows that spending money on entertainment isn't how you get votes in the legislature to begin with.

The "old-time" lobbyists wouldn't recognize today's Texas legislature. It is incredibly diverse in its interests and constituencies. Its responsibilities have grown tremendously as the federal government has become gridlocked and punted critical decisions back to the states. The state budget is straining to keep up with Texas's exploding population growth, much of which is in poorer areas of the state. Court cases have come down requiring the state to build 100,000 new prison beds, clean up its mental health services, and equitably fund public schools. At the same time, the Texas economy has diversified away from the traditional agricultural and energy base, though they are still important players. There are now widely diversified business interests in the state, each with its own particular legislative interests and regulatory concerns. These businesses often have conflicting interests, and most big lobbying projects involve business interests fighting one another for competitive advantage.

Government entities have also become major players in the legislative process. It is not widely appreciated that among the most powerful lobby groups in Texas are universities and municipalities. Public education is also a traditional lobby power, but it has become fragmented in recent years as teachers and administrators, as well as rich and poor districts, have split up and developed antagonistic interests. This is one reason I am always amused when I see the media talking about the influence of "special interests." Government spends just as much time (and money) lobbying the legislature as private interests do.

One thing the press is right about is that it is expensive to lobby the Texas legislature. And it keeps getting more expensive because of the complexity of the issues and the growing plurality and fragmentation of the process. It is virtually impossible to pass controversial legislation through the legislature. There are too many competing interests, too much political heat, and too little time to sit down and work something out in a deliberate way. Passing, amending, or killing legislation for a particular client is an all-consuming activity during the precious 140 days every two years that the legislature comes to town.

Here are a few things a lobbyist has to do or understand if he or she hopes adequately to represent a client:

■ **Work the members.** This is the cardinal rule of lobbying. Never assume that a legislator will vote your way. You never know who the legislator has talked to, what might be most important politically, or what constituents are saying unless you find out. And you can't find out without talking directly to the legislator.

■ **Be prepared.** If you don't know your issue, you don't have a chance. Master the facts. Reduce your case to the bare minimum. You will probably have only one or two minutes to make your argument, so you had better do it right.

■ **Tell the whole truth, and nothing but the truth.** A lobbyist's credibility is the coin of the realm. One misrepresentation can be devastating. If you don't know the answer, admit it, and then get it. An unethical lobbyist won't last very long in the business.

■ **Don't let the lobby become the issue.** Issues are won or lost on the merits. The easiest way to lose an issue in the legislature is for the lobby activities associated with the issue to become bigger than the issue itself. The rule of thumb here is don't do anything that you wouldn't want to see on the front page of the *Dallas Morning News*.

■ **Legislators vote based on the views of their constituents, not the lobbyist.** A good lobbyist will always seek support for an issue in the legislator's home district. Legislators respond to the voters who elect them, and it doesn't do any good to be best friends with a legislator if the people back home are against you.

■ **Compromise is the name of the game.** If there is any controversy at all on an issue, then you can expect to have to compromise eventually.

The legislature almost never gives one party everything it asks for at the expense of another. Its job is to balance the interests as best it can, and most legislators are looking for ways to give both sides something that allows them to declare victory and go home.

■ **Politic only during the political season.** When the legislature comes to town, it is to legislate. Never mix campaign matters and legislative matters. It is common for lobbyists to help legislative candidates raise money for their campaigns, but there is a time and place for that, and it is not during the legislative session.

■ **Don't be partisan.** Thanks to the tone set by the legislative leadership since the rise of a genuine two-party system in Texas, most legislators leave partisan politics at the door when they come to Austin. It is extremely bad form for a lobbyist to play partisan politics in the legislative process. Issues are neither Democratic nor Republican, and a lobbyist has to make sure that they stay that way.

■ **You must be present to win.** A million things can happen to derail your issue. You have to be there all the time to keep things on track. If that means going to a committee hearing and staying all night, that's what you do. Legislators appreciate it when lobbyists go through the same ordeal as they do. The corollary to this rule is never let your client find out about something from any other source but you, especially if it's bad news.

The Texas legislature can't operate without lobbyists, whether they are "hired guns," association executives, or ordinary citizens who care about the issues, write letters, and make phone calls. Things move too fast and there is too much information for legislators to assimilate without the focus lobbyists bring to an issue. If you keep these principles in mind and approach the legislature with the respect it deserves, just about anyone can gain access to the legislative process.

It is possible to succeed in lobbying without ever having been in the legislature. I came to it through legislative staff experience and legal training. Others start out in completely different business careers and end up lobbying. Still others come from political campaigns or journalism. Just like anything else, there is no magic formula. And also just like anything else, personal integrity, mutual respect for one's colleagues, hard work, and a little luck are the keys to long-term success.

INFORMAL CONTACTS You can see how overwhelming the frantic the pace of a legislative session can be for both lobbyist and legislator. Days filled with floor sessions, committee meetings, visits from constituents, and the myriad other chores of a regular session can leave little time for extended communication between interest groups and policy makers. At this juncture, many groups seek to provide such opportunities through what can be called informal contacts. These allow for the cultivation of relationships in a more leisurely and personable way than do formal meetings and committee hearings.

Most groups who develop such contacts use social occasions to do so. Interest groups will often host various kinds of parties and get-togethers on a regular basis during a legislative session. At these parties, group members and lobbyists can mix and mingle with legislators, committee staffers, even secretaries in a relaxed, depressurized atmosphere. Issues can be discussed in detail and subtle nuances of policy explored. Perhaps most important, lobbyists can get to know legislators as people and can begin to cultivate personal relationships with them. As most people know, talking to a friend is much easier than talking to a stranger.

The importance of these contacts is underscored by the number of groups who engage in such activities and the amount of money they spend on them. In the course of trying to shape legislation, interest groups spend hundreds of thousands of dollars for wining and dining legislators during (as well as before and after) a regular session. Although new ethics legislation has helped to curb some of the more egregious examples of such spending (see the "Regulating Interest Groups" section below), the words of Charles Deaton still ring true. Deaton, the founding editor of the *Texas Government Newsletter*, was speaking to a group of college students who were in Austin for a field trip. He suggested that if a legislator went to every breakfast, brunch, lunch buffet, cocktail party, and sit-down banquet hosted by scores of interest groups during a regular session, at the end of the 140 days, that legislator ran the very real risk of becoming a 700-pound alcoholic!

So how are we to regard such efforts by interest groups? Are they blatant attempts to buy a member's vote with fun, food, and frivolity? Or are they merely gatherings where people with common interests get together to relax, and that have no material influence on policy? As is usually the case in politics, the truth probably lies somewhere between these two extremes. No one who has watched Texas politics over the years can deny that such contacts often prove beneficial to the group that initiates them. Yet to say that such events "buy" votes for that group is an oversimplification. The vast majority of legislators don't have their votes on the market. Even if one did, it's doubtful that a steak dinner or a plate of barbeque could affect such a purchase. No, these events don't buy votes. But they may help a lobbyist gain access, and that can be crucial. In an atmosphere where both time and information are in short supply, having the time to make your point is often the difference between success and failure. The best information in the world is useless if you don't have access to those who can use that information to help you and your group. They may not agree with what you tell them. They may even wind up voting against you. But it won't be because they never knew what you had to say on the issue.

This question of access brings up another point for consideration. While all kinds of groups are free to organize as interest groups and attempt to influence public policy, not all are able to compete equally in the social arena. Many groups simply can't afford to wine and dine legislators to the same extent as others. And legislators, if they aren't very careful, may find themselves paying more attention to the suggestions of their friends across the dinner table than to those (meritorious though they may be) who can't afford to throw a party. Once again, it becomes obvious that the resources available to an interest group have a direct bearing on the group's success.

Membership Mobilization

Much of the attention we've given to interest groups has focused on the activities of their lobbyists in Austin, but there are times when groups orchestrate activities around the state in an attempt to exert influence on policy makers. Such attempts to mobilize a broad outpouring of unified opinion on an issue can sometimes move a legislator who has resisted other appeals made by the group.

Typically, such an effort would begin with the group's lobbyist communicating with group members about the need to contact certain policy makers. This usually happens when a committee is considering a bill of particular interest or before a bill is to come up for a vote on the floor. Group supporters will be urged to express their thoughts on the bill by writing, phoning, faxing, or e-mailing messages to committee members, especially if these members are their own representatives. Legislators do tend to listen to their constituents, and a well-organized campaign, such as we've described, can often help in the overall attempt to persuade members to the group's point of view.

However, such **membership mobilization** needs to be carefully crafted. Effective grassroots efforts take a lot of work and oversight, and the better organized a group is, the more likely such actions will succeed. Obviously, groups with small memberships may find themselves at a disadvantage here, and those where decision making is concentrated at the top with little membership input may also have trouble enlisting enthusiastic support from those members.

membership mobilization
The act of enlisting the rank-and-file members of an interest group in attempting to sway policymakers; often includes massive letter-writing efforts and may also include marches and demonstrations.

Tea Party activists protest in Austin against the Obama administration. How can such events help mobilize members?

Even the means of membership communication need to be carefully monitored. Nothing will so quickly guarantee that a legislator will ignore a group's plea as the receipt of 500 or so e-mails or photocopied letters, all saying exactly the same thing. Most legislators will rightly conclude that a troop of reasonably bright chimpanzees could be trained to produce such letters and will discount completely any such effort. Groups that hope to be successful in mobilizing large numbers of people have to be able to convince their members to sit down and write a personal letter expressing each individual's feelings. Guidelines may give the members ideas about what to say, but how that is said should be left up to each member. Legislators tend to pay more attention to these kinds of communication.

Other more dramatic methods of membership mobilization can include marches and demonstrations, often on the steps of the state capitol and usually during a legislative session. Rank-and-file group members often like such activities because they can draw the media's attention to the group's cause and may expand public awareness of the group's issues. Moreover, many ex-hippie baby boomers, who now belong to perfectly respectable interest groups, never have quite gotten that urge to protest out of their systems! A striking example of such a demonstration was seen when motorcyclists from all over Texas descended on the Capitol several years ago to urge the legislature to repeal the state's "helmet law." Such efforts may get you on the six o'clock news, but they rarely have a lasting impact on legislators (although in the instance just cited, lawmakers did make some changes for which the group had lobbied). In truth, most legislators simply don't have time for such exercises. Even efforts to blanket the legislature and blitz members with flyers and position papers on a group's "day" at the Capitol usually are only marginally successful. Again, the hectic schedule maintained by most senators and representatives makes it difficult to gain their time and attention through such grandstanding tactics.

Interim Oversight

Just because the legislature adjourns and goes home after a regular session does not mean that an interest group's work is done for another 19 months. In the past this interim may have brought a measurable slowdown in group efforts, but most veteran lobbyists will tell you that today the work goes on, in session or out. For many groups, the job may only be starting once your bill has passed.

State agencies and departments will be responsible for implementing the provisions of most bills. (For more on the executive branch, see Chapters 7 and 8.) Many groups will seek to monitor the actions of these agencies, verifying that they are indeed doing what the law requires. This is especially true of those interest groups representing professions that are licensed, regulated, or funded by the state. For example, teachers' organizations will constantly monitor the actions of the Texas Education Agency and of local school boards to make sure those bodies are doing what they're supposed to with regard to teacher rights and responsibilities.

interim oversight
Various actions by an interest group aimed at protecting its gains and promoting its goals between sessions of the legislature.

Another **interim oversight** strategy draws from the idea of membership mobilization mentioned above. Although mass meetings and group demonstrations during the legislative session are rarely effective, encouraging a group's members to contact legislators during the interim can be useful in building support for the group's agenda. When the legislature is out of session, members have time to sit down with the public and discuss issues of concern. They can look at what was done as well as at what might be on the political horizon, and interest group members can get to know their representatives on a personal level. Such personal relationships can be extremely helpful once the legislative circus is back in town.

For the same reasons, interest groups may continue to host legislators at various outings during the interim. These activities have been restricted by new ethics legislation, but they remain a useful tool for cultivating legislators' goodwill. Likewise, lobbyists may find themselves doing research and even offering testimony before committees during this "down" time. Even though the legislature may be adjourned, numerous interim committees, appointed to explore various issues prior to the next sessions, remain at work. (For a further discussion of such committees, see Chapter 6.) Lobbyists frequently use these meetings to stake out their group's position early. One of this book's authors, David Clinkscale, did that very thing on several occasions while serving as president of the Texas Community College Teachers Association, offering testimony on funding recommendations for higher education and opposing the offering of freshman and sophomore courses by junior- and senior-level institutions. As you can see, interest groups in Texas have to work year-round in order to be effective.

Regulating Interest Groups

For years, interest groups and the lobbyists who represented them were virtually free of any kind of meaningful regulation. Following the Sharpstown Scandal in the early 1970s, however, the Texas legislature did enact the Lobbyist Registration Act. This law, one of Common Cause's first legislative successes in Texas, sought to identify those who were attempting to influence legislation on behalf of a client group. Until recently, the basic thrust of interest group regulation in Texas has tended to focus primarily on such registration as a means of controlling interest group actions. However, since the mid-1990s, tighter restrictions have been placed on certain kinds of expenditures by interest groups and their representatives, and the responsibility for monitoring their activities and expenditures has been vested with the Texas Ethics Commission, to whom all interest groups and their lobbyists must report periodically.

Under current law, a person must register with the Ethics Commission as a lobbyist if he or she receives more than $1,000 in a calendar quarter as compensation for engaging in communications with legislative or executive branch members that are intended to influence the passage of laws or the formulation of administrative rules. A person also must register if he or she expends more than $500 in a calendar quarter on such communications aimed at such influence.[14] "Communications" here refers to a rather broad array of activities, including the provision of food and beverages, entertainment expenses, gifts, awards and mementos, mass media advertising, and fund-raisers.

WHAT CAN YOU DO?

Texans for Public Justice is an Austin-based non-profit organized in 1997 to take on political corruption and corporate abuses in Texas. TPJ aspires to serve as a "clear voice to debates on political reform, consumer protection, civil justice and corporate accountability" through the organization's intensive research and public advocacy.

Access Texans for Public Justice (http://www.tpj.org) and locate its link to Lobby Watch, which gives the public an unusual and thorough glimpse into, as the TJP states, "the influence of money and corporate power in Texas politics." Also included on TPJ's Web site is a link to its Major Reports, such as *Money in PoliTex: A Guide to Money in the 2008 Texas Legislative Elections*.

After you have reviewed Texans for Public Justice and its links, you will have a far greater understanding about how and to what extent lobbyists and their clients influence state and local elections and bureaucratic decision making in Texas.

The reporting of these activities, generally on a monthly basis, must specify the recipient of the "communication."

In addition to these rather detailed reporting requirements, certain activities are specifically prohibited, such as providing loans, transportation and lodging (with certain exceptions), and expenditures for entertainment, awards, and/or gifts that exceed $500 per person in a calendar year.[15] These regulations certainly have helped to reduce the kind of freewheeling lobby spending that characterized Texas politics during most of the 20th century. However, experienced advocates representing a wide array of influential businesses and associations can still drop a lot of money in a short period of time in the pursuit of successful legislation.

Money and Interest Groups

Money may not be the only thing in Texas politics, but as political consultant Bill Emory once remarked, "It's way ahead of whatever's in second place." Indeed, money is often referred to as the "mother's milk" of politics. This is obviously the case with interest group activity, because much of what such groups accomplish depends on funding, both internal and external.

Internal Funding

Internal funding refers to the processes by which a group raises money for its ongoing political operations. All interest groups must raise some money for such activities, but the amount the group can raise in most cases depends on the size and composition of the group. Obviously, larger groups have a greater capacity to raise money for operations than do smaller ones. Still, small groups made up of more affluent members can often compete on an equal financial footing with larger, but less affluent groups.

Most groups raise money for internal operations by levying membership dues. Not every dollar raised in this manner will be earmarked for political activity, but many will be used to promote the group's interests in the political arena. Here again, organizational structure may be decisive in determining how much money a group can raise. Those groups with high levels of membership commitment to group goals (such as the NRA) usually have no trouble raising the money they need. The less cohesive the group, the more difficult it will be to raise such funds. Groups with memberships that wax and wane may have better luck holding garage sales and car washes rather than attempting to collect annual dues from a tenuously allied membership.

When you recall all the possible activities in which an interest group may engage, you can see how important money is to that group and its success. The differences in money-raising capabilities among groups translate into significant differences in the kinds of activities in which groups may be able to participate. Not all groups can afford to hire a George Christian or a Mike Toomey to lobby on their behalf. Not all groups can afford to offer a daily (or even weekly or monthly) lunch buffet for legislators. Not all groups can afford to underwrite the costs of mass mailings on behalf of the group's members. The Texas Constitution says all citizens have an equal right to join together and pursue group goals before policy makers. The reality of Texas politics says such efforts are rarely equal when it comes to money.

External Funding: PACs

Interest groups raise money not only to fund their own operations but also, increasingly, to contribute to election campaigns. To anyone seeking elected office, money talks. That being the case, it can be safely said that in Texas interest groups often monopolize the conversation. The relationship between interest groups and campaign contributions is tricky in this state. Texas law specifically forbids labor unions and corporations (or groups composed of such entities, often referred to as trade associations) from contributing money directly to individual political campaigns. That would seem to bar any interest groups representing such entities from giving money to a person running for office. However, there is a huge loophole through which interest groups of all sorts have poured hundreds of thousands of dollars. That loophole is the **political action committee**, or **PAC**.

A PAC is a voluntary association of individuals who band together for the purpose of raising and distributing money for political campaigns. The key word here seems to be "voluntary." For example, under state law, Compass Bancshares, Inc., one of the largest banking companies in Texas, could not set aside corporate money to be contributed to Rick Perry's campaign for lieutenant governor. However, employees of Compass Bancshares could contribute their own money to a political action committee that they have voluntarily joined, and this money could then be disbursed to the Perry campaign or others.

Such groups are perfectly legitimate. However, to many people they give the appearance of being a very obvious way around legal restrictions on giving to campaigns. Questions are often raised, for example, regarding just how "voluntary" membership is in such organizations. Even if nothing specific is said to an employee or union member, a sense of coercion may be present if "everyone" at work is joining the PAC and you haven't. Such pressures may lead some people to go along in order to get along.

political action committee (PAC)
A voluntary association of individuals who band together for the purpose of raising and distributing money for political campaigns.

TABLE **5.1** **PACs with Contributions of $250,000 or More, 1/1/2008–6/30/2008**

POLITICAL ACTION COMMITTEE	AMOUNT CONTRIBUTED
Texans For Lawsuit Reform PAC	$2,763,351.00
Compass Bancshares, Inc. PAC	$792,915.13
Texas and Southwestern Cattle Raisers Association State PAC	$685,799.71
Blue Texas	$579,640.67
Stars Over Texas PAC	$502,100.00
MetroTex PAC	$449,410.45
Annie's List	$427,065.66
Texas Credit Union League PAC	$321,724.14
First Command Political Action Committee	$321,182.44
Texans for Economic Development	$310,141.47
Best for Texas PAC	$302,364.98
Associated General Contractors of Texas PAC	$288,444.28
Texans for Insurance Reform	$282,162.16

SOURCE: Texas Ethics Commission, *July 2008 Semiannual Report*, http://www.ethics.state.tx.us/tedd/c&e0708c.html.

As they proliferate, political action committees are playing a larger and larger role in electoral politics in Texas. In recent election cycles, PACs have collected millions of dollars to invest in Texas political races, and that trend will likely continue in the future (see Table 5.1). As PACs pour more and more money into state elections, they contribute to the upward spiral in the cost of getting elected. That trend may send candidates for public office scurrying in search of more PAC contributions, which, in turn, may further drive up the costs of running for office. Such a vicious circle may make it difficult for a person without ties to PACs to have a realistic chance to run for office. It also means that interest groups without the financial base to play PAC politics may increasingly find themselves outside the policy-making process.

PAC money may also contribute to a subtle but very real erosion of access to elected representatives by the citizenry. Let's say you decide to run for a seat in the Texas House. At today's rates, that race will cost about $250,000, if you can catch one on sale. Unless your family is filthy rich or you just won the lottery, you won't have that kind of discretionary money floating around, so you'll have to try and solicit contributions to your campaign. Well, let's suppose that PACs representing 25 different interest groups each give you $2,000. That will account for 20 percent of your campaign budget. If you get elected, and a representative of one of those interest groups then wants to talk to you, will you take the call? Of course you will. By giving you a substantial portion of what you needed to get elected, those groups have gained the kind of access that Judy Doe from Lampasas, Texas, can't come close to matching. How ironic, then, that a device originally conceived to expand participation in and access to the political process may be restricting these more and more with each passing year.

The Iron Triangle

The "Iron Triangle" is a coalition formed among interest groups, the legislature, and government departments that accounts for the creation of much public policy in Texas. The triangle, as illustrated in Figure 5.1, operates because each point on the model has something that it can give to each of the others. In return, each expects to receive something from the others.

As we have said, interest groups have two primary means at their disposal for use in obtaining favorable policies. One is campaign contributions. Legislators need money in order to run for office, and an interest group's PAC can help the legislator meet these needs. The other is information. Because the legislature is understaffed, lobbyists for interest groups can provide information, formulate position papers, and even draft bills. Anything that makes a legislator's job easier makes him or her more likely to support an interest group's viewpoint, especially if that legislator has no strong opinions in that area.

In return for this help, the interest group expects favorable consideration by legislators. In its interaction with government departments, legislators expect to receive staff services. The staff of a department will help members of the legislature gather information about that agency. Again, a factor in the success of this process is the understaffing of the legislature: it makes information a valuable commodity. In return for this assistance, the department expects funding from the legislature. Legislative appropriations are the lifeblood of government. Without them, an agency cannot exist.

It is the department's job to implement policy passed by the legislature. They turn policy into programs. Interest groups hope that programs are shaped to their benefit. To ensure that this occurs, interest groups can arrange expert testimony at legislative committee hearings that involve a particular agency. Because these hearings help determine an agency's funding, favorable testimony can be helpful.

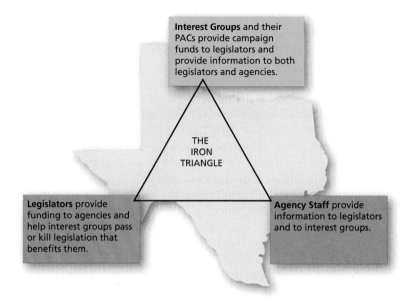

FIGURE **5.1** **The Iron Triangle.**

Agencies realize this and work to keep interest groups on their side as they implement legislation. In a sense, many agencies see interest groups as their clients.

In order to understand better how this works, let's plug in some real entities. The legislative point will be filled by the House Public Education Committee because most legislation is shaped in committee. The interest group will be the Texas State Teachers Association (TSTA), which represents elementary and secondary teachers in the state. The logical government department would be the Texas Education Agency (TEA). First and foremost, TSTA wants the legislature to provide higher salaries for teachers. Through its PAC, it will deliver campaign contributions to committee members. Additionally, it will provide committee members with information that supports its arguments. For example, the group might provide information that compares Texas with other states, showing that states with higher teacher salaries have higher standardized test scores.

The legislature provides funding to TEA. In return, TEA provides information on its activities to the understaffed legislature. If TEA has an ally on the Public Education Committee, a representative from TEA and that member might even script out questions and answers prior to committee hearings on the agency's budget. This would make both the legislator and the agency look good during the hearings because the member would know what to ask and the agency would know how to answer.

Beyond salary concerns, two chief complaints of teachers are classroom overcrowding and excessive paperwork. TEA can provide relief by enforcing teacher-student ratios and restricting state-mandated paperwork. In return, TSTA can find an expert from a university with a highly regarded education department, like the University of North Texas, and send a Ph.D. to tell the legislature, "TEA is doing a wonderful job. They would do even better if they had more funding."

Why, then, does TSTA not always get its way? Because dozens of interest groups compete in the area of education policy alone. Some want lower taxes. Businesses want graduates who can read, write, and do math. Others, like the Texas Association of School Administrators (TASA), want increased education funding, but they don't want the money dedicated exclusively to teacher salary increases. "Let *us* decide where the money should be spent," administrators say as they stand outside the newly renovated weight room for the football team, "and we'll take care of the teachers." In their relations with TEA, administrators want waivers from teacher-student ratios. This allows them more discretion over spending. TASA favors more paperwork because it helps them keep tabs on teachers. Besides, paperwork on a desk helps justify an administrator's salary.

Left out of this triangle are the governor, the public, and the courts. By vetoing, or threatening to veto a bill, the governor inserts him- or herself into the equation. Governor Perry vetoed only 35 of the 1459 bills passed by the 80th legislature in 2009. Even Governor Perry's Father's Day Massacre (see Chapter 7) killed only a small percentage of bills. Governors generally become personally involved with perhaps a couple of dozen bills. The rest are passed without direct gubernatorial involvement. In 1991, when Lieutenant Governor Bob Bullock suggested the need for an income tax, public opposition was so overwhelming that a triangle never had a chance to form. That we must go back to 1991 to find such an example denotes the fact that public involvement is rare, although the public can have some involvement through choosing legislators and by joining interest groups. Of course, the courts can become involved when they declare a law to be unconstitutional. Although such occurrences are often dramatic, they are usually quite rare.

Interest Groups and You

What are you going to do with your newfound knowledge about interest groups? You could use it as another avenue of participation in the political system here in Texas. Yes, you're "just" a student. But you might have more than a passing interest in things like tuition costs, residence requirements, and curriculum mandates. Changes in any of these areas could have an enormous impact on your life. So it might be to your advantage, when such issues are being discussed, to work through an interest group in order to make sure you get in your two cents worth.

Moreover, by participating in interest group activities now, you'll be ready to take an expanded role in such activities when you're out of school and have entered a business or profession that is represented by such groups. If you're going to be an accountant, you can be sure that you'll need to interact with the government regarding your profession at some time during your career. If you go into business, the same is true. Decisions by government will directly affect your livelihood, and you'll want to have some input into those decisions. Health care professionals will face ever-increasing interaction with government in the coming years. Even when you retire, you and all your friends will still need to keep an eye on what the government does with things like state retirement accounts and tax breaks for senior citizens. So get used to it, and get involved. The interest you protect will probably be your own.

Summary

Interest groups are made up of people who share a common set of ideas or principles and who attempt to advance those ideas by influencing public policy makers. Such groups and their activities are protected by constitutional guarantees of the rights to assemble and to petition our government. They play a very important role in Texas politics and provide citizens with magnified voices and multiplied choices. There are many types of interest groups and they evidence a wide variety of internal organization. The most influential interest groups in Texas represent the business community, but labor, professions, and ethnic groups, as well as others, also organize themselves to protect and advance their causes. These groups use a number of strategies to reach their goals, but providing information to policy makers is the most important of these. Interest groups also use entertainment, membership mobilization, and continuing oversight of the political process to gain what they want. An increasingly important aspect of interest group activity is the formation of political action committees used to contribute money to political campaigns. PACs have a significant impact on both campaign finance and access to elected officials. Finally, interest groups try to establish a close working relationship with key legislative committees and relevant state agencies in order to further their goals. Even as a student, you have the opportunity to become involved with the interest group of your choice, which could lead to a lifetime commitment to the causes that matter to you.

Chapter Test

1. An interest group is best defined as an organized entity sharing common ideas that
   a. Tries to get its members elected to public office.
   b. Tries to influence public policy makers to adopt the group's ideas.
   c. Tries to do both a and b.
   d. Tries to do neither a nor b.

2. Interest groups that concentrate decision making at or near the top of the group's structure and exercise leadership through a small group at that level are said to have a _____ organizational structure.
   a. centralized
   b. decentralized
   c. amorphous
   d. polymorphous

3. The most powerful interest community in Texas is that of
   a. labor.
   b. ethnic groups.
   c. single-issue groups.
   d. business.

4. One of the most powerful single-issue interest groups in Texas is
   a. the Texas Medical Association.
   b. the Texas State Teachers Association.
   c. the National Rifle Association.
   d. the Nature Conservancy.

5. The most important commodity that interest groups provide to the legislature during a session is
   a. information.
   b. gifts.
   c. access.
   d. pizza.

6. A person who works on behalf of an interest group and serves as the point of contact between the group and policy makers is a
   a. staff member.
   b. gubernatorial aide.
   c. client.
   d. lobbyist.

7. When an interest group organizes its members to hold a rally on the steps of the Capitol in order to highlight an issue important to the group, it is engaging in
   a. information dissemination.
   b. membership mobilization.
   c. interim oversight.
   d. none of the above.

8. The body responsible for monitoring the activities of interest groups in Texas is the
   a. Texas Public Employees Association.
   b. Texas Research League.
   c. Texas Attorney General's Office.
   d. Texas Ethics Commission.

9. A voluntary association of individuals who band together for the purpose of raising and distributing money for political campaigns is called a
   a. special interest.
   b. lobby guild.
   c. political action committee.
   d. political party.

10. The so-called Iron Triangle includes
    a. interest groups.
    b. legislators.
    c. government agencies.
    d. all of the above.

Answers: 1. b 2. a 3. d 4. c 5. a 6. d 7. b 8. d 9. c 10. d

Critical Thinking Questions

1. Discuss the several roles that interest groups play in Texas politics and identify their positive and negative influences.

2. Discuss the various types of interest group found in Texas and give examples of each type.

3. Discuss the various methods employed by interest groups in Texas and evaluate the role that money plays in interest group politics.

Key Terms

access, **p. 128**
amorphous, **p. 122**
centralized, **p. 121**
decentralized, **p. 121**
"hired gun," **p. 129**
information dissemination, **p. 127**

interest group, **p. 118**
interim oversight, **p. 136**
lobbyist, **p. 128**
membership mobilization, **p. 135**
political action committee (PAC), **p. 139**
single-issue groups, **p. 124**

Notes

1. *United States Constitution*, Amendment One, Clause 1.
2. *Texas Constitution*, Article I, Section 27.
3. Will Rogers, "Breaking into the Writing Game," *Illiterate Digest* (1924).
4. To learn more about this interest group, visit http://www.tgrta.com.
5. You can find out more about this powerful interest group and examine some of its policy goals by accessing its Web site at http://www.ttara.org.
6. If you're curious to see labor's perspective on the issues confronting Texans today, go to http://www.texasaficio.org. Then compare that view with the one found on the TTARA site noted above.
7. You can check the pulse of the Texas Medical Association at http://www.texmed.org, see what the trial lawyers are arguing at http://www.ttla.com, and review TSTA activities at http://www.tsta.org.
8. You can examine the issues important to this interest group at http://www.texasnaacp.org.
9. You can find out more about this interest group, which was organized in San Antonio in 1968, if you go to http://www.maldef.org.
10. You can check out the group's ideas and issues at http://www.nra.org.
11. You can obtain information on MADD by going to their Web site, http://www.madd.org.
12. Check out the Nature Conservancy at the group's Web site, http://www.nature.org/texas.
13. Take a look at the information provided by the League of Women Voters at http://www.lwvtexas.org or read about Common Cause and its goals at http://www.commoncause.org/states/texas.
14. You can examine the statutes, legal opinions, and TEC rules at the Web site of the Texas Ethics Commission, http://www.ethics.state.tx.us.
15. Ibid.

The Legislature in Texas Politics

6

Texas becomes a part of the Mexican state of Coahuila y Tejas and is given two representatives in its legislative assembly.

1824   **1836**

After winning independence from Mexico, the Republic of Texas forms its own legislative body, the Congress of the Republic.

By the end of this chapter on the legislature, you should be able to . . .

★ Explain the structure and composition of the legislature.
★ Differentiate between redistricting and gerrymandering.
★ Analyze the role of the presiding officers and "The Team."
★ Discuss the importance of the committee system.
★ Describe the process of how a bill becomes a law.
★ Analyze the dynamics of the legislative process.

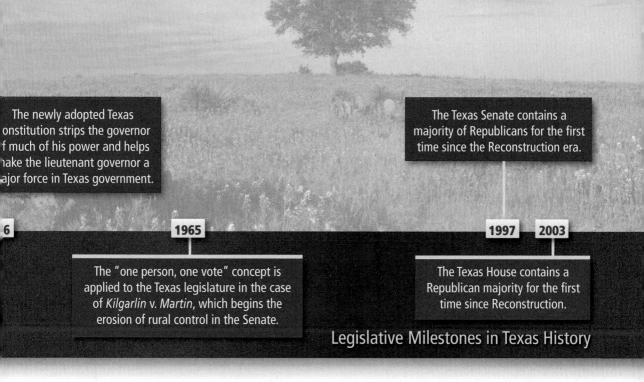

The newly adopted Texas Constitution strips the governor of much of his power and helps make the lieutenant governor a major force in Texas government.

The Texas Senate contains a majority of Republicans for the first time since the Reconstruction era.

6

1965

1997 **2003**

The "one person, one vote" concept is applied to the Texas legislature in the case of *Kilgarlin* v. *Martin*, which begins the erosion of rural control in the Senate.

The Texas House contains a Republican majority for the first time since Reconstruction.

Legislative Milestones in Texas History

No Person's Life, Liberty, or Property Is Safe
When the Texas Legislature Is in Session!

—PLAQUE ON THE WALL OF A MEMBER OF THE TEXAS
HOUSE OF REPRESENTATIVES

The Texas legislature is the lawmaking branch of Texas government, and as such it assumes a certain primacy in the state's political scheme. After all, before the courts can interpret the laws and before the executive branch can put the laws into effect, someone has to create the laws. Actions by the legislature touch virtually every aspect of our lives from health and safety regulations to educational curricula, from crime prevention and criminal justice to environmental protection. The legislature in essence oversees a multibillion dollar "corporation" by virtue of the fact that it approves the state's biennial budget.

To find out virtually anything you want to know about "the Lege," take a look at one of the best Web sites available for delving into Texas government. Log on to and check out http://www.capitol.state.tx.us. When everything is said and done, this deliberative body is the biggest dog in the Texas political kennel.

The Texas Constitution:
A Closer Look

Both the U.S. and the Texas constitutions create lawmaking entities as part of a tripartite (three-element) scheme of government. In both documents, these lawmaking entities—the U.S. Congress and the Texas legislature—are given primacy. By the way, the terms "Congress" and "legislature" are not interchangeable. For example, it is improper to speak of the "Texas Congress" unless, of course, you are referring to that deliberative body that made laws for the Republic of Texas between 1836 and 1846! At any rate, both basic documents address the powers and limitations of these two deliberative bodies. Some areas of policy formulation are shared. For example, both the U.S. Congress and the Texas legislature can tax, borrow money, establish courts, enact criminal laws, protect the environment, and raise and support armed forces. In the case of the latter power, the armed forces raised and supported by the Texas legislature include the Texas National Guard and the Texas Air National Guard. Both can appropriate money for the operation of government, but whereas Congress's expenditures may (and routinely do) exceed revenues, the legislature is prohibited from doing so, except under emergency conditions. Some lawmaking powers are exclusively those of the U.S. Congress. Only the Congress can regulate **interstate** commerce (that which takes place among or between the states), although the legislature can regulate **intrastate** commerce (that which takes place solely within the boundaries of Texas). Congress alone can coin money, establish rules of naturalization, declare war, and enter into relations with other nations. Finally, some things are prohibited to both bodies. Neither Congress nor the legislature can suspend the right of habeas corpus (except in an extraordinary circumstance), neither can either body enact bills of attainder (laws that impose a criminal punishment without a judicial proceeding) or ex post facto laws (retroactive laws). One last point of contrast: the U.S. Constitution takes slightly more than 2,200 words to enumerate the powers of Congress; the Texas Constitution describes the workings of the legislature in a mind-boggling 29, 392 words!

Visitors who observe the legislature in action are either appalled by the apparent chaos that seems to reign on the floor of the House or puzzled by the apparent lack of any meaningful activity on the floor of the Senate. Members who may have spent hundreds of thousands of dollars to win an office that pays $600 a month before taxes may find themselves mentally and emotionally overwrought by the hectic end of a regular session.

Further, these legislators must also endure the jibes of a public that little understands what they do or how they do it. One frequently sees displayed on vehicles in and around Austin a bumper sticker that warns, "Lock Up the Women and Children and Bury Your Money! The Legislature's Back in Town!" As the late House Speaker Billy Clayton, who spent 20 years on the west (House) side of the

Capitol building, was fond of saying, There are two things you should never watch being made: sausage and laws. Doing so can easily cause you to lose your taste for both. Yet what happens on the second floor of that domed building in the middle of Austin remains the essential expression of the concept of representative democracy in Texas. So despite the warnings of tacky bumper stickers and former presiding officers, we're going to take a close look at the structure and dynamics of this intriguing institution.

The Legislature in Texas

Structure

The Texas Constitution specifies that the Texas legislature is to be a bicameral body. This means that legislative power is vested in a two-house assembly. The Senate, called by some people (mostly its own members) the upper house, is composed of thirty-one people. The House of Representatives numbers 150 members. Both of these figures represent the maximum for each chamber allowed by the constitution. The legislature meets in **regular session** for not more than 140 days every two years, beginning in January of odd-numbered years. Other meetings of this assembly for lawmaking purposes, referred to as **special sessions**, may only be called by the governor, are limited to an agenda determined by the governor, and can last no longer than 30 (although there is no limit on the number of special sessions a governor may call).[1]

regular session
The constitutionally scheduled, biennial session of the legislature.

special sessions
Extra legislative sessions called by the governor.

The structure of the Texas legislature clearly reveals the suspicion with which the authors of the constitution viewed government in general and lawmaking bodies in particular. Created to handle the political business of a sparsely populated, largely rural state in the late 19th century, this body was designed to do its job and then get out of town. Although Texas has become one of the largest, most complex urban states in the nation, that same attitude prevails today. Remember that plaque in the House member's office? Overseeing the operation of anything the size of Texas is a full-time job; yet, as we pointed out in the last chapter, serving in the Texas legislature is a full-time job only part of the time. For 19 months out of every two years, legislators pursue their careers and live somewhat more normal lives, although there is still a good bit of intrusion from the legislature. But for five months, they come together in a gigantic political and governmental pressure cooker and attempt to govern a $90-billion-a-year monster. It is this constant constraint of time more than anything else that shapes the people of the legislature and what they do.

Membership

The citizens of the state elect members of the Texas legislature in partisan elections.

Members of the House of Representatives serve two-year terms and there is no limit on the number of terms one may serve. To serve in the House, a person must:

- be a U.S. citizen and a registered voter;
- reside in Texas two years prior to election;
- reside in the district one year prior to election; and
- be at least 21 years old.

Legislators are an easy target for political science professors, authors and editorial cartoonists. Would you consider taking that type of job for $600 months?

House members receive a salary of $600 per month as well as a per diem (living expense) during the most recent legislative session of $168 daily.[2]

Senators are elected to four-year terms and they too are not limited regarding how many terms they may serve. In order to ensure some degree of membership continuity from session to session, one-half of the Senate is elected every two years. The exception to this rule occurs after each decennial (ten year) reapportionment, when all Senate seats are contested. Following such an election, lots are drawn to determine which 15 senators will serve a single two-year term before reverting back to the normal term of four years. In order to serve in the Senate you must:

- be a U.S. citizen and a registered voter;
- reside in Texas five years prior to election;
- reside in your district one year prior to election; and
- be at least 26 years old.

Senators receive the same salary and the same per diem as House members.[3]

Legislators enjoy a number of privileges as elected representatives of the people, including constitutional guarantees that they may not "be questioned in any other place for words spoken in debate in either house." This is to ensure free and unfettered discussion in the process of conducting public business. Another interesting privilege accorded legislators is freedom from arrest (except for treason, felony, or breach of the peace) during a legislative session and while going to or coming from a regular or special session. This is intended to protect members from intimidation or retaliation because of their legislative activities.[4]

We can look at the demographic makeup of the legislature in order to gain a better understanding of its aggregate membership. One obvious measure of its internal composition is party affiliation. In 2009, the House of Representatives contained 76 Republicans and 74 Democrats. This represents a significant increase in seats for Democrats over the party's nadir in 2003. Also in 2009, the Senate numbered 19 Republicans and 12 Democrats, an increase of one Democrat over the previous session.[5] In 2010, however, Republicans dramatically reversed the gains that Democrats made in 2008. Although Senate composition remained the same, Republicans captured 99 seats in the Texas House of Representatives, leaving the Democrats with only 51 seats. That is an all-time high for Republicans in the House.

The diversity found in the Texas population is not as readily apparent in the legislature. The membership tends to over represent middle- and upper-income groups, and relatively few of what might be called "working Texans" (people with "8-to-5" jobs or who punch a time clock every day) will be found among legislative ranks. The largest single professional group among legislators has always been lawyers. Business is also well represented in the legislature. The popular (though largely unfounded) notion that only lawyers can create laws may account for the former, and a desire to protect the climate in which their businesses operate can explain the latter. Yet the predominance of these two occupation groups may be due to that key element we mentioned before—time. Lawyers and businesspeople who can more closely control their own schedules, especially if they're in some kind of partnership, are more likely to be able to adapt to the "full-time part of the time" nature of the legislature. Those who must be at work on a regular basis likely will not be able to consider legislative service seriously.

Over the past several decades, the Texas legislature has slowly begun to more closely approximate the state's ethnic mosaic. The 81st legislature that convened in January of 2009 included 32 Hispanic, 14 African American, and 2 Asian American members in the House.[6] The membership of the Senate included six Hispanics and two African Americans.[7] Gains in minority legislative seats are attributable in part to the use of single-member districts since the 1970s (for a discussion of legislative redistricting, see "Apportionment" section below). Although encouraging, these numbers still lag behind the overall percentages of each group in the general population. Moreover, federal court rulings questioning the constitutionality of race-based apportionment schemes, coupled with persistent Republican electoral strength up and down the ballot, may not be good news for those who seek to increase minority representation in the legislature.

More startling is the discrepancy between the legislature and the general population with regard to gender. Currently, there are 37 female House members and 6 female senators.[8] While these numbers represent high-water marks for women, they are still underrepresented in the legislature. However, it should be pointed out that the rising tide of Republican fortunes resulted in a significant number of female Republican candidates winning election up and down the ballot in recent elections, and this trend may continue in the future. Yet the state's conservative political culture, which responds slowly and reluctantly to change, may cause this development to lag behind other states.

Apportionment

Apportionment refers to dividing the population into districts for purposes of election and representation. The Texas Constitution stipulates that the House and the Senate, respectively, are responsible for dividing the state into such districts.[9] These districts must be contiguous, which means you can't have part of a Senate district in Brownsville and the other part of it in Amarillo. And they are to be redrawn (or redistricted) every ten years following publication of the federal census.

apportionment
Dividing the population into districts for purposes of election and representation.

The last day of the 2009 legislative session found many bills still pending, a byproduct of cramming two years of law-making into 140 days. Do you believe that Texas should continue to have biennial sessions?

redistricting
The process of redrawing district lines to maintain the concept of "one person, one vote."

The process of **redistricting** is one of the most troublesome issues to confront the legislature. Redrawing district lines is necessary because as people move from place to place, each district's population ebbs and flows. Some districts gain population and become quite crowded; others lose people and become under populated. Neither situation is fair. People who live in a district with only one-half or one-third the population of another district wield more political influence than their more crowded neighbors. Think about it: Would you rather be one out of 50,000 or one out of 250,000? If you're part of the less populous district, your voice has a better chance of being heard. Your vote is five times more powerful than that of the those in the larger district. In this way, people in an overpopulated district wind up casting a diluted vote.

The remedy for such inequities would seem to be simple—just move a few lines on a map and instant fairness results. It's never that easy in Texas politics.

The very people who are charged with the responsibility of redrawing these lines are usually the most reluctant to do so. Senators and representatives become such by winning in their own districts. So regardless of whether that district is over- or underpopulated, they usually want to keep it just like it is. This reluctance caused redistricting to go undone in many states for many years. However, in the early 1960s, the federal courts began ordering redistricting at a number of levels of government, and Texas soon came under the reapportionment gun.

"one person, one vote"
A principle of representation that means the vote of one citizen should be worth no more or no less than the vote of another citizen; districts with equal population ensure this.

The 1964 U.S. Supreme Court case of *Reynolds* v. *Sims*[10] ruled that in a bicameral state legislature, both houses had to be apportioned on the basis of equal population among districts. This principle has best been expressed in the phrase **"one person, one vote."** Very simply, this means the vote of one citizen should be worth no more or no less than the vote of another citizen. Districts with equal population assure this. Texas was not involved in the *Reynolds* case, but the precedent it set was soon applied to this state and its district-drawing practices.

THE SENATE The 1876 Constitution of Texas has always required that both House and Senate districts reflect an equal division of the population, but it also stipulated "no single county shall be entitled to more than one Senator." As urban growth progressed, several counties such as Harris (Houston), Dallas, Bexar (San Antonio), and Tarrant (Fort Worth) experienced booming population growth but remained limited to one senator each and thus increasingly underrepresented. Mindful of the *Reynolds* case, a Houston attorney, Bill Kilgarlin (who later served on the Texas Supreme Court) filed suit in a Houston federal district court seeking to overturn the "one senator per county" limit. The court, citing *Reynolds*, found that particular constitutional restriction to be in violation of the "one person, one vote" principle and struck it down.

The implications of this case, *Kilgarlin* v. *Martin*,[11] were enormous. Because the most populous urban counties had been restricted to one senator, power in the Texas Senate had remained largely in the hands of rural senators, even though their population base had steadily eroded. Once new Senate districts were ordered, a significant shift in power began. Urban counties gained more Senate seats and acquired more influence over the agenda and actions of the senate. Today's Senate districts may vary greatly in geographic size (District 26 in San Antonio is one of the smallest; District 19 in West Texas, one of the largest), but each now must average 672,639 constituents and thus adhere to the principle of "one person, one vote." Of course, it would be practically impossible to create 31 districts, each of which would contain the exact number of constituents in an "ideal" district. Therefore, the courts have allowed the legislature some leeway in this process, and in general, districts may deviate from the "ideal" district size by about 5 percent.

THE HOUSE The Texas House suffered its share of headaches on the redistricting front. Senate districts had always been **single-member districts**; that is, each specific geographic area contained the same number of people and elected one person (a "single member") to represent that area in the Senate. The House, however, in response to court pressures to redistrict, had created several multimember districts in the largest urban counties. Such districts seemed to adhere to the letter of the "one person, one vote" pronouncement, but they actually subverted its spirit. Here's how they worked. Instead of taking a large urban county and dividing it into individual districts with each electing one representative, the House declared these counties to be giant districts in and of themselves, and every voter in that county could choose a number of representatives, all of whom would represent them in the legislature. Consider this example. Assume that a fair calculation of the "one person, one vote" rule would produce a ratio of one elected representative for every 50,000 citizens. Then say that a particular county has 300,000 citizens. That county would thus be entitled to six representatives under "one person, one vote." The simplest and the fairest way to do that would be to count out 50,000 people, draw a line around them, and let each group elect their own representative. However, if the

single-member district
A specific geographic area with a population equal to that of other districts that elects one person (a single member) to represent that area.

county were a multimember district, then all the citizens in the county could vote in six different races to choose six different representatives, all of whom would supposedly represent all of the county's citizens.

Such an arrangement might seem like a good idea, but it presents serious problems. Under these multimember schemes, nothing would prevent all the district's representatives from living in one area, one neighborhood, or even on one street. This could make it difficult for other areas of the county to have their concerns voiced. Moreover, this system makes it difficult for those outside the power structure to gain a foothold. Because they had to appeal to voters countywide, minority candidates like Hispanics and African Americans (and in the 1960s, liberals and Republicans) stood little chance of being elected, even though they might have enjoyed overwhelming support in their own communities. In truth, these multimember districts were simply a kind of rearguard action to help the ruling rural conservative Democrats preserve their power in the House for as long as possible, in the face of changing demographic and political forces. Such action is, of course, entirely consistent with the traditionalistic political culture that is so prevalent in Texas. (See the discussion of political culture in Chapter 1.)

These multimember districts began to disappear in the early 1970s. First the Legislative Redistricting Board, charged with redrawing district lines when the legislature fails to do so (this group is described in more detail below), ordered the replacement of a 23-seat multimember district encompassing all of Harris County with 23 single-member districts. Court cases challenging multimember districts in Bexar and Dallas counties, then Tarrant, Nueces (Corpus Christi), and Jefferson (Beaumont) counties soon followed. In each case, single-member districts were ordered and subsequent elections saw more minorities and Republicans winning House seats than ever before. As had been the case in the Senate, the rural power bloc in the House was thus forced to share power with a more diverse group within the legislature. Today, all 150 House districts in Texas are single-member districts and each now must contain an average of 139,012 constituents. Again, deviations of 5 percent are allowed in creating these districts.

GERRYMANDERING: ROUND ONE By the early 1980s, single-member districts were used across the entire state for choosing legislators. By then, another aspect of apportionment was coming under closer scrutiny, the phenomenon of **gerrymandering**. This involves drawing districts so as to either help or hurt a person's or a party's chances of winning election. For example, if you know you can do well among labor unions, you would try to have your district drawn to include as many union members as possible. Conversely, if you wanted to minimize a group's political influence, you would try to split its members up among several districts, thus denying them sufficient numbers to win any one seat.

gerrymandering
The act of drawing representative districts in order to help or hinder a person, or a political party, to win an election.

Gerrymandering is about as old a practice as electing representatives. However, in recent years it has become a more complex political problem because of both the sophistication of political data available and the heightened political awareness of more groups in society. Whereas before, arguments involved whether one county should or should not be in a particular district, those arguments now center on whether one census tract or even one side of a block should be included or excluded. Combine this with more widely available data as a result of the Internet revolution, and it's no wonder that charges of gerrymandering are routinely tossed about after every redistricting plan is revealed.

Such charges were exaggerated by the growing partisanship of Texas elections and by the willingness of Republicans to challenge the legality of districts drawn primarily by Democrats in the 1990s. Because many recent reapportionment plans created by the legislature have been challenged in (and often overturned by) the courts, many people have found themselves in a different Senate or House district in almost every election. The redistricting plan enacted following the 2000 census exemplifies this trend. The Legislative Redistricting Board—made up of the attorney general, lieutenant governor, Speaker of the House, comptroller of public accounts, and land commissioner—stepped in to redraw district lines when the House and the Senate failed to do so in the 2001 session of the legislature. Four of the five members of this body were Republicans, hence the resultant legislative districts took on a decidedly Republican tone in their makeup. As a direct result of this redrawing, the Republicans gained control of both houses of the legislature. Obviously, who draws the districts is as important as how they are drawn.

GERRYMANDERING: ROUND TWO The most controversial issue before the legislature in 2003 was the proposed redistricting of the state's delegation to the U.S. Congress. 2003 was not supposed to be a redistricting year. Under normal circumstances, redistricting is a once-a-decade phenomenon, concluded the year after the U.S. Census and, thankfully, not revisited for ten years.

In 2001, the Texas House and Senate failed to create a redistricting map and, eventually, responsibility for congressional redistricting fell to a panel of federal judges. Republicans were not happy with the results. After the 2002 elections, Democrats held 17 of the 32 Texas congressional seats, despite the fact that Republican candidates captured 60 percent of the congressional vote statewide. The short version of how this came to pass is that the judges drew lines that protected incumbent congresspeople, reiterating in many ways the pro-Democratic lines drawn by the Democratic dominated legislature in 1991. But because Texas had two more congressional seats after reapportionment, thus leading to the creation of two new districts, Republicans were able to gain those new seats.

In the 2002 legislative elections, Republicans made great strides. By controlling the legislative redistricting process in 2001, Republicans had been able to carve maps that gave them large majorities in both the Texas House and Senate. Since nothing in Texas law or the state constitution *prohibits* redistricting at any time, Republican leaders decided to push forward with the effort. Most of the impetus for this unprecedented maneuver came from the majority leader of the U.S. House at that time, Representative Tom DeLay of Sugarland. DeLay was committed to enlarging the Republican majority in the U.S. House and saw Texas as a fertile ground for such an endeavor. It was at his urging that the controversial redistricting process was begun. As was to be expected, Democrats were outraged.

In the 2003 regular session, redistricting never got legs, largely due to two main obstacles. First and foremost, the Senate in general and Lieutenant Governor Dewhurst in particular seemed less than committed to visiting the issue. A huge factor was the Senate's long-standing "two-thirds rule," an internal mechanism that requires the support of two-thirds of the members in order for a bill to reach the floor (see the discussion of this odd rule below). With Democrats comprising more than a third of the Senate, and with no push from Dewhurst, redistricting was dead on arrival in the Senate.

Not taking any chances, House Democrats ensured the issue would die when 55 of them walked out of the chamber and headed to Oklahoma, thereby preventing a quorum. Without two-thirds of its members present—100 representatives—the House could not do business. They didn't return to Austin until after the deadline for all bills to be out of **committee**, thereby killing the redistricting plan and, along with it, dozens of other bills. The entire controversy left ruffled feathers all around, with Democrats believing that Republicans had destroyed the bipartisan atmosphere that had historically prevailed in the legislature (most recently under former Republican Governor George W. Bush) and Republicans believing that Democrats had thwarted the will of the people of Texas by running to Oklahoma (an act some Texans compared to 1960s-era "draft dodgers" fleeing to Canada).

Undeterred, Governor Perry called a special session for late June, extending into July. Again, the two-thirds rule prevented redistricting from reaching the floor, but by the end of the first special session, Dewhurst was perturbed at House and Senate Democrats and was feeling pressure from his fellow Republican leaders. He believed that Senate Republicans had offered a reasonable redistricting plan and wondered why Democrats wouldn't accept a plan that would protect most of their incumbents. He began sounding ominous warnings about the two-thirds rule, reminding senators that it was an internal Senate regulation that could be rescinded by the majority—meaning Republicans—at any time. It was clear, the Democrats thought, that the first order of business in a second special session would be to suspend the rule and allow legislation to reach the floor by a majority vote. This time, Senate Democrats considered leaving.

Republicans anticipated their move. Governor Perry devised a plan to end the first session a day early, immediately convene a second and catch the Democrats still in Austin. Democrats were quicker, though. Eleven immediately left for the Marriott in Albuquerque, New Mexico—perhaps demonstrating better judgment than their House cohorts, who earlier had fled to the Holiday Inn in Ardmore, Oklahoma. (Why flee out of state? Legislative rules require senators and representatives to be on the job during session. If they are absent within the state—see the Texas Mosaic on the "Killer Bees" in this chapter—the Texas Rangers can compel them to return. Once they cross state lines, though, they are beyond the Rangers' jurisdiction.)

With Democrat Ken Armbrister remaining in Austin, the 11 had the bare majority they needed to block a quorum. But the defection of just one would be enough to get the Senate up and running again. Through the second special session, the boycott held. As the session ended, however, Houston Senator John Whitmire returned to Austin, saying that the he believed Governor Perry would continue calling sessions until redistricting passed. The boycott crumbled and the remaining Democrats returned as well.

Even then, redistricting was not a sure thing. Republicans began fighting among themselves as House members favored one plan and senators favored another. The House version won out—it included a separate congressional district

committees
Divisions of a legislative body charged with initial deliberations on legislative proposals.

for Midland and another in DFW tailor-made for Speaker Tom Craddick's ally Kenny Marchant—and that plan resulted in a huge gain in congressional seats for Republicans in the 2004 general election. Thus, the precedent was set for the legislature to undertake redistricting just about any time it chose to do so and for just about any reason. The implications of such actions and their impact on representation in Texas in the coming years remain to be seen, but it seems a safe bet that the result will be more, rather than less, partisan wrangling over the always divisive issue of redistricting.

The Presiding Officers

Many people have observed that the candidates who run for elected office tend to have extremely—how shall we put this?—*healthy* egos. This is nowhere more evident than in the Texas legislature. When you bring together 150 such egos in the House and then stir in 31 more in the Senate, the potential for chaos and confrontation is enormous. In order to get anything accomplished in the legislative arena, someone has to organize these people and get them moving in the same direction. That responsibility falls to the presiding officers in each house, two of the most important and powerful figures in Texas politics.

Most Texans are shocked to find out that their governor isn't all that powerful in the great cosmic scheme of Texas politics (for a further discussion of this interesting observation, see Chapter 7). Many Texas political observers will argue that the most powerful officeholder in the state is in fact the lieutenant governor, who presides over the Senate. Only slightly less powerful is the presiding officer of the House of Representatives, the Speaker. Their power derives in part from the 1876 Texas Constitution, which, in stripping away many of the governor's prerogatives, tended to bolster these two positions. It also derives in part from the rules under which the two bodies operate. Perhaps most importantly, however, their power grows out of custom and tradition, out of a time-honored realization by individual legislators that they each must yield some of their individual power in order to be able to work together collectively. The beneficiaries of this arrangement are the presiding officers, who thus become a combination head coach and referee for their respective houses. In this role they can exert more influence over legislation than anyone in Texas. Let's take a closer look at each of these officers and how they function.

The Lieutenant Governor

Although nominally a member of the executive branch of Texas government, the lieutenant governor is charged by the constitution with presiding over the Senate. It is in this capacity that he fills his most important role. The occupant of this office is chosen in a statewide election and serves a four-year term with no limit on reelection (former Lieutenant Governor Bill Hobby set a longevity record by holding the office from 1973 to 1991). Although elected at the same time as the governor, these two officials don't run as a team and don't constitute a "ticket" as do the president and vice president at the national level. Indeed, it is entirely possible for the governor to be from one party while the lieutenant governor is from another. The lieutenant governor receives a salary of $7,200 per year, the same as all other members of the legislature. The powers given the lieutenant governor are quite significant.

To begin with, he may recognize individual members who wish to speak from the floor of the Senate. Now at first glance, this may not seem significant. After all, how much political savvy does it take to point at someone and say, "The chair recognizes the senator from Harris [County]"? But if you think about it, you'll realize that the lieutenant governor could easily use this power to mold the direction and tone of debate on an issue. Even the order of business in the Senate can be affected by whom the lieutenant governor chooses to recognize. If a senator who is "carrying" a bill in the Senate on behalf of a colleague in the House cannot gain the floor, there's little chance the bill will survive. Without being recognized, a senator may not formally participate in Senate debate and thus may not be able to make a point she deems vital to that debate or to express the views of her constituents. Most recent holders of this office have made a good faith effort to give everyone who wishes to speak the opportunity to do so, but the fact that they do *not* have to do so can be a potentially powerful factor in shaping legislation.

The lieutenant governor also appoints the members of all Senate committees as well as their chairs and vice chairs. As will be discussed in more detail later in this chapter, committees form the backbone of the legislature. They have the power to make or break legislation. By determining *who* serves on each committee, the lieutenant governor can go a long way toward shaping *how* each committee deals with legislation. This is especially true when it comes to naming committee chairs. These appointees are usually close friends of the lieutenant governor, senators with whom he has worked and whom he can trust. The personal dimension of such appointments allows the lieutenant governor to contribute to a committee's deliberations routinely. Occasionally this is done directly. More often, it happens through the expression and implementation of political views shared among the committee's chair, its key members, and the presiding officer. Because of this, it's safe to say that most legislation opposed by the lieutenant governor never makes it out of committee.

Not only does the lieutenant governor appoint members of Senate committees, he also appoints the Senate members of all conference committees. These groups must resolve the differences between Senate and House versions of a bill, and their ability to do so often depends on the personalities of the five senators and five representatives who make up each committee. The lieutenant governor chooses people on whom he can depend to safeguard the interests of the Senate in any deliberations leading to a compromise. No one held the office of lieutenant governor of Texas longer than Bill Hobby, who presided over the Senate from 1973 to 1991. A quiet, scholarly man, Hobby often surprised people with his quick, dry wit. Once, when addressing a group of college students that was visiting Austin during a legislative session, he was asked if it were true (as their professor had told them) that the lieutenant governor was the most powerful elected official in Texas. Without missing a beat, Hobby replied that that honor belonged to the district attorney of Travis County. When the student looked puzzled, Hobby pointed out, with a twinkle in his eye, that the Travis County DA was the official responsible for bringing charges against elected state officials (including, of course, the lieutenant governor)! The DA aside, even the lieutenant governor doesn't always get his way, as illustrated in the Texas Mosaic on the "Killer Bees."

The lieutenant governor determines the jurisdiction of all committees, and then refers all bills to those committees. A committee's jurisdiction simply refers to the kinds of bills it can consider. Most of the time, these boundaries are rather broadly drawn. In fact, most bills could go to any number of committees, depending on the interpretation of the bill's intent and on each committee's "turf." As you can see, this enhances the lieutenant governor's control over the fate of bills. With a good bit of discretion in this matter, he can send a bill to a "friendly" committee or to a "hostile" committee that will likely kill it. If this happens (and it does with some regularity), a bill opposed by the lieutenant governor will for all practical purposes be "dead on arrival" when it gets to a committee.

Finally, the lieutenant governor holds several *ex officio* positions that further strengthen his role in Texas politics. These are offices he holds automatically because he occupies another office (in this case, that of lieutenant governor). One of the most important of these *ex officio* positions is chair of the **Legislative Budget Board (LBB)**. This body oversees a staff whose recommendations become a kind of working document for the state's biennial budget. And since its members are all appointed either directly or indirectly by the presiding officers, you can be sure that the final budget will bear a striking resemblance to the one proposed by the LBB. As its chair, the lieutenant governor thus becomes *the* major player in the budgetary process. He or she also serves on the Texas Legislative Council, which directs the research services of the legislature. In addition, the lieutenant governor appoints members to numerous boards, including the Sunset Advisory Commission, which recommends the re-creation or abolition of most administrative agencies of the state.

Legislative Budget Board
A body made up of members of the house and senate, including the two presiding officers, which oversees a staff responsible for preparing the basic working budget for the legislature's consideration.

Texas **MOSAIC**

The Killer Bees
Rattling the Texas political cage

Rarely can an individual legislator challenge the power of a presiding officer and get away with it. In 2003, disgruntled Democrats in both the House and the Senate tried but ultimately failed to prevent Republicans from gerrymandering Texas's congressional districts (see above). But this was not the first time such tactics were used in Texas politics. A group of Senate mavericks did clash with then Lieutenant Governor Bill Hobby in May 1979, and, to the surprise of many veteran political observers, prevailed. This incident, known as "the attack of the Killer Bees," has assumed the status of legend in Texas politics. It all began late in the legislative session when Hobby tried to push through the Senate a bill that would establish separate-day presidential and state primary elections. He hoped this would enable conservative Democrats to vote for former Texas governor and Republican presidential hopeful John Connally in a Republican presidential primary before returning to the regular state Democratic primary to choose candidates for state offices. However, Hobby could not bring the bill up for consideration because 12 senators refused to vote to suspend the rules to do so. In a rare

fit of pique on the part of the lieutenant governor, he announced that he was going to supersede the rules and bring the bill up anyway. The 12 senators who had opposed him on the dual-primary bill then turned the rules against their own presiding officer.

Knowing that a *quorum* (the minimum number of members required to be present on the floor of the Senate in order to conduct business) was 21, they realized that if they didn't show up on the floor, the Senate could not meet and transact business. Because the end of the session loomed, such a halt would throw that body into a panic that could in turn pressure Hobby into relenting. So, these guys went "over the wall" (so to speak). They disappeared and, sure enough, the Senate ground to a standstill for lack of a quorum. Furious, Hobby invoked his power as lieutenant governor, ordering the Department of Public Safety and the Texas Rangers to begin an all-out search for the missing dozen senators. Of course, word quickly spread, and soon the media joined in the hunt for the wayward 12, fueling rumors of "sightings" all over the state.

While the media circus expanded and Hobby grew more frustrated, the missing senators were hiding out

(continued)

(continued from page 159)

in a garage apartment in Austin, playing cards, and generally beginning to get on one another's nerves. One of the fugitives, Gene Jones, decided that he'd had enough of his colleagues. He sneaked back to his Houston district, but word leaked out that he had been spotted in that city. Hobby sent a Texas Ranger, Charlie Cook, in a DPS helicopter to snag the wayward senator and "escort" him back to the Senate. When Gene Jones spotted the Texas Ranger approaching his door, he asked his brother, Clayton, to go out and pick up the morning paper. Ranger Cook, armed with a photo of Senator Jones, confronted the senator's brother and told him he had orders to return him to Austin. Clayton Jones would only say that the Ranger was making a mistake, to which Cook replied that Jones would have to come with him.

When they got to Austin and Clayton Jones was brought into the Senate, the sergeant-at-arms, Kelly Arnold, immediately pointed out that this man was *not* Senator Gene Jones. When questioned as to why he had

not clarified his identity, the senator's brother responded that he'd never ridden in a helicopter before and it sounded like a really fun thing to do!

Needless to say, the Texas Rangers found themselves with considerable egg on their faces, and Lieutenant Governor Hobby still lacked the necessary quorum to conduct business. Under increasing pressure from other senators, Hobby finally relented and announced that the dual-primary bill was dead for the session. The 12 wayward senators, given assurances that they would not face retaliation for their actions, shortly thereafter returned in triumph to the Senate chamber and the session ended without further incident.

The name "Killer Bees"? It was given the missing senators by one of Hobby's aides who said they reminded him of the characters who dressed up in bumblebee outfits in a *Saturday Night Live* skit starring John Belushi. Hobby, more familiar with the classics than with pop culture, later admitted sheepishly that he'd never seen or heard of the show.

Because the real power of the lieutenant governor lies in his role as president of the Senate, not much thought is usually given to his role as successor to the governor should that office become vacant. However, it has not been business as usual in Texas politics of late. Governor George W. Bush's overwhelming reelection victory in 1998 served as the launch pad for his 2000 presidential campaign, and it set off an interesting chain reaction within the corridors of Texas government. The Texas Constitution as it was then written provided that the lieutenant governor (at that time, Rick Perry) would assume the governor's office on the swearing-in of President Bush. However, the constitution was unclear as to whether or not the lieutenant governor was required to give up that office on assuming the duties and responsibilities of the governorship, and here's where things really got interesting. The Texas Constitution states that the president pro tempore of the Senate, elected from among the Senate's members at the beginning of a session, is to perform the duties of the lieutenant governor in the latter's absence. A constitutional amendment adopted in 1999 requires that the lieutenant governor resign his office on succession to the governor's office. If the lieutenant governor's office thus becomes vacant, then the president pro tempore must convene the Senate within 30 days of the vacancy. The senate is then charged with electing a sitting senator to perform the duties of the lieutenant governor *in addition to his duties as senator* until the next general election.[12]

This is exactly what transpired following the 2000 presidential election. Prior to his swearing in as president, George W. Bush resigned the governorship of Texas. Lieutenant Governor Rick Perry succeeded to the office of governor and, in keeping with the 1999 constitutional amendment, resigned his position as lieutenant governor. The Texas Senate then elected one of its own, Senator Bill Ratliff from Mount Pleasant, as the new lieutenant governor. This election could have positioned Ratliff to make a run for that office in 2002 when he technically would

Lt. Governor David Dewhurst crosses the capitol to visit with house members. Why is it important for the head of the senate to reach out to house members?

have been the incumbent. But Ratliff declined to run, and the lieutenant governor's race pitted former state comptroller John Sharp against incumbent land commissioner David Dewhurst. Dewhurst won handily and assumed control of the Senate in January of 2003, a position he continues to hold today.

The Speaker of the House

The presiding officer of the House of Representatives is the Speaker. His powers are similar to those of the lieutenant governor, with some important differences. For example, the Speaker is chosen from among the House members by the House members themselves. So if you want to be the Speaker, you have to win two elections: one in your district and one in which you persuade a majority of your colleagues in the House that they can't possibly live another session without you as their leader. Until the 1940s, most Speakers served a single two-year term and did not seek reelection. From the 1950s to the 1970s, two terms became the norm. Then, in 1975, Billy Clayton, a veteran legislator from west Texas, was elected to the first of four terms in the office. Gib Lewis of Fort Worth succeeded Clayton and went him one better by serving five terms as Speaker. As the average tenure has increased, so has the competition for the office. Candidates seek early pledges of support from their colleagues, even to the extent of having them sign pledge cards expressing their loyalty. They raise and spend thousands of dollars and crisscross the state in search of votes. An example of such a campaign that produced some surprising results came in 1991–1992 and pitted two veteran west Texas representatives against each other. The initial favorite appeared to be Jim Rudd, chair of the powerful House Appropriations Committee. However, his close ties with outgoing Speaker Gib Lewis, who at the time was beset with charges of ethics violations, may have proved costly. In a somewhat surprising development, Representative Pete Laney, who promised a more "open" speakership, won the office.

Elected in the 1993 legislative session, Speaker Laney hoped to be elected to an unprecedented sixth term in the 2003 session. Even the possibility of Republican control of the House after the 2002 election did not prevent his gathering much support from members of both parties. However, Laney's district was one of those substantially redrawn by the Republican-dominated Legislative Redistricting Board and his reelection was by no means a sure thing. Although he did manage to hold on to his own seat, the magnitude of the Republican victory in the House led him to release those members who had pledged their support to him. This cleared the way for the election of Tom Craddick of Midland, then the senior Republican in the House, as that party's first Speaker since Reconstruction.

In the past, a sitting Speaker was usually guaranteed reelection if he sought it. This process was aided enormously by the fact that, well in advance of the election, the Speaker would hand out the aforementioned pledge cards, on which members were encouraged to express their support for him and "join the team" (see the following section for a fuller explanation of this concept). Take the power inherent in the office, add to it the enormous pressure brought to bear by the pledge card system, stir in the fact that this is an open ballot election for all to see (including the sitting Speaker), and you have a recipe that makes it difficult for a House member to oppose an incumbent Speaker and have any kind of meaningful legislative career thereafter.[13] Craddick's election did not deviate substantially from this time-honored formula.

Once elected, the Speaker shares many powers and prerogatives with the lieutenant governor. Like the lieutenant governor, the Speaker determines the jurisdiction of committees, refers all bills, and designates committee chairs. However, in naming committee members, the Speaker is more restricted than his counterpart in the Senate. This came about in response to some rather heavy-handed tactics used by Speaker Gus Mutscher during the Sharpstown Scandal of the early 1970s. After Mutscher left office in disgrace, the House instituted a **limited seniority system** for choosing committee members. Under this plan, with the very important exception of the Appropriations Committee, one-half the membership of standing substantive committees in the House (excluding the committee chairs and vice-chairs) must be appointed on the basis of seniority. Take the example of the Natural Resources Committee, which has 11 members. The Speaker appoints the chair and vice-chair, leaving 9 members to be named. Five are appointed based on their seniority (i.e., how long they have served in the House) and the remaining members are named at the Speaker's discretion. This means that someone who's been around for a long time may be able to get a desired committee assignment even if he or she happens to be a political enemy of the Speaker. This system doesn't place severe limitations on the Speaker, but it does diminish his or her power slightly in comparison with that of the lieutenant governor. In fact, many consider the Speaker to be second only to the lieutenant governor in terms of the power he wields in Texas politics.

limited seniority system
A method of committee selection used in the house that limits the Speaker to appointing half the members of most standing committees (plus the chairs); the other members gain their seats by seniority.

The Speaker also holds a number of *ex officio* positions in state government. Like the lieutenant governor, he is a member of the Legislative Budget Board and the Texas Legislative Council, on both of which he serves as vice chair, and he can also appoint members to various other boards, including the Sunset Advisory Commission. As is the case with the lieutenant governor, the Speaker may use these *ex officio* positions to enhance his already considerable legislative powers.

"The Team"

Those who hang around the legislature long enough will hear repeated references to "the team." The team refers to those legislators who are supporters and allies of the presiding officers. The Speaker's team in the House and the lieutenant governor's team in the Senate help these two presiding officers run their respective shows. Team members have developed a good working relationship with the presiding officer; have earned trust, they often are called on to help with implementation of his or her legislative strategy.

The relationship between team members and presiding officers is a complex one. To begin with, it is not a completely servile one on the part of the members. As powerful as they are, presiding officers can't routinely operate in a dictatorial manner (though they may get away with doing so on occasion). If one does, his or her colleagues may very well not reelect the Speaker, or a lieutenant governor may see that the Senate change its rules to strip him or her of powers. Prior to the 1998 and 2002 elections, there was speculation that such rule changes might be effected for purely partisan reasons if voters gave control of the Senate to Republicans but elected Democrat John Sharp as lieutenant governor. Rick Perry's victory in 1998 and David Dewhurst's win in 2002 and 2006 have stilled such speculation for now. On the other hand, most observers credit the heavy-handed tactics of Speaker Craddick, particularly toward the end of the 2007 legislative session, with helping to foment a rebellion that led to the election of Joe Straus as speaker at the beginning of the 2009 session (see the discussion below). In fact, a complicated system of rewards and punishments, rather than pure partisanship, enables these officers to exercise their powers and helps build and nurture the legislature's "teams."

Legislators know better than most the fundamental rule of Texas politics: You never get something for nothing. Therefore, if you want the presiding officer's help in trying to pass a bill or achieve some other legislative goal, you have to be willing to help him or her when called on to do so. This system has been described in many ways—quid pro quo, "You scratch my back and I'll scratch yours," and "Go along to get along." It simply boils down to this reality: the people who consistently help the presiding officers are usually named as committee chairs, appointed to the committees they desire, and wind up with close-in parking and the best office space at the Capitol. Their bills get good committee referrals and favorable calendar placement. Those who don't do these things wind up in committee "twilight zones," never quite seem to be able to get their bills processed, and have to park a long way off!

One last thing that needs to be said about **"the team"** is that, until the 21st century, traditionally it has not operated on a partisan basis. Political party affiliation has rarely been a factor in determining team membership, and the presiding officers have been remarkably nonpartisan in how they have run their respective houses.

"the team"
Unofficial term for those legislators who are supporters and allies of presiding officers and who form the leadership core of the legislature.

Even during the 1970s and 1980s, when Republicans still constituted a minority in both houses, they regularly were appointed to chair committees and regularly were consulted by both presiding officers. One reason for this was the fact that the presiding officers during that era were conservative Democrats who found it easy to work with Republicans. For example, during his tenure as lieutenant governor, Bob Bullock (himself a conservative Democrat) actively sought Republican input in developing the Senate's legislative agenda and, during his last term, appointed GOP senators to chair five of the Senate's 13 standing committees, including the powerful Education and Jurisprudence Committees.[14] In like manner, Lieutenant Governor Perry resisted calls for increased partisanship in the Senate and named Democrats to chair five such committees. His successor, Bill Ratliff, divided 12 committee chairs evenly between Republicans and Democrats in the 2001 legislative session. On the House side of the Capitol, increasing partisan rhetoric (and, in particular, partisan attacks on former Speaker Laney by some Republican members) contributed to more tension than had usually been the case. Nevertheless, Laney named 12 Republicans to chair committees in the Democrat-controlled House. However, upon his accession to the office of Speaker, Tom Craddick promoted a decidedly more partisan (some would say confrontational) style of leadership in the House. Straus reverted to a much more collegial method of running the House, but he still appointed a disproportionate number of Republican chairs, especially to key committees.

Evidence of a resultant breakdown of the "team" concept in the House can be seen in the events that transpired in the closing days of the 2007 regular session of the legislature. At that time, the already strained atmosphere in the House threatened to explode in a revolt against Speaker Craddick. A group of frustrated lawmakers, Democrats and Republicans alike, reacted to what they saw as the heavy-handed tactics of the Speaker by offering a motion to remove Craddick from his office. This led to a parliamentary storm which saw: (1) the Speaker

Tom Craddick spent three decades amassing a Republican majority in the Texas house and was rewarded with the speakership. After three terms, though, his seemingly abrasive manner wore on some members and he was ousted from power.

Republican Joe Straus brought a more congenial style to the speaker's office. Leadership styles vary, often evolving during a speaker's service.

refuse to recognize the members who sought to make the motion, (2) the House parliamentarian overruling of the Speaker's action, (3) the refusal of Craddick to abide by the parliamentarian's ruling and, finally, (4) the resignation of the parliamentarian in protest over what the Speaker asserted to be his "absolute right of recognition." The entire affair left bad feelings all around on the part of many House members (both Republican and Democrat) and this animosity carried over to the beginning of the 2009 session of the legislature, when a coalition of moderate Republicans and Democrats succeeded in forcing Craddick's resignation as Speaker and replacing him with the aforementioned Straus, himself a moderate Republican from San Antonio.

The Committee System

Committees function as little legislatures. Because of the immense volume of legislation routinely introduced each session, some sort of system for dividing labor and making an efficient use of limited time is needed. The committee system has evolved to meet these needs. Every piece of legislation introduced is referred to a committee and no legislation will be debated on the floor of either house unless a committee has first considered it. Moreover, the House and Senate almost always follow their recommendations, so committees exercise what amounts to life or death control over legislation.

Committees have attained this power in part because they allow the legislature to make better use of its time. As we have already noted, time limitations are *the* decisive factor in the legislative process. By dividing the membership into multiple smaller bodies, the committee system allows the legislature to consider more bills and to deliberate more fully on those bills that are introduced. In effect, the committee system acts as a screening mechanism, allowing the legislature to differentiate the good, the bad, and the ugly among bills and to do so more efficiently and effectively than would be the case if every bill had to be considered by the entire membership of each house.

Committees also provide a way for a somewhat transitory body like the legislature to develop institutional expertise and memory. Remember, the legislature is not a *continuously* full-time institution. It's in business for five months every two years, then, barring special sessions, it disappears. (However, we should point out that even when the legislature is out of session, many of its committees continue to work.) Add to this the high rate of turnover (sometimes 25 percent or more) from session to session, and you have a potential problem. Not only does a new session open more than a year and a half after the last one adjourned, but also many of the faces in this latest legislative crowd will be brand new, and a newly elected member is usually as lost as a goose when it comes to the intricacies of the legislative process. The committee system helps prevent the legislature from having to reinvent the wheel each session. Even though there may be many newcomers, there are always a number of veteran legislators around. These veterans typically are assigned to the same committee each session, thus they develop a depth of knowledge on specific topics that can be invaluable in wading through the legislative swamp. Each committee therefore builds a core of experts on whom other members, both inside and outside that committee, can depend for reliable guidance. The fact that some of these veterans come back session after session gives the legislature a kind of topical memory it might not otherwise have.

A good example of this expertise can be seen in the career of former State Senator Bill Ratliff. Senator Ratliff served in the Senate for many years before retiring from public life, and for most of that time he was a member of the Senate Education Committee. The knowledge he developed regarding colleges, universities, and professional schools in Texas was so extensive that he was routinely consulted regarding all aspects of this topic. His presence on the Education Committee served to give that body credibility among Senate members, who might not have known the difference between a contact hour and a happy hour, but knew they could find answers to pertinent questions by asking Ratliff. Ironically, one of the unintended consequences of the movement to limit legislators' terms in office would be the eventual loss of such valuable expertise.

Standing Committees

standing committee
A deliberative body formed each time a legislature meets that deals with topics of recurring interest.

The most important committees in the legislature are **standing committees**. Formed each time the legislature meets, these bodies deal with topics of recurring interest. It is through service on these standing committees that members develop that expertise just discussed. All members will be appointed to these committees, with most serving on two or three of them each session. In the 2009 session of the Texas legislature, the House formed 35 such committees and the Senate formed 19, as noted in Table 6.1. These numbers may vary slightly from session to session as the issues with which the legislature is confronted change. But, by and large, these bodies will be around every time the House and the Senate convene.

SUBSTANTIVE COMMITTEES The more numerous of the standing committees are the substantive committees, which deal with specific public policy topics. These include the House Appropriations and the Senate Finance Committees, which handle state spending and budgetary matters and are the most powerful committees of this type in the legislature. Other important substantive committees include the House Public Education and Higher Education Committees, the Senate Education and Higher Education Committees, the House Criminal Jurisprudence Committee, the Senate Jurisprudence Committee, and the State Affairs Committees in both houses. These bodies hammer out the specifics of legislation that can affect the lives of every Texan, from the amount of money it takes to run state government to the curriculum in our schools to the amount of time people will spend in prison for the crimes they commit. These committees address the complex issues that face Texas time and again.

PROCEDURAL COMMITTEES Procedural committees seem at first glance to be of lesser importance than their higher-profile siblings, the substantive committees. Yet these bodies, which deal with the internal operations of the two houses, can play a vital role in the legislature. Keeping the House and the Senate going is a difficult task and procedural committees help to do that. They may coordinate the distribution of office space among the members, a job carried out by the administration committees of the two houses. They may establish the parameters of debate when bills are considered, a task that falls to the Rules and Resolutions Committee in the

TABLE **6.1** **Standing Committees of the Senate and House, 81st Texas Legislature**

SENATE COMMITTEES[15]

Administration	Higher Education
Agriculture and Rural Affairs	Intergovernmental Relations
Business and Commerce	International Relations and Trade
Committee of the Whole Senate	Jurisprudence
Criminal Justice	Natural Resources
Economic Development	Nominations
Education	State Affairs
Finance	Transportation and Homeland Security
Government Organization	Veteran Affairs and Military Installations
Health and Human Services	

HOUSE COMMITTEES[16]

Agriculture and Livestock	Insurance
Appropriations	Judiciary and Civil Jurisprudence
Border and International Affairs	Land and Resource Management
Business and Industry	Licensing and Administrative Procedures
Calendars	Local and Consent Calendars
Corrections	Natural Resources
County Affairs	Pensions, Investments and Financial Services
Criminal Jurisprudence	Public Education
Culture, Recreation, and Tourism	Public Health
Defense and Veterans' Affairs	Public Safety
Elections	Redistricting
Energy Resources	Rules and Resolutions
Environmental Regulation	State Affairs
Federal Economic Stabilization Funding	Technology, Economic Development, and Workforce
General Investigating and Ethics	Transportation
Higher Education	Urban Affairs
House Administration	Ways and Means
Human Services	

House. They may determine the order in which bills will be taken up for discussion and debate, a role undertaken by the House Calendars Committee. And lest you think that such committees are a kind of legislative swamp into which powerless senators and representatives disappear, never to be heard from again, think again. If you were one of a handful of House members who could decide the fate of a bill merely by its placement on a list of pending legislation, you could exert tremendous influence over the kinds of laws that are ultimately passed. Members of the House Calendars Committee, the most powerful procedural committee in the legislature, can do just that. Not surprisingly, these committees tend to be well stocked with team members loyal to the presiding officers.

Special Committees

From time to time, the legislature has to create temporary committees to deal with special situations. The most common of these **special committees** are the conference committees. The presiding officers appoint five representatives and five senators to the **conference committee**. These committees attempt to iron out differences

special committee
A temporary committee formed by the legislature for limited or nonroutine purposes.

conference committee
Joint committee of house and senate members whose purpose is to iron out the differences between house and senate versions of a bill.

between House and Senate versions of a bill. It is rare for any bill to pass one house in the exact form as in the other, so these bodies are a routine part of legislative business. On occasion, one house's conferees may convince their counterparts to accept their version of a bill, but the more common scenario has both sides giving and taking in order to reach a compromise acceptable to all. Most conference committee work tends to concentrate near the end of legislative sessions, so service on such a body can be nerve wracking.

interim committee
A special committee formed to study a topic or problem between sessions of the legislature.

Another kind of special committee frequently seen in the legislature is the **interim committee**. An interim committee is given a particular assignment to be carried out between sessions of the legislature. This can be done either by appointing existing standing committees to act as interim bodies or by creating new committees for specific purposes (these are sometimes referred to as select committees). Meeting while the legislature is out of session, such committees are usually asked to study a specific problem and make recommendations at the next legislative session. In carrying out these duties, committees frequently hold hearings in various parts of the state and allow public testimony on their assigned topics. In recent years, such bodies have studied the TASP program (a testing program to determine the need for remediation among college freshmen), juvenile justice, payment of health care providers, state employee compensation and benefits, and public school funding. Prior to the 2009 regular session, such committees were charged with examining the impact of changes in the state tax system on businesses as well as the effect of reforms to the Texas Youth Commission enacted during the 2007 session. Interim committees give the legislature a head start on upcoming issues, but depending on the topic, serving on these bodies can create an additional burden of time and expense for legislators.

How Committees Work

The fate of every piece of legislation introduced is in the hands of committees. They can change, rearrange, pass, or kill bills as they see fit. Legislators spend more time in committee meetings than in any other facet of the legislative process. Visit the legislature and observe a daily session of the full House or Senate and you'll wonder *if* they ever get anything done. Visit a committee during testimony or "mark-up" and you'll see *how* they get things done. The legislature in committee is the legislature at work.

COMMITTEE CHAIRS The chair of each committee exerts enormous influence over the actions of that body. This person, usually a close friend or political ally of the presiding officer, is responsible for organizing the committee, overseeing its general operation, and presiding over its meetings. The chair recognizes members to speak, determines the order in which bills referred to the committee will be considered, and, in general, acts as a kind of "minor league" presiding officer. It is no exaggeration to say that if a committee chair opposes a bill, that bill's outlook will be very bleak. There have been instances when a chair took exception to the way a committee member voted on a favorite bill and thereafter refused even to bring up that member's bills for consideration at any time during the remainder of the session. Such behavior may not be the norm, but it happens often enough to make members wary of crossing swords with the chair.

Ursula Parks, then a member of the Legislative Budget Board's Public Educations Team testifies before a meeting of the House Public Education Committee. Often, state agency staff appear at legislative committee meetings.

SUBCOMMITTEES If committees represent an attempt by the legislature to create an efficient division of labor, then subcommittees represent a furtherance of that aim. Some committees formally divide themselves into smaller groups, with each such group having its own formal structure. For example, in the 81st Legislature, the Senate Intergovernmental Relations Committee created a Subcommittee on Flooding and Evacuations. This was in response to the confusion and displacement that followed the battering of the Texas Gulf Coast by several recent hurricanes. Bills that came to the full committee were passed on to this subcommittee if they dealt with this specific topic. Such subcommittees study the bills given them, then recommend action to the full committee, which in turn can accept or reject the recommendation. In most cases, they go along with the subcommittee. Even those committees that don't adopt such a formal structure may nevertheless divide into informal working groups during "mark-up" (see the "Committee Action" section below for an explanation of this process) in order to consider their bills more effectively. Subcommittees simply enable the committees to get more work done.

COMMITTEE STAFFS Most standing committees are provided with a minimal staff to facilitate their work, although the size and importance of a committee may have some bearing on the size of its staff. In most cases, this staff will include a committee clerk and perhaps one or two assistants. These people often are the unsung heroes of the legislative process. Usually underpaid and consistently overworked, they conduct research, help clarify legislation, keep track of where the committee is in its agenda, make coffee, and provide all kinds of other support services to committee members, all of whom seem to want to call on staff members at the same time. Of crucial importance among these staffers is the clerk of the committee.

These clerks often are the most knowledgeable people regarding a committee's business and some of them are bona fide experts in the matters that come before their committee. As was noted in Chapter 5, most successful lobbyists will be quick to tell you that they regularly depend on the information and expertise of these people in tracking legislation important to their cause. Although rarely recognized for their work, these staff members usually are the difference between a smoothly running committee and one in which the wheels come off on a regular basis.

How a Bill Becomes a Law

The path taken by a bill as it becomes a law is long and torturous, and although many are called, few are chosen. The percentage of those that never become law is extremely high, usually in the 80 percent range, and the vast majority of bills never make it much beyond their introduction. In the 2009 regular session of the legislature, a total of 7,419 bills were filed, but only 1,459 bills eventually reached the governor's desk for his action, an attrition rate of greater than 80 percent.[17] Passing a bill into law requires a shifting combination of skill, perseverance, nerve, flexibility, and plain old-fashioned luck. Yet this act lies at the heart of the legislative process, and watching it unfold can provide a fascinating glimpse into the dynamics of Texas politics.

Introduction of a Bill

Any member of the legislature (but only members) may introduce a bill, although the real author may be anyone from a constituent to a lobbyist to a staff assistant to an actual member. Bills may be introduced in both houses, but the constitution stipulates that all revenue bills must originate in the House of Representatives. Since 1989, the legislature's rules have allowed for the prefiling of bills. This simply means that members may begin filing bills for an upcoming regular session as soon as the November general election is concluded. This can be advantageous because bills filed early generally have a better chance of passage.

Multiple copies of each bill introduced are filed with the appropriate clerks in each house. Bills are designated "HB" (House Bill) or "SB" (Senate Bill) and then assigned a number in the general order in which they are filed. Of late it has become fashionable for the leadership in both houses to "reserve" numbers, usually single digits, for the more important bills. For instance, in 2009, the general appropriations bill was designated as HB 1. After filing, the clerks see that every bill is reproduced and distributed to all members. This begins a paper barrage. *Every* time changes are made in a bill, those changes are noted and new copies distributed. The ability to access bills online would seem to have mitigated this problem somewhat, but members still complain that they are drowning in paper. After filing and numbering, a bill moves to first reading and referral. All bills must be read three times on separate days, a practice dating to medieval England when most members of Parliament were illiterate. This is probably not the case in today's Texas legislature, so the "readings" usually consist only of stating the number, author, and title of the bill. And many bills routinely contain an emergency clause suspending this three-day rule. The presiding officer then refers the bill to the committee of his choice.

Committee Action

The way committees work has already been discussed in general terms; now let's look at some specifics of what goes on when bills get to committee. The chair of each committee is largely responsible for deciding the order in which bills are considered. Once that order is determined, the Texas Open Meetings Law requires that advanced public notice of committee hearings on a bill must be posted. Anyone may appear at these hearings and offer testimony on a particular bill or on a number of bills. Those who wish to do so simply fill out a witness affidavit card that calls for some basic personal information, and then wait their turn. Witnesses may testify for a bill, against a bill, or on a bill, and committee members may in turn question witnesses. Depending on the bill, such hearings may last a few minutes or stretch over several days.

Once testimony has been taken, the committee moves into "mark-up." In this intensive work session, committee members roll up their sleeves and go through the bill with a fine-tooth comb. Although it is technically possible for a bill to emerge from mark-up in its exact original form, this rarely happens. Committees usually make some kind of changes in bills. These can be minor but can also be major, ranging up to rewriting bills completely or combining them with bills of a similar nature. They also may decide to do nothing and simply set a bill aside and consider it no further. Such a practice, known as **pigeonholing** a bill, effectively kills the bill and is the most common committee action taken.

After a committee finishes marking up a bill, it must vote on what to do with the bill. Committee votes are by majority, and if the bill meets with the group's approval, it will be referred to the entire House with a recommendation that it be enacted. This committee recommendation is crucial because the House and Senate almost always go along with what their committees suggest. Getting your bill out of committee puts you a long way down the road to passage.

Bills that require the state to spend money face a couple of extra hurdles. They must be "certified" by the state's comptroller of public accounts; that is, the comptroller's office must verify that if the bill were to pass, sufficient revenue would be available to fund its operation for the budget period. This obviously gives the comptroller a great deal of influence over fiscal legislation. Then, bills that require money also must be approved by the Appropriations Committee in the House and by the Finance Committee in the Senate. These enormously powerful bodies can't change the content of such bills coming from other committees, but they can (and often do) alter the amount of money called for in a bill.

At the point where bills come out of final committee action, Senate and House procedures differ. Bills in the Senate go on a single calendar in the general order in

WHAT CAN YOU DO?

Although you might think that giving testimony before a legislative committee is something reserved for high-priced lobbyists and other political "big guns," it's not. Any citizen may do so by following some relatively simple procedures. If you wish to offer testimony on a bill, you will need to contact the committee to which the bill has been referred and find out when a hearing has been scheduled. This hearing will almost certainly take place in one of the committee meeting rooms in the state capitol. You can access information on the schedules of all House and Senate committees at http://www.capitol.state.tx.us. Try to get there well before the meeting begins and ask the committee clerk for a witness affidavit. This card asks for your name, address, group you represent, and whether you wish to speak for the bill, against the bill, or on the bill. After that, it's just a matter of waiting your turn. When you address the committee, keep your remarks succinct and be prepared to answer any questions from the members of the committee. Good luck!

pigeonholing
The act of a setting aside a bill in committee and refusing to consider it, thereby "killing" it.

which they are received. In the House, bills go to the Calendars Committee, which is responsible for placing them on one of several calendars used by the House. This committee can arrange the bills in any order they wish and can also rearrange calendar orders if they so desire. The Calendars Committee basically serves as the House's gatekeeper by deciding what bills will make it to the floor. As such, it is one of the most powerful bodies in the legislature.

Floor Action

The House and the Senate differ significantly in their floor action procedures. Because it contains almost five times as many members as the Senate, the House more rigorously regulates debates on bills. Calendar orders in the House are followed faithfully, and more procedural controls are imposed. When a bill hits the House floor, it is read a second time and then the debate begins. House members may speak no more than ten minutes on each bill, although the bill's author is given 20 minutes at the beginning and 20 minutes at the conclusion of the debate. Discussion usually alternates between those for and those against the bill, with the Speaker controlling the flow of the debate. At the conclusion of deliberations, a vote is taken and if a majority favors the bill, it passes. However, as was noted above, if the bill doesn't contain an emergency clause, it must be carried over to the next day, read a third time (with no debate), then voted on a final time.

Note that the House rules do not allow for members to filibuster (see below for a fuller discussion of this Senate tactic). However, a kind of multi-member, "tag team" quasi-filibuster is used on rare occasions, especially during divisive House debates. This procedure, known as "chubbing," involves a large number of members, each of whom uses his full time period allotted for debate and many of whom stall the proceedings with obscure parliamentary inquiries and motions. Chubbing can drastically slow down debate, and can be especially effective at the end of a legislative session when certain deadlines for considering and adopting legislation come into play. An example of this tactic can be seen in the action of some Democrats in the House at the end of the 2009 regular session. The House was debating a voter identification bill, one of the most volatile and divisive issues to confront the 81st Legislature and one to which most Democrats were adamantly opposed. By chubbing the bill, they succeeded in delaying its consideration past the deadline for adoption specified in the House rules. They succeeded in killing the bill, but in doing so, they ignited a firestorm of anger among other House members, many of whose bills were effectively killed by this parliamentary delaying tactic.

The Senate does things differently. For one thing, its debate is more relaxed. Discussions on the Senate floor seem more personal, and senators often speak to an issue several times. Moreover, the Senate places no limits on debate, so senators may engage in **filibustering**. This amounts to talking endlessly on a particular bill in the hope of delaying a vote. A senator may not be interrupted as long as he or she stands at his or her desk and makes remarks that pertain to the bill. Such action can be a crucial element in legislative tactics, especially near the end of a session.

filibustering
The practice of delaying or killing a bill by talking at great length; grows out of the senate's rule allowing unlimited debate.

The Senate also differs in the way it goes about calling up bills for debate. Like the House, the Senate for many years had a rule that required bills to be taken up in calendar order. Unlike the House, however, the Senate would routinely suspend that rule in order to conduct its business. To force such a suspension, a bill that no one wished to consider would be placed at the top of the Senate calendar. In a number of sessions of the legislature, this "blocking" bill was one that dealt with county compost! Custom and tradition dictated that this piece of legislation never be considered. Thus, every other bill taken up by the Senate was technically out of order, even if they followed each other on the calendar, because this first one had been skipped. The Senate eventually simplified its procedures by adopting a rule that required an absolute two-thirds majority vote—21 of 31—to bring a bill to the floor (this is the rule that became a source of contention during the gerrymandering brouhaha discussed previously). Once a bill is brought up and debated, then a simple majority—16 of 31—is all that is required to pass it. Historically, then, the Senate has required more people to agree to talk about a bill than it has required to pass that bill.

This may seem puzzling, but there really is a reason for this practice. Over the years, the Senate decided it should use precious debate time on those bills that have the greatest likelihood of passage. After all, nothing is more frustrating to a legislator than to spend hours or even days debating a bill only to reach some impasse that prevents passage. Requiring a two-thirds vote to call up a bill forces its author and supporters to seek consensus before the bill gets to the floor. Compromises made to get the bill up for discussion make it more likely that the bill will pass once it is brought up. Conversely, issues that create sharp, often irreconcilable differences among senators usually don't even make it to the floor. Seen in this light, the Senate's peculiar way of doing business makes a bit more sense. However, critics of this process charge that the "two-thirds" rule precludes many important issues from Senate deliberation simply because they are controversial and not readily amenable to the kinds of compromises need to secure the necessary number of votes to allow debate. This in turn may allow problems to grow and thus may place the legislature in more of a crucial policy quandary at a later date. Moreover, the increased spirit of partisanship manifested in both regular and special sessions in recent years have led some in the Senate to at least consider abolishing this time-honored means of regulating the agenda.

As in the House, the Senate votes on a bill at the conclusion of debate and a majority vote passes the bill. But remember: once a bill passes one house, it must be sent to the other and undergo the rites of passage once again. Some legislators attempt a shortcut here by lining up a member of the other house to introduce an identical bill in that chamber. With both bills working their way through the House and Senate at the same time, final passage sometimes can be hastened.

If the versions of a bill passed by the two houses differ, then a conference committee must be appointed to work out those differences. Composed of five representatives and five senators, this body tries to reach a compromise agreeable to both houses. Any such compromise must be arrived at by majority vote of both groups of conferees. The agreed-on compromise is then sent back to the respective houses for their reactions. They may accept or reject the committee's recommendation, but they may not amend it. If accepted by both houses, the bill goes to the governor for

This diagram displays the sequential flow of a bill from the time it is introduced in the House to final pasage and transmittal to the governor. A bill introduced in the Senate would follow the same procedure in reverse.

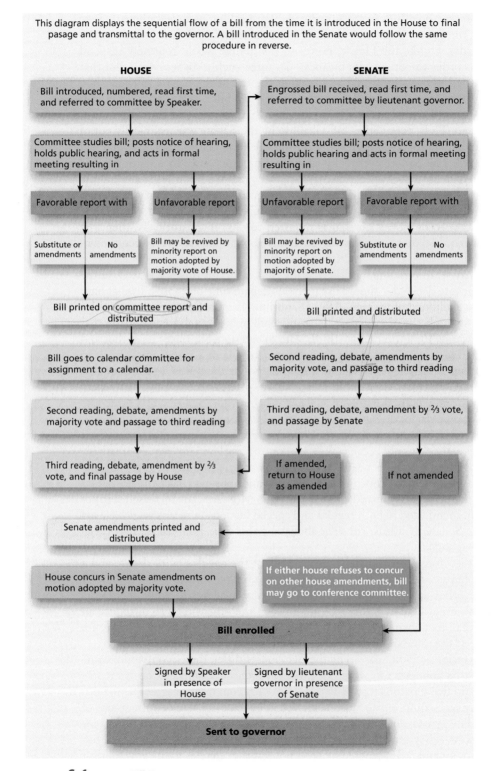

FIGURE **6.1** How a Bill Becomes a Law.

his or her action. If he doesn't veto it, the bill becomes a law, and the bill's author can relax for the first time in months.

Ways to Kill a Bill

Of course, the process we've just described seems rather orderly when viewed on paper as part of a nice, neat flowchart. Remember, however, that hundreds of bills are at various points on that chart at any given time. Committees may be juggling scores of bills in various stages of study. Members rush from floor session to committee meeting and back numerous times in a day.

In the midst of such frantic activity, it becomes very difficult to keep track of one bill, much less several. It also becomes very easy to kill a bill in all the confusion. In fact, if bills were birds, they'd be on the endangered species list. The reason is fairly simple: to pass a bill you have to do several hundred things right, but to kill one you only have to mess up one of those several hundred things. Let's look at only a few of the ways a bill can be killed. The presiding officer can effectively kill a bill by referring it to a hostile committee. So, if the Speaker or the lieutenant governor doesn't like you or your bill, you lose even before you've had a chance to play. If you make it by the presiding officer, you've got to deal with a committee. If a committee chair doesn't like you, your bill will get pigeonholed and never see the light of legislative day. Or the committee could amend your bill to death, incorporating so many changes that it no longer does what you wanted it to do the way you wanted it to be done. In such a situation, the author usually withdraws the bill from consideration, effectively killing it.

If your bill makes it out of committee, it may run afoul of the House Appropriations or Senate Finance Committees, which could decide to gut the funding for it. In that case, even if your bill passed, it couldn't be implemented and you'd still lose. Then there's the Calendars Committee in the House. If one of its members recalls the time you embarrassed her at a cocktail party, she may even the score by placing your bill so far down on the calendar that it will never reach the floor. During floor action, your bill may be saddled with crippling amendments. And the Senate provides some added opportunities for legislative homicide at this point. Remember the "two-thirds" rule? Make 11 senators mad and they'll vote not to call your bill up. No debate, no vote, no bill. Or let one senator get bent out of shape and he's likely to start talking. Such a filibuster in the waning days of a session can prove fatal. Then there's "**tagging**." Under this rule, any senator may request in writing a 48-hour delay in considering a bill in order to allow for adequate public notification. Although a bill may only be "tagged" once, when this happens at the end of a session, it also can deal a deathblow to a bill.

Finally, your bill may not find a sponsor in the opposite house. Or a conference committee might not be able to find a compromise both houses can live with. Or the governor could veto it. So the wonder of the legislative process is not that a bill is ever killed; the wonder is that some do occasionally make it through this labyrinth and actually become laws. In the Texas Mosaic nearby, you will find a listing of some of the more interesting bills that passed, or failed, in the 2009 session.

"tagging"
A senate rule that allows a senator to postpone committee consideration of a bill for forty-eight hours in hopes of killing it.

Texas MOSAIC

There Oughta Be a Law . . .
And now there is!

The 81st Texas legislature adjourned its regular session *sine die* on June 1, 2009. By that time, legislators had sent 1459 bills to the governor, of which he eventually vetoed 35. These new laws dealt with a multitude of issues both old and new, including those discussed below.[18]

Money. The biennial state budget enacted by the legislature called for spending $182.3 billion. This amount was achieved without members having to tap into the state's $9.1 billion rainy day fund, thus ensuring something of a financial cushion going into the next budget cycle.

Public Education. The state's public education budget was increased by some $1.9 billion over current levels of funding. This included an increase in the per capita allotment for students each district receives and an across-the-board $800 pay increase for teachers. Also, reforms in the public school accountability system will now emphasize mastery of such frontline subjects as English, math, science, and social studies, and will focus on greater career and/or college preparation.

Higher Education. Funding for public higher education was increased by $1.2 billion over current levels. An additional $250 million in financial aid is now available to enable approximately 35,000 more students to attend college. A framework was created to facilitate the emergence of so-called tier one research universities in the state, and the top 10 percent college admission rule was modified to give universities more control over their admission policies.

Health. The legislature modified the state's Children's Health Insurance Program (CHIP) and Medicaid procedures to provide payment to doctors and hospitals based on outcome quality rather than number of procedures performed. They also implemented a uniform patient health care information system.

Criminal Law. Penalties for gang-related offenses were enhanced and now certain gang members may be subjected to increased electronic monitoring. New programs were also authorized to prevent the initial involvement of young people in gang activity.

Natural Disasters. Members enacted legislation to improve the state's ability to prepare for and respond to natural disasters in reaction to the devastation visited on the Texas Coast by Hurricane Ike. And improvements in the Texas Windstorm Insurance Association program are aimed at providing better financial protection to Gulf Coast residents and communities.

And now there isn't . . . Several controversial pieces of legislation did not make it through the meat grinder that is the Texas legislature during the most recent session, and these included bills on the following topics:

Voter Identification. Several bills requiring voters to show alternate forms of identification in addition to a voter registration card were introduced, but died in the last days of the session due to a chubbing effort by House Democrats.

Transportation. Members from the Fort Worth–Dallas metropolitan area struggled mightily to pass legislation that would give local governments the authority to enact additional taxes to fund alternative mass transit systems (including greatly expanding light rail options). A coalition of antitax members doomed their effort in the waning days of the session.

Concealed Handguns. Several bills to allow holders of concealed handgun licenses to carry their weapons onto the campuses of public colleges and universities were introduced. The bills specifically forbade these institutions from prohibiting such actions, and each bill listed dozens of cosponsors. However, late session opposition from a number of groups, including law enforcement organizations, student associations, and college faculties helped to bring about the bills' demise.

The Legislature in the Political Arena

The internal complexities of the legislative process are enough to drive a reasonably sane person to the point of distraction. But legislation does not occur in a vacuum. Numerous elements from the larger political arena also affect the making of laws, and these factors can prove to be crucial at times.

Legislative Support

As was pointed out in Chapter 5, information is the most valuable commodity in the legislature. During the hectic pace of a regular session, members need as much information as they can get. For this, they often rely on a number of governmental support groups.

Aside from their own staff members, legislators can also call on the resources of the **Texas Legislative Council**. This body was created to provide research and bill-drafting services to members. Overseen by a group of legislators, including the two presiding officers, the staff of the council can help legislators with legal and other kinds of research and with the actual writing of bills. Legislators also have access to the Legislative Reference Library, an extensive collection of materials including up-to-date compilations of Texas and U.S. legal codes. The Legislative Budget Board provides members with a working budgetary document each session, and the Legislative Clipping Service furnishes them a daily anthology of political news items taken from newspapers around the state. You can see what's happening at the Legislative Council, the Reference Library, and the LBB by logging on to the previously mentioned Texas legislature Online Web site at http://www.capitol.state.tx.us and navigating to their respective home pages.

Texas Legislative Council
The legislature's research and bill-drafting service.

Another source of support for legislators is information received from state agencies. These agencies depend on the legislature for their very existence, so they manage to develop a kind of mutually beneficial relationship with members over time. This is especially true of agency heads and the committees with which they regularly interact. For example, Commissioner of Higher Education Dr. Raymund Paredes regularly represents the interests of the agency he heads, the Higher Education Coordinating Board, before House and Senate committees. These committees and their chairs have frequently called on Paredes as well as the Coordinating Board staff for timely information, or have asked them to study and make recommendations with regard to higher education policies and practices. Such relationships can give legislators the information they need and provide the agencies involved with familiar (and friendly) faces at budget time.

Last, but certainly not least, are interest groups. As we've discussed previously, interest groups can often generate far more accurate and detailed information than the various in-house groups on which legislators frequently depend. And, as is the case with veteran agency heads, members often ask experienced lobbyists to provide data from the interest group's information storehouse. In fact, veteran observers of the legislature note that sometimes it's difficult, if not impossible, to tell the lobbyists from the legislators without name tags. Over the years, as legislators, lobbyists, and agency heads find themselves spending hours together hammering out public policy, certain bonds of respect and dependence develop. (For a discussion of this "iron triangle," see Chapter 5.) Such relationships are important for the information they can provide members, but they also can create problems when the narrow, parochial interests of agencies and interest groups are promoted over the broader interests of the general public.

Other Players

The final group of players in the legislative game comes from many areas. One of the more important is the governor. Although the office of governor in Texas is constitutionally weak, a governor with the right kind of personality can have a significant impact on the legislative process. A governor who shows a willingness to work with the legislature usually stands a good chance of seeing some of his or her own programs adopted. Successful governors carefully choose issues with which the legislature is already sympathetic, quietly cultivate personal relationships with House and Senate members, and avoid confrontations with the presiding officers.

In this regard, Governor George W. Bush gave a clinic in gubernatorial-legislative relations during his tenure in office. For example, as he prepared to assume the office for the first time in 1995, he noted which issues—tort, welfare, and education reforms, along with revising juvenile justice—had been the focus of legislative attention prior to the regular session. Realizing that these issues would probably be around for some time, he endorsed them as his own. During the course of that session, he managed to invite every Senate and House member to the mansion for informal visits. And early on, he made clear his willingness to work with Lieutenant Governor Bullock and Speaker Laney in achieving mutually agreed-on goals. This strategy resulted in a clean sweep for Bush and his legislative allies in those areas.

However, his successor, Rick Perry, has not been as successful in his dealings with the legislature. His perceived aloofness from the legislative process has produced a distinctly cool relationship with members of the House and Senate, and he is viewed by a number of legislators as being unwilling to get involved in the hammering out of tough policy solutions. His ill-fated attempt to mandate human papillomavirus (HPV) immunizations for young girls in 2007 gave members an excuse to "put him in his place" by rebuffing the proposed policy.

Another player of significance is the comptroller of public accounts. The constitution requires that the state maintain a balanced budget. In 2009, as discussed in the Inside the Federalist System box nearby, the national government's stimulus package played a big role in helping Texas balance the budget. The legislature is prohibited from spending more money than the comptroller certifies as being available during a biennium. This gives her some powerful leverage in the budgetary process. The legislature says how the money will be spent, but the comptroller says how much will be spent. (For a fuller discussion of the role of the comptroller in Texas politics, see Chapter 8.)

Within the House and Senate, the various legislative caucuses occasionally have an impact on the formulation of public policy. In this context, a caucus is simply a group of legislators who share a common bond or interest and who come together to promote or protect that interest. Examples in the Texas legislature include the House Republican and House Democratic Caucuses, which are obviously partisan-based; the Texas Conservative Coalition, uniting conservative

INSIDE
THE FEDERALIST SYSTEM

The 2009 Stimulus Act

That the relationship between the national government and the state governments is constantly changing is almost a given. This can readily be seen in the economic recession that began in 2008, and the resultant policy initiatives that have come from the federal government to assist financially strapped state governments. The 2009 economic stimulus package passed by Congress provided hundreds of millions of dollars to state governments to enable them to meet their current obligations and/or expand their services in response to the human needs engendered by the downturn. While some state officials, including Governor Rick Perry, quickly sought to make political hay with conservative supporters by threatening to refuse such federal funds, it became apparent early in the 2009 legislative session that members of the Texas House and Senate would not be so quick to reject such stimulus money. Several members of the legislature publically called the governor out on such threats, and the House even went so far as to create a select (temporary) committee, the Federal Economic Stabilization Funding Committee, to direct the use of the federal largesse that was due the Lone Star State.

Democrats and Republicans alike; and groups like the Mexican American Legislative Caucus and the Legislative Black Caucus, whose organizational basis is the ethnicity of their members. Such groups try to build coalitions and rally support for issues of particular concern to their members.

Another force to which legislators occasionally respond is constituents, who provide input from time to time. Unfortunately, this is not always as important a source of information and ideas as it should be. In an ideal world, an informed, interested electorate would regularly communicate its wishes to elected representatives. If experience is any indicator, Texas is no ideal world in this respect. House and Senate members rarely hear from their constituents at all, and often the messages they do receive are indecipherable. The simple fact is this: a legislative session usually is not a good time to try contacting a senator or representative to express your concerns. Things are just too hectic during that time, and your representative probably won't be able to give you the attention you deserve.

The Legislature and You

So how are you supposed to relate to these men and women elected to act in your behalf? We've already seen that they are impossibly busy during a legislative session. And the demographic reality of modern Texas is such that you're not likely to run into them in the express checkout lane at H-E-B or Wal-Mart. As we have seen, each Texas senator represents more than half a million people and each representative counts more than 139,000 people as constituents. Making yourself heard in such a crowd might seem to be difficult, but it's not impossible. Make contact. Communicate with your legislators and express your concerns, then maintain this contact. One communication from a constituent may be easy to ignore; regular correspondence from that constituent isn't. All legislators have e-mail addresses, and you can find these at the Web site for the legislature, Texas Legislature Online. *Regular* communication with your elected representatives is as close and convenient as a personal computer.

Finally, a communication strategy that may set you apart from other constituents is to tell your representative what you like about his or her actions. Most legislators get both ears full when they do something people don't like, but they rarely hear from folks when they get it right. Make an effort to meet your senator or representative in person, preferably between sessions of the legislature when his or her schedule is less hectic. And after you've had your say, listen to them. You might learn something. Most importantly, hold them accountable. Monitor what happens during the session and see if they do what they promised. If they don't, call their hand. Remember, they work for you. Will this sort of citizen response (and responsibility) take place? We hope so, but it will take a concerted effort on your part because democracy is neither quick nor easy. In any event, you can't claim ignorance of the process. The next move is up to you.

Summary

The legislature is the primary branch of government in Texas. A bicameral (two-house) body, it is composed of the 31-member Senate and the 150-member House of Representatives.

Senators are elected to four-year terms and representatives serve two-year terms. Through the process or redistricting and the practice of gerrymandering, legislators draw their own district lines. The lieutenant governor presides over the Senate and the Speaker presides over the House. "The team," a group of friends and political allies among each house's membership, aids them. The main work of the legislature is done by committees, which allow the two houses to divide their labor efficiently and thus get more work done. The most important of these bodies are the standing committees, which are formed each time the legislature meets. All bills introduced will be referred by the presiding officer to a standing committee. The committees will take action on the bills by recommending passage, or they will refuse to consider them. Bills reported out go to the floor for debate and vote. If a bill passes in one house, it is then sent to the other house for consideration. If the House and Senate pass different versions of a bill, a conference committee tries to reach a compromise. Legislators must deal with agency heads, lobbyists, the governor, and other players while engaged in the legislative process. Citizens can also be a factor if they are patient and persistent.

Chapter Test

1. A law-making assembly made up of two deliberative bodies is called a _____ legislature.
   a. unicameral
   b. bicameral
   c. multicameral
   d. tricameral

2. Members of the Texas House of Representatives must be at least _____ years of age in order to hold office.
   a. 21
   b. 26
   c. 30
   d. 35

3. Members of the Texas Senate must reside in the state _____ years prior to their election.
   a. 2
   b. 3
   c. 5
   d. 10

4. The process of drawing legislative districts so as to either help or hurt a person's or a party's chances of winning election is known as
   a. chubbing.
   b. filibustering.
   c. salamandering.
   d. gerrymandering.

5. The case of _____ applied the "one person, one vote" concept to the Texas legislature.
   a. *Reynolds* v. *Simms*
   b. *Kilgarlin* v. *Martin*
   c. *White* v. *Regester*
   d. *Grovey* v. *Townsend*

6. The _____ is elected by the members of the legislative body over which he presides.
   a. governor
   b. lieutenant governor
   c. Speaker of the House
   d. comptroller of public accounts

7. Committees enable the legislature to
   a. provide for an efficient division of labor.
   b. develop legislative expertise.
   c. maintain an institutional "memory."
   d. all of the above.

8. The so-called two-thirds rule is used by _____ in order to bring bills to the floor for discussion.
   a. both the House and the Senate
   b. neither the House nor the Senate
   c. the House
   d. the Senate

9. The delaying tactic known as _____ grows out of the Senate's rule providing for unlimited debate.
   a. filibustering
   b. gerrymandering
   c. chubbing
   d. schmoozing

10. A _____ committee is used to resolve the differences between House and Senate versions of a bill.
    a. standing
    b. procedural
    c. conference
    d. interim

Answers: 1. b   2. a   3. a   4. d   5. b   6. c   7. d   8. d   9. a   10. c

Critical Thinking Questions

1. Discuss the basic structure of the Texas legislature and identify the roles played by the presiding officers and "The Team."

2. Discuss the committee system in the Texas legislature, including the different types of committee and how they work.

3. Discuss the process whereby a bill becomes a law, noting the various ways in which a bill can be killed during this process.

Key Terms

apportionment, **p. 151**
conference committee, **p. 167**
committees, **p. 156**
filibustering, **p. 172**
gerrymandering, **p. 154**
interim committee, **p. 168**
Legislative Budget Board (LBB), **p. 159**
limited seniority system, **p. 162**
"one person, one vote," **p. 152**
pigeonholing, **p. 171**

redistricting, **p. 152**
regular session, **p. 149**
single-member districts, **p. 153**
special committee, **p. 167**
special sessions, **p. 149**
standing committees, **p. 166**
"tagging," **p. 175**
Texas Legislative Council, **p. 177**
"the team," **p. 163**

Notes

1. Texas Constitution, art. 3.
2. Ibid.
3. Ibid.
4. Ibid.
5. Legislative Reference Library of Texas, *81st Legislature (2009)–Statistical Profile.* http://www.lrl.state.tx.us/legis/profile81.html.
6. Texas House of Representatives, *Office of the Chief Clerk.*
7. Texas Legislature Online, *Texas Senators of the 81st Legislature.* http://www.senate.state.tx.us/75r/senate/Members.htm.
8. Legislative Reference Library of Texas, *81st Legislature (2009)– Statistical Profile.* http://www.lrl.state.tx.us/legis/profile81.html.
9. Texas Constitution, art. 3.
10. *Reynolds* v. *Sims*, 377 U.S. 533 (1964).
11. *Kilgarlin* v. *Martin*, 252 F. Supp. 404 (1966).
12. Texas Constitution, art. 3.
13. The contemporary poster boy for wandering in the political wilderness as a result of openly opposing the election of a speaker would have to be Representative Lon Burnam of Fort Worth. Burnam resolutely voted against the election of Tom Craddick as House Speaker,

and this open defiance of the speaker resulted in Burnam being sentenced to service on committees whose jurisdiction only rarely coincided with the interests and concerns of his constituents. Moreover, Burnam routinely was unable to get even a hearing in committee on most of the bills that he proposed and almost never succeeded in passing legislation. Obviously, openly opposing the Speaker comes at a tremendous price.

14. Bob Bullock was one of the most colorful and controversial figures in Texas politics. His life and legacy are brilliantly treated in Dave McNeely and Jim Henderson, *Bob Bullock: God Bless Texas* (Austin, TX: University of Texas Press, 2008).

15. Texas Legislature Online, *Senate Committees, 81st Legislature.* http://www.capitol.state.tx.us/Home.aspx.

16. Texas Legislature Online, *House Committees, 81st Legislature.* http://www.capitol.state.tx.us/Home.aspx.

17. Legislative Reference Library of Texas, *81st Legislature (2009)–Bill Statistics.* http://www.legis.state.tx.us/Reports/Report.aspx?ID=legislativestatistics.

18. Texas Legislature Online, *Office of the Lieutenant Governor.* http://www.ltgov.state.tx.us/prview.php?id=225.

The Governor

7

Texas secedes from the Union. Sam Houston refuses to take a loyalty oath to the Confederacy and is removed as governor

Jose Felix Trespalacios becomes the first governor of the Mexican state of Texas.

1822   **1846**   **1**

J. Pickney Henderson becomes the first governor of the state of Texas under the U.S. flag

By the end of this chapter on the governor, you should be able to . . .

★ Describe the most significant powers possessed by the governor, including the ability to call special sessions and a veto that is very difficult to override.

★ Explain how the governor has an integral role in the legislative process.

★ Analyze the effectiveness of the governor's appointive powers.

★ Explain how the governor's military, clemency, and judicial powers are insignificant compared to the powers of other state's chief executives.

★ Analyze how the governor shares power with several independently elected executive officials.

★ Explain the governor's use of informal powers.

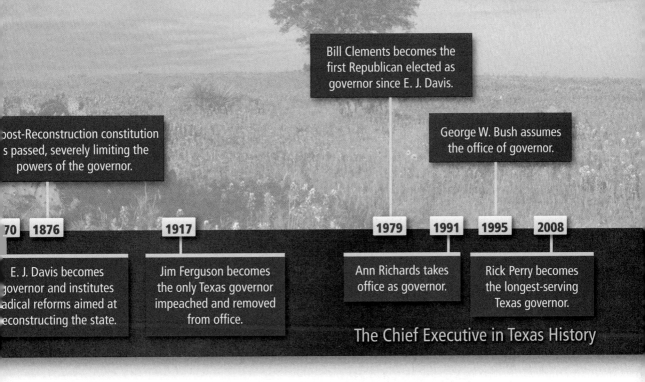

Bill Clements becomes the first Republican elected as governor since E. J. Davis.

George W. Bush assumes the office of governor.

post-Reconstruction constitution s passed, severely limiting the powers of the governor.

70 1876   1917   1979 1991 1995 2008

E. J. Davis becomes governor and institutes adical reforms aimed at econstructing the state.

Jim Ferguson becomes the only Texas governor impeached and removed from office.

Ann Richards takes office as governor.

Rick Perry becomes the longest-serving Texas governor.

The Chief Executive in Texas History

You can put lipstick and earrings on a hog and call it Monique, but it's still a pig.

—FORMER GOVERNOR ANN RICHARDS, ON FAILED GOVERNMENT PROGRAMS

When candidates run for **governor**, they naturally campaign on bold, broad themes regarding how they will transform Texas. Most governors *want* to be involved in the decision-making process. If asked who is the head of state government, the average Texan would likely answer, "the governor." Most citizens view the office as the head of the executive branch, if they think about it at all. They believe that, acting as a chief executive, the governor has wide-ranging powers that allow him or her to exert control over the state's bureaucracy. In Texas, nothing could be further from the truth.

At the 1875 constitutional convention, members of the Texas Grange and other opponents of former Governor E. J. Davis were determined to rein in the power of the executive (see Chapter 2). Reacting in part to the perceived abuses by the Davis administration, they split executive power among several elected officials, reverting to a method used prior to 1869. By creating this plural executive, they ensured that

governor
The state's highest elected executive official.

no one person could ever exercise the broad powers that Davis had. Major executive offices would be independently accountable to the voters. Additionally, a system of boards and commissions has evolved that further restricts the governor's power. As a result, newly elected governors are saddled with boards comprised of members appointed by their predecessor.

In order for a governor to succeed in implementing legislative initiatives within this environment, he must use informal powers effectively. It is not enough for the governor to wait at his or her desk until a bill arrives that he or she can sign or veto. Instead, the governor must communicate with legislative leaders, offer advice, listen to the concerns of others, and establish his or her agenda in order to affect legislative outcomes.

Qualifications, Term, and Salary

A person must be at least 30 years old, a resident of Texas for five years, a U.S. citizen, and a registered voter in order to be elected to any executive office in Texas. In reality, successful candidates for governor tend to be financially well-off and have spent years building credibility and name recognition within their party. Running for governor is an expensive endeavor, and even wealthy candidates need financial assistance from PACs and interested individuals.

In 2002, in a race that will likely prove to be an aberration, the top two candidates combined spent almost $100 million on their election efforts. The independently wealthy Democrat, Tony Sanchez, ponied up more than $60 million of his own money in his losing effort. Incumbent governor Rick Perry, spending less than half of his opponent's total, still won by about 18 percentage points. Even under normal circumstances, however, it cost $20 million for a candidate to fund a serious race. In 2006, Perry's campaign spent over $30 million, more than his four competitors combined. Historically, governors in Texas have been white men. Ann Richards is the most recent exception.

Governor Bush was unique in that he had never held elective or appointive public office before winning the governorship in 1995. Most Texas governors are married, Protestant, and between their late 40s and early 60s when first elected to office. The term of office is four years. Attempts to limit terms have repeatedly failed. This lack of term limits gives the Texas governor an advantage over colleagues in other states. Term limits make governors instant lame ducks, allowing the legislature to discount their significance because of their upcoming departure. Likewise, some governors have two-year terms, forcing them to run for reelection on an almost continuous basis.

Prior to Governor Bush's reelection in 1998, no Texas governor had ever been elected to consecutive four-year terms. In a state where incumbents generally fare well in statewide races, this office was the exception. The primary factor in the governor's inability to retain office has been the divergence between the public's expectations and the governor's actual power. Voters expect much from the governor and hold him accountable when things go wrong. The Texas Constitution, meanwhile, limits his ability to act in an effective manner. Governors can seldom live up to their promises or to the people's expectations. Nonetheless, in 2006, Perry became the first Texas incumbent governor to be twice reelected to four year terms.

The governor's salary is $115,345. This makes him or her one of the highest-paid governors in the nation. You can visit the governor's Web site at: http://www.governor.state.tx.us.

The Governor's Powers

Most experts consider the powers of the Texas governor to be limited. Keith Mueller's classic study attempted to compare the power of governors by ranking them according to four criteria (see Table 7.1). He concluded that only two states, South Carolina and Mississippi, have less powerful governors than Texas. Texas falls well below the mean score of state chief executives. Such studies may be interesting from a comparative perspective, but they nonetheless contain serious shortcomings. For instance, in determining total power ranking, the index weights all four factors equally. In reality, some powers are more important than others. Furthermore, the study only considers constitutional or statutory powers without considering the way in which the powers are used within the political environment in each specific state (see the "Veto Power" section below).

TABLE 7.1 Ranking of Selected Governors Using Mueller's Scale

STATE	TENURE	APPOINTIVE	BUDGET	VETO	TOTAL
Massachusetts	5	5	5	5	20
New York	5	4	5	5	19
California	5	3	5	5	18
Ohio	4	4	5	5	18
Michigan	5	2	5	5	17
Alabama	4	3	5	4	16
Oklahoma	4	2	5	5	16
Arkansas	2	4	5	4	15
Texas	5	1	3	3	12
Mississippi	3	1	1	5	10
Mean:16.18					

SOURCE: Keith J. Mueller, "Explaining Variation and Change in Gubernatorial Powers, 1960–1982," *Western Political Quarterly* 38 (1985). Reprinted by permission of the University of Utah, copyright holder.

formal powers
Powers granted by the constitution or statutes.

It is clear, though, that compared to many states, the **formal powers** of the Texas governor are limited. For instance, the governor has little budgetary authority. In 41 other states, the governor has the primary responsibility for creating the budget.

Although the governor has thousands of opportunities to make appointments to various boards and commissions in a single four-year term, two factors limit this power. First, overlapping terms ensure that the former governor continues to affect Texas politics after leaving office. Second, the most important executive offices in the state are elected by voters, not appointed. Still, the governor has several notable formal powers that he can use to influence government operations. More importantly, the governor must use his or her informal powers pragmatically in order govern effectively.

Executive Powers

The primary purpose of the executive branch is to carry out laws. In this capacity, the governor can appoint executive boards and commissions, as well as exercise law enforcement and military responsibilities. The governor has little control over the day-to-day operations of the executive branch, however, as most government employees are picked through a merit selection process that precludes their removal for political reasons. From a positive perspective, this ensures that competent workers cannot be removed because of political differences. From a negative one, it prevents a governor from dismissing public employees who work to thwart his or her agenda.

Appointment Powers

The governor of Texas has significant power to appoint board and commission members. It is common practice in Texas for governors to appoint major campaign contributors to these positions. For example, when openings occurred on the Parks and Wildlife Commission, Governor George W. Bush appointed Richard Heath, who had contributed $114,849 to his campaign, and Lee Bass, who gave $47,500. Likewise, many of Perry's appointees had contributed to his campaign; a *Houston Chronicle* report tabbed the total at about $5 million. Conversely, though, only about 1 in 10 appointees had contributed to the governor.[1]

Governors' appointments often receive close scrutiny as to the segments of the population represented. Hispanics made up only 11 percent of Bush's first-term appointments; African Americans, 7 percent. In each case, this represented substantially less than the representation given to the respective minority groups through Richards' appointments.[2] Richards tried to mirror the racial and ethnic diversity of Texas in her appointments, and she came close to doing so. In fairness to Bush, his appointments more nearly reflected the election returns. During his initial run for governor, his deepest support came from, and most of his early appointments went to, white males. Likewise, Perry's appointments have mirrored his supporters. Several years into his service, 16 percent of his appointments had been Hispanic—11 percent black and 3 percent from other minority groups. During this period, 36 percent of Perry's appointees were female.

senatorial courtesy
A discretion allowing senators to derail a governor's nomination from within their home district.

One legislative restraint on the governor's appointment power is the practice of **senatorial courtesy**. Under this informal practice, state senators can derail appointees from their home district. If the senator disapproves of the choice, tradition dictates that the appointment be defeated. Another constraint is that all appointments must be approved by two-thirds of the Senate. The importance of this is heightened by the evolution of Texas into a two-party state. Because neither party will control a two-thirds majority in the foreseeable future, no governor can ignore the opposition during the appointment process. Realistically, though, few appointees are rejected, as many have been serving for months before the legislature comes into session. Rejecting them after the fact would create chaos for the board or commission on which they served. 2009 was something of an exception, as two high-profile appointees, one to chair the State Board of Education and one to serve on Pardons and Paroles, were rejected by the Senate.[3]

overlapping terms
Terms of appointed board members that are staggered to ensure continuity of experience.

The major restraint on the governor's power in the appointment process is the six-year **overlapping terms** of board members. For at least the first two years of a term, a new governor interacts with agency boards dominated by appointees of the previous governor. Texas law makes no provision for the chief executive to remove seated board members who were appointed by his predecessor.

Essentially, this means that when Governor Bush entered office, he had to deal with a bureaucratic structure dominated by board members appointed by Governor Richards, the person he defeated in the previous gubernatorial election.

The governor is restricted even in efforts to remove his own appointees—he can do so only with two-thirds approval of the Senate. This limits the governor's control over state agencies. Once appointed, board members are all but free to ignore the governor's wishes. These restrictions are intentional. Conservative policy makers wanted to ensure that no governor would have absolute control over boards and commissions. One hundred and thirty-five years after E. J. Davis left the governor's office, his legacy lives on in a system designed to limit power.

Unlike many states, Texas has a plural executive, a concept that will be more fully explored in the following chapter. Key executive department heads, such as the attorney general and the comptroller, are elected independent of the governor. As a result, the governor has no formal control over their actions or their agencies. All of these officials have the primary responsibility for implementing policy within their respective agencies. Although they may listen to the governor's advice, they are under no obligation to follow it. The governor has no formal or constitutional power that would allow him or her to override the decisions of other elected executives. This significantly weakens the governor, who is thereby reduced to a figurehead in respect to bureaucratic oversight, being unable to review and control the actions of these agencies.

From 1991–1999, governors had to deal with major department heads who were from the opposition party. During his first term, Bush, a Republican, worked with a Democratic lieutenant governor, comptroller, attorney general, and land commissioner. In his second term, however, all department heads were Republican. When Rick Perry took office in 2000, and after he was reelected governor in 2002, 2006, and 2010, Republicans continued to hold all statewide executive offices. Perry's third straight four-year term is unprecedented in Texas gubernatorial history.

Military Power

The Texas Constitution gives the governor specific military powers. He can declare **martial law**. In the case of rioting or looting, the governor has extensive power to enact and enforce curfews and take other unconventional actions, although these powers are rarely used. He can also call out the Texas Guard in an emergency. Most often, this occurs when there is a natural disaster, such as the flooding that often accompanies hurricanes on the Gulf Coast. These powers are limited because significant military power resides with the national government.

martial law
The power to impose military rule during a crisis.

Law Enforcement Powers

The governor also has limited law enforcement powers. He appoints the public safety commissioner. He may also take control of the Texas Rangers (not the baseball team) in certain situations. Additionally, he can introduce legislation aimed at combating crime.

The Texas Army National Guard at a deployment ceremony at Baylor University. This deployment, of course, was at the behest of the president, not the governor.

Legislative Powers

Session-Calling Power

One of the governor's most significant powers is the ability to call special sessions. Not only does he have the sole authority to call these special legislative sessions, he also sets the agenda. This allows the governor to put the legislature in the spotlight and pressure it into action. If it fails to perform in a special session, where performance often translates into endorsing the governor's proposals, the legislature runs the risk of incurring the wrath of voters.

In most states, the legislature can call itself into session, but not in Texas. Reserving this power for the governor not only strengthens the executive, it also limits the legislature. The Grange gave the governor this power exclusively in order to create a roadblock for overzealous legislators.

The governor has sole power to set the agenda for such a session. The legislature cannot bring any issue to a vote in special session unless the governor gives approval. An astute governor can use this power to increase his or her influence, especially when the legislature has an issue it wishes to pass. Because the governor can add issues to the agenda, he or she can insist that the legislators pass the governor's program first. In 1984, for example, Governor Mark White knew that the legislature was not particularly interested in passing his controversial and expensive education reform bill in an election year. He also knew that highway construction programs are always popular with campaigning politicians. Therefore, he promised to open the session to highway construction if education reform was passed first. His plan worked.

The governor can keep the legislature in session indefinitely, providing another incentive for it to cooperate. Although each special session can last no more than 30 days, the governor may call an unlimited number of sessions. The threat of a special session can likewise be used to encourage the legislature to enact the governor's agenda during the regular session. With pay of only $600 per month, legislators don't want to spend more time in Austin than is absolutely necessary. In 1995, when his education reform package seemed to be foundering, Bush encouraged the legislature to pass a bill by issuing such a threat. As a result, the package passed in regular session. Throughout the 1990s, special sessions, common in the 1980s, became less frequent as legislators learned the value of finishing their business on time.

The early 21st century would be a different story. After having no special sessions from 1991–2001; comprising the entire Bush administration, Governor Perry called three sessions in 2003, one in 2004 and two in 2005. The three sessions of 2003, discussed in detail in Chapter 4, dealt primarily with redistricting. The 2004 session—a spectacular failure, tried to restructure the state's education financing system. When the 2005 regular session likewise failed in its reform efforts, Governor Perry called the House and Senate back into special session twice, producing no significant results. The legislature's repeated refusal underscores an important point: In Texas, the governor can't *make* anyone do anything. However, in 2006, facing a Texas supreme court order to reform funding or face a school system shutdown, the legislature did enact reform; significantly cutting local property taxes while expanding business taxes. We'll look at the reform package more closely in Chapter 12. In 2009, a special session was required after the legislature failed to complete legislation renewing several major agencies, including the departments of Transportation and Insurance.

Message Power

The state constitution requires the governor to address the legislature on the condition of Texas. This "State of the State" address occurs at the beginning of each legislative session. It gives the governor the opportunity to address the entire legislature directly and to make suggestions, presenting his or her legislative agenda. The significance of this power is directly related to the governor's persuasive ability (see "Informal Powers" section below).

Veto Power

Studies of gubernatorial powers routinely rank the Texas governor among the lowest. As noted earlier, the mid-1980s study by Mueller placed the Texas chief executive 48th out of the 50 states. The low scores for appointive and budget powers are essentially correct, and only seven governors ranked below Texas in **veto power**.[4] Yet, in the past 60 years, the legislature overrode only one veto by a Texas governor, as we discuss in the Inside the Federalist System box. Few other states' governors can make such a claim. In fact, the one override came under unique circumstances.

In 1979, during the first legislative session under Republican Bill Clements, Democrats still controlled both the House and Senate with more than a two-thirds majority. When the governor vetoed a relatively minor local bill, the Democratic legislature used the opportunity to send two messages. First, despite the change at

veto power
The ability of the governor to strike down legislation, subject to override.

the governor's mansion, the Democrats were still firmly in control of the legislature. Second, a rookie governor should not interfere with a legislative tradition: local bills, which affect only a limited area, generally do not garner opposition.

Under normal circumstances, obtaining a two-thirds majority to override a veto is a daunting task. However, many bills pass the House and Senate with overwhelming margins, yet still fall victim to the governor's veto pen. A major difficulty in overriding the governor's veto lies in the structure of the legislative session. Meeting for only 140 days every two years means that a great deal of legislation must be created in a short time-span.

Because of legislative rules, most bills that pass do so toward the end of the session. The Texas Constitution gives the governor ten days, excluding Sundays, to decide whether to veto a bill, sign it, or let it become law without his or her signature. If that time frame extends beyond the end of the session, the governor may hold the bill for an additional 20 days. Unlike the Louisiana legislature, which can call itself into session for the sole purpose of overriding a veto, the Texas legislature cannot override a **post-adjournment veto**. Such vetoes are absolute. The great majority of bills are passed within the last two weeks of the session, so this enables the governor to kill most legislation with which he or she disagrees.

post-adjournment veto
A veto administered after the legislature has adjourned; in Texas, it cannot be overridden.

In 2001, Governor Perry used the post-adjournment veto to kill HB 660, a measure that would have established a career and technology education advisory board. He vetoed the bill despite the fact that it passed overwhelmingly—139:2 in the House and 30:0 in the Senate. Nonetheless, Perry was able to stop the legislation by holding his veto until after the legislature had left Austin.

The governor can often accomplish more with the threat of the veto than with the actual use of it. The fact is that, under normal circumstances, few bills are vetoed. In 1999, for instance, fewer than 2 percent of the bills that passed the legislature were vetoed. The rest became law. Nonetheless, legislators know that the governor has almost absolute power to kill a bill. They also realize that because of biennial sessions, a dead bill stays dead for two years. (The governor will not allow a bill that he or she opposes to be considered in special session.) Therefore, if the governor expresses opposition to provisions of a bill, the sponsors of that bill are likely to attempt a compromise. Because of this, and because the governor wants to maintain cordial relations with the legislature so that his or her agenda will be given proper consideration, the overwhelming majority of bills that pass are signed into law.

The year 2001 was an entirely different story. New governor Rick Perry vetoed 82 of the 1,600 bills passed by the legislature in what became known as the Father's Day Massacre. Eighty of the 82 were applied on the third Sunday in June, after the legislature had adjourned. More than 5 percent the legislature's bills were killed by the governor' pen. It was not, however, the *number* of vetoes that was remarkable; that percentage isn't that much above the historical norm (1999 was unusual for the low percentage of vetoes issued). It was the *manner* in which Perry went about killing the legislation.

Normally, Texas governors indicate what they are going to veto. Perry, however, killed numerous bills that legislators thought he was going to sign, infuriating many, including several within his own party. Major fence-mending was needed as the former rancher entered his first full-term in office. Perry vetoed 48 of 1384 bills passed in 2003, only 19 of 1389 in 2005, 51 of 1481 in 2007, and 34 of 1459 in 2009.[5]

In 1995, Governor Bush showed that he knew how to use gubernatorial power despite the fact that he was new to political office. One of the cornerstones of his legislative program was welfare reform. Among the items that Bush considered vital were limits on the time a person could spend on welfare and a freeze-out period that would keep applicants from reapplying for a specified period of time. The bill that entered the conference committee did not meet his standards regarding a freeze-out, so he let it be known that he would veto it unless the three-year exclusionary period was lengthened. He would either call the legislature into special session in order to pass an acceptable welfare reform bill or use his executive power to petition the federal government grant Texas a waiver, so that it could impose stricter rules on a trial basis. One opponent of the freeze-out ended up supporting it in conference committee, pointing out that welfare reform might become even more restrictive in a special session or under a federal government waiver. He acknowledged that Bush had managed a victory on the issue by threatening to veto the bill.[6]

In 1991, Ann Richards wielded power in a unique way when she decided not to veto a controversial bill. The legislature had passed a redistricting bill favored by Democrats in the Texas Senate. In most cases, a Democratic governor would be happy to sign such a measure, but representatives of many minority interest groups believed the bill was unfair to minority voters, who had been a big part of Richards' 1990 electoral victory. They pressured her to veto. Senate Democrats let it be known that a veto would derail the advancement of her future legislative initiatives. Richards solution was to let the bill become law without her signature—if a Texas governor does nothing with a bill, it becomes law. As a result, she could tell minority groups that she sympathized with their argument and therefore refused to sign the bill, yet still give Senate Democrats the redistricting plan they wanted.

In 2007, there was a notable increase in filing statements attached to bills that passed without the Governor Perry's signature. All 20 bills that passed without the governor's affirmation included his specific objections or constitutional concerns. Because of the governor's lack of executive power, it would be difficult for him to use these statements as a basis for thwarting implementation of policy.

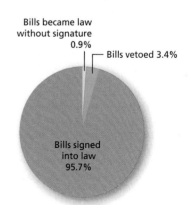

Note: the overwhelming number of bills passed by the legislature become law without interference from the governor.

FIGURE **7.1** **The Governor's Vetoes, 2007–2009.**

Governor Rick Perry works the floor of the Texas House for votes. How can personal appeals from the governor impact the legislative agenda?

Budgetary Powers

Line Item Veto Power

line item veto
The governor's ability to delete individual items in the appropriations bill.

In addition to a standard veto, the governor also has a **line item veto**. This allows him or her to veto one or more items in the appropriations bill while signing the rest into law. Although it technically has the authority, the legislature has not overridden a line item veto in state history. Appropriations bills are always passed at the end of the session, allowing the governor to hold the bill past the legislature's adjournment and issue a post-adjournment veto, which cannot be overridden. This gives the governor an extraordinary amount of negotiating power on spending bills. The Texas governor does not, however, have a reduction veto, which would allow him or her to reduce an appropriations item without eliminating it. In those states that allow the governor to reduce a spending item without vetoing it, the legislature usually has the opportunity to override the reduction and reinstate the original spending figure.

Generally, the line item veto is used as incremental budget management—that is, the governor cuts a small percentage of overall state spending. In 2005, however, Perry vetoed the entire $33.6 billion public education budget, forcing the legislature into special session with orders to reform education finance so that schools could open in the fall. Under attack in some quarters for a perceived lack of leadership, Perry took a bold step to put himself at the center of the political storm. In fact, the action ended up being more show than substance as the governor signed a reintroduced version of the $33.6 billion when significant education reform failed to materialize. Perry did, however, make about a half a billion dollars in legitimate cuts to the $139 billion document.

In 2007, Perry line item vetoed $647million, including $153 million for community college worker health insurance—funding that was later restored through a compromise with the Legislative Budget Board. Prior use of the line item veto has been more typical. In 2003, Perry vetoed about $79 million from the final budget; in 2001, he line item vetoed a little more than half a billion dollars from the $113.8 billion biennium budget. Most of the axed items were appropriations for bills that either failed to pass or were vetoed. They had to be included in the budget because their fate was unclear when the final appropriations bill was put together. Over the past several sessions, most such vetoes have been of items that were dead anyway, so the action is usually more of a housekeeping measure than a substantive political action. In 2009, none of his legislative vetoes were substantive, as all were either of bills that failed to pass or bills that the governor vetoed.

Budget Creation Power

In 42 states, the governor has full responsibility for drafting the budget. Texas is one of only 8 states in which the governor shares this power with the legislature. In practice, not much sharing occurs. The Legislative Budget Board (see chapters 6 and 12) controls the budget process in Texas. In fact, the legislature pays no attention to the governor's budget at all. In 2003, Governor Perry submitted a budget containing nothing but zeros. Although he caught significant flak from the media, his broader point was that the legislature should start with a blank slate while preparing the state's appropriations bill. The House and Senate paid no attention.

This lack of budgetary power contributes significantly to the governor's weakness, at least in comparison to his counterparts in other states. The governor can transfer or withhold funds from an agency only on approval by the LBB. Legislation in 1991 further weakened the executive's budgetary authority by allowing the LBB to initiate such changes, then seek approval from the governor. This allowed legislators to ignore the governor during initial deliberations on such transfers or withholding. Remember, however, that the line item veto helps the governor retain a significant role in spending decisions.

Judicial Powers

Appointment Power

Although the Texas Constitution requires the popular election of state judges, the governor nonetheless has a significant role in shaping the judiciary. Because the governor appoints judges to fill vacancies at the district level or above, more than half of Texas judges were originally appointed. Like all other appointments, the Senate must approve the governor's nominee by at least a two-thirds concurrence.

Clemency Power

The **clemency powers** of the Texas governor are quite restricted. Unlike the chief executive in many states, the governor of Texas has no independent power to pardon or parole.

clemency power
Power to pardon, commute, or parole.

The governor can make recommendations to the Board of Pardons and Paroles and can approve or reject their recommendations of pardon or sentence reduction. A 1934 constitutional amendment, which we discuss in the Constitution box, stripped the governor of independent power. This amendment came in the wake of a scandal. During Miriam Ferguson's term as governor, the easiest way to win a loved one's freedom was to visit Ferguson's husband, Jim, with cash in hand (see Texas Mosaic: James E. Ferguson). Removing pardoning powers from the governor lessened the chance that the chief executive would be directly involved in graft or corruption.

The only independent clemency power that the governor possesses is the ability to grant a 30-day reprieve in a death penalty case. In today's law-and-order society, the reprieve is seldom granted. Politicians cannot afford to appear soft on crime if they wish to win reelection. One notable case of a granted reprieve took place in 1979 when Governor Clements issued a stay for Randall Dale Adams. Adams, who

The Texas Constitution: A Closer Look

Compared to the President, who has unlimited power to pardon those accused of federal offenses, the governor's clemency powers are rather limited. The primary reason for the limits, of course, was the perceived abuses that occurred during the tenures of James E. and Miriam Ferguson. The governor is encumbered with a Board of Pardons and Paroles, as provided for below.

ARTICLE IV

Sec. 11. BOARD OF PARDONS AND PAROLES; PAROLE LAWS; REPRIEVES, COMMUTATIONS, AND PARDONS; REMISSION OF FINES AND FORFEITURES.

(a) The Legislature shall by law establish a Board of Pardons and Paroles and shall require it to keep record of its actions and the reasons for its actions. The Legislature shall have authority to enact parole laws and laws that require or permit courts to inform juries about the effect of good conduct time and eligibility for parole or mandatory supervision on the period of incarceration served by a defendant convicted of a criminal offense.

(b) In all criminal cases, except treason and impeachment, the Governor shall have power, after conviction, on the written signed recommendation and advice of the Board of Pardons and Paroles, or a majority thereof, to grant reprieves and commutations of punishment and pardons; and under such rules as the Legislature may prescribe, and upon the written recommendation and advice of a majority of the Board of Pardons and Paroles, he shall have the power to remit fines and forfeitures. The Governor shall have the power to grant one reprieve in any capital case for a period not to exceed thirty (30) days; and he shall have power to revoke conditional pardons. With the advice and consent of the Legislature, he may grant reprieves, commutations of punishment and pardons in cases of treason.

sat for years on death row, was later released from prison when further evidence exonerated him. The governor can issue only one such reprieve per prisoner. In 1993, after Ann Richards issued a stay in the Leonel Herrera case, Herrera was rescheduled for execution (see Chapter 10). With no further reprieves possible, the prisoner was put to death.

Informal Powers

Because of limited formal powers granted by the constitution or state law, the governor often relies on **informal powers** to affect government operations. These powers lie outside the constitutional mandate of the office. Nonetheless, they are an important part of the total arsenal of weapons that the governor has at his or her disposal.

informal powers
Powers not specifically granted in the constitution or statutes.

Partisan Leader

The governor is the leader of his or her political party. It is the governor's responsibility, as the party's most visible member, to articulate political positions. In effect, and with apologies to the state chairs, the governor speaks for the party. The governor can introduce a legislative package that reflects the values of his or her party. He or she must be able to convince members to vote the party line on key votes. Concurrently, the governor must be able to work with members of the opposition party and not appear to be so partisan as to alienate the public. While some Republicans criticized Bush for not being partisan enough, the governor managed to forge an effective relationship with Democratic leaders. Governors do not always take the partisan role as seriously as do other party members. When asked about the controversial Republican state platform during the 1994 campaign, Bush claimed he had not even read it. Perry's election in 2002 marked the first time since Reconstruction that the Republicans won both the governorship and control of both houses of the legislature.

Persuasive Power

Most people, both in and out of Texas, see the governor as the state's leader. This perception allows the governor to achieve goals in areas that may be beyond the office's constitutional or statutory reach. As a representative of Texas, the governor strives to project a positive image for the state. Former Governor Richards effectively used the platform of her office to induce businesses to move to Texas, as we discuss in the nearby Texas Mosaic on her. In a weak governor system, acting as an advocate for the state is one of the most valuable roles the governor can assume.

More than any other state official, the governor can influence public opinion. The governor's speeches are more likely to receive media coverage. The governor has access to a statewide network of newspapers and television stations. Through effective manipulation of the media, a governor can bring pressure on both the legislature and other members of the executive branch. Television and the Internet give contemporary Texas governors an advantage that their predecessors did not have: the ability to go into the living room of virtually every home in the state.

Texas MOSAIC

Two for the Price of One:
James E. Ferguson

James E. "Pa" Ferguson rose from humble beginnings to be twice elected governor of Texas. Despite his sparse formal education, Ferguson was both a lawyer and a bank president before entering politics in 1914. A political unknown, he vaulted to the governor's office through his astute handling of the hot prohibition topic: he refused to take a side. He argued that Texans had been hung up on the wet/dry issue long enough, and were tired of it, and that there were other, more important issues that the state needed to address.

Pa was something of a populist, advocating and signing into law a provision that limited the rent landowners could charge tenant farmers. The law made him popular with poor Texans, although it would ultimately be overturned by the Texas supreme court. Ferguson also worked to improve the education system and oversaw the creation of the state highway department. His first term was a legislative success.

His second term was not as smooth. In June 1917, after serious quarrels with the faculty and administration of the University of Texas at Austin, Ferguson line-item vetoed the entire appropriation for the school. Although a technicality created by the attorney general kept the university open, Ferguson had committed a political blunder. Antagonizing the University of Texas alumni association is not exactly a swift political move. Repercussions followed quickly.

Texas House Speaker Franklin Fuller called a special session of the Texas legislature in order to consider the impeachment of Ferguson. This, of course, was not a legal action, as only the governor can call a special session. Having just been indicted on criminal charges for the misappropriation of state funds, Ferguson took the bizarre step of endorsing the session, making it

legal. Had he not given his approval, he could not have been impeached.

The House impeached Ferguson on 21 charges. The Senate found him guilty on 10, removed him from the governorship, and barred him from holding office again. The day before he was removed, Pa resigned, claiming this action enabled him to run again. He did attempt to run in 1918, but was handily defeated by William Hobby in the Democratic primary.

Jim Ferguson wielded power even after he was no longer governor.

The Hobby defeat did not mark the end of Pa Ferguson in Texas politics. Although initially an opponent of women's suffrage, Ferguson took advantage of the newly enfranchised gender by running his wife, Miriam "Ma" Ferguson, for governor in 1924. Working as a team, the Fergusons campaigned against the Ku Klux Klan, which controlled Texas politics at the time. Miriam won, becoming the first woman governor of Texas, and Jim set up office in the Capitol. Clearly the power behind the throne, Pa established policy and made a bit of money on the side as he did his best to ease prison overcrowding.

Ma was defeated in her 1926 reelection bid. In 1932, however, as the Great Depression spread through the state, Miriam was elected again. When she—or he—chose not to seek reelection in 1934, the Ferguson era finally came to an end.

SOURCES: Rupert N. Richardson, Adrian Anderson, and Ernest Wallace, *Texas: The Lone Star State* (Englewood Cliffs, NJ: Prentice Hall, 1993). *Seymour* v. *Conner, Texas: A History* (Arlington Heights, IL: Harlan Davidson, 1971).

Texas governors have failed to exploit this power to its full advantage, however. They have seldom made effective use of the media in order to prod the legislature into action. Rather, most seem to prefer a hands-on approach to legislative influence. Governor Perry, more media savvy than most, was the first Texas governor to have a blog, Twitter, Facebook and Flickr presence.

Governor Bush used his personality to inject himself into the governmental process. Through frequent meetings with legislators, Bush tried to maintain a presence within the system. By the end of his first legislative session, almost all members of the Texas House and Senate had visited the governor's mansion for lunch.

Even the state Supreme Court justices had dined with the governor. Bush displayed a willingness to listen to those with more governmental experience. As a result, he integrated himself into the legislative process and earned favorable reviews from state leaders, even those within the opposing party.

Furthermore, interacting with a cross-section of legislative members helps ensure that the governor does not become isolated. All too often, chief executives at both the state and national level surround themselves with like-minded individuals—this happened with Bush during his presidency. If all the governor's closest advisers share common views, he or she can become isolated from dissenting opinion. This can lead to a policy mistake that would have appeared obvious to outsiders.

As governor, Bush avoided these types of problems by maintaining connections that transcend both political ties and branches of government. His successor, Rick Perry, has had problems getting along even with members of his own party. He did not maintain the close legislative ties that Bush had created, and actions like the Father's Day Massacre further strained legislative relations.

Congressional Liaison

Governors Richards and Bush actively lobbied Congress for programs that benefited Texas. Richards worked to ensure that the state would receive proper reimbursement after the cancellation of the Super Collider project. Often, she worked with Republican U.S. Senator Kay Bailey Hutchison in lobbying for fairness in federal funding for Texas. Likewise, Bush used the power of the governor's office to plead with Congress for a just allocation of Medicaid money. Both governors realized that the visibility of their office entitled them to speak on Texas's behalf regarding state interests. Governors have a unique opportunity to influence members of the U.S. House and Senate, especially those from their home state.

International Relations

With the growing importance of international trade to the Texas economy, the governor also plays an important role in international relations, especially with Latin America in general and Mexico in particular. Governors Bush and Perry have both worked to improve the relationship with our neighbor to the south. Implementation of the North American Free Trade Agreement (NAFTA) has pushed trade to the forefront of relations between Texas and Mexico, but the state and nation have also worked closely on water resource questions and other border issues. Although the relationship is much friendlier than it was a decade ago, points of tension remain. In late summer 2002, for example, President Vicente Fox canceled a trip to meet with Bush at the "Texas White House" to protest Perry's refusal to stop the execution of a Mexican citizen convicted of capital murder. No permanent damage occurred, however, as Fox almost immediately scheduled a meeting with Perry shortly thereafter. Perry also stood in opposition to those in his party who wanted to build a wall along the entire border between Texas and Mexico, believing that the proposal was impractical and unworkable. It is important to realize that because of Texas's special relationship with Mexico, the job of the governor has evolved to include informal ambassador as well.

Leadership Style

In Texas, a governor's approach to his job has a significant impact on how much power he wields. In the past, some governors have approached the office in a manner consistent with the wishes of the creators of the Texas Constitution. They chose not to involve themselves heavily in day-to-day operations. As a result, their impact on government was minimal. During Bill Clements's second term, for example, the governor failed to fill hundreds of vacancies on boards and commissions. Dolph Briscoe ran the governor's office like it was a part-time job he did not really need. He seemed more interested in playing the role of a gentleman rancher.

In contrast, governors Richards and Bush threw themselves into the political fray. Richards played the part of the political veteran, an insider who had all the answers. She was an expert on Texas government and let those around her know it. She was not afraid to rub political opponents, or allies, the wrong way. Bush, on the other hand, first played on the perception that he was a newcomer to Austin, soliciting advice and opinions. More congenial in the role than Richards, he took care not to criticize members of the opposition party openly, and he attempted to build consensus. It was a quality Bush maintained through his second term and into his run for the White House. His bipartisan approach was not as easy to maintain once he arrived in Washington.

Another difference between Richards and Bush is that Richards involved herself in more policy decisions. Bush, during his first legislative session, concentrated on four key issues. His agenda included welfare reform, juvenile justice reform, education reform, and tort reform. The legislature passed measures acceptable to Bush on each of these, but he realized that he would expend too much political capital fighting every fight. Instead, he concentrated on battles he either knew he could win or believed were of fundamental importance. On other issues he let his opinion be known. Rather than creating political showdowns over relatively minor bills, he knew he could issue a post-adjournment veto to stop those that he opposed. The important common denominator between the leadership styles of these two successful governors is that each created a distinct, comfortable working environment and stuck to it.

Perry ascended to the office after Bush became president. Although he had been elected as lieutenant governor in 1998, Perry had neither the benefits nor the limitations of having established an agenda while running for governor. This is part of what led to tensions with the legislature; no one was sure where the new governor stood on issues, and Perry wasn't quick to stake out his stands. The Father's Day Massacre (see above "Veto Power" section) strained relations even more. However, when running for the office on his own, Perry put forth an agenda that would set the course for the 2003 term, giving himself a set of goals and his opponents a set of targets. Hit by a huge budgetary shortfall not of his making, but was a result of a nationwide recession and economic downturn, the 2003 session was tough on the new Republican leadership. Perry's endorsement of Speaker of the House Tom Craddick's and U.S. Congressman Tom DeLay's efforts for a midcensus redistricting of Texas congressional seats damaged the office's bipartisan perception. In both the 2004 called and 2005 regular sessions, Perry failed to shepherd through an education finance reform package, leading to the 2005 special sessions, which failed just as miserably. However, education finance reform finally passed in 2006, as we discussed earlier in this chapter.

The Governor's Staff

A competent **staff** is critical to effective governing. In the early 1990s, the governor's staff in Texas grew to be among the largest in the nation. In 1994, and again in the early days of the Bush administration, the office was downsized. Some functions were transferred from the governor's office to executive departments and agencies and others were eliminated. Examples of transferred programs include Headstart, which was moved to the Health and Human Services Commission; and the governor's energy office, which now resides in the General Services Commission. Nonetheless, the staff of about 270 remains large enough to serve the governor's needs effectively, giving him or her a substantial advantage over counterparts in other states. Many governors' offices are significantly understaffed.[7]

The governor's office is divided into several separate entities, such as the Administrative Office, the Criminal Justice Division, and the Policy Office. Staff members are chosen by the governor and serve at the governor's discretion. Unlike other

staff
The governor's aides; not subject to legislative approval.

Texas MOSAIC

Increasing Gender Diversity:
Ann Richards

For years, the executive branch of Texas government was a males-only club. Although Miriam "Ma" Ferguson held the office, she did not hold the power. Ann Richards helped bring down the ceiling that blocked women from holding some of the highest offices in the state.

After six years as a Travis county commissioner, Richards ran for state treasurer. During her two terms she did much to modernize the office. She shortened the time between the receipt of funds and their deposit in interest-bearing accounts, began the process of tax flow analysis for the state, and ensured that more state funds were deposited in interest-bearing accounts. Richards also introduced computerization, a big step in allowing for the treasury's eventual merger into the comptroller's office.

In 1990, Richards ran for governor. Her steady, enthusiastic campaign, although underfunded in relation to Republican opponent Clayton Williams, managed to capture a close race. Richards won because, unlike Williams, she made few mistakes along the way. An experienced campaigner, she took advantage of the Republican's political naïveté. Williams had a practice of saying the wrong things to the press at the wrong time. His statements made great headlines, but they helped Richards look like the more savvy and stable candidate.

As governor, Richards worked to bring businesses to Texas. She was so successful that the state of California began to run anti-Texas ads in nationwide business magazines. Although less successful in helping the state preserve the federally funded Super Collider project, she did manage a financial settlement on terms favorable to Texas.

An iconic shot of Governor Ann Richards.

Her legislative efforts were less productive. She successfully blocked both limitations on abortion rights and a bill allowing Texans to carry concealed weapons, but the former schoolteacher was unable to pass comprehensive education reform. She did manage to ram through a funding equalization bill that passed state Supreme Court scrutiny, but it won her few friends among voters who had defeated a similar proposal in a statewide vote less than three months before.

Richards, who lost her reelection bid in 1994, appointed more minorities and women to state boards and commissions than any other governor. While her rhetoric often sounded liberal, she would become the first governor in years to sign a budget without a tax increase. She believed that the Texas government could be responsive, efficient, and inclusive. Richards passed away in September 2006.

gubernatorial appointments, no legislative approval is necessary. The staff is accountable to the governor alone and must look after his or her best interests as they give advice.

In addition to carrying out the governor's policies, staff members are often involved in intergovernmental relations. They work with national or local levels of government to aid in the implementation of laws and policies. One of the most important offices within the governor's staff is the Legislative Office. These staff members are, in effect, the governor's lobbyists. They present the governor's views and advocate his or her positions to the legislature. They help develop policy initiatives.

The governor has little time to take broad ideas, such as reforming welfare policy, and turn them into concrete programs. Staff help decide what specific measures the proposals should contain. In addition, the staff advises the governor on how to get the most out of the legislative process, helping to bring proposals forward when they are most likely to pass.

Over the course of a four-year term, the governor will make about 3,000 appointments to various boards, commissions, and judicial vacancies. No individual can know the best potential appointee for each position, so an able staff is invaluable. Two sections of the governor's staff, the Office of Governmental Appointments and the Policy Office, share primary responsibility for assisting with appointments. The Office of Governmental Appointments also works as a liaison between the governor and the agencies, boards, and commissions. Members of the Policy Office bear the responsibility of ensuring that the governor's policies are implemented.[8]

Options for Reform

Any discussion of reform in the Texas executive branch should begin with the realization that the writers of the Texas Constitution deliberately sought to create a weak executive. Despite the problems encountered by a weak governor in modern political administration, many Texans to this day would be suspicious of efforts to give the governor more power. So, just because several proposed reforms may be interesting intellectually, it is unlikely many will ever be enacted. While some reforms may be desirable to many in the state, it should be noted that simply changing the powers of the governor would not, in itself, guarantee better government.

One way to increase the governor's power would be to give him or her removal power over executive department appointees. Likewise, board terms should conform to the governor's term, allowing former appointees to remain on the job only until the new governor appoints new people. In this way, board members are directly accountable to the governor, and the voters can justifiably hold the governor responsible when board members prove either incompetent or at odds with public opinion.

The plural executive could be changed to a cabinet form of government. The governor could appoint the attorney general, comptroller, and other executive offices with policy-making powers. With these offices serving at the governor's pleasure, a team concept would develop in the executive branch. Infighting would be reduced (though not eliminated). The endless squabbles occurring within any presidential administration in Washington, as an example, mean that Politics, among other things, Happens.

Another option to increase the governor's power would be to return all budget preparation authority to him or her. This is the norm in most states. In Texas, however, the Legislative Budget Board's handling of the budget during the past several years has been so astute that such a change makes little sense simply in order to give the governor more power.

The reforms suggested here, no doubt, would strengthen the governor. More importantly, they would increase accountability while simultaneously giving the governor power to make government operate more effectively. It would give the governor the tools to meet the expectations placed on the chief executive by the voters.

WHAT CAN YOU DO?

According to a rating system devised by Professor Thad Beyle, Texas has the twenty-fourth most powerful governor in the U.S. The ratings are based on institutional and personal powers including a governor's tenure potential, interparty control, and appointment, budget, veto, and organizational powers.

Read Beyle's report, Gubernatorial Power: The Institutional Power Ratings for the 50 Governors of the United States (http://www. unc.edu/~beyle/gubnewpwr.html), and consider how constitutional and other restrictions placed on the Texas governor inhibit his or her ability to govern a state that has evolved dramatically since 1876. Consider writing a letter to your state senator or representative asking them to propose a constitutional amendment that will permit the governor to become more efficient within "the plural executive."

TEXAS GOVERNORS SINCE 1899

Joseph D. Sayers	Jan. 1899–Jan. 1903
S. W. T. Lanham	Jan. 1903–Jan. 1907
Thomas Mitchell Campbell	Jan. 1907–Jan. 1911
Oscar Branch Colquitt	Jan. 1911–Jan. 1915
James E. Ferguson[1]	Jan. 1915–Aug. 1917
William Pettus Hobby	Aug. 1917–Jan. 1921
Pat Morris Neff	Jan. 1921–Jan. 1925
Miriam A. Ferguson	Jan. 1925–Jan. 1927
Dan Moody	Jan. 1927–Jan. 1931
Ross S. Sterling	Jan. 1931–Jan. 1933
Miriam A. Ferguson	Jan. 1933–Jan. 1935
James V. Allred	Jan. 1935–Jan. 1939
W. Lee O'Daniel[2]	Jan. 1939–Aug. 1941
Coke R. Stevenson	Aug. 1941–Jan. 1947
Beauford H. Jester[3]	Jan. 1947–July 1949
Allan Shivers	July 1949–Jan. 1957
Price Daniel	Jan. 1957–Jan. 1963
John Connally	Jan. 1963–Jan. 1969
Preston Smith	Jan. 1969–Jan. 1973
Dolph Briscoe	Jan. 1973–Jan. 1979
William P. Clements	Jan. 1979–Jan. 1983
Mark White	Jan. 1983–Jan. 1987
William P. Clements	Jan. 1987–Jan. 1991
Ann W. Richards	Jan. 1991–Jan. 1995
George W. Bush[4]	Jan. 1995–Dec. 2000
Rick Perry	Dec. 2000–

SOURCE: *Texas Almanac, 2006–07* (Dallas, TX: *Dallas Morning News*, 2006), pp. 423–424.

[1] *Impeached and resigned.*
[2] *Resigned from office to join U.S. Senate.*
[3] *Died in office.*
[4] *Resigned from office to become president of the United States.*

Summary

The Texas Grange intended to create a weak executive when they molded the 1876 Constitution. They succeeded in their goals. The Texas governor has weaker formal powers than those of counterparts in almost any state. Gubernatorial power is hampered by the independent selection of the plural executive, an institution that is discussed thoroughly in Chapter 8. Nonetheless, astute use of these limited formal powers, the post-adjournment veto and session-calling aspects in particular, can enhance the governor's ability to play a vital role in policy development.

For a governor to be most effective, though, the position requires the judicious use of informal powers. The governor must be a lobbyist, a spokesperson for the state, and a party leader. Each governor must create a leadership style that enhances his or her ability to govern. A governor who understands these principles, as well as the office's inherent limitations, can have an important impact on Texas politics.

Chapter Test

1. Regarding boards and commission appointments, the governor can
   a. appoint members independently.
   b. remove his or her own appointees with two-thirds Senate approval.
   c. remove a previous governor's appointees with thirds Senate approval.
   d. all of the above.

2. The most significant aspect of veto power is
   a. the veto cannot be overridden.
   b. the threat of a veto can influence legislation.
   c. the governor can veto portions of nonappropriations bills.
   d. it is automatically applied to any bill the governor does not sign.

3. In Texas, the governor appoints
   a. all judges.
   b. all appellate judges.
   c. Supreme Court justices only.
   d. district court and higher judges in the case of a vacancy.

4. The first woman governor of Texas was
   a. Miriam Ferguson.
   b. Ann Richards.
   c. Barbara Jordan.
   d. Martha Whitehead.

5. During a four-year term, a governor makes about
   a. 100 appointments.
   b. 500 appointments.
   c. 4,000 appointments.
   d. 10,000 appointments.

6. All are true of Ann Richards *except* she
   a. supported abortion rights.
   b. modernized the treasurer's office.
   c. was the second elected Republican governor since Reconstruction.
   d. was defeated in her reelection bid.

7. The Texas governor has significant veto power because
   a. there is no provision to override.
   b. a three-fourths vote is required to override.
   c. a postadjournment veto cannot be overridden.
   d. of the appropriations reduction power.

8. The special session agenda is determined by the
   a. governor.
   b. legislature.
   c. Speaker of the House.
   d. Legislative Budget Board.

9. The governor can serve
   a. unlimited four-year terms.
   b. unlimited two-year terms.
   c. only two four-year terms.
   d. only two consecutive four-year terms.

10. The governor's most important budgetary power is the
    a. budget creation power.
    b. line item veto.
    c. ability to control agency spending.
    d. ability to transfer funds independently.

Answers: 1. b 2. b 3. d 4. a 5. c 6. c 7. c 8. a 9. a 10. b

Critical Thinking Questions

1. Should the governor of Texas be given more power?

2. Which of the governor's powers is most important?

3. What is the biggest weakness of the Texas governor's office?

Key Terms

clemency power, **p. 195**
formal powers, **p. 187**
governor, **p. 185**
informal powers, **p. 197**
line item veto, **p. 194**
martial law, **p. 189**

overlapping terms, **p. 188**
post-adjournment veto, **p. 192**
senatorial courtesy, **p. 188**
staff, **p. 201**
veto power, **p. 191**

Notes

1. Stiles, Matt, Records Show Appointees Gave Texas Governor $5 Million, *Houston Chronicle.* May 4, 2009, http://www.chron.com/disp/story.mpl/metropolitan/6406108.html.

2. "Bush Trails Richards in Naming Minorities to State Boards and Agencies, Review Finds," *Dallas Morning News*, June 12, 1998, p. 22A.

3. R. J. Ratcliffe, "Perry Works with Texas Lawmakers to Salvage Bad Year," *Houston Chronicle.* May 14, 2009, http://www.chron.com/disp/story.mpl/headline/metro/6439800.html.

4. Keith J. Mueller, "Explaining Variation and Change in Gubernatorial Powers, 1960–1982," *Western Political Quarterly* (September 1985), pp. 42–47.

5. Vetoed Bills, 1860–2007, Legislative Reference Library of Texas. http://www.lrl.state.tx.us/legis/vetoes.

6. Sylvia Moreno, "Conference Committee Toughens Welfare Bill," *Dallas Morning News*, May 24, 1995, p. 20A.

7. *Fiscal Size-Up: 2006–07 Biennium*, Legislative Budget Board, p. 86.

8. *Fiscal Size-Up*, pp. 86–87.

The Plural Executive and the Bureaucracy

8

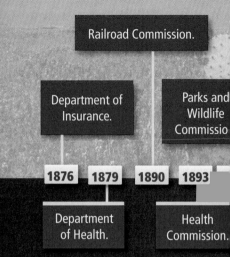

Railroad Commission.

Department of Insurance.

Parks and Wildlife Commissio

| 1876 | 1879 | 1890 | 1893 |

Department of Health.

Health Commission.

*Although some Texas agencies have changed names since their inception, their origins can be traced back to these years.

By the end of this chapter on the plural executive and the bureaucracy, you should be able to . . .

★ Differentiate between cabinet and plural executive forms of government.

★ Explain the roles of the Lieutenant Governor, Attorney General, Comptroller, Land Commissioner and Commission of Agriculture

★ Explain the selection process for the State Board of Education and the Railroad Commission.

★ Differentiate among the functions of various types of boards and commissions.

★ Explain how appointed boards can limit the governor's power.

★ Describe the purpose and process of The Sunset Advisory Commission.

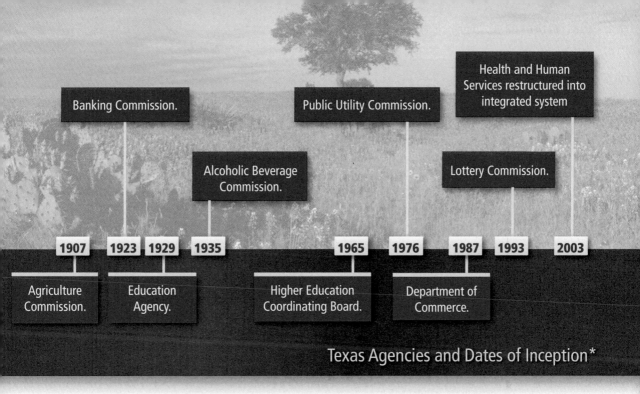

Texas Agencies and Dates of Inception*

Banking Commission. 1923 · *Agriculture Commission. 1907* · *Education Agency. 1929* · *Alcoholic Beverage Commission. 1935* · *Higher Education Coordinating Board. 1965* · *Public Utility Commission. 1976* · *Department of Commerce. 1987* · *Lottery Commission. 1993* · *Health and Human Services restructured into integrated system 2003*

Giving government money and power is like giving whiskey and car keys to teenage boys.

—P. J. O'ROURKE

As the chief executive of the United States, the president selects his or her top department officers—or **cabinet**—in order to help him run the nation. (See the Inside the Federalist System box nearby) At the state level, the cabinet system is also the normal structure. Thirty-nine states have such a form of government.

In Texas, however, there is no cabinet system. Rather, the state has a **plural executive**, whereby the governor, lieutenant governor, attorney general, comptroller, land commissioner, and agriculture commissioner are elected independently, as we illustrate in Figure 8.1. This reflects the state's conservative tradition, which feared the concentration of power in too few hands.

As a result, power is dispersed. One decidedly negative consequence is that most citizens are not aware of the identity of a comptroller or land commissioner, neither do they realize the talents needed to perform these jobs well. Yet citizens are

cabinet
A form of government where the chief executive appoints other major executive department heads.

plural executive
A political system whereby major executive officers are elected independent of the governor.

INSIDE
THE FEDERALIST SYSTEM

United States

One of the most important structural differences between the Texas and U.S. governmental systems is the limited executive power of the Texas governor. Most notably, the president appoints his or her cabinet, while the governor is encumbered with a plural executive. The chart below shows the disparity of power.

THE PRESIDENT APPOINTS:

Secretary of Agriculture
Secretary of Commerce
Secretary of Defense
Secretary of Education
Secretary of Energy
Secretary of Health and Human Services
Secretary of Homeland Security
Secretary of Housing and Urban Development
Secretary of Interior
Secretary of Labor
Secretary of State
Secretary of Transportation
Secretary of Treasury
Secretary of Veterans Affairs
The Attorney General
EPA Administrator
U.S. Trade Representative
U.S. Ambassador to the United Nations

NATIONAL OFFICIALS INDEPENDENTLY ELECTED:

None

Texas

THE GOVERNOR APPOINTS:

Secretary of State
Insurance Commissioner
Adjutant General

TEXAS OFFICIALS INDEPENDENTLY ELECTED:

Attorney General
Agriculture Commissioner
Commissioner of the General Land Office
Comptroller
Lieutenant Governor
Railroad Commission

still responsible for choosing the best person through the elective process. It is a safe bet that a majority of voters can neither name the executive officers they voted into office nor define the responsibilities of these leaders. A consequence of the plural executive is that consistency and teamwork are sacrificed.

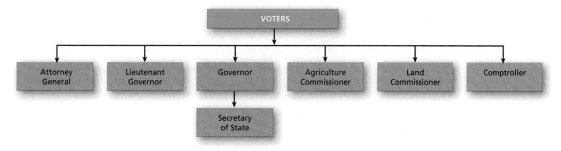

FIGURE **8.1** The Executive Branch Offices.

In addition to the inter- and intraparty rivalries, each executive won election by pushing his or her own agenda, which might not be consistent with the plans of the governor or fellow officers. This certainly acts as a check on the governor's power, but it also makes efficient government much more difficult to achieve. Independently elected executive officials limit the power of the governor. These offices have independent constituencies that they need to serve. The governor's opportunity to appoint executive officials is limited. A primary objective of the executive branch is to carry out laws. This is accomplished through an extensive bureaucracy, which employs a large number of workers. The governor has little direct control over this aspect of the executive branch.

Elected Officials

The Lieutenant Governor

Many political scientists believe that the office of lieutenant governor is the most powerful position in the state. Ironically, the greatest powers are in the legislative arena because of the office's role in the Texas Senate and the Legislative Budget Board (see Chapter 6). From an executive perspective, the lieutenant governor's role is to succeed the governor in the case of death, removal, or resignation. The lieutenant governor also serves in the governor's capacity when the latter is out of the state. In Texas, as is the case in about half of the states, the governor and lieutenant governor run for office independently. This creates the possibility that these executive officers will be from different parties, as was the case following the 1994 elections, but that has not been an issue over the last decade, as Republicans have won all statewide races.

In 1998 Rick Perry became the first Republican elected to hold the office, succeeding, the colorful Bob Bullock, profiled in the nearby Mosaic. Perry ascended to the governor's office when Bush became president. For two years, the office was technically vacant, although Senator Bill Ratliff served as acting lieutenant governor after being selected from among his peers. In 2002, Republican David Dewhurst was elected to the post. The former land commissioner, a self-made millionaire who made his fortune in real estate and investments after serving as a CIA agent, defeated Democratic stalwart John Sharp by five percentage points, the closest of the statewide elections that year. His 2006 and 2010 reelections were by landslides.

Lt. Governor David Dewhurst speaks with members of the press. Why are most of the office's powers considered legislative in nature?

Once an Election Day obscurity, despite being perhaps the state's most powerful office, the lieutenant governor's race has certainly entered the big leagues of Texas politics. The Dewhurst campaign spent close to $30 million on the 2002 election—at least $10 million from the candidate's own pocket—and started running television ads 18 months prior to the election. Sharp spent less, but still was in the eight-digit neighborhood, which is quite a lot for a position that pays $7,200 a year. The lieutenant governor's Web site can be accessed at http://www.senate.state.tx.us/75r/LtGov/LtGov.htm.

The Attorney General

attorney general
The state's lawyer; elected.

The **attorney general** (AG) is the state's lawyer. The office defends the state and its constitution in court and represents Texas in any litigation that the office initiates. As is the case in most states, the attorney general is elected. In Texas, he or she serves a four-year term.

The attorney general's position, while among the most prominent, is one of the least understood. In the past, most candidates for AG ran on a platform promising to be tough on crime, although the state's chief litigant has little to do with criminal prosecution. In Texas, prosecution is routinely handled by the county or district attorney's office (see Chapter 9). In most states, the attorney general can initiate criminal proceedings. Here, the chief legal officer has no such power. In fact, the Texas attorney general is one of the few who cannot, of his or her own initiative, intervene in local prosecutions. Campaigning as a tough-on-crime candidate, then, was quite cynical. It pandered to the public's fear of crime and insinuates that the

Texas **MOSAIC**

Old-Style Texas Politics:
Bob Bullock

"This morning, God got the first of many performance reviews from Bob Bullock. I'm sure heaven will become a much more efficient place, now that he is there," said Sen. David Sibley on the day Bullock died.

Bob Bullock was by no means a warm and cuddly politician. But he knew more about Texas government than anyone else. And he got things done. Sometimes through fear and intimidation, other times through doggedly finding the right answer and stubbornly sticking with it until others fell into line. During his 16 years as comptroller, he single-handedly modernized the office, giving it computers and professional financial analysis. He created the Texas Performance Review, which enabled the comptroller to save the state billions of dollars by recommending cost-saving measures at various state agencies. He parlayed that position into an 8-year stint as lieutenant governor, where he ran the state with an iron fist. He was at the forefront of efforts to revamp the state's education funding system. He helped reform welfare and criminal justice and won passage of legislation that limited lawsuits.

To call Bob Bullock a Texas legend is an understatement. Although there were many significant political leaders in Texas during the 20th century, none wielded power in quite the same way as the former lieutenant governor. Controversial, stubborn, and outspoken, Bullock gave "colorful" a whole new meaning in Texas politics. Bullock wouldn't have agreed with that

particular adjective; he said, "I just had a propensity for getting into trouble." A reformed alcoholic, he battled a lifelong addiction to cigarettes, had numerous health problems, was treated for depression and anxiety, endured a heart attack and a bypass operation, and married numerous times. His temper was quick and legendary. And you didn't ever want to end up on his bad side because he had a tendency to remember. He worked impossibly long hours and expected the same devotion from his staff.

Lt. Governor Bob Bullock was an icon in Texas politics. He wielded the gavel like it was a sledgehammer.

A lifelong Democrat, he once circulated a photo of former governor John Connally's head on the body of a turkey when the latter switched parties. Nonetheless, Bullock was one of the first political leaders to discern the national appeal of Republican George W. Bush. As early as 1997, he was touting Bush as a future president. He endorsed the governor's reelection bid in 1998, despite the fact that Bush's opponent was a former employee and the father of Bullock's goddaughter.

Bullock's signature expression was "God Bless Texas," a sentiment he felt so strongly about that, coming from him, it was part prayer, part demand.

average voter doesn't know enough to see through this approach. In the last three elections, however, candidates have run on issues actually related to the office.

The Office of the Attorney General (OAG) has about 4,200 employees. It employs some 400 attorneys and has 70 regional offices. One of the most important and active of the departments is the Consumer Protection Division. This office seeks to protect consumers from deceptive trade practices and citizens from unsafe conditions.[1] In the past decade, attorneys general from several states, including Texas, have joined together to sue companies such as Quaker Oats for making unsubstantiated health claims regarding their products. The Consumer Protection Division also investigates unfair and anticompetitive practices of businesses within the state. This enforces a state constitutional mandate to ban monopolies and protect consumers. In the late 1990s, attorneys general successfully pursued cases against tobacco companies for damages incurred by citizens who end up receiving state-financed medical care. These cases resulted in significant revenue for the state.

Through such lawsuits, the attorney general can significantly increase his name recognition. In 1994, as his reelection bid approached, former Attorney General Dan Morales filed a lawsuit against several fast-food chains operating in the state. He claimed that their smoking sections created unreasonable health dangers to children, whose business they were attempting to solicit. Morales not only reached an out-of-court settlement, whereby the franchises agreed to ban smoking, he also saw his name splashed across newspaper headlines throughout the state.

The primary purpose of the highly visible Child Support Enforcement Division is collecting child support. It works to establish paternity and locate absent parents. Funding for the office comes from a mixture of federal and state funds because child care enforcement is mandated under federal law. As a result, the office is somewhat limited as to how it operates because case priority is set by federal regulation. Former AG John Cornyn made a highly visible effort to publicize parents who are delinquent in their child support payments. His "Top Ten Evaders" posters were popular with the media.

As is the case in most states, the Texas attorney general has a significant role in tax collection and antitrust law. The Collections Division works to recover delinquent taxes. If a business is behind in its tax payments, the OAG can intervene. The OAG also has the responsibility of providing legal counsel to all state agencies, centralizing a service that was earlier provided by the individual agencies.

One of the most important branches of the OAG is the Opinion Committee, which provides interpretations of laws and regulations, or of the U.S. or Texas constitutions, for government agencies and the legislature. The opinions may either attempt to clarify existing laws or rules, or they may assess the constitutionality of proposed laws or rules. In 2003, for example, General Abbott issued an opinion in regard to a whether Texas could operate video lottery terminals under the state's constitution. In effect, "video lottery" machines can be set up to mimic slot machines. Abbott ruled that, short of a constitutional amendment, the Constitution bars such devices. You can read the entire opinion by going to: http://www.oag.state.tx.us/opinions/GA/GA0103.pdf.

These opinions can be overturned by Texas courts, but they carry significant weight with the Texas court system. The Texas Supreme Court and Court of Criminal Appeals have shown a willingness to follow the attorney general's opinions in most situations. The opinions carry the force of law unless overturned by the courts.

Traditionally, Texas attorneys general used the office as a stepping-stone to a higher position. Former Governor Mark White, elected in 1982, had previously served as the state's attorney general. Likewise, former attorney general Jim Mattox ran for governor in 1990 and Dan Morales ran in 2002. Both were defeated in the Democratic primary. Of the last nine governors, only White had previously served as attorney general.

In 1998, John Cornyn became the first Republican elected to the office. He had served on the state's Supreme Court prior to becoming the state's top lawyer. During his term in the office, Cornyn concentrated his efforts on lessening federal controls on the prison system, modernizing the state's child support collection efforts, and strengthening Texas's Open Meeting Laws, which keep the government from operating without public scrutiny.

Greg Abbott was first elected to the office in 2002. Also a Republican, he had served on the state Supreme Court. He pledged that he wouldn't carry a political

my turn

Open Government

by Greg Abbott

Attorney General of Texas

Among the most vital law enforcement duties of the attorney general of Texas is to serve as the public's watchdog for government in the sunshine and to defend against abuses of our open government laws.

That can range from answering questions about open meetings and public records to bringing enforcement action in the courts. For example, my office obtained the first-ever indictments by a Texas attorney general for violations of both the Public Information Act and the Open Meetings Act, in separate cases involving local officials in Texas.

My belief in aggressive enforcement of open government laws is based on my personal and professional commitment to the rule of law, to making certain that every citizen receives equal, fair, and transparent treatment under our system of justice.

Related to that are two appropriately balanced principles that are deeply ingrained in our democracy: Our system of government depends on a fully informed electorate, and a knowledgeable electorate depends on an open and accessible government.

These ideas predate both our nation and our state. Founding father James Madison, who was one of the principal drafters of the Bill of Rights, said: "A popular Government without popular information or the means of acquiring it, is but a Prologue to a Farce or a Tragedy or perhaps both. Knowledge will forever govern ignorance, and a people who mean to be their own Governors, must arm themselves with the power knowledge gives."

That attitude toward government eventually found its way to Texas. Reflecting the fact that Texas was settled by hardy individualists and won her independence through the shedding of patriots' blood, a commitment to the authority of man over government has always been part of the fabric of our political process.

In 1836, the Constitution of the newly independent Republic of Texas included this clear and uncompromising statement: "All political power is inherent in the people, and all free governments

Attorney General Greg Abbott, on the right.

are founded on their authority, and instituted for their benefit."

When Texas entered the Union in 1845, that precise language was included in the Bill of Rights of its new Constitution. The Constitution of 1876, adopted after Reconstruction and which remains the basic law of Texas today, uses exactly the same words. In fact, you'll find them chiseled in granite over the entrance to the State Archives in Austin. They are virtually sacrosanct in the Lone Star State.

Today, that spirit of government for and by the people is codified in what are known as the Texas Open Meetings Act (Texas Government Code, Chapter 551) and the Texas Public Information Act (Texas Government Code, Chapter 552).

Legislation requiring that meetings of most governmental bodies be open to the public and that the public be given proper notice was first adopted by the Texas legislature in 1967. With some changes, it continues to be our basic guarantee of open meetings and open decision making.

The role of the attorney general's office is to interpret the Open Meetings Act in written legal opinions and, when the law is ignored, to work with county and district attorneys to make sure it is enforced.

(continued)

(continued from page 213)

What was at first known as the Open Records Act, later the Public Information Act (PIA), was adopted by the Texas legislature in 1973, a landmark year for open government in Texas.

The catalyst for change was the Sharpstown stock-fraud scandal, in which Houston businessman Frank W. Sharp was alleged to have made loans to a number of state officials. Loan proceeds were used to purchase stock in his bank, stock which would increase in value once favorable legislation was approved. There were a number of convictions and several officials, while not directly accused or convicted, had their careers tainted as a result.

The 1972 elections saw turnover in most statewide offices and, most significantly for open government, the 1973 Texas legislature met in what has been called "a spirit of reform," with almost half of the House made up of newcomers.

James R. Nowlin, then a member of the Texas House and later a U.S. District judge, wrote at the time that the scandals "brought unusual and encouraging political pressures from a large segment of the general public for substantive action [and] closer statutory supervision" of government officials.

Led by House Speaker Price Daniel Jr., the son of a former attorney general (and the great-great-great-grandson of Sam Houston), a number of bills were introduced to reform the way government and elected officials did business. One of them, House Bill 6, became the Texas Open Records Act, signed into law by Governor Dolph Briscoe on June 14, 1973.

Language in the legislation, now codified in Texas statutes, was clear and to the point. It says that government is the servant and not the master of the people and that all citizens are entitled to complete information about what their government and public officials are doing.

Perhaps most emphatically, the legislation established as public policy for all time that "the people, in delegating authority, do not give their public servants the right to decide what is good for the people to know and what is not good for them to know. The people insist on remaining informed so that they may retain control over the instruments they have created."

In other words, our freedom limits government, but government can never limit our freedom.

The attorney general's office is frequently asked to interpret the parameters of open meeting laws and even more frequently required to rule on whether a public agency must release information.

Fortunately for the people of Texas, the enthusiasm with which the legislature approached open government in the early 1970s did not diminish once the bills became law. Between 1973 and 2005, open government laws were amended and refined, often to reflect changes in society or in technology, but they were never weakened and the principles that underlie them remained strong.

Today, in fact, Texas open government laws are recognized to be among the best in the nation. The national Freedom of Information Center often cites Texas as an example of how things should work.

The process is fairly straightforward. Any person can ask a governmental body for information. That information is presumed to be open, unless it falls within one of the PIA's specific exemptions or is confidential under another state law. The government agency must promptly release the information or ask the attorney general for a ruling.

Most observers consider the Texas law to be even tougher than the federal Freedom of Information Act, because it doesn't give government agencies the ability to decide for themselves what is public information and what is not. Texas law begins with the assumption that everything is public, with certain fairly narrow exceptions (such as information about active police investigations or corporate trade secrets).

Keeping up with open records requests is a mammoth undertaking. The Office of the Attorney General maintains a special hotline—(877) OPEN-TEX—just to answer open records questions. By 2004, it was getting 10,000 calls a year. Also in 2004, we received more than 11,000 requests from governmental bodies for rulings on the withholding of information, requests that we must rule on within a specific period of time.

The number of requests for rulings quadrupled between 2000 and 2004. In fact, we will issue more open records letter rulings in a typical two-week period (about 500) today than the office did in a full year (396) two decades ago.

It is not just numbers, however. As government agencies become more aware of their obligations, the requests for rulings are more sophisticated and more complex and take more time to answer.

Most of the increase can be attributed to the public's interest in knowing what government is doing and, in turn, government's desire to do what is right.

In a state as big as Texas, law can be lengthy, complex, complicated, and confusing. As a result, no matter how conscientious a public servant may be, and how dedicated to fulfilling his or her responsibilities, there are always opportunities for missteps. A big part of my job is to make sure government agencies and officials at all levels are aware of their obligations.

Our prosecution efforts confirmed several reasons why people don't comply with open government laws. First, some simply don't want to follow the law; they want to hide information. Second, some are foot-draggers who want to impede access to information by building barriers between themselves and the public's right to know. Third, and most frequently, the great majority of public officials simply didn't know the rules to follow.

To help make everyone's job easier, I asked the 2005 legislature to pass legislation requiring open records and open meetings training for more than 35,000 state and local officials in Texas. When the governor signed the bill mandating such training, it marked an important and positive step forward for open government.

This training will ensure that all public officials know the rules. It will reduce violations, increase compliance, and speed the time in which government responds to public requests for information. Most importantly, it will remove any excuses government officials might have had for not complying with the law, and they will know there are consequences for not following it.

The 2005 Texas legislature also passed a bill—the first in the nation—that requires more disclosure of information about how the public's money is invested in private funds. In the years ahead, I am confident that Texas open government laws will continue to adapt to changing public needs.

In the past three decades, each Texas attorney general has left a unique mark on the ideal of open government and public information. I am confident that will continue, because it is in the public interest. As the state's chief law enforcer, my commitment to open government will never waver. It is important to our democracy that the sun always shines on government in Texas.

agenda into office, saying that the attorney general's job is to enforce the law regardless of whether he agrees with it. His My Turn essay on open government appears in this chapter. The OAG's Web address is http://www.oag.state.tx.us. Abbott was elected to the office for a third time in 2010.

Comptroller of Public Accounts

Texas is one of only 13 states to elect the **comptroller** of public accounts. The comptroller is the state's accountant and chief tax collector. Significantly, the comptroller estimates state revenue and certifies that the legislature's appropriations bill falls within the revenue estimate. This is a by-product of the balanced budget provision of the state's constitution (see Chapter 12).

comptroller
The state's chief accountant and financial officer.

The comptroller's office exercises important powers. The position of state accountant may not sound like an enticing job and in most states, it's not, but in Texas, the office carries power for three primary purposes: (1) the comptroller tells the legislature how much money it has to spend, (2) the comptroller finds ways to save the state money and to spend funds more efficiently, and (3) the comptroller fills out federal grant paperwork. If the forms are filled out correctly, the state, with little or no additional effort, can end up with considerably more federal money. The office employs about 3,000 workers.[2]

Susan Combs, a former state representative and the previous agriculture commissioner, was elected comptroller in 2006. She defeated her Democratic opponent with 60 percent of the vote and did not draw a Democratic challenger in 2010. Combs worked to make the comptroller's office more transparent by giving the office a more navigable and inclusive online presence.

Prior to 2003, the comptroller had significant performance review power, allowing her to investigate state agencies and public schools, looking for inefficient

Comptroller Susan Combs at a press conference. Why is the comptroller an integral part of the budgetary process in Texas?

practices and searching for ways to save public money. It had been a successful endeavor, saving the state more than $10 billion during its dozen-year lifespan. Most of those review powers were stripped, however, when the previous comptroller, former Republican Carole Strayhorn, got into a political dust-up with Governor Perry, who she would unsuccessfully challenge in an independent bid for his office in 2006. Performance review was transferred to the Legislative Budget Board.

One of the most interesting revolutions in Texas politics occurred in the 1995 session, when the legislature opted to abolish the treasurer's office. In 1994, Democrat Martha Whitehead was elected treasurer, when she made the unusual promise to abolish her office. Whitehead was able to shepherd her proposal through the legislature even though it required two-thirds approval, because abolishing the office required a constitutional amendment. In November 1995, the voters approved the amendment and the treasurer's functions were folded into the comptroller's office. Although the monetary savings have been minimal, actually closing a state agency is an important symbolic step in a politically conservative state.

With the addition of the treasury functions, the comptroller's office now receives and manages all state money from the time of collection until the state's bills came due. Former state treasurer Ann Richards ensured that all state monies were deposited in interest-bearing accounts. Prior to that, some state funds essentially served as welfare for bankers, who were the major contributors to candidates running for the treasurer's office.

The Unclaimed Properties Division of the comptroller's office is the depository for unclaimed property. In addition to providing a public service, the comptroller uses this function to gain political recognition. The office annually publishes a list of people with property, such as valuables left in safe

WHAT CAN YOU DO?

Do you think you might have left money in a forgotten bank account or failed to claim a utility deposit? Perhaps you are owed insurance benefits or corporate dividends. If this might apply to you, call (800) 654-3463 or check on the Internet at http://www.window.state.tx.us/up/.

deposit boxes or a dormant bank account, which is unclaimed. Not coincidentally, the annual Sunday newspaper supplement is published in late October, just prior to the November elections. People finding that they have money coming are happy with the comptroller as a result. The comptroller also benefits from reinforced name recognition among those who merely skim the publication but do not find their names.

The Commissioner of the General Land Office

The commissioner of the General Land Office has the responsibility for leasing and use of the state's public land. Like the other positions we have discussed, the **land commissioner** serves a four-year term. Much of the state's public land is dedicated to the Permanent School Fund (PSF), which receives income from leases as well as from oil and mineral production. The PSF has a market value of about $24 billion.[3] The land commissioner also serves as the chair of the Veterans Land Board, which provides low-interest loans to veterans wishing to buy land.

land commissioner
State official responsible for overseeing the leases and uses of state-owned land; elected.

Republican Jerry Patterson won the 2002 land commissioner's race by about a dozen percentage points. He was reelected in 2006 and 2010. The conservative former state senator, who won with a strong grassroots effort, vows to increase oil and gas production in the state, which would bring more money to Texas schools.

The Commissioner of Agriculture

The agriculture commissioner is the one statewide elected executive office that is not constitutionally mandated, as noted in the nearby Texas Constitution feature.

Todd Staples, Texas Commissioner of Agriculture (c) speaks with John Whitmire (l) of Houston and Lt. Governor David Dewhurt (r) in the Texas Senate. Why is it important for executive officials to meet with legislative leaders?

WHAT CAN YOU DO? Are you a member of a group interested in adopting a beach? Call the land commissioner's office at (877) TXCOAST for more information or use the Internet and go to http://www.glo.state.tx.us/adopt-a-beach/cleanup.html.

WHAT CAN YOU DO? Have a question about pesticides or another agriculture issue? Call the Texas Department of Agriculture at (800) TELL-TDA.

The agriculture commissioner's Web site is http://www.agr.state.tx.us/.

It was created by statute in 1907. The commissioner' job requires the candidate to be a practicing farmer. This simply means that when filing for election, the candidate must claim to be an experienced farmer. Texas is one of only 11 states to elect this position.

The commissioner oversees the 650-employee Texas Department of Agriculture (TDA), which is responsible for regulating the use of pesticides and providing information, training, and licenses for their use. Along with being a regulatory agency, the office also promotes the consumption of Texas-grown food, wine, fiber, and nursery plants through its Marketing and Agribusiness Development Division. TDA has helped Texas farmers sell products throughout the world, involving itself in projects as diverse as kicking off ceremonial cattle drives and promoting the sale of long-stem bluebonnets.[4]

An interesting function of the office is its responsibility for establishing the accuracy of weights and measures. Under this mandate, the agriculture commissioner certifies that gasoline pumps work properly. Commissioners have had the political savvy to put their names on the gas pump inspection stickers so that motorists see it every time they fill up their vehicles.

The Texas Constitution: A Closer Look

The Texas Constitution mandates the creation of the major offices of the executive branch, requiring the election of all but the secretary of state. The Agriculture Commission is created by state law.

ARTICLE IV. EXECUTIVE DEPARTMENT

Sec. 1. OFFICERS CONSTITUTING THE EXECUTIVE DEPARTMENT. The Executive Department of the State shall consist of a Governor, who shall be the Chief Executive Officer of the State, a Lieutenant Governor, Secretary of State, Comptroller of Public Accounts, Commissioner of the General Land Office, and Attorney General. (Amended November 7, 1995)

Sec. 2. ELECTION OF OFFICERS OF EXECUTIVE DEPARTMENT. All the above officers of the Executive Department (except Secretary of State) shall be elected by the qualified voters of the State at the time and places of election for members of the Legislature.

Texas MOSAIC

Increasing Diversity in the Executive Branch:
The Secretaries of State

Like most of the executive branch in Texas, the secretary of state's office was long a bastion of white, male Democrats. In recent years, that profile has been altered drastically.

With the advent of Republican governors in 1979, the party barrier fell. The racial barrier was first cracked in 1968, when Governor John Connally appointed Roy Barrera Sr., a Hispanic, to the office. In 1983, Governor Mark White named Myra McDaniel to the post, making her the third woman and the first African American to hold the office. The two other women served in the 1920s, shortly after women were given the right to vote.

Recent secretaries of state such as Democrat Ron Kirk and Republicans Tony Garza and Alberto Gonzales reflect the more inclusive nature of contemporary Texas politics. Governors realize that reaching out to the minority community in making high-profile appointments can bring political gains. The almost universal respect afforded to these men helps open doors for other minority aspirants in jobs both in and out of government.

Kirk, an African American, replaced Governor Ann Richards's initial secretary of state, who resigned to become a federal judge. Kirk, a lawyer, had served as the chair of the state's General Services Commission. Popular before becoming secretary of state, Kirk used the additional exposure gained in the office to propel himself into the Dallas mayor's seat in 1995. He brought together a group of supporters that included liberals, conservatives, Republicans, and Democrats, and he scored an easy victory over a field of opponents. As mayor, Kirk tried to be a mediator among the various factions within the fractured Dallas city council. He was reelected in 1999 and staged a high-profile but unsuccessful race for the U.S. Senate in 2002.

Garza, a Hispanic, already had a career in Republican politics before accepting the secretary of state appointment. A tough conservative, he had served

Tony Garza served as U.S. ambassador to Mexico after being Texas's secretary of state.

seven years as county judge in Cameron County. Garza served two and a half years as secretary of state, before Governor Bush appointed him to a vacant seat on the Texas Railroad Commission, a position to which he was subsequently reelected. He later became the U.S. ambassador to Mexico. His replacement in the secretary of state post was Alberto Gonzales, whom Bush appointed to the Texas Supreme Court in 1999. When Bush became president, Gonzales resigned to become White House legal counsel. In 2005, Gonzales became attorney general for the United States, resigning after a controversial two years of service.

Rick Perry's first secretary of state was Henry Cuellar. The new governor reached across party lines to appoint the Democrat, the fourth Hispanic to hold the office. Gwen Shea, a Republican and the fourth woman to hold the office, replaced Cuellar in January 2002. She was replaced by Geoffrey Conner in 2003. Dallas–Fort Worth car dealer and major Republican contributor Roger Williams followed him in 2005. Phil Wilson took office in 2007.

Current agriculture commissioner Todd Staples was elected in 2006 and reelected in 2010. A Republican, he previously served in both the Texas House and Senate. He has followed in the footsteps of former Commissioner Susan Combs, continuing an emphasis on providing schoolchildren with healthy food choices. He has tried to help farmers and ranchers improve their profit margins and has been an advocate of property rights.

Appointed Offices

Although the most important department heads are independently elected, the governor appoints the secretary of state, the insurance commissioner and the adjutant general. Additionally, the governor selects the education, as well as the health and human services commissioners, which are discussed in more detail later in this chapter.

Secretary of State

secretary of state
The state's chief election officer; appointed by the governor.

For a state obsessed with electing every possible official, Texas is ironically one of the few states that does not elect the **secretary of state**. The governor's appointment is subject to Senate confirmation. The chief election officer for Texas, the secretary of state interprets the election code. The office provides training for election clerks and maintains a master roll of all registered voters in the state. The office also issues charters for businesses incorporated in the state. The office has been a state-level entry point for many Texas political figures, as discussed in the nearby Texas Mosaic. The *Texas Register*, which reports administration agency rules, attorney general opinions, and other government information, is published by the secretary of state's office. The *Texas Register* Web site is available at http://www.sos.state.tx.us/texreg/index.shtml.

Insurance Commissioner

With skyrocketing home insurance rates, the insurance commissioner's office became a political lightning rod in the early 21st century. The department, with about 1,700 employees regulates insurance company practices and helps ensure that these companies have financial resources to cover potential claims.[5] The insurance department was initially overseen by a three-member board, but it was replaced by a single commissioner, appointed by the governor, in 1994. It's easier to target one person than a group, hence the department's head has come under intense scrutiny as rates have increased.

Although the department is supposed to cap insurance rates, recent deregulatory efforts left most homeowners policies, as well as auto insurance rates, outside of the state's regulatory reach. Through a constitutional amendment, Texans have capped medical malpractice liability and it has become progressively harder to collect damages in the state.

Adjutant General

The governor appoints the adjutant general for a two-year term. The appointment is subject to Senate approval. With the exception of the governor, the adjutant general is the highest-ranking state military leader. Along with two assistants, the general oversees the Army National Guard, the Air National Guard, and the Texas National Guard.

The Bureaucracy

bureaucracy
Executive branch departments that carry out the law.

When the legislature passes a law, government policy does not magically change. Laws must be carried out—that is, executed—by the executive branch. That's where the **bureaucracy** comes into the picture. To most people, "bureaucracy" is a bad word. Citizens tend to believe that faceless bureaucrats are lazy or power hungry, or both. They associate bureaucracy with "red tape" and inefficiency. Almost everyone has had a bad experience with a government agency. There are rumors that even state colleges are imperfect. (Registration procedures may be inefficient, bookstores may run out of textbooks, financial aid departments might mess up your grants, and professors may be detached and arrogant. Finding no research that bolsters these claims, we dismiss them.)

For the most part, the sinister reputation attributed to government departments is too harsh. Generally, Texans take government services for granted. When the traffic on a state-built and state-financed road flows smoothly, when state-financed traffic lights work, when government regulations keep chemical plants from blowing up, and when professors show up for class, we don't stop and think, "Wow, the government did a great job today." But these desirable occurrences are not automatic. Without myriad government agencies working in cooperation with each other, no public policy goal would ever be accomplished. But when things go wrong, we notice immediately and blame the government and its workers. These employees, constrained by rules and regulations intended to ensure efficiency and fairness, are often doing the best job possible.

Size

About 150,000 employees (not counting education workers) labor for the state's bureaucracy.[6] While that may seem like an extraordinarily large number, it pales in comparison to the almost 3 million employees in the civilian federal work force. Local governments in Texas employ almost three-quarters of a million additional workers. In comparison to other states, the employee level of the state government is reasonable. Texas has the second-largest number of state employees, but one must bear in mind that Texas also has the second-largest state population. Table 8.1 shows Texas's rank among selected states in the number of state employees per 10,000 people in its

TABLE **8.1** **Number of Full-Time Equivalent State Employees per 10,000 Population for Selected States**

STATE	EMPLOYEES
Alaska	376
Delaware	292
Utah	197
Alabama	188
New Jersey*	177
Idaho	160
Oregon	159
Virginia*	158
50-State Average	142
Tennessee	139
Massachusetts*	138
Georgia*	132
Michigan*	130
Pennsylvania*	129
New York*	127
Texas*	120
Ohio*	119
California*	107

*15 most populous states
SOURCE: U.S. Bureau of the Census: Statistical Abstract (GPO 2008), p. 300.

population. Almost 90 percent have a higher rate of full-time state employees.[7] Realize, however, that states with large populations tend to have fewer state employees per capita. There are efficiencies associated with having a large population.

Hierarchy and Expertise

hierarchy
Chain of command.

One characteristic of a bureaucracy is its hierarchical nature. In a **hierarchy**, there is a definite chain of command. A person at the lower level of the pyramid-shaped structure does not report directly to the agency head, but rather to his or her boss, who is at the next highest level. Likewise, this person reports to a boss at the next highest level. Each boss has a span of control—the number of people who work under him or her—established at a level intended to make the organization operate efficiently. In most cases, the span of control will number between 5 and 12 workers.

The bureaucracy is intended to create experts and therefore instill efficiency in government. Each person, whether a typist, an accountant, or an engineer, should be an expert in his or her field. With each person paired with the job for which he or she is best prepared, there should be no waste of effort. Of course, this is an idealized version of how government operates. In reality, waste and mismanagement occur in government just as in every other aspect of life. In government, however, this waste is more controversial because "our money" (i.e., tax dollars) is involved.

In the past, a person needed "connections" to get a government job. The "spoils system" all but ensured that jobs went to workers within the winning political party. While this patronage system still exists for appointed board and commission positions, the trend in government is toward a merit system of hiring for most government employees. This means selecting the best person for a job, based on skills and qualifications. Such a system also allows for affirmative action, the practice of giving preferential treatment to members of groups discriminated against in the past. The goal of this highly controversial practice is to make the workforce more closely mirror the demographic makeup of the state.

Accountability

In Texas, most of the bureaucracy is decentralized. The governor does not exercise direct control over agencies, and most state boards and commissions are directly accountable to no one. Elected executive heads provide some measure of accountability for certain agencies. For example, employees of the agriculture department are, in at least some small way, accountable to the agriculture commissioner, who is accountable to the voters. The 3,500 employees of the Texas Workforce Commission, however, are removed from direct accountability. The governor appoints the commission members, but, as discussed earlier, has limited power over any board, because he or she cannot remove prior appointees from office and because board members' terms overlap. As a result, the average citizen can do little to direct displeasure toward a particular agency. These agencies are, however, more accountable to interest groups. The agency's "clients" have an important impact on its ability to receive adequate funding from the legislature (see "The Iron Triangle" section in Chapter 5).

Despite being part of the executive branch, agencies are much more accountable to the legislature than to the governor. First, funding is the lifeblood of these agencies, so they depend on the legislature for appropriations. Without money, no agency can survive. Without funding increases, no agency can grow. Second, agencies are subject to the sunset review process, which ultimately allows the legislature to close an agency. The governor can, of course, use line item veto power to punish agencies that fail to cooperate with his or her agenda, as Pa Ferguson did in 1917, when he vetoed the entire appropriation for the University of Texas. Most governors have not been willing to use such heavy-handed tactics.

Elected Boards and Commissions

TEXAS RAILROAD COMMISSION One of the enduring truths of the nation's capital is that bureaucrats survive. Agencies don't fold their tents and quietly fade away after their work is done. They find something new to do. Invariably, that something new involves more people with more power and more paperwork—all involving more expenditures.[8]

When former-president Gerald Ford wrote these words, he was talking about national government agencies. No organization in the country, however, fits this description better than the **Texas Railroad Commission (TRC)**. Most Texas voters are not aware of what the commissioners really do. Established by an 1890 amendment to the Texas Constitution, the original intent of the agency was to regulate rail rates within Texas. However, the national government's Interstate Commerce Commission (ICC) so greatly controls railroads that the Railroad Commission has had very few railroad-related responsibilities for years.

But the agency has found other things to do. Over the years, the Railroad Commission gained control over pipelines, oil and gas production, and trucking. Federal legislation took away the commission's power to set intrastate trucking rates in the mid-1990s and gave control to the ICC. In response to the federal changes, remaining transportation regulation has been transferred to the state departments of transportation and public safety.

The most important aspect of the TRC is its control over oil and natural gas. Production levels are set by the agency. The Railroad Commission sets the rates for gas utility companies. Liquid petroleum gas and compressed natural gas are also regulated by the TRC.

The Railroad Commission has three members, elected in a partisan manner to overlapping six-year terms. Current members, who are all Republican, include Michael Williams, who has served on the commission since 1999, David Porter, who was elected in 2010, and Elizabeth Jones, who was elected in 2006. The Chair of the Commission is the member next up for election; an honor that significantly helps with campaign fund-raising. The Railroad Commission's Web address is http://www.rrc.state.tx.us/.

STATE BOARD OF EDUCATION Texans also elect the **State Board of Education (SBE)**, which has limited oversight of the Texas Education Agency. The 15 board members serve overlapping four-year terms and are elected by district, not statewide. In selecting the education commissioner, the SBE forwards three suggestions to the governor. The governor chooses from among the nominees, and with the Senate's consent, the commissioner serves a four-year term.

The SBE has seen their authority reduced in recent years as a group of far-right conservatives ran a series of "stealth" candidates for the board. Their strategy was to run

Texas Railroad Commission
State commission that oversees oil and gas production; elected.

State Board of Education
Elected board that oversees the Texas Education Agency.

well-financed campaigns in the Republican primary elections for these low-profile positions, then take advantage of the ascendancy of the party to win the general elections. Although they comprised an outright majority on the board, the group's members have comprised a sizable faction. In 1995, the legislature and Governor Bush moved to strip the board of much of its power before the group could enact its antipublic education agenda. However, the SBE reasserted itself in 2002, with a strict reading of its charge to ensure against errors in textbooks. In essence, anything that the SBE disagreed with became an "error." The board used this provision to exert significant pressure on publishers in social, political, economic, and science texts. Additionally, the board has restructured public high school curriculum in a decidedly conservative direction. In the 2010 elections, however, the right wing of the board lost control of a couple of seats, which may have a moderating impact in the future.

The legislature has tried to decentralize school administration. Local schools can petition for campus charters under the reforms, allowing for easier creation of magnet schools and escaping from many state requirements. Additionally, independent charter schools can apply for and receive state funds with SBE approval. The results of the charter school law have been somewhat mixed. Hundreds of applications for charter schools were filed, but by the end of 2008 barely 200 schools were in operation. The SBE revoked, rescinded, or failed to renew the charters of several schools and more were on questionable financial footing or had gone bankrupt; these schools garnered more media attention than the charter schools that were apparently succeeding.[9] Although most charter schools underperform when compared with traditional public schools, one must keep in mind that many charters cater to at-risk students. Further, on average, charter schools spend less per student than their traditional counterparts. On the other hand, several charter schools were ranked exemplary or recognized in the top rankings awarded by the Texas Education Agency.

As boards that are elected rather than appointed, the SBE and the Railroad Commission are exceptions. This denotes their importance, as Texans want to retain direct control over the key components of government in order to ensure accountability.

Administrative Boards

Some of the more significant appointed boards are discussed in the following sections.

PARKS AND WILDLIFE DEPARTMENT One type of board oversees administrative agencies, such as the Parks and Wildlife Department, the Department of Health, and the Department of Human Services. The Parks and Wildlife Department is overseen by a nine-member board appointed by the governor and is headed by an executive director, who is appointed by the board. The purpose of the department is to protect wildlife, maintain parks, and provide for recreational opportunities. The department publishes *Texas Parks and Wildlife* magazine. Game wardens enforce hunting and fishing laws, as well as water safety provisions. The department also manages the state's historic sites and public parks.

HEALTH AND HUMAN SERVICES COMMISSION Health and Human Services underwent a major overhaul and consolidation in 2004. Eleven agencies were merged into four, with each reporting to the Health and Human Services Commission. The departments include Aging and Disability, Assistive and Rehabilitative Services, Family and

Protective Services, and State Health Services. Consolidation should make it easier for Texans to find where to turn for services. An Executive Commissioner oversees the commission with the assistance of a nine-member council, appointed by the governor.

DEPARTMENT OF TRANSPORTATION   The Texas Department of Transportation (TxDOT) is one of the largest agencies in the state and employs about 15,000 full-time workers.[10] TxDOT's executive director, who is appointed by the three-member board, must be an engineer. The department was created in 1917, as the State Highway Department. Over the years, it has evolved so that it covers land, water, and air transportation. It is responsible for developing a statewide transportation plan. A second appointed board within the TxDOT structure, the six-member Motor Vehicle Board, regulates motor vehicle registration.

University Boards and the Coordinating Board

There is a dual system of oversight for public universities in Texas. Each system has its own board, each with members appointed by the governor. For systems like the University of Texas, all individual universities are governed by a single board. These boards are responsible for setting policy and hiring top administrators. Many universities, such as Stephen F. Austin University, have their own boards.

The Texas Higher Education Coordinating Board oversees all higher education in the state. The 18-member board administers the Texas Higher Education Assessment (THEA) program. It also sets standards for course transferability both among universities and from community colleges to universities. The board is influential in determining the allocation of higher education funding. The Legislative Budget Board gives significant weight to the coordinating board's funding priorities, if not its funding levels, when the LBB puts together the budget.

The overlapping functions of these boards provide insight into how government operates. In any given policy area, many bureaucratic entities and boards may have some responsibility. Coordination becomes imperative for government to function efficiently. All too often, however, the involved organizations do not work well together and policy bogs down.

Occupational Licensing Boards

A significant number of boards in Texas set standards for occupational licensing. Examples include the Texas State Board of Plumbing Examiners and the Board of Nurse Examiners for the State of Texas. Most boards are comprised of both workers in that field and members of the public, with the former having the majority of the seats. Licensing is regulated in areas as diverse as cosmetology, dentistry, occupational therapy, psychology, polygraphy, and audiology.

Regulatory Boards

Many commissions in the state are involved in business regulation. Among the most significant are the **Public Utility Commission (PUC)** and the Texas Alcoholic Beverage Commission (TABC).

Public Utility Commission
Agency that regulates utility companies; appointed.

The main function of the PUC is setting utility rates. Utility companies make rate hike requests based on their expenses. The commission holds public hearings on the proposed increases before setting rates. The PUC has authority over privately owned utility companies, but not those operated by city governments. The PUC regulates electric and phone companies. It became most controversial in the late 1980s when an appointee of Democratic Governor Mark White and an appointee of Republican Governor Bill Clements publicly clashed over philosophical and personal differences. The *CBS Evening News* televised a tape of one of the more contentious shouting sessions, embarrassing many state government officials. Although meetings are often still volatile, most discussions are now limited to policy matters. As a result, the commission has not attracted as much attention in recent years. Nonetheless, because of its regulatory power over the utility industry, it remains one of the most significant boards in the state.

The TABC oversees alcohol-related commerce in Texas. Day-to-day operations are carried out by administrators hired by the commission. The TABC regulates both liquor stores and establishments that serve alcoholic beverages. Liquor licenses and "happy hours" fall under their jurisdiction. Over a decade ago, happy hours became a point of controversy. Mothers Against Drunk Driving (MADD) has lobbied to ban such promotional practices, arguing that they lead to increased inebriation resulting in traffic accidents. Restaurant and bar owners, along with alcohol manufacturers, lined up in opposition. TABC banned two-for-one drink promotions as a result of pressure from MADD, but happy hours were not been eliminated. Neither side was able to win complete victory.

The TABC inspects alcohol manufacturers, including the state's expanding beer and wine production industry. One division of the commission monitors the collection of alcohol-related taxes.

The Sunset Advisory Commission

Sunset Advisory Commission
Appointed joint commission that reviews state agencies.

In recognition of the enormous growth in the number and scope of state agencies, the **Sunset Advisory Commission** was created in 1977 to help determine if agencies had outlived their usefulness. The commission is composed of five senators appointed by the lieutenant governor, five representatives appointed by the Speaker, and two members of the public, one appointed by the Speaker and the other by the lieutenant governor. The commission has a full-time staff that aids in the research and review processes. Additionally, the commission can make recommendations to agencies, including those not currently under review, in order to increase efficiency and save the state money. It also has the authority to bring an agency up for review out of order. As a result, these recommendations are taken seriously and usually implemented.

Under the review process, all nonconstitutionally mandated agencies must be renewed by the legislature every 12 years. The Sunset Commission plays a vital role in this process. When an agency is up for review, it must first complete a self-evaluation. Next, public hearings take place. Finally, the commission will make its recommendations to continue, abolish, or merge the agency. The recommendation is not binding; the legislature has the final say as to the fate of an agency.

In most cases, the legislature must reauthorize an agency under review in order for it to continue. Constitutionally mandated agencies are not subject to this automatic abolishment. Most agencies survive the review process: only about one in seven are eliminated. As a result of sunset recommendations, 54 were abolished, 12 combined with existing agencies, and 2 split apart. Additionally, several committees and boards have been abolished or restructured.[11] You can learn more about the Sunset Advisory Commission at their Web site, located at http://www.sunset.state.tx.us.

Summary

In Texas, the executive department is fragmented, fractured, and weakened. Due to influences from the state's past, including the Texas Grange and the state's traditionalistic political structure, the Texas Constitution limits the power of the governor. It seeks to keep any one person from exercising too much power.

Instead of a cabinet system of government, Texas has a plural executive. The lieutenant governor, attorney general, comptroller, treasurer, land commissioner, and agriculture commissioner are all independently elected. As a result, these officers are not directly accountable to the governor.

The governor's influence is also weakened by the system of boards and commissions, which can be administrative, licensing or regulatory. Some, like the Railroad Commission and the State Board of Education, are elected by voters. This shields these members from the governor's influence. Others, appointed by the governor, are selected for six-year overlapping terms. This means that during the first term, a governor must operate within a board system dominated by someone else's appointees. Because a governor cannot remove a person chosen by a predecessor, the bureaucratic system often operates independently from him or her. This system was no accident. It was deliberately created to weaken the power of the chief executive.

Chapter Test

1. Duties of the attorney general include all *except*
   a. child support enforcement.
   b. enforcing antitrust legislation.
   c. appointing county attorneys.
   d. giving counsel to state agencies.

2. The state treasurer's office
   a. collects tax revenue.
   b. issues currency.
   c. was abolished by the voters.
   d. estimates revenue.

3. Which of the following is *not* a constitutionally mandated office?
   a. land commissioner
   b. governor
   c. comptroller
   d. agriculture commissioner

4. Which of the following is appointed by the governor?
   a. attorney general
   b. secretary of state
   c. comptroller
   d. treasurer

5. The executive who collects taxes and is the state's accountant is the
   a. comptroller.
   b. treasurer.
   c. auditor.
   d. governor.

6. What is not typical of the cabinet form of government?
   a. concentrated power
   b. independently elected officials
   c. the governor is more accountable
   d. the governor appoints most executives

7. The executive responsible for ensuring the accuracy of weights and measures is the
   a. comptroller.
   b. land commissioner.
   c. attorney general.
   d. agriculture commissioner.

8. The official responsible for enforcing the Open Records Act is the
   a. governor.
   b. attorney general.
   c. public records commissioner.
   d. comptroller.

9. The state's official revenue estimates come from the
   a. LBB.
   b. comptroller.
   c. lieutenant governor.
   d. governor.

10. About how many noneducation workers does Texas employ?
    a. 10,000
    b. 21,000
    c. 160,000
    d. 230,000

Answers: 1. c 2. c 3. d 4. b 5. a 6. b 7. a 8. b 9. b 10. c

Critical Thinking Questions

1. How has the Sunset Advisory Commission impacted Texas government ?

2. How are the Railroad Commission and State Board of Education part of the plural executive?

3. Should the governor be allowed to appoint new board members on taking office?

Key Terms

attorney general, **p. 210**
bureaucracy, **p. 220**
cabinet, **p. 207**
comptroller, **p. 215**
hierarchy, **p. 222**
land commissioner, **p. 217**
plural executive, **p. 207**

Public Utility Commission (PUC), **p. 225**
secretary of state, **p. 220**
State Board of Education (SBE), **p. 223**
Sunset Advisory Commission, **p. 226**
Texas Railroad Commission (TRC), **p. 223**

Notes

1. *Legislative Budget Board Fiscal Size-Up*, Texas Legislative Budget Board, 2008, p. 67.

2. *Fiscal Size-Up*, p. 75.

3. *Fitch Affirms Texas Permanent School Fund's IFS at 'AAA,'* *Reuters News Service*, http://www.reuters.com/article/pressRelease/idUS265373+20-Jan-2009+BW20090120.

4. *Fiscal Size-Up*, p. 323.

5. Ibid., p. 409.

6. Ibid., p. 10.

7. *U.S. Statistical Abstract*, U.S. Census Bureau, 2008, p. 300.

8. Gerald R. Ford, *A Time to Heal* (New York, NY: Berkeley, 1980), p. 265.

9. Texas Education Agency Division of Charter Schools Summary of Charter Awards and Closures, p. 1.

10. *Fiscal Size-Up*, p. 384.

11. *Guide to the Texas Sunset Process*, Sunset Advisory Commission, July 2008, p. 12.

The Texas Courts System

9

The Texas Supreme Court holds its first term.

1840   1845

A constitutional amendment requires justices to be elected.

By the end of this chapter on the Texas courts system, you should be able to . . .

★ Identify the Texas judicial system network of courts.

★ Differentiate between civil and criminal law.

★ Differentiate between original and appellate jurisdiction.

★ Analyze how the Texas judiciary plays an important role in shaping public policy.

★ Explain why the method for selecting Texas judges is under constant criticism.

★ Evaluate the merits of suggested judicial reforms.

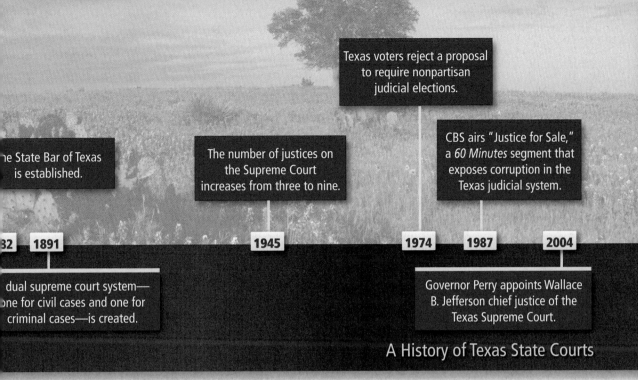

Texas voters reject a proposal to require nonpartisan judicial elections.

e State Bar of Texas is established.

The number of justices on the Supreme Court increases from three to nine.

CBS airs "Justice for Sale," a *60 Minutes* segment that exposes corruption in the Texas judicial system.

32 1891   1945   1974   1987   2004

dual supreme court system—
one for civil cases and one for
criminal cases—is created.

Governor Perry appoints Wallace B. Jefferson chief justice of the Texas Supreme Court.

A History of Texas State Courts

*The question is, how much justice
can you afford?*

Conflict is an inevitable and necessary element of any democracy. The judicial system was created to resolve conflicts arising among individuals, groups, corporations, and the government. Some conflicts stem from broken contracts, disputes over property ownership, or personal injury; others might originate from police action or from the interpretation of a statute, a law, or a phrase contained in a legislative act.

The very concept of justice creates conflict. It is indeed rare when two opposing parties who have gone to court are both satisfied with the verdict. More often than not, at least one side believes that justice was not served. This is especially true in criminal cases, where victims frequently express dissatisfaction with the "system." While it is true that inconsistencies abound in the Texas court system, Texas and the rest of the nation have made great strides in recent years to make justice more accessible and more equitable.

The Texas Court System

Determining Jurisdiction

jurisdiction
The power of a court to hear a case.

The term **jurisdiction** means the court's authority to hear a particular case. A court must have jurisdiction over the matter before it can hear it. For example, a criminal case cannot be filed in a court that has only civil jurisdiction. By the same standard, a civil case in which a billion dollars is in dispute cannot be heard by your neighborhood small claims court, which has jurisdiction only up to $10,000. Cases are assigned to specific courts based on the type of law and on the type of court.

Texas has more than 3,000 courts that settle more than 10 million disputes per year.[1] As daunting as it sounds, determining which court will hear a particular case is a relatively simple task because each court is set up to hear specific types of cases. By understanding a few basic concepts about the judicial system, you'll be able to determine which court will hear a particular case. The fact that the Texas judicial system consists of six types of courts makes it especially simple.

The first step in determining which court will hear a case is to know whether the case is civil or criminal. If the case is civil in nature, and if you know what or how much is being disputed, you'll be able to name the court that will hear the case. If the case is criminal, all you'll have to know is what level of crime is under consideration.

All cases, civil and criminal, originate at the trial court level. Think of the trial as the first contest, or the "original." For this reason, trial courts are also known as courts of original jurisdiction. All subsequent hearings stemming from the original trial are known as appeals, and appeals are heard, as you may have figured out by now, in the appellate courts.

In this section we will explore the two types of law as well as the two types of court. The two types of law are criminal law and civil law; and the two types of courts are trial (original) courts and appellate courts.

Two Types of Law

civil law
Law that deals with private rights and seeks damages rather than punishment.

plaintiff
The person or entity that initiates a civil lawsuit.

defendant
Person charged with a crime or the subject of a civil suit.

Civil law exists to protect rights and property and to hold individuals accountable for their actions. Civil lawsuits usually involve two private entities, at least one of which is attempting to recover damages or to correct a situation that the party perceives as unfair. All civil cases, regardless of which court hears them, have two sides; namely, a plaintiff and a defendant. The **plaintiff** is the person or party that initiates the lawsuit and is always listed first. For example, in the case of *Smith* v. *Jones*, we know that Smith is the plaintiff because her name appears first. Ms. Smith is suing the defendant, Mr. Jones. The **defendant** is the person or party that is being sued. Among the more frequently heard civil cases are contract disputes. For example, a dissatisfied homeowner may sue a remodeler for monetary damages in civil court. Other civil cases may involve inheritances, divorces, and product liability. With few exceptions, anyone may file a civil lawsuit if the plaintiff believes that the defendant has caused some type of monetary, emotional, or physical harm. You may have heard the expression: "Anyone can sue anyone for anything." This is for the most part true, as evidenced by the civil lawsuit filed against the drive-through restaurant by a woman who claimed that she was harmed by coffee that was served much hotter than industry standards of reasonableness. In winning her case she introduced evidence that management knew the coffee was being served hotter than necessary and failed to take corrective action.

Criminal law, as illustrated in Table 9.1, focuses on regulating people's conduct and protecting society from the unlawful actions of individuals. If you are a criminal justice major, you know this to be "prohibitive law." All criminal law is prohibitive in nature. There are no laws that allow conduct, but there are plenty of laws that ban certain acts. For example, there is no law that says it is legal to proceed through a green light at an intersection, but there are laws that prohibit running a red light. We sometimes hear of people who want the government to "legalize marijuana," but in reality, they're asking for a repeal of the law that makes marijuana illegal. Other criminal acts include theft, robbery, assault, and identity theft. Criminal law is further distinguished from civil law by the fact that it is structured and codified, meaning that the criminal laws are contained in various "codes," such as the Penal Code, Education Code, Elections Code, Transportation Code, and about a dozen others. These codes clearly define what conduct is criminal, and they provide for specific penalties.

Because criminal law reflects societal values, it is subject to change and revision. In recent years the laws against driving while intoxicated were modified in order to prosecute persons whose blood-alcohol content is .08, down from the previous level of .10. This revision was made to further discourage drinking and driving and was largely the result of lobbying by Mothers Against Drunk Driving and other groups committed to fighting Driving While Intoxicated (DWI). A society's criminal laws also reflect the changing social climate. In 2009 Texas DWI laws were further strengthened, making it a felony to drive drunk with a child in the car and requiring defendants to submit to blood tests when they drive drunk with a child passenger.[2]

criminal law
Laws that regulate individual conduct and seek to protect society by punishing criminal acts.

TABLE **9.1** Types of Law

	CIVIL	CRIMINAL
Purpose	Protect property	Regulate conduct
Plaintiff	Aggrieved	Government
Source of Law	Unrestricted	Criminal codes
Burden of Proof	Preponderance	Beyond reasonable doubt
Final Remedy	Usually monetary	Fine or incarceration

Other Distinctions Between Civil and Criminal Law

A critical distinction between civil and criminal law is the burden of proof. Civil cases are decided on a preponderance of the evidence. The plaintiff must convince the jury that his or her argument is more reasonable than the defendant's, in order to prevail in a civil lawsuit. This practice of "weighing" the evidence and testimony is known as **preponderance**. If the plaintiff proves, in the minds of the jurors, that the defendant is mostly at fault, the plaintiff wins. By contrast, a person prosecuting a criminal case must convince all the jurors that the defendant is guilty beyond a reasonable doubt. This is a fairly lofty standard; if even one juror does not vote "guilty," the defendant cannot be convicted. The term "**beyond a reasonable doubt**" does not mean absolute certainty, but it does suggest that, under the circumstances, any reasonable person would conclude that the defendant did commit the crime.

Civil cases can be initiated by an individual, group, or corporation. In contrast, criminal cases are initiated by a **prosecutor** who is employed by the state. It is the prosecutor's job to prove the case in court. In a criminal case, the victim does not

preponderance
The majority of evidence in a civil case.

beyond a reasonable doubt
Burden of proof on the state in a criminal case.

prosecutor
A government employee who initiates criminal cases against individuals.

need to retain an attorney, as the prosecutor fills this role. In contrast, most of the litigants in a civil case are represented by attorneys they personally hire.

Can an Act Be Both Civil and Criminal?

In a word, yes. Sometimes an event, such as a crime of violence, can be the cause for both civil and criminal actions. For example, a person who injures another may be prosecuted for assault because there is a specific law prohibiting this conduct. The victim would also be entitled to sue the assailant in civil court to recover medical expenses, lost wages, and monetary damages for pain and suffering.

Two Types of Courts

original jurisdiction
The authority of a court to try a case for the first time.

THE TRIAL COURTS Trial courts, or courts of **original jurisdiction,** hear a case for the first time. The trial court's function is twofold: (1) it determines the facts of the case, and based on those facts, (2) it applies the existing law to reach a verdict. The trial court is where witnesses testify, evidence is introduced, objections are raised, and juries determine whether there is liability or guilt. There are four levels of trail courts in Texas: municipal, justice, county court-at-law, and district. We will visit each of these courts later in this chapter.

appellate court
Courts that hear appeals from lower courts.

THE APPELLATE COURTS If the verdict of a trial court is appealed, an **appellate court** reviews the case. Appellate courts exist to determine whether the trial courts have correctly applied the law. These courts review both the manner in which the law was applied and whether established legal procedures were followed. A party appealing a trial court verdict cannot introduce new or additional evidence at the appellate level. The party can only question whether the evidence introduced at trial was sufficient to support the trial court's findings of fact.

uphold
Higher court leaves ruling intact.

reverse and render
The high court overturns the lower court and enacts a final verdict.

reverse and remand
The high court overturns lower court and orders a new trial.

After an appellate court reviews a case it can come to one of three conclusions. The most common finding of the appellate court is to **uphold.** This means the appellate court did not find cause to change the verdict of the trial court and thus the trial court's verdict stands. The opposite happens when the appellate court's decision is to **reverse and render.** This means the verdict of the trial court is overturned (reversed) and the verdict now favors the other party (the decision is rendered in favor of the appealing party). The third possible outcome of an appeal is **reverse and remand.** This means the appellate court has found that errors were made in the trial, but it does not want to render its own verdict. In this case, the appellate court remands (sends back) the case so that another trial can be held. The new trial, obviously, will use a new jury. There are two levels of appellate courts in Texas: the courts of appeal and the supreme courts. Each of these will be examined later in this chapter.

Structure of the Texas Courts System

By now, you should understand the basics of the court system. You know that some cases are civil and some are criminal; and you know that some are trials and some are appeals. Armed with this knowledge, we can outline the structure of the Texas courts system. There are over 3,000 courthouses across the state, but determining which courts hear which cases is a relatively simple task. We will examine each of Texas's six levels of courts as illustrated in Figure 9.1; namely, four trial and two

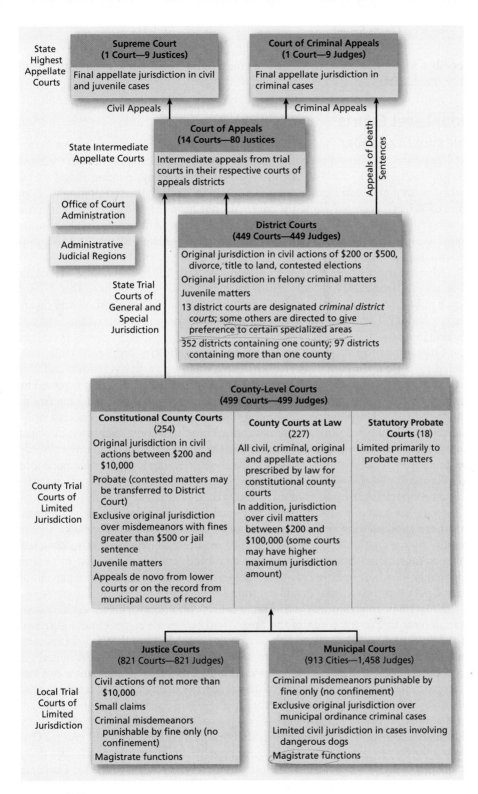

FIGURE **9.1** **The Texas Court System.** The courts and their jurisdictions.

appellate levels, starting with the lowest court and working our way up to the Texas Supreme Court.

Trial-Level Courts

THE MUNICIPAL COURT There are some 1,325 municipal courts throughout Texas[3] and they have jurisdiction over all Class C misdemeanors occurring within the city's geographic limits. Violations of this type include speeding, making illegal turns, failing to stop at a stop sign or at a red light, parking illegally, and driving with an expired driver's license. Municipal courts do not have the authority to hear more severe traffic offenses, such as those involving injuries or intoxication. The maximum punishment the court can order for any traffic-related offense is $500, plus court costs.

Municipal courts are further empowered to hear Class C state law violations that are punishable by fine only. These include simple assault (those that do not result in bodily injury), petty theft (under $50), and public intoxication and disorderly conduct. Like the traffic offenses, these crimes carry fines that may not exceed $500.

Other cases heard by the municipal court include city ordinance violations, including noise disturbances, fireworks-related offenses, curfew violations and violations of the city or town building codes. A city **ordinance** is a law that is passed by the city council and is enforceable only within that particular city. Cities are free to enact and enforce ordinances, and many Texas cities have recently enacted ordinances prohibiting cell phone communications in school zones. Because municipal courts have exclusive original jurisdiction to hear these cases, a defendant's only recourse is to plead his or her case in this court. Although municipal courts can assess a maximum fine of $500 for all other Class C offenses, violations of city ordinances are punishable by fines of up to $2,000.

ordinances
Laws enacted by incorporated cities and towns; violations punishable by fine only and heard in municipal court.

State law allows a city to determine qualifications for its municipal judges. Most are appointed by the city council, and most cities require the judge to live within the city. Although state law does not require municipal judges to have law degrees, most larger cities and towns that retain full-time municipal judges require them to be attorneys or have extensive legal training. Statewide, about 50 percent of municipal court judges have graduated from law school.

Most small-town municipal courts are courts of nonrecord, meaning there is no official recording or transcript of the cases heard before the court. Courts of record maintain tape recordings or transcripts of court proceedings so that appellate courts can determine whether any errors were made during the original trial. Where there is no official record, there can be no appeal. In the event that a defendant is not satisfied with the verdict from a court of nonrecord, the defendant may request a **trial de novo**, which, literally translated from Latin means "new trial." These trials are held at the county court at law level, which is a court of record. Until recently, many defendants paid lawyers to file their traffic tickets at the higher-level courts. This caused the county courts at law to become bogged down with cases and forced them to dismiss many of the tickets. To counter this, many municipal courts have become courts of record, and this has eliminated the defendant's option of requesting a trial de novo.

trial de novo
Cases that are retried by the county court after being heard in lower courts of non-record.

There are two ways in which a municipal court may become a court of record. One method requires the city to conduct a special election. The other, more common method requires legislative action. Under this approach, city administrators ask a member of the state legislature to sponsor a bill making its municipal court a court of record. If the bill is passed by both the Texas House and Senate, the city can create the new court without holding a local election. Cities seeking to establish a court of record are allowed to determine for themselves which approach to take.

THE JUSTICE COURT This court goes by many names, including "small claims" and "the people's court." Each of the state's approximately 1,000 justice courts is presided over by a justice of the peace (JP), a locally elected judicial official. These courts are highly versatile because they are empowered to hear both criminal and civil cases. Each of Texas's 254 counties has a justice of the peace and—depending on the county's population—can have as many as eight.

The criminal cases heard by these courts are of the same level as the municipal court: Class C misdemeanors. The answer to the question How do I know whether the municipal court or the justice court will hear my ticket? depends on the agency that gave you the ticket. If you are charged with running that stop sign in the city by a city police officer, the local municipal court will have jurisdiction. On the other hand, if a county sheriff's deputy or a state trooper presents with a citation, the case will be heard in justice court by the local JP.

The justice court's jurisdiction in civil matters is extensive, since it is the lowest court in the state having civil jurisdiction. These courts hear most of the civil cases in which the amount in dispute is under $10,000. If a plaintiff wishes to sue someone for more than that amount, he must file the case in a higher court. A person that wants to file a civil case valued at less than $10,000 may file in justice court or in a higher court. What's the difference? Since the justice court is somewhat informal, plaintiffs and defendants are not required to hire attorneys to state their cases. For this reason, the court is often referred to as "small claims court" or "the people's court." Filing a case in justice court is less costly and usually gets on the docket much sooner than do cases in the higher courts.

The Texas Constitution empowers JPs to perform a variety of other judicial duties, including arraignments of prisoners and issuance of criminal arrest warrants at the request of law enforcement officers. Justice courts possess exclusive jurisdiction for issuing peace bonds against people whom the judge believes may become hostile or violent toward another individual. A **peace bond** is a court order designed to keep the peace by protecting someone who has been threatened, but not harmed. When a justice of the peace issues a peace bond he or she is ordering the person who made the threats to deposit money with the court. If the person who made the threats commits the threatened criminal action then the deposited money will be given to the state.

peace bond
A court order providing a jail sentence issued by a justice of the peace against a person who had threatened another person.

One does not need a law degree to become a justice of the peace, neither does one need any previous legal training or experience. The law requires JPs who are not licensed attorneys to complete extensive civil and criminal training programs. Justices of the peace may be removed from office if they do not complete the required training successfully. Some critics (most of them unemployed or

Texas MOSAIC

Judge Roy Bean

Perhaps he had never heard of the Texas Bar, but that's exactly where Judge Roy Bean held court. From his saloon called the Jersey Lilly in the town of Langtry, Texas, Judge Bean meted out more than justice—he was the Law of the West. That saloon/courtroom in the small town on the banks of the Rio Grande is now a Texas shrine. For 19 years, Judge Bean presided over a territory so wild and vast that it hadn't even been named. Langtry hasn't grown much since the days when the legendary judge would operate his saloon and hold court in the same building. Today, the town has about 25 inhabitants.

Many myths have been written about the "hanging judge" who sentenced many to death by lynching, but in reality he was quite lenient. He never sentenced anyone to death by hanging or otherwise. On one occasion, the sheriff brought a man charged with carrying a concealed weapon to the Jersey Lilly. Judge Bean told the sheriff that the charges wouldn't stick. He reasoned that if the man was just standing, he wasn't "carrying" anything. And if the accused was walking, well then, "he was a travelin', and travelin' men have the right to possess a weapon." Although he was relatively merciful in the punishment he administered, there was something about Bean's brand of justice that was unattractive to the criminal element. Perhaps it was the sign that hung in the courtroom that read, "Argumentum Adjudicum." Judge Bean told anyone who asked what it meant, "Don't argue with the judge." Legend has it that Bean was about as tolerant of the state government as he was of criminals; which is to say, he wasn't. On receiving a letter from then-Governor Jim Hogg that Judge Bean's court had failed to transfer money from fines to Austin, Judge Bean responded with his

Judge Roy Bean in front of his courthouse, the Jersey Lilly Archives Division—Texas State Library.

own letter: "Dear Governor, Why don't you run things in Austin and let me run them down here?" Austin neither received any money from nor appropriated any for Judge Bean's court. Evidently, the arrangement suited both parties just fine.

From the many stories one hears about Judge Bean, one may presume that the stages of arrest as outlined in this chapter and in Chapter 10 were not followed to the letter, if at all. We do know that he was regarded as fair, swift, and impartial, and for that very reason the criminals feared him.

How many modern-day judges can make that same claim?

underemployed attorneys), have argued that JPs should be required to earn law degrees and be practicing attorneys. Although it is true that some justices of the peace, especially in rural areas, may not be as qualified as some attorneys in the legal education arena, the fact remains that most are highly competent in performing their duties. In addition to issuing search and arrest warrants and peace bonds, JPs also perform marriages and, in counties without a medical examiner's office, serve as coroner. Most modern JPs don't have quite as colorful of a resume as that of the legendary Roy Bean, featured in the Mosaic.

THE COUNTY COURTS In Texas, there are county courts at law and there are county commissioner's courts. Although similar in name, there is a world of difference. The county courts discussed in this chapter are judicial courts, meaning they are part of the Texas judicial system. By contrast, the county commissioner's courts, discussed in Chapter 11, are legislative bodies and are not judicial in scope.

There are three categories of county-level courts: the county court-at-law, the constitutional county court, and the probate court. The first two are the only courts in the state to have both original and appellate jurisdiction. The courts' appellate jurisdiction is limited and stems from cases that are appealed from municipal courts and justice courts. Cases that have been decided by lower courts of nonrecord are retried de novo at this level. This is not an appeal, but rather a brand new trial heard at this (the county court) level.

The Texas Constitution provides for one constitutional county court in each of the state's 254 counties. As some of Texas's counties grew more urbanized, it became clear that these courts could not handle the volume of cases generated by an ever-increasing population. In response, the Texas legislature created county courts-at-law, which serve as county-level courts authorized to hear cases of both criminal and civil nature. To date, the legislature has authorized about 200 of these county courts-at-law. In creating these courts, the legislature established more stringent qualifications for the judges. For example, county court-at-law judges are required to be licensed attorneys, whereas judges presiding over constitutional county courts are required only to be "well informed in the law." As in the justice court, criminal cases typically dominate the docket, accounting for nearly three-quarters of the county court-at-law's activity. The court's original jurisdiction in criminal cases includes driving while intoxicated, assault resulting in bodily injury, possession of marijuana (under 4 ounces), and other Class A and B misdemeanors.

The types of civil cases heard in the county court-at-law and in the constitutional county court include personal injury lawsuits and tax disputes. The legislature authorizes some county courts-at-law to hear cases involving up to $200,000, but the constitutional county courts are generally limited to cases in which the plaintiff seeks considerably less. In criminal cases, defendants have the option of choosing either a bench trial or a jury trial. A **bench trial** is a trial without a jury, in which the judge determines issues of fact. If the defendant elects to have a bench trial, no jury is selected and the judge alone renders a verdict. In recent years, fewer than 5 percent of the defendants in criminal trials conducted in the state's county courts-at-law opted for jury trials.

bench trial
A criminal trial that is held without jury, as requested by the person charged.

Also at the county level are the probate courts, which hear matters involving wills and estates. There are 16 of these courts, all of them located in the more populous counties. Like justices of the peace, all county-level judges are chosen in countywide partisan elections and serve four-year terms. All candidates for these courts must possess a law degree and be licensed to practice law in Texas.

THE DISTRICT COURTS The district courts are the state's highest-level trial courts. They have both criminal and civil jurisdiction, although many of them are set up to hear exclusively one or the other. There are about 450 of these courts, most of them located in the state's more populous areas. A "district" can be as small as a county, and some counties have eight or more district courts. In the less densely populated areas a district may encompass many counties. Since this is the highest trial court in the state, it hears the most serious of cases—felonies. Statewide, a majority of the court's criminal cases are disposed of by **plea bargaining**, a process in which the lawyer for the accused negotiates a relatively lighter sentence in return for a guilty plea. Plea bargaining is controversial but necessary, especially in the urban areas where the dockets are stacked with thousands of cases. The practice saves taxpayers millions of dollars each year—money that would otherwise be spent prosecuting the accused.[4]

plea bargaining
A process in which the accused receives a lighter sentence than could be expected from a trial verdict in exchange for a guilty plea.

In the civil arena, there is no limit as to the monetary damages a plaintiff may seek in the district court. Each year we see more cases in which the amount in dispute is in the billions of dollars. The most common type of civil cases heard in district court are divorce, child custody, and family law matters. Other civil cases include state tax disputes, personal injury lawsuits, workers' compensation claims, and contract disputes. District court judges are elected to 4-year terms and run in partisan elections. Candidates must be at least 25 years of age and must either be a licensed attorney or have served as a judge in another court for at least 4 continuous years.

Appellate Courts

The state's appellate court system is comprised of two levels: intermediate and supreme. These courts' jurisdiction extends only to cases that have already been tried in the courts of original jurisdiction. Appellate justices hear cases in odd-numbered panels. In other words, three, five, up to nine justices preside over every appellate case and they vote on the outcome. In most instances, a panel of three judges will hear a particular case, allowing the courts to hear several cases simultaneously and thus resolve many cases at the same time. About two-thirds of the cases heard by the intermediate courts are criminal in nature, and these courts generally make dispositions in all cases in fewer than two years. All Texas justices are elected to six-year terms in partisan elections, a practice that has come under fire and is discussed in greater detail later in this chapter.

INTERMEDIATE COURTS OF APPEAL The intermediate courts hear all appeals from the state's county and district courts, except capital murder cases in which the defendant is sentenced to death. Death penalty cases bypass the intermediate courts and get an automatic review to the Court of Criminal Appeals, but in all other cases, one of the litigants must request an appeal. Candidates for these courts are required to be at least 35 years of age and must have practiced law for 10 or more years or have served as a judge in a court of record for 10 or more years. There are 14 Courts of Appeals, arranged by geographic region (see Figure 9.2).

FIGURE **9.2** **Texas Courts of Appeals.**

The appellate courts review the transcripts of the lower courts and briefs of the lawyers to determine if the trial court followed the law or violated any rules during the trial. At times, these appellate courts find themselves the target of public criticism, especially when they overturn a trial court's conviction on what the public perceives as a "technicality." This was the case in Amarillo, where an appellate court reversed a 62-year prison sentence given to a woman convicted of suffocating her young daughter. The appellate court ruled that the trial court erred on several important points, namely, allowing inadmissible evidence to be introduced. Most appeals are based on the allegation that the judge made a mistake during the trial stage. The judge, for instance, may have disallowed admissible evidence or misinterpreted a law. The facts of the case are not subject to appeal, only the application of the law. In other words, one cannot appeal a case merely on the grounds that there is a disagreement on the outcome. In order to have a successful appeal, the party must demonstrate that an error may have been made by the judge during the trial.

DUAL SUPREME COURTS Texas is one of only two states that has a "dual" Supreme Court system (Oklahoma is the other). The Supreme Court actually consists of two separate and distinctive entities; the Texas Supreme Court, which hears civil cases, and the Texas Court of Criminal Appeals, which hears criminal cases, with such exceptions as spelled out in the nearby Constitution box. All other states use the federal model, in which a single Supreme Court hears both criminal and civil cases. Neither the Texas Court of Criminal Appeals nor the Texas Supreme Court are "superior" to the other. These courts are the highest appellate courts in the state, thus any appeals beyond these courts must be heard in the federal appellate court system.

The Texas Constitution: A Closer Look

AN EXCEPTION TO THE RULE

This chapter points out that Texas has a dual Supreme Court System: The Supreme Court hears cases that are civil in nature and the Court of Criminal Appeals, as its name implies, hears cases that are criminal in nature. There is an exception, however. From a legal standpoint, crimes committed by juveniles (individuals age 16 and under) are civil actions and are tried in civil courts. Technically, juveniles are not arrested, they are "taken into custody"; and they are not jailed, but "detained." Consequently, the state's highest appellate court for hearing criminal cases involving juvenile defendants is the Texas Supreme Court, and not the Court of Criminal Appeals.

WHAT CAN YOU DO?

The schedule of public activities of the Texas Supreme Court can be accessed through the court's Web site. Attend one of the oral arguments over which the court presides to understand more fully how the court works. Most of its business occurs between September and April. On the calendar you can see the days on which the court conducts oral arguments between disputing parties (typically on Tuesdays, Wednesdays, and Thursdays of selected weeks of the month), holds conferences between the justices (usually on Mondays and Tuesdays), and issues its orders (on Fridays). The Texas Supreme Court is located in the Supreme Court Building at 201 W. 14th Street in Austin. Office hours are 8:00 A.M. to 5:00 P.M., Monday through Friday, except on holidays.

A chief justice and eight associate justices preside over each court, although they are referred to as judges in the criminal court. Supreme Court Chief Justice Wallace Jefferson is profiled in the Mosaic nearby. Most of the time, cases at this level are heard **en banc**, meaning that all nine members of the court sit in on the case. In death penalty cases, all nine members of the Court of Criminal Appeals must be present. Justices of the Supreme Court and Court of Criminal Appeals are selected in partisan statewide elections and serve six-year terms. Terms are staggered to ensure that a majority have appellate court experience.

Criminal cases heard in any of the state's 14 courts of appeals may be appealed to the Court of Criminal Appeals by the defendant, in limited circumstances by the state, or by both. The Texas Constitution requires cases in which the defendant is given the death penalty to be reviewed by the Texas Court of Criminal Appeals. This is often referred to as an "automatic appeal," but that term is erroneous because the court is *required* to review the case even if the defendant does not wish to appeal his or her death sentence.

en banc
When an appellate court convenes all of its members to hear an appeal.

The Texas Supreme Court has the exclusive authority to issue licenses to practice law and has established a Board of Law Examiners to administer this function. The Texas Constitution granted the Texas Supreme Court the responsibility for establishing civil procedural rules and for overseeing the efficient administration of the state's entire judicial system. The Supreme Court's administrative responsibilities include overseeing the administration of all criminal courts as well, even though the court itself does not hear criminal cases.

The Court's Role in Public Policy Making

Most Americans are taught to view the major government institutions (the executive, the legislative, and the judiciary) as three distinct entities with separate and narrow powers.

We might have learned in high school that the U.S. government has "three branches" and that the legislative branch makes the laws and the courts interpret the laws. This view is somewhat oversimplified. The fact is that the courts often modify and even create laws, although that is not their prescribed function.

judicial activism
A philosophical approach dictating that the purpose of the courts is to take an active role in public policy making.

For decades, legal experts have discussed the merits of **judicial activism**, a philosophy that promotes court intervention in policy making. The debate continues today, as fierce as ever and fueled by federal and state court decisions that often contradict—and thus overrule—the expressed desires of the legislative branch and popular opinion. Over the years, both the Texas Supreme Court and the Texas Court of Criminal Appeals have rendered decisions that have in practice had the same effect as legislation. The Texas high courts have declared unconstitutional much legislation, including that relating to the financing of public schools. In these cases, the courts have taken it upon themselves to establish guidelines that have had the effect of law. Critics of judicial activism claim that policies created by the courts are in themselves unconstitutional because the policies were not made by the process of representative democracy. Actually, this claim is only partially valid because the members of the court are elected, albeit not for the express purpose of making laws. The argument goes that when the courts create legislation, they deprive citizens of the right to participatory democracy. On the other hand, proponents of judicial activism claim that the courts have the responsibility to protect the interests of all sides, even if one side happens to be in the minority in terms of public opinion.

Selection of Judges

The process used by Texans for selecting judges is highly politicized and thus a source of criticism. Although municipal court judges can be appointed by city councils or by other city officials, the judges presiding in every other level of the Texas court system—from justice of the peace to chief justice of the Supreme Court—are selected by the process of popular election.

Texas is one of only seven states requiring its judges to run in partisan elections. Most other states follow the federal model of executive appointment with legislative confirmation, eliminating some of the politics that are inherent in any partisan election. Texas's system makes it necessary for judicial candidates to identify with a political party and to hit the campaign trail, much like as if they were running for a legislative seat.

There are two reasons why Texas elects, rather than appoints, most of its judges. The first, and probably the most influential, reason stems from Texas's own traditionalistic and individualistic political culture (discussed in Chapter 1). This culture is still prevalent today, as evidenced by the resistance to judicial reform. So strong is the resistance that reformists have experienced remarkable difficulty in getting the legislature even to discuss, much less adopt, some of the proposals. The second reason stems from the first. Even before the current Texas Constitution was drafted, Texans held a basic distrust of government in general and politicians in particular. The framers of the Texas Constitution, as we note in the Inside the Federalist System box, reasoned that a popularly elected judiciary would be more responsive to the people, rather than to the full-time politicians and special interests. This is truly one of the greatest ironies in Texas politics because modern-day voter apathy has caused judicial candidates to recognize (some would say "and to serve") the special interests—from whom they get the majority of campaign contributions—more than most voters. The fact is that most judges raise most of their campaign money from attorneys who do business before their court, creating at least the perception of impropriety. The people who wrote the Texas Constitution were relying on an informed and active electorate to choose our judges.

The framers of the Texas Constitution established a system of electing judges in large part to curtail the governor's appointment powers. There is a great irony here, too, because the same system allows the governor to make judicial appointments in the event that a vacancy occurs between elections. Table 9.2 indicates that five of the nine Texas Supreme Court justices first assumed office by means of gubernatorial appointment. Given the framers' distrust of government generally and their disdain for governors specifically, it is doubtful that they anticipated such a high rate of appointments to the state's highest courts. Being appointed to fill a term of office provides a huge advantage to the appointee, because it allows the justice to run as an incumbent in the next election.

TABLE **9.2** **Method of Initial Judicial Selection**

	SUPREME COURT	COURT OF CRIMINAL APPEALS	COURT OF APPEALS	DISTRICT COURT (ALL)	COUNTY COURT AT LAW	JUSTICE COURT	MUNI. COURT
Appointment	5	1	42	185	80	213	1303
Election	4	8	37	244	137	578	18

INSIDE
THE FEDERALIST SYSTEM

Federalism allows each state to determine how its Supreme Court justices are to be chosen. You learned in this chapter that the method of selecting Texas Supreme Court justices is through regularly scheduled partisan elections. Most states follow the federal model, which is appointment through a process of executive selection and legislative confirmation. Some states use hybrid systems that combine appointments and regular elections. While the system used in Texas is highly controversial, we can take comfort in the fact that federalism allows us to change it through proper channels, and federal approval is not required.

The Supreme Court of Texas. Do you think judges should be appointed for life, selected by voters or chosen through some other method?

First Assumed Office

The positive consequence of judicial appointment has been a striking increase in the number of women and minorities sitting on the bench. Governor Ann Richards kept her campaign promise to appoint persons who better reflect the actual demographics of the state. Governors Bush and Perry embraced that policy too, and the effect is a more diverse judicial system. In 2004 Perry appointed Wallace B. Jefferson the state's first African American Texas Supreme Court chief justice. The former chief justice, Tom Phillips, resigned his post after serving for 17 years.

Justices running in statewide elections must raise hundreds of thousands of dollars in order to pay for campaign advertisements, and because they have even less name recognition, challengers often must raise even more. Some Supreme Court candidates have raised more than $1 million, most of which came from political action committees.

Judicial candidates are prohibited from discussing pending cases while on the campaign trail, but that prohibition hasn't stopped some judges from violating this

Texas **MOSAIC**

Justice Wallace B. Jefferson

In 2004, Governor Perry appointed Wallace B. Jefferson to Chief Justice of the Texas Supreme Court. Justice Jefferson grew up in San Antonio and earned his law degree at the University of Texas. Besides being one of the youngest chief justices, he is the first African American to serve in that capacity. Justice Jefferson was no stranger to high courts, having argued and won two cases in the U.S. Supreme Court there while practicing in his San Antonio law firm.

Justice Jefferson was named the Outstanding Young Lawyer by the San Antonio Young Lawyers Association in 1997. In 1998, he served as president of the San Antonio Bar Association which, during his tenure, hired personnel whose sole mission was to coordinate the provision of legal services to the poor. He was named a "40 Under 40 Rising Star" in 1996 by the *San Antonio Business Journal*, and in 2001 by the *Texas Lawyer*. Justice Jefferson was recognized as a "Pillar" of the Northside Independent School District in 1999, and received the Distinguished Alumni Award from James Madison College at Michigan State University in 2002. His professional activities have included serving on the Supreme Court of Texas Advisory Committee, the Texas State Commission on Judicial Conduct and chairing the host committee for the 2000 Fifth Circuit Judicial Conference. He is past

Wallace Jefferson is the first African American to serve as Chief Justice of the Texas Supreme Court. How was his appointment indicative of the changing political landscape in Texas?

president of the William S. Sessions American Inns of Court. Justice Jefferson has lectured across the country on appellate advocacy and received national recognition from the American Bar Association. Justice Jefferson has previously served as a director of the San Antonio Public Library Foundation, the San Antonio Bar Foundation, and the Alamo Area Big Brothers/Big Sisters organization.

prohibition. Law clerks, attorneys, and even former Supreme Court justices have testified that the rules are routinely broken.

In the late 1980s, allegations of power abuses made against Texas Supreme Court justices brought an array of investigative reporters to Austin. The Texas high courts received nationwide publicity and were even featured in a *60 Minutes* segment. Justices were accused of trading votes for campaign contributions and for changing liability law in favor of the plaintiffs' attorneys in return for large campaign contributions. The implicated justices were all voted out of office or left the bench.

The Call for Judicial Reform

The fact that candidates for Texas's highest courts are elected on an at-large basis has also created controversy, particularly among minority groups. The 18 justices comprising the two most powerful courts hardly mirror the racial and ethnic makeup of the state. There is widespread agreement that were it not for the fact that recent governors have appointed minorities to fill judicial vacancies, there would be much less diversity in the Texas judicial system. Reformists have suggested a process that uses single-member districts in order to provide Hispanics and African Americans equal opportunity to select and to serve as members of the state courts. These reformists even include former and current judges serving on Texas's highest courts. Former Texas Supreme Court Chief Justice Tom Phillips has said that Texas has "the most expensive judicial races in the world and the most politicized judicial races in the world." Former Lieutenant Governor Bob Bullock's plan, which was ultimately rejected, called for district judges to be elected in nonpartisan elections in county commissioner districts. The plan would have meant fewer costly elections and would have ensured more minority representation.

A reform measure called the Missouri Plan would once and for all alleviate the rising costs of campaigning, depoliticize the judicial system, and provide opportunities for qualified minority representation on the courts. Versions of the plan have been successfully adopted by a majority of the states. It combines the features of appointment while preserving the right of the voters to remove judges. A typical Missouri Plan system begins with a list of qualified candidates submitted to the governor by a panel consisting of legislators, judges, and citizens. The governor then appoints judges from the list to serve a term, which is usually four years. At the end of the term, the voters are given the opportunity to vote on whether to keep the judge in office. If the majority of the votes are to retain the judge, he or she serves an additional term of seven years. If the voters choose to remove the judge, the governor selects another candidate from the panel's list. Under this system, judicial candidates are required neither to identify with a political party nor to raise campaign contributions. Many of Texas's presiding judges favor implementation of the Missouri Plan. The greatest opposition has been from certain special interest groups that have been effective in promoting their own candidates.

Additional reforms have been proposed in recent years by various groups, elected officials, and judges:

- *Court Structure.* Proposed reforms include abolishing the Texas Court of Criminal Appeals, making the Texas Supreme Court the highest court for all civil and criminal cases.

- *Judicial Selection.* Reformists argue that justice would be better served if judges presiding in courts of original jurisdiction were appointed by the appropriate legislative bodies, such as the city council and county commissioners. Others argue that a system of appointing judges would make the selection process even more political than it already is and would take control away from the voters.
- *Nonpartisan Judicial Elections.* The most persuasive argument posed by reformists favoring this measure is that judicial candidates will no longer need to "conform" to a single political ideology and can thereby exercise a greater degree of judicial freedom. Many reformists also argue that nonpartisan elections would cost much less and would allow women and minority candidates to compete on a more equitable plane.
- *No Straight-Ticket Voting.* This proposal would virtually eliminate the "coattail effect" that takes place in major elections. Over the past ten years, many sitting judges (and other locally elected officials) have switched parties not for ideological reasons, but for the purpose of capturing the votes of straight-ticket voters in state and national elections.

Most Texans cannot name more than two or three justices on the Supreme Court or Court of Criminal Appeals. (And we are probably being optimistic when we say two or three.) Nonetheless, voters are more likely to recognize the name of a sitting justice than the name of a political newcomer. Name recognition is an important advantage for an incumbent seeking judicial office in Texas. This advantage, combined with the fact that most citizens pay little or no attention to the politics of the judiciary, virtually ensures reelection. Occasionally, however, judges do make the news. In Houston, for example, a county court-at-law judge was publicly reprimanded after he allegedly consumed alcoholic beverages and fondled female prosecutors while on the bench. In a DWI case being heard in his court, the judge allegedly drank the evidence and later commented to prosecutors, "I am sure glad you lost so that I don't have to preserve this evidence."

Summary

At first glance, the Texas judicial system appears to be immense and complex. On closer examination, one may conclude that each of the courts in the intricate system serves an important and specific purpose. As Texas moves toward reform, we realize that each level becomes increasingly more difficult to resolve to the satisfaction of the majority of people. The most controversial practices include the method of selecting judges and the role of the court in making public policy. Because these issues are so abstract and philosophical, and there are so many ways in which reform can be made, it is safe to presume that a majority of the people will never be completely satisfied with the outcome.

Chapter Test

1. The term **jurisdiction** means
   a. the court's authority to hear a particular case.
   b. the elected official's term of office.
   c. sending the case to a higher court for review.
   d. a system of selecting judges.

2. A **trial de novo** is
   a. trying a misdemeanor as a felony.
   b. an examination of a trial by an appellate court.
   c. a new trial.
   d. a trial without a jury.

3. The state's highest trial court is the
   a. Court of Appeals.
   b. Supreme Court.
   c. District Court.
   d. Justice Court.

4. Which of the following statements is true?
   a. Texas has two highest courts.
   b. All municipal judges are elected.
   c. The term of office for a Supreme Court justice is four years.
   d. All of the above.

5. A justice of the peace
   a. can issue peace bonds.
   b. hears both civil and criminal cases.
   c. is elected in a partisan election.
   d. all of the above.

6. The current Chief Justice of the Texas Supreme Court is
   a. Tom Phillips.
   b. Harriet Meyers.
   c. Wallace Jefferson.
   d. Alberto Gonzales.

7. One way to resolve the controversial nature of the Texas judicial system would be to
   a. require justices of the peace to have law degrees.
   b. allow municipal judges to hear civil cases.
   c. prohibit straight-ticket voting in judicial elections.
   d. televise all district court proceedings.

8. A philosophy that promotes court intervention in policy making.
   a. judicial noncompliance.
   b. judicial activism.
   c. judicial restraint.
   d. judicial review.

9. A trial without a jury is called a
   a. a bench trial.
   b. an appellate proceeding.
   c. an automatic appeal.
   d. a suppression hearing.

10. A negotiated settlement in a criminal case is called
    a. judicial activism.
    b. bench trial.
    c. trial de novo.
    d. plea trial.

Answers: 1. a 2. c 3. c 4. a 5. d 6. c 7. c 8. b 9. a 10. d

Critical Thinking Questions

1. How would you address the controversial nature of the judicial selection process?

2. Should plea bargaining be eliminated or reformed to include automatic minimum sentences?

3. Should juries be given less discretion in determining sentences?

4. Should the Texas Court of Criminal Appeals be merged with the Supreme Court?

Key Terms

appellate court, **p. 234**

jurisdiction, **p. 232**

bench trial, **p. 239**

beyond a reasonable doubt, **p. 233**

civil law, **p. 232**

criminal law, **p. 233**

defendant, **p. 232**

en banc, **p. 242**

judicial activism, **p. 242**

jurisdiction, **p. 232**

ordinances, **p. 236**

original jurisdiction, **p. 234**

peace bond, **p. 237**

plaintiff, **p. 232**

plea bargaining, **p. 240**

preponderance, **p. 233**

prosecutor, **p. 233**

reverse and remand, **p. 234**

reverse and render, **p. 234**

trial de novo, **p. 236**

uphold, **p. 234**

Notes

1. http://www.courts.state.tx.us/. Texas Courts Online

2. Texas Penal Code, Chapter 49, 2009–2-11.

3. http://www.txmca.com/. Texas Municipal Courts Association

4. Amir Efrati, "Nobody . . . Is Ever Going to Plead Guilty Again." The *Wall Street Journal*, June 29, 2009.

The Judicial System and Due Process

Stephen F. Austin forms the Texas Rangers. Originally composed of only ten men who "rode across the range," the group's purpose was to protect settlers from Mexicans and Indians.

1837

10

By the end of this chapter on the judicial system and due process, you should be able to . . .

★ Explain why crime rates are among the most important statistical data generated by government.

★ Analyze how the role of law enforcement has evolved, involving more citizen input and cooperation.

★ Evaluate how the Texas prison system has become one of the largest in the world.

★ Explain how an individual's right to due process extends through all stages of the criminal justice system.

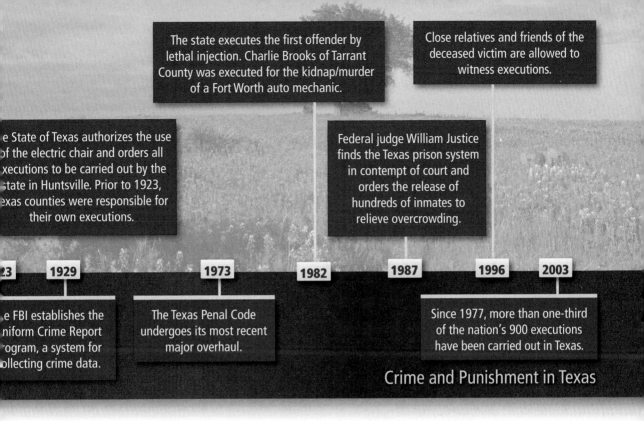

The state executes the first offender by lethal injection. Charlie Brooks of Tarrant County was executed for the kidnap/murder of a Fort Worth auto mechanic.

Close relatives and friends of the deceased victim are allowed to witness executions.

e State of Texas authorizes the use of the electric chair and orders all executions to be carried out by the state in Huntsville. Prior to 1923, exas counties were responsible for their own executions.

Federal judge William Justice finds the Texas prison system in contempt of court and orders the release of hundreds of inmates to relieve overcrowding.

23   1929   1973   1982   1987   1996   2003

e FBI establishes the niform Crime Report ogram, a system for ollecting crime data.

The Texas Penal Code undergoes its most recent major overhaul.

Since 1977, more than one-third of the nation's 900 executions have been carried out in Texas.

Crime and Punishment in Texas

Texas is the poster boy state of judicial horrors.

—DEFENSE ATTORNEY ALAN DERSHOWITZ

*Capital punishment.
Those without the capital get the punishment.*

—LAST WORDS OF A TEXAS DEATH ROW INMATE

ssues of crime and punishment pervade virtually all discussions of state and local government and dominate many political campaigns. Being "tough on crime" is important to people seeking elected office, and candidates take advantage of the opportunity to have their photograph taken with law enforcement officials.

Crime and Punishment

If there is a fundamental concern that Texans share with the rest of the country, it's crime and punishment. The fear of being victimized is real to anyone who has read about criminal street gangs, auto theft, carjackings, or drive-by shootings.

What to do about all this crime is a political question and the jury is split. Nearly everyone agrees on the importance of prevention, but few agree on how to go about it. Some say that a good education keeps people from committing street crimes out of necessity; others believe that crime prevention means educating potential victims about how to maintain their property and personal safety.

Do we have enough police officers to address the demand for service? Is the selection and training process for police officers, prosecutors, judges, and juries adequate, or is that part of the problem? Should the prison system administer punishment, reform, or a combination? Do defendants and criminals really "get all the rights," or are many disadvantaged defendants charged and convicted without the benefit of due process? As relevant as these questions are, Texas lawmakers are starting to look beyond these reactive issues, asking questions such as, What can be done to diminish the need for more police, courts, and prisons?" This new proactive style of public service is only in its formative stages, but it appears to be very promising. Aside from these new approaches, the incidence of crime in Texas has been on a downward trend since its peak in the early 1990s.[1]

Reporting Crime

Each year, the Federal Bureau of Investigation (FBI) publishes *Crime in the United States*, a comprehensive statistical breakdown of crime categorized by type, region, rates, and even time-of-day. The publication is prepared according to a standard called the Uniform Crime Reports (UCR). Measuring crime across America is a highly ambitious task. After all, each of the states has its own version of criminal laws, and which crimes should be included in the report. There are literally hundreds, maybe thousands, of different crimes on the books, and tracking all these would be a daunting task. To simplify things, the UCR devised a list of eight index crimes. The index works much like the Dow Jones stock market index, which tracks a handful of selected stocks representing the entire market. **Index crimes** are those eight offenses that the state and national governments use to perform statistical studies. They include murder, rape, robbery, aggravated assault, burglary, theft, auto theft, and arson. Index statistics are used to establish and compare crime rates among states and regions.[2]

WHAT CAN YOU DO?

Many police and sheriff's departments offer a variety of programs designed to get citizens more involved. These programs include Neighborhood Watch, National Night Out, the Citizen Police Academy, and Citizens on Patrol. To find out if these programs are available in your area, call your local law enforcement agency.

Crime in Texas

index crimes
Seven categories of crime used for statistical study by the federal and state governments.

Although the overall crime rate in Texas has been decreasing, each year more than 1 million people are arrested in Texas for the commission of major crimes. Despite significant decreases in murder, rape, and other assaultive offenses, the number of arrests continues to escalate, primarily due to the flourishing illicit drug trade.

In the mid-1980s thousands of people connected to the manufacture of metham-phetamine were jailed and given the maximum 20-year sentences. Now they're coming out of hibernation—so to speak—and the manufacturing of these home-made drugs is on the rise. So prevalent is this that in 2007 the legislature passed laws requiring retailers to keep certain cold remedies (used to manufacture meth) behind their counters. Other legislation empowers police and social workers to physically remove children found in the presence of dope labs.

Factors in the Crime Rate

A number of elements contribute to the crime rates. Most criminal justice experts agree that one of the factors is the increased age of the average Texan over the past decade, meaning there are fewer individuals in the "crime-prone" years of 17 to 24. Another factor is the efforts of the legislature to keep violent and repeat offenders behind bars for a longer period of time. Texas now has more prison beds than ever before. In fact, the state of Texas has a larger prison system than most countries. In 2005 and again in 2007, the legislature passed laws mandating longer sentences for the more serious and violent offenders, and has greatly expanded the punishment for domestic and "dating" violence. The punishments have also increased dramati-cally for repeat offenders.

Perhaps technology is the foremost reason for the reduction in crime. With knowledge that the overall incidence of crime is down and arrests are up, we can conclude that the justice system is getting more efficient.[3] The use of computers has had dramatic effect on crime fighting efforts on the streets and in the courtrooms. A generation ago, identifying a suspect through fingerprints was an agonizing and tedious task. Today, all the police have to do is scan a small portion of a print found at a crime scene and the computers will reveal the suspect's name, location, and photograph.

Corrections

The corrections system is costly, largely due to the expense of housing individuals convicted of committing criminal acts. Other factors are contributing to the rising cost of corrections: the actual cost of housing the inmates and the increasing volume of the jail population. By a substantial margin, Texas leads the rest of the nation in the state inmate rate. How big is "the system"? It is astonishing. Texas leads the nation in the number of people under some form of supervision, with nearly 1 million people in jail, prison, probation, or parole. This means that 1 in nearly every 20 adults is on the bad side of the justice system, with as many as 5 percent of adult males in Texas cur-rently incarcerated, on probation, or on parole. Both criminal justice agencies and lawmakers acknowledge that better education and employment opportunities would play an important part in reducing the number of incarcerated Texans. According to the Texas Department of Criminal Justice, almost 80 percent of Texas's prison inmates did not complete high school and half were not employed when they were arrested.[4] Legislators, educators, and criminal justice officials are working coopera-tively to address these and other problems. By the most conservative estimates, it costs more than $16,000 per year to keep an adult behind bars, compared to $354 for one year of adult education. The annual cost estimates of housing prisoners do not take into account the money spent investigating, arresting, trying, and convicting the individual offender.[5]

CAPITAL PUNISHMENT The use of capital punishment dates back to the beginnings of recorded history. During the colonial period, each of the 13 colonies used it to some extent, and some had dozens of capital offenses on the books. In modern times, the states get to determine whether or not the death penalty is an option, but the parameters have been severely restricted. Where some colonies, and later the states, prescribed death for crimes ranging from horse thievery to witchcraft, today the states are limited to just a few of the more heinous crimes.

No state executes more prisoners than Texas. It is becoming increasingly difficult for Texas death row inmates to be granted clemency or stays of execution, even when evidence exists that may suggest their innocence. Well-known criminal defense attorney Alan Dershowitz has said that he could teach an entire course on abuse of justice using Texas as a case study. Every capital punishment case generates a degree of controversy, but few have ever been as contentious as that of Leonel Herrera, who was convicted in 1982 of killing a police officer. Eight years after his trial, Herrera's attorneys presented new evidence that suggested his brother actually committed the crime. His brother had died shortly before this new evidence came to light. The state denied the request for a new trial, citing a Texas law that required new evidence to be presented 30 days after the initial trial. The U.S. Supreme Court upheld the Texas law as constitutional, over the objections of Herrera's attorneys who argued that executing an individual when there was still doubt about his guilt violates the provision against cruel and unusual punishment. Since Herrera's execution, the state has revised the law to allow the admission of new evidence even after the 30-day time period has passed.

Capital punishment is one of the most controversial contemporary issues. Much of this controversy stems from myriad of myths believed and often cited by individuals arguing for and against. For example, supporters of the death penalty claim that much-needed prison space would be available if the state expanded the list of capital crimes and executed more prisoners. This belief is invalid, as is the popular notion that putting the condemned to death would save the taxpayers money. At any given time, there are about 400 individuals on Texas death row. This comparatively small number of prisoners hardly would make a dent in the total inmate population even if all these individuals were executed tomorrow. Moreover, it costs taxpayers much more money—in some cases, several millions—to get a death penalty conviction. In almost all cases, the guilt of the accused is well-established, and the appeals address the constitutionality of the death penalty.

The myths abound as to the reason why nearly 40 percent of the executions performed in the United States occur on Texas. You may have heard some people say it is because Texas is such a large, populated state, or because Texas has a higher-than-average criminal element. Not true. There is no correlation between a state's population and its execution rate. California has a much higher population yet it performs very few executions. On the other hand, Oklahoma has a comparatively low population yet ranks number two in the number of executions. Statistically speaking, Texans are a relatively law-abiding people. Violent crime rates statewide are the envy of many other states. Someone may tell you Texas executes more people because it has stricter laws. You might remind that person that Texas's laws are no stricter than that of other states. So why then does Texas have such a high execution rate? The answer to that question can be found in the title page of Chapter 1 of this textbook: political culture. The state's individualistic and traditionalistic natures explain why prosecutors are more prone to seek the death penalty and why juries are more apt to give it.

CAPITAL CRIMES IN TEXAS Capital offenses in Texas include:

- murder of a person whom the defendant knows to be a peace officer, firefighter, or employee of a penal institution who is acting in his official capacity;
- murder of a person while the defendant is in the course of committing or attempting to commit kidnapping, burglary, robbery, aggravated sexual assault, or arson;
- murder for hire (any party agreeing to participate);
- murder committed while escaping or attempting to escape from a penal institution;
- serial and mass murder; or
- murder of a child under six years of age;
- the retaliatory murder of any Texas judge;
- any doctor performing a third-trimester abortion or an abortion on a minor without parental consent; and
- certain repeated sex crimes against children.

"QUESTIONS OF LIFE AND DEATH" In Texas death penalty cases, jurors determine the punishment by following a specific formula set by the law. The judge asks the jury to answer the following three questions. Depending on the answers, the sentence is life or death.

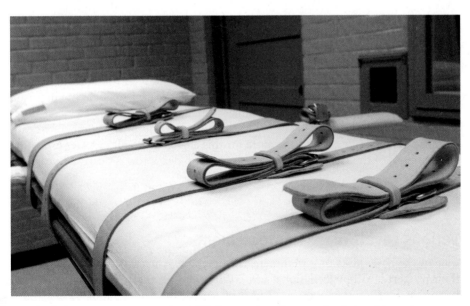

Texas leads the nation in executions since 1977, but even here the pace of capital punishment has slowed. Should the state continue to push for the death penalty in capital cases?

1. Was the defendant's conduct that caused the death of the victim committed deliberately and with the reasonable expectation that the victim's death would ensue?
2. Is it probable that the defendant would commit additional criminal acts of violence that would constitute a continuing threat to society?
3. Is there anything in the circumstances of the offense and the defendant's character and background that would warrant a sentence of life imprisonment rather than the death sentence?

If the answers are yes/yes/no, the sentence is death. If the answers are anything but yes/yes/no, the sentence is life without the possibility of parole.

EXECUTIONS ON THE DECLINE As a result of recent U.S. Supreme Court rulings and changes to the Texas laws made in 2005 and 2007, criminal justice analysts predict a slow but steady decline in the number of executions carried out in Texas. Two of the three reasons why such a decrease in the use of the death penalty are U.S. Supreme Court decisions affecting juveniles and mentally retarded individuals. The third reason is the most significant. The legislature has empowered juries to sentence defendants to life without the possibility of parole.

The U.S. Supreme Court held that persons who were 17 years old or younger at the time the capital crime was committed could not be executed. Consequently, several death row inmates were transferred to the general prison population and are now serving life terms, meaning most will one day be eligible for parole. In another case, the U.S. Supreme Court ruled that states could not execute persons found to be mentally retarded. As a result, Governor Perry commuted the sentences of 28 death row inmates to life.

An even more significant factor in explaining why there will be fewer executions in the future stems from changes made in how juries sentence convicted individuals. Prior to September 2005, juries had two choices in a capital case: the death penalty or life in prison. Over the years, many jurors who pronounced death were troubled by the fact that a sentence of life in prison meant a chance for parole after 40 years. The jurors said that they opted for the death penalty because it was the only way to ensure that the convict would never be loose again. Now, juries still have only two choices, but they are very different: the death penalty or life in prison without the possibility of parole. Criminal justice officials cite the fact that other states making similar moves have experienced a reduction in the number of death sentences. It will take a decade or more for this change to result in lower execution rates, in light of the fact that the average tenure on death row is nearly 11 years.

Law Enforcement

Various Levels of Law Enforcement

One of the basic tasks of government is to provide protection for its citizens and their property. Although national law enforcement agencies such as the Federal Bureau of Investigation and the Drug Enforcement Administration garner much publicity in their efforts to enforce the law, state and local governments provide by far the majority of police services.

In 1965, the Texas legislature took steps toward elevating professionalism among its law enforcement ranks by creating the Texas Commission on Law Enforcement. The commission mandated that all state, county, and local law enforcement officers complete basic training in order to be licensed. Today, the commission sets the criteria for licensing more than 80,000 police officers, reserves, jailers, and corrections officers throughout the state. To be eligible for a license, candidates must complete an 800-hour basic police academy and must be physically and mentally fit. In addition, the commission requires licensed officers to attend regular in-service training on topics of current interest, which now include identity theft, family violence, racial profiling, and other specialized investigative topics.

STATE LEVEL The state law enforcement agency most visible to Texans is the Department of Public Safety (DPS) Highway Patrol. The DPS provides a wide array of police services, ranging from ensuring the safety of commercial vehicles (License and Weight) to tracking con artists who travel across the state (Bunco Division). A division of the DPS known even to non-Texans is the **Texas Rangers,** an elite group of 100 state troopers that investigates major crimes and allegations of police misconduct. The subject of Texas folklore and even some movies, the Rangers were formed in 1837, when the Republic of Texas needed an inexpensive yet effective police force because Texas was an economically depressed and dangerous place to live.[6] "Captain Bill" McDonald remains a Ranger legend. In the 1870s, he was said to have come face-to-face with a mob of 20 angry men, all with shotguns leveled at him. Demonstrating great presence of mind, he told the mob, "I'm here to investigate a foul murder you scoundrels have committed—now, put up them guns."[7] After the men did as they were told, one witness observed, "Captain Bill would charge Hell with a bucket of water." Today, the Texas Rangers have evolved into a respected force of specially trained investigators who probe some of the state's most intricate crimes and are often called in to investigate allegations of police misconduct at the county and municipal level.

Texas Rangers
An elite division of the Department of Public Safety that investigates major crimes and allegations of police misconduct.

More than a dozen other law enforcement agencies operate at the state level. The licensed peace officers assigned to these state agencies are empowered to enforce all state and local laws, but they serve in specialized fields. For example, the Texas Alcoholic Beverage Commission regulates the manufacturing, transportation, distribution, and sale of alcoholic beverages throughout the state.

COUNTY LEVEL Each of Texas's 254 counties has a **sheriff,** whose duty it is to maintain a county jail and to provide police service in the rural, nonincorporated areas of the county. Sheriffs are elected to four-year terms. In some rural areas, the sheriff and his appointed deputies must provide police services for the entire county because there are no cities or towns large enough to have police departments. In such cases, the state police may be called to assist the sheriff's office in the performance of these services. Like the sheriff, the constable is a county-level law enforcement official who is elected to four-year terms of office and empowered to provide police services. The constable's primary mission is to provide assistance and administrative support to the justices of the peace by serving subpoenas and other types of summons.

sheriff
The county's chief law enforcement officer; elected to four-year terms.

Although each county elects only one sheriff, as many as eight constables may be authorized, depending on population. Constables and their deputies generally carry

A police officer arrests a college student.

out their duties in plain clothes, although in some precincts they wear distinctive uniforms much like other peace officers. Because they are licensed peace officers, they often assist the sheriff and local police by providing patrol services in high-crime areas.

SPECIAL DISTRICTS The Texas Constitution authorizes the formation of law enforcement districts to provide specialized police services for specific areas. Most Texas colleges and universities have their own police departments, as do airports and public transportation systems. These specialized agencies are composed of licensed peace officers who are responsible for preventing crime and ensuring the safety of the citizens within their district and the surrounding area. Contrary to popular belief (and to the consternation of many college students), the "campus cops" are empowered and obligated to take the appropriate police action when the situation calls for it. They are not merely "rent-a-cops" or "the dream police." Nearly all areas of the state are served by narcotics task forces, which are made up of specially trained peace officers who gather information about the manufacturing, transportation, and sale of illegal drugs. These special districts often transcend city and county lines, and some are partially funded by state and federal grants. Some of these drug task forces are so effective that they fund themselves through the sale of the seized homes, vehicles, and other property previously owned by drug dealers. Indeed, these seizures have allowed law enforcement agencies to purchase high-tech equipment at no cost to the taxpayers.

LOCAL LEVEL Texas's urban and most populous counties may have as many as two dozen municipal police departments to provide citizens with law enforcement services. These police departments vary in size, from as few as one or two people to several thousand. Salaries, training, and benefits for municipal police officers also vary greatly. Despite the efforts of the Texas Commission on Law Enforcement, some Texas peace officers receive little standardized professional training. Technology has already begun to remedy this dilemma. Beginning in 1999, the state approved distance learning forms of training, such as Internet and CD-ROM programs containing the latest laws and crime-fighting techniques. Training tools such as these have brought state-of-the-art technology to even the smallest and most remote police agencies.

The late 1990s brought a major change in the way municipal police departments deal with crime and the way they relate with members of the community. Often called community-based policing (CBP), this innovative style of law enforcement empowers home and business owners, community leaders, and members of all segments of the community to participate actively in the day-to-day operations of their police departments. CBP programs, such as Citizen's Police Academies and Citizens on Patrol, have fostered a better understanding of the police role. Programs such as these thrive in cities and towns throughout Texas, contributing to positive and productive police-community relationships.

Due Process

Most of the commonly cited state laws that regulate the conduct of individuals and groups can be found in the **Texas Penal Code,** which defines and categorizes crimes and provides for a range of punishment. The Penal Code classifies offenses as misdemeanors, which are relatively minor offenses punishable by a fine and up to one year in county jail, and felonies, more serious crimes in which a convicted person may serve time in the state penitentiary. Table 10.1 illustrates the categories of selected crimes and their scheduled punishments as contained in the Texas Penal Code.

Due process is the rights guaranteed to individuals accused of committing criminal acts. These rights include equal treatment and protection under the law, safeguards against cruel and unusual punishment, the right to trial by jury, the right to a court-appointed attorney if the defendant cannot afford to pay an attorney, and the right to face the persons who have made the accusation. Many of these rights are spelled out in the U.S. and Texas constitutions; others, such as the exclusionary rule, have evolved from past practice and court decisions.

Texas Penal Code
The state's definitions and categorizations of crimes and punishments.

due process
Constitutionally protected rights of persons accused of committing criminal acts.

TABLE **10.1** Crime Classifications and Selected Offenses

MISDEMEANORS			
CATEGORY	MAXIMUM FINE	SENTENCE[1]	EXAMPLES[2]
Class C[3]	$500	none	simple assault; theft under $50; most traffic violations; city ordinance violations; public intoxication; disorderly conduct
Class B	$2,000	180 days	DWI (first offense); prostitution; harassment; possession of marijuana (under 2 oz.)
Class A	$4,000	1 year	assault causing injury; resisting arrest; some weapons violations

FELONIES			
CATEGORY	MAXIMUM FINE	SENTENCE[4]	EXAMPLES
State Jail	$10,000	180 days–2 yrs.	unauthorized use of vehicle; vehicle burglary
3rd Degree	$10,000	2-10 years	deadly conduct; kidnapping; escape; aggravated assault
2nd Degree	$10,000	2-20 years	sexual assault; robbery; intoxication manslaughter; burglary of a habitation
1st Degree	$10,000	5-99 years	indecency with a child; murder; attempted capital murder; aggravated sexual assault
Capital	N/A	life/death[5]	murder of a peace officer; serial or mass murder; murder for hire; murder of a child under 6

Notes:
[1]Misdemeanor sentences are served in the county jails.
[2]Many classifications of crime span a wide range of punishment categories, depending on value and the defendant's prior record.
[3]City ordinance violations carry fines of up to $2,000.
[4]Felony sentences are served in the state jails or state penitentiaries.
[5]Punishment for a capital felony is either life in prison without parole or death by lethal injection.

exclusionary rule

A due process right that makes it illegal for the government to use evidence gathered during an unlawful police search.

The **exclusionary rule** demands that any items or evidence gathered during an illegal search of a person's private property be excluded as evidence against the defendant at the time of trial. Say a police officer pulls a motorist over for speeding and demands to search the car for drugs. Although this officer lacks probable cause to believe the driver is carrying drugs, and the motorist objects to the search, the officer searches the car anyway and discovers 100 kilos of cocaine and a stolen copy of *Lone Star Politics* in the trunk. At the trial, the evidence against the defendant (the cocaine and the book) will be inadmissible if the officer cannot establish why he or she stopped and searched the motorist. For more the exclusionary rule, see Inside the Federalist System.

That's why it is important that police follow the rules every step of the way and uphold due process, observing the constitutionally protected rights of persons accused of committing criminal acts. (And in case you're wondering, the motorist will get neither his drugs nor his stolen book back.) In recent years, the U.S. Supreme Court has reviewed the merits of the exclusionary rule and has retained it by a slim margin. Some citizens want to do away with it, citing case after case where defendants are caught "red-handed" only to be released because the police failed to observe their due process rights. They claim that it shouldn't matter *how* the evidence was seized, as long as the bad guys get punished.

Proponents of the rule point out that police already have a great deal of, perhaps too much, discretionary power. They argue that doing away with the rule would result in police conducting arbitrary searches. The Court compromised by establishing what has come to be known as the "good faith" exception to the exclusionary rule, whereby incriminating evidence may be admissible if the police acted

INSIDE

THE FEDERALIST SYSTEM

Search and Seizure

The 2009 U.S. Supreme Court case *Arizona* v. *Gant* provides a prime example of how judicial review can profoundly affect long-standing practices. Prior to this case, police in every state, including Texas, were authorized to search motor vehicles whenever a recent occupant had been arrested. It did not matter what the arrest was for. The police had blanket authority to search.

These searches "incident to arrest" often turned up evidence of other crimes, and the defendants were charged and convicted accordingly. For example, a motorist may have been arrested for an unpaid traffic ticket, and if during a search the police discovered drugs, or weapons, or any other items that offends the laws, that motorist was charged and convicted of the much higher crime.

Arizona v. *Gant* changed all that. Now the police can search a car only with the consent of the driver, unless they have reason to believe the car contains evidence that is directly connected to the crime for which the occupant was arrested.

While this is not the first time the federal courts have overturned Texas laws and practices, it certainly has changed the way local Texas police and sheriffs conduct their business. Opponents of the change claim that a lot more drugs will be left on the streets, while proponents are praising the high court's preservation of privacy rights.

in good faith. For example, an officer pulls up to a traffic accident where several victims are in critical condition. The officer opens a woman's purse in an effort to find the name of her doctor or next of kin and stumbles on a ski mask, handgun, robbery note, and marked currency connected to a recent bank robbery. This evidence would be admissible under the good faith exception.

Crime victims and law-abiding citizens often vent frustration when an individual who has been charged with a crime is provided with an attorney at no cost and that attorney manages to produce a successful defense. Frequently heard complaints about the system include, "The criminal has all the rights," and "The courts let the criminal go because of a technicality." These "technicalities" are often actually gross violations of the accused's due process guarantees, and, if the concepts of equal protection and civil liberties are to be preserved, the courts have no choice but to let the defendant go.

Stages of Due Process

ARREST, SEARCH, AND SEIZURE For the accused, the first formal stage of the criminal justice process is the arrest. Both the U.S. and Texas constitutions guarantee that no person shall be arrested unless **probable cause** has been established. The concept of probable cause is one of the most important in the entire legal system. Probable cause can be said to exist when it appears more likely than not that an individual has committed a criminal act. When it exists, the government is authorized to restrain an individual's freedom and liberties. Probable cause can be determined by a peace officer who makes the apprehension or by a judge who issues a warrant of arrest. Unless an individual is charged with the crime of capital murder, he or she is allowed the opportunity to post bail. **Bail** is a cash deposit posted by the accused as a guarantee that he or she will return to court when summoned. The amount of bail is determined by a judge, who must consider the nature of the crime, the accused's past record, and other factors.

Arrests are usually accompanied by one or more types of searches. The Fourth Amendment of the U.S. Constitution provides all citizens the right to be free from unreasonable searches and seizures of property by the government. The police and prosecutors may not abridge this important safeguard while they are collecting evidence against a person accused of violating the law. Conditions under which police may lawfully conduct a search of an individual's property are highly regulated by law. Police can thoroughly search any person who has been arrested, provided the arrest was legal. Searches of homes, cars, and other private premises often require a search warrant, and the officers must show sufficient cause in order to obtain one. Many search warrant requests are denied because the officers fail to convince the judge that there are good reasons, or enough probable cause, to search.

Police officers may seize one or more categories of evidence during a lawful search. The first category, *fruits of a crime*, includes any items stolen or otherwise illegally obtained by the accused. The second category, *tools of a crime*, may be any item or instrument used during the commission of a criminal act. For example, a screwdriver used to steal a car would be considered a tool of a crime. Another category is called *contraband*. Mere possession of items considered contraband is illegal. Child pornography, some types of drugs, and gambling equipment fall under this category. The final category, *mere evidence*, pertains to items that tend to connect an individual with a crime. An example of mere evidence would be fingerprints or blood splatters found at the scene of a crime.

probable cause
The total set of facts and circumstances that would lead a reasonable person to believe that an individual committed a specific criminal act.

bail
A cash deposit or other security given by the accused as a guarantee that he will return to court when summoned.

"I was robbed!" Is it theft, burglary, or robbery?

Suppose you walk out to your car today only to discover that someone has broken in and stolen your favorite textbook. You might call the campus police and tell them you were robbed. You weren't robbed, you were burglarized.

Most Americans are somewhat familiar with the eight index crimes, but few have difficulty differentiating the subtleties among theft, burglary, and robbery. The common element is theft, which is the simple act of stealing. Shoplifting is a prime example of theft. Burglary and robbery amount to "theft plus." In the case of burglary, the offender commits a theft after breaking into or unlawfully entering a vehicle or structure. Burglary is defined as "theft plus" illegal entry.

Robbery is the most serious of the three because it is a crime against persons. You cannot be robbed unless you were present when the theft or attempted theft took place. In addition, a robbery requires the victim to be injured or placed in fear of imminent injury during the encounter. Robbery is "theft plus" a threatening or violent act.

So as bad as it would be to have your car burglarized, you may find comfort in the fact that you weren't the victim of a robbery. Don't let this happen to you—carry your textbook with you!

Grand Jury and Indictment

grand jury
A panel composed of twelve citizens who determine whether enough evidence exists to charge a person with a felony and make him or her stand trial.

For individuals accused of committing a felony, a critical component of due process is the right to have the facts of the case heard by a **grand jury.** The grand jury is comprised of 12 citizens who serve for three to six months and are chosen by judges of the district courts. The grand jury determines whether there is sufficient evidence for the accused to stand trial. After the facts and circumstances of a felony case are heard, the grand jury votes. If nine or more members find that the case should proceed to the trial stage, an **indictment** (also called a "true bill") is issued and a trial is scheduled. A nonindictment, or "no-bill," is declared if the grand jury determines that no crime was committed or the accused was justified in his actions. For example, the grand jury often concludes that homeowners who kill or seriously injure intruders were merely exercising their right to protect themselves. When an individual is no-billed by the grand jury, all criminal proceedings stop and the case is dropped.

indictment
A finding by the grand jury that the case will proceed to the trial stage; also called a true-bill.

The grand jury process has been controversial since its inception, not because of its role but because of the way the proceedings take place. Because grand jurors volunteer to serve for as long as six months, they are often not representative of the community as a whole. Most are financially secure. Another criticism is that grand juries operate in secrecy. Neither the person charged nor his attorneys are allowed to attend the proceedings, and it is illegal for jury members to discuss the cases with anyone. Because only the prosecutors and other government agents are allowed to present evidence, there is really no way of knowing what evidence was presented or withheld. For these reasons, the grand juries have been labeled as the "rubber stamp" of the police and prosecutor, meaning that they will conclude whatever the government wants them to conclude. Attempts have been made to reform the Texas grand jury system. Over a decade ago, then Texas Speaker of the House Gib Lewis introduced a bill that would have allowed an accused to have an attorney present

The Texas Constitution: A Closer Look

Mention the "Bill of Rights" to people and they will naturally think of the first ten amendments to the U.S. Constitution. Many people do not know that all state constitutions also contain a bill of rights. You might be pleased to know that the Texas Constitution affords us with even greater liberty than does the U.S. document. Here are two examples of constitutional protections provided by the State of Texas:

Sec. 18. IMPRISONMENT FOR DEBT.
No person shall ever be imprisoned for debt.

Sec. 20. OUTLAWRY OR TRANSPORTATION FOR OFFENSE.
This provision prohibits the state from requiring an individual to leave the state as part of his sentence or punishment.

during the grand jury proceedings. Not surprisingly, this occurred shortly after he was indicted by a Travis County grand jury.

Trial

After the indictment, the case is assigned to a prosecutor and prepared for trial. The **prosecutor** is an attorney representing the victim and the state against the accused. In felony cases, the accused has the right to an attorney who will represent his or her side. If the accused cannot afford one, the court appoints one for him or her. Most criminal cases are disposed of by way of **plea bargain**, the process of negotiating a settlement, usually for a lesser charge or less jail time. The plea bargain is another controversial issue in today's justice system. The fact is that there are not enough trial courts or prison beds in the state to handle all the cases, and plea bargaining has become a necessity. Due process rights at the trial stage include the right to a trial by jury, although the defendant often waives this right and elects to have a **bench trial**, wherein his or her case is heard by a judge and no jury. When a defendant opts for a bench trial, the judge hears the testimony and determines the verdict. Six jurors hear misdemeanor cases (those heard in municipal, justice, and county courts-at-law). Twelve jurors are required for felony jury cases, which are tried in the district courts.

Before 1992, jurors were selected exclusively from voter registration lists, and this practice tended to exclude many young, minority, and less affluent individuals. Today, in an effort to make juries reflect a true cross-section of Texans, the courts select prospective jurors from the driver's license rolls. The courts may request lists of potential jurors from the secretary of state's office, which in turn provides randomly selected names from driver's license, state identification card, and voter

prosecutor
A government employee who initiates criminal cases against individuals.

plea bargaining
A process in which the accused receives a lighter sentence than could be expected from a trial verdict in exchange for a guilty plea.

bench trial
A criminal trial that is held without jury, as requested by the person charged.

registration rolls. To be eligible for jury duty, an individual must be at least 18 years old, not convicted of or under indictment for a felony crime, mentally competent, and a U.S. citizen. Potential jurors are entitled to automatic exemption if they are 65 years old or older, a full-time college or secondary school student, or the sole caretaker of a child 10 years of age or younger.

voir dire
Trial jury selection process conducted by attorneys for both sides.

Prior to the trial, a jury panel is interviewed by the defense and prosecution (or plaintiff and defense, in a civil case). This process is called **voir dire,** and its purpose is to ensure that none of the jurors is predisposed to making a decision until after all the evidence is heard. The term "voir dire" means, literally, to "tell the truth." In order to make this determination, lawyers on both sides often ask questions of a personal nature. In 1994, a Denton County woman, Dianna Brandborg, went to jail for refusing to answer a jury questionnaire sent to her by a district court. After writing "not applicable" to 12 of the 110 questions, the judge declared that Brandborg was in contempt of the court and sentenced her to three days in jail. The questions she refused to answer pertained to her income and political affiliation. She won an appeal in federal court in 1995. The federal judge ruled that the trial court did not balance the defendant's right to a fair trial with Brandborg's right to privacy and that questions asked of prospective jurors must be applicable to the case if a juror is required to answer.[8]

The trial begins with opening statements from both sides. Next, the prosecution presents its case. The defense then has the opportunity to present its own version of the incident and to introduce witnesses and evidence that might indicate the defendant's innocence. At no time does the defendant have to speak or testify before the jury. But, if the defendant wishes to address the court in self-defense , the prosecutor then has a right to cross-examine him or her. The fact that the accused does not have to answer any questions is an important example of due process rights under the Fifth Amendment to the U.S. Constitution. The Fifth Amendment prevents the government from compelling a person to testify against him- or herself (this is known as self-incrimination). Moreover, the Fifth Amendment also provides for an attorney to represent the accused at no cost if certain conditions are met. Of course, the Texas Constitution also contains a Bill of Rights, and many of these rights are the same as those found in the U.S. Constitution. One interesting amendment contained in the Texas Constitution is a prohibition against outlawry. To be "outlawed" means to be banished from the state as part of one's punishment. Texans can rest assured that they can never be forced to leave the state, no matter what they do.

double jeopardy
A criminal defendant's due process right to be protected from being tried a second time (after receiving a not-guilty verdict the first time).

A conviction in a criminal jury trial requires that all members of the jury agree on a verdict of "guilty." Likewise, a unanimous vote is required for a finding of "not guilty." After the jury reaches a unanimous verdict of not guilty, the defendant cannot be tried again for the same crime. Doing so would violate the defendant's due process right against **double jeopardy.** The double jeopardy rule does not allow the government to prosecute an individual more than once for a specific charge. For this reason, the state must present its best possible case because, as some judges have observed, "The prosecution gets only one bite from the apple." If the final verdict is not unanimous, or if the jury fails to render a verdict at all, the judge declares a **hung jury** (a nonunanimous verdict) or mistrial, and the prosecutor has the option of requesting a second trial using another jury. Some of the factors the district or county attorney must consider when deciding whether to try a defendant again are cost and public sentiment.

hung jury
Term describing the failure to render a verdict in a criminal case.

my turn

Essay from a Texas Death Row Inmate

Martin Allen Draughon

Texas Death Row Inmate Martin Allen Draughon was convicted of capital murder in a Harris County Court when he was 24 years old and served 20 years before he was released. He eventually proved, through ballistics evidence, that he did not commit the crime for which he was charged and convicted. He agreed to write this essay for *Lone Star Politics* in hopes that readers will gain a better understanding of what it is like to be on Texas death row.

At the time of this writing I'm a 33-year-old death row prisoner. Been here since the summer of '87, long enough that I've become an "old timer." And that's a scary thought when you live on death row, for each year is both a victory and a threat. There are now many more on death row than when I got here, yet I am more lonely than ever. I know it's because my soul is slowly being strangled each time I have to deal with death here—and dealing with death is an everyday thing on death row.

I remember, before I got here, I was really scared about coming to this place. I had no idea what death row was going to be like, but I naturally expected the worst. I had absolutely no concept of death row. I had never even thought about death row or capital punishment before this mess I'm in. I didn't even know it existed. One by one over the years, each one of these special friends has been murdered by the State of Texas. As a free man I never experienced the depth of friendship as I have here on death row. I thought I had friends "out there." Turns out it was all superficial. They have all long ago vanished from my life. These friendships I have had on death row have survived the harshest psychological strain possible, yet still maintained their sincerity. It's a hard thing to do . . . to say "good-bye" to a friend because tomorrow he goes to his planned death. Yet I've uttered the "good-bye" many times already.

And this place became a little lonelier. I want so badly to have the depth of such friendship again, but it could never be the same. There seems to be that unwilling deadness inside me that makes it nearly impossible for me to put my trust and feelings on the line again when I know that this friend will probably be killed also, and again another piece of me will die with him. I wonder how much

more of me can die along with my friend before I become something less than alive, something less than human?

You lose a lot more than your freedom when you come to prison. You lose all ties to a life you once lived. Poof! It's gone—forever. Who and what you always thought yourself to be no longer matters, no longer exists. You lose your sense of individuality when you come into this place. The continual degradation and humiliation we endure day in and day out only further strips us of what humanity and dignity we have left. You become even less than a number here on death row. Another file in someone's office. An unfeeling shell of the man who once was.

There is no compassion on death row. You are never even allowed to touch your family at a visit. Not even before you are taken away to be executed are you allowed to touch and hug your family. When I was sentenced to death, my mother was in the courtroom. I wasn't even allowed to hug her before I was taken away. Nor my sisters, for that matter. One day during the trial my sister brushed against my back while walking past me in the courtroom . . . if I'd known that would be the very last touch I'd ever get from her I would have fully relished the moment.

The first few years I just settled into a prisoner existence, made friends and learned from each new experience. These were friendships that had developed and matured under the extreme hardships of this environment and with a death sentence hanging over our heads. I'd shared some very private and painful moments with a number of them.

Death row is a very cold and lonely place. With each passing year, things get more stressful. More restrictions are placed on us. More is taken away

(continued)

(continued from page 265)

from us. More laws are made to speed us toward our deaths a little faster. More of the public is inflamed by the media [they] hate us even more and [want to] do even worse things to us. With each passing year, more men are killed and I have grown and matured. I have become much more of a man than I ever would have become if this had not happened to me, but I'm afraid all the good there is to get from all this has already come and gone.

When I knew I was headed to death row I started trying to prepare myself for it psychologically. I had already gotten past the stage of wanting to kill myself. Now I was getting ready. I knew life as I'd known it was officially over. My life now is 100 percent separate from the life I had before prison, before death row. With the exception of family and relatives, I don't know anyone now that I knew before I came to prison. And this is not all that is lost when you come to death row. Not only do you usually lose all your friends, this whole ordeal also puts an unbearable strain on family and relatives. In a lot of cases, the family of the death row prisoner also fades from his life.

1994 was probably the hardest year for me. In January, I was moved into the Death Watch Cell and all my belongings were taken away and inventoried. I had an execution date fast approaching. One day I was taken to the Captain's office where I had to answer a bunch of questions, provide a lot of details, make up my list of witnesses to watch me die, decide what I wanted for my last meal, what I wanted to wear when I was executed, who to release my body to, and what to do with all the personal property I have accumulated over the years. All this to help make preparations for my own death. (I didn't have an answer for more than half what I was asked!) What to do now? Write some letters maybe . . .? Could you have enough presence of mind to "write" when you knew plans were being made to kill you in 24 hours? Maybe I should write my family and friends, tell them "something." I'm telling you, your mind shuts down completely at such [a] time. I could barely formulate a complete sentence, let alone write my "last words" to someone. The morning of the day of my scheduled execution a sergeant came to tell me I received a "stay."

Whew!

Over the years, out of necessity, I have learned at least a little about the law and capital appeals. At various times, this or that guy would share his legal

papers with me and I couldn't believe what I was reading. Inaccurate police reports, outright lies, and, in one case, a man was sentenced to death in a case where there was no physical evidence. But it happens. I've read it for myself.

There have been several times when the actual killer is known to the authorities and still an execution is carried out—for any number of reasons. Could be because it's the easiest way to go and it "settles" unsolved crimes, or the prosecution grants a favor to the other criminal, or it could be election year and to admit a mistake would be a bad "career move." For the purpose the death penalty was created, it is not working. The death penalty hasn't served to deter crime in the least, yet the public, through the help of the media fanning the flames of fear and prejudice, are still being duped into supporting it.

The only way to avoid getting caught in the criminal justice snare is if you or your family is influential and has lots of money. Feel free to refer to the O. J. Simpson trial. I'm not saying he's guilty, but I am saying this: I know a great MANY men who were convicted, sent to death row, and EXECUTED on A LOT LESS evidence than they had on O.J.!

Once I accepted that my life was over, I began to develop a desire to try to help other young people learn from the mistakes I made with drugs, money, life in the fast lane, and being "naive about the criminal (in)justice system," mistakes I am paying for with my life. I hope that if I can save at least a few others from treading the same path, then I'll leave behind at least a little something good in this world.

When my death row journey began, I quickly learned the power of the pen and that if I wanted to maintain any contact with the outside world, I'd have to develop my writing skills. So, I learned to express myself in the written form, and I began to write. But not for just this reason alone. I knew that I had thrown my life away and was wounded to the very core of my soul at such a loss. I was filled with so much regret and sorrow. Writing became my release valve and my legacy.

But no longer do the words flow as easily as they once did. Don't know what the problem is. Is it because I've already said all there is to say? Or is it because the deaths of over 115 men I've known has created such a dead place that words can't get past it anymore?

Who will listen anyway?

Texas is one of a handful of states in which the jury decides the amount of time the accused will serve. When a jury trial results in a "guilty" verdict, a separate proceeding, with the same jury, is held to determine the sentence. No matter the outcome in a criminal trial, the defendant can still be sued in civil court by the victim or the victim's family. Because the civil trial is initiated by a private party and not the government, this practice does not violate the double jeopardy rule.

Summary

The incidence of crime has been decreasing in Texas, and it is widely held that an increase in professional training, innovative management techniques, and an increase in citizen involvement are the primary factors contributing to this trend. Major reforms have been made in the Texas correctional system, although it is clear that further modifications are necessary.

Enforcing the laws is one of the fundamental roles of government and in Texas, a highly traditional state, there is great resistance to change. Progressive and innovative reforms are being implemented slowly, and these measures are expected to spread throughout Texas and the nation.

A wave of U.S. Supreme Court decisions and legislative changes will make a significant impact on the number of death sentences, and ultimately, the number of executions carried out in Texas.

Both the U.S. and Texas constitutions guarantee individuals certain due process rights, and these rights pervade all stages of the criminal justice system. Although the judicial system is often condemned for being too technical and criticized for being too "soft" on suspected criminals, our due process rights are among the most precious liberties we enjoy as a free people.

Chapter Test

1. The eight crimes that governments use for their official crime statistics are known as
   a. index crimes.
   b. uniform crimes.
   c. status crimes.
   d. statutory crimes.

2. The rights guaranteed to individuals accused of committing a crime
   a. Miranda rights.
   b. elementary rights.
   c. due process.
   d. exclusionary rights.

3. The use of the capital punishment in Texas is expected to
   a. increase slightly.
   b. skyrocket due to the rising crime rate.
   c. remain constant over time.
   d. decrease in the next decade.

4. Fingerprints, DNA, and hair fibers are examples of this category of evidence.
   a. tools
   b. fruits
   c. mere
   d. contraband

5. The county official responsible for maintaining a county jail.
   a. constable
   b. police chief
   c. justice of the peace
   d. sheriff

6. A process by which prospective jurors are interviewed and required to be truthful.
   a. voir dire
   b. res gestae
   c. corpus delecti
   d. habeas corpus

7. Texas executes more than any other state because
   a. it has much higher crime rates.
   b. of its political culture.
   c. the laws are comparatively stricter than other states.
   d. explosive population gains in urban areas.

8. Evidence taken during an unlawful police search may not be used in court because of
   a. the Contraband Principle.
   b. the Voir Dire Exception.
   c. the Evidentiary Doctrine.
   d. the Exclusionary Rule.

9. A plea bargain is
   a. a negotiated settlement in a criminal case.
   b. a measure of the crime rates.
   c. an agreement among law enforcement officials.
   d. a term defining community-based policing.

10. Jurors are selected from
    a. a pool of volunteers.
    b. a list of persons required to perform community service.
    c. driver's license holders.
    d. voter registration rolls.

Answers: 1. a 2. c 3. d 4. c 5. d 6. a 7. b 8. d 9. a 10. c

Critical Thinking Questions

1. How has community-based policing affected law enforcement in Texas?

2. Should grand jury proceedings be open record?

3. Should sheriffs be appointed?

Key Terms

bail, **p. 261**
bench trial, **p. 263**
double jeopardy, **p. 264**
due process, **p. 259**
exclusionary rule, **p. 260**
grand jury, **p. 262**
hung jury, **p. 264**
index crimes, **p. 252**

indictment, **p. 262**
plea bargaining, **p. 263**
probable cause, **p. 261**
prosecutor, **p. 263**
sheriff, **p. 257**
Texas Penal Code, **p. 259**
Texas Rangers, **p. 257**
voir dire, **p. 264**

Notes

1.   Elliott Cochran, "Crime in State, County Down," *Courier of Montgomery County*. June 15, 2009).

2.   Uniform Crime Reports, http://www.fbi.gov/ucr/ucr.htm.

3.   Mile Little, "Sometimes Just a Touch Is Enough," *Liberty County Vindicator*, July 1, 2009

4.   Michelle Deitch, "Prison Statistics Should Make Texans Feel Uneasy," *Dallas Morning News*, September 8, 2002, p. 5J.

5.   Adam Liptak, "1 in 100 U.S. Adults Behind Bars, New Study Says," *New York Times*, February 28, 2008.

6.   Walter Prescott Webb, *The Story of the Texas Rangers* (Austin, TX: Encino Press, 1971), p. 8.

7.   Walter Prescott Webb, *The Texas Rangers: A Century of Frontier Defense* (Austin, TX: University of Texas Press, 1965), p. 458.

8.   Nita Thurman, "Woman Wins Battle over Juror's Right to Privacy," *Dallas Morning News*, June 18, 1995, p. 37A.

Local and County Governments and Special Districts

11

Stephen F. Austin, in his effort to populate Texas, offers an exemption from all general taxes for the first ten years to people moving from the United States.

Houston was the capi of the Republic from 1837 to 1840.

1820s   **1836**   **1837**

Houston is founded by brothers Augustus C. and John K. Allen, w pay a little more than $1.40 per a for 6,642 acres of land near the headwaters of Buffalo Bayou.

By the end of this chapter on local and county governments and special districts, you should be able to . . .

★ Identify how Texans can have an impact on their local governments.

★ Differentiate among the two types of cities and several forms of city government.

★ Explain the impact of grassroots politics on local government.

★ Explain why counties were established and how they have evolved.

★ Analyze the importance of special districts abound in Texas.

★ Explain the impact of regional councils of governments.

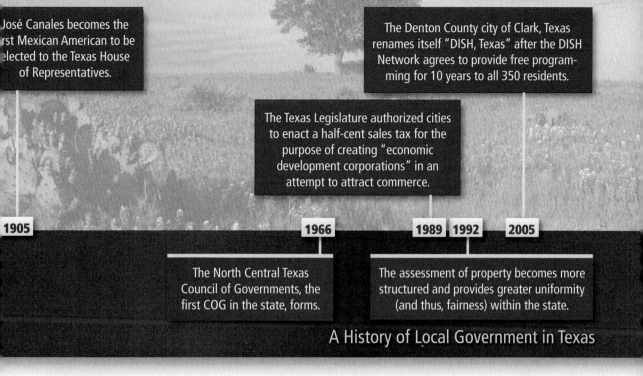

José Canales becomes the first Mexican American to be elected to the Texas House of Representatives.

The Denton County city of Clark, Texas renames itself "DISH, Texas" after the DISH Network agrees to provide free programming for 10 years to all 350 residents.

The Texas Legislature authorized cities to enact a half-cent sales tax for the purpose of creating "economic development corporations" in an attempt to attract commerce.

1905   1966   1989   1992   2005

The North Central Texas Council of Governments, the first COG in the state, forms.

The assessment of property becomes more structured and provides greater uniformity (and thus, fairness) within the state.

A History of Local Government in Texas

You're not remembered on how much power you had—you're remembered on how you used it.

—DALLAS COUNTY COMMISSIONER JOHN WILEY PRICE

Former U.S. Speaker of the House Thomas "Tip" O'Neill once declared, "All politics is local." He was explaining how the problems and concerns across America affect the actions of elected government officials at the national level. This saying has endured, perhaps because the people who study government understand that the decisions that most affect the lives of citizens are made by the local school board, in the city hall, and in the county courthouses. Government at the local or "grassroots" level is the fountainhead of state, national, and global politics. Our system of federalism depends on the dynamics of intergovernmental relationships at all levels, and thus an understanding of how local government is structured is essential to anyone wishing to participate.

Local government is defined as any level of government below the state level. Specifically, it includes three levels: municipal (or city), county, and special district. Although local government is the essence of American democracy, most people cannot identify the type of local government in their own hometowns, much less name their county commissioners or city council members. The profound irony of American democracy is that although participation in local government affords citizens the most control over their own lives, voter turnout for local elections is lower than that for any other level. Texas citizens insist on local control, yet a turnout of

10 percent of the qualified voters for a municipal election is common and a turnout of 20 percent is celebrated.

Local government is where many of the state's top public figures launched their political careers. There, they put their ideas and ideals to the test and acquire political skills. Former governor Ann Richards started her highly successful political journey as a Travis County commissioner. Before long, she ran for and won the statewide offices of treasurer and then governor. Former San Antonio city councilman Henry Cisneros also served as the city's mayor, and was later chosen by President Clinton to serve as the secretary of housing and urban development. Had Cisneros not established a track record as both an able politician and an effective administrator at the local level, he probably would not have been considered for a cabinet position.

Texas **MOSAIC**

Increasing Texas Diversity:

Henry Cisneros

Henry Cisneros personifies several of the key points of this chapter. Once among the most talked about and popular U.S. political figures, for many years he represented the strengthening political clout of the Hispanic community both in Texas and throughout the country. Cisneros has never forgotten his grassroots beginnings. His life's work has not changed in the least—but the scale has multiplied. Thirty years ago he was struggling for sidewalks in his west San Antonio council district. Later, as secretary of Housing and Urban Development, he made the most out of his agency's $1.6 billion budget, a budget he managed to double within two years of being appointed. Cisneros's vision, coupled with his energy and ability to get things done, made him a formidable force in urban policy. He seems to be as at ease with the people on the streets of any U.S. city as he was when he was a city councilman in San Antonio during the 1970s. During those years, he would drive his battered Volkswagen Beetle into the neighborhoods of his district and conduct his version of the town hall meeting. In a time and place where politicians were generally distrusted, Henry Cisneros demonstrated that he could and would get things done. He brought participatory democracy to some of the poorest districts in the city, and he listened to the concerns of the residents. After serving his district for several years, he was twice elected mayor of San Antonio, a sprawling and diverse city with immense needs, especially in the area of housing and development. As mayor, he was instrumental in the passage of the bond package for and the construction of the Alamodome, a state-of-the-art sports arena that exemplifies the city's own prosperous future. He is also fondly remembered and especially well appreciated by many in San Antonio for his contribution in making the city a major tourist attraction. Cisneros played a key role in the renovation of the Riverwalk and in the construction of the SeaWorld theme park complex.

Former San Antonio mayor Henry Cisneros was chosen by President Clinton to serve as Secretary of Housing and Urban Development.

He has served as president for the Spanish-language television network Univision. Will Henry Cisneros seek higher elected office? Will he become the first Hispanic to serve as a U.S. senator from Texas? He has been vague about his own political aspirations, and his personal and marital issues have cast a shadow on his otherwise brilliant political acumen. One thing about Henry Cisneros remains clear: he understands the wants and needs of his constituents, and he will do what it takes to attain them.

Former Governor Ann Richards started her career in politics at the grassroots level. Her first elected office was as a Travis County commissioner, and she was later elected state treasurer and then governor.

Today, local governments perform a wide range of services, from building roads and keeping them clean and safe to collecting garbage and providing health care for the homeless. Many students are astounded to learn how much local government costs. For example, in 2008 the City of Houston spent over $1 billion on the police, fire, and city courts alone.[1]

In an era of ever-increasing demands and limited resources, many of today's successful local government leaders are managing and operating more like business-people than politicians. The field of public administration has grown as tomorrow's leaders seek professional training in order to deliver expected services more effectively. Colleges and universities across the country offer advanced degrees in public administration and related fields to prepare our leaders for challenges ranging from long-term waste disposal, education, and infrastructure improvement to water management, and homeland security. No matter where in Texas you live, you are soon likely to be logging more miles on toll roads. Although the planning, funding, and construction of these roads remain primarily a state and national issue, supervision and enforcement will always be a responsibility of local government.

Three very broad levels of local government exist: municipal, county, and special district. The cities, towns, and villages throughout the state operate as municipalities. Four of five Texans live within the boundaries of a municipality, but every Texan lives in—and is therefore affected by—one of the state's 254 counties. Special districts, including the approximately 1,100 independent school districts, are specially created units of government that may encompass only part of a city or several counties.

Municipal Government

About 80 percent of Texans live within the boundaries of some 1,200 municipalities. Municipal governments, performing a variety of services, uniquely reflect the citizens who reside within them. The term "municipal government" applies to cities, towns, and villages that are recognized by the legislature as being a governmental entity. Although a municipality can only be classified in one of two ways, general law or home rule, countless variations in the form of government operate in these cities.

Types of Municipalities

There are in essence two types of cities: general law and home rule. Both types of government are of great importance to Texans because although a majority of the cities operate under general law, a majority of Texans reside in cities with a home rule charter as indicated in Figure 11.1.

general law
A highly restrictive, and the most fundamental type of, legal status for municipal government.

GENERAL LAW **General law** cities have limited autonomy. These cities are more closely regulated by the state government and do not provide a wide array of services. These cities tend to have lower taxes, smaller populations, and fewer employees.

Three-fourths, or approximately 900, of Texas's municipalities are classified as general law cities. General law cities are not heavily populated and do not usually provide "big city" services such as libraries, public recreation facilities, and public housing. These cities are limited by the generic laws pertaining to local governments in the Texas Constitution, as noted in the box nearby. General law cities are less autonomous than home rule cities because the Texas Constitution limits their local tax rates and compels them to a limited form of government. In other words, general law cities are governed more by state regulation than by the local population.

home rule
A legal status that gives municipalities more autonomy in establishing tax rates and providing services; must be approved by a majority of the voters in municipalities consisting of 5,000 or more persons.

HOME RULE For the most part, **home rule** have the opposite characteristics. Unlike general law cities, home rule cities are highly autonomous and thus able to provide a greater array of services, such as libraries and parks. These services, of course, come at the cost of higher local taxes. When you consider the fact that some 80 percent of Texans live in home rule cities, you may conclude that these people don't mind paying higher tax rates in return for services such as water and sewage, parks, libraries, and senior citizens centers. Many Texans regard these and other city-funded projects, like convention centers, municipal pools, golf courses, youth centers, and museums, as enhancements to the quality of life. It's a trade-off, and it gives Texans a choice.

FIGURE **11.1** Texas Cities with More Than 50,000 People.

The Texas Constitution: A Closer Look

The Texas Constitution sets limitations on the amount of taxes a city can levy. Article XI, Section 4 prohibits cities with fewer than 5,000 residents from becoming home rule, and it places strict limitations on the amount of taxes that can be levied.

Section 5 allows cities with home rule charters to levy significantly higher local taxes, but sets a cap and sets further restrictions. One of the most notable is a prohibition against adopting local laws inconsistent with state law.

In order to obtain home rule status, a municipality must have a population of at least 5,000 citizens and the eligible voters must approve a city charter in a popular election.[2] The charter specifies the name of the municipality and the form of government to be implemented.

A home rule charter allows a municipal government greater independence in devising a tax rate structure and in determining the form of government best suited for its citizenry. A charter is essentially a constitution for the city: a contract setting out the powers and the limitations of municipal government. Home rule cities have a greater degree of flexibility in setting local tax rates, deciding which services to provide, and determining the form of government to be used.

Forms of Municipal Government

Essentially three forms of municipal government exist in Texas: mayor-council, council-manager and commission. Each home rule city can create and modify its form of government based on the desires or needs of the community. General law cities may make some modifications to suit the needs of the citizens, but to a much lesser extent.

MAYOR-COUNCIL This type of arrangement is widely used in most of Texas's less populated and rural cities.

It is a simple form of government in which most of the day-to-day executive operations are carried out by either the mayor or by a city council. Most mayor-council municipalities have only a few departments; therefore, the salary of a full-time, professional administrator or manager is not justified.

These smaller cities often do not have police or fire departments; the county sheriff's department and volunteer firefighters usually see to these public safety needs. Public utilities are frequently provided by cooperatives or special districts, not the local government. Two main variations to the mayor-council form of government can be found in Texas: weak mayor and strong mayor. In a weak mayor system, the mayor has limited policy implementation and no veto powers. Mayors working within this system cannot, for example, establish policies without the consent of the city council, neither can they appoint or remove department heads such as the police chief or fire marshal.

In the strong mayor cities, the mayor is often empowered to veto policies and ordinances passed by the council and to hire and fire city personnel as he or she deems appropriate. This form of local government is neither common nor popular in Texas, a state that traditionally avoids giving much power to any single person. In addition to these powers, mayors of strong mayor municipalities also have more extensive budgetary powers than do their counterparts in weak mayor systems.

The mayor-council form of municipal government is used primarily by the smaller cities of Texas, with one significant exception. Houston, the largest city in Texas and fourth-largest American city, operates under this form of government with great efficiency. Houston's strong mayor sets the city council agenda and presides over council meetings. He or she also has veto power that in practice is often final. Former Dallas mayor Laura Miller attempted to have her city's government changed from council-manager to the mayor-council form. She failed in this attempt.

COUNCIL-MANAGER The council-manager form of government is used by most medium- and larger-sized cities in Texas, as noted in the table nearby, and throughout the United States. The qualified voters who reside in the city elect a city council and a mayor, which in turn hire a **city manager** to carry out the council's policies. This system allows for both professional management and local political control. City managers usually are formally trained in urban studies or public administration and have extensive knowledge of budgeting, finance, and personnel laws. Typically the highest-paid city employees earn salaries comparable to CEOs of mid-sized corporations. Dallas's city manager earns $263,000, Ft. Worth's earns $189,000, and Lubbock's earns $161,000. Mayors under this system have limited powers and, somewhat like the governor, must rely on the force of their personality to have an impact. Some, like former San Antonio mayor Henry Cisneros, profiled in the Mosaic nearby, have made their presence known on the state or national stage.

city manager
Professional political appointee who oversees city operations on a day-to-day basis

The city manager hires other qualified professionals to oversee the various departments, although in most cities, the council must approve the hiring and removal of department heads. Because the city manager is appointed based on his or her training, ability, and merit, the position is apolitical (at least in theory). This means that the manager is allowed to make policy decisions based on need and in the best interest of the community as a whole. For this very reason, the council-manager form of municipal government has its advocates and critics.[3]

The strongest argument in favor of this system is that there is very little waste. The professional qualifications of the city administrators and their staffs allow them to carry out the council's—and the people's—desires in a cost-effective, efficient manner without considering the political implications. Proponents point out that professional municipal administration results in lower tax rates and an optimum level of service because the administrators are trained to research policy decisions thoroughly prior to implementation.

TABLE **11.1 Form of Municipal Government in Selected Texas Cities**

CITY	FORM OF GOVERNMENT	YEAR ADOPTED
Abilene	Council-Manager	1981
Amarillo	Commission	1913
Arlington	Council-Manager	1990
Austin	Council-Manager	1991
Benbrook	Council-Manager	1990
College Station	Council-Manager	1992
Commerce	Commission	1954
Conroe	Mayor-Council	1992
Corpus Christi	Council-Manager	1993
Corsicana	Commission	1956
Dallas	Council-Manager	1907
Denton	Council-Manager	1959
Dumas	Commission	1991
Fort Worth	Council-Manager	1986
Friendswood	Council-Manager	1971
Galveston	Council-Manager	1991
Hillsboro	Council-Manager	1981
Houston	Mayor-Council	1946
Huntsville	Council-Manager	1992
Keller	Council-Manager	1982

(continued)

TABLE **11.1** (continued)

CITY	FORM OF GOVERNMENT	YEAR ADOPTED
Kingsville	Council-Manager	1986
Laredo	Council-Manager	1982
McAllen	Commission	1980
Pasadena	Mayor-Council	1992
Richardson	Council-Manager	1989
San Angelo	Council-Manager	1915
San Antonio	Council-Manager	1951
Texarkana	Council-Manager	1969
Texas City	Mayor-Council	1946
Tyler	Council-Manager	1937
Waco	Council-Manager	1958

SOURCE: *Dallas Morning News; Texas Almanac.*

COMMISSION Only a handful of municipalities in Texas use this type of local government. It provides for the direct supervision and executive powers over a specific department by an elected commissioner. In other words, there is an elected "commissioner" for each of the city's departments. Rather than using a council to oversee the operation of the city as a whole, the commission form of government requires officeholders to oversee the day-to-day operations of their respective departments.

The commission system is often criticized for being too fragmented, as there is usually no single individual who is accountable for the overall responsibility of the local government. This system most closely resembles the plural executive system found at the state level (see Chapter 7). It was first was implemented in Galveston shortly after the devastating hurricane of 1900 that claimed an estimated 8,000 lives and effectively wiped out the local government. The city has since abandoned the commission system in favor of a council-manager form of municipal government.

WHAT CAN YOU DO? Nearly every municipality in Texas, regardless of the form of government, provides citizens the opportunity to serve as members on various planning, land use, zoning, and other boards and commissions. Service on these boards and commissions allows citizens to have a more direct influence on their local governments. Contact your city or town secretary for more information about how you can serve.

Municipal Elections

All municipal elections in Texas are nonpartisan, meaning that the political party affiliation of the candidates is not identified during the campaign or on the ballot. The mayor and council members of your city do not run as Republicans, Democrats, or by any other party label.

Membership on a city council is one way of getting involved in local politics at the grassroots level. Because political parties generally play little or no role in council elections, the cost of running a successful campaign is relatively low. The candidates do not receive support or funding from "the party." In the larger cities, successful candidates attempt to form **coalitions**; that is, they try to garner the support of members associated with various civic and professional groups such as parent-teacher associations, neighborhood associations, and chambers of commerce.

coalitions
Alliances consisting of a variety of individuals and groups in support of a particular candidate for elected office.

In most cases, individuals who seek elected office at the grassroots level do so because they wish to fulfill a sense of civic duty. To be sure, it is not the money that attracts city council candidates. In most cases, members are paid $10 to $50 per council session. The type of election system adopted by the local government determines the composition of the city council. The three types of city council elections are the at-large system, the place system, and the single-member district system.

Types of Municipal Elections

AT-LARGE SYSTEM The **at-large system** is the most common type of local election because it works best for small towns, and the majority of Texas's 1,200 towns have populations of less than 5,000. The term "at-large" means citywide. Since there are no precincts or districts, voters are free to choose whomever they wish to represent them. The candidates essentially all run against one another and the top vote-getters sit on the city council.

at-large system
A method of electing representatives where there are no districts or wards drawn, and the candidate may draw votes from the entire area to be governed.

PLACE SYSTEM The **place system** is most often used in the medium-sized, more homogeneous cities of Texas. In this variation of the at-large system, the seats on the city council are distinguished by numbers, such as "places" one, two, three, and so on. Candidates filing for office are required to run for a particular place, and only one council member is selected per place by way of popular vote. The place system most benefits political newcomers because it does not force them to compete against established, popular incumbents. Rather, candidates may choose the seat for which they would like to run.

place system
A system of electing local government leaders whereby the candidates must campaign for a particular seat on the city council.

SINGLE-MEMBER DISTRICTS The state's larger cities tend to be more diverse and thus prefer to have diversity on the city councils. The way to achieve diversity is through **single-member districts** (sometimes called "wards"). Under this system, the city is divided into districts, and voters within these districts only may vote for candidates who reside within them. The system is the best way of ensuring that ethnic or political minorities receive representation on the city council. Usually, the mayoral candidate runs at large, because the mayor represents the city as a whole.

single-member district
A specific geographic area with a population equal to that of other districts that elects one person (a single member) to represent that area.

The Effects of Group Participation

The impact of special interest groups in politics and public policy at the state and national levels is well known (see Chapter 5). The effect of locally based groups on public policy at the local level can be equally as profound. Locally based groups have made great strides in determining the course of local government by affecting some of the most important decisions made by city leaders. Ethnic groups, neighborhood associations, and municipal employee associations continue to play a major role in formulating local government policy.[4]

ETHNIC GROUPS When compared with the struggles faced in addressing discriminatory practices at other levels of government, ethnic and race-based groups have found that local government is relatively more accessible. Many larger cities are seeing greater equality in the hiring and promotion of minorities, in part due to the implementation of single-member district elections and the resulting election of minority representatives. This more-inclusive representation in elected and appointed positions has fostered ordinances and other mandates to award minority-owned businesses more opportunities to participate in bidding on government work contracts, such as the construction and maintenance of roads, buildings, parks, and other public facilities.

NEIGHBORHOOD ASSOCIATIONS Homeowners and neighborhood associations, chambers of commerce, civic organizations, and coalitions formed by these groups have discovered that the key to change is political involvement. Through their numbers, resources, and activities (including endorsements of candidates willing to voice the groups' interests), these groups have gained for themselves an array of benefits that otherwise may not have come their way. Throughout Texas, active and well-organized neighborhood associations have lobbied the city council for road improvements, parks, lighting, and even the placement of additional fire department substations.

Often, these groups take advantage of low voter turnout by ensuring that their own members and their families and friends vote. The general voter apathy often enables groups to control virtually all aspects of local governments. Members of these groups are more prone to vote and to entice others to vote in the same manner. In addition, members often attend the council meetings and stay informed of decisions that might affect them.

MUNICIPAL EMPLOYEE GROUPS Employee groups have realized incredible gains from political participation at the local level. In San Antonio, for example, the local police officer's association campaigned hard for city council candidates who promised to support better pay and better working conditions. The association enlisted literally hundreds of volunteers to promote their interests, resulting in the redirection of millions of dollars to fund these benefits. As a direct result of this grassroots participation in Texas, more than 100 local police associations have banded together and hired lobbyists to support the passage of bills favorable to them.[5]

Municipal Finance

ad valorem
A system of taxation that is assessed "according to value," whereby the more a property is worth, the higher the tax to be paid on it.

The majority of Texas municipalities rely heavily upon property taxes to fund the services they provide. The tax rates are determined by each of the cities' governing bodies, using guidelines established by the Texas Constitution, city policy, and the needs of the community. Property taxes are assessed using an **ad valorem** structure, meaning that each property is taxed "according to value." Values are determined by the county property assessment office. Most Texas home rule cities have established an ad valorem rate of between 50¢ and 75¢ per $100 of assessed value. Home rule cities may tax at a rate of up to $2.50 under state law, but such a move would be detrimental to attracting businesses and housing developments. A home owner whose property is valued at $100,000 and who lives in a municipality with a 50¢ tax rate would pay $500 per year in property tax. By law, the ad valorem tax rate cannot exceed $1.50 per $100 of assessed value in general law cities.

In Texas, everyone who pays for housing is affected by the local property tax rates, whether they own a home or pay rent on a house or apartment. Landlords and apartment management companies figure taxes into tenants' lease agreements. Many renters hold the mistaken notion that since they do not own property, they are not affected by the property tax rates.

Other revenue generated by Texas municipalities includes a sales tax rebate from the state. Businesses and services operating within the municipalities collect state sales tax and forward the proceeds to the state's comptroller of public accounts. After the funds are certified, the comptroller's office sends each city a rebate check that amounts to the taxable product collected by the city's merchants. Cities also collect franchise taxes from utility companies that place lines or wires along and under city streets.

Like the sales tax rebate, the **franchise tax** is collected on a percentage of the total sales collected. In addition to the state sales tax rebates, cities are allowed to collect their own sales tax of 1 percent. Like the half-cent rebate, these funds are collected by the merchants and sent to Austin, where the state comptroller certifies the taxes and sends the city a rebate check. Almost every municipality in the state takes full advantage of this opportunity.

User fees, such as admittance charges to public golf courses, amusement parks, boat ramps, and other government-owned facilities, may comprise 30 percent or more of the revenue of some of Texas's municipalities. Court fees and fines collected by municipal courts and permit fees collected by city hall are also sources of revenue for the cities.

In addition to the general sales taxes, some cities implement special taxes to fund or supplement specific projects or services. Examples include Fort Worth's "Crime District Tax," a half-cent levy that pays for crime prevention and after school programs. Other examples include library taxes and stadium taxes. Growing cities may implement an "economic development tax," which is an add-on sales tax that is used to offer business economic incentives in return for locating stores or offices in the city, thereby creating jobs and sales tax revenues. Before implementing these special taxes, the city must call an election and voters must approve them.

Cities are bound by law to fund their day-to-day operations, like paying employees and purchasing fuel, with money collected from taxes and fees. In most circumstances, the cities must borrow money for major expenditures, such as flood control systems, buildings, street construction and repair, or major equipment. Large expenses that are not part of the day-to-day operations of the city are known as **capital improvements**. In order to raise the money necessary for these and other capital projects, the city may sell municipal bonds. Individuals purchase these bonds as investments through private brokers. Like paying a mortgage, the city pays off the bonds in small increments that include interest payments.

BONDS Two types of bonds are sold by Texas municipalities: general obligation and revenue.

General obligation bonds are sold when the city needs to raise money to build or improve city-owned facilities. They are paid back gradually from the usual sources of revenue available to the city. **Revenue bonds** are sold for the construction or improvement of a city-owned property that is expected to generate revenue, such as a sports arena or public water park. These bonds are paid back from the revenue generated by the capital improvement.

franchise tax
A specific tax paid by businesses operating in Texas.

user fees
Monies paid to local governments by citizens who utilize a particular government service (e.g., tuition at a state school or fees at a public boat ramp).

capital improvements
Long-term infrastructure improvements, such as roads, that are often built with bond money

general obligation bond
A bond issued by a local government for the purpose of making capital improvements and, like a mortgage, are paid off in small, yearly payments.

revenue bond
Issued by local governments for the purpose of capital improvements and repaid by revenue generated by the improvement; examples include sports arenas and public facilities for which there is an admission charge.

This extension of the bikeway in Austin over Cesar Chavez Street was funded with bond money. Why do governmental entities generally borrow funds for projects such as this?

EMINENT DOMAIN: CAN IT BE USED IN THE NAME OF ECONOMIC DEVELOPMENT? The Texas Constitution allows municipalities the right to reclaim private property in the name of the government if the property is needed for the greater public good. This power, called "eminent domain," has been used to displace landowners in the interest of constructing highways, airports, shopping malls, and military installations. The laws governing eminent domain require the government to compensate the landowner for "fair market value." The City of Hurst, Texas, made national headlines when it chose to use eminent domain for the purpose of expanding a shopping center. In 1997, the city made plans to allow developers to expand North East Mall into an existing residential neighborhood. With proceeds generated from a special half-cent sales tax, the city sought to purchase 127 homes. The owners of 117 of these homes agreed to the city's offer, which in some cases was nearly twice the current market value.

The remaining ten home owners fought the city to the end, but lost. The hold-outs claimed that the city should compensate the home owners at a much higher commercial, rather than residential, property rate. They filed an unsuccessful lawsuit against the city. Meanwhile, the home owners in Hurst have been forced out by city officials, who condemned their homes. The city claims that the mall must be expanded because major tenants, such as department stores, will move elsewhere and the revenue lost would inhibit the city's ability to provide essential services.

Dallas Cowboys owner Jerry Jones and Arlington officials wisely avoided eminent domain issues when clearing the way for the new stadium.

The loss of tax revenue would devastate the city's budget and cripple the local economy, according to city officials. Area residents are divided over the matter. Those who side with the city want convenient shopping and the economic benefits brought about by the sales tax revenue, which will be in the millions. Those opposed say the city has overstepped its bounds and has selectively interpreted the Texas Constitution in an unfair manner. They argue that the purpose of the Constitution is to protect private property, and that the City of Hurst has stolen it.

In 2007 the Texas legislature passed a bill that prevents local governments from using eminent domain solely for the purpose of generating a larger tax base. As a result of the Hurst case and a redevelopment proposal in downtown El Paso, a constitutional amendment limited eminent domain takings for private use and dramatically curtailed instances in which property could be condemned as a public nuisance. Since then, at least 32 other states have passed or considered similar bills.

BUDGETING The budgeting process for municipal governments requires extensive research and planning, as cities strive to maintain the lowest tax rates possible while maintaining the highest level of service. Most Texas cities put their yearly budgets into effect on the first day of October, and planning for the next year starts on the second day of the same month, if not earlier. Providing municipal services to residents is just one of many challenges facing Texas's cities. City officials must create a favorable climate for business because businesses provide important benefits to the community.

INSIDE THE FEDERALIST SYSTEM

In Step

Although public safety is primarily a function of state and local government, it is hardly exclusive of federal government intervention. The federal Strategic Traffic Enforcement Program (STEP) provides us with an example of how federal funds assist cities across Texas. Under the program, local governments may seek federal dollars to fund special enforcement efforts, such as are seat belt violators and speeders. Many cities have shown an increasing reliance on these grants to assist them in their efforts at keeping us safe.

A large shopping center can create hundreds of jobs in the community and generate thousands of dollars in local sales tax rebates, so it is often considered to be in the city's best interest to attract retailers to the area. In smaller cities that have many businesses, homeowners often enjoy lower ad valorem rates because the businesses generate enough revenue to provide basic services. Of course, increased commerce also fosters the need for additional services such as road repair and public safety, all of which require additional funding. In order to attract business and commerce, many municipalities offer financial incentives, called **abatements**. Abatements come in the form of lower taxes for a specified time and are often instrumental in a corporation's decision to locate an office or plant within the limits of a particular city. Abatements are hardly new to Texas; in fact, the state was a pioneer in offering incentives. In the 1820s, Stephen F. Austin, in his effort to populate Texas, offered an exemption from all general taxes for the first ten years to people moving from the United States.

> **abatement**
> A financial incentive offered by governments to business and commercial concerns as a means of luring them to set up operations within the borders of a particular city.

Today, two trends are apparent in financial incentives: first, abatements offered by municipalities have escalated in both frequency and monetary amounts, and second, more businesses are seeking these tax incentives in order to reduce their costs. The practice of offering incentives to business concerns has become widespread as citizens have come to appreciate the positive economic benefits and conveniences that industry and retail establishments bring. In 1989, the Texas legislature authorized cities to enact a half-cent sales tax for the purpose of creating "economic development corporations." Revenue from this special tax is used for advertising, purchasing land, and developing infrastructure intended to attract commerce.

County Government

The Texas Constitution calls counties "administrative arms of state government"; we find this to be a most brilliant definition. Everything the counties do is on behalf of the state. For example, your Texas license plates are distributed by the county tax office, state law violators are prosecuted in the county courts, and state health services are administered through county-run facilities.

my turn

Is County Government Antiquated?

by Former Tarrant County Commissioner Dionne Bagsby

If county government did not already exist, it would have to be invented. Antiquated? Hardly. Counties are the governments of the future. County government in Texas is not perfect. There is much that is outdated and old-fashioned. But the potential is there. No other unit of local government is better suited to meet the evolving needs of our increasingly complex urban society.

The problems that our metropolitan areas face no longer fit neatly into compact municipal boundaries. Transportation, pollution, health care, and crime are just a few of the issues that clearly spill across neighborhood and city boundaries.

Any success in solving these or any of the other problems challenging us today rests, in no small way, on how well and how soon counties assume their proper role as full partners in the area of public service and public policy decision making. Of all of the local units of government, only the county level is large enough to marshal the resources and efforts of the entire community when the need arises.

Other states have long recognized the role counties can play. Counties operate under home rule charters in nearly half the states and offer a full array of local services. Where they have home rule, counties do not detract from municipal authority but rather complement cities and other local jurisdictions. When issues or problems start to overlap city boundary lines, the county is there with the ability to step in and help coordinate areawide efforts and resources.

Many of the defects of Texas county government have been remedied elsewhere. Other states have reduced the number of lawmaking bodies and have professionalized county administration. Texas needs to move in similar directions. We need to make counties up-to-date instruments of local government. The 19th-century idea of a county as merely an administrative branch of the state has long passed away in most of the country.

Despite the legal restrictions that Texas places on county government, Tarrant County has been in the forefront among the state's counties in adapting to the needs of our rapidly changing community. Among other innovations, Tarrant County has taken a leadership role in coordinating the community development and planning efforts of the smaller municipalities within its boundaries; in joining Dallas County and the North Texas Tollroad Authority in forming an employee benefits consortium; in coordinating the development of the countywide 911 emergency telephone service; and by serving as a catalyst for the implementation of countywide programs run by community-based nonprofits to eliminate the ravaging impacts of poverty within our borders.

County government in Texas is not without its faults. It can and must be improved and modernized. We need to streamline county administration, professionalize county staff, put teeth into the ability of counties to deal with local problems, and make county government more accessible to all of our citizens.

Structure of County Government

Although counties act as branch offices of state government, they are considered "local governments" because county officials are elected locally from within the county they serve. This system allows the community to determine how best to deliver state resources to the local area. While each of Texas 254 counties serve the same purpose, the system allows for some individuality.

Compared to cities, counties are relatively weak in terms of autonomy. That's because unlike home rule cities, counties do not have home rule charters and cannot adopt ordinances. County government is much like the plural executive model of government that exists at the state level in that no single executive or officer controls or is accountable for the county's policy-making personnel.

Texas's 254 counties are as diverse as the people who inhabit them. Unlike cities, which regularly see geographical expansion, the counties boundaries are permanent. In fact, many Texas cities extend into as many as 4 counties. County populations range from fewer than 70 (Loving County in far west Texas) to more than 3 million (Harris County). Some counties are smaller than large cattle ranches, and others are larger than some small states. Obviously, each county has specific needs according to its size, location, population density, and other factors.

Despite the stunning geographical and population diversity among the counties, the Texas Constitution mandates that all 254 counties be governed in essentially the same manner. Each county is governed by a commissioners court and all elected county officials serve four-year terms of office.

COMMISSIONERS COURT Each county, regardless of size and demographic composition, is governed by a five-member county commissioners court composed of four commissioners and presided over by a county judge. The county is divided into four precincts of equal population, with each precinct electing its own commissioner.[6] The county judge is elected at large, meaning countywide. Although it is called a "court," the function of this body is strictly administrative. That is, no trials are held in the Commissioners Court and its members serve no judicial functions. The Commissioners Court acts as a city manager more than it does a court.

The Commissioners Court appoints key administrators and other personnel; sets the county tax rates; adopts the county budget; awards contracts for construction, repair, and maintenance of county buildings and roads; provides medical care for the indigent, and performs other related administrative tasks as required by the Texas Constitution and legislature.

Harmony among the various elected county officials is especially vital because of the fragmented nature of county government. For example, the Commissioners Court provides the sheriff with the funds to purchase equipment and provide public safety services. Yet, the commissioners enjoy little, if any, oversight on how these funds are used. Since the sheriff is elected independently, he or she might choose to implement policies that are not approved by the commissioners. Fortunately, such conflicts are rare and last only a few years—until the next elections.

Other Elected Officials

DISTRICT OR COUNTY ATTORNEY The district or county attorney is the county's legal officer and adviser. Not every county has its own elected attorney, and those not having one contract these services from neighboring counties. The office provides legal services for county agencies and officials acting in a public service capacity, and it provides representation when a lawsuit is brought against the county. On the recommendation of the Commissioners Court, the district or county attorney may initiate a lawsuit against another governmental agency or private concern.

The office of the district attorney presents a vivid example of the degree of discretion given to our locally elected officials. As the criminal prosecutor, the district or county attorney has sole discretion in determining whether an individual will be held accountable for committing a crime. Although all prosecutors enforce the same state laws, they have tremendous discretionary powers, and these powers are often driven by the wants of the community. For example, the decision on whether to seek the death penalty in a capital murder trial is made by the elected district or county attorney.

SHERIFF The sheriff's primary responsibilities are to provide law enforcement services to areas of the county that are not served by a police department and to oversee the county jail. Most Texans live in incorporated cities and towns that are served by municipal police departments and thus are seemingly unaffected by the sheriff. Most sheriff offices have small staffs because they serve small populations. Indeed, most Texas counties do not even have a county jail. For the approximately 20 percent of Texans who live in the rural areas of the state, the sheriff's department is the only law enforcement agency available.

Although vested with law enforcement powers, there is no provision that requires a sheriff to be a licensed peace officer when seeking office and this has been the cause of some concern. Essentially, any person eligible to vote in a given county may run for and be elected sheriff. This is an additional reason that we should pay attention to the qualifications of persons running for local office.

DISTRICT CLERK The district clerk is the official custodian of county records, including all filings and proceedings for the District Courts and County Courts at Law they serve. The clerk is registrar, recorder and custodian of all documents that are part of criminal, juvenile, family court, and civil actions. Since most court proceedings are public record, the office must store, manage, and disseminate court-related data efficiently. For many Texans, the first encounter with the district clerk is a jury duty notice. The district clerk's staff manages these notices and assigns prospective jurors to the various courts. In the larger counties, the office collects filing fees and other funds on behalf of the courts.

COUNTY CLERK The functions of the county clerk vary greatly, depending on the county. The office is responsible for maintaining the county's legal records and vital statistics, such as birth and death certificates, marriage licenses, and real estate transactions. Unless the Commissioners Court has appointed other individuals to perform these specific tasks, the county clerk records the court's minutes and certifies all candidates running for countywide office. Many county officials agree that the county clerk is the busiest person on the county payroll.

TAX ASSESSOR–COLLECTOR In the past, tax assessors were burdened with tremendous pressure from property owners seeking lower property values. The reason was clear: the lower the property value, the lower the taxes due. Due to changes in the method used to determine the value of property, the title of this office no longer reflects the officeholder's primary duties. Although the tax assessor–collector no longer "assesses" property value, he or she does have the important responsibility of identifying taxable property and collecting taxes that are due to the state and county.

Prior to 1992, each assessor–collector was free to develop his or her own criteria for determining the value of taxable property. Needless to say, this led to inconsistency throughout the state. As a result of state constitutional amendments passed in recent years, the assessment of property is now more structured and provides greater uniformity (and thus, fairness) within the state.

Most Texans are familiar with their county tax assessor–collectors because that office collects registration renewal fees and issues titles for motor vehicles. The office also registers voters in some counties. In the most rural counties of Texas, the office of tax assessor-collector is not filled, and the sheriff carries out the duties.

TREASURER   The county treasurer, or the person who performs the treasurer's duties, has been referred to as the county's official bookkeeper. He or she is responsible for tracking all collections and expenditures and has considerable input in formulating the county's budget.

Most urban counties have eliminated this elected office (a process that requires a constitutional amendment) and have allowed the Commissioners Court to appoint a county auditor to perform these tasks. Obviously, the appointed auditors generally have greater qualifications than do the elected treasurers, and this has worked well in counties having budgets that run into the tens of millions of dollars. People looking to reform county government cite the appointed auditors as positive proof that appointed officials can be held to higher standards than can elected officials.

County Government Finance

Compared to municipalities and special districts, counties are subject to stringent restrictions when it comes to raising revenue. Because ad valorem taxes are the counties' largest single source of revenue, the constitutionally imposed maximum tax rate of 80¢ per $100 valuation is a significant restriction. In order for the counties to raise the tax rate beyond 80¢, the Commissioners Court must first obtain legislative approval by both the House and Senate. After obtaining approval, the proposed tax rate increase must be approved by the qualified voters in the county. Many municipalities, particularly in urban areas, are allowed to assess much higher property tax rates without such legislative approval.

County ad valorem tax rates typically fall between 25¢ and 30¢ per $100 of valuation. This means that a homeowner with a property valued at $100,000 in a county where the tax rate was 25¢ per $100 would pay $250 yearly in county property tax.

Counties may, under certain circumstances, issue bonds just like the municipalities. Here again, they must comply with constitutional requirements that are more stringent than those for the cities. The county cannot, for example, issue bonds for an amount that exceeds 35 percent of the total countywide assessed valuation.

In addition to selling bonds to generate revenue, many counties are eligible for federal grants-in-aid for the construction of hospitals, airports, flood control projects, and other capital improvements. Much of this grant money is used by the counties for optional services (those not required by law but that provide services to residents) such as parks, libraries, airports, and sports complexes.

All Texas counties operate on a yearly budget cycle, which is usually prepared by the county auditor or budget officer with input from all department heads and interested residents. Much like the case of municipal budgeting, the public hearings are sparsely attended. The final draft of the budget is then forwarded to the Commissioners Court for review and acceptance before it is put into effect.

Firework stands often locate just outside of city limits, escaping the reach of municipal law. Should county government be granted ordinance making powers?

Criticism of County Government and Proposed Reform

Texans have been critical of the constitutional limitations imposed on counties ever since the counties were created. They have been suggesting ways of making county government more effective and more responsive to local needs. The major stumbling block on the path to reform is, of course, the Texas Constitution. The constitutional prohibition against the counties establishing home rule charters, ordinances, and the constitutionally mandated plural executive system severely limits any reform measures by citizens. The following section lists the most common complaints about county government.

THE LONG BALLOT One of the reasons voters are apathetic about county government is that they are required to elect as many as six individuals to perform executive and administrative functions, yet no single person can be held accountable for the efficiency of the overall operation. Reformists have suggested implementing a system modeled after the council-manager form of municipal government. Such a system would allow the elected commissioners to appoint a professional county manager who in turn would hire a professional staff. Accountability would be placed in the office of the county manager and there would be a greater likelihood that the people in executive and administrative positions would be well qualified and properly trained.

INABILITY TO ESTABLISH HOME RULE Unlike the cities and special districts, counties are constitutionally prohibited from tailoring their system to the needs and desires of local residents. Ironically, a provision in the Texas Constitution would have allowed counties to enact home rule charters. That provision was eliminated in

1969, and because it was so complex, not a single county had been able to establish a charter before it was taken off the books.

INABILITY TO PASS ORDINANCES The Commissioners Court is not empowered to create countywide ordinances to serve the safety, convenience, and moral expectations of the citizens. For example, nearly every incorporated city in the state has ordinances banning the sale and possession of fireworks and regulating the operation of sexually oriented businesses. For this reason, people traveling through the state often see these types of businesses in clusters within a few feet of the city limits. Some reform has been seen in this area. By an act of the Texas legislature in 1995, Harris County was granted permission to establish a teen curfew. Although such acts clearly demonstrate reform, they are difficult to attain because they require action by the state legislature.

spoils system
A system in which elected officials provide jobs and promotions to personal affiliates; see civil service.

SPOILS SYSTEM Although it does not exist to the extent that it did a few decades ago, the **spoils system** is still a fact of life in many counties. This system awards government jobs and contracts to individuals and firms who have helped in the elected person's political campaign. Many elected officeholders are permitted to hire personnel to assist them in their duties. These jobs often go to individuals who were friendly and loyal to the elected official, without regard to the person's qualifications, skills, or abilities.

civil service
Merit-based system of selecting government employees.

In order to alleviate the effects of the spoils system and to attract the most qualified persons, many counties have established a **civil service** system. Under this system, individuals seeking a job with the county government must meet specified job related requirements and are hired and promoted based on merit. Most of the larger counties require applicants to take written exams and to compete for entry-level positions and promotions. Another advantage of the civil service system is that county employees are not subject to losing their positions if the person who hired them is defeated in an election. This ensures continuity not only in the employees' careers but also in government operations.

Special Districts

special district
A type of local government established for a specific geographic area and for a specific purpose such as education, flood control, or public utility service.

A **special district** is the third classification under the broad title of "local government." A special district is a government entity established to deliver a specific service to a limited geographic area. They vary tremendously in terms of size, function, and scope, but all special districts share three unique features. First, they are substantially independent from other governments. In other words, they provide a product or service that no other government does. For example, the Dallas Independent School District (DISD) is totally independent from Dallas's city government. They have separate boundaries, budgets, and governing bodies. A second common feature among special districts is that they have "governmental character," which is another way of saying they have a source of funding. Some special districts, such as ISDs, are funded primarily by property taxes. Others, such as regional transportation districts, are funded by local sales taxes and tolls. A third shared feature is a "recognized existence." The special district must be chartered by the state or

Rush hour in Austin, only partially alleviated by a city bus. How does the individualistic nature of most Texans ingrain resistance toward mass transit?

otherwise approved by the state legislature. Recognition includes the requirement that business is conducted openly as it is in all other governments.

The Nature of Special Districts

Only California and Illinois have more special districts than does Texas. In fact, special districts comprise the fastest growing form of government in the nation today. There are more than 2,800 special districts in Texas, more governments than the number of cities and counties combined. Although some special districts are bounded by city limits or by county lines, most transcend these political boundaries and serve larger regions of the state.

Types of Special Districts

EDUCATION DISTRICTS The most common form of special district in Texas is the **independent school district** (ISD). During the Davis administration (see Chapter 2), the state controlled the entire public education system and all discretionary power was in the hands of the governor. As a reaction to this centralization, the framers of the current constitution allowed for the creation of ISDs to ensure more local control of Texas's public schools.

independent school district
Local-level limited purpose government that determines public school policy.

Texas public school expenditures are astonishing and growing by the year. The Dallas ISD's 2008 budget is more than $2 billion. This includes money raised in local districts and contributions from the state's Foundation School Program, as well as other state and federal grants. Because some districts have much greater property wealth than others, wealthier districts have been ordered by both the state courts and the legislature to share some of their property tax revenue with the poorer districts.

Each of Texas's approximately 1,000 ISDs is governed by a school board consisting of between four and nine members chosen in local nonpartisan elections. Most school board members are not paid for their service, and there is no requirement that members have children attending public schools in their district. The school board hires a professional manager, sometimes called a **superintendent**, to oversee the day-to-day operations of the school system. Other duties of the school board members include establishing a school calendar, setting teacher salaries, establishing teacher qualifications and standards, constructing and maintaining school buildings, vehicles, and other equipment, establishing the property tax rate, and selecting textbooks. Most public school education funding comes from the property taxes levied by the ISDs.

superintendent
The appointed manager of a public school system.

Texas has approximately 50 community college districts that offer academic and vocational programs. Until recently, state grants were the primary source of operating revenue for the community colleges, but today, a majority of the funding comes from property taxes and tuition. Virtually all community colleges throughout the state have been forced to raise tuition and tax rates to offset the reduction in state dollars. A typical community college district's tax rate is between ten and twenty cents per $100 valuation. Using the hypothetical $100,000 home in a district with a tax rate of ten cents, the home owner would pay a yearly community college tax of $100.

NONEDUCATION DISTRICTS Throughout the state, hundreds of special districts have been established for delivering services ranging from water and utilities, public housing, and hospitals, to public transportation and flood control. Some areas of Texas have even established "noxious weed control" and "wind erosion" districts to provide these specific services to those areas in need.

As is the case in school districts, most of the funding for noneducational special districts comes in the form of property taxes. Other sources of revenue include user fees (fares, licensing, etc.), special sales taxes, and grants from the state and federal governments.

Councils of Government

Although the needs of the local governments vary depending on a variety of factors, the basics of providing governmental services are the same for virtually all local governments. For this reason, nearly all municipal and county governments, as well as most special districts, participate in a **council of government** (COG). The 24 COGs in Texas, as shown in Figure 11.2, represent distinct regions. All local governments within their respective regions are eligible for membership. COGs have been created to allow cooperation and communication by local governments within a specific region. Because COGs are not governments, they have no taxing power and cannot pass laws, rules, or ordinances; nor can they impose sanctions against any government. The COGs provide training for city managers, council members, mayors, public safety officers, and other elected and appointed officials. They are also useful in assessing the future environmental, transportation, economic development, labor, and land use issues, as well as other social needs of the region. In addition, they often prevent unnecessary duplication of research or work.

council of government (COG)
A regional voluntary cooperative with no regulatory or enforcement powers; consists of local governments and assesses the needs of the area as a whole.

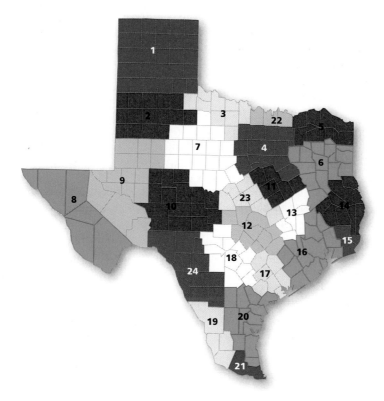

FIGURE **11.2** Boundaries of the 24 Texas Councils of Government (CoGs).

Summary

Texas has myriad local governments that provide citizens countless opportunities to participate in and affect public policy. Local government continues to be a springboard for future state and national leadership careers. True to the prevailing traditionalistic political culture that existed when the current Texas Constitution was drafted, local government was meant to be controlled by the local populace. Implementation of many of the recommended reform measures outlined in this chapter would require action on the part of the legislature.

Cities and towns are generally free to adopt and modify the structure of their own local governments as needs require. These local governments are attracting formally trained professionals to manage the day-to-day operations and are using innovative budgetary techniques to ensure the most services for the taxpayers. As local governments are being run more like businesses, waste is being eliminated and solutions to old problems are being discovered and shared.

Due in large measure to the constitutional constraints placed on the counties, special districts have grown in number and scope. Councils of government not only provide local governments at all levels the opportunity to conduct cooperative studies, they also act as a training ground for future leaders.

Chapter Test

1. Local government is defined as
   a. only cities smaller than 1 million.
   b. state-level government that affects rural areas.
   c. any level of government below the state level.
   d. cities and special districts, but not counties.

2. Most Texas cities are classified as
   a. general law.
   b. home rule.
   c. type III chartered.
   d. council-manager.

3. Usually, these officials are formally trained in urban studies or public administration.
   a. mayors
   b. aldermen
   c. county commissioners
   d. city managers

4. In Texas, all municipal elections are nonpartisan, meaning
   a. elections are held in even-numbered years.
   b. there is no political party affiliation.
   c. citizens are not allowed to contribute funds to candidates.
   d. these elections are nonbinding.

5. These governmental units act as administrative arms of state government.
   a. cities
   b. counties
   c. special districts
   d. all of the above

6. Which of the following is an example of a special district?
   a. the City of Austin
   b. the County of Travis
   c. the Austin Independent School District
   d. the Hill Country Chamber of Commerce

7. A government entity established to deliver a specific service to a limited geographic area.
   a. special district
   b. home rule status
   c. at-large system
   d. home rule charter

8. A system by which government employees are hired and promoted based on merit.
   a. spoils
   b. ad valorem
   c. general law
   d. civil service

9. This official's constitutional duties include maintaining a county jail.
   a. district attorney
   b. constable
   c. sheriff
   d. police chief

10. All elected county officials
    a. serve four-year terms of office.
    b. must run in partisan elections.
    c. may run for unlimited terms.
    d. all of the above.

Answers: 1. c 2. a 3. d 4. b 5. b 6. c 7. a 8. d 9. c 10. d

Critical Thinking Questions

1. How do Councils of Government impact local entities?

2. Should cities be allowed to impose eminent domain to promote economic development?

3. How can grassroots activities impact local government?

Key Terms

abatement, **p. 284**

ad valorem, **p. 280**

at-large system, **p. 279**

capital improvements, **p. 281**

city manager, **p. 277**

civil service, **p. 290**

coalitions, **p. 278**

council of government (COG), **p. 292**

franchise tax, **p. 281**

general law, **p. 274**

general obligation bond, **p. 281**

home rule, **p. 274**

independent school district (ISD), **p. 291**

place system, **p. 279**

revenue bond, **p. 281**

single-member district, **p. 279**

special district, **p. 290**

spoils system, **p. 290**

superintendent, **p. 292**

user fees, **p. 281**

Notes

1. FY2010 Operating Budget Schedule. http://www.houstontx.gov/budget/index.html.

2. Texas Constitution, art. 11, sec. 4.

3. Robert P. McGowan and John M. Stevens, "Survey of Local Government Officials: Analysis of Current Issues and Future Trends," *The Urban Interest* 4 (spring 1992), p. 55.

4. John L. Pape, "Sonora's Adopt a Neighborhood Program: Building a Stronger Community," *Texas Town and City* (January 1994), p. 16.

5. Anthony Giardino, "Membership Has Its Privileges," *Texas Police Star* (spring 1992), p. 12.

6. *Avery* v. *Midland County*.

Finance, Budgeting, and Public Policy

12

This was the last year that the state budget was less than $1 million. Ironically, "budget buster" E. J. Davis was governor.

The state budget exceeds $10 millio

| 1871 | 1876 | 1910 | 19 |

The current Texas Constitution is ratified. It requires the state's budget to be balanced.

The state budget exceeds $1 million.

By the end of this chapter on finance, budgeting, and public policy, you should be able to . . .

★ Explain what is meant by the term 'public policy.'
★ Describe the steps in the public policy model.
★ Analyze the constraints on the budget process in Texas.
★ Explain the role of the Legislative Budget Board.
★ Differentiate among the major source of tax revenue in Texas.
★ Explain how nontax revenue has surpassed tax revenue.
★ Describe the top three areas of expenditure in Texas.
★ Explain how some policy-making decisions have few or no fiscal implications.

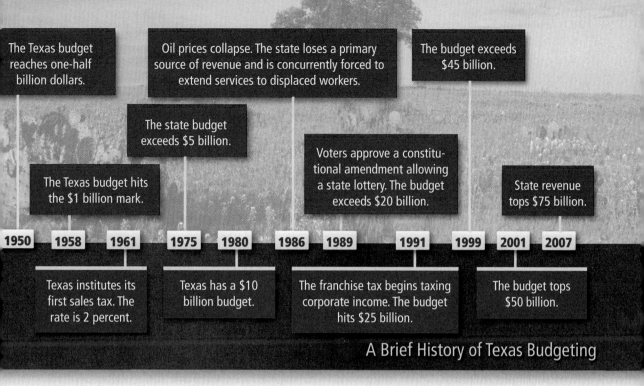

A Brief History of Texas Budgeting

| 1950 | 1958 | 1961 | 1975 | 1980 | 1986 | 1989 | 1991 | 1999 | 2001 | 2007 |

Above the timeline:

1950 — The Texas budget reaches one-half billion dollars.

1958 — The Texas budget hits the $1 billion mark.

1961 — The state budget exceeds $5 billion.

1980 — Oil prices collapse. The state loses a primary source of revenue and is concurrently forced to extend services to displaced workers.

1989 — Voters approve a constitutional amendment allowing a state lottery. The budget exceeds $20 billion.

1999 — The budget exceeds $45 billion.

2007 — State revenue tops $75 billion.

Below the timeline:

1961 — Texas institutes its first sales tax. The rate is 2 percent.

1975 — Texas has a $10 billion budget.

1986 — The franchise tax begins taxing corporate income. The budget hits $25 billion.

2001 — The budget tops $50 billion.

Government is 90 percent budget, the rest is poetry.

—THE LATE BOB BULLOCK, LIEUTENANT GOVERNOR OF TEXAS

The budget is the guts of government,
and all the rest is feathers.

—MOLLY IVINS, *FORT WORTH STAR-TELEGRAM*

In politics, things change fast. Just a few years ago, new revenue resulting from a surging state economy was plentiful enough to increase spending and cut taxes at the same time. An elected official could be everything to everybody: friend of education, protector of the poor, cutter of taxes. Not that the Texas legislature was going to go on a wild spending spree and fund every proposal that came along. That would go against the state's traditionalistic character. Still, the fiscal good times of the 1990s contrasted sharply with both the economic chaos of the 1980s and the brewing economic storm of the new millennium.

State funding crises are largely cyclical. In the early 1980s, financial difficulty was far from the minds of most Texas leaders. Oil prices were headed up and with them, state revenues. Texas is a historically miserly state when it comes to expenditures, but it seemed reasonable then to bank on increased revenue for additional spending in the areas of highways, welfare, and public schools. Oil prices were at

$36 a barrel. Some experts predicted they would soar to $90. Instead, they plunged to $10. The effect of the drop in oil prices on revenue was staggering. Oil tax revenue dropped, followed by sales tax revenue as workers lost their jobs and oil-dependent cities were devastated. Add in the savings and loan collapse and agricultural problems, and the entire state soon faced economic chaos. Plus, state spending increased as displaced workers put a strain on the state's public aid resources.

In order to keep up with increasing demands for revenue, the state sales tax increased from 4¢ on the dollar in the early 1980s to 6¢ by 1989. A motor fuels tax that was 5¢ per gallon in 1984 was 15¢ five years later. Beer taxes increased from $5 to $6 per barrel; cigarette taxes, from 18½¢ to 26¢ per pack. Tax revenue, which had been stagnant through the mid-1980s, began to grow again toward the end of the decade.

As the economy improved and tax rates either rose or remained the same, tax revenue increased tremendously in the 1990s. However, taxes once borne by Texas's oil industry were now firmly on the backs of working Texans. Additionally, education funding once provided by the state government was increasingly pushed to the local districts, resulting in a mammoth increase in local property taxes, a problem addressed by the legislature in 1997 and again in 1999 and 2006. State officials counted on the economy to continue to grow at a rapid rate and based their projections on these beliefs. With the economic downturn of 2002 and the state facing a $10 billion deficit, revenues failed to keep up with spending increases, leaving state officials with tough fiscal decisions. Elected officials managed the problems by cutting programs, not raising taxes.

Faced with a Supreme Court order to change the state's method of financing schools, the legislature significantly altered the state's tax structure in a 2006 special session. It is such a fundamental shift that, while comparing taxing and spending prior to and after 2007 might not exactly be comparing apples to oranges, at least it will be comparing two very different types of apples. Almost immediately following this budgeting shift, Texas followed the rest of the nation into a major recession. Although the state seemed poise to emerge more quickly from the downturn than its counterparts, Texas still entered the 2011 regular session facing a $18 billion budget gap simply to retain current levels of service, a deficit that could rise if the national recovery slowed or stopped.

Public Policy

public policy
Any act, law, legislation, or program enacted by a public entity.

Public policy can be defined as any course of action taken by the government that affects any segment of the public. It takes its form in laws, statutes, regulations, rules, and legislation. Although the legislative branch is formally responsible for "making the laws," public policy is actually created by every branch of government. The executive branch, through executive orders and policy initiatives, produces public policy, often without the input—or the approval—of the legislative branch. The courts, through judicial review and precedent, establish public policies that affect all Texans.

Public policy is the very essence of government because it is made at all levels of government. The federal government regulates foreign trade and domestic spending. State governments create public policies such as speed limits and motorcycle helmet laws. Local governments, county commissioners' courts, city councils, and school districts affect public policy by determining how land should be used, what hours the public library should operate, and how many students should be allowed to enroll in a particular class.

The study of public policy represents an entire subfield of political science. Public policy analysts probe the interaction resulting from the dynamics among the institutions of government and the public. Like politics itself, public policy analysis is the study of power, distribution, and outcomes. Public policy takes into consideration the various choices available to solve a problem or issue. We often find that the final product—the resulting policy—represents a compromise among competing interests.

Types of Policy

Political scientists have identified three broad categories of public policy: redistributive, distributive, and regulatory. Redistributive polices are usually the most controversial because they often cause divisions among social classes. Examples of redistributive policies include most forms of welfare and subsidized school lunches. Recently, funding for the Children's Health Insurance Program (CHIP) has been a source of legislative debate, and with declining federal dollars for federal programs like Medicaid, more parents will be relying on state-funded programs like CHIP to cover their children's medical needs.

Distributive policies are those that are intended to be neutral for taxpayers. Everyone pays, and everyone benefits. Gasoline tax used to build and maintain highways are a classic example of distributive polices. While local governments occasionally provide redistributive policies, such as city-subsidized housing, these policies are more frequently put into place by state government. By and large, cities implement distributive policies by providing parks, public safety, and public works projects. In the case of local governments, everyone pays for these services through property taxes, and all enjoy the results.

Regulatory policies are the most common and are enacted by state and local governments alike. As the name implies, they are created to regulate, and often to limit, specific activities. At the state level, policies that relate to environmental issues, legalized gambling, sales and distribution of alcoholic beverages, and motor vehicle registration provide examples of the state's regulatory power. Cities create zoning boards, inspection services, and ordinances restricting the operations of certain businesses, all in an effort to protect property values, enhance safety, or ensure a better quality of life.

	Redistributive	Distributive	Regulatory
Types of Public Policy	Policies that shift resources from the "haves" to the "have nots."	Policies funded by all taxpayers that address the desires of particular groups.	Policies designed to restrict or monitor the actions of certain groups or individuals.

FIGURE **12.1** **Types of Public Policy.**

The Policy Model

Understanding public policy is vital to appreciating the nature of policy. Political scientists have created a four-stage model for how an idea becomes an actual policy or law. These four stages are agenda setting, formulation, adoption/implementation, and evaluation. We will illustrate the actual dynamics of the process by taking a closer look at Texas's "Castle Law" and how it developed through the process.

Agenda Setting

Before any government agency initiates action, the need for such action must be recognized. During the agenda-setting stage, the matter is brought to the attention of the government and a resolution is sought. Sometimes a single event can place an issue on the government's agenda. For example, in 1999, the Texas legislature passed a bill that became known as the "Amber Alert," which required law enforcement agencies to coordinate with local media outlets for the purpose of alerting citizens about child abductions. In other instances, pressure from ordinary citizens and interest groups like the National Rifle Association can put issues on the front burner. Such was the case with the "Castle Law" passed by the Texas legislature in 2007. Prior to the Amber Alert's passage, several police departments and local media outlets established a voluntary program that was widely successful. The Texas Amber Alert made this a statewide network, and it was so successful that it was adopted by the U.S. Congress and extended nationwide. The bill is named after Amber Haggerman, a young Texas girl whose abduction caused an outcry among citizens.

The agenda-setting stage is important not only to those who wish to create new policies, but also to those who oppose governmental action. An individual, corporation, or group opposed to governmental intervention will often attempt to abort the policy process at this stage. Sometimes these groups are successful in the short term.

For example, although public opinion polls identified the popularity of a law allowing Texans to carry concealed handguns in their cars, various groups—including law enforcement and educational groups—managed to keep the issue on the back burner, or "off the agenda."

Despite such organized opposition, or perhaps in response to the popularity of the legislation, Governor Perry promised to sign the bill into law if he was reelected in 2006. He did just that, and the "Castle Law" was one of the first bills passed in the new session. The agenda-setting stage is also responsible for updating, or modifying bills. For example, after some interest groups pointed out that the bill, as originally proposed, allowed persons convicted of family violence to carry concealed weapons, the legislature acted quickly and closed this and other loopholes.

Formulation

After a problem has been recognized and defined, the next step is deciding what will be done about it and who will do it. In the formulation stage, options are explored. Policy makers may decide that a new public policy is needed or that an existing one can be modified to correct a problem. The level and degree of government involvement are also established during this stage. For example, after the legislature passed the Castle Law, the state's law enforcement officials and prosecutors were trained in the law's application. Texas lawmakers use this stage most effectively by learning from what other states have done. Such research prevents our state from making the same mistakes others may have made. For example, Texas copied Maryland's "Give Them a Break Laws" when in 2001 it implemented laws that doubled the traffic fines for certain moving violations committed where men and women are working on public roadways. In 2003 Texas copied, nearly word-for-word, provisions for a "Move Over Law" that requires motorists to move one lane over for emergency vehicles parked on shoulders and roadsides.

Often, a legislative body, such as Congress or a city council, determines the formulation of a public policy. Sometimes the courts make this determination, as has been the case in the areas of public school financing and prison overcrowding. Such was the case in 2005, when three special sessions failed to produce education finance reform. The legislature resolved to let the Texas Supreme Court settle certain issues before meeting again to redraft an appropriations bill. At other times, decisions are made by bureaucrats in government agencies.

Adoption and Implementation

At this stage, a government response to an issue is finalized. Conflicts with existing policies are considered, as are costs and funding. Specific roles are defined for the government agency or agencies that will be responsible for carrying out the policy. Moreover, these agencies review past policy adoptions by Texas and other states. Chances are that other states have already adopted similar policies, and we can learn from their successes and failures.

Policy is implemented when it is carried out. Timing, public education, and opinion regarding the policy have an impact on the success at this phase. Policy and perceived fairness are among the issues addressed here. It is important that the agencies responsible for implementing public policy thoroughly understand and adhere to the letter and spirit of the law or inconsistencies will surely develop. The input into and acceptance by teachers of any education reform package will have a huge impact on its ultimate success.

The media are often involved here. When the state government implements a major new public policy, such as the sales tax holiday for school clothes and supplies, newspapers and television stations provided the public with a rundown of the rules and regulations. The state agencies often generate press releases and conduct interviews with members of the media to advertise and to clarify the new policy. When the Castle Law was implemented, the Texas Department of Public Safety and other agencies saw to it that the public had easy access to the terms and conditions of the new law.

Evaluation

In theory, all public policies are evaluated periodically to determine whether they have had the desired effect. Problems arise here if the desired effect is not clear or the method for making these measurements is ill-conceived. Policy makers may discover during the evaluation process that the policy is in need of some change in order to be effective, and this may necessitate going back to the first or second stage of the process.

There is often disagreement on the effectiveness of public policies. For example, both opponents and proponents of affirmative action programs cite statistics to justify their position. One side calls for abolishing the programs; the other side indicates a need for their expansion.

More often than not, evaluation is carried out in a superficial manner. Government tends to evaluate what is easy to evaluate rather than those factors that show the effectiveness of a program. It is easier, for instance, to count the number of people or claims a government agency processes than it is to determine the effect of a policy. Texas does a better job than most states, thanks in part to the built-in evaluation process known as the Sunset Advisory Commission (see Chapter 8). Although the commission does not review the specific policies that are carried out by the agencies, it does conduct a comprehensive review of the agencies themselves.

An excellent example of how the evaluation stage works is found in the changes made to the Ashley Laws. In this case, the new law seems to be working well. The new public laws allowing local police to publish the names, addresses, and photographs of convicted child molesters is popular with everyone except the offenders. The Right to Carry (a concealed handgun) Law has been modified in every legislative session since it was introduced in 1995. Recent changes in the law empower municipal judges and justices of the peace to instantly revoke the licenses of those who commit, and in some cases even are accused of, family violence. The most recent change included the expansions provided by the Castle Law.

WHAT CAN YOU DO?

The Communication Area of the Texas comptroller's office publishes interesting and pertinent data about Texas financial policies.

To be placed on the *Fiscal Notes* mailing list, go to https://www.window.state.tx.us/fnotes/.

The Texas Budget

Constraints on Budgeting

Creating the state's budget is the hardest thing the Texas legislature does. The fact that total state revenue rose from just under $17 billion in 1985 to $53.8 billion in 2001, and almost $91 billion in 2010 does not mean that monetary concerns vanished. The very nature of budgeting in Texas guarantees that the process will be difficult. Some of the constraints are placed on all or most states, while others are peculiar to Texas.

Balanced Budget Provision

balanced budget
A means to keep the government from spending more than it receives in revenues.

The Texas Constitution mandates that the state must have a **balanced budget,** as noted in the constitution box. This provision greatly affects how the state operates. It requires, for instance, that if the state is to meet increased spending demands during a recession, it must increase tax rates. Most economists would argue that increasing taxes during a recession is detrimental to a weak economy's health, often prolonging the economic downturn because it removes money from the taxpayers' pockets when there is a shortage of spending in the first place.

The Texas Constitution:
A Closer Look

The best way to limit government power is to limit the government's power to spend. With the balanced budget provision, the writers of the Texas Constitution did just that. This provision's impact is more pronounced in Texas than in many of the other states that have similar restrictions, because of the state's strong antitaxation sentiment. It reads as follows:

Sec. 49. STATE DEBTS.

(a) No debt shall be created by or on behalf of the State, except:

    (1) to supply casual deficiencies of revenue, not to exceed in the aggregate at any one time two hundred thousand dollars;

    (2) to repel invasion, suppress insurrection, or defend the State in war;

    (3) as otherwise authorized by this constitution; or

    (4) as authorized by Subsections (b) through (f) of this section.

Sections b–f are somewhat wordy, but in a nutshell they require the same process as a constitutional amendment before the state takes on bonded indebtedness. Bonds can be issued only for specifically stated purposes and only with the approval of two-thirds of the house, two-thirds of the senate, and the majority of voters who participate in the election called to consider constitutional amendments.

The balanced budget provision makes the comptroller of public accounts an integral part of the budget-making process. The comptroller must certify revenue and estimate how much money will come into state coffers. Technically, the legislature can override his or her projection with a four-fifths vote in both the House and the Senate. Realistically, the comptroller's estimate is a concrete limit that can't be raised unless the House and Senate increase tax rates. The conservative nature of Texas politics ensures that the 80 percent override threshold cannot be met. Even if the legislators know that the comptroller's estimate is low, many conservative legislators would use the voting procedure to block additional spending.

A 1978 state constitutional amendment provides a further restriction on state fiscal policy. State tax revenues are constitutionally barred from rising faster than the estimated growth of the Texas economy—although the amendment doesn't apply to dedicated funds (art. 8, sec. 22). This provision can be overridden if a simple majority declares and specifies an emergency that requires higher tax revenue. Although seemingly an easy obstacle to overcome, the provision requires a public, recorded vote that might come back to haunt legislators who opt to raise taxes. At the same time, it allows the legislature to access additional funds if a true emergency exists. The comptroller's budget estimates can be found at http://www.window.state.tx.us/finances/.

The Biennial Budget System

The ability of the comptroller to accurately predict revenue is limited. In order to project state revenue, a person would have to know oil prices, inflation rates, unemployment rates, personal income, gross state product, and a host of other economic numbers in each month from the beginning of the two-year economic cycle until the end. Furthermore, because national budgets are on a yearly cycle, it is difficult to know how much federal money will flow into the state over a two-year period. All together, 30 months elapse from the first revenue projection until the end of the budget period. Texas comptrollers are traditionally conservative in nature, almost always underestimating revenues. As a result, the state—with some notable exceptions over the last decade -usually has surplus funds. Often, the legislature will pass an additional spending bill contingent on revenue exceeding projections. When the comptroller is comfortable in certifying additional revenue, these programs are activated.

Nonetheless, the biennial nature of the Texas budget poses difficulties. Uncertain revenue flow restricts the ability of the legislature to spend effectively. The legislature faces challenges in mapping out priorities over a 30-month period. Changing social, political, economic, and technological conditions can quickly make policy inadequate or obsolete. It is problematic for the legislature to react to change when they meet only 5 months out of 24.

Public Sentiment

Like most Americans, Texans don't like paying taxes, but in this state, the antitax sentiment is more ingrained. Citizens might expect quality education, good highways, and an effective prison system, but they believe this can be achieved while keeping spending to a minimum. For instance, most Texans equate an "effective" prison system with one that keeps criminals off the streets. There is little sentiment for rehabilitative spending.

The individualistic nature of Texans makes many suspicious of social spending. Even programs that might save money in the long term, like prenatal care and the Children's Health Insurance Program, are subject to intense scrutiny. Under such constraints, tax increases are an unpopular way to enhance revenue. Politicians recognize this. In the 2006 and 2008 elections, it was rare to find a candidate from either party and for any office who strayed from the "no new taxes" philosophy.

Dedicated Funds

dedicated funds
Revenues set aside for specific expense categories.

An additional constraint on the legislature is that much of the Texas budget is comprised of **dedicated funds.** These are revenues earmarked for a certain purpose from the moment they are collected. A portion of the gasoline tax, for instance, can only be used for highway construction. Money from oil and gas leases goes into the Permanent University Fund and can only be used by the University of Texas and Texas A&M systems. Texas has about 200 separate dedicated funding categories. A portion of the sales tax on sporting goods goes to the parks and wildlife account.

A twelfth of the state hotel tax is dedicated for advertising and marketing. Funds dedicated by the state constitution or state laws totaled over $42 billion each biennium.[1] Dedicated funds began as a conservative phenomenon. The idea was to restrict runaway spending by limiting the legislature's ability to spend freely. Such funds can only be spent for certain purposes. Additionally, dedicating ensures that at least some money will be available for important expenditures.

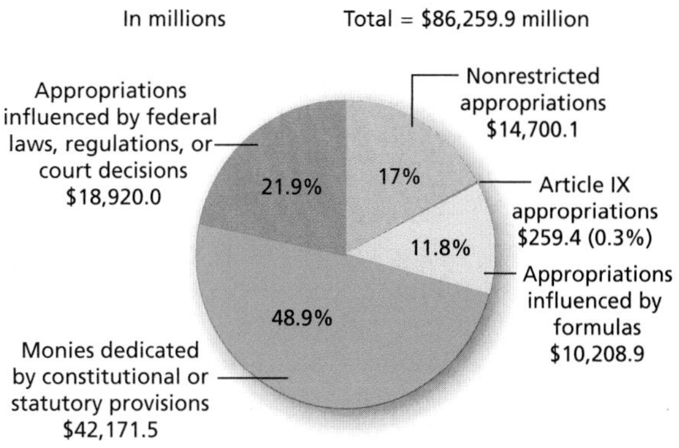

A problem for the Texas legislature is that such a high percentage of state revenue is restricted. Dedicated funds and state spending influenced by federal mandates, which will be discussed in the next section, account for over 80 percent of the state's general revenue. The legislature therefore has limited flexibility in deciding how to budget. In 1995, legislation that removed more than $3.3 billion per biennium from dedicated sources took effect. Revenues not dedicated within the state constitution or rededicated by the legislature were freed for discretionary spending.[2] Two years later, however, the state fell back into the same trap as the move to dedicate funds began anew. Almost all lottery revenue was dedicated to education, although most of it was flowing to that purpose anyway. The legislature tied the hands of future lawmakers with this action.

FIGURE **12.2 Restricted Appropriations from General Revenue Funds and General-Revenue Dedicated Funds Budget 2008–2009 Biennium.**

Congressional and Court Mandates

The federal government mandates much of the state's spending, requiring that minimum standards be met in a variety of areas. With the growth of federal **mandates**, state and local governments have found it necessary to bear much of the costs of providing services. Federal laws, such as those concerning health care, access for the disabled, and landfills and other environmental concerns, cost hundreds of millions of dollars. Federally mandated programs ate up almost $19 billion of the 2008–2009 budget, while another $10 billion in state spending was influenced by federal matching fund formulas.[3] States bear the majority of the cost for health-related mandates. Local government pays most of the price for environmental mandates. With Congress more cognizant of state spending constraints, federal legislation must now take into account the costs associated with unfunded mandates.

mandates
Regulations set by Congress that state and local government must meet.

In addition to meeting congressional spending mandates, Texas must meet federal court-ordered standards. Recently, the state has been under federal court orders to improve its prison and mental health and mental retardation services, as well as to equalize spending at the public university level of higher education. Concurrently, state courts have ordered Texas to equalize spending in its public secondary and elementary education, further restricting the legislature's discretion. Every dollar spent as a result of congressional mandate or court-ordered reform is a dollar that cannot be spent elsewhere.

The Budget-Making Process

In theory, Texas has a dual budget process. The governor draws up one budget while the **Legislative Budget Board** (LBB) creates a competing one. In reality, the LBB dominates the process. The LBB is a joint House and Senate committee that has the primary responsibility for creating the state's preliminary appropriations bill. The board is cochaired by the lieutenant governor and the Speaker of the House. Ex-officio officers, those who are on the LBB by virtue of the positions they hold, include the chairs of the Senate Finance Committee, the Senate State Affairs Committee, the House Appropriations Committee, and the House Ways and Means Committee. In addition, the lieutenant governor appoints two senators and the Speaker appoints two House members. Inasmuch as the lieutenant governor appoints all of the committee chairs in the Senate and the Speaker does likewise in the House, the legislative leaders have tremendous power over the purse. The LBB also has a sizable, professional and permanent staff that aids in the budget-making process.

Budget creation begins at the agency level. Each agency makes an appropriations request based on past expenditures and anticipated needs. Often, the LBB directs agencies to hold current spending levels, reduce spending, or produce separate budgets for various levels of spending. For instance, an agency might be asked to produce a budget allocating resources at current levels, at a 5 percent funding reduction, and at a 3 percent funding increase. The LBB would therefore receive three different budget proposals from the agency. Using the agency recommendations, the LBB begins to construct the budget.

Through this process, legislative leaders have much power. The Speaker and lieutenant governor are, in essence, the cochairs of the committee that decides where the state's revenue will be spent. The House and Senate will alter the LBB blueprint, but the basic priorities usually remain intact. True political power is defined by a person's ability to control the flow of government spending. As cochairs of the LBB, the lieutenant governor and Speaker have greater control over the process than any other players.

The House and Senate adjust the LBB's budget. The Appropriations Committee in the House and the Finance Committee in the Senate create spending bills. Individual lawmakers have the opportunity to affect spending both through these committees and through floor debate. The Senate and House will inevitably have some different spending priorities, so the final bill will emerge from the conference committee (see Chapter 6). Even after the legislature approves the conference bill, the governor can veto individual line items from the budget (see Chapter 7).

The LBB, working with the governor, has the power to transfer or impound funds when the legislature is out of session. Either the governor or the LBB can begin the process by proposing that certain funds either not be spent or be shifted. No action can be taken unless both participants approve. When funds are transferred, they can either be used within the original agency or shifted to a different agency altogether. This process allows changes to be made in the budget without necessitating a special session of the legislature. It saves the state both time and money. Visit the Legislative Budget Board's Web site at http://www.lbb.state.tx.us.

Democratic house members Elliot Naishtat and Patrick Rose listen to testimony on CHIPs and Medicaid.

State Revenue

The $182 billion biennial budget for 2010–2011 is vastly different from more constrained state fiscal habits of the past. In 1977, the total revenue of the state of Texas was $7.37 billion. Yearly state income would not double until 1984, when it reached $14.92 billion. Following some ups and downs due to economic turbulence in the mid-1980s, state revenue exceeded $18 billion in 1987. From that point forward, the growth was explosive. By 1991, total revenue was $26.2 billion. In 1998, it had risen to $44.5 billion. By 2009, revenue was almost $80 billion. A more accurate measure of state budget growth can be gained by adjusting the current budget for population growth and inflation. Accounting for these adjustments, state spending increased from $73 billion in 1994–1995 biennium to $91 billion—in 1994 dollars—in 2008–2009. Although still a significant increase, it is dramatically less than the almost 250 percent increase that occurs when these factors are not considered.[4]

This explosive growth brought much more money into the state coffers. However, it did not bring an end to the state's fiscal concerns. Most states entered 2009 facing a real budget crisis. State revenues had dried up because of the stagnant economy. At the same time, state resources were strained like never before as more people sought government aid. Texas's coffers were not exactly overflowing with money as the legislature gathered in Austin, but the state faced more favorable conditions than most. Restrained spending in the past had kept current and future obligations in check. And while the recession hit Texas, it didn't have the impact it had in other places where the economy was weaker. Still, with an extended downturn likely, lawmakers were reluctant to embark on big spending programs, even with the $12 billion grant that the state received as part of President Barack Obama's 2009 federal stimulus package. They feared that increased spending now could be costly in the long run, especially if the federal government is not as generous two years down the road. Instead, they moderately increased the state's budget by 7.4 percent—or about 3.6 percent per year—an amount almost equal to the President's stimulus boost. In fact, the state cut general revenue spending by almost 2 percent from the previous biennium, preparing itself for leaner times when the legislature convenes in 2011. Texas did this without tapping into its "Rainy Day Fund," which should grow to $9 billion by the 2011 legislative session and will be available at that point to help cover any temporary shortfalls.

In January 2010, Governor Perry, Lieutenant Governor Dewhurst and Speaker Straus ordered most state agencies to but their annual budgets by 5% for the second half of the biennium. Although public education, employee retirement programs and some health care programs were exempted, colleges and universities, the courts and most other state agencies had to comply. This intervention saved over $1 billion in 2011 spending.

The Obama stimulus package was part of a long-term trend toward greater federal grants. These grants are controversial, since they carry the stipulation that spending be carried out under stricter federal scrutiny. More often than not, nontax revenue has accounted for more than half of the state's budget since the mid-1990s. For a historical perspective on state revenue broken down by source, visit http://www.window.state.tx.us/taxbud/revenue.html.

Tax Collection

regressive tax
A system of taxation whereby the tax rate increases as income decreases.

progressive tax
A system of taxation whereby the tax rate increases as income increases.

The Texas sales tax has often been criticized for its alleged regressive tendencies. We will argue that this viewpoint is, at best, incomplete. First, let's define some terms. A **regressive tax** places a higher burden on the poor than the wealthy. In other words, the poor would pay a higher percentage of their income in taxes. A **progressive tax**, on the other hand, places a higher burden on the wealthy. Table 12.1 shows the effect of a flat sales tax on two families of four, one that makes $10,000 a year; the other, $100,000 a year.

TABLE **12.1** **Effects of a Regressive Sales Tax on Two Families**

	FAMILY A	FAMILY B
Total income	$10,000	$100,000
Sales tax rate	8%	8%
Family spending	$9,259	$80,000
Tax paid	$741	$6,400
Percent of income paid in taxes	7.4%	6.4%

In this simplistic model—*which is not how the Texas system operates*—the sales tax applies to all purchases, including housing, food, utilities, and medicine. The presumption is that the low-income family must spend all of its money in order to make ends meet. The wealthier family, meanwhile, saves and invests a portion of its income. It does not pay a sales tax on this portion. Therefore, although Family B pays $5,659 more in sales tax than Family A, the economically disadvantaged family actually pays a higher percentage of its income in taxes than the wealthy family does: 7.4 percent to 6.4 percent. The fact that wealthy people find other uses for a portion of their income makes an all-inclusive sales tax regressive. But the Texas sales tax is nothing like this.

An example of a progressive tax is a graduated income tax. Look at the same families in Table 12.2. This presumes a tax system under which no deductions are allowed. The 8 percent paid by Family B is, of course, a higher percentage than the 1 percent paid by Family A. The $8,000 in total taxes is also much more than the $100 incurred by the poorer family. This tax system is progressive, placing a higher burden on the wealthier family.

TABLE **12.2** **Effects of a Progressive Tax on Two Families**

	FAMILY A	FAMILY B
Total income	$10,000	$100,000
Income tax rate	1%	8%
Tax paid	$100	$8,000

SALES TAX The largest source of **tax revenue** in Texas is the **sales tax**. It is such a significant part of the tax structure that it brings in about 55 percent of the state's tax revenue. The second highest source of tax revenue, the franchise tax, brings in about11 percent of the total. Because of the recession, and contrary to the norm, tax revenue dropped from 2008 to 2009, and seemed certain to drop again in 2010.

In 2009, the state collected $21 billion through the sales tax. One of the highest sales tax rates in the nation, the 6.25 percent tax is on the retail price of selected goods and services sold in the state. Only Mississippi, Nevada, Rhode Island, and Washington have higher actual rates. Rates appear higher in Minnesota, but a portion of that rate must be distributed to the local governments. In Texas, cities can assess their own 1 percent tax, which is added to the state levy. Special districts, such as those for parks, crime control, or sport facility construction, often add another penny or so to the actual tax rate.

tax revenue
Funds generated through the tax system.

sales tax
Tax paid on goods and services; collected at the point of sale and forwarded to the state treasury.

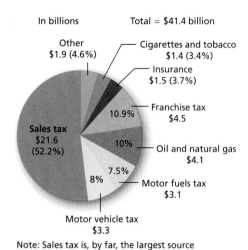

In billions   Total = $41.4 billion

Note: Sales tax is, by far, the largest source of Texas tax revenue.

FIGURE **12.3 Texas Collections by Major Tax, 2009.**

Texas is one of 26 states to completely exempt non-prepared food from the sales tax. If a person buys meat, lettuce, tomatoes, and bread, he does not pay a sales tax on the purchase. If, on the other hand, a person purchases a sandwich already prepared, she does pay the tax. Therefore, a meal prepared at a restaurant incurs the sales tax, but one prepared at home does not. The law is a little quirky. Buy six or more donuts and it is nontaxable; five or fewer and it is taxable. (There's no truth to the rumor that the law enforcement lobby was behind this exemption.)

What dampens the regressivity of the Texas sales tax is the fact that many of the expenses of a financially disadvantaged family are sales tax–exempt. In addition to food and prescription drugs, medical services, housing, and utilities are all free from the state portion of the sales tax. The family earning more money would be likely to eat out more often, incurring a sales tax on a higher-priced meal. If you consider the motor vehicle sales tax—see below—to be a part of the broader tax, the system becomes even less regressive.

One of the more controversial aspects of the state sales tax is in the area of services. Some are taxable, others are not. If you hire an engineer to create computer software or a lawn service to cut your yard, you are required to pay a sales tax on the purchase. On the other hand, if you hire a lawyer or accountant, you don't pay a sales tax on the services provided. It is worth remembering that within the Texas legislature, the most prevalent occupation is being a lawyer. As such, they use their power to protect their own interests.

In 1999, the legislature enacted more sales tax exemptions. Electronic data processing, nonprescription drug sales, and Internet access are not subject to sales tax. Additionally, a back-to-school sales tax holiday creates a three-day period each August during which most clothing and shoes priced under $100 per item are tax-free.

FRANCHISE TAX In 2006, the Texas legislature fundamentally altered the structure of business taxes in the state. The new, broader tax significantly reduced tax loopholes and brought many businesses under the tax system for the first time. The new system will eventually bring more than twice as much into state coffers as the previous one; much of the significantly increased revenue from the new structure will be dedicated to a property tax relief fund, which mandates lower property tax rates in local school districts.

Such a significant change usually has an outside impetus. In this case, the shove came from the Texas Supreme Court, which had declared the state's method of financing public education unconstitutional. Texas has long had a constitutional prohibition against a statewide property tax. Previous school financing law, however, had left 90 percent of the state's districts taxing within pennies of $1.50 per $100 of property value. State recapture of dollars from property-rich districts had created a situation where practically all districts had to tax at the maximum. The state Supreme Court ruled that the system had created a *de facto* statewide property tax and ordered the legislature to fix the financing structure before schools opened in the fall of 2006. Under the gun, with elections approaching, the legislature opted for the creation of a Property Tax Relief Fund, paid for through a restructuring of the franchise tax.

In its original incarnation, the **franchise tax** was levied on a business's inventory. Some Texans are old enough to remember "inventory reduction sales," which occurred prior to a business's official inventory date. In 1991, however, the legislature changed the tax so that a business would pay either $2.50 per $1,000 of taxable capital or 4.5 percent of its earned surplus, whichever is greater. ("Earned surplus" meant income; the legislature simply chose to employ a more politically acceptable phrase.) From a business standpoint, the franchise tax was worse than a true income tax. The earned surplus tax almost doubled franchise tax revenue. Still, that altered tax left many Texas businesses outside of the tax umbrella. Corporations paid the tax, but limited partnerships and professional associations did not. Although limited partnerships like the Texas Rangers Baseball Club at least paid sales tax on their ticket and concession sales, most law firms and medical associations escaped state business taxes altogether. In 1997, Governor Bush tried and failed to extend corporate taxes to these entities, despite his then-ownership interest in the Rangers. The lawyer-laden legislature opposed this proposal. Many corporations turned themselves into partnerships in the ensuing years. However, in the 2006 special session, the specter of facing angry voters and closed schools was enough to make legislators opt for broader business taxes.

franchise tax
A specific tax paid by businesses operating in Texas.

The new franchise tax is a "margin tax," assessed on the lesser of the following:

- 70 percent of a business's total revenue;
- a business's revenue minus its cost of goods sold;
- a business's revenue minus employee compensation.

Businesses engaged primarily in wholesale or retail trade pay a 1/2 percent tax on that margin rate. Other businesses pay 1 percent on the margin rate. Sole proprietorships are exempt from the tax, but professional associations, partnerships, and corporations all pay.

Only three states have no corporate income tax. Of the 32 states with flat tax rates, none have an effective rate lower than that of Texas. The franchise tax generates almost 11 percent of tax revenue, bringing in about $4.3 billion in 2009.

MOTOR VEHICLE SALES AND RENTAL TAX The tax on sales and rental of motor vehicles is listed as a separate source of state revenue, although it is essentially no different from the sales tax. The state's share of the revenue is the same 6.25 percent on sales and long-term leases. However, short-term car rentals, which are defined as those lasting fewer than 30 days, are subject to a 10 percent tax. Manufactured homes are taxed at just over 3 percent of their value. The motor vehicle tax brought in just over $2.6 billion in 2009. This is the state's fourth-largest tax source, bringing in just under 7 percent of tax revenue.

MOTOR FUELS TAX In 2009, the **motor fuels tax** produced just over $3 billion in revenue for the state. The state's share of the gas tax is 20 percent per gallon on both diesel and gasoline, and 15 percent per gallon on liquefied gas. The gasoline tax rate has increased 400 percent since 1981, but total revenue from the motor fuels taxes has increased even more. Gas pump taxes provide about 8 percent of tax revenue.

motor fuels tax
A tax on gasoline, diesel, and other motor fuels.

OIL AND GAS PRODUCTION TAXES In 1985, the oil production tax and the gas production tax each brought more than $1 billion into the state coffers. The tax, paid by oil and gas producers, is in addition to the gasoline tax paid by consumers. In 1998, the combined revenue of the two sources was less than $900 million. These taxes once provided 28.3 percent of the state's total revenue. By 1998, their contribution fell to 2.3 percent. Both the oil and the gas taxes are levied on market value: 4.6 percent for oil and 7.5 percent for gas. When oil and gas prices dipped, Texas was hit twice. The tax brought in less revenue per barrel of oil when the price of a barrel dropped. As prices fell, oil production became less profitable and fewer barrels were produced in Texas, causing a further reduction in revenue. Although oil and gas revenue experienced a brief spike mid-decade spike, natural gas revenue was about $1.4 billion in 2009, while the oil production tax reached $880 million. Oil and gas production brought in less than 3 percent of total state revenue; a percentage that is certain to drop over the coming years as natural gas production in Texas has again slowed.

"SIN" TAXES Taxes levied on those habits that are seen as detrimental by many are often dubbed **"sin" taxes**. The most significant of these are the taxes on cigarettes, tobacco products, and alcoholic beverages.

"sin" taxes
Taxes levied on selected goods and services, such as alcoholic beverages and tobacco products.

Tobacco taxes produced just over $1.3 billion in revenue in 2007, a 144 percent increase over the previous year, primarily due to a significant hike in cigarette taxes. The state tax on a pack of cigarettes rose from 41 percent per pack to $1.41. Smokeless tobacco or tobacco sold for pipes or self-rolled cigarettes is taxed at 40 percent of the manufactures' list price. Cigar taxes are significantly lower as a percentage of their sales price. By 2009, tobacco tax income reached almost $1.6 billion.

With higher oil prices the rule over the last several years, working oil wells have, once again, become a common sight. Why do oil prices have less impact on the Texas budget than they had three decades ago?

The rising cost of cigarettes, a result of successful lawsuits against the tobacco industry and increased state and federal taxes, has had a detrimental effect on tobacco sales in Texas. This trend should accelerate in the future with the full effect of tobacco legislation. It has had a mitigating impact on rising tobacco revenue. Most of the increased revenue from cigarette and tobacco tax increases is targeted for the Property Tax Relief Fund.

Alcoholic beverage taxes generated just almost $800 million dollars in 2009. The tax rate ranges from $6 a barrel for beer to $2.40 a gallon for liquor. The state also receives 14 percent of the gross receipts from mixed-drink sales. Alcohol income has steadily, but slowly, increased, while the tax rate has remained the same. It was not lost on political observers that legislators increased taxes on cigarettes, but not on cigars or alcoholic beverages.

In the 2007 legislative session, a sin tax was enacted on patrons of adult entertainment establishments. This $5 entry fee was dubbed the "pole tax" by political pundits and is not to be confused with the poll tax, which we discussed in Chapter 3 and was struck down by the U.S. Supreme Court. The Texas pole tax was also struck down by a state appeals court on the grounds that it discriminatorily infringed on a single form of free expression. The state appealed to the Texas Supreme Court and collection of the tax has been suspended in the interim.[5] The Court had heard the case, but not issued a decision, as of this writing.

"Sin" taxes have been criticized as the most regressive aspect of Texas taxes because poor people tend to spend a higher percentage of their income on tobacco and alcohol products than do the wealthy. This is not an argument that evokes great sympathy from the average Texan.

INSURANCE AND UTILITY TAXES The insurance occupation tax has increased dramatically in recent years, bringing in almost $1.3 billion in 2009. The tax rate varies due to the type of insurance involved and the amount of the individual insurance company's investment within the state. Likewise, utility taxes are based on a company's gross receipts. This tax generated about $500 million in state revenue in 2009.

OTHER TAXES A small percent of state tax revenue is generated from other taxes. These include inheritance taxes, hotel and motel taxes, amusement fee taxes, and a number of other minor revenue sources. In total, these taxes brought in about $500 million in 2009.

Tax Notes

Texans are subject to many taxes other than those imposed by the state. It is important to differentiate among the state taxes discussed above, the local taxes discussed in the previous chapter, and federal taxes, such as the income and social security taxes deducted from an individual's paycheck. Alcohol, tobacco, and gasoline are subject to both federal and state taxes.

Even with the school property tax relief granted during the 2006 special session, Texans pay more in property taxes than do the citizens in most states. Higher property values have put severe financial strains on many homeowners. Technically, these taxes are part of the local tax structure, not the state system, but they add significantly to the total taxes paid by Texans.

On a per-person basis, the state of Texas receives only about 4.2 percent of the average citizen's income in taxes. Despite the fact that many Texas tax rates have been raised in recent years, state tax revenue as a percentage of overall personal income is the same as it was in the late 1970s. Texas has the second-lowest tax rate as a percentage of income among the 50 states.[6]

Texas is one of only seven states without a personal income tax. This has many consequences, some positive and some negative, for the state and its citizens. First, the absence of an income tax makes it more difficult for the state to raise tax rates. Many Texans see that as a good thing. Common sense dictates that the current state sales tax, especially in tandem with local government add-ons, is so high that raising it more would likely have a negative impact on the state economy. (If a sales tax becomes too high, it eventually discourages spending. Items that were otherwise obtainable become too expensive because of tax considerations. When spending drops, workers lose jobs, compounding revenue problems. Therefore, because of the effect on economic activity, raising a tax can sometimes result in a drop in state revenue.) As it is, only eight states have a higher sales tax than Texas,[7] but that may be a little misleading because of the state's broad sales tax exemptions that we discussed earlier.

Without a major rewriting of the tax code—or a major influx of revenue from some other source—state government is restrained. With revenue constrained by the tax structure, tax-based expenditures are essentially limited to current revenues plus increases that result from economic growth. Conservatives might see this positively because, when coupled with the balanced budget provision, it limits the growth of government.

Conservatives fear that an income tax rate would be too easy to raise and therefore oppose allowing such a tax. Many liberals, on the other hand, would argue that the current system is far too restrictive. Some government programs, such as education, are so vital that they deserve more government funding even if nontraditional forms of financing, such as an income tax, are needed.

The Texas Constitution, as a result of a 1993 amendment, prohibits the state from instituting an income tax unless voters give their approval. Even then, the uses for income tax revenue are restricted. Two-thirds would go to provide school property tax relief (see Chapter 11), and the other third would be dedicated to education. Such a system would multiply the dedicated funds restrictions with which the state has grappled for decades. The provision also requires voter approval for any rate increase.

Historically, one of the best arguments put forward by income tax advocates was that state income tax, unlike the sales tax, was deductible from federal taxes. Texans were leaving money in the federal treasury because of an inefficient taxing mechanism. In 2004, the U.S. Congress made sales tax deductible for Texans who itemize. That legislation was scheduled to expire in 2005, but has been extended through successive sessions of Congress. If it is permanently renewed, and that is possible, but by no means certain, it would undercut one of the arguments for a state income tax.

Taxation Summary

Texas has a low state tax burden. Of the 15 most populous states, Texas has the lowest level of state tax revenue per capita. Only two of those 15 have no personal income tax. When you include local taxes, the burden on most Texans increases considerably.

It is important to understand that the above-mentioned fiscal constraints on the state have pushed many government programs to the local level. For instance, many states heavily fund education construction programs. In Texas, most funding is local. Almost half of the total state and local tax burden on Texans goes to local governments, not the state. Nonetheless, Texans pay fewer than 22 percent out of every dollar in combined state and local taxes—more than 10 percent lower than the citizen of an average state. See Table 12.3 for a comparison of Texas taxes with those of other states.

TABLE **12.3** **State Taxes per Person in Various States**

STATE	YEARLY TAXES PER CAPITA
Alabama	$1,510
Minnesota	$2,715
California	$2,614
New York	$2,351
Connecticut	$2,881
Oklahoma	$1,828
Hawaii	$2,859
Pennsylvania	$1,835
Massachusetts	$2,691
Texas	$1,377
Louisiana	$1,610
Virginia	$1,818
Michigan	$1,790
U.S. average	$1,966

SOURCE: U.S. Census Bureau, *Statistical Abstract* (Washington, DC: U.S. GPO, 2005), p. 278.

Reforming Texas Taxes

Texas certainly saw dramatic tax reform in 2006. However, one idea that has generated significant revenue for other states—casino gambling—has never quite got out of the gate in Texas. Staring at an $18 billion shortfall, and with a Speaker of the House whose family is in the racing business, the prospective extension of legalized gambling faces short odds than ever. Additionally, the largest horse track in Texas is now owned by the same holding company that runs the Winstar casino across the Oklahoma border, and they'd love to see slot machines at the track. The last time casino-style gambling received serious legislative consideration, Winstar was one of the biggest interests fighting *against* legalization, fearing that it would cut into their Oklahoma profits.

The Casino Option

Saturday, October 30, 2004 was the biggest day in the history of Texas horse racing. Lone Star Park in Grand Prairie hosted the equine equivalent of the Super Bowl—the Breeder's Cup. In many ways, it is more like eight Super Bowls, with championships being determined in eight different divisions. The Cup brought over 53,000 fans and an estimated economic impact of over $35 million. What remains to be seen is whether that day was the real beginning of racing in Texas—or the beginning of the end.

As an industry, horse racing is in trouble. It's no secret that Americans like to gamble. Until a few years ago, most Americans could legally gamble only in Vegas, Atlantic City, or at the racetrack. After a brief period of legalization during the Depression, Texans could not legally bet on horses until the late 1980s. Even then, opponents of gambling promised that this was only the beginning. Pari-mutuel betting today, one-armed bandits tomorrow. Horsemen said they had no interest in slots, just horses. So why, 20 years later, are the same horse forces begging for slots?

The nature of the game has changed. When gambling options were limited, a full 40 percent of America's legally wagered dollars were bet on horses. Now it's less than 3 percent. As more states have approved casinos, more betting money—and tax revenue—have gone other places. In other states, tracks—with the approval of state legislatures—have been able to supplement their track purses with slot money. Slots are a losing proposition for the gambler. Over the long term, the casino always wins. With a portion of those winnings, some "racinos" have added to their purses—the payout for the winning horses. Bigger payouts attract better horses and more bettors. And we are talking about a lot of money. Casino supplements to race purses totaled close to $200 million nationwide in 2004. Total purses were just over a billion dollars, and that includes states like Texas that don't allow slot supplementation. Oklahoma, Louisiana, New Mexico, and Arkansas all allow tracks to supplement purses with slot income. But not Texas.

The Texas Thoroughbred industry is not the only one facing problems. In July 2005, Churchill Downs sold fabled Hollywood Park (think Seabiscuit). The new owners threatened to tear down the track unless the state of California legalized the racino format within three years; although they have backed off that timetable, Hollywood Park's future hangs by a fraying thread. With California voters approving more Indian casinos, Hollywood Park faces stiffer competition for limited betting dollars without the benefit of operating their own slots. Likewise, the future of the Pimlico racecourse in Maryland is up in the air. The home of the Preakness—the second leg of racing's Triple Crown—suffers from competing with surrounding states where racinos are the norm. Except for Preakness weekend, racing is quickly becoming a losing proposition in Maryland.

Of course, the racing industry is just part of this story. Slot machines in Texas could bring upward of $1.5 billion a year into state coffers. That means a billion and a half dollars that doesn't come from cutting spending or raising the sales tax or other fees. Cross the Oklahoma border, visit the Winstar Casino, and try to find a car that doesn't have Texas plates. Good luck. Or head east to Shreveport for a more realistic comparison. Visit the racino at Louisiana Downs. Ninety percent of the cars are from Texas.

And that's where this controversy plays out in its starkest terms. Seven years ago, Louisiana Downs was all but dead. No one went to the races. Betting totals were down; therefore, purses were in freefall. But LA Downs has had slots since May 2003. By 2005, they had extended their race season and upped their purses. Lone Star Park, on the other hand, has cut purses, then cut them again. Horse owners follow the money; horse players follow the horses. As a result, owners are taking their best horses, if not their entire stables, out of Texas. Wagering money follows. By the summer of 2009, Lone Star was cutting stakes races from its schedule. The slots at LA Downs bring in about $100 million a year in revenue—of which 15 percent went to supplement purses and 15 percent went to the state. Louisiana operates two other

Ghostzapper—shown here in the lead—won the Breeder's Cup Classic at Lone Star Park in 2004. How are Texas horse tracks on unequal footing when compared to operations in neighboring states?

racinos—one of which creates about 40 percent more slot revenue, one about 20 percent less. Together, they put a major strain on the Texas racing industry and provide a major boon to Louisiana state coffers.

As it stands, the Texas racing business model is unsustainable. Texas tracks are not attracting enough betting money to cover the purses they pay out. In late 2010, the racing industry was considering the radical approach of eliminating racing dates at the tracks in San Antonio and Houston in 2011, consolidating all thoroughbred racing at Lone Star Park. By cutting the total number of races and running from one track, per race purses could be increased, potentially drawing better horses and more horse players. Industry officials see this as a one year bridge, stretching to the legalization of on-site slot machines. If the legislature doesn't cooperate, though, all future bets are off.

Other Revenue Raising Options

Any single tax increase in a $182 billion biennial budget—or about $91 billion a year—will have only a marginal impact on revenue. But let's look at some revenue options. A nickel increase in the gas tax would generate over a half a billion dollars a year. Adding a dollar a gallon tax on beer and wine would bring in $400 million. Sales taxes on doctors and lawyers would generate about $1 billion a year. The same taxes on auto repair service would create a quarter of a billion a year. Doubling utility taxes would bring in an additional quarter billion as well. A full-penny sales tax increase would garner almost $2 billion annually. There are other choices, of course, but keep in mind that almost any tax increase is going to generate significant opposition.

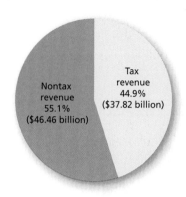

FIGURE **12.4** 2009 Texas
Revenue by Source.

Of all of the statistics regarding Texas state revenue, perhaps the most interesting and relevant is this: in recent years, the state has received more revenue from nontax than from tax sources. Through most of the 1990s, nontax revenues outstripped state tax income by a small margin. Through the early 21st century, nontax revenue has consistently comprised about 54 percent of state spending. In 1982, taxes provided 64.4 percent of all state revenue. Tax revenue exceeded 60 percent of state income as late as 1989. In 2009, tax revenue fell just below 45% of total state revenue. The largest source of this **nontax revenue** is **federal grants**, but significant income also comes from licenses, fees, interest income, and the lottery.

FEDERAL GRANTS In 2008, federal grants produced over 30 percent of state revenue. This amounted to over $26 billion in federal funding.[8] In the 2010–11 budget, with the Obama stimulus package (see the Federalism box about the money Texas turned down), grants skyrocketed to 36 percent of the budget, an average of almost $33 billion a year. Nowhere in state government has there been a more significant financial impact than in the area of federal grants. Federal revenue in 1994 roughly equaled total state spending in 1980, which was $10.66 billion. Total federal funding for Texas in 1977 was $1.88 billion. The federal contribution to the state budget increased more than 1833 percent from 1977 to 2010.

Federal funding grew steadily through the 1980s. Opening the decade at $2.6 billion, federal grants did not exceed $3 billion until 1984. Funding surpassed $4 billion in 1986, and eclipsed $5 billion in 1989. The explosion in federal revenues began in the early 1990s. Since then, these funds have increased an average of almost $1 billion per year. Much of this funding increase came as a result of expanded Medicaid grants.

nontax revenue
Revenue derived from non-tax sources, such as the lottery and fees paid to the state.

federal grants
Revenue distributed to states from the federal government.

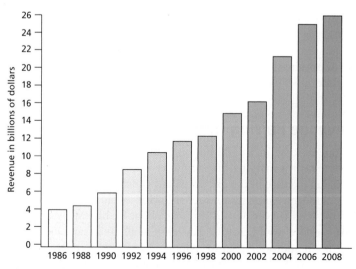

FIGURE **12.5** Growth in Federal Revenue Coming to Texas.

INSIDE
THE FEDERALIST SYSTEM
Left on the Table

As we discussed more thoroughly in Chapter 2, federal grants come with strings attached. Usually, state governments bite the bullet and accept the requirements that come with the cash. And certainly, that's what happened with more than $12.1 billion that Texas took from the 2009 federal stimulus package. Texas did not, however, take everything it was offered.

Governor Perry turned down some $555 million in additional unemployment benefits that would have gone to out-of-work Texans. Although the funds would have provided a significant boost to the Texas economy, Perry thought the residual costs were too high. Taking the funds would have required Texas to change its unemployment tax requirements, inevitably leading to higher taxes on Texas businesses even as the recession deepened.

Not all Texans agreed with Perry's call to reject the funds, with even a significant number of Republicans voicing their objections. There were, in fact, enough votes in the legislature to pass a bill accepting the funds, but there would not have been enough votes to override the governor's inevitable veto; so the effort died in the legislature.

Texas wasn't the only state to reject the unemployment funds. A handful of Republican governors did the same. Unemployment wasn't the only portion of the stimulus package that Perry rejected; in addition, he turned down a much smaller energy grant that also came with strings. It is worth noting, however, that although the rejections drew the press coverage, Texas took more than 95 percent of the stimulus plan money, along with all the strings that came wrapped around that package.

Another significant factor was the state's restructuring of existing programs in order to qualify for matching funds. Former comptroller John Sharp deserves much of the credit for this as it was his performance reviews that made the changes possible. Over the 1994–1995 biennium, restructuring of existing programs raised an additional $1.23 billion in federal Medicaid funding alone without additional state expenditures. Still, on a per capita basis, federal spending in Texas is only 89 percent of the national average.[9] That translates to about $2.5 billion less than what equitable funding would produce.

In the 2008–2009 budget, federal grants made up 58 percent of the health and human services budget. They accounted for 43 percent of business and economic development. Although the federal share of education funding has increased dramatically over the last few years, it still comprises only about 16 percent of state public education spending.[10]

LICENSES, FEES, AND PERMITS The second-largest source of nontax revenue comes from licenses, fees, permits, fines, and penalties. This fund created about $7.2 billion in revenue in 2009. It includes such items as higher-education tuition and professional licenses, as well as hunting, fishing, and driver's licenses.[11]

INTEREST AND INVESTMENT INCOME The state's investments and cash on hand produced over $1.3 billion in revenue in 2009.[12]

The state clears over a billion dollars a year in net lottery revenue. What effect do you think legalized casino gambling would have on lottery sales?

lottery
Revenue raising method of the state involving games of chance.

THE LOTTERY In its early days, the Texas **lottery** exceeded all expectations for raising revenue. In 1997, it provided $1.86 billion in net state income, after administrative expenses. Even after the big winnings were paid, the lottery pulled in $1.2 billion in profit for the state. The Texas lottery was the best-selling lottery in the nation. All that would change quickly.

KILLING THE CASH COW: A QUICK LESSON IN BUDGET POLICY CONSEQUENCES In the 1997 session, the Texas legislature took ill-advised steps that drastically undercut the ability of the lottery to increase its revenue stream. Put bluntly, the legislature got greedy, and Texas paid for it. Part of the damage was calculated: some conservatives opposed to the lottery on moral grounds knew their actions would have a negative impact. Others were just foolish. They reasoned they could make more profit for the state by cutting the lottery's advertising budget and reducing the gambler's return on lottery purchases.

First, this ignores the essential fact practiced by corporate America—advertising attracts customers. Cutting the ad budget reduced the number of players. Second, it ignores basic human nature: if the odds are bad, people won't play as much. Whether players were cognizant of the fact that payments had dipped from 57 percent on the dollar to 53 percent, or whether they just realized they were winning less, ticket sales and profits dropped. The state lost more than $100 million in net revenue in 1998 alone, and ticket sales were off by $600 million. Once the leader in lottery sales, Texas dropped to third among the states. In 1999, sales and profits dipped even more, prompting the legislature to try to correct its mistake. They increased the payout share. As a result, the slumping revenue trend reversed. The 2001 revenue numbers were $500 million below 1997 numbers. They edged up slightly in 2002, bringing in just under $1 billion in profit. In 2003, Texas joined the Mega Millions multi-state lottery in an effort to revive interest. By 2004, net revenue—after prizes have been paid—edged back over $1 billion. By 2008, the state retained over $1 billion from the lottery.[13] By cutting off crucial momentum during its formative years, however, legislators permanently damaged lottery revenue.

OTHER SOURCES In 2009, all other sources produced about $5.5 billion. These sources include sales of goods and services, land income, and revenue from the settlement of legal claims.[14]

Expenditures

The Big Three

The best insight into public policy can be gained by gauging government expenditures. Spending levels show priorities, even when these priorities are mandated by politicians in Washington, DC, rather than in Austin. Government spending has been rising steadily ever since government started providing services. Political scientists believe that both social and technological factors have been responsible for most of these increases. Social considerations include labor-management relations, urbanization, and an expansion of the notion that government should provide, or at least regulate, basic social services. Technological advances, such as air and ground transportation and mass communication, have necessitated some degree of governmental intervention. Highway and air safety, privacy rights, and environmental concerns are among the relatively modern issues faced by government. Social and technological changes have ushered in a host of regulatory agencies that have sent state government expenditures soaring.

It is vital to note, however, that Texas spends much less on government services, per person, than the average state. Texas ranks last in total per capita state government spending, 46th in welfare spending, 44th in education expenditures, and 45th in public health spending. Texas ranks 75th in highway spending and spends more per capita than the average state.[15]

Texas spends more on education than on any other government service, accounting for 41.4 percent of the 2010–2011 budget, or over $75 billion. This includes public education, which accounts for over 70 percent of the total, and higher education, which takes the remainder. Public Health and Human Services come in second, taking up 32.7 percent of the budget. In fact, the social services budget closed to within a percentage point of education spending in 1997, but education has pulled back in front in the wake of welfare reform and an increased state commitment to education. Business and Economic Development, of which transportation spending is the largest component, runs a distant third in terms of total expenditures. Still, it accounts for over 11.4 percent of total state spending. These "big three" expenditure items claim almost 86 percent of total state spending.[16]

For a historical perspective on state expenditures by function, go to http://www.window.state.tx.us/taxbud/expend.html.

Education

Funding Texas's public schools has sparked political debate for over a century. It will likely continue to do so. Despite numerous rounds of education reform, the issue of how to provide equal funding to the state's 1,031 independent school districts will continue to be controversial. The school districts are diverse in size. Of those districts, 860 have fewer than 1,600 students. These districts combined, however, contain less than 11 percent of total school enrollment.[17]

The total cost of the Texas public education system, including local, state, and federal monies, is about $41 billion per year.[18] Education spending has increased an average of 6 percent per year over the last decade, although the constant dollar increase has been much less dramatic. The state's share of public education spending is a little over $25 billion. Yet only 60 percent of every dollar goes to classroom expenditures; the rest goes to administration, buildings, extracurricular activities, and other costs. Critics argue that a higher percentage should go to instruction, which is the purpose of an education system in the first place. In late summer 2005, Governor Perry, through the TEA commissioner, mandated that schools spend 65 percent of their funds on classroom purposes, phased in over the next few years. The order quickly sparked debate over what exactly comprises "instruction." In 2009, a bill to override the executive order died in committee.

From the mid-1980s to the mid-1990s, arguments over the extent of education equalization were at the forefront of the education reform movement in Texas. The controversy began because some districts spent much more per student than others. Often, this variance was due to property value differences. Local property taxes are a major source of education revenue, and those districts with a large tax base have more wealth to draw on. In 1986, the state Supreme Court ruled that these funding discrepancies violated the state constitutional provision mandating an "efficient" public education system.

On three separate occasions, in fact, the Texas Supreme Court declared the state's public school financing method unconstitutional. Finally, in early 1995, the Court approved an equalization plan, freeing the legislature to address other education reform measures. Senate Bill 7, which was signed into law in 1993, garnered concessions from the richest school districts. The funds surrendered by these wealthier districts subsidize those districts with lower tax bases; districts that otherwise have inadequate means of raising revenue. In terms of total spending for public education, Texas spends less per student than most states, an average a bit more

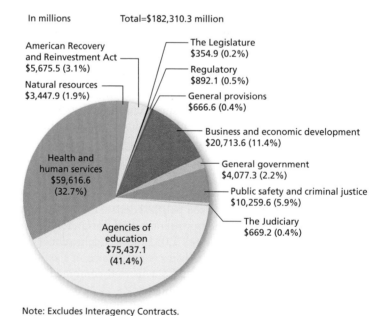

In millions   Total=$182,310.3 million

American Recovery and Reinvestment Act — $5,675.5 (3.1%)

Natural resources — $3,447.9 (1.9%)

The Legislature $354.9 (0.2%)

Regulatory $892.1 (0.5%)

General provisions $666.6 (0.4%)

Business and economic development $20,713.6 (11.4%)

Health and human services $59,616.6 (32.7%)

General government $4,077.3 (2.2%)

Public safety and criminal justice $10,259.6 (5.9%)

The Judiciary $669.2 (0.4%)

Agencies of education $75,437.1 (41.4%)

Note: Excludes Interagency Contracts.

FIGURE **12.6** **State Expenditures for 2009–2010.**

SOURCE: Legislative Budget Board

than $7,500 per student per year. That's about $1,500 per student behind the average state in annual education spending.[19]

Higher Education

About one and a quarter million students attend Texas's 144 public and private colleges and universities each year, with the state pumping a bit over $11 billion a year into the system. In 2003, the legislature deregulated tuition at state colleges and universities, pushing more of the cost onto students, but allowing universities to recruit prominent faculty and upgrade programs. The results have been dramatic. At the University of Texas, tuition alone for 12 hours cost students more than $3,500. The same class load at a community college would cost about $500. That is one reason that most undergraduate students from Texas take advantage of the state's 49 public community colleges. These schools, which receive a portion of their funding from the state, account for the majority of the total semester credit hours earned by Texas students. In the past decade, community college enrollment has increased by about a third.

One of the biggest events in Texas higher education in recent years was the *Hopwood* decision, a ruling by the Fifth Circuit Court of the United States, which essentially dismantled the state's affirmative action program in higher education. In *Hopwood* v. *Texas*, the court ruled that denying admission of Cheryl Hopwood and her coplaintiffs, who were white, to the University of Texas School of Law was reverse discrimination because their law school admission test scores and undergraduate grade-point averages were higher than those of some minority applicants who gained admission. Texas had created a minority preference system in an effort to make the racial makeup of the state's higher education student body more reflective of the state's overall population. Because of a fear that *Hopwood* would result in a significant drop in minority enrollment, the state adopted other measures aimed at helping lower-income students gain admission. The state adopted a rule requiring all public universities to admit students from the top 10 percent of their graduating classes, assuring that some students from poor school districts receive spots in the state's top universities. By concentrating on economic status, Texas avoids conflict with *Hopwood*, which spoke to the issue of racial discrimination and preferences. Although the U.S. Supreme Court ultimately upheld the use of racial preferences initially used by Texas, the state continued to use the 10 percent rule, modifying it in 2009 by allowing University of Texas to limit its application to 75 percent of its incoming class. So many University of Texas students were admitted under the rule that it threatened to cut off access for everyone else. That could have been a big problem for the school's athletic programs within a couple of years.

Health and Human Services

Let's start with this basic fact. On a per-person basis, Texas spends less on health and human services (HHS) than practically any other state. Relatively few qualify for any public assistance, and those who do generally receive much lower benefits than their counterparts in other states. Nonetheless, health and human services expenditures have exploded over the last 20 years. Spending increased substantially from the mid-1980s to the mid-1990s. Factors that contributed to the growth were increases in Medicaid—health care for the poor—and welfare spending. For example, the number of Medicaid recipients has grown from 790,826 in 1986 to more than 2.9 million in 2009.[20] The number of families receiving cash assistance increased from 410,423 to 810,707 between 1986 and 1994.[21] From 1994 on, though, the number of families receiving cash assistance dramatically dropped to below a quarter of a million in 2005, before rising slightly in the following years. Much of the initial decrease was due to the robust Texas economy that had more people working than ever before. The remainder resulted from welfare reform measures on both the state and national level. State assistance became more difficult to obtain for aliens and the terminally dependent.

As the economy faltered at the beginning of this century, Medicaid recipients reached record numbers. The overwhelming number of residents on Medicaid are children—they comprise about three out of five recipients. Notably, however, only about a fifth of Medicaid spending is on children. Most Medicaid funds are expended on the elderly and disabled. Medicaid costs alone are about $22 billion a year, almost four-fifths of the overall HHS budget.[22]

The health and human services budget exceeds $30 billion a year, about 60 percent of which comes from federal government grants. This contrasts starkly to the early 1990s, when total health and human services spending was a little more than $4 billion.

In the mid-1990s, massive welfare reform took place in Texas. What was once called "Aid to Families with Dependent Children" became "Temporary Assistance for Needy Families" (TANF). The emphasis here is on the word "temporary," because the purpose of the change is to wean long-term recipients off the welfare rolls. This transition has been a joint state and federal effort. Texas began the move toward restricting welfare eligibility during the 1995 legislative session by setting time limits for physically able recipients to find jobs. The federal government, which provides most of the funding for public assistance in Texas, imposed more stringent requirements in 1996, which Texas adopted in 1997. Maximum TANF payments amount to about $249 a month for a parent and two children.[23]

As a result of the restructuring and economic expansion, welfare caseload rates have dropped dramatically. From the beginning of 1995 to 1999, the number of recipients dropped by 47 percent, ranking Texas near the top in caseload reduction.[24] As time and work restrictions came into full force, TANF recipients plunged, dropping to less than 100,000 in April 2009.[25] TANF payments comprise less than 150 million dollars a year—less than 1 percentage of the HHS budget.

Federal guidelines make qualifying for food assistance easier than qualifying for TANF. Nonetheless, Texas makes it more difficult to qualify than almost any other state. Even those who qualify receive a smaller monthly benefit, because Texas makes fewer funds available than do the other states. In an effort to curtail abuse and to better monitor the program, Texas implemented the Lone Star Card program in 1994. Rather than receiving food stamps, recipients are provided with what is essentially a debit card. The card is used to purchase food and the recipient's account is electronically adjusted, unspent benefits remaining as a credit on the card. Savings have been realized because of a reduction in fraud. The centralized, computerized system has evidently scared off some unscrupulous people who were afraid of getting caught making a fraudulent application.

Altogether, food assistance expenditures dropped so dramatically that the private contractor who administers the card program was losing money because of the unexpectedly small volume of business. The number of food stamp recipients in

Texas dropped from about 2.5 million in 1994 to less than 1.5 million in 2000. By 2007, recipients edged close to 2.5 million again and continued to rise. Food stamp funding comes entirely from federal grants. A family receiving both TANF and the Lone Star Card will live at about 77 percent of the federal poverty level.

A longtime public policy challenge for Texas has been the large percentage of Texas children who are uninsured. Although Medicaid provides coverage for many, that system can be frustrating for poor working parents who make too much to qualify for state aid, yet don't have insurance through their employers. Medicaid phases out at the poverty level, leaving hundreds of thousands of children uninsured. Using monies won in the state's settlement with the tobacco industry, Texas created the Children's Health Insurance Program (CHIP) in 1999. CHIP provided coverage to children under the age of 18 whose parents make less than twice poverty-level income and who are not covered by Medicaid or private insurance. CHIP is one of the most generous federal matching programs, providing more than $2.50 in federal monies for every dollar the state puts in. That's a better matching ratio than Medicaid. Shortly after its inception, CHIP covered more than half a million Texas children.

In 2003, facing that aforementioned $10 billion current funds deficit, the legislature made substantive changes in CHIP, making qualification much more difficult and raising copays. As a result, participation dropped dramatically, falling by more than 150,000 enrollees. Although Texas saved significant state funds by cutting its rolls by 30 percent, it lost significantly more in federal money. Additionally, more of a burden was placed on county-operated emergency rooms, which saw a huge influx of uninsured children, many of whom really only needed primary care. As is often the case in Texas, costs were transferred to local governments. Many conservatives, who by their nature seldom support big government programs, were highly critical of the cuts. As a result, the 2005 legislature increased CHIP spending by 41 percent. This almost immediately increased program participation to about 400,000; by July 2010, enrollment was back above 520,000.[26]

Business and Economic Development

Business and Economic Development is third on the state's budget list, accounting for about 11.5 percent of total spending—over $10 billion per year. About 43 percent of these expenditures come from federal grants. Four-fifths of the total allotment goes to a single state agency: the Texas Department of Transportation (TxDOT). Over the years, legislative action eliminated waste and duplication by merging several state agencies and creating TxDOT. The agency oversees the budget and operation of transportation planning, highway design, the purchase of right-of-way, public transportation systems, aviation safety, motor vehicle registrations, and a host of other functions related to transportation. Texas is a large state, so it requires many miles of highways. In recent years, more than 90 percent of the TxDOT budget has gone to the design, construction, and maintenance of 79,000 miles of state highways. The state's transportation budget is almost $7 billion per year. Federal funding makes up almost half of the total, most of the rest comes from the state's motor fuel tax and vehicle registration fees. In the last few years, Texas has moved toward the creation of more toll roads, the idea being that the people who use the highways should pay a higher percentage of their construction costs.

Other offices funded through Business and Economic Development included the lottery commission and the Department of Economic Development. Only the Texas Workforce Commission, which helps provide worker training, has an annual budget of over a billion dollars.

Other Expenditures

Prisons, public safety, and the operations of the general government and administration of the various regulatory agencies are among the other major state expenditures. Combined, these expenditures comprise less than 12 percent of total state spending.

Public safety ranks fourth in expenditures, taking up about 6 percent of the budget. Expenditures at the state level include funding for the Department of Public Safety (DPS) and for the Department of Criminal Justice (see Chapter 10) to administer the state's prison system. The DPS employs more than 2,200 commissioned peace officers, most of whom provide uniformed police services, such as traffic enforcement and safety, throughout the state. The Department of Criminal Justice houses some 155,000 inmates in approximately two dozen prisons throughout the state. Since 1984, the cost of incarcerating prisoners has doubled. The cost of treating prisoners for substance abuse is significant. In addition to those incarcerated, almost 350,000 Texans are under some form of probation or parole. Although prison costs more, even minimal supervision is a strain on state resources.

The offices of the governor, attorney general, judicial agencies, comptroller, and other state officials constitute the budgetary item "general government." Together with spending for legislative operations, these items take up about 2½ percent of the budget.

For a comparison of total Texas expenditures with those of other states, see Table 12.4.

TABLE **12.4 State Government Expenditures per Capita**

Texas	$3,011
Florida	$3,110
Virginia	$3,692
Oklahoma	$3,711
Alabama	$3,894
Louisiana	$3,996
U.S. average	$4,126
New Jersey	$4,153
Michigan	$4,603
California	$4,773
Massachusetts	$5,252
Hawaii	$5,611
New York	$5,614

SOURCE: U.S. Census Bureau, *Statistical Abstract* (Washington, DC: U.S. GPO, 2008), p. 286.

Nonfiscal Policy

Some policy decisions do not have a direct impact on the state's fiscal plan. Recent examples include the Castle Law, abortion policy, and tort reform. Sometimes, the policy process is fueled by ideological values, as is the case in the first two examples.

More often, there is a tangible, economic interest, even if it has no bearing on state finances, as with tort reform. In 2007 the legislature passed the Castle Law, allowing Texans to carry concealed handguns almost anywhere. The issue was high on the agenda during the previous legislature, but apparently not high enough. Through negotiation with opponents and compromise, supporters of the bill carried the day.

For years, the business community in Texas complained about its potential liability in civil lawsuits. Texas was one of the easiest states in which to win a lawsuit and collect damages. In 1995, their grievance was addressed by the legislature. The legislature attempted further reform in 2003. Tort reform makes it more difficult to win a lawsuit.

Potentially, this has saved businesses millions of dollars annually, and consumers have been protected from some of the more outrageous increases in insurance premiums. The financial impact on the state's budget itself is limited. The impact on Texas businesses and on persons who believe they have been wronged by corporate negligence has been significant.

Summary

Establishing a state budget is a complex endeavor requiring careful planning and coordination. The procedure must take into account the needs of the state while complying fully with an array of constraints imposed by state and federal mandates. The Legislative Budget Board, the governor, the comptroller of public accounts, and others play a significant role in the process. Changes in the primary sources of revenue have fostered changes in both fiscal and public policies across the state. The challenge in Texas is greater than in most other states because of its size and its biennial budget.

Fiscal and public policies are created through a series of stages. Each stage provides advocates and opponents with opportunities to affect policy. Public education still receives the lion's share of the state's money, followed by health and human services. The state's priorities in most major policy issues can be determined by examining the budget.

If an issue has no effect on fiscal policy, the state's priorities cannot be so easily discerned.

Chapter Test

1. The first step in the policy-making process is
   a. implementation
   b. Adoption
   c. Evaluation
   d. Agenda setting

2. The annual Texas budget is about
   a. $9 million
   b. $9 billion
   c. $90 billion
   d. $900 billion

3. The Texas budget is balanced by
   a. State law
   b. A provision in the state constitution
   c. Tradition
   d. Federal mandate

4. The Texas budget cycle is
   a. 6 months
   b. One year
   c. Two years
   d. Five years

5. The most important player in creating the Texas budget is the
   a. Legislative Budget Board
   b. Governor
   c. Comptroller
   d. Legislative Resource Council

6. Which comprises the largest source of Texas tax revenue?
   a. Franchise tax
   b. Income tax
   c. Sales tax
   d. Motor fuels tax

7. The largest source of non-tax revenue is
   a. Federal grants
   b. The lottery
   c. Casinos
   d. Licenses, fees and permits

8. The largest category of expenditure by the state of Texas is
   a. Human services
   b. Transportation
   c. Federal aid
   d. Education

9. Funding prompted by federal mandates and dedicated funds accounts for about what percentage of the Texas budget?
   a. 7
   b. 25
   c. 60
   d. 80

10. In Texas, you pay sales tax on
    a. Medical services
    b. Legal services
    c. Unprepared food
    d. A meal at a restaurant

Answers: 1. d 2. c 3. b 4. c 5. a 6. c 7. a 8. d 9. d 10. d

Critical Thinking Questions

1. Should Texas have an income tax?

2. Does Texas spend an appropriate amount of its budget on education, human services, and transportation?

3. Should lottery money be dedicated to education?

Key Terms

balanced budget, **p. 302**
dedicated funds, **p. 304**
federal grants, **p. 318**
franchise tax, **p. 311**
Legislative Budget Board (LBB), **p. 306**
lottery, **p. 320**
mandates, **p. 305**

motor fuels tax, **p. 311**
nontax revenue, **p. 318**
progressive tax, **p. 308**
public policy, **p. 298**
regressive tax, **p. 308**
sales tax, **p. 309**
"sin" taxes, **p. 312**
tax revenue, **p. 309**

Notes

1. *Fiscal Size-Up: 2008–09 Biennium*, Legislative Budget Board, 2008, p. 5.

2. Mike Reissig, "Revenues on a Roll," *Fiscal Notes* (January 1995), p. 11.

3. *Fiscal Size-Up*, 5.

4. Ibid., p. 8.

5. Jim Vertuno, "Texas Appeals to Keep Pole Tax," *Houston Chronicle* June 12, 2009, http://www.chron.com/disp/story.mpl/metropolitan/6473888.html.

6. *Fiscal Size-Up*, p. 44.

7. Ibid., p. 49.

8. Comptroller, http://www.window.state.tx.us/taxbud/revenue.html.

9. *Fiscal Size-Up*, p. 51.

10. Ibid., pp. 2–6.

11. *Revenue by Source for Fiscal Year 2009*, Texas Comptroller of Public Accounts, http://www.window.state.tx.us/taxbud/revenue.html.

12. *Revenue by Source for Fiscal Year 2009*, Texas Comptroller of Public Accounts, http://www.window.state.tx.us/taxbud/revenue.html.

13. Ibid.

14. Ibid.

15. *Fiscal Size-Up*, pp. 50–51.

16. *Summary of Conference Committee Report for Senate Bill 1*, Legislative Budget Board, 2009, 1.

17. *Fiscal Size-Up*, 200.

18. Ibid., 197–99.

19. Ibid., 199.

20. Ibid., 181.

21. Texas Legislative Budget Board, *Summary of Legislative Budget Estimates for the 1996–97 Biennium* (January 1995), p. 9.

22. *Summary of Conference Committee Report for Senate Bill 1*, Legislative Budget Board, 2009, p. 66.

23. *Fiscal Size-Up*, p. 186.

24. "On Welfare, Legislature Goes for Carrot, Not Stick," *Houston Chronicle*, May 30, 1999, http://proquest.umi.com.

25. "Texas TANF and SNAP Statistics," *Texas Health and Human Services Commission*, April 2009, http://www.hhsc.state.tx.us/research/index.html.

26. "CHIP Enrollment, Renewal and Disenrollment Rates," Texas Health and Human Services Commission, July 2010, http://www.hhsc.state.tx.us/research/CHIP/ChipRenewStatewide.html.

The Constitution of the United States of America*

(Preamble)

We the People of the United States, in Order to form a more perfect Union, establish Justice, insure domestic Tranquility, provide for the common defence, promote the general Welfare, and secure the Blessings of Liberty to ourselves and our Posterity, do ordain and establish this Constitution for the United States of America.

ARTICLE I.

(The Legislature)

SECTION 1. All legislative Powers herein granted shall be vested in a Congress of the United States, which shall consist of a Senate and House of Representatives.

SECTION 2. The House of Representatives shall be composed of Members chosen every second Year by the People of the several States, and the Electors in each State shall have the Qualifications requisite for Electors of the most numerous Branch of the State Legislature.

No person shall be a Representative who shall not have attained to the Age of twenty five Years, and been seven Years a Citizen of the United States, and who shall not, when elected, be an Inhabitant of that State in which he shall be chosen.

Representatives and direct [Taxes][1] shall be apportioned among the several States which may be included within this Union, according to their respective Numbers [which shall be determined by adding to the whole Number of free Persons, including those bound to Service for a Term of Years, and excluding Indians not taxed, three fifths of all other Persons].[2] The actual Enumeration shall be made within three Years after the first Meeting of the Congress of the United States, and within every subsequent Term of ten Years, in such Manner as they shall by Law direct. The Number of Representatives shall not exceed one for every thirty Thousand, but each State shall have at Least one Representative; and until such enumeration shall be made, the State of New Hampshire shall be entitled to chuse three, Massachusetts eight, Rhode-Island and Providence Plantations one, Connecticut

---

*This text retains the spelling, capitalization, and punctuation of the original. Brackets indicate passages that have been altered by amendments.

[1] See Amendment XVI.

[2] See Amendment XIV.

five, New-York six, New Jersey four, Pennsylvania eight, Delaware one, Maryland six, Virginia ten, North Carolina five, South Carolina five, and Georgia three.

When vacancies happen in the Representation from any State, the Executive Authority thereof shall issue Writs of Election to fill such Vacancies.

The House of Representatives shall chuse their speaker and other Officers; and shall have the sole Power of Impeachment.

SECTION 3. The Senate of the United States shall be composed of two Senators from each State [chosen by the Legislature thereof],[3] for six Years; and each Senator shall have one Vote.

Immediately after they shall be assembled in Consequence of the first Election, they shall be divided as equally as may be into three Classes. The Seats of the Senators of the first Class shall be vacated at the Expiration of the second year, of the second Class at the Expiration of the fourth Year, and of the third Class at the Expiration of the sixth Year, so that one third may be chosen every second Year [and if Vacancies happen by Resignation, or otherwise, during the Recess of the Legislature of any State, the Executive thereof may make temporary Appointments until the next Meeting of the Legislature, which shall then fill such Vacancies].[4]

No Person shall be a Senator who shall not have attained to the Age of thirty Years, and been nine Years a Citizen of the United States, and who shall not, when elected, be an Inhabitant of that State for which he shall be chosen.

The Vice President of the United States shall be President of the Senate, but shall have no Vote, unless they be equally divided.

The Senate shall chuse their other Officers, and also a President pro tempore, in the Absence of the Vice President, or when he shall exercise the Office of President of the United States.

The Senate shall have the sole Power to try all Impeachments. When sitting for that Purpose, they shall be on Oath or Affirmation. When the President of the United States is tried, the Chief Justice shall preside: And no Person shall be convicted without the Concurrence of two thirds of the Members present.

Judgment in Cases of Impeachment shall not extend further than to removal from Office, and disqualification to hold and enjoy any Office of honor, Trust or Profit under the United States; but the Party convicted shall nevertheless be liable and subject to Indictment, Trial, Judgment and Punishment, according to Law.

SECTION 4. The Times, Places and Manner of holding Elections for Senators and Representatives, shall be prescribed in each State by the Legislature thereof; but the Congress may at any time by Law make or alter such Regulations, except as to the Places of chusing Senators.

[The Congress shall assemble at least once in every Year, and such Meeting shall be on the first Monday in December, unless they shall by Law appoint a different Day.][5]

SECTION 5. Each House shall be the Judge of the Elections, Returns and Qualifications of its own Members, and a Majority of each shall constitute a Quorum to do Business; but a smaller Number may adjourn from day to day, and

---

[3] *See Amendment XVII.*

[4] *See Amendment XVII.*

[5] *See Amendment XX.*

may be authorized to compel the Attendance of absent Members, in such Manner, and under such Penalties as each House may provide.

Each House may determine the Rules of its Proceedings, punish its Members for disorderly Behaviour, and, with the Concurrence of two thirds, expel a Member.

Each House shall keep a Journal of its Proceedings, and from time to time publish the same, excepting such Parts as may in their judgment require Secrecy; and the Yeas and Nays of the Members of either House on any question shall, at the Desire of one fifth of those present, be entered on the Journal.

Neither House, during the Session of Congress, shall, without the Consent of the other, adjourn for more than three days, nor to any other Place than that in which the two Houses shall be sitting.

SECTION 6. The Senators and Representatives shall receive a Compensation for their Services, to be ascertained by Law, and paid out of the Treasury of the United States. They shall in all Cases, except Treason, Felony and Breach of the Peace, be privileged from Arrest during their Attendance at the Session of their respective Houses, and in going to and returning from the same; and for any Speech or Debate in either House, they shall not be questioned in any other Place.

No Senator or Representative shall, during the Time for which he was elected, be appointed to any civil Office under the Authority of the United States, which shall have been created, or the Emoluments whereof shall have been encreased during such time; and no Person holding any Office under the United States, shall be a Member of either House during his Continuance in Office.

SECTION 7. All Bills for raising Revenue shall originate in the House of Representatives; but the Senate may propose or concur with Amendments as on other Bills.

Every Bill which shall have passed the House of Representatives and the Senate, shall, before it becomes a Law, be presented to the President of the United States; If he approves he shall sign it, but if not he shall return it, with his Objections to that House in which it shall have originated, who shall enter the Objections at large on their Journal, and proceed to reconsider it. If after such Reconsideration two thirds of that House shall agree to pass the Bill, it shall be sent, together with the Objections, to the other House, by which it shall likewise be reconsidered, and if approved by two thirds of that House, it shall become a Law. But in all such Cases the Votes of both Houses shall be determined by yeas and Nays, and the Names of the Persons voting for and against the Bill shall be entered on the Journal of each House respectively. If any Bill shall not be returned by the President within ten Days (Sundays excepted) after it shall have been presented to him, the Same shall be a Law, in like Manner as if he had signed it, unless the Congress by their Adjournment prevent its Return, in which Case it shall not be a Law.

Every Order, Resolution, or Vote to which the Concurrence of the Senate and House of Representatives may be necessary (except on a question of Adjournment) shall be presented to the President of the United States; and before the Same shall take Effect, shall be approved by him, or being disapproved by him, shall be repassed by two thirds of the Senate and House of Representatives, according to the Rules and Limitations prescribed in the Case of a Bill.

SECTION 8. The Congress shall have Power To lay and collect Taxes, Duties, Imposts and Excises, to pay the Debts and provide for the common Defence and general Welfare of the United States; but all Duties, Imposts and Excises shall be uniform throughout the United States;

To borrow Money on the credit of the United States;

To regulate Commerce with foreign Nations, and among the several States, and with the Indian Tribes;

To establish a uniform Rule of Naturalization, and uniform Laws on the subject of Bankruptcies throughout the United States;

To coin Money, regulate the Value thereof, and of foreign Coin, and fix the Standard of Weights and Measures;

To provide for the Punishment of counterfeiting the Securities and current Coin of the United States;

To establish Post Offices and post Roads;

To promote the Progress of Science and useful Arts, by securing for limited Times to Authors and Inventors the exclusive Right to their respective Writings and Discoveries;

To constitute Tribunals inferior to the supreme Court;

To define and punish Piracies and Felonies committed on the high Seas, and Offences against the Law of Nations;

To declare War, grant Letters of Marque and Reprisal, and make Rules concerning Captures on Land and Water;

To raise and support Armies, but no Appropriation of Money to that Use shall be for a longer Term than two Years;

To provide and maintain a Navy;

To make Rules for the Government and Regulation of the land and naval Forces;

To provide for calling forth the Militia to execute the Laws of the Union, suppress Insurrections and repel Invasions;

To provide for organizing, arming, and disciplining, the Militia, and for governing such Part of them as may be employed in the Service of the United States, reserving to the States respectively, the Appointment of the Officers, and the Authority of training the Militia according to the discipline prescribed by Congress;

To exercise exclusive Legislation in all Cases whatsoever, over such District (not exceeding ten Miles square) as may, by Cession of particular States, and the Acceptance of Congress, become the Seat of the Government of the United States, and to exercise like Authority over all Places purchased by the Consent of the Legislature of the State in which the Same shall be, for the Erection of Forts, Magazines, Arsenals, dock-Yards, and other needful Buildings;—And

To make all Laws which shall be necessary and proper for carrying into Execution the foregoing Powers, and all other Powers vested by this Constitution in the Government of the United States, or in any Department or Officer thereof.

SECTION 9. The Migration or Importation of such Persons as any of the States now existing shall think proper to admit, shall not be prohibited by the Congress prior to the Year one thousand eight hundred and eight, but a Tax or duty may be imposed on such Importation, not exceeding ten dollars for each Person.

The Privilege of the Writ of Habeas Corpus shall not be suspended, unless when in Cases of Rebellion or Invasion the public Safety may require it.

No Bill of Attainder or ex post facto Law shall be passed.

[No Capitation, or other direct, Tax shall be laid, unless in Proportion to the Census or Enumeration herein before directed to be taken.][6]

No Tax or Duty shall be laid on Articles exported from any State.

No Preference shall be given by any Regulation of Commerce or Revenue to the Ports of one State over those of another; nor shall Vessels bound to, or from, one State, be obliged to enter, clear, or pay Duties in another.

No Money shall be drawn from the Treasury, but in Consequence of Appropriations made by Law; and a regular Statement and Account of the Receipts and Expenditures of all public Money shall be published from time to time.

No Title of Nobility shall be granted by the United States: And no Person holding any Office of Profit or Trust under them, shall, without the Consent of the Congress, accept of any present, Emolument, Office, or Title, of any kind whatever, from any King, Prince, or foreign State.

SECTION 10. No State shall enter into any Treaty, Alliance, or Confederation; grant Letters of Marque and Reprisal; coin Money; emit Bills of Credit; make any Thing but gold and silver Coin a Tender in Payment of Debts; pass any Bill of Attainder, ex post facto Law, or Law impairing the Obligation of Contracts, or grant any Title of Nobility.

No State shall, without the Consent of the Congress, lay any Imposts or Duties on Imports or Exports, except what may be absolutely necessary for executing its inspection Laws: and the net Produce of all Duties and Imposts, laid by any State on Imports or Exports, shall be for the Use of the Treasury of the United States; and all such Laws shall be subject to the Revision and Controul of the Congress.

No State shall, without the Consent of Congress, lay any Duty of Tonnage, keep Troops, or Ships of War in time of Peace, enter into any Agreement or Compact with another State, or with a foreign Power, or engage in War, unless actually invaded, or in such imminent Danger as will not admit of delay.

ARTICLE II.

(The Executive)

SECTION 1. The executive Power shall be vested in a President of the United States of America. He shall hold his Office during the Term of four Years, and, together with the Vice President, chosen for the same Term, be elected, as follows.

Each State shall appoint, in such Manner as the Legislature thereof may direct, a Number of Electors, equal to the whole Number of Senators and Representatives to which the State may be entitled in the Congress; but no Senator or Representative, or Person holding an Office of Trust or Profit under the United States, shall be appointed an Elector.

---

[6]*See Amendment XVI.*

[The Electors shall meet in their respective States, and vote by Ballot for two Persons, of whom one at least shall not be an Inhabitant of the same State with themselves. And they shall make a List of all the Persons voted for, and of the Number of Votes for each; which List they shall sign and certify, and transmit sealed to the Seat of the Government of the United States, directed to the President of the Senate. The President of the Senate shall, in the Presence of the Senate and House of Representatives, open all the Certificates, and the Votes shall then be counted. The Person having the greatest Number of Votes shall be the President, if such Number be a Majority of the whole Number of Electors appointed; and if there be more than one who have such Majority, and have an equal Number of Votes, then the House of Representatives shall immediately chuse by Ballot one of them for President; and if no Person have a Majority, then from the five highest on the List the said House shall in like Manner chuse the President. But in chusing the President, the Votes shall be taken by States, the Representation from each State having one Vote; A quorum for this Purpose shall consist of a Member or Members from two thirds of the States, and a Majority of all the States shall be necessary to a Choice. In every Case, after the Choice of the President, the Person having the greatest Number of Votes of the Electors shall be the Vice President. But if there should remain two or more who have equal Votes, the Senate shall chuse from them by Ballot the Vice President.][7]

The Congress may determine the Time of chusing the Electors, and the Day on which they shall give their Votes; which Day shall be the same throughout the United States.

No Person except a natural born Citizen, or a Citizen of the United States, at the time of the Adoption of this Constitution, shall be eligible to the Office of President; neither shall any Person be eligible to that Office who shall not have attained to the Age of thirty five Years, and been fourteen Years a Resident within the United States.

[In Case of the Removal of the President from Office, or of his Death, Resignation, or Inability to discharge the Powers and Duties of the said Office, the Same shall devolve on the Vice President, and the Congress may by Law provide for the Case of Removal, Death, Resignation or Inability, both of the President and Vice President, declaring what Officer shall then act as President, and such Officer shall act accordingly, until the Disability be removed, or a President shall be elected.][8]

The President shall, at stated Times, receive for his Services, a Compensation, which shall neither be encreased nor diminished during the Period for which he shall have been elected, and he shall not receive within that Period any other Emolument from the United States, or any of them.

Before he enter on the Execution of his Office, he shall take the following Oath or Affirmation:—"I do solemnly swear (or affirm) that I will faithfully execute the Office of President of the United States, and will to the best of my Ability, preserve, protect and defend the Constitution of the United States."

SECTION 2. The President shall be Commander in Chief of the Army and Navy of the United States, and of the Militia of the several States, when called

---

[7] *See Amendment XII.*
[8] *See Amendment XXV.*

into the actual Service of the United States; he may require the Opinion, in writing, of the principal Officer in each of the executive Departments, upon any Subject relating to the Duties of their respective Offices, and he shall have Power to grant Reprieves and Pardons for Offences against the United States, except in Cases of Impeachment.

He shall have Power, by and with the Advice and Consent of the Senate, to make Treaties, provided two thirds of the Senators present concur; and he shall nominate, and by and with the Advice and Consent of the Senate, shall appoint Ambassadors, other public Ministers and Consuls, Judges of the supreme Court, and all other Officers of the United States, whose Appointments are not herein otherwise provided for, and which shall be established by Law: but the Congress may by Law vest the Appointment of such inferior Officers, as they think proper, in the President alone, in the Courts of Law, or in the Heads of Departments.

The President shall have Power to fill up all Vacancies that may happen during the Recess of the Senate, by granting Commissions which shall expire at the end of their next Session.

SECTION 3. He shall from time to time give to the Congress Information of the State of the Union, and recommend to their Consideration such Measures as he shall judge necessary and expedient; he may, on extraordinary Occasions, convene both Houses, or either of them, and in Case of Disagreement between them, with Respect to the Time of Adjournment, he may adjourn them to such Time as he shall think proper; he shall receive Ambassadors and other public Ministers; he shall take Care that the Laws be faithfully executed, and shall Commission all the Officers of the United States.

SECTION 4. The President, Vice President and all civil Officers of the United States, shall be removed from Office on Impeachment for, and Conviction of, Treason, Bribery, or other high Crimes and Misdemeanors.

ARTICLE III.

(The Judiciary)

SECTION 1. The judicial Power of the United States, shall be vested in one supreme Court, and in such inferior Courts as the Congress may from time to time ordain and establish. The Judges, both of the supreme and inferior Courts, shall hold their Offices during good Behaviour, and shall, at stated Times, receive for their Services, a Compensation, which shall not be diminished during their Continuance in Office.

SECTION 2. The judicial Power shall extend to all Cases, in Law and Equity, arising under this Constitution, the Laws of the United States, and Treaties made, or which shall be made, under their Authority;—to all Cases affecting Ambassadors, other public Ministers and Consuls;—to all Cases of admiralty and maritime Jurisdiction;—to Controversies to which the United States shall be a Party;—to Controversies between two or more States; [—between a State and Citizens of another State;—][9] between Citizens of different States,—between Citizens of the same State claiming Lands under Grants of different States, [and between a State, or the Citizens thereof, and foreign States, Citizens or Subjects.][10]

In all Cases affecting Ambassadors, other public Ministers and Consuls, and those in which a State shall be Party, the supreme Court shall have original Jurisdiction. In all the other Cases before mentioned, the supreme Court shall have appellate Jurisdiction, both as to Law and Fact, with such Exceptions, and under such Regulations as the Congress shall make.

The Trial of all Crimes, except in Cases of Impeachment, shall be by Jury; and such Trial shall be held in the State where the said Crimes shall have been committed; but when not committed within any State, the Trial shall be at such Place or Places as the Congress may by Law have directed.

SECTION 3. Treason against the United States, shall consist only in levying War against them, or in adhering to their Enemies, giving them Aid and Comfort. No Person shall be convicted of Treason unless on the Testimony of two Witnesses to the same overt Act, or on Confession in open Court.

The Congress shall have Power to declare the Punishment of Treason, but no Attainder of Treason shall work Corruption of Blood, or Forfeiture except during the Life of the Person attainted.

ARTICLE IV.

(Interstate Relations)

SECTION 1. Full Faith and Credit shall be given in each State to the public Acts, Records, and judicial Proceedings of every other State. And the Congress may by general Laws prescribe the Manner in which such Acts, Records and Proceedings shall be proved, and the Effect thereof.

SECTION 2. The Citizens of each State shall be entitled to all Privileges and Immunities of Citizens in the several States.

A Person charged in any State with Treason, Felony, or other Crime, who shall flee from Justice, and be found in another State, shall on Demand of the executive Authority of the State from which he fled, be delivered up, to be removed to the State having Jurisdiction of the Crime.

[No Person held to Service or Labour in one State under the Laws thereof, escaping into another, shall, in Consequence of any Law or Regulation therein, be discharged from such Service or Labour, but shall be delivered up on Claim of the Party to whom such Service or Labour may be due.][11]

SECTION 3. New States may be admitted by the Congress into this Union; but no new State shall be formed or erected within the Jurisdiction of any other

---

[9] *See Amendment XI.*
[10] *See Amendment XI.*
[11] *See Amendment XIII.*

State; nor any State be formed by the Junction of two or more States, or Parts of States, without the Consent of the Legislatures of the States concerned as well as of the Congress.

The Congress shall have Power to dispose of and make all needful Rules and Regulations respecting the Territory or other Property belonging to the United States; and nothing in this Constitution shall be so construed as to Prejudice any Claims of the United States, or of any particular State.

SECTION 4. The United States shall guarantee to every State in this Union a Republican Form of Government, and shall protect each of them against Invasion, and on Application of the Legislature, or of the Executive (when the Legislature cannot be convened) against domestic Violence.

ARTICLE V.

(Amending the Constitution)

The Congress, whenever two thirds of both Houses shall deem it necessary, shall propose Amendments to this Constitution, or, on the Application of the Legislatures of two thirds of the several States, shall call a Convention for proposing Amendments, which, in either Case, shall be valid to all Intents and Purposes, as Part of this Constitution, when ratified by the Legislatures of three fourths of the several States, or by Conventions in three fourths thereof, as the one or the other Mode of Ratification may be proposed by the Congress; Provided that no Amendment which may be made prior to the Year One thousand eight hundred and eight shall in any Manner affect the first and fourth Clauses in the Ninth Section of the first Article; and that no State, without its Consent, shall be deprived of its equal Suffrage in the Senate.

ARTICLE VI.

(Debts, Supremacy, Oaths)

All Debts contracted and Engagements entered into, before the Adoption of this Constitution, shall be as valid against the United States under this Constitution, as under the Confederation.

This Constitution, and the laws of the United States which shall be made in Pursuance thereof; and all Treaties made, or which shall be made, under the Authority of the United States, shall be the supreme Law of the Land; and the Judges in every State shall be bound thereby, any Thing in the Constitution or Laws of any State to the Contrary notwithstanding.

The Senators and Representatives before mentioned, and the Members of the several State Legislatures, and all executive and judicial Officers, both of the United States and of the several States, shall be bound by Oath or Affirmation, to support this Constitution; but no religious Test shall ever be required as a Qualification to any Office or public Trust under the United States.

ARTICLE VII.

(Ratifying the Constitution)

The Ratification of the Conventions of nine States, shall be sufficient for the Establishment of this Constitution between the States so ratifying the Same.

Done in Convention by the Unanimous Consent of the States present the Seventeenth Day of September in the Year of our Lord one thousand seven hundred and Eighty seven and of the Independence of the United States of America the Twelfth. IN WITNESS whereof we have hereunto subscribed our Names.

Go. Washington
Presid't. and deputy from Virginia

ATTTEST
William Jackson
Secretary

DELAWARE
Geo. Read
Gunning Bedford jun
John Dickinson
Richard Basset
Jaco. Broom

MASSACHUSETTS
Nathaniel Gorbam
Rufus King

CONNECTICUT
Wm. Saml. Johnson
Roger Sherman

NEW YORK
Alexander Hamilton

NEW JERSEY
Wh. Livingston
David Brearley
Wm. Paterson
Jona. Dayton

PENNSYLVANIA
B. Franklin
Thomas Mifflin
Robt. Morris
Geo. Clymer
Thos. FitzSimons
Jared Ingersoll
James Wilson
Gouv. Morris

NEW HAMPSHIRE
John Langdon
Nicholas Gilman

MARYLAND
James McHenry
Dan of St. Thos. Jenifer
Danl. Carroll

VIRGINIA
John Blair
James Madison Jr.

NORTH CAROLINA
Wm. Blount
Richd. Dobbs Spaight
Hu. Williamson

SOUTH CAROLINA
J. Rutledge
Charles Cotesworth Pinckney
Charles Pinckney
Pierce Butler

GEORGIA
William Few
Abr. Baldwin

Articles in addition to, and amendment of the Constitution of the United States of America, proposed by Congress and ratified by the Legislatures of the several states, pursuant to the Fifth Article of the original Constitution.

(The first ten amendments were passed by Congress on September 25, 1789, and were ratified on December 15, 1791.)

Amendment I—Religion, Speech, Assembly, Petition

Congress shall make no law respecting an establishment of religion, or prohibiting the free exercise thereof; or abridging the freedom of speech, or of the press; or the right of the people peaceably to assemble, and to petition the Government for a redress of grievances.

Amendment II—Right to Bear Arms

A well regulated Militia, being necessary to the security of a free State, the right of the people to keep and bear Arms, shall not be infringed.

Amendment III—Quartering of Soldiers

No Soldier shall, in time of peace be quartered in any house, without the consent of the Owner, nor in time of war, but in a manner to be prescribed by law.

Amendment IV—Searches and Seizures

The right of the people to be secure in their persons, houses, papers, and effects, against unreasonable searches and seizures, shall not be violated, and no warrants shall issue, but upon probable cause, supported by Oath or affirmation, and particularly describing the place to be searched, and the persons or things to be seized.

Amendment V—Grand Juries, Double Jeopardy, Self-incrimination, Due Process, Eminent Domain

No person shall be held to answer for a capital, or otherwise infamous crime, unless on a presentment or indictment of a Grand Jury, except in cases arising in the land or naval forces, or in the Militia, when in actual service in time of War or public danger; nor shall any person be subject for the same offence to be twice put in jeopardy of life or limb; nor shall be compelled in any criminal case to be a witness against himself, nor be deprived of life, liberty, or property, without due process of law; nor shall private property be taken for public use, without just compensation.

Amendment VI—Criminal Court Procedures

In all criminal prosecutions, the accused shall enjoy the right to a speedy and public trial, by an impartial jury of the State and district wherein the crime shall have been committed, which district shall have been previously ascertained by law, and to be informed of the nature and cause of the accusation; to be confronted with the witnesses against him; to have compulsory process for obtaining witnesses in his favor, and to have the assistance of counsel for his defence.

Amendment VII—Trial by Jury in Common-Law Cases

In Suits at common law, where the value in controversy shall exceed twenty dollars, the right of trial by jury shall be preserved, and no fact tried by a jury, shall be otherwise re-examined in any Court of the United States, than according to the rules of the common law.

Amendment VIII—Bails, Fines, and Punishment

Excessive bail shall not be required, nor excessive fines imposed, nor cruel and unusual punishments inflicted.

Amendment IX—Rights Retained by the People

The enumeration in the Constitution, of certain rights, shall not be construed to deny or disparage others retained by the people.

Amendment X—Rights Reserved to the States

The powers not delegated to the United States by the Constitution, nor prohibited by it to the States, are reserved to the States respectively, or to the people.

Amendment XI—Suits Against the States (Ratified February 7, 1795)

The Judicial power of the United States shall not be construed to extend to any suit in law or equity, commenced or prosecuted against one of the United States by Citizens of another State, or by Citizens or Subjects of any Foreign State.

Amendment XII—Election of the President and Vice-President (Ratified June 15, 1804)

The Electors shall meet in their respective states, and vote by ballot for President and Vice-President, one of whom, at least, shall not be an inhabitant of the same state with themselves; they shall name in their ballots the person voted for as President, and in distinct ballots the person voted for as Vice-President, and they shall make distinct lists of all persons voted for as President, and of all persons voted for as Vice-President, and of the number of votes for each, which lists they shall sign and certify, and transmit sealed to the seat of the government of the United States, directed to the President of the Senate;—The President of the Senate shall, in the presence of the Senate and House of Representatives, open all the certificates and the votes shall then be counted;—The person having the greatest number of votes for President, shall be the President, if such number be a majority of the whole number of Electors appointed; and if no person have such majority, then from the persons having the highest numbers not exceeding three on the list of those voted for as President, the House of Representatives shall choose immediately, by ballot, the President. But in choosing the President, the votes shall be taken by states, the representation from each state having one vote; a quorum for this purpose shall consist of a member or members from two-thirds of the states, and a majority of all the states shall be necessary to a Choice. [And if the House of Representatives shall not choose a President whenever the right of choice shall devolve upon them, before the fourth day of March next following, then the Vice-President shall act as President, as in the case of the death or other constitutional disability of the President.][12]—The person having the greatest number of votes as Vice-President, shall be the Vice-President, if such number be a majority of the whole number of Electors appointed, and if no person have a majority, then from the two highest numbers on the list, the Senate shall choose the Vice-President; a quorum for the purpose shall consist of two-thirds of the whole number of Senators, and a majority of the whole number shall be necessary to a choice. But no person constitutionally ineligible to the office of President shall be eligible to that of Vice-President of the United States.

Amendment XIII—Slavery (Ratified on December 6, 1865)

SECTION 1. Neither slavery nor involuntary servitude, except as a punishment for crime whereof the party shall have been duly convicted, shall exist within the United States, or any place subject to their jurisdiction.

SECTION 2. Congress shall have power to enforce this article by appropriate legislation.

Amendment XIV—Citizenship, Due Process, and Equal Protection of the Laws (Ratified on July 9, 1868)

SECTION 1. All persons born or naturalized in the United States, and subject to the jurisdiction thereof, are citizens of the United States and of the State wherein they reside. No State shall make or enforce any law which shall abridge the privileges or immunities of citizens of the United States; nor shall any State deprive any person of life, liberty, or property, without due process of law; nor deny to any person within its jurisdiction the equal protection of the laws.

SECTION 2. Representatives shall be apportioned among the several States according to their respective numbers, counting the whole number of persons in each State, excluding Indians not taxed. But when the right to vote at any election for the choice of electors for President and Vice President of the United States, Representatives in Congress, the Executive and Judicial officers of a State, or the members of the Legislature thereof, is denied to any of the male inhabitants of such State, being twenty-one years of age, and citizens of the United States, or in any way abridged, except for participation in rebellion, or other crime, the basis of representation therein shall be reduced in the proportion which the number of such male citizens shall bear to the whole number of male citizens twenty-one years of age in such State.

---

[12]*Amendment XX.*

SECTION 3. No person shall be a Senator or Representative in Congress, or elector of President and Vice President, or hold any office, civil or military, under the United States, or under any State, who, having previously taken an oath, as a member of Congress, or as an officer of the United States, or as a member of any State legislature, or as an executive or judicial officer of any State, to support the Constitution of the United States, shall have engaged in insurrection or rebellion against the same, or given aid or comfort to the enemies thereof. But Congress may by a vote of two-thirds of each House, remove such disability.

SECTION 4. The validity of the public debt of the United States, authorized by law, including debts incurred for payment of pensions and bounties for services in suppressing insurrection or rebellion, shall not be questioned. But neither the United States nor any State shall assume or pay any debt or obligation incurred in aid of insurrection or rebellion against the United States, or any claim for the loss or emancipation of any slave, but all such debts, obligations and claims shall be held illegal and void.

SECTION 5. The Congress shall have power to enforce, by appropriate legislation, the provisions of this article.

Amendment XV—The Right To Vote (Ratified on February 3, 1870)

SECTION 1. The right of citizens of the United States to vote shall not be denied or abridged by the United States or by any State on account of race, color, or previous condition of servitude.

SECTION 2. The Congress shall have power to enforce this article by appropriate legislation.

Amendment XVI—Income Taxes (Ratified on February 3, 1913)

The Congress shall have power to lay and collect taxes on incomes, from whatever source derived, without apportionment among the several States, and without regard to any census or enumeration.

Amendment XVII—Election of Senators (Ratified on April 8, 1913)

The Senate of the United States shall be composed of two Senators from each State, elected by the people thereof, for six years; and each Senator shall have one vote. The electors in each State shall have the qualifications requisite for electors of the most numerous branch of the State legislatures.

When vacancies happen in the representation of any State in the Senate, the executive authority of such State shall issue writs of election to fill such vacancies: *Provided*, That the legislature of any State may empower the executive thereof to make temporary appointments until the people fill the vacancies by election as the legislature may direct.

This amendment shall not be so construed as to affect the election or term of any Senator chosen before it becomes valid as part of the Constitution.

Amendment XVIII—Prohibition (Ratified on January 16, 1919)

SECTION 1. After one year from the ratification of this article the manufacture, sale, or transportation of intoxicating liquors within, the importation thereof into, or the exportation thereof from the United States and all territory subject to the jurisdiction thereof for beverage purposes is hereby prohibited.

SECTION 2. The Congress and the several States shall have concurrent power to enforce this article by appropriate legislation.

SECTION 3. This article shall be inoperative unless it shall have been ratified as an amendment to the Constitution by the legislatures of the several States, as provided in the Constitution, within seven years from the date of the submission hereof to the States by the Congress.[13]

Amendment XIX—Women's Right to Vote (Ratified on August 18, 1920)

The right of citizens of the United States to vote shall not be denied or abridged by the United States or by any State on account of sex.

Congress shall have power to enforce this article by appropriate legislation.

Amendment XX—Terms of Office, Convening of Congress, and Succession (Ratified February 6, 1933)

SECTION 1. The terms of the President and Vice President shall end at noon on the 20th day of January, and the terms of Senators and Representatives at noon on the 3d day of January, of the years in which such terms would have ended if this article had not been ratified; and the terms of their successors shall then begin.

SECTION 2. The Congress shall assemble at least once in every year, and such meeting shall begin at noon on the 3d day of January, unless they shall by law appoint a different day.

SECTION 3. If, at the time fixed for the beginning of the term of the President, the President elect shall have died, the Vice President elect shall become President. If a President shall not have been chosen before the time fixed for the beginning of his term, or if the President elect shall have failed to qualify, then the Vice President elect shall act as President until a President shall have qualified; and the Congress may by law provide for the case wherein neither a President elect nor a Vice President elect shall have qualified, declaring who shall then act as President, or the manner

---

[13]*Amendment XXI.*

in which one who is to act shall be selected, and such person shall act accordingly until a President or Vice President shall have qualified.

SECTION 4. The Congress may by law provide for the case of the death of any of the persons from whom the House of Representatives may choose a President whenever the rights of choice shall have devolved upon them, and for the case of the death of any of the persons from whom the Senate may choose a Vice President whenever the right of choice shall have devolved upon them.

SECTION 5. Sections 1 and 2 shall take effect on the 15th day of October following the ratification of this article.

SECTION 6. This article shall be inoperative unless it shall have been ratified as an amendment to the Constitution by the legislatures of three-fourths of the several States within seven years from the date of its submission.

Amendment XXI—Repeal of Prohibition (Ratified on December 5, 1933)

SECTION 1. The eighteenth article of amendment to the Constitution of the United States is hereby repealed.

SECTION 2. The transportation or importation into any State, Territory, or possession of the United States for delivery or use therein of intoxicating liquors, in violation of the laws thereof, is hereby prohibited.

SECTION 3. This article shall be inoperative unless it shall have been ratified as an amendment to the Constitution by conventions in the several States, as provided in the Constitution, within seven years from the date of the submission hereof to the States by the Congress.

Amendment XXII—Number of Presidential Terms (Ratified on February 27, 1951)

No person shall be elected to the office of the President more than twice, and no person who has held the office of President, or acted as President, for more than two years of a term to which some other person was elected President shall be elected to the office of the President more than once. But this Article shall not apply to any person holding the office of President when this Article was proposed by the Congress, and shall not prevent any person who may be holding the office of President, or acting as President, during the term within which this Article becomes operative from holding the office of President or acting as President during the remainder of such term.

Amendment XXIII—Presidential Electors for the District of Columbia (Ratified on March 29, 1961)

SECTION 1. The District constituting the seat of Government of the United States shall appoint in such manner as the Congress may direct:

A number of electors of President and Vice President equal to the whole number of Senators and Representatives in Congress to which the District would be entitled if it were a State, but in no event more than the least populous State; they shall be in addition to those appointed by the States, but they shall be considered, for the purposes of the election of President and Vice President, to be electors appointed by a State; and they shall meet in the District and perform such duties as provided by the twelfth article of amendment.

SECTION 2. The Congress shall have power to enforce this article by appropriate legislation.

Amendment XXIV—Poll Tax (Ratified on January 23, 1964)

SECTION 1. The right of citizens of the United States to vote in any primary or other election for President or Vice President, for electors for President or Vice President, or for Senator or Representative in Congress, shall not be denied or abridged by the United States or any State by reason of failure to pay any poll tax or other tax.

SECTION 2. The Congress shall have power to enforce this article by appropriate legislation.

Amendment XXV—Presidential Disability and Vice Presidential Vacancies (Ratified on February 10, 1967)

SECTION 1. In case of the removal of the President from office or of his death or resignation, the Vice President shall become President.

SECTION 2. Whenever there is a vacancy in the office of the Vice President, the President shall nominate a Vice President who shall take office upon confirmation by a majority vote of both Houses of Congress.

SECTION 3. Whenever the President transmits to the President pro tempore of the Senate and the Speaker of the House of Representatives his written declaration that he is unable to discharge the powers and duties of his office, and until he transmits to them a written declaration to the contrary, such powers and duties shall be discharged by the Vice President as Acting President.

SECTION 4. Whenever the Vice President and a majority of either the principal officers of the executive departments or of such other body as Congress may by law provide, transmit to the President pro tempore of the Senate and the Speaker of the House of Representatives their written declaration that the President is unable to discharge the powers and duties of his office, the Vice President shall immediately assume the powers and duties of the office as Acting President.

Thereafter, when the President transmits to the President pro tempore of the Senate and the Speaker of the House of Representatives his written declaration that no inability exists, he shall resume the powers and duties of his office unless the Vice President and a majority of either the principal officers of the executive department or of such other body as Congress may by law provide, transmit within four days to the President pro tempore of the Senate and the Speaker of the House of Representatives their written declaration that the President is unable to discharge the powers and duties of his office. Thereupon Congress shall decide the issue, assembling within forty-eight hours for that purpose if not in session. If the

Congress, within twenty-one days after receipt of the latter written declaration, or, if Congress is not in session, within twenty-one days after Congress is required to assemble, determines by two-thirds vote of both Houses that the President is unable to discharge the powers and duties of his office, the Vice President shall continue to discharge the same as Acting President; otherwise, the President shall resume the powers and duties of his office.

Amendment XXVI—Eighteen-Year-Old Vote (Ratified on July 1, 1971)

SECTION 1. The right of citizens of the United States, who are eighteen years of age or older, to vote shall not be denied or abridged by the United States or by any State on account of age.

SECTION 2. The Congress shall have power to enforce this article by appropriate legislation.

Amendment XXVII—Congressional Salaries (Ratified on May 18, 1992)

SECTION 1. No law varying the compensation for the services of the Senators and Representatives, shall take effect, until an election of Representatives shall have intervened.

Selected Excerpts from the Texas Constitution

ARTICLE I: Bill of Rights

That the general, great, and essential principles of liberty and free government may be recognized and established, we declare:

SECTION 1. FREEDOM AND SOVEREIGNTY OF STATE Texas is a free and independent State, subject only to the Constitution of the United States, and the maintenance of our free institutions and the perpetuity of the Union depend upon the preservation of the right of local self-government, unimpaired to all the States.

SECTION 2. POLITICAL POWER INHERENT IN THE PEOPLE All political power is inherent in the people, and all free governments are founded on their authority, and instituted for their benefit. The faith of the people of Texas stands pledged to the preservation of a republican form of government, and, subject to this limitation only, they have at all times the inalienable right to alter, reform or abolish their government in such manner as they may think expedient.

SECTION 3. EQUAL RIGHTS All free men, when they form a social compact, have equal rights, and no man, or set of men, is entitled to exclusive separate public emoluments, or privileges, but in consideration of public services.

SECTION 3A. EQUALITY; SEX, RACE Equality under the law shall not be denied or abridged because of sex, race, color, creed, or national origin. This amendment is self-operative.

SECTION 4. NO RELIGIOUS TEST No religious test shall ever be required as a qualification to any office, or public trust, in this State; nor shall any one be excluded from holding office on account of his religious sentiments, provided he acknowledge the existence of a Supreme Being.

SECTION 5. WITNESSES; RELIGION, OATH No person shall be disqualified to give evidence in any of the Courts of this State on account of his religious opinions, or for the want of any religious belief, but all oaths or affirmations shall be administered in the mode most binding upon the conscience, and shall be taken subject to the pains and penalties of perjury.

SECTION 6. FREEDOM OF WORSHIP All men have a natural and indefeasible right to worship Almighty God according to the dictates of their own consciences. No man shall be compelled to attend, erect or support any place of worship, or to maintain any ministry against his consent. No human authority ought, in any case whatever, to control or interfere with the rights of conscience in matters of religion, and no preference shall ever be given by law to any religious society or mode of worship. But it shall be the duty of the Legislature to pass such laws as may be necessary to protect equally every religious denomination in the peaceable enjoyment of its own mode of public worship.

SECTION 7. NO APPROPRIATIONS FOR SECTARIAN PURPOSES No money shall be appropriated, or drawn from the Treasury for the benefit of any sect, or religious society, theological or religious seminary; nor shall property belonging to the State be appropriated for any such purposes.

SECTION 8. FREEDOM OF SPEECH AND PRESS Every person shall be at liberty to speak, write or publish his opinions on any subject, being responsible for the abuse of that privilege; and no law shall ever be passed curtailing the liberty of speech or of the press. In prosecutions for the publication of papers, investigating the conduct of officers, or men in public capacity, or when the matter published is proper for public information, the truth thereof may be given in evidence.

And in all indictments for libels, the jury shall have the right to determine the law and the facts, under the direction of the court, as in other cases.

SECTION 9. SEARCHES AND SEIZURES The people shall be secure in their persons, houses, papers and possessions, from all unreasonable seizures or searches, and no warrant to search any place, or to seize any person or thing, shall issue without describing them as near as may be, nor without probable cause, supported by oath or affirmation.

SECTION 10. RIGHTS OF CRIMINAL DEFENDANTS In all criminal prosecutions the accused shall have a speedy public trial by an impartial jury. He shall have the right to demand the nature and cause of the accusation against him, and to have a copy thereof. He shall not be compelled to give evidence against himself, and shall have the right of being heard by himself or counsel, or both, shall be confronted by the witnesses against him and shall have compulsory process for obtaining witnesses in his favor, except that when the witness resides out of the State and the offense charged is a violation of any of the anti-trust laws of this State, the defendant and the State shall have the right to produce and have the evidence admitted by deposition, under such rules and laws as the Legislature may hereafter provide; and no person shall be held to answer for a criminal offense, unless on an indictment of a grand jury, except in cases in which the punishment is by fine or imprisonment, otherwise than in the penitentiary, in cases of impeachment, and in cases arising in the army or navy, or in the militia, when in actual service in time of war or public danger. (Amended Nov. 5, 1918.)

SECTION 11. BAIL All prisoners shall be bailable by sufficient sureties, unless for capital offenses, when the proof is evident; but this provision shall not be so construed as to prevent bail after indictment found upon examination of the evidence, in such manner as may be prescribed by law.

SECTION 11A. DENIAL OF BAIL (a) Any person (1) accused of a felony less than capital in this State, who has been theretofore twice convicted of a felony, the second conviction being subsequent to the first, both in point of time of commission of the offense and conviction therefor, (2) accused of a felony less than capital in this State, committed while on bail for a prior felony for which he has been indicted, (3) accused of a felony less than capital in this State involving the use of a deadly weapon after being convicted of a prior felony, or (4) accused of a violent or sexual offense committed while under the supervision of a criminal justice agency of the State or a political subdivision of the State for a prior felony, after a hearing, and upon evidence substantially showing the guilt of the accused of the offense in (1) or (3) above, of the offense committed while on bail in (2) above, or of the offense in (4) above committed while under the supervision of a criminal justice agency of the State or a political subdivision of the State for a prior felony, may be denied bail pending trial, by a district judge in this State, if said order denying bail pending trial is issued within seven calendar days subsequent to the time of incarceration of the accused; provided, however, that if the accused is not accorded a trial upon the accusation under (1) or (3) above, the accusation and indictment used under (2) above, or the accusation or indictment used under (4) above within sixty (60) days from the time of his incarceration upon the accusation, the order denying bail shall be automatically set aside, unless a continuance is obtained upon the motion or request of the accused; provided, further, that the right of appeal to the Court of Criminal Appeals of this State is expressly accorded the accused for a review of any judgment or order made hereunder, and said appeal shall be given preference by the Court of Criminal Appeals.

In this section: (1) "Violent offense" means: (A) murder; (B) aggravated assault, if the accused used or exhibited a deadly weapon during the commission of the assault; (C) aggravated kidnapping; or (D) aggravated robbery.

(2) "Sexual offense" means: (A) aggravated sexual assault; (B) sexual assault; or (C) indecency with a child.

SECTION 12. HABEUS CORPUS The writ of habeas corpus is a writ of right, and shall never be suspended. The Legislature shall enact laws to render the remedy speedy and effectual.

SECTION 13. EXCESSIVE BAIL; OPEN COURTS Excessive bail shall not be required, nor excessive fines imposed, nor cruel or unusual punishment inflicted. All courts shall be open, and every person for an injury done him, in his lands, goods, person or reputation, shall have remedy by due course of law.

SECTION 14. NO DOUBLE JEOPARDY No person, for the same offense, shall be twice put in jeopardy of life or liberty, nor shall a person be again put upon trial for the same offense, after a verdict of not guilty in a court of competent jurisdiction.

SECTION 15. TRIAL BY JURY The right of trial by jury shall remain inviolate. The Legislature shall pass such laws as may be needed to regulate the same, and to maintain its purity and efficiency. Provided, that the Legislature may provide for the temporary commitment, for observation and/or treatment, of mentally ill persons not charged with a criminal offense, for a period of time not to exceed ninety (90) days, by order of the County Court without the necessity of a trial by jury. (Amended Aug. 24, 1935.)

SECTION 15A. EVIDENCE FOR COMMITMENT; APPEAL No person shall be committed as a person of unsound mind except on competent medical or psychiatric testimony. The Legislature may enact all laws necessary to provide for the trial, adjudication of insanity and commitment of persons of unsound mind and to provide for a method of appeal from judgments rendered in such cases. Such laws may provide for a waiver of trial by jury, in cases where the person under inquiry has not been charged with the commission of a criminal offense, by the concurrence of the person under inquiry, or his next of kin, and an attorney ad litem appointed by a judge of either the County or Probate Court of the county where the trial is being held, and shall provide for a method of service of notice of such trial upon the person under inquiry and of his right to demand a trial by jury.

SECTION 16. NO EX POST FACTO LAWS No bill of attainder, ex post facto law, retroactive law, or any law impairing the obligation of contracts, shall be made.

SECTION 17. TAKINGS FOR PUBLIC USE No person's property shall be taken, damaged or destroyed for or applied to public use without adequate compensation being made, unless by the consent of such person; and, when taken, except for the use of the State, such compensation shall be first made, or secured by a deposit of money; and no irrevocable or uncontrollable grant of special privileges or immunities, shall be made; but all privileges and franchises granted by the Legislature, or created under its authority shall be subject to the control thereof.

SECTION 18. NO IMPRISONMENT FOR DEBT No person shall ever be imprisoned for debt.

SECTION 19. DUE COURSE OF LAW No citizen of this State shall be deprived of life, liberty, property, privileges or immunities, or in any manner disfranchised, except by the due course of the law of the land.

SECTION 20. NO OUTLAWRY OR TRANSPORTATION FOR OFFENSE No citizen shall be outlawed. No person shall be transported out of the State for any offense committed within the same. This section does not prohibit an agreement with another state providing for the confinement of inmates of this State in the penal or correctional facilities of that state.

SECTION 21. NO CORRUPTION OF BLOOD No conviction shall work corruption of blood, or forfeiture of estate, and the estates of those who destroy their own lives shall descend or vest as in case of natural death.

SECTION 22. TREASON Treason against the State shall consist only in levying war against it, or adhering to its enemies, giving them aid and comfort; and no person shall be convicted of treason except on the testimony of two witnesses to the same overt act, or on confession in open court.

SECTION 23. RIGHT TO KEEP AND BEAR ARMS Every citizen shall have the right to keep and bear arms in the lawful defense of himself or the State; but the Legislature shall have power, by law, to regulate the wearing of arms, with a view to prevent crime.

SECTION 24. SUBORDINATION OF MILITARY The military shall at all times be subordinate to the civil authority.

SECTION 25. QUARTERING OF SOLDIERS No soldier shall in time of peace be quartered in the house of any citizen without the consent of the owner, nor in time of war but in a manner prescribed by law.

SECTION 26. NO PERPETUITIES OR MONOPOLIES Perpetuities and monopolies are contrary to the genius of a free government, and shall never be allowed, nor shall the law of primogeniture or entailments ever be in force in this State.

SECTION 27. RIGHT OF ASSEMBLY The citizens shall have the right, in a peaceable manner, to assemble together for their common good; and apply to those invested with the powers of government for redress of grievances or other purposes, by petition, address or remonstrance.

SECTION 28. SUSPENSION OF LAWS No power of suspending laws in this State shall be exercised except by the Legislature.

SECTION 29. BILL OF RIGHTS INVIOLATE To guard against transgressions of the high powers herein delegated, we declare that everything in this "Bill of Rights" is excepted out of the general powers of government, and shall forever remain inviolate, and all laws contrary thereto, or to the following provisions, shall be void.

SECTION 30. RIGHTS OF CRIME VICTIMS

(a) A crime victim has the following rights: the right to be treated with fairness and with respect for the victim's dignity and privacy throughout the criminal justice process; and the right to be reasonably protected from the accused throughout the criminal justice process.

(b) On the request of a crime victim, the crime victim has the following rights: the right to notification of court proceedings; the right to be present at all public court proceedings related to the offense, unless the victim is to testify and the court determines that the victim's testimony would be materially affected if the victim hears other testimony at the trial; the right to confer with a representative of the prosecutor's office; the right to restitution; and the right to information about the conviction, sentence, imprisonment, and release of the accused.

(c) The legislature may enact laws to define the term "victim" and to enforce these and other rights of crime victims.

(d) The state, through its prosecuting attorney, has the right to enforce the rights of crime victims.

(e) The legislature may enact laws to provide that a judge, attorney for the state, peace officer, or law enforcement agency is not liable for a failure or inability to provide a right enumerated in this section. The failure or inability of any person to provide a right or service enumerated in this section may not be used by a defendant in a criminal case as a ground for appeal or post-conviction writ of habeas corpus. A victim or guardian or legal representative of a victim has standing to enforce the rights enumerated in this section but does not have standing to participate as a party in a criminal proceeding or to contest the disposition of any charge.

ARTICLE III: Legislative Departments

SECTION 1. LEGISLATURE COMPOSED OF SENATE AND HOUSE OF REPRESENTATIVES
The Legislative power of this State shall be vested in a Senate and House of Representatives, which together shall be styled "The Legislature of the State of Texas."

SECTION 2. NUMBER OF SENATORS AND REPRESENTATIVES The Senate shall consist of thirty-one members, and shall never be increased above this number. The House of Representatives shall consist of ninety-three members until the first apportionment after the adoption of this Constitution, when or at any apportionment thereafter, the number of Representatives may be increased by the Legislature, upon the ratio of not more than one Representative for every fifteen thousand inhabitants; provided, the number of Representatives shall never exceed one hundred and fifty.

SECTION 3. ELECTION AND TERM OF OFFICE OF SENATORS The Senators shall be chosen by the qualified electors for the term of four years; but a new Senate shall be chosen after every apportionment, and the Senators elected after each apportionment shall be divided by lot into two classes. The seats of the Senators of the first class shall be vacated at the expiration of the first two years, and those of the second class at the expiration of four years, so that one half of the Senators shall be chosen biennially thereafter. Senators shall take office following their election, on the day set by law for the convening of the Regular Session of the Legislature, and shall serve thereafter for the full term of years to which elected and until their successors shall have been elected and qualified.

SECTION 4. ELECTION AND TERM OF OFFICE OF REPRESENTATIVES The Members of the House of Representatives shall be chosen by the qualified electors for the term of two years. Representatives shall take office following their election, on the day set by law for the convening of the Regular Session of the Legislature, and shall serve thereafter for the full term of years to which elected and until their successors shall have been elected and qualified.

SECTION 5. SESSIONS OF LEGISLATURE The Legislature shall meet every two years at such time as may be provided by law and at other times when convened by the Governor. When convened in regular Session, the first thirty days thereof shall be devoted to the introduction of bills and resolutions, acting upon emergency appropriations, passing upon the confirmation of the recess appointees of the Governor and such emergency matters as may be submitted by the Governor in special messages to the Legislature; provided that during the succeeding thirty days of the regular session of the Legislature the various committees of each House shall hold hearings to consider all bills and resolutions and other matters then pending; and such emergency matters as may be submitted by the Governor; provided further that during the following sixty days the Legislature shall act upon such bills and resolutions as may be then pending and upon such emergency matters as may be submitted by the Governor in special messages to the Legislature; provided, however, either House may otherwise determine its order of business by an affirmative vote of four-fifths of its membership.

SECTION 6. QUALIFICATIONS OF SENATORS No person shall be a Senator, unless he be a citizen of the United States, and, at the time of his election a qualified elector of this State, and shall have been a resident of this State five years next preceding his election, and the last year thereof a resident of the district for which he shall be chosen, and shall have attained the age of twenty-six years.

SECTION 7. QUALIFICATIONS OF REPRESENTATIVES No person shall be a Representative, unless he be a citizen of the United States, and, at the time of his election, a qualified elector of this State, and shall have been a resident of this State two years next preceding his election, the last year thereof a resident of the district for which he shall be chosen, and shall have attained the age of twenty-one years.

SECTION 8. EACH HOUSE IS JUDGE OF QUALIFICATIONS Each House shall be the judge of the qualifications and election of its own members; but contested elections shall be determined in such manner as shall be provided by law.

SECTION 9. PRESIDENT PRO TEMPORE OF SENATE; SPEAKER OF THE HOUSE

(a) The Senate shall, at the beginning and close of each session, and at such other times as may be necessary, elect one of its members President pro tempore, who shall perform the duties of the Lieutenant Governor in any case of absence or disability of that officer.

If the said office of Lieutenant Governor becomes vacant, the President pro tempore of the Senate shall convene the Committee of the Whole Senate within 30 days after the vacancy occurs. The Committee of the Whole shall elect one of its members to perform the duties of the Lieutenant Governor in addition to his duties as Senator until the next general election. If the Senator so elected ceases to be a Senator before the election of a new Lieutenant Governor, another Senator shall be elected in the same manner to perform the duties of the Lieutenant Governor until the next general election. Until the Committee of the Whole elects one of its members for this purpose, the President pro tempore shall perform the duties of the Lieutenant Governor as provided by this subsection.

(b) The House of Representatives shall, when it first assembles, organize temporarily, and thereupon proceed to the election of a Speaker from its own members.

Each House shall choose its other officers.

SECTION 11. RULES OF PROCEDURE Each House may determine the rules of its own proceedings, punish members for disorderly conduct, and, with the consent of two-thirds, expel a member, but not a second time for the same offense.

SECTION 13. VACANCIES IN LEGISLATURE When vacancies occur in either House, the Governor, or the person exercising the power of the Governor, shall issue writs of election to fill such vacancies; and should the Governor fail to issue a writ of election to fill any such vacancy within twenty days after it occurs, the returning officer of the district in which such vacancy may have happened, shall be authorized to order an election for that purpose.

SECTION 14. LEGISLATORS PRIVILEDGED FROM ARREST Senators and Representatives shall, except in cases of treason, felony, or breach of the peace, be privileged from arrest during the session of the Legislature, and in going to and returning from the same, allowing one day for every twenty miles such member may reside from the place at which the Legislature is convened.

SECTION 15. DISRESPECTFUL OR DISORDERLY CONDUCT Each House may punish, by imprisonment, during its sessions, any person not a member, for disrespectful or disorderly conduct in its presence, or for obstructing any of its proceedings; provided, such imprisonment shall not, at any one time, exceed forty-eight hours.

SECTION 16. SESSIONS TO BE OPEN The sessions of each House shall be open, except the Senate when in Executive session.

SECTION 24. COMPENSATION LEGISLATORS; SESSIONS

(a) Members of the Legislature shall receive from the Public Treasury a salary of Six Hundred Dollars ($600) per month, unless a greater amount is recommended by the Texas Ethics Commission and approved by the voters of this State in which case the salary is that amount. Each member shall also receive a per diem set by the Texas Ethics Commission for each day during each Regular and Special Session of the Legislature.

(b) No Regular Session shall be of longer duration than one hundred and forty (140) days.

(c) In addition to the per diem the Members of each House shall be entitled to mileage at the same rate as prescribed by law for employees of the State of Texas.

SECTION 25. SENATORIAL DISTRICTS The State shall be divided into Senatorial Districts of contiguous territory according to the number of qualified electors, as nearly as may be, and each district shall be entitled to elect one Senator; and no single county shall be entitled to more than one Senator.

SECTION 26. APPORTIONMENT OF REPRESENTATIVES The members of the House of Representatives shall be apportioned among the several counties, according to the number of population in each, as nearly as may be, on a ratio obtained by dividing the population of the State, as ascertained by the most recent United States census, by the number of members of which the House is composed; provided, that whenever a single county has sufficient population to be entitled to a Representative, such county shall be formed into a separate Representative District, and when two or more counties are required to make up the ratio of representation, such counties shall be contiguous to each other; and when any one county has more than sufficient population to be entitled to one or more Representatives, such Representative or Representatives shall be apportioned to such county, and for any surplus of population it may be joined in a Representative District with any other contiguous county or counties.

SECTION 26A. COUNTIES WITH MORE THAN SEVEN REPRESENTATIVES Provided however, that no county shall be entitled to or have under any apportionment more than seven (7) Representatives unless the population of such county shall exceed seven hundred thousand (700,000) people as ascertained by the most recent United States Census, in which event such county shall be entitled to one additional Representative for each one hundred thousand (100,000) population in excess of seven hundred thousand (700,000) population as shown by the latest United States

Census; nor shall any district be created which would permit any county to have more than seven (7) Representatives except under the conditions set forth above.

SECTION 30. NO CHANGE IN PURPOSE OF BILL No law shall be passed, except by bill, and no bill shall be so amended in its passage through either House, as to change its original purpose.

SECTION 31. BILLS MAY ORIGINATE IN EITHER HOUSE Bills may originate in either House, and, when passed by such House, may be amended, altered or rejected by the other.

SECTION 32. THREE READINGS; EXCEPTION No bill shall have the force of a law, until it has been read on three separate days in each House, and free discussion allowed thereon; but in cases of imperative public necessity (which necessity shall be stated in a preamble or in the body of the bill) four-fifths of the House, in which the bill may be pending, may suspend this rule, the yeas and nays being taken on the question of suspension, and entered upon the journals.

SECTION 33. REVENUE BILLS All bills for raising revenue shall originate in the House of Representatives, but the Senate may amend or reject them as other bills.

SECTION 34. NO RECONSIDERATION OF DEFEATED BILLS AND RESOLUTION After a bill has been considered and defeated by either House of the Legislature, no bill containing the same substance, shall be passed into a law during the same session. After a resolution has been acted on and defeated, no resolution containing the same substance, shall be considered at the same session.

SECTION 35. SUBJECT OF BILLS
(a) No bill, (except general appropriation bills, which may embrace the various subjects and accounts, for and on account of which moneys are appropriated) shall contain more than one subject.

(b) The rules of procedure of each house shall require that the subject of each bill be expressed in its title in a manner that gives the legislature and the public reasonable notice of that subject. The legislature is solely responsible for determining compliance with the rule.

A law, including a law enacted before the effective date of this subsection, may not be held void on the basis of an insufficient title.

SECTION 36. NO REVIVAL OR AMENDMENT OF REFERENCE No law shall be revived or amended by reference to its title; but in such case the act revived, or the section or sections amended, shall be re-enacted and published at length.

SECTION 37. REFERENCE OF BILLS TO COMMITTEE No bill shall be considered, unless it has been first referred to a committee and reported thereon, and no bill shall be passed which has not been presented and referred to and reported from a committee at least three days before the final adjournment of the Legislature.

SECTION 38. SIGNING BY PRESIDING OFFICER The presiding officer of each House shall, in the presence of the House over which he presides, sign all bills and joint resolutions passed by the Legislature, after their titles have been publicly read before signing; and the fact of signing shall be entered on the journals.

SECTION 39. NO LAW TO TAKE EFFECT FOR NINETY DAYS; EXCEPTION No law passed by the Legislature, except the general appropriation act, shall take effect or go into force until ninety days after the adjournment of the session at which it was enacted, unless in case of an emergency, which emergency must be expressed in a preamble or in the body of the act, the Legislature shall, by a vote of two-thirds of all the members elected to each House, otherwise direct; said vote to be taken by yeas and nays, and entered upon the journals.

SECTION 40. SPECIAL SESSIONS When the Legislature shall be convened in special session, there shall be no legislation upon subjects other than those designated in the proclamation of the Governor calling such session, or presented to them by the Governor; and no such session shall be of longer duration than thirty days.

SECTION 41. VOTES TO BE VIVA VOCE In all elections by the Senate and House of Representatives, jointly or separately, the vote shall be given viva voce, except in the election of their officers.

SECTION 49. CREATION OF STATE DEBT

(a) No debt shall be created by or on behalf of the State, except: (1) to supply casual deficiencies of revenue, not to exceed in the aggregate at any one time two hundred thousand dollars; (2) to repel invasion, suppress insurrection, or defend the State in war; (3) as otherwise authorized by this constitution; or (4) as authorized by Subsections (b) through (f) of this section.

(a) The legislature, by joint resolution approved by at least two-thirds of the members of each house, may from time to time call an election and submit to the eligible voters of this State one or more propositions that, if approved by a majority of those voting on the question, authorize the legislature to create State debt for the purposes and subject to the limitations stated in the applicable proposition. Each election and proposition must conform to the requirements of Subsections (c) and (d) of this section.

(b) The legislature may call an election during any regular session of the legislature or during any special session of the legislature in which the subject of the election is designated in the governor's proclamation for that special session. The election may be held on any date, and notice of the election shall be given for the period and in the manner required for amending this constitution. The election shall be held in each county in the manner provided by law for other statewide elections.

(c) A proposition must clearly describe the amount and purpose for which debt is to be created and must describe the source of payment for the debt. Except as provided by law under Subsection (f) of this section, the amount of debt stated in the proposition may not be exceeded and may not be renewed after the debt has been created unless the right to exceed or renew is stated in the proposition.

(d) The legislature may enact all laws necessary or appropriate to implement the authority granted by a proposition that is approved as provided by Subsection (b) of this section. A law enacted in anticipation of the election is valid if, by its terms, it is subject to the approval of the related proposition.

(e) State debt that is created or issued as provided by Subsection (b) of this section may be refunded in the manner and amount and subject to the conditions provided by law.

(f) State debt that is created or issued as provided by Subsections (b) through (f) of this section and that is approved by the attorney general in accordance with applicable law is incontestable for any reason.

SECTION 49A. FINANCIAL STATEMENT BY COMPTROLLER It shall be the duty of the Comptroller of Public Accounts in advance of each Regular Session of the Legislature to prepare and submit to the Governor and to the Legislature upon its convening a statement under oath showing fully the financial condition of the State Treasury at the close of the last fiscal period and an estimate of the probable receipts and disbursements for the then current fiscal year. There shall also be contained in said statement an itemized estimate of the anticipated revenue based on the laws then in effect that will be received by and for the State from all sources showing the fund accounts to be credited during the succeeding biennium and said statement shall contain such other information as may be required by law. Supplemental statements shall be submitted at any Special Session of the Legislature and at such other times as may be necessary to show probable changes.

From and after January 1, 1945, save in the case of emergency and imperative public necessity and with a four-fifths vote of the total membership of each House, no appropriation in excess of the cash and anticipated revenue of the funds from which such appropriation is to be made shall be valid. From and after January 1, 1945, no bill containing an appropriation shall be considered as passed or be sent to the Governor for consideration until and unless the Comptroller of Public Accounts endorses his certificate thereon showing that the amount appropriated is within the amount estimated to be available in the affected funds. When the Comptroller finds an appropriation bill exceeds the estimated revenue he shall endorse such finding thereon and return to the House in which same originated. Such information shall be immediately made known to both the House of Representatives and the Senate and the necessary steps shall be taken to bring such appropriation to within the revenue, either by providing additional revenue or reducing the appropriation.

For the purpose of financing the outstanding obligations of the General Revenue Fund of the State and placing its current accounts on a cash basis the Legislature of the State of Texas is hereby authorized to provide for the issuance, sale, and retirement of serial bonds, equal in principal to the total outstanding, valid, and approved obligations owing by said fund on September 1, 1943, provided such bonds shall not draw interest in excess of two (2) per cent per annum and shall mature within twenty (20) years from date.

ARTICLE IV: Executive Departments

SECTION 1. OFFICERS OF THE EXECUTIVE DEPARTMENT The Executive Department of the State shall consist of aGovernor, who shall be the Chief Executive Officer of the State, a Lieutenant Governor, Secretary of State, Comptroller of Public Accounts, Commissioner of theGeneral LandOffice, and AttorneyGeneral.

SECTION 2. ELECTION OF EXECUTIVE OFFICERS All the above officers of the Executive Department (except Secretary of State) shall be elected by the qualified voters of the State at the time and places of election for members of the Legislature.

SECTION 3A. SUCCESSION If, at the time the Legislature shall canvass the election returns for the offices of Governor and Lieutenant Governor, the person receiving the highest number of votes for the office of Governor, as declared by the Speaker, has died, fails to qualify, or for any other reason is unable to assume the office of Governor, then the person having the highest number of votes for the office of Lieutenant Governor shall become Governor for the full term to which the person was elected as Governor. By becoming the Governor, the person forfeits the office of Lieutenant Governor, and the resulting vacancy in the office of Lieutenant Governor shall be filled as provided by Section 9, Article III, of this Constitution.

If the person with the highest number of votes for the office of Governor, as declared by the Speaker, becomes temporarily unable to take office, then the Lieutenant Governor shall act as Governor until the person with the highest number of votes for the office of Governor becomes able to assume the office of Governor. Any succession to the Governorship not otherwise provided for in this Constitution, may be provided for by law; provided, however, that any person succeeding to the office of Governor shall be qualified as otherwise provided in this Constitution, and shall, during the entire term to which he may succeed, be under all the restrictions and inhibitions imposed in this Constitution on the Governor.

SECTION 4. SWEARING IN OF GOVERNOR; QUALIFICATIONS The Governor elected at the general election in 1974, and thereafter, shall be installed on the first Tuesday after the organization of the Legislature, or as soon thereafter as practicable, and shall hold his office for the term of four years, or until his successor shall be duly installed. He shall be at least thirty years of age, a citizen of the United States, and shall have resided in this State at least five years immediately preceding his election.

SECTION 5. COMPENSATIONS OF GOVERNOR The Governor shall, at stated times, receive as compensation for his services an annual salary in an amount to be fixed by the Legislature, and shall have the use and occupation of the Governor's Mansion, fixtures and furniture.

SECTION 7. GOVERNOR AS COMMANDER-IN-CHIEF He shall be Commander-in-Chief of the military forces of the State, except when they are called into actual service of the United States. He shall have power to call forth the militia to execute the laws of the State, to suppress insurrections, repel invasions, and protect the frontier from hostile incursions by Indians or other predatory bands.

SECTION 8. GOVERNOR MAY CONVENE LEGISLATURE The Governor may, on extraordinary occasions, convene the Legislature at the seat of Government, or at a different place, in case that should be in possession of the public enemy or in case of the prevalence of disease thereat. His proclamation therefor shall state specifically the purpose for which the Legislature is convened.

SECTION 9. GOVERNOR'S ADDRESS The Governor shall, at the commencement of each session of the Legislature, and at the close of his term of office, give to the Legislature information, by message, of the condition of the State; and he shall recommend to the Legislature such measures as he may deem expedient. He shall account to the Legislature for all public moneys received and paid out by him, from any funds subject to his order, with vouchers; and shall accompany his message with a statement of the same. And at the commencement of each regular session, he shall present estimates of the amount of money required to be raised by taxation for all purposes.

SECTION 10. GOVERNOR SHALL CAUSE EXECUTION OF LAWS He shall cause the laws to be faithfully executed and shall conduct, in person, or in such manner as shall be prescribed by law, all intercourse and business of the State with other States and with the United States.

SECTION 11. PARDONS AND PAROLES

(a) The Legislature shall by law establish a Board of Pardons and Paroles and shall require it to keep record of its actions and the reasons for its actions. The Legislature shall have authority to enact parole laws and laws that require or permit courts to inform juries about the effect of good conduct time and eligibility for parole or mandatory supervision on the period of incarceration served by a defendant convicted of a criminal offense.

(b) In all criminal cases, except treason and impeachment, the Governor shall have power, after conviction, on the written signed recommendation and advice of the Board of Pardons and Paroles, or a majority thereof, to grant reprieves and commutations of punishment and pardons; and under such rules as the Legislature may prescribe, and upon the written recommendation and advice of a majority of the Board of Pardons and Paroles, he shall have the power to remit fines and forfeitures. The Governor shall have the power to grant one reprieve in any capital case for a period not to exceed thirty (30) days; and he shall have power to revoke conditional pardons. With the advice and consent of the Legislature, he may grant reprieves, commutations of punishment and pardons in cases of treason.

SECTION 12. VACANCIES IN STATE OR DISTRICT OFFICES TO BE FILLED BY APPOINTMENT

(a) All vacancies in State or district offices, except members of the Legislature, shall be filled unless otherwise provided by law by appointment of the Governor.

(b) An appointment of the Governor made during a session of the Senate shall be with the advice and consent of two-thirds of the Senate present.

(c) In accordance with this section, the Senate may give its advice and consent on an appointment of the Governor made during a recess of the Senate. To be confirmed, the appointment must be with the advice and consent of two-thirds of the Senate present.

If an appointment of the Governor is made during the recess of the Senate, the Governor shall nominate the appointee, or some other person to fill the vacancy, to the Senate during the first ten days of its next session following the appointment. If the Senate does not confirm a person under this subsection, the Governor shall nominate in accordance with this section the recess appointee or another person to fill the vacancy during the first ten days of each subsequent session of the Senate until a confirmation occurs. If the Governor does not nominate a person to the

Senate during the first ten days of a session of the Senate as required by this subsection, the Senate at that session may consider the recess appointee as if the Governor had nominated the appointee.

(d) If the Senate, at any special session, does not take final action to confirm or reject a previously unconfirmed recess appointee or another person nominated to fill the vacancy for which the appointment was made: (1) the Governor after the session may appoint another person to fill the vacancy; and (2) the appointee, if otherwise qualified and if not removed as provided by law, is entitled to continue in office until the earlier of the following occurs: (A) the Senate rejects the appointee at a subsequent session; or (B) the Governor appoints another person to fill the vacancy under Subdivision (1) of this subsection.

(e) If the Senate, at a regular session, does not take final action to confirm or reject a previously unconfirmed recess appointee or another person nominated to fill the vacancy for which the appointment was made, the appointee or other person, as appropriate, is considered to be rejected by the Senate when the Senate session ends.

(f) If an appointee is rejected, the office shall immediately become vacant, and the Governor shall, without delay, make further nominations, until a confirmation takes place. If a person has been rejected by the Senate to fill a vacancy, the Governor may not appoint the person to fill the vacancy or, during the term of the vacancy for which the person was rejected, to fill another vacancy in the same office or on the same board, commission, or other body.

(g) Appointments to vacancies in offices elective by the people shall only continue until the next general election.

(h) The Legislature by general law may limit the term to be served by a person appointed by the Governor to fill a vacancy in a state or district office to a period that ends before the vacant term otherwise expires or, for an elective office, before the next election at which the vacancy is to be filled, if the appointment is made on or after November 1 preceding the general election for the succeeding term of the office of Governor and the Governor is not elected at that election to the succeeding term.

(i) For purposes of this section, the expiration of a term of office or the creation of a new office constitutes a vacancy.

SECTION 14. PRESENTATION FOR APPROVAL OF GOVERNOR; BILLS Every bill which shall have passed both houses of the Legislature shall be presented to the Governor for his approval. If he approve he shall sign it; but if he disapprove it, he shall return it, with his objections, to the House in which it originated, which House shall enter the objections at large upon its journal, and proceed to reconsider it. If after such reconsideration, two-thirds of the members present agree to pass the bill, it shall be sent, with the objections, to the other House, by which likewise it shall be reconsidered; and, if approved by two-thirds of the members of that House, it shall become a law; but in such cases the votes of both Houses shall be determined by yeas and nays, and the names of the members voting for and against the bill shall be entered on the journal of each House respectively. If any bill shall not be returned by the Governor with his objections within ten days (Sundays excepted) after it shall have been presented to him, the same shall be a law, in like manner as if he had signed it, unless the Legislature, by its adjournment, prevent its return, in which case it shall be a law, unless he shall file the same, with his objections, in the office of the Secretary of State and give notice thereof by public proclamation within twenty days after such adjournment. If any bill presented to the Governor contains several items of appropriation he may object to one or more of such items, and approve the other portion of the bill. In such case he shall append to the bill, at the time of signing it, a statement of the items to which he objects, and no item so objected to shall take effect. If the Legislature be in session, he shall transmit to the House in which the bill originated a copy of such statement and the items objected to shall be separately considered.

If, on reconsideration, one or more of such items be approved by two-thirds of the members present of each House, the same shall be part of the law, notwithstanding the objections of the Governor. If any such bill, containing several items of appropriation, not having been presented to the Governor ten days (Sundays excepted) prior to adjournment, be in the hands of the Governor at the time of adjournment, he shall have twenty days from such adjournment within which to file objections to any items thereof and make proclamation of the same, and such item or items shall not take effect.

SECTION 15. PRESENTATION FOR APPROVAL OF GOVERNOR; ORDERS, RESOLUTIONS, OR VOTES

Every order, resolution or vote to which the concurrence of both Houses of the Legislature may be necessary, except on questions of adjournment, shall be presented to the Governor, and, before it shall take effect, shall be approved by him; or, being disapproved, shall be re-passed by both Houses, and all the rules, provisions and limitations shall apply thereto as prescribed in the last preceding section in the case of a bill.

SECTION 16. LIEUTENANT GOVERNOR

(a) There shall also be a Lieutenant Governor, who shall be chosen at every election for Governor by the same electors, in the same manner, continue in office for the same time, and possess the same qualifications. The electors shall distinguish for whom they vote as Governor and for whom as Lieutenant Governor.

(b) The Lieutenant Governor shall by virtue of his office be President of the Senate, and shall have, when in Committee of the Whole, a right to debate and vote on all questions; and when the Senate is equally divided to give the casting vote.

(c) In the case of the temporary inability or temporary disqualification of the Governor to serve, the impeachment of the Governor, or the absence of the Governor from the State, the Lieutenant Governor shall exercise the powers and authority appertaining to the office of Governor until the Governor becomes able or qualified to resume serving, is acquitted, or returns to the State.

(d) If the Governor refuses to serve or becomes permanently unable to serve, or if the office of Governor becomes vacant, the Lieutenant Governor becomes Governor for the remainder of the term being served by the Governor who refused or became unable to serve or vacated the office. On becoming Governor, the person vacates the office of Lieutenant Governor, and the resulting vacancy in the office of Lieutenant Governor shall be filled in the manner provided by Section 9, Article III, of this Constitution.

SECTION 17. DISABILITY WHILE GOVERNOR'S OFFICE VACANT

(a) If, while exercising the powers and authority appertaining to the office of Governor under Section 16(c) of this article, the Lieutenant Governor becomes temporarily unable or disqualified to serve, is impeached, or is absent from the State, the President pro tempore of the Senate, for the time being, shall exercise the powers and authority appertaining to the office of Governor until the Governor or Lieutenant Governor reassumes those powers and duties.

(b) The Lieutenant Governor shall, while acting as President of the Senate, receive for his or her services the same compensation and mileage which shall be allowed to the members of the Senate, and no more unless the Texas Ethics Commission recommends and the voters approve a higher salary, in which case the salary is that amount; and during the time the Lieutenant Governor exercises the powers and authority appertaining to the office of Governor, the Lieutenant Governor shall receive in like manner the same compensation which the Governor would have received had the Governor been employed in the duties of that office, and no more. An increase in the emoluments of the office of Lieutenant Governor does not make a member of the Legislature ineligible to serve in the office of Lieutenant Governor.

(c) The President pro tempore of the Senate shall, during the time that officer exercises the powers and authority appertaining to the office of Governor, receive in like manner the same compensation which the Governor would have received had the Governor been employed in the duties of that office.

SECTION 20. COMMISIONS IN THE NAME OF THE STATE All commissions shall be in the name and by the authority of the State of Texas, sealed with the State Seal, signed by the Governor and attested by the Secretary of State.

SECTION 21. SECRETARY OF STATE There shall be a Secretary of State, who shall be appointed by the Governor, by and with the advice and consent of the Senate, and who shall continue in office during the term of service of the Governor. He shall authenticate the publication of the laws, and keep a fair register of all official acts and proceedings of the Governor, and shall, when required, lay the same and all papers, minutes and vouchers relative thereto, before the Legislature, or either House thereof, and shall perform such other duties as may be required of him by law. He shall receive for his services an annual salary in an amount to be fixed by the Legislature.

SECTION 22. ATTORNEY GENERAL The Attorney General elected at the general election in 1974, and thereafter, shall hold office for four years and until his successor is duly qualified. He shall represent the State in all suits and pleas in the Supreme Court of the State in which the State may be a party, and shall especially inquire into the charter rights of all private corporations, and from time to time, in the name of the State, take such action in the courts as may be proper and necessary to prevent any private corporation from exercising any power or demanding or collecting any species of taxes, tolls, freight or wharfage not authorized by law. He shall, whenever sufficient cause exists, seek a judicial forfeiture of such charters, unless otherwise expressly directed by law, and give legal advice in writing to the Governor and other executive officers, when requested by them, and perform such other duties as may be required by law. He shall reside at the seat of government during his continuance in office.

He shall receive for his services an annual salary in an amount to be fixed by the Legislature.

SECTION 23. TERMS OF COMPTROLLER; COMMISSIONER OF GENERAL LAND OFFICE The Comptroller of Public Accounts, the Commissioner of the General Land Office, and any statutory State officer who is elected by the electorate of Texas at large, unless a term of office is otherwise specifically provided in this Constitution, shall each hold office for the term of four years and until his successor is qualified. The four-year term applies to these officers who are elected at the general election in 1974 or thereafter. Each shall receive an annual salary in an amount to be fixed by the Legislature; reside at the Capital of the State during his continuance in office, and perform such duties as are or may be required by law. They and the Secretary of State shall not receive to their own use any fees, costs or perquisites of office. All fees that may be payable by law for any service performed by any officer specified in this section or in his office, shall be paid, when received, into the State Treasury.

SECTION 24. ACCOUNTS OF PUBLIC MONEYS An account shall be kept by the officers of the Executive Department, and by all officers and managers of State institutions, of all moneys and choses in action received and disbursed or otherwise disposed of by them, severally, from all sources, and for every service performed; and a semi-annual report thereof shall be made to the Governor under oath.

The Governor may, at any time, require information in writing from any and all of said officers or managers, upon any subject relating to the duties, condition, management and expenses of their respective offices and institutions, which information shall be required by the Governor under oath, and the Governor may also inspect their books, accounts, vouchers and public funds; and any officer or manager who, at any time, shall wilfully make a false report or give false information, shall be guilty of perjury, and so adjudged, and punished accordingly, and removed from office.

ARTICLE V: Judicial Department

SECTION 1. JUDICIAL POWER; COURTS IN WHICH VESTED The judicial power of this State shall be vested in one Supreme Court, in one Court of Criminal Appeals, in Courts of Appeals, in District Courts, in County Courts, in Commissioners Courts, in Courts of Justices of the Peace, and in such other courts as may be provided by law. The Legislature may establish such other courts as it may deem necessary and prescribe the jurisdiction and organization thereof, and may conform the jurisdiction of the district and other inferior courts thereto. (Amended Aug. 11, 1891, Nov. 8, 1977, and Nov. 4, 1980.)

SECTION 2. SUPREME COURT; JUSTICES; SECTIONS; ELIGIBILITY; ELECTION; VACANCIES The Supreme Court shall consist of the Chief Justice and eight Justices, any five of whom shall constitute a quorum, and the concurrence of five shall be necessary to a decision of a case; provided, that when the business of the court may require, the court may sit in sections as designated by the court to hear argument of causes and to consider applications for writs of error or other preliminary matters. No person shall be eligible to serve in the office of Chief Justice or Justice of the Supreme Court unless the person is licensed to practice law in this state and is, at the time of election, a citizen of the United States and of this state, and has attained the age of thirty-five years, and has been a practicing lawyer, or a lawyer and judge of a court of record together at least ten years. Said Justices shall be elected (three of them each two years) by the qualified voters of the state at a general election; shall hold their offices six years, or until their successors are elected and qualified; and shall each receive such compensation as shall be provided by law. In case of a vacancy in the office of the Chief Justice or any Justice of the Supreme Court, the Governor shall fill the vacancy until the next general election for state officers, and at such general election the vacancy for the unexpired term shall be filled by election by the qualified voters of the state. The Justices of the Supreme Court who may be in office at the time this amendment takes effect shall continue in office until the expiration of their term of office under the present Constitution, and until their successors are elected and qualified.

SECTION 3. JURISDICTION OF SUPREME COURT The Supreme Court shall exercise the judicial power of the state except as otherwise provided in this Constitution. Its jurisdiction shall be coextensive with the limits of the State and its determinations shall be final except in criminal law matters. Its appellate jurisdiction shall be final and shall extend to all cases except in criminal law matters and as otherwise provided in this Constitution or by law. The Supreme Court and the Justices thereof shall have power to issue writs of habeas corpus, as may be prescribed by law, and under such regulations as may be prescribed by law, the said courts and the Justices thereof may issue the writs of mandamus, procedendo, certiorari and such other writs, as may be necessary to enforce its jurisdiction. The Legislature may confer original jurisdiction on the Supreme Court to issue writs of quo warranto and mandamus in such cases as may be specified, except as against the Governor of the State.

The Supreme Court shall also have power, upon affidavit or otherwise as by the court may be determined, to ascertain such matters of fact as may be necessary to the proper exercise of its jurisdiction.

The Supreme Court shall appoint a clerk, who shall give bond in such manner as is now or may hereafter, be required by law, and he may hold his office for four years and shall be subject to removal by said court for good cause entered of record on the minutes of said court who shall receive such compensation as the Legislature may provide.

SECTION 4. COURT OF CRIMINAL APPEALS; JUDGES The Court of Criminal Appeals shall consist of eight Judges and one Presiding Judge.

The Judges shall have the same qualifications and receive the same salaries as the Associate Justices of the Supreme Court, and the Presiding Judge shall have the same qualifications and receive the same salary as the Chief Justice of the Supreme Court. The Presiding Judge and the Judges shall be elected by the qualified voters of the state at a general election and shall hold their offices for a term of six years.

In case of a vacancy in the office of a Judge of the Court of Criminal Appeals, the Governor shall, with the advice and consent of the Senate, fill said vacancy by appointment until the next succeeding general election.

For the purpose of hearing cases, the Court of Criminal Appeals may sit in panels of three Judges, the designation thereof to be under rules established by the court. In a panel of three Judges, two Judges shall constitute a quorum and the concurrence of two Judges shall be necessary for a decision. The Presiding Judge, under rules established by the court, shall convene the court en banc for the transaction of all other business and may convene the court en banc for the purpose of hearing cases. The court must sit en banc during proceedings involving capital punishment and other cases as required by law.

When convened en banc, five Judges shall constitute a quorum and the concurrence of five Judges shall be necessary for a decision. The Court of Criminal Appeals may appoint Commissioners in aid of the Court of Criminal Appeals as provided by law.

SECTION 5. JURISDICTION OF COURT OF CRIMINAL APPEALS; TERMS OF COURT; CLERK

The Court of Criminal Appeals shall have final appellate jurisdiction coextensive with the limits of the state, and its determinations shall be final, in all criminal cases of whatever grade, with such exceptions and under such regulations as may be provided in this Constitution or as prescribed by law.

The appeal of all cases in which the death penalty has been assessed shall be to the Court of Criminal Appeals. The appeal of all other criminal cases shall be to the Courts of Appeal as prescribed by law. In addition, the Court of Criminal Appeals may, on its own motion, review a decision of a Court of Appeals in a criminal case as provided by law. Discretionary review by the Court of Criminal Appeals is not a matter of right, but of sound judicial discretion.

Subject to such regulations as may be prescribed by law, the Court of Criminal Appeals and the Judges thereof shall have the power to issue the writ of habeas corpus, and, in criminal law matters, the writs of mandamus, procedendo, prohibition, and certiorari.

The Court and the Judges thereof shall have the power to issue such other writs as may be necessary to protect its jurisdiction or enforce its judgments. The court shall have the power upon affidavit or otherwise to ascertain such matters of fact as may be necessary to the exercise of its jurisdiction.

The Court of Criminal Appeals may sit for the transaction of business at any time during the year and each term shall begin and end with each calendar year. The Court of Criminal Appeals shall appoint a clerk of the court who shall give bond in such manner as is now or may hereafter be required by law, and who shall hold his office for a term of four years unless sooner removed by the court for good cause entered of record on the minutes of said court.

The Clerk of the Court of Criminal Appeals who may be in office at the time when this Amendment takes effect shall continue in office for the term of his appointment.

SECTION 6. COURTS OF APPEALS; TERMS OF JUSTICES; CLERKS

The state shall be divided into courts of appeals districts, with each district having a Chief Justice, two or more other Justices, and such other officials as may be provided by law.

The Justices shall have the qualifications prescribed for Justices of the Supreme Court.

The Court of Appeals may sit in sections as authorized by law. The concurrence of a majority of the judges sitting in a section is necessary to decide a case. Said Court of Appeals shall have appellate jurisdiction co-extensive with the limits of their respective districts, which shall extend to all cases of which the District Courts or County Courts have original or appellate jurisdiction, under such restrictions and regulations as may be prescribed by law. Provided, that the decision of said courts shall be conclusive on all questions of fact brought before them on appeal or error. Said courts shall have such other jurisdiction, original and appellate, as may be prescribed by law.

Each of said Courts of Appeals shall hold its sessions at a place in its district to be designated by the Legislature, and at such time as may be prescribed by law. Said Justices shall be elected by the qualified voters of their respective districts at a general election, for a term of six years and shall receive for their services the sum provided by law. Each Court of Appeals shall appoint a clerk in the same manner as the clerk of the Supreme Court which clerk shall receive such compensation as may be fixed by law.

All constitutional and statutory references to the Courts of Civil Appeals shall be construed to mean the Courts of Appeals.

SECTION 7. JUDICIAL DISTRICTS; DISTRICT JUDGES; TERMS OR SESSIONS; ABSENCE; DISABILITY OR DISQUALIFICATION OF JUDGE The State shall be divided into judicial districts, with each district having one or more Judges as may be provided by law or by this Constitution. Each district judge shall be elected by the qualified voters at a General Election and shall be a citizen of the United States and of this State, who is licensed to practice law in this State and has been a practicing lawyer or a Judge of a Court in this State, or both combined, for four (4) years next preceding his election, who has resided in the district in which he was elected for two (2) years next preceding his election, and who shall reside in his district during his term of office and hold his office for the period of four (4) years, and who shall receive for his services an annual salary to be fixed by the Legislature. The Court shall conduct its proceedings at the county seat of the county in which the case is pending, except as otherwise provided by law. He shall hold the regular terms of his Court at the County Seat of each County in his district in such manner as may be prescribed by law. The Legislature shall have power by General or Special Laws to make such provisions concerning the terms or sessions of each Court as it may deem necessary.

The Legislature shall also provide for the holding of District Court when the Judge thereof is absent, or is from any cause disabled or disqualified from presiding.

SECTION 8. JURISDICTION OF DISTRICT COURT District Court jurisdiction consists of exclusive, appellate, and original jurisdiction of all actions, proceedings, and remedies, except in cases where exclusive, appellate, or original jurisdiction may be conferred by this Constitution or other law on some other court, tribunal, or administrative body. District Court judges shall have the power to issue writs necessary to enforce their jurisdiction.

The District Court shall have appellate jurisdiction and general supervisory control over the County Commissioners Court, with such exceptions and under such regulations as may be prescribed by law.

SECTION 10. TRIAL BY JURY In the trial of all causes in the District Courts, the plaintiff or defendant shall, upon application made in open court, have the right of trial by jury; but no jury shall be empaneled in any civil case unless demanded by a party to the case, and a jury fee be paid by the party demanding a jury, for such sum, and with such exceptions as may be prescribed by the Legislature.

GLOSSARY

1876 Constitution the current Texas Constitution, written after Reconstruction.

abatement a financial incentive offered by governments to business and commercial concerns as a means of luring them to set up operations within the borders of a particular city.

access the ability of an interest group to contact policymakers in an attempt to enlist their help. Access is crucial, for without it an interest group's information is largely useless.

ad valorem a system of taxation that is assessed "according to value," whereby the more a property is worth, the higher the tax to be paid on it.

amendments additions or deletions to the constitution; passed in a prescribed manner.

amorphous groups with tenuously connected interests.

appellate courts courts that hear appeals from lower courts.

apportionment dividing the population into districts for purposes of election and representation.

at-large system a method of electing representatives where there are no districts or wards drawn, and the candidate may draw votes from the entire area to be governed.

attorney general the state's lawyer; elected.

bail a cash deposit or other security given by the accused as a guarantee that he will return to court when summoned.

balanced budget a means to keep the government from spending more than it receives in revenues.

bench trial a criminal trial that is held without jury, as requested by the person charged.

beyond a reasonable doubt burden of proof on the state in a criminal case.

Bill of Rights the portion of the constitution limiting the government and empowering the individual.

Black Codes post–Civil War laws restricting the freedom of African Americans.

bureaucracy executive branch departments that carry out the law.

cabinet a form of government where the chief executive appoints other major executive department heads.

capital improvements long-term infrastructure improvements, such as roads, that are often built with bond money.

centralized groups with decision making concentrated near the top.

city manager professional political appointee who oversees city operations on a day-to-day basis.

civil law law that deals with private rights and seeks damages rather than punishment.

civil service merit-based system of selecting government employees.

clemency power power to pardon, commute, or parole.

coalitions alliances consisting of a variety of individuals and groups in support of a particular candidate for elected office.

committees divisions of a legislative body charged with initial deliberations on legislative proposals.

comptroller the state's chief accountant and financial officer.

conference committee joint committee of house and senate members whose purpose is to iron out the differences between house and senate versions of a bill.

constitution the basic document under which a state or nation's government operates.

conventions formal party meetings to select leadership, delegates, and create a platform.

cooperative federalism era of expanded national government power, mandates, and funding.

council of government (COG) a regional voluntary cooperative with no regulatory or enforcement powers; consists of local governments and assesses the needs of the area as a whole.

criminal law laws that regulate individual conduct and seek to protect society by punishing criminal acts.

Davis, E. J. the Republican governor of Texas during the era of Reconstruction.

decentralized groups with decision making widely dispersed.

dedicated funds revenues set aside for specific expense categories.

defendant person charged with a crime or the subject of a civil suit.

"Democrats of Texas" a liberal faction of Democrats formed in the 1950s.

devolution the transfer of government programs from the national to the state level.

disfranchised persons who cannot vote, or who believe their votes don't count.

double jeopardy a criminal defendant's due process right to be protected from being tried a second time (after receiving a not-guilty verdict the first time).

down-ballot races statewide races below the level of president, U.S. Senator, or governor.

dual federalism well-defined divisions between national and state powers and responsibilities.

due process constitutionally protected rights of persons accused of committing criminal acts.

election burnout occurs when citizens believe there are too many elections, and thus, fail to vote.

en banc when an appellate court convenes all of its members to hear an appeal.

exclusionary rule a due process right that makes it illegal for the government to use evidence gathered during an unlawful police search.

factions divisions within a political party.

federal grants revenue distributed to states from the federal government.

federalism a constitutional sharing of powers between the national and state governments.

filibustering the practice of delaying or killing a bill by talking at great length; grows out of the senate's rule allowing unlimited debate.

formal powers powers granted by the constitution or statutes.

franchise tax a specific tax paid by businesses operating in Texas.

general election the process through which officeholders are elected from among party nominees.

general law a highly restrictive, and the most fundamental type of, legal status for municipal government.

general obligation bond a bond issued by a local government for the purpose of making capital improvements and, like a mortgage, are paid off in small, yearly payments.

gerrymandering the act of drawing representative districts in order to help or hinder a person, or a political party, to win an election.

government composed of public institutions acting with authority to levy taxes and to allocate things for society.

governor the state's highest elected executive official.

grand jury a panel composed of twelve citizens who determine whether enough evidence exists to charge a person with a felony and make him or her stand trial.

Grange a populist farmers' alliance influential in the creation of the 1876 Constitution.

gubernatorial election the election for governor and other executive offices.

hierarchy chain of command.

"hired gun" refers to a professional, outside lobbyist employed by an interest group to represent its interests on a particular issue. The relationship lasts until the issue is settled.

home rule a legal status that gives municipalities more autonomy in establishing tax rates and providing services; must be approved by a majority of the voters in municipalities consisting of 5,000 or more persons.

hung jury term describing the failure to render a verdict in a criminal case.

ideological a group or party built around a unifying set of principles.

independent school district (ISD) local-level limited purpose government that determines public school policy.

index crimes seven categories of crime used for statistical study by the federal and state governments.

indictment a finding by the grand jury that the case will proceed to the trial stage; also called a true-bill.

informal powers powers not specifically granted in the constitution or statutes.

information dissemination the ability of a lobbyist to provide information to elected officials.

interest group a collection of individuals who share a common set of ideas or principles and who attempt to advance those ideas or principles by influencing public policymakers.

interim committee a special committee formed to study a topic or problem between sessions of the legislature.

interim oversight various actions by an interest group aimed at protecting its gains and promoting its goals between sessions of the legislature.

judicial activism a philosophical approach dictating that the purpose of the courts is to take an active role in public policymaking.

judicial review the power of the courts to strike down laws that violate the state or national constitution.

jurisdiction the power of a court to hear a case.

land commissioner state official responsible for overseeing the leases and uses of state-owned land; elected.

Legislative Budget Board (LBB) a body made up of members of the house and senate, including the two presiding officers, which oversees a staff responsible for preparing the basic working budget for the legislature's consideration.

legislative law law passed by the legislature.

limited seniority system a method of committee selection used in the house that limits the Speaker to appointing half the members of most standing committees (plus the chairs); the other members gain their seats by seniority.

line item veto the governor's ability to delete individual items in the appropriations bill.

lobbyist a person who works on behalf of an interest group and who serves as a point of contact between the group and policymakers.

long ballot a system under which many officials are up for election at the same time.

lottery revenue raising method of the state involving games of chance.

mandates regulations set by Congress that state and local government must meet.

martial law the power to impose military role during a crisis.

membership mobilization the act of enlisting the rank-and-file members of an interest group in attempting to sway policymakers; often includes massive letter-writing efforts and may also include marches and demonstrations.

mosaic the joining of small pieces of material, varied in shape and color, to produce a whole image; often used describe the social and cultural diversity that defines Texas.

motor fuels tax a tax on gasoline, diesel, and other motor fuels.

new federalism greater discretion to state governments in the use of federal grants.

non-tax revenue revenue derived from non-tax sources, such as the lottery and fees paid to the state.

"Obnoxious Acts" the derisive name given to the legislation included in E. J. Davis' agenda.

"one person, one vote" a principle of representation that means the vote of one citizen should be worth no more or no less than the vote of another citizen; districts with equal population ensure this.

ordinances laws enacted by incorporated cities and towns; violations punishable by fine only and heard in municipal court.

original jurisdiction the authority of a court to try a case for the first time.

overlapping terms terms of appointed board members that are staggered to ensure continuity of experience.

peace bond A court order providing a jail sentence issued by a justice of the peace against a person who had threatened another person.

pigeonholing the act of a setting aside a bill in committee and refusing to consider it, thereby "killing" it.

place system a system of electing local government leaders whereby the candidates must campaign for a particular seat on the city council.

plaintiff the person or entity that initiates a civil lawsuit.

platform the statement of principles passed by a political party's convention.

plea bargaining a process in which the accused receives a lighter sentence than could be expected from a trial verdict in exchange for a guilty plea.

plural executive a political system whereby major executive officers are elected independent of the governor.

plurality exists when a candidate has more votes than any other candidate, even if the total is less than 50 percent.

political action committee (PAC) a voluntary association of individuals who band together for the purpose of raising and distributing money for political campaigns.

political culture the attitudes, beliefs, and behavior that shape an area's politics; often a product of various historical and social factors unique to that area.

political party a group of people who share common goals and attempt to control government by winning elections.

politics the process of seeking or maintaining power.

poll tax a tax paid for registering to vote (this tax no longer exists).

post-adjournment veto a veto administered after the legislature has adjourned; in Texas, it cannot be overridden.

precinct a political subdivision through which elections are carried out.

precinct convention the basic or grassroots level at which delegates are selected to the county party convention.

preponderance the majority of evidence in a civil case.

primary election the process through which major parties choose their nominees for the general election.

probable cause the total set of facts and circumstances that would lead a reasonable person to believe that an individual committed a specific criminal act.

Progressive Era a period of time (1890-1910) during which Texas enacted numerous laws designed to protect ordinary citizens and to prevent their being taken advantage of by large monopolies such as the railroads.

progressive tax a system of taxation whereby the tax rate increases as income increases.

prosecutor a government employee who initiates criminal cases against individuals.

public policy any act, law, legislation, or program enacted by a public entity.

Public Utility Commission (PUC) agency that regulates utility companies; appointed.

Reconstruction post-Civil War period (1865–1877) during which former Confederate states had restrictive laws applied to them by the federal government; it (and E. J. Davis) led to Texas becoming a one-party Democratic state.

redistricting the process of redrawing district lines to maintain the concept of "one person, one vote."

regressive tax a system of taxation whereby the tax rate increases as income decreases.

regular session the constitutionally scheduled, biennial session of the legislature.

Republic of Texas the independent nation created by Texans that lasted from 1836 to 1846; its status as an independent country has contributed to (and continues to influence) an independent spirit in its politics.

resolutions proposed planks in the party platform; formed and submitted through the convention system,

revenue bond issued by local governments for the purpose of capital improvements and repaid by revenue generated by the improvement; examples include sports arenas and public facilities for which there is an admission charge.

reverse and render the high court overturns the lower court and enacts a final verdict.

reverse and remand the high court overturns lower court and orders a new trial.

sales tax tax paid on goods and services; collected at the point of sale and forwarded to the state treasury.

secretary of state the state's chief election officer; appointed by the governor.

senatorial courtesy a discretion allowing senators to derail a governor's nomination from within their home district.

sheriff the county's chief law enforcement officer; elected to four-year terms.

"sin" taxes taxes levied on selected goods and services, such as alcoholic beverages and tobacco products.

single-issue groups interest groups, such as the NRA and MADD, that devote their energies to pursuing a single, narrowly defined policy goal.

single-member district a specific geographic area with a population equal to that of other districts that elects one person (a single member) to represent that area.

Smith v. Allright U.S. Supreme Court case that overturned the white primary.

special committee a temporary committee formed by the legislature for limited or nonroutine purposes.

special district a type of local government established for a specific geographic area and for a specific purpose such as education, flood control, or public utility service.

special election an election held to fill a vacancy, ratify a state constitutional amendment, or approve a local bond issue.

special sessions extra legislative sessions called by the governor.

spoils system a system in which elected officials provide jobs and promotions to personal affiliates; see civil service.

staff the governor's aides; not subject to legislative approval.

standing committee a deliberative body formed each time a legislature meets that deals with topics of recurring interest.

State Board of Education (SBE) elected board that oversees the Texas Education Agency.

state senatorial district convention mid-level party meeting between precinct and state; same level as county convention.

Sunset Advisory Commission appointed joint commission that reviews state agencies.

superintendent the appointed manager of a public school system.

"tagging" a senate rule that allows a senator to postpone committee consideration of a bill for forty-eight hours in hopes of killing it.

tax revenue funds generated through the tax system.

"the team" unofficial term for those legislators who are supporters and allies of presiding officers and who form the leadership core of the legislature.

Texas Legislative Council the legislature's research and bill-drafting service.

Texas Penal Code the state's definitions and categorizations of crimes and punishments.

Texas Railroad Commission (TRC) state commission that oversees oil and gas production; elected.

Texas Rangers an elite division of the Department of Public Safety that investigates major crimes and allegations of police misconduct.

"Texas Regulars" a conservative faction of the Democratic party during the 1940s.

trial de novo cases that are retried by the county court after being heard in lower courts of non-record.

turnout percentage of registered voters who cast ballots.

universal suffrage the concept that holds that virtually all adult citizens (felons and illegal aliens are excluded) have the right to vote.

unfunded mandates congressional directives that are issued without corresponding federal funding.

user fees monies paid to local governments by citizens who utilize a particular government service (e.g., tuition at a state school or fees at a public boat ramp).

veto power the ability of the governor to strike down legislation, subject to override.

voir dire trial jury selection process conducted by attorneys for both sides.

Voting Rights Act of 1965 national act protecting minorities from discrimination in the voting or the registration process.

white primary the practice of allowing only whites to vote in the Democratic primary (discontinued).

PHOTO CREDITS

INDEX

Page numbers followed by *f* or *t* indicate material in figures or tables, respectively. Page references containing *n* refer to notes.

A

abatements, 284
Abbott, Greg, 212–213, 213*f*
ab initio, 49
abortion
  interest groups and, 125
  policy on, 326
absentee ballots, 74
access, of interest groups, 128
accountability, of bureaucracy,
  222–223
activism, judicial, 242–243
Adams, Randall Dale, 196–197
adjutant general, 220
administrative boards, 224–225
Administrative Office, 201
adult entertainment, tax on, 313
ad valorem, 280, 288
advertising
  campaign, 83
  state lottery, 320
affirmative action, 323
African American Texans
  civil rights of
    Black Codes and, 48
    Civil War amendments and,
      39–40
    Reconstruction and, 13,
      48–53
  discrimination against, 16, 27,
    48
  gubernatorial appointments of,
    188, 219
  interest groups of, 124
  in judicial system, 245, 246
  in legislature, 151
  lynching of, 51
  political offices held by, 27–28,
    68, 151, 219, 245, 246
  political participation by
    in 19th century, 48–53
    voter turnout, 70
  political party support from,
    101
  population of, 26*f,* 27–28
  redistricting and, 154, 193
  slavery of, end of, 13, 39–40
  voting rights of, 39–40, 48, 49,
    66–68
    poll tax and, 29, 40, 67
    Voting Rights Act of 1965
      and, 67–68
    white primary and, 29,
      66–67
agencies, state
  abolition *vs.* reauthorization of,
    226–227
  budgetary role of, 306
  bureaucracy of, 220–226

  dates of inception, 206*f*–207*f*
  interest groups and, 129*f,*
    136–137, 140–142
  iron triangle and, 140–142,
    141*f*
  legislature and, 177, 222–223
  performance review of,
    215–216
agenda setting, for policy, 300
Agrarians, 100
Agriculture, Texas Department of,
  218
agriculture commissioner,
  217–219
Aid to Families with Dependent
    Children, 324
Air National Guard, 220
Alabama, constitution of, 44, 45
Alamo, 8*f,* 9–10, 107
alcoholic beverages
  regulation of, 225–226, 257
  taxes on, 298, 312–313, 317
Alger, Bruce, 103
Allred, James V., 100, 203
amendments. *See also specific*
    amendments
  definition of, 39
  to state constitutions, 45, 45*t*
  to Texas Constitution, 45, 45*t,*
    57, 57*f*
  to U.S. Constitution, 39–40
American GI Forum, 16
American Independent Party, 91
Americans with Disabilities Act
    of 1990, 43
amorphous interest groups, 122
amusement fee tax, 313
Anahuac skirmish (1832), 9
Angelo, Ernest, 89
Anglo Texans
  colonists, 8–10
  population of, 26, 26*f*
annexation, by U.S., 11, 18, 46, 48
antitrust law, 212
appellate courts, 232, 234–236,
    235*f,* 240–242, 240*f*
appointed boards and commis-
    sions, 187, 188–189
appointments
  gubernatorial, 187, 188–189,
    202
  to legislative committees,
    158–159, 162–163
apportionment, 151–157. *See also*
    redistricting
Appropriations Committee,
    House, 162, 166, 171, 175,
    306

B

Aristotle, 65
Arizona v. *Gant,* 260
Armbrister, Ken, 156
Armstrong, Gaylord, 129–130
Army National Guard, 190*f,* 220
Arnold, Kelly, 160
arrest, 258*f,* 261
Article I of U.S. Constitution
  Section 8 (congressional pow-
    ers), 40
  Section 10 (state powers), 37
Article IV of U.S. Constitution,
    37, 38
Ashley Laws, 302
Asian American Texans, 28, 151
at-large system, in local elections,
    279
attorney general, 189, 210–215
  Abbott as, 212–215, 213*f*
  law interpreted by, 212
  name recognition of, 212
  as stepping-stone position, 212
  in Texas Constitution, 218
  Web site of, 215
auditor, county, 288
Austin
  bikeway funding in, 282*f*
  location of, 19
  mass transit in, 291*f*
Austin, Moses, 8
Austin, Stephen F., 8, 284

B

Bagsby, Dionne, 285
bail, 261
Baker Botts (law firm), 130
balanced budget, 54, 178, 215,
    302–303
Balcones Escarpment, 18, 19*f,* 20
ballot(s)
  absentee, 74
  alternative, 74
  bilingual, 49, 72
  computerized, 71*f*
  local races on, 78–80
  long, 73, 289
  trilingual, 72
Baptist General Convention of
    Texas, 125
Barber, Joshua, 104–105
Barnes, Ben, 128–129
Barnett shale, 19
Barrera, Roy, Sr., 219
Barton, Joe, 29
Bass, Lee, 188
Baylor University, 190*f*
Bay of Pigs, 106
beach adoption, 218
Bean, Roy, 238, 238*f*

Becker, Kelly, 98–99
Ben Barnes Group, 128–129
bench trial, 239, 263
Bentsen, Lloyd, 76, 108
Beyle, Thad, 203
beyond a reasonable doubt, 233
bicameral legislature, 149
biennial budget system, 304
biennial legislature, 53, 54,
    126–127, 149, 152*f,* 192
Big Bend National Park, 21
Big Bend Ranch State Natural
    Area, 21
Big Thicket, 19
bilingual ballots, 49, 72
bill(s)
  committee action on, 171–172
  comptroller certification of, 171
  conference committees and,
    167–168, 173
  designation of, 170
  filing statements with, 193
  floor action on, 172–175
  gubernatorial action on,
    173–175, 190–191,
    191–193
  introduction of, 170
  killing, methods of, 175
  mark-up of, 171
  passed in 2009 session, 176
  pigeonholing of, 171
  procedural committees and,
    166–167
  process for, 170–175, 174*f*
  reading of, 170
  scheduling of, 166–167,
    171–172
  tagging of, 175
  testimony on, 171
Bill of Rights, Texas, 54–56, 213,
    263, 264
Bill of Rights, U.S., 39–40
  definition of, 39
  nationalization of, 40
"birders," 19
Black Codes, 48
Black Prairie, 19
blacks. *See* African American
    Texans
Blakely, William, 105–106
Blanton, Annie Webb, 16
block grants, 42
"blocking" bill, 173
"blue laws," 29
Board of Law Examiners, 242
Board of Nurse Examiners for the
    State of Texas, 225
Board of Pardons and Paroles,
    196

boards and commissions. *See also*
 specific boards
 administrative, 224–225
 elected, 223–225
 gubernatorial appointments to,
  187, 188–189
 occupational licensing, 225
 overlapping terms on, 187,
  188–189
 regulatory, 225–226
 university, 225
boards of education
 local, 292
 state, 223–224
bonds, 281, 282*f,* 288
Brandborg, Dianna, 264
Breeder's Cup, 315, 317*f*
Briscoe, Dolph, 200, 203, 214
Bryan, William Jennings, 91
budget, county, 288
budget, municipal, 283–284
budget, Texas, 296–298, 302–326
 balanced, 54, 178, 215,
  302–303
 biennial system of, 304
 comptroller and, 171, 178,
  215–217, 303–304
 constraints on, 302–303
 creation of, 195, 203, 302, 306
 dedicated funds in, 304–305,
  305*f*
 expenditures in, 321–327, 322*f*
 federal stimulus package and,
  178, 179, 308, 319
 general government in, 326
 governor and, 194–195, 203,
  306
 history of, 296*f*–297*f*
 individualistic culture and, 304
 Legislative Budget Board and,
  169*f,* 177, 195, 306
 legislature and, 171, 178,
  302–306
 mandates and, 43–44, 305
 process of, 306
 public sentiment and, 304
 revenue in, 307–320
 in Texas Constitution, 53, 54,
  303
budgetary powers, in federalism,
 40–44
buffalo, 14
Bullock, Bob, 183*n*14, 211, 211*f*
 and budget, 297
 and "God Bless Texas," 3, 211
 and income tax, 142
 and judicial reform, 246
 and Republicans, 112, 164, 178
burden of proof, 233
bureaucracy, 220–226
 accountability of, 222–223
 chronology of, 206*f*–207*f*
 decentralized, 222
 definition of, 220
 expertise of, 222
 hierarchy in, 222
 negative reputation of, 220–221
 size of, 221–222, 221*t*
burglary, 262
Burnam, Lon, 182*n*13
burnout, election, 73

Bush, George H. W., 17, 106
Bush, George W.
 as governor, 203
 appointments of, 188–189,
  219, 245
 bipartisan approach of, 112,
  178, 197, 200
 Bullock and, 211
 constitutional revision and,
  60
 downsized staff of, 201
 and education, 191, 224
 election of (1994), 17, 72,
  84–85, 109, 197
 international relations of,
  199
 leadership style of, 200
 as liaison to Congress, 199
 persuasive power of, 198–199
 plural executive and, 189
 reelection of (1998), 17, 72,
  85, 101, 186
 successor to, 160, 209
 tax policy of, 311
 threat of special session by,
  191
 unique background of, 186
 veto threat by, 193
 as president, federal spending
  under, 43
Bush, Jeb, 85
Business and Economic
 Development expendi-
 tures, 321, 325–326
business interests, 122–123, 129*f*
businesspeople, as legislators, 151

C

Cabeza de Vaca, Alvar Nuñez,
 5–6
cabinet, 202–203, 207, 208
Caddo Indians, 6, 7
Calendars Committee, House,
 167, 172, 175
California
 capital punishment in, 254
 constitution of, 45
 special districts in, 291
campaigns, election, 81–85, 81*f*
 advertising in, 83
 distance factor in, 81–82
 emotional costs of, 80, 84
 financing for, 80, 81–85,
  139–140, 139*t,* 186
 for local offices, 78–80
 negative *vs.* positive, 84–85
Campbell, Thomas Mitchell, 203
campus police, 258
Caperton, Kent, 128–129
capital improvements, 281
capital punishment, 254–256,
 255*f*
 controversy over, 254–255
 Court of Criminal Appeals
  and, 240, 242
 Death Row inmate's essay on,
  265–266
 decline of executions in Texas,
  256
 high rate of executions in
  Texas, 254–255

offenses for, 255
 political culture and, 255
 "questions of life and death" in,
  255–256
 stays of execution, 196–197,
  254
Caprock escarpment, 20
carpetbagger, 50
Carrillo, Victor, 223
cash crops, 21
casino option, for state revenue,
 315–317
Castle Law, 300–302, 326–327
Castro, Fidel, 106
categorical grants, 42
Catholicism, and land grants, 8
cattle and cattle ranches, 5*f*
 frontier state and, 14
 Hispanic colonists and, 7
 history of, 21
caucus, party, 66
caucuses, in legislature, 178–179
Center for Responsive Politics,
 128
central government, *vs.* federalism, 37
centralized interest groups, 121
chair, legislative committee, 168
chair, party
 county, 95*f,* 96–97
 precinct, 95–96, 95*f*
 state, 95*f,* 97
Chamber of Commerce, 121–122
charter, home rule, 274–276
charter schools, 224
checks and balances, 39
chemical industry, 23
child labor law, 100
child molesters, public information on, 302
Children's Health Insurance
 Program (CHIP), 176,
 299, 304, 307*f,* 325
Child Support Enforcement
 Division, 212
chili cook-off, 21
CHIP. *See* Children's Health
 Insurance Program
Christian, George, 129, 138
Christian, George Scott, 129,
 132–133
Christian Life Commission, 125,
 126*f*
"chubbing," 172
Churchill Downs, 316
cigarette tax, 298, 310*f,* 312–313
cigar tax, 313
Cisneros, Henry, 272, 272*f,* 277
cities. *See* municipal government;
 municipalities
citizen-legislators, 127
Citizens on Patrol, 252, 259
Citizen Police Academy, 252,
 259
city manager, 277
civic duty, voting as, 70–71
civil law, 232–234
 burden of proof in, 233
 criminal law *vs.,* 233–234,
  233*t*
 definition of, 233

civil rights
 of African American Texans
  Black Codes and, 48
  Civil War amendments and,
   39–40
  Reconstruction and, 13,
   48–53
 of Hispanic Texans, 16, 49
 of women, 54
civil service, 290
Civil War, 11–14, 99
Class A misdemeanors, 239, 259*t*
Class B misdemeanors, 239, 259*t*
Class C misdemeanors, 236, 237,
 259*t*
Clayton, Billy, 129, 148–149, 161
clemency power, 195–196, 254
Clements, William P.
 appointments of, 226
 leadership style of, 200
 Republican Party and, 17, 101,
  107, 108
 stay of execution by, 196–197
 terms as governor, 203
 and Toomey, 131
 veto use by, 191–192
Clinkscale, David, 137
Clinton, Bill, 72, 109, 272
Clinton, Hillary, 102–103
Coahuila y Tejas, 46
Coahuiltecan Indians, 7
coalition(s)
 definition of, 90, 278
 in municipal elections, 278–279
coalitional parties, 90
Coastal Plains, 18–19, 19*f*
"coat-tail effect," 247
codes, and criminal law, 233
coercive federalism, 42
COG. *See* councils of government
Coke, Richard, 12–13, 52
Collections Division, 212
college funding, 304, 323
colonists, 7–10
 Anglo, 8–10
 Hispanic, 7
Colquitt, Oscar Branch, 203
Comanche, 7
Combs, Susan, 215, 216*f,* 219
commerce
 interstate, 148
 intrastate, 148
commission(s). *See* boards and
 commissions
commissioner of agriculture,
 217–218
commissioner of general land
 office, 217, 218
Commissioners Court, 286
commission government,
 277*t*–278*t,* 278
Commission on Law
 Enforcement, Texas, 257
committees, legislature, 130–131,
 156, 165–170
 action on bills, 171–172
 appointment to, 158–159,
  162–163
 chairs of, 168
 conference, 158, 167–168, 173
 efficiency of, 165

committees, legislature (*continued*)
  expertise of, 165–166
  House, 162–163, 165–170
  interim, 168
  jurisdiction of, 158–159
  lieutenant governor and, 158–159
  limited seniority system in House and, 162–163
  methods of, 168–170
  procedural, 166–167
  Senate, 158–159, 165–170
  Speaker of House and, 162–163
  special, 167–168
  staffs of, 169–170
  standing, 166–167, 167*t*
  subcommittees of, 169
  substantive, 166
Common Cause, 125, 137, 145*n*13
communication, with legislators, 179–180
community-based policing (CPB), 258–259
community colleges, 292, 323
commutation of sentences, 195–196, 256
comptroller of public accounts, 189, 215–217
  budgetary role of, 171, 178, 215–217, 303–304
  information from, 302
  review power of, 215–216
  in Texas constitution, 218
  treasurer's duties assumed by, 216
  Unclaimed Properties Division of, 216–217
computers, for voting, 71*f*
concealed handguns, 176, 300–302, 326–327
Confederacy, 11–14, 48, 99
conference committees, 158, 167–168, 173
Congress, U.S.
  enumerated powers of, 40
  legislature *vs.*, 148
  seniority in, 16
  Texas governor and, 199
Connally, John, 203, 211, 219
Conner, Geoffrey, 219
conquistadores, 6
conservatism, 29–30
conservatives
  in Democratic Party, 100–101, 103, 111
  in legislature, 178–179
  lottery opposition from, 320
  in Republican Party, 110–112
  tax position of, 314
constable, 257–258
constituents, and legislature, 179–180
constitution(s)
  definition of, 39
  purpose of, 39
Constitution, Texas, 46–60
  1836 (Republic of Texas), 46, 54, 213
  1846, 46–47, 54
  1861, 48
  1866, 48

1869, 48–53
1876 (current), 53–56
  amendments to, 45, 45*t*, 57, 57*f*
  Bill of Rights in, 54–56, 213, 263, 264
  clemency powers in, 196
  Closer Look, 31, 56, 69, 111, 119, 148, 196, 218, 241, 263, 275, 303
  counties in, 284, 286, 289–290
  court system in, 237, 239, 241, 243
  death penalty in, 242
  eminent domain in, 282
  executive branch in, 53–54, 185–186, 218
  governor in, 185–186, 189
  Grange influence on, 53, 57, 185–186
  home rule in, 275
  independent school districts in, 291
  interest groups in, 119, 138
  legislative law in, 45
  legislature in, 53–54, 148, 149, 153, 157
  length of, 44
  limits on government power in, 54
  as model of disarray, 57–58
  political parties in, 111
  state budget in, 53, 54, 303
  suffrage in, 69
  Web site for, 56
  chronology of, 34*f*–35*f*
Coahuila y Tejas, 46
  revision of, 57–60
  Constitutional Convention of 1974 and, 58–59, 59*f*
  need for, 57–58
  obstacles to, 60
  prospects for, 59–60
Constitution, U.S.
  amendments to, 39–40
  federalism in, 36–39
  interstate relations in, 37, 38
  length of, 44
  limits on states in, 37
constitution(s), state, 44–45
  amendments to, 45, 45*t*
  effective dates of, 44, 44*t*
  legislative law in, 44–45
  lengths of, 44, 44*t*
  structure of, 44–45
Constitutional Convention of 1866, 12
Constitutional Convention of 1868, 48–49
Constitutional Convention of 1869, 12
Constitutional Convention of 1875, 35, 47*f*, 53, 185
Constitutional Convention of 1974, 58–59, 59*f*
constitutional county courts, 235*f*, 239
constitutional republic, 39
Consumer Protection Division, 211
contraband, 261

contribution limits, for campaigns, 82–83, 85
conventions, constitutional
  of 1866, 12
  of 1868, 48–49
  of 1869, 12
  of 1875, 35, 47*f*, 53, 185
  of 1974, 58–59, 59*f*
conventions, party, 92–94, 93*f*
  county or district, 93–94, 93*f*, 96*f*
  precinct, 92–93, 93*f*
  resolutions of, 92
  state, 93*f*, 94
Cook, Charlie, 160
cooperative federalism, 42
Cornyn, John, 27, 109, 212
Coronado, Francisco Vásquez de, 6, 6*f*
corrections system, 253–256, 326
Corsicana oil field, 22
cotton
  growing region for, 20
  history of production, 21, 22
  "Cotton Capital," 20
council-manager government, 277, 277*t*–278*t*
councils of government (COG), 292, 293*f*
counsel, right to, 259
county attorney, 286–287
county auditor, 288
county chair, of party, 95*f*, 96–97
county clerk, 287
county conventions, 93–94, 93*f*
county court-at-law, 235*f*, 239
county courts, 235*f*, 239
county executive committee, 95*f*, 97
county government, 284–290
  Commissioners Court in, 286
  criticism and reform of, 289–290
  elected offices in, 286–288
  finance in, 288
  structure of, 285–286
  in Texas Constitution, 284, 286, 289–290
county law enforcement, 257–258, 287
county manager, 289
county treasurer, 288
court fees, 281
court of appeals, 235*f*
Court of Criminal Appeals, 235*f*, 241–242
  attorney general and, 212
  death penalty review by, 240, 242
  proposed abolition of, 246
courts, federal, orders from, 41–42, 305
courts, in Texas, 230–247, 235*f*
  appellate, 232, 234–236, 235*f*, 240–242, 240*f*
  county, 235*f*, 239
  district, 235*f*, 239–240
  jurisdiction of, 232
  justice, 235*f*, 237–238
  municipal, 235*f*, 236–237, 243
  in policy-making, 242–243, 298
  of record *vs.* nonrecord, 236–237

reform of, call for, 246–247
selection of judges, 243–244, 244*t*, 247
structure of system, 234–236, 235*f*
trial, 232, 234–240, 235*f*
cowboy image, 8*f*, 29
CPB. *See* community-based policing
Craddick, Tom, 164*f*
  heavy-handed tactics of, 163, 164
  Perry's endorsement of, 200
  Republican Party and, 68, 107, 157, 162, 164
  resignation as speaker, 165
  revolt against (2007), 163, 164–165
  selection as Speaker of House, 68, 162, 182*n*13, 200
crime(s)
  capital, in Texas, 255
  classification of, 259, 259*t*
  index, 252, 262
  rate of, factors in, 253
  reporting of, 252
  in Texas, 252–253
crime and punishment, 251–259
  chronology of, 250*f*–251*f*
  concern over, 252
  corrections system in, 253–256
  due process in, 259–267
  law enforcement in, 256–259
  legislative action on, 2009, 176
  Texas Penal Code in, 233, 259, 259*t*
Crime in the United States (FBI), 252
Criminal Jurisprudence Committee, House, 166
Criminal Justice, Texas Department of, 326
Criminal Justice Division, 201
criminal law, 233–234
  burden of proof in, 233
  civil law *vs.*, 233–234, 233*t*
  definition of, 233
cruel and unusual punishment, 259
Crystal City, 19
Cuellar, Henry, 219
culture, political. *See* political culture
Cuney, Norris Wright, 50–51

D
Daiell, Jeff, 76
Dallas
  form of government, 277
  location of, 19
  population of, 25
Dallas Cowboys, 283*f*
Dallas Independent School District (DISD), 290
Daniel, Price, 203
Daniel, Price, Jr., 105–106, 214
Davis, Anne Elizabeth Britton, 52
Davis, Edmund J. "E. J.", 12–14, 49–53, 52*f*
  diversity of thought, 52
  and Obnoxious Acts, 51

reaction against, 14, 51, 56, 185
and Republican Party, 12–14,
17, 103
death penalty. *See* capital punishment
Deaton, Charles, 134
debt, imprisonment for, 263
decentralized bureaucracy, 222
decentralized interest groups,
121–122
Declaration of Independence
(Texas), 10, 27, 46
dedicated funds, 304–305, 305*f*
de facto segregation, 16
defendant, 232
defense manufacturing, 23
de jure segregation, 16
Delaware, constitution of, 45
DeLay, Tom, 155, 200
Delco, Wilhelmina, 28
delegates, to party conventions,
92–94
democracy
Jacksonian, 47–48
pure, 39
Democratic Party, 99–103
affiliation with, personal explanation of, 98–99
Clinton (Hillary) and, 102–103
dominance of, 99–101, 103
challenges to and demise of,
17, 89, 101–110
Reconstruction and, 14,
51–53
and seniority in Congress, 16
factions in, 99–101, 111
foundations of, 99
general elections and, 75–76
governor as leader of, 197
Johnson and, 100, 103–106
in legislature, 112–113,
150–151, 155–157,
178–179
liberals *vs.* conservatives in,
100–101, 103, 111–112
minority support for, 101, 112
in new millennium, 110–113
Obama and, 102–103
platform of, 91, 94, 102
primaries and, 66–67, 75
Reconstruction and, 12–14,
48–53, 99, 103
and redistricting, 112, 155–157
retrenchment of, 101–103
Web site of, 94, 103
Democrats of Texas, 100–101
demographics, 24–28
population distribution, 25–26,
26*t*
population diversity, 26–28, 26*f*
population growth, 24–25, 25*t*
population size, 24
demonstrations, 135*f*, 136
Department of Agriculture, Texas,
218
Department of Criminal Justice,
Texas, 253
Department of Economic
Development, Texas, 326
Department of Health, 224
Department of Human Services,
224

Department of Public Safety
(DPS), 257, 326
Department of Transportation,
Texas, 225, 325
departments, state. *See also specific
departments*
interest groups and, 136–137,
140–142
iron triangle and, 140–142,
141*f*
legislature and, 177
Depression, 16, 38, 42
deputy registrar, voter, 69
deregulation, 24
Dershowitz, Alan, 251, 254
de Soto, Hernando, 6
devolution, 43, 80
Dewhurst, David, 161*f*, 210*f*, 217*f*
and budget, 308
elections as lieutenant governor
(2002, 2006), 161, 163,
209–210
and redistricting, 112–113,
155–156
and Republican Party, 112–113,
163
direct mail, 79–80
disaster preparedness, 176
discrimination, 16, 27, 48
DISD. *See* Dallas Independent
School District
disfranchised, 72
distributive policy, 299, 299*f*
district attorney, 286–287
district clerk, 78–80, 287
district conventions, 93–94, 93*f*,
96*f*
district courts, 235*f*, 239–240
districts, judicial, 246
districts, legislative
apportionment of, 151–157
battle over, 2003, 112, 155–157
gerrymandering of, 154–157
House, 153–154, 154*f*
multimember, 153–154
"one person, one vote" and,
152–154
redistricting of, 112–113,
151–157
Senate, 153, 153*f*
single-member, 151, 153–154
districts, municipal, 279
districts, special, 290–292
definition of, 290
education, 290, 291–292
governmental character of, 290
independence of, 290
law enforcement, 258
nature of, 291
recognized existence of,
290–291
taxes of, 309
types of, 291–292
diversity, 4, 26–28, 26*f*, 30–31
early, in Texas, 50–51
in elections (Jordan, Barbara),
68
in executive branch, 219
gender (Richards, Ann), 201,
201*f*
in judicial system, 245–246
in local government, 272

in local government (Cisneros,
Henry), 272, 272*f*
of thought (Davis, E. J.), 52
division, of Texas, 19, 49
doctors
interest groups of, 123
sales tax on, 317
Dole, Bob, 72
double jeopardy, 55, 264
down-ballot races, 78–80, 108
DPS. *See* Department of Public
Safety
Draughon, Martin Allen,
265–266
driving while intoxicated (DWI),
125, 226, 233
drop-off factor, in local elections,
79
Drug Enforcement
Administration, 256
drug task forces, 258
drunk driving, 125, 226, 233
dual federalism, 42
dual-primary bill, 159–160
due process, 40, 259–267
arrest, 261
definition of, 259
grand jury and indictment,
262–263
search and seizure, 260–261
stages of, 261–262
trial, 263–267
dues, for interest groups, 138
Dukakis, Michael, 108
DWI. *See* driving while intoxicated

E

early voting, 74
economic conservatives, 111
economic development
eminent domain for, 282–283
state expenditures on, 321,
325–326
Economic Development, Texas
Department of, 326
economic development corporations, 284
economic development tax, 281
economy, 21–24
confidence in, 23–24
education and, 24
first stage of (take it, extraction), 21–23
second stage of (make it, manufacturing), 23
third stage of (serve it, service),
23–24
education
boards of
local, 292
state, 223–224
and economy, 24
federalism and, 36
funding of, 298, 304, 310–311,
313–314, 321–323
classroom *vs.* administration
in, 322
debate over, 321–322
Permanent School Fund and,
49, 217
Permanent University Fund
and, 60, 304

Texas Supreme Court ruling
on, 298, 310–311, 322
total costs of, 321
interest groups and, 118, 121,
123, 125, 130, 136,
141–142
legislative action on, 2009, 176
reform of
Bush (George W.) and, 191
Perry and, 194–195, 322
Richards and, 57
White and, 190
special districts in, 290,
291–292
and voter turnout, 70
Education Agency, Texas, 136,
141–142, 223–224, 322
Education Code, 233
Education Committee, Senate,
166
Edwards Plateau, 19*f*, 20
Eisenhower, Dwight, 103
Elazar, Daniel J., 28–29
elected boards and commissions,
223–225
elected offices, in counties,
286–288
elected offices, in political parties,
92, 95–97, 95*f*
county, 95*f*, 96–97
precinct, 95–96, 95*f*
state, 95*f*, 97
elected officials, in executive
branch, 209–219
election(s), types of, 75–77. *See
also specific types*
election burnout, 73
election campaigns, 81–85, 81*f*
advertising in, 83
distance factor in, 81–82
emotional costs of, 80, 84
financing for, 80, 81–85,
139–140, 139*t*
for local offices, 78–80
negative *vs.* positive, 84–85
Elections Code, 233
El Paso, eminent domain in,
283
Emancipation Proclamation, 13
emergency clause, and reading of
bills, 170
eminent domain, 282–283, 283*f*
Emory, Bill, 138
employee groups, municipal, 279,
280
en-banc, 242
Enron, 23
enumerated powers, of Congress,
40
environmental interest groups,
125
equal protection, 40, 259
Equal Rights Amendment, 54
Ethics Commission, Texas, 81,
128, 137–138, 145*n*14
ethnic groups, in municipal elections, 279–280
ethnic interest groups, 124
exceptionalism, Texas, 11
exclusionary rule, 259, 260–261
executions, in Texas, 196–197,
254–256, 255*f*

executive branch. *See also specific offices*
  appointed offices of, 220
  bureaucracy in, 206*f*–207*f*,
    220–226
  diversity in, increasing, 219
  elected officials in, 209–219
  governor's powers in, 187–188
  plural nature of, 185–186, 189,
    207–220, 209*f*
  public policy produced in, 298
  purpose of, 187
  reform of, options for, 202–203
  in Texas Constitution, 53–54,
    185–186, 218
executive committee
  county, 95*f*, 97
  state, 95*f*, 97
executive powers, of governor,
  187–188
ex officio positions
  of lieutenant governor, 159,
    306
  of Speaker of the House, 163,
    306
expenditures, state, 321–327
  for big three, 321–326
  in budget, 2011-2012, 322*f*
  business and economic devel-
    opment, 321, 325–326
  comparison with other states,
    321, 326*t*
  education, 298, 321–323
  health and human services,
    321, 323–325
  per capita, 321, 326*t*
  political culture and, 297, 304
expertise
  of bureaucracy, 222
  of legislative committees,
    165–166
explorers
  French, 6–7
  Spanish, 5–6, 6*f*
extractive economies, 21–23

F

factions
  definition of, 99
  in Democratic Party, 99–101, 111
  interest groups and, 119
  in Republican Party, 111
fair market value, in eminent
  domain, 282
family tradition, and voting,
  70–71, 72
Farabee, Ray, 129, 132
farmer, agriculture commissioner
  as, 218
"Farmer Jim." *See* Ferguson, James
  E. "Jim, Pa"
Farmers' Alliance, 100
fast-food companies, state action
  against, 212
Father's Day Massacre, 142, 193,
  199, 200
Federal Bureau of Investigation
  (FBI), 252, 256
Federal Economic Stabilization
  Funding Committee, 179
federal funding, 40–44
  for counties, 288

state revenue from, 318–319, 318*f*
  for traffic enforcement, 284
federalism, 36–44. *See also*
    Inside the Federalist
    System
  application of, 36–37
  budgetary powers in, 40–44
  coercive, 42
  cooperative, 42
  definition of, 36
  devolution in, 43, 80
  dual, 42
  history of, 42
  mandates and, 43–44
  national gains in, 38, 39–40
  new, 42
  "new" new, 42–44
  shared powers in, 38–39
  in U.S. Constitution, 36–39
Federalist No. 10, 119
fees, revenue from, 319
felonies, 259*t*
Ferguson, H. C., 51
Ferguson, James E. "Jim, Pa," 15,
  198, 198*f*
  Democratic Party and, 100
  gubernatorial powers reduced
    after, 196
  impeachment of, 15, 33*n*14, 198
  and University of Texas, 15,
    198, 223
  years of gubernatorial term, 203
Ferguson, Miriam "Ma," 15–16,
  100, 196, 198, 201, 203
Fields, Jack, 77
Fifteenth Amendment, U.S.,
  39–40, 66
Fifth Amendment, U.S., 264
filibustering, 172
filing statements, 193
finance (financing)
  campaign, 80, 81–85, 139–140,
    139*t*
  county, 288
  cycles in, 297–298
  interest group, 138–140
  mandates and, 43–44, 305
  municipal, 280–284
  special district, 290
  state, 296–298, 302–326.
    See also budget, Texas;
    expenditures, state;
    revenue, state
Finance Committee, Senate, 166,
  171, 175, 306
firework sales, 289*f*
First Amendment, U.S., 40
Fiscal Notes, 302
Fisher, Richard, 77
flag burning, as free speech, 40
floor action, on bill, 172–175
Folklife Festival, 27
food stamps, 324–325
football, high school, 108
Ford, Gerald, 223
formal contacts, of lobbyists,
  130–131
formal powers, of governor, 187
Fort Worth
  crime district tax in, 281
  form of government, 277
  location of, 19

Foundation School Program, 291
Fourteenth Amendment, U.S.,
  40, 41, 48
Fourth Amendment, U.S., 261
Fox, Vicente, 199
franchise tax, 281, 309, 310–311,
  310*f*
fraud, voter, 74
Freedom of Information Act, 214
Freedom of Information Center,
  214
French explorers, 6–7
frontier, 14–15
fruits of a crime, 261
Fuller, Franklin, 198
full faith and credit, 38

G

Galveston, form of government,
  278
gambling, 29, 45, 126*f*, 315–317
game wardens, 224
Garcia, Hector P., 16
Garner, John Nance, 16, 100
Garza, Tony, 219, 219*f*
gasoline tax, 298, 299, 304, 310*f*,
  311–312, 317
gay and lesbian groups, 125
gender diversity, Richards and,
  201, 201*f*
general election, 75–76
general government, expenditures
  on, 326
general law, 274
general obligation bonds, 281
General Services Commission,
  201, 219
geographic center, of Texas, 18
geography
  regions of Texas, 18–21, 19*f*
  size of Texas, 18, 18*f*
Georgia, constitutions of, 46
German settlers, 10, 11, 20
gerrymandering, 68, 109,
  154–157
"Give Them a Break Laws," 301
Gonzales, Alberto, 219
Gonzales, Henry B., 105
Gonzales, Raul, 111
Gonzales v. Raich, 43
Gonzalez, Raul, 27
GOP. *See* Republican Party
government
  definition of, 3–4
  distrust/trust in, 29
  open, 213–215
  politics *vs.*, 3–4
  as watchdog, 213
governor(s), 184–204. *See also specific governors*
  appointment powers of, 187,
    188–189, 202
  budgetary powers of, 194–195,
    203, 306
  chronology of, 184*f*–185*f*
  clemency power of, 195–196
  election of, 76
    campaign spending in, 186
    campaign themes in, 185
  executive powers of, 187–188
  expectations for v. reality, 186
  formal powers of, 187

impeachment of, 15, 33*n*14, 198
informal powers of, 186,
  197–200
international relations of, 199
judicial powers of, 195–197,
  243, 244*t*
law enforcement powers of, 189
leadership style of, 200
legislative powers of, 173–175,
  178, 190–191, 191–193
as liaison to Congress, 199
limited powers of, 187, 187*t*
listing, since 1899, 203
message power of, 191
military power of, 189
Mueller's scale of powers, 187,
  187*t*, 191
as partisan leader, 197
persuasive power of, 197–199
plural executive and, 185–186,
  189
qualifications of, 186
reform of office, options for,
  202–203
salary of, 186
session-calling power of, 149,
  190–191
staff of, 201–202
successor to, 43, 160, 209
terms of, 186
in Texas Constitution, 53–54,
  186, 189, 218
veto power of, 142, 175,
  191–193, 193*f*
Web site of, 186
Gramm, Phil, 108
grand jury, 262–263
Grand Old Party. *See* Republican
  Party
Grand Prairie, 19
Grange
  definition of, 53
  and Democratic Party, 100
  and Texas Constitution, 53, 57,
    185–186
Granger, Gordon, 13
Grant, Ulysses S., 52
grants, federal, 40–44, 215, 288,
  318–319, 318*f*
Great Society, 16–17, 42
Green Party, 76, 91, 94, 99
Grovey v. Townsend, 66
Guadalupe Peak, 21
Gulf Lowlands, 18–19, 19*f*

H

Haggerman, Amber, 300
Hall County, 20
Hamilton, A. J., 49
handguns, concealed, 176,
  300–302, 326–327
Harris County, trilingual ballots
  in, 72
Headstart, 201
Health, Department of, 224
health, legislative action on, 2009,
  176
Health and Human Services
  Commission, 201, 224–225
Health and Human Services
  expenditures, 321,
  323–325

Heath, Richard, 188
helmet law, 136
Herrera, Leonel, 197, 254
hierarchy
    in bureaucracy, 222
    definition of, 222
Higher Education Committee,
    House, 166
higher education funding, 304,
    323
High Plains, 19*f*, 20–21
Hightower, Jim, 91
Highway Department, 225
highway funding, 41, 122, 129*f*,
    325
Highway Patrol, 257
Hill, John, 107
hired guns, 129, 133
Hispanic Texans
    civil rights of, 16, 49
    colonists, 7
    discrimination against, 16, 27
    gubernatorial appointments of,
        188, 219
    interest groups of, 124
    in judicial system, 246
    language barriers for, 72
    in legislature, 151
    political offices held by, 27,
        151, 219, 246, 272
    political party support from, 101
    population of, 26*f*, 27
    redistricting and, 154
    in Republic of Texas, 11
    in Texas Revolution, 9
    voter turnout of, 70, 71*f*, 72
    voting rights of, 49
history, Texas, 2*f*–3*f*, 5–17. *See also
    specific events and individu-
    als*
Hobbes, Thomas, 11
Hobby, Bill, 108, 157, 158,
    159–160
Hobby, William Pettus, 198, 203
Hogg, James Stephen, 14–15, 100
Hollywood Park, 316
home rule, 274–276, 280,
    289–290
Hopwood v. *Texas,* 323
horse racing, 315–317, 317*f*
hotel and motel tax, 305, 313
House of Representatives, Texas.
    See also legislature
    "chubbing" in, 172
    committees of, 165–170
        appointment to, 162–163
        procedural, 166–167
        special, 167–168
        standing, 166–167, 167*t*
        substantive, 166
    demographic makeup of,
        150–151
    districts for, 153–154, 154*f*
    floor action in, 172–175
    limited seniority system in,
        162–163
    membership of, 149–150
    political parties in, 112–113,
        150–151
    presiding officer of, 157,
        161–163. *See also* Speaker
        of the House, Texas

qualifications for, 149
salary in, 150
structure of, 149
terms in, 149
Houston
    form of government, 276
    population of, 25
Houston, Sam, 9–11, 46, 46*f*
Houston Ship Channel, 22
HPV immunization, 178
Hughes and Luce (law firm), 130
human papillomavirus (HPV)
    immunization, 178
Human Services, Department of,
    224
hung jury, 264
Hurst, eminent domain in,
    282–283
Hutchison, Kay Bailey, 77, 77*f*,
    109, 199

I

ICC. *See* Interstate Commerce
    Commission
identification, required for voting,
    74, 112, 172, 176
ideological parties, 90–91
Illinois, special districts in, 291
impeachment, of Ferguson, 15,
    33*n*14, 198
incentives, financial or tax, 284
income tax
    lack of, in Texas, 142, 314
    as progressive tax, 309, 309*t*
independent school district (ISD),
    290, 291–292
index crimes, 252, 262
Indians. *See* Native Americans
indictment, 262–263
individualistic culture, 29, 30, 31,
    35
    and budget, 304
    and business interests, 122
    and capital punishment, 255
    and election of judges, 243
    and frontier, 14
    and mass transit, 291*f*
informal contacts, of lobbyists,
    134–135
informal powers, of governor, 186,
    197–200
information, for legislature, 127,
    177
information dissemination, by
    interest groups, 127
inheritance tax, 313
Inside the Federalist System
    Bill of Rights, Texas *vs.* U.S.,
        55
    cabinet *vs.* plural executive, 208
    campaign contribution limits,
        82–83
    federal funds for traffic
        enforcement, 284
    federal stimulus money (2009),
        179, 319
    interest groups (lobbyists), 128
    justices of Texas Supreme
        Court, 244
    party platforms, 102
    presidential *vs.* gubernatorial
        veto, 192

Reconstruction-era governor,
    12–13
search and seizure, 260
unemployment funds, 319
Institute of Texan Cultures, 27
insurance commissioner, 220
insurance tax, 310*f*, 313
interest groups, 9, 116–143
    access for, 128
    activities specifically prohibited
        for, 138
    amorphous, 122
    business, 122–123, 129*f*
    centralized, 121
    choices multiplied by, 119–120
    chronology of, 116*f*–117*f*
    clash among, 123–124
    decentralized, 121–122
    definition of, 118
    divisiveness of, 120
    ethics of, 128, 134, 137–138
    external funding for, 139–140
    focus of, 118
    information dissemination by,
        127
    interim oversight by, 136–137
    internal funding for, 138
    in iron triangle, 140–142, 141*f*
    legislature and, 117, 126–138,
        126*f*, 177–178
    membership mobilization by,
        135–136, 135*f*
    methods of, 126–138
    money and, 138–140
    negative effects of, 120–121,
        120*f*
    organizational structure of,
        121–122
    participation in, 142
    perceptions of, 117
    persuasion by, 118
    political parties *vs.*, 118
    positive effects of, 119–120
    regulation of, 134, 137–138
    roles of, 118–121
    single-issue, 118, 124–125
    spontaneous activity of, 122
    Texas Constitution and, 119,
        138
    types of, 121–125
    unequal representation by, 120*f*,
        121
    voices magnified by, 119
interest income, for state, 319
interim committee, 168
intermediate courts of appeal,
    240–241, 240*f*
international relations, of gover-
    nor, 199
Internet
    campaigning via, 80, 83, 84
    voting via, 74
interstate commerce, regulation
    of, 148
Interstate Commerce
    Commission (ICC), 223
interstate relations, U.S.
    Constitution on, 37, 38
intrastate commerce, regulation
    of, 148
investment income, for state, 319
iron triangle, 140–142, 141*f*

ISD. *See* independent school dis-
    trict
Ivins, Molly, 297

J

Jackson, Andrew, 48
Jacksonian democracy, 47–48
jails and prisons, 253–256
Jefferson, Wallace B., 28, 242,
    245, 245*f*
Jester, Beauford H., 203
Johnson, Gregory Lee, 40
Johnson, Lyndon
    and Democratic Party, 100,
        103–106
    as president, 16–17, 42
    as U.S. senator, 16
Jones, Clayton, 160
Jones, Elizabeth, 223
Jones, Gene, 160
Jones, Jerry, 283*f*
Jordan, Barbara, 28, 67, 68
JP. *See* justice of the peace
judges
    bench trial by, 263
    municipal, 236
    selection of, 243–244, 244*t*, 247
judicial activism, 242–243
judicial review, 39
judicial system, 230–247. *See also*
    courts, in Texas
    chronology of, 230*f*–231*f*
    constitutional revision and,
        60
    corrections in, 253–256
    crime and punishment in,
        250*f*–251*f*, 251–259
    criticism of, 231
    diversity in, 245–246
    due process in, 259–267
    governor and, 195–197, 243,
        244*t*
    law enforcement in, 256–259
    purpose of, 231
    reform of, call for, 246–247
    selection of judges, 243–244,
        244*t*, 247
    in Texas Constitution,
        53–54
Junell, Rob, 60
Juneteenth celebration, 13
jurisdiction
    of courts, 232
    definition of, 232
    original, 232, 234
    of legislative committee,
        158–159
jury
    grand, 262–263
    hung, 264
    selection of, 264
    trial by, 259, 263
jury duty
    eligibility for, 264
    exemption from, 264
    voter registration and, 73,
        263–264
justice, concept of, 231, 247
justice courts, 235*f*, 237–238
justice of the peace, 237–238
justices, Texas Supreme Court,
    242, 244

K

Kelley, Russell "Rusty," 129
Kennedy, John F., 16, 105, 106
Kentucky, constitution of, 45
Kilgarlin, Bill, 153
Killer Bees, 159–160
Kirk, Ron, 28, 101, 219
Know-Nothing Party, 99
Krueger, Bob, 76–77, 107
Ku Klux Klan, 16, 198

L

labor unions
  interest groups of, 123
  membership in, 30
  political party support from, 101
Lamar, Mirabeau Buonaparte,
    10–11
land commissioner, 217, 218
land grants, 8
Laney, Pete, 112, 162, 178
Lanham, S. W. T., 203
La Salle, Robert de (René-Robert
    Cavelier, Sieur de La
    Salle), 2f, 6–7
Lasswell, Harold, 33n1
law enforcement, 256–259
  county, 257–258, 287
  governor's power in, 189
  local, 258–259
  professionalism in, 257, 258
  special district, 258
  state, 257
  traffic, federal funds for, 284
lawyers
  county, district attorney as,
    286–287
  interest groups of, 123
  as legislators, 151
  as lobbyists, 129–130, 132–133
  right to have, 259
  sales tax on, 317
  state, attorney general as, 210
LBB. *See* Legislative Budget
    Board
leadership style, of governors, 200
League of United Latin American
    Citizens (LULAC), 124
League of Women Voters, 125,
    145n13
Legislative Black Caucus, 179
Legislative Budget Board (LBB),
    169f, 177, 195, 306
  Higher Education
    Coordinating Board and,
    225
  lieutenant governor on, 159,
    209, 306
  performance review by, 216
  Speaker of the House on, 163,
    306
Legislative Clipping Service, 177
legislative law, in state constitu-
    tions, 44–45
Legislative Office, 202
Legislative Redistricting Board,
    154, 155, 162
Legislative Reference Library, 177
legislature, 146–180
  bicameral, 149
  biennial, 53, 54, 126–127, 149,
    152f, 192

budgetary role of, 178, 302–306
committees of, 130–131, 156,
    162, 165–170
  action on bills, 171–172
  appointment to, 158–159,
    162–163
  chairs of, 168
  conference, 158, 167–168, 173
  efficiency of, 165
  expertise of, 165–166
  House, 162–163, 165–170
  interim, 168
  jurisdiction of, 158–159
  lieutenant governor and,
    158–159
  limited seniority system in
    House and, 162–163
  methods of, 168–170
  procedural, 166–167
  Senate, 158–159, 165–170
  Speaker of House and,
    162–163
  special, 167–168
  staffs of, 169–170
  standing, 166–167, 167t
  subcommittees of, 169
  substantive, 166
Congress *vs.*, 148
constituents and, 179–180
criticism of, as easy option,
    150f
demographic makeup of,
    150–151
districts for
  apportionment of, 151–157
  battle over, 2003, 155–157
  gerrymandering of, 154–157
  House, 153–154, 154f
  multimember, 153–154
  "one person, one vote" and,
    152–154
  redistricting of, 112–113,
    151–157
  Senate, 153, 153f
  single-member, 151,
    153–154
ego of members, 157
expenditure for operations of,
    326
floor action in, 172–175
gubernatorial address to, 191
information for, need for, 127,
    177
interest groups and, 117,
    126–138, 126f, 177–178
  access of, 128
  establishing link between,
    128–130
  ethics of, 128, 134, 137–138
  formal contacts between,
    130–131
  informal contacts between,
    134–135
  information dissemination
    by, 127
  interim oversight by,
    136–137
  in iron triangle, 140–142,
    141f
  membership mobilization by,
    135–136, 135f
  regulation of, 134, 137–138

Killer Bees and, 159–160
lawmaking in, 147–149
  bills passed in 2009 session,
    176
  conference committees and,
    158, 167–168, 172–173
  governor's power in,
    173–175, 178, 190–193,
    194f
  procedures and scheduling
    in, 166–167, 171–172
  process of, 170–175, 174f
membership of, 149–150
methods of operation, 126–127
milestones in history of,
    146f–147f
in political arena, 177–179
political parties in, 112–113,
    150–151, 163–164,
    178–179
presiding officers of, 157–163
primacy of, 147, 148
privileges of members, 150
qualifications for, 149–150
quorum in, 112, 156, 159–160
regular sessions of, 149
salaries in, 150
special sessions of, 149,
    190–191, 200
and state agencies, 177,
    222–223
structure of, 149
support for, 177–178
"team" in, 162, 163–165
terms in, 149–150
in Texas Constitution, 53–54,
    148, 149, 153, 157
volume of work for, 126–127,
    152f
Web site of, 147, 177
Leland, Mickey, 28
Lewis, Gib, 128, 161–162,
    262–263
"Lexington of Texas," 9
liberals, in Democratic Party,
    100–101, 103, 111–112
libertarian conservatives, 111
Libertarian Party, 75, 76, 91
licenses, revenue from, 319
licensing boards, 225
lieutenant governor, 157–161,
    209–210
  Bullock as, 211, 211f
  committee control by, 158–159
  election of, 157
  ex officio positions of, 159, 306
  on Legislative Budget Board,
    159, 209, 306
  powers of, 157–158, 209
  recognition from, 158
  salary of, 157
  as successor to governor, 160,
    209
  on Sunset Advisory
    Commission, 159, 226
  "team" for, 163–165
  term of, 157
  in Texas constitution, 218
  Web site of, 210
life and death questions, in capital
    punishment, 255–256
limited seniority system, 162–163

Lincoln, Abraham, 12, 13
line-item veto, 194–195
Llano Uplift, 19f, 20
lobbyist(s), 120f, 128–138,
    177–178
  access for, 128
  activities specifically prohibited
    for, 138
  definition of, 128
  ethics of, 128, 134, 137–138
  federal *vs.* Texas, 128
  formal contacts of, 130–131
  former legislators as, 129
  former staff members as, 129
  as hired guns, 129, 133
  informal contacts of, 134–135
  interim oversight by, 136–137
  in iron triangle, 140–142, 141f
  lawyers as, 129–130, 132–133
  Legislative Office as, 202
  money and, 138–140
  My Turn on (Christian, George
    Scott), 132–133
  registration of, 128
  regulation of, 134, 137–138
  Texas Mosaic on (Toomey,
    Mike), 131
local courts, 235f
local elections, 78–80, 108
  municipal, 278–280
  voter turnout for, 271–272
local government, 270–293
  definition of, 271
  diversity in, 272
  history of, 270f–271f
  as launch for political careers,
    272
  levels of, 274
  services of, 273
Lone Star Card, 324–325
Lone Star Park, 315–317, 317f
long ballot, 73, 289
lottery, state, 45, 320, 320f
Louisiana
  constitutions of, 46
  gambling in, 316–317
Louisiana Downs, 316–317
lowest unit rate (LUR), 83
Lubbock, form of government,
    277
Lucas, A. F., 15
LULAC. *See* League of United
    Latin American Citizens
LUR. *See* lowest unit rate
lynching, 51

M

MADD. *See* Mothers Against
    Drunk Driving
Madison, James, 90, 119
magnet schools, 224
mail
  campaigning via, 79–80, 83
  interest groups use of, 135–136
  voter registration via, 74
majority rule, constraints on, 35
MALDEF. *See* Mexican-
    American Legal Defense
    and Educational Fund
malpractice, 123
manager, city, 277
manager, county, 289

mandates, 43–44, 305
  definition of, 43, 305
  unfunded, 43–44, 305
Manifest Destiny, 11
manufacturing, 23
Marchant, Kenny, 157
marches, 135*f,* 136
margin tax, 311
marijuana, medical, 43
marital property, 58
Marketing and Agribusiness
    Development Division, 218
mark-up, of bills, 171
martial law, 189
Maryland, horse racing in, 316
mass transit, 291*f*
matching funds, 319
Mattox, Jim, 212
mayor(s)
  strong, 276
  weak, 276
mayor-council government, 276,
    277*t*–278*t*
McDaniel, Myra, 219
McDonald, "Captain Bill," 257
McGinnis, Lochridge, and
    Kilgore, 129–130
media, and governor, 197–199
Medicaid, 199, 299, 307*f,*
    318–319, 323–324
medical malpractice, 123
medical marijuana, 43
membership mobilization,
    135–136, 135*f*
mere evidence, 261
message power, of governors, 191
"messing with Texas," 108
Mexican-American Legal
    Defense and Educational
    Fund (MALDEF), 124
Mexican-American Legislative
    Caucus, 179
Mexico
  Anglo settlers and, 8–10
  republic of, founding of, 7
  revolution of (1810), 7
  Texan revolt against, 9–10
  Texas governors and, 199
"middle of the road," 91
Midland, 20
military power, of governor, 189
Miller, Laura, 276
misdemeanors
  Class A, 239, 259*t*
  Class B, 239, 259*t*
  Class C, 236, 237, 259*t*
missions, Spanish, 7
Mississippi
  gubernatorial power in, 187
  sales tax in, 309
Missouri Plan, for judicial reform,
    246
mobilization, by interest groups,
    135–136, 135*f*
monopolies, ban on, 211
Moody, Dan, 203
Morales, Dan, 27, 212
moralistic culture, 30
mortgage crisis (2008), 23
mosaic. *See also* Texas Mosaic
  definition of, 4
  Texas as, 4

Mothers Against Drunk Driving
    (MADD), 125, 145*n*11,
    226, 233
motorcyclists, helmet law for, 136
motor fuels tax, 298, 299, 304,
    310*f,* 311–312, 317
Motor Vehicle Board, 225
motor vehicle sales and rental tax,
    310, 310*f,* 312
motor voter law, 69–70, 71
mountain ranges, 21
"Move Over Law," 301
Mueller, Keith, 187
Mueller's scale, of gubernatorial
    powers, 187, 187*t,* 191
multiculturalism, 28
multimember districts, 153–154
municipal bonds, 281, 282*f*
municipal courts, 235*f,* 236–237,
    243
municipal elections, 278–280
  at-large system of, 279
  employee groups and, 279, 280
  ethnic groups and, 279–280
  group participation in, effects
    of, 279–280
  neighborhood associations and,
    279, 280
  place system of, 279
  single-member districts in,
    279–280
  types of, 279
municipal employee groups, 279,
    280
municipal government, 274–284
  budgets in, 283–284
  commission, 277*t*–278*t,* 278
  council-manager, 277,
    277*t*–278*t*
  finance in, 280–284
  forms of, 276–278
  mayor-council, 276, 277*t*–278*t*
municipalities, 274–284
  general law, 274
  home rule, 274–276, 280
  Texas cities with more than
    50,000 people, 275*f*
municipal police, 258–259
Mutscher, Gus, 162
My Turn, 31
  county government (Bagsby,
    Dionne), 285
  Death Row inmate (Draughon,
    Martin Allen), 265–266
  Democratic Party (Becker,
    Kelly), 98–99
  down-ballot races (Wilder,
    Tom), 78–80
  lobbyists and legislature
    (Christian, George Scott),
    132–133
  open government (Abbott,
    Greg), 213–214
  Republican Party (Barber,
    Joshua), 104–105

N

NAACP. *See* National Association
    for the Advancement of
    Colored People
NAFTA. *See* North American
    Free Trade Agreement

Naishtat, Elliott, 307*f*
National Association for the
    Advancement of Colored
    People (NAACP), 124
National Guard, 190*f,* 220
National Night Out, 252
National Rifle Association
    (NRA), 118, 124, 300
Native Americans
  frontier state and, 14–15
  Hispanic colonists and, 7
  Reconstruction and, 13
  Republic of Texas and, 11
  Spanish explorers and, 5–7, 6*f*
natural gas
  deposits of, 19
  Railroad Commission and, 223
  state revenue from, 304, 310*f,*
    312
Natural Resources Committee,
    162
Nature Conservancy, 125, 145*n*12
Navarro, José Antonio, 27
Navarro family, 9
Neff, Pat Morris, 203
negative campaigning, 84–85
neighborhood associations, 279,
    280
Neighborhood Watch, 252
Nevada, sales tax in, 309
New Deal, 100
new federalism, 42
"new" new federalism, 42–44
Newton, Sir Isaac, 17
Nineteenth Amendment, U.S.,
    40, 66
Nixon, Richard, 42, 107
Nixon v. *Herndon,* 66
no-bill (nonindictment), 262
nonindictment, 262
nonpartisan (special) election,
    76–77
nonpartisanship, in legislature,
    112, 163–164
nonrecord, courts of, 236–237
nontax revenue, state, 318–320,
    318*f*
no pass-no play rule, 108
Noriega, Rick, 27
North American Free Trade
    Agreement (NAFTA),
    199
Nowlin, James R., 214
NRA. *See* National Rifle
    Association

O

OAG. *See* Office of the Attorney
    General
Obama, Barack
  Democratic Party and, 102–103
  federal spending under, 43
  stimulus package of, 178, 179,
    308, 319
  Tea Party rally against, 135*f*
Obnoxious Acts, 51, 52
obscenity, definition of, 4
occupational licensing boards, 225
O'Daniel, W. Lee, 203
Odessa, 20
Office of Governmental
    Appointments, 202

Office of the Attorney General
    (OAG), 211–215
Ogallala aquifer, 20
oil
  collapse of industry (1970s and
    1980s), 17, 23
  Depression and, 16
  discovery of, 15, 22
  history of production, 21,
    22–23, 22*f*
  production region for, 20
  Railroad Commission and, 223
  Spindletop field, 15, 22, 22*f*
  state revenue from, 297–298,
    310*f,* 312, 312*f*
oil refineries, 22–23
Oklahoma
  capital punishment in, 254
  gaming competition in,
    316–317
O'Neill, Thomas "Tip," 271
one-party system, 99–101
  and down-ballot races, 79
  Reconstruction and, 14, 51–53,
    99
  Republican resurgence and, 17,
    89, 101–110
  and seniority in Congress, 16
  voter turnout in, 73
"one person, one vote," 152–154
OPEC. *See* Organization of
    Petroleum Exporting
    Countries
Open Meetings Law, 171, 212,
    213–215
open primary, 75
Open Records Act of 1973, 214
Opinion Committee, 212
ordinances
  county empowerment for, 289*f,*
    290
  definition of, 236
  violations of, 236
Oregon, voter registration in, 74
Organization of Petroleum
    Exporting Countries
    (OPEC), 17
original jurisdiction, 232, 234
O'Rourke, P. J., 207
outlawry, 263, 264
overlapping terms, on
    boards/commissions, 187,
    188–189
override, of gubernatorial veto,
    192
Overstreet, Morris, 27

P

Packwood, Robert, 74
PACs. *See* political action com-
    mittees
Padre Island, 18–19
Paine, Thomas, 102
Paluxy River, 119–120
Panhandle, 20
pardons, 195–196
Paredes, Raymund, 177
Parent Teacher Association
    (PTA), 118, 125
Parks, Ursula, 169*f*
Parks and Wildlife Commission,
    188

Parks and Wildlife Department, 224
parole, 195–196
participation, political. *See* political participation
parties. *See* political parties
Partners in Mobility, 129*f*
party caucus, 66
Patterson, Jerry, 217
Paynter, Suzii, 126*f*
peace bond, 237–238
Pease, Elisha M., 12
Penal Code, 233, 259, 259*t*
Pennzoil-Texaco conflict, 123
people's (justice) courts, 235*f*, 237–238
Permanent School Fund, 49, 217
Permanent University Fund (PUF), 60, 304
Permian Basin, 16, 20
permits, revenue from, 319
Perry, Rick
  as agriculture commissioner, 109
  as governor, 194*f*, 203
    appointments of, 188, 219, 245
    and budget, 194–195, 308
    and comptroller, 216
    and concealed handguns, 300
    and death penalty cases, 256
    election of (2002), 84, 186, 197
    and federal stimulus money, 179, 319
    international relations of, 199
    leadership style of, 200
    and legislature, 178, 194*f*, 199, 200
    media use by, 198
    persuasive power of, 199
    plural executive and, 189
    and redistricting battle, 156
    special sessions called by, 200
    as successor to Bush, 160
    and Toomey, 131
    veto use by, 142, 192, 193, 194–195, 200
  as lieutenant governor, 163, 164, 209–210
persuasive power, of governor, 197–199
Phillips, Tom, 245, 246
phone banks, 80, 84
Pickens, T. Boone, 20–21
pigeonholing, of bill, 171
Pimlico, 316
Piney Woods, 19, 19*f*
place system, in local elections, 279
plaintiff, 231
planks, of party platforms, 94
platform, 94
  definition of, 91
  of Democratic Party, 91, 94, 102
  of Republican Party, 94, 102
plea bargaining, 240
pledge cards, for Speaker of House, 161–162

plural executive, 185–186, 189, 207–220, 209*f*
  appointed offices of, 220
  cabinet system *vs.*, 202–203, 207, 208
  definition of, 207
  elected officials in, 209–219
  negative consequences of, 207–209
plurality
  definition of, 76
  in general elections, 76
"pole tax," 313
police. *See* law enforcement
policy. *See* public policy
Policy Office, 201, 202
political action committees (PACs), 139–140, 186
  with contributions of $250,000 or more, 139*t*
  definition of, 139
political culture, 28–31
  definition of, 28
  individualistic, 29, 30, 31, 35
    and budget, 304
    and business interests, 122
    and capital punishment, 255
    and election of judges, 243
    and frontier, 14
    and mass transit, 291*f*
  moralistic, 30
  and policy, 30–31
  traditionalistic, 29–30, 31, 35
    and capital punishment, 255
    and election of judges, 243
    and legislative districts, 154
    and voter turnout, 73
  types of, 28–30
political participation
  African American, in 19th century, 48–53
  in municipal elections, 279–280
  voter qualifications, 68–70
  voter registration, 69–70, 70*f*, 73–75
  voter turnout, 65, 70–75
  voting chronology, 64*f*–65*f*
  voting rights, 66–68
political parties, 88–113. *See also* Democratic Party; Republican Party
  African Americans and, 50–51
  chronology of, 88*f*–89*f*
  coalitional, 90
  conventions of, 92–94, 93*f*
    county or district, 93–94, 93*f*, 96*f*
    precinct, 92–93, 93*f*
    state, 93*f*, 94
  definition of, 90
  and down-ballot races, 79, 108
  elected offices of, 92, 95–97, 95*f*
    county, 95*f*, 96–97
    precinct, 95–96, 95*f*
    state, 95*f*, 97
  general elections and, 75–76
  governor as leader of, 197
  ideological, 90–91
  interest groups *vs.*, 118
  in judicial elections, 243, 246–247

in legislature, 112–113, 150–151, 155–157, 163–164, 178–179
local elections and, 79
Madison on, 90
in new millennium, 110–113
one-party system of, 99–101
  and down-ballot races, 79
  Reconstruction and, 14, 51–53, 99
  Republican resurgence and, 17, 89, 101–110
  and seniority in Congress, 16
  voter turnout in, 73
platforms of, 91, 94
primaries and, 66–67, 75
purpose of, 89
Reconstruction and, 12–14, 48–53, 103
and redistricting, 112, 155–157
structure of, 90–92
in Texas Constitution, 111
in Texas legislature, 112–113
third, 90–91
two-party system of, emergence of, 17, 89, 108
political science, 299
politics
  all as local, 271
  definition of, 3, 33*n*1
  as game, 89
  government *vs.*, 3–4
poll tax, 29, 40, 67
population, 24–28, 33*n*19
  distribution of, 25–26, 26*t*
  diversity of, 26–28, 26*f*
  growth of, 24–25, 25*t*
  size of, 24
Populist Party, 91
positive campaigning, 84–85
postadjournment veto, 192
Post Oaks and Prairies, 19, 19*f*
Preakness, 316
precinct, definition of, 92
precinct chair, of party, 95–96, 95*f*
precinct convention, 92–93, 93*f*
preponderance, of evidence, 233
President, in Republic of Texas, 46
president pro tempore, of Senate, 160
presiding officers, of legislature, 157–163
press, freedom of, 55
Price, John Wiley, 271
primary, 75
  dual, legislative dispute over, 159–160
  open, 75
  white, 29, 66–67
prisons, 253–256, 326
probable cause, 261
probate courts, 235*f*, 239
professional interests, 123–124
Progressive Era
  definition of, 14
  reforms of, 14–15, 66–67
Progressive Party, 91
progressive tax, 308–309, 309*t*
Prohibition, 16
prohibitive law, 233
Project Rescue, 125

property rights
  eminent domain *vs.*, 282–283
  marriage and, 58
property taxes, 280–281
  assessment of, 280, 287–288
  education funding from, 291–292, 310–311, 313–314, 322–323
  municipal revenue from, 280–281
  relief from, 311, 313–314
Property Tax Relief Fund, 311
prosecutor, 233, 286–287
protests, 135*f*, 136
public administration, 273
public assistance, low levels of, 30
Public Education Committee, House, 166
Public Information Act, 213–215
public policy, 298–302
  adoption of, 301
  agenda setting for, 300
  courts and, 242–243, 298
  definition of, 298
  distributive, 299, 299*f*
  as essence of government, 298
  evaluation of, 301–302
  fiscal, 303–326
  formulation of, 300–301
  implementation of, 301
  model of, 300–302
  nonfiscal, 326–327
  redistributive, 299, 299*f*
  regulatory, 299, 299*f*
  study of, 299
  types of, 299, 299*f*
public policy analysts, 299
Public Safety, Department of, 257, 326
public safety expenditures, 326
Public Utility Commission (PUC), 225–226
PUC. *See* Public Utility Commission
PUF. *See* Permanent University Fund

Q
Quaker Oats, 211
"questions of life and death," in capital punishment, 255–256
quid pro quo, in legislature, 163
quorum, in legislature, 112, 156, 159–160

R
racism, 16
Radical Republicans, 12, 13, 48–53
Railroad Commission, Texas, 223–224
railroads
  building of, 14, 22
  regulation of, 14–15
"Rainy Day Fund," 308
Ratliff, Bill, 60, 160–161, 164, 166, 209
Rayburn, Sam, 16
reading, of bills, 170
Reagan, Ronald, 42, 107–108
Reagan Revolution, 107–108

reasonable doubt, beyond, 233
Reconstruction, 12–14, 48–53, 103
record, courts of, 236–237
records, open, 212, 213–215
Redeemers, 99–100
redistributive policy, 299, 299f
redistricting
  2003 fight over, 112, 155–157
  definition of, 152
  gerrymandering in, 68, 109, 154–157
  of legislative districts, 151–157
  Legislative Redistricting Board and, 154, 155
  minority rights in, 67–68, 154, 193
  "one person, one vote" and, 152–154
  political parties and, 109
  Speaker of House and, 162
reduction veto, 194
registrar, voter, 69
registration, lobbyist, 128
registration, voter, 69–70, 70f, 73–75
  jury duty and, 73, 263–264
  motor voter law and, 69–70, 71
regressive tax, 308–309, 309t, 310
regular session, of legislature, 149
regulatory boards, 225–226
regulatory policy, 299, 299f
religion, freedom of, 55
religious interest groups, 125
Remington, Frederic, 6f
removal
  of governors, 15, 198
  of gubernatorial appointments, 189, 202
republic, constitutional, 39
Republican Party, 103–110
  affiliation with, personal explanation of, 104–105
  African Americans and, 50–51
  constitutional revision and, 60
  factions in, 111
  and federalism, 42–44
  gains of, 109–110, 110f
  general elections and, 75–76
  governor as leader of, 197
  in legislature, 112–113, 150–151, 155–157, 178–179
  local elections and, 79, 108
  in new millennium, 110–113
  one-party system vs., 14, 89
  platform of, 94, 102
  primaries and, 75
  Reagan Revolution and, 107–108
  Reconstruction and, 12–14, 48–53, 103
  and redistricting, 112, 155–157
  resurgence of, 17, 89, 101–110
  slow growth of, 107
  in Texas legislature, 112–113
  Tower and, 105–107, 108
  Web site of, 94, 110
Republic of Texas, 10–11
  annexation by U.S., 11
  constitution of, 46, 54, 213
  definition of, 10

difficulties in, 10, 11
  and Texas Exceptionalism, 11
reserved powers, 43
resolutions, of party convention, 92
"retail politics," 80
revenue, state, 307–320
  casino option and, 315–317
  dedicated funds in, 304–305, 305f
  increasing, options for, 315–320
  nontax, 318–320, 318f
  tax, 308–317, 310f
revenue bonds, 281
reverse and remand, in appellate court, 234
reverse and render, in appellate court, 234
review power, of comptroller, 215–216
Reynolds v. Sims, 152–153
Rhode Island
  constitution of, 45
  sales tax in, 309
Richards, Ann, 201f, 273f
  as county commissioner, 272, 273f
  as governor, 186, 201, 203
    appointments of, 189
    education reform of, 57
    election of (1990), 76
    judicial appointments of, 245
    leadership style of, 200
    as liaison to Congress, 199
    loss to Bush (1994), 17, 72, 84–85
    minority support for, 72
    and redistricting, 193
    stay of execution by, 197
    as state treasurer, 216
robbery, 262
"Robin Hood" school reform, 57
Rogers, Will, 120
Roosevelt, Franklin, 100
Rose, Patrick M., 307f
Ruby, George, 50, 50f
Rudd, Jim, 162
Ruiz, Francisco, 27
Ruiz family, 9
Rules and Resolution Committee, House, 166–167
runoff elections, 75

S

sales tax, 281, 284, 298, 309–310
  dedicated funds from, 304–305
  on doctors and lawyers, 317
  exemptions from, 310
  motor vehicle, 310, 311
  as regressive tax, 308–309, 309t, 310
  revenue from, 308–310, 310f
San Antonio
  Cisneros and, 272, 272f, 277
  Institute of Texan Cultures in, 27
  location of, 19
  population of, 25
Sanchez, Tony, 27, 84, 101, 186
San Jacinto, battle of, 9–10
Santa Anna, Antonio López de, 9–10, 9f, 46

Sargent, Ben, 120f
Saudi Arabia, 17
Sayers, Joseph D., 203
SBE. See State Board of Education
school(s). See education
school district, independent, 290, 291–292
school lunches, 299
search and seizure, 55, 259, 260–261
secession, Texas ordinance of, 48
secretary of state, 220
  diversity in office, 219
  Senate confirmation of, 220
  in Texas constitution, 218
Secretary of State, Texas, 81
segregation, 16
Seguin family, 9
self-incrimination, 264
self-reliance, 30
Senate, Texas. See also legislature
  approval of
    for gubernatorial appointments, 188–189, 195
    for secretary of state, 220
  committees of, 165–170
    appointment to, 158–159
    procedural, 166–167
    special, 167–168
    standing, 166–167, 167t
    substantive, 166
  demographic makeup of, 150–151
  districts for, 153, 153f
  filibustering in, 172
  floor action in, 172–175
  membership of, 149
  political parties in, 112–113, 150–151
  president pro tempore of, 160
  presiding officer of, 157–161. See also lieutenant governor
  salary in, 150
  structure of, 149
  terms in, 150
  two-thirds rule in, 112, 156, 173, 175
Senate, U.S.
  contest for Bentsen's seat, 76–77
  contest for LBJ's seat, 103–106
senatorial courtesy, 188
seniority
  in Texas House, limited system of, 162–163
  in U.S. Congress, for Texans, 16
sentencing, 267
service economy, 23–24
Seventeenth Amendment, U.S., 40
shared powers, in federalism, 38–39
Sharp, Frank W., 17, 214
Sharp, John, 111, 161, 163, 209, 319
Sharpstown Scandal (1970s), 17, 33n16, 58, 107, 162, 214
Shea, Gwen, 219
Sheridan, Philip H., 3

sheriff, 257–258, 286, 287
Shivers, Allan, 203
signs, campaign, 80
single-issue groups, 118, 124–125
single-member districts
  judicial, 246
  legislative, 151, 153–154
  municipal, 279–280
"sin" taxes, 312–313
slavery, end of, 13, 39–40
slot machines, 316
small claims (justice) courts, 235f, 237–238
Smith, Preston, 203
Smith v. Allwright, 66–67
smoking sections, 212
"snowbirds," 19
social conservatives, 111
South Carolina
  constitution of, 45
  gubernatorial power in, 187
South Dakota v. Dole, 41
South Plains, 20
South Texas Prairie, 19, 19f
Southwest Voter Education and Registration Project, 72
Spanish colonists, 7
Spanish explorers, 5–6, 6f
Speaker of the House, Texas, 157, 161–163
  ex officio positions of, 163, 306
  on Legislative Budget Board, 163, 306
  pledge cards for, 161–162
  political culture and, 30
  powers of, 161
  revolt against Craddick (2007), 164–165
  on Sunset Advisory Commission, 163, 226
  "team" for, 162, 163–165
  tenure of, 161
special committees, 167–168
special districts, 290–292
  definition of, 290
  education, 290, 291–292
  governmental character of, 290
  independence of, 290
  law enforcement, 258
  nature of, 291
  recognized existence of, 290–291
  taxes of, 309
  types of, 291–292
special election, 76–77
special sessions, of legislature, 149, 190–191, 200
special taxes, 281
speech, freedom of, 40, 55
speed limits, state power over, 43
spending. See expenditures
Spindletop oil field, 15, 22, 22f
spoils system, 222, 290
stadium finance, 281, 282f
staff
  gubernatorial, 201–202
  legislative committee, 169–170
standing committees, 166–167, 167t
Staples, Todd, 217f, 219

state(s)
constitutions of, 44–45
effective dates of, 44, 44*t*
lengths of, 44, 44*t*
federalism and, 36–44
limitations on, in U.S. Constitution, 37
powers of, in U.S. Constitution, 37
reserved powers of, 43
State Affairs Committees, 166, 306
State Board of Education (SBE), 223–224
state chair, of party, 95*f,* 97
state conventions, 93*f,* 94
state executive committee, 95*f,* 97
State Highway Department, 225
state law enforcement, 257
"State of the State" address, 191
state senatorial district convention, 93–94, 93*f,* 96*f*
statutory probate courts, 235*f,* 239
stay of execution, 196–197, 254
STEP. *See* Strategic Traffic Enforcement Program
Stephen A. Austin University, 225
Sterling, Ross S., 203
Stevenson, Adlai, 103
Stevenson, Coke R., 100, 203
Stewart, Potter, 4
stimulus package, federal, 178, 179, 308, 319
Stockard, Paul, 65
Stockton Plateau, 21
straight-ticket voting, 247
Strategic Traffic Enforcement Program (STEP), 284
Straus, Joe, 30, 68, 163, 165
Strayhorn, Carole, 216
strong mayors, 276
Sturns, Louis, 27
subcommittees, legislature, 169
substantive committees, 166
suffrage. *See also* voting; voting rights
in Texas Constitution, 69
universal, 65, 69
Sunset Advisory Commission, 159, 163, 226–227, 302
Super Collider, 199, 201
superintendent, school, 292
Super Tuesday primary, 75
Supreme Court, Texas, 235*f,* 241–242, 244*f*
on adult entertainment tax, 313
attorney general and, 212
diversity on, 245, 245*f*
on education funding, 298, 310–311, 322
power abuse allegations against, 246
selection of justices, 243, 244, 247
in state constitution, 53–54
Web site of, 242
Supreme Court, U.S.
on capital punishment, 256
on federal funding, 41
interpretation of Constitution by, 36
judicial review by, 39
on redistricting, 152–154
on reserved powers, 43
on voting rights, 66–67
supreme courts, Texas, dual, 235*f,* 241–242

T
TABC. *See* Texas Alcoholic Beverage Commission
tagging, of bill, 175
TANF. *See* Temporary Assistance for Needy Families
Tarrant County
district clerk of (Wilder, Tom), 78–80, 78*f*
operations of (Bagsby, Dionne), 285
TASA. *See* Texas Association of School Administrators
tax(es)
alcohol, 298, 312–313, 317
business interests and, 122–123
city/municipal, 275, 280–284
collection of, 212, 215, 287–288, 308–313
comparison with other states, 313–315, 315*t*
dedicated funds from, 304–305
franchise, 281, 309, 310–311, 310*f*
income, 142, 309, 309*t,* 314
insurance, 310*f,* 313
margin, 311
motor fuels, 298, 299, 304, 310*f,* 311–312, 317
motor vehicle sales and rental, 310, 310*f,* 311
nontax revenue *vs.,* 318, 318*f*
oil and natural gas, 310*f,* 312, 312*f*
on per-person basis, 314
poll, 29, 40, 67
progressive, 308–309, 309*t*
property, 280–281
assessment of, 280, 287–288
education funding from, 291–292, 310–311, 313–314, 322–323
municipal revenue from, 280–281
relief from, 311, 313–314
reform in, 315
regressive, 308–309, 309*t*
sales, 281, 284, 298, 304–305, 308–310, 309*t,* 317
"sin," 312–313
special, 281
state revenue from, 308–317, 310*f*
tobacco, 298, 310*f,* 312–313
utility, 313, 317
tax abatements, 284
tax assessor-collector, 287–288
TDA. *See* Texas Department of Agriculture
TEA. *See* Texas Education Agency
teacher salaries, 141–142
"team," in legislature, 162, 163–165
Tea Party, 135*f*
TEC. *See* Texas Ethics Commission

Tejanos, 9. *See also* Hispanic Texans
Temple State Bank, Ferguson and, 15
Temporary Assistance for Needy Families (TANF), 324–325
Tenth Amendment, U.S., 43
Terlingua, 21
term limits, 166, 186
Texans for Public Justice, 137
Texas. *See also specific entries*
changing face of, 30–31
demographics of, 24–28, 33*n*19
diversity of, 4, 26–28, 26*f,* 30–31
economy of, 21–24
geography of, 18–21, 18*f,* 19*f*
history of, 2*f*–3*f,* 5–17
as mosaic, 4
perceptions of, 4
political culture of, 28–31
size of, 18, 18*f*
Texas Abortion Rights League, 125
Texas Alcoholic Beverage Commission (TABC), 225–226, 257
Texas A&M University System
constitutional revision and, 60
funding for, 304
Texas Association of School Administrators (TASA), 142
Texas Commission on Law Enforcement, 257, 258
Texas Community College Teachers Association, 121, 130
Texas Conservative Coalition, 178–179
Texas Department of Agriculture (TDA), 218
Texas Department of Criminal Justice, 253
Texas Department of Transportation (TxDOT), 225, 325
Texas Education Agency (TEA), 136, 141–142, 223–224, 322
Texas Ethics Commission (TEC), 81, 128, 137–138, 145*n*14
Texas Exceptionalism, 11
Texas Folklife Festival, 27
Texas Good Roads and Transportation Association, 122
Texas Government Newsletter, 134
Texas Higher Education Assessment (THEA), 225
Texas Legislative Council, 159, 163, 177
Texas Medical Association, 123, 145*n*7
Texas Mosaic, 31
Bean (Judge Roy), 238, 238*f*
bills passed in 2009 session, 176
diversity in elections (Jordan, Barbara), 68
diversity in executive branch, 219

diversity in local government (Cisneros, Henry), 272, 272*f*
diversity of thought (Davis, E. J.), 52
early diversity in Texas, 50–51
Ferguson (James E.), 198, 198*f*
gender diversity (Richards, Ann), 201, 201*f*
Killer Bees, 159–160
lobbyist's tale (Toomey, Mike), 131
old-style politics (Bullock, Bob), 211, 211*f*
Republic of Texas, 10
Supreme Court (Jefferson, Wallace B.), 245, 245*f*
Texas National Guard, 220
Texas Panhandle, 20
Texas Parks and Wildlife (magazine), 224
Texas Penal Code, 233, 259, 259*t*
Texas Railroad Commission (TRC), 223–224
Texas Rangers, 159–160, 189, 257
Texas Rangers Baseball Club, 311
Texas Register, 220
Texas Regulars, 100
Texas Research League, 122
Texas Revolution, 9–10
Texas State Board of Plumbing Examiners, 225
Texas State Teachers Association, 16, 118, 123, 141–142
Texas Taxpayers and Research Association (TTARA), 122–123
Texas Taxpayers Association, 122
Texas Tourism Board, 28
Texas Trial Lawyers Association, 123
Texas Workforce Commission, 222, 326
textbook errors, 224
THEA. *See* Texas Higher Education Assessment
theft and theft plus, 262
third parties, 90–91
Thirteenth Amendment, U.S., 39–40
three Cs, of economy, 21
Tidelands controversy, 103
timber industry, 19, 22
tobacco companies, damages from, 211
tobacco tax, 298, 310*f,* 312–313
toll roads, 325
tools of a crime, 261
Toomey, Mike, 129, 131, 138
tort reform, 326
tourism, 19
Tower, John, 105–107, 106*f,* 108
trade associations, 122
traditionalistic culture, 29–30, 31, 35
and capital punishment, 255
and election of judges, 243
and legislative districts, 154
and state expenditures, 297
and voter turnout, 73
transit, mass, 291*f*

Transportation, Texas Department of, 225, 325
Transportation Code, 233
transportation funding, 41, 122, 129f, 176, 325
Travis, William B., 107
Travis County, Richards as commissioner of, 272, 273f
TRC. *See* Texas Railroad Commission
treasurer, county, 288
treasurer, state, abolition of, 216
trial(s), 263–267
  bench, 263
  by jury, right to, 259, 263
trial courts, 232, 234–240, 235f
trial de novo, 236
trilingual ballots, 72
true bill (indictment), 262–263
Truman, Harry, 103
trust, in government, 29
TTARA. *See* Texas Taxpayers and Research Association
Turner, Sylvester, 28
turnout, voter, 30, 65, 70–75
  of African Americans, 70
  education and, 70
  family tradition and, 70–71, 72
  of Hispanics, 70, 71f
  individual factors in, 72–73
  language barriers and, 72
  in local elections, 271–272
  Texas factors in, 73–75
  trends in, 71–72
  type of election and, 71
  of young people, 73
Twenty-fourth Amendment, U.S., 40, 67
Twenty-sixth Amendment, U.S., 40
two-party system, emergence of, 17, 89, 108
two-thirds rule, in Texas Senate, 112, 156, 173, 175
TxDOT. *See* Texas Department of Transportation

U

UCR. *See* Uniform Crime Reports
Unclaimed Properties Division, 216–217
unemployment benefits, 319
unfunded mandates, 43–44, 305
Uniform Crime Reports (UCR), 252

Union League, 50
unions
  interest groups of, 123
  membership in, 30
  political party support from, 101
unitary system, 37
United States, annexation by, 11, 18, 46, 48
United States v. *Lopez,* 43
United States v. *Morrison,* 43
United States v. *Texas,* 67
universal suffrage, 65, 69
university boards, 225
university funding, 304, 323
University of Texas
  affirmative action and, 323
  board of, 225
  constitutional revision and, 60
  Ferguson (James E.) and, 15, 198, 223
  funding for, 304, 323
  Institute of Texan Cultures, 27
university police, 258
unreasonable search and seizure, 261
uphold, in appellate court, 234
urban population, 25–26, 26t, 275f
user fees, 281
utility regulation, 225–226
utility taxes, 313, 317

V

Veramendi family, 9
Vermont, constitution of, 45
Veterans Land Board, 217
veto
  gubernatorial power of, 142, 175, 191–193, 193f
  line-item, 194–195
  override of, 192
  postadjournment, 192
  presidential *vs.* gubernatorial, 192
  reduction, 194
Vietnamese Texans, trilingual ballots for, 72
Vietnam War, 16–17
voir dire, 264
voter fraud, 74
voter identification, requirement for, 74, 112, 172, 176
voter registrar, 69
voter registration, 69–70, 70f, 73–75
  jury duty and, 73, 263–264
  motor voter law and, 69–70, 71

voter turnout, 30, 65, 70–75
  of African Americans, 70
  education and, 70
  family tradition and, 70–71, 72
  of Hispanics, 70, 71f
  individual factors in, 72–73
  language barriers and, 72
  in local elections, 271–272
  Texas factors in, 73–75
  trends in, 71–72
  type of election and, 71
  of young people, 73
voting
  absentee, 74
  alternative methods of, 74
  chronology of, 64f–65f
  computers for, 71f
  early, 74
  qualifications for, 68–69
  straight-ticket, 247
  Web site for information on, 75
voting rights
  of African Americans, 39–40, 48, 49, 66–68
  poll tax and, 29, 40, 67
  Voting Rights Act of 1965 and, 67–68
  white primary and, 29, 66–67
  federal court intervention in, 67
  of Hispanic Texans, 49
  history of, 66–68
  in Texas Constitution, 69
  universal suffrage and, 65
  of women, 16, 40, 66
Voting Rights Act of 1965, 67–68

W

Waco, location of, 19
Wainwright, Dale, 28
Wallace, George, 91
Washington State, sales tax in, 309
watchdog, government as, 213
Watergate, 58
water resources, 20–21
Ways and Means Committee, House, 306
weak mayors, 276
welfare
  as redistributive policy, 299
  reform of, 193, 324
  state expenditures on, 323–325
West, Royce, 28
Western Highlands, 19f, 20–21
West Texas, potential state of, 49
West Texas basins and ranges, 21

What Can You Do?, 31
  beach adoption, 218
  comptroller information, 302
  crime prevention, 252
  gubernatorial power, 203
  Institute of Texan Cultures, 27
  local government, 278
  marital property, 58
  party participation, 94
  testimony in legislature, 171
  Texans for Public Justice, 137
  Texas Department of Agriculture, 218
  Texas Supreme Court, 242
  Unclaimed Properties Division, 216
  voter registration, 69
Whig Party, 99
White, Mark, 108, 190, 203, 219, 226
Whitehead, Martha, 216
white primary, 29, 66–67
Whitmire, John, 156, 217f
Wichita Prairie, 19f, 20
Wilder, Tom, 78–80, 78f, 81
Williams, Clayton, 76, 109, 201
Williams, Michael, 28, 223
Williams, Roger, 219
Williamson, Robert McAlpin, 10
will of the people, 39
Wilson, Phil, 219
wind power, 21
wining and dining, by lobbyists, 134–135
Winstar Casino, 316–317
Winter Garden, 19
women
  equal rights in Texas Constitution, 54
  voting rights of, 16, 40
Workforce Commission, Texas, 222, 326
Wright, Jim, 105–106

Y

Yarborough, Ralph, 100–101
yellow dog Democrats, 101
youth
  Democratic affiliation of, 98–99
  Republican affiliation of, 104–105
  voter turnout of, 73